Sixth Edition

Creating Writers

6 Traits, Process, Workshop, and Literature

VICKI SPANDEL

INDEPENDENT WRITING CONSULTANT

PEARSON

Boston Columbus Indianapolis New York San Francisco Upper Saddle River
Amsterdam Cape Town Dubai London Madrid Milan Munich Paris Montreal Toronto
Delhi Mexico City Sao Paulo Sydney Hong Kong Seoul Singapore Taipei Tokyo

This book is dedicated to the all the students who have so generously shared their writing with me—and to every student who writes so that his or her voice may be heard.

Vice President, Editor-in-Chief: Aurora Martínez Ramos
Associate Sponsoring Editor: Barbara Strickland
Editorial Assistant: Katherine Wiley
Senior Marketing Manager: Christine Gatchell
Production Editor: Janet Domingo
Editorial-Production Service: Kathy Smith
Manufacturing Buyer: Megan Cochran
Design and Electronic Composition: Schneck-DePippo Graphics
Cover Designer: Jennifer Hart
Author Photo: Lynn Woodward Photography
Cover Art: "Four Season Tree" by Stephanie Brooks, Library Street & Dr. H. O. Smith Schools

Printed in the United States of America
10 9 8 7 6 5 4 3 2   EBM   15 14 13 12

www.allynbaconmerrill.com

ISBN 10: 0-13-294410-3
ISBN 13: 978-0-13-294410-6

Contents

CHAPTER 1

Getting Acquainted with the 6 Traits   1

CHAPTER 2

Setting the Stage with Writing Process and Writing Workshop   30

CHAPTER 9

Going INFORMATIONAL 266

CHAPTER 10

Exploring the World of BEGINNING WRITERS 308

Contents

Foreword
by Jeff Anderson

She's done it again. Vicki Spandel has expertly honed her seminal work in writing assessment and instruction, making it better than ever. With the six traits of writing as ubiquitous as they are, you'd think that impossible. Not for Vicki. Nearly 30 years ago, she helped start a movement that showed writing instruction was about more than merely assigning writing—craft lessons, purposeful revision and feedback could all be harnessed to create writers. What Vicki told us years ago research has now borne out: Young writers learn by assessing and talking about models, and by receiving feedback that helps them identify what is or is not working in their own writing. In a time of common core curriculum and testmania, we need Vicki's voice, calm and true, keeping us on track, staying the course.

When I first encountered Vicki's work almost fifteen years ago, I was struck by its simplicity, good sense, and practicality. As a writing project graduate, I was able to easily integrate and tweak my instruction to incorporate concrete language about writing and examples showing good detail, strong word choice, or moving voice. Talking about students' writing with colleagues helped me clarify what I valued and also unveiled what really matters in writing and instruction. But what has been most moving for me is seeing young writers discuss, evaluate, and improve—as *they* figure out what it means to write well.

Over the years, I became increasingly aware of how voice, sentence fluency, word choice and conventions supported each other—I even wrote two books about it. I give a lot of credit to Vicki and her emphasis on language and models as a catalyst for the whole mentor text movement. And in this sixth edition, Vicki maintains the original simplicity of trait-based instruction while continuing to evolve *Creating Writers* to align with what she and others have discovered about effectively teaching writing.

The underlying message is consistent: Kids can and will write well when they know what quality looks like. Some educators have overlooked this message, equating the six traits to an almost mechanical use of rubrics, completely missing Vicki's thoughtful ties to writing workshop and mentor texts. In this edition, that's harder to do. The connection to writing process is brought right into the spotlight—and the chapter on writing process and work-shop (Chapter 2) enhanced by authentic teacher voices is a welcome addition. In her practical and inspiring way, Vicki clears away the fog, showing how process, workshop, and traits fit together. And the emerging conclusion could hardly be more clear: We cannot just clip rubrics to students' work and say we are teaching the traits. It goes deeper than that.

Too many teachers have focused so literally on rubrics that they cannot see beyond them to the concepts that define good writing—and it's these concepts that we want to teach. In doing so, we help students see their writing as never before, recognizing strengths as writers that they didn't even know they possessed. As Vicki so eloquently says, "We are looking for what writers *can* do, rather than what they cannot do. Rubrics, or writing guides, are a map of discovery, reminding us to see what we might otherwise overlook." Viewed this way, rubrics don't limit teachers—they set us free. Katie Wood Ray advocates that students name what they know in order to own a concept. The traits give us meaningful names for concepts that take the mystery out of writing—allowing students to think and talk about writing just as writers do. This creates a real power shift in the classroom.

If you own a previous edition of this book, get ready for a revised edition that is truly *new*. I love—and you will, too—the new easy-to-follow organization. Everything you need to teach a given trait is in one place, easy to find, and every trait-connected chapter follows a similar format—starting with books and more books. The Warming Up with Literature feature expands any reader's view of what it means to write well. Vicki and I share a book addiction, and she loads us up with helpful, ready-to-use excerpts, lists, and summaries. As writing teachers, we are continually looking for new literature to inject life and voice into our classrooms. I was happy to see familiar titles—and encountered others I wound up ordering within minutes.

Outstanding student samples are still here (along with some new voices), now with fresh Write Connection suggestions to help us extend students' learning. Vicki's commentaries and suggested ways of responding to writers help us remember that careful, well-selected feedback is the lynchpin to growing writers. New craft lessons—with strong emphasis on modeling—simplify the teaching of any trait. The thoughtful end-of-chapter questions are excellent and offer many ideas I plan to try not only with colleagues but with students as well.

The expanded chapter on nonfiction is just what teachers are hungry for today. It shows nonfiction as a search for questions—*and* answers. Vicki models everything from teaching children to take notes to discovering sources and integrating quotations.

These new additions give the same interactive feel to the book that you experience in one of Vicki's workshops. And her Author's Notes give you that side by side coaching that you always long for with any instructional resource. Vicki somehow anticipates your next question even as you're reading the text. Her insight takes you a bit deeper—no matter your level of development.

Steeped in meaningful quotes and research, *Creating Writers* takes the reader on a journey of what works in teaching writing. The lively prose is packed with ready-to-use examples and trusted voices: children's authors, writing experts, and—as always—teachers. The tapestry Vicki weaves from these voices will leave no writing teacher unchanged. If this is your first dabbling in the traits, get ready to have your mind blown. If you're revisiting or recalibrating, as we all need to do from time to time, your brilliant writing teacher friend is back to share what she knows to be true about creating writers. This edition could well be called *Creating Writing Teachers*.

Jeff Anderson
Author of *10 Things Every Writer Needs to Know*

Preface

It's an honor being asked to write a 6th edition. After all, you don't see *Moby Dick*, 6th edition—the one where Ahab survives and launches a whale protection program. (True enough, novels—especially classics—are different. But still.) On the other hand . . . it's also a bit daunting.

Once you're five editions in, what more can there be to say? It isn't like we're discovering new traits every year. Even if we count presentation—the "Pluto" trait (is it really a trait or isn't it?)—we only have seven. (Well, maybe eight—I'll save that surprise for later.) But you know what happens once you start to write—it so happens there really *was* more to say and maybe a new perspective from which to say it. So let's get to it: What's different in edition six?

New to This Edition

If you're familiar with previous editions, the very first thing you'll notice when you peek inside (or review the Table of Contents) is that the *whole book* is reorganized. And the most important feature of this reorganization is that *everything* pertaining to a given trait—sample papers, writing guides, lessons, recommended trade books, *the works*—is now *all in one place*. This makes the book easy to navigate—whether you're reading it on your own, as part of a study group, or in a college class.

Second, I've always hoped to make it clear that the six traits—despite their potential to illuminate revision—cannot and *do not* exist in a vacuum. They're often taught as if they do. As if stacking up trait-based lessons like cordwood will make all the difference. It won't. Like all shortcuts, this approach is doomed. It takes three things working together: writing process, writing workshop—*and* traits—to make trait-based writing instruction successful. Chapter 2 shows you how to set the stage for success by creating an atmosphere in which traits can flourish.

Third, this edition emphasizes the need to use rubrics—or writing guides—with intelligence. Rubrics don't own or control us—like Hal in "2001: A Space Odyssey." We wrote them, and *we own them*. We can, and must, interpret them to suit ourselves, revise them as necessary to reflect new thinking, and quite often step outside their boundaries to say things written criteria alone cannot capture. To be honest, I always thought this was obvi-

ous. Apparently, it wasn't. Believe it or not, some people find rubrics intimidating—and restrictive. Don't be one of them. Throughout this book, I will show you how to work with writing guides inventively and fearlessly, as part of a more expansive and effective approach to assessment.

Here are twelve additional changes I hope you'll love:

1. The **literature** sections for every trait are *greatly* expanded, including many more book recommendations and lesson suggestions that reveal what you've probably long suspected—that the traits are as much about reading as about writing.

2. Many **new papers** make their debut in this edition (and as always, others had to go). I brought back some old favorites—like *Sand Dollar* and *Metamorphosis*—and added new writing I am confident you and your students will enjoy discussing, including numerous **expository** and **persuasive** pieces. Each paper has lessons to teach.

3. **Lessons and strategies** are also expanded, now emphasize **modeling**, and include more of the thinking behind each lesson to help you see what specific skills you're helping students build.

4. **Author's notes**, inserted throughout the text, suggest ways of adapting lessons to meet the needs of challenged writers—and those who *need* a challenge.

5. The **informational writing** chapter (Chapter 9) has grown to include not only more papers, but also a wickedly good list (if I do say so) of books for teaching informational writing—along with lessons specific to that genre.

6. Instead of loading you down with endless sets of writing guides, I show you how to create your own checklists for **persuasive writing**—or for **any genre** that suits you.

7. Because many teachers are now going beyond print, I've included a section on **technology** that will, I hope, give you confidence to make podcasts, videos, blogs, wikis, and other multimedia formats part of your curriculum.

8. Chapter 10, which focuses on **primary writing**, now includes the Early Guides from *Creating Young Writers* (revised in 2011), primary-level checklists to help you document what even the youngest writers can do.

9. Everyone is talking about the **Common Core Standards for Writing** these days, and you may be

wondering whether these Standards are closely connected to the six traits. They are, and I will show you how—right up front in Chapter 1.

10. **Study Group Questions and Activities** have all been revised to make this book ideal for use in a college classroom or with a study group.

11. The **writing guides** (aka, rubrics) are all updated, but continue to follow the "leap the river" format that makes them easy to use and to teach.

12. Writing guides for teachers now appear in a **one-page format**, making them easier to use than ever.

Teachers always want **more lessons**—more than you can possibly put into one book, so let me suggest two additional sources. First, if you want to focus on revision specifically, have a look at *Creating Revisers and Editors*, a series of lessons that show students how to do focused editing or revision—doing small things like adding detail, spicing up verbs, knowing when to use *it's* or *its*. These complementary editions, also published by Pearson Education, are grade-specific and range from grades 2 through 8. Second, if you are currently using the *Write Traits Kits* (written by my co-author Jeff Hicks and me, and published by Great Source Education), please know that both this book and *Creating Revisers and Editors* fully complement lessons in those kits—and *neither is a repetition of what you will find there*. If I were to describe the difference, I'd say that this book (while it contains many lessons) is a conversation; it is, in essence, *everything* I say in workshops and seminars—only in far more detail.

On a personal note, if you teach writing, *thank you*. Your work, while joyful and rewarding, is also extraordinarily difficult—for so many reasons. Writing is complex, and getting truly proficient takes a lifetime. But they don't give you a lifetime to show results. You get a few months. And it isn't as if you're working under cover. Everyone is watching. Even people who are neither teachers nor writers are only too happy to tell you what you need to do differently. You are expected to be gracious (and creative) through all this. And guess what? You are. Not every single blessed second of every blooming day, probably—teachers are human, after all—but *most* of the time. Even when battered by results from tests that have almost no relevance to the *best things* that are happening in your classroom, you remain resilient—and flexible. Willing to try just one more thing. And every now and then—usually when no one else is watching—magic happens, and maybe you think to yourself, "Oh . . . if only they could see me *now*." You find, after oh-so-many attempts, the just-right way to say it, do it, show it, and a small face lights up. For a second or two

you forget the critics—because it's those faces that matter. They're the reason you teach—and keep teaching.

In this book, I share a few faces with you—but mostly I share voices. Voices of students who, in many cases, defied boundaries—going beyond conventions, beyond rubrics, beyond rules. They are an amazing gift—first to me, and now to you. I hope they remind you of all the things you love about teaching: students suddenly getting it, students writing their hearts out because they know someone (maybe *you*) will read it, students gaining the confidence that comes with knowing they can do something *really* well and that no one (test in hand or not) can take that away from them.

If you are new to trait-based teaching, I want to say two things to you. First, the six traits support and enrich writing process at every step. They're a catalyst. Traits are the spark that ignites passionate, meaningful revision. There is only one reason to teach the traits at all: They work. If you want your students to taste writing success—success you can see and measure—this is your book. Second, because the traits are *not a curriculum* in any sense or form, they will not take over your classroom or replace *anything you are doing now*. Rather, they will fit in with, adapt to, accommodate, and expand your current practice. They will help your students become the independent writers and revisers you always wanted them to be. And, together with the best of writing process and writing workshop, they will help you become what every 21st-century teacher needs to be: unstoppable.

If we meet someday, I hope your 6th edition is looking a little dog-eared, marginalia blossoming everywhere, sticky notes poking out top and sides. If so, I'll know that every moment spent on this revision was worth it.

Acknowledgments

Countless people have contributed to the development of this book—to mention everyone, I would need another book, but know you are loved and appreciated even if your name is not on these pages. First and foremost, I want to acknowledge how much all teachers, including myself, owe to the tens of thousands of student writers who have taught us all so much. The original six-trait model was built upon their voices, and without them, neither this book nor the six traits themselves would exist.

Special thanks to the many student writers whose work appears in this edition—and to those for whom we could not make room, much as we wanted to. Your contributions were greatly valued. We have sought permission for each paper and copyrighted selection in this book. If for any reason you feel your work has been published without permission, we will happily correct that oversight.

Thank you to all of the teachers who invited me into their classrooms to share lesson ideas and work with their students, and who shared instructional strategies or lessons with me.

My deepest thanks to *all* those people who have been my personal teachers through the years: in particular, to Jeff Anderson (who wrote the Foreword for this edition), a writing teacher so brilliant he should have (probably will have) his own reality show; to Cindy Marten, who knows that genius is hollow without compassion, and whose spirit (*"Work hard, Be kind, Dream big"*) will guide—I believe—our nation's very destiny in literacy; to Don Graves, the gentle man (whom we now miss so much) who taught us the importance of voice, and who shaped a view of assessment that dared to look beyond conventions to the soul of writing; to the remarkable Judy Mazur, who has brought writing process, workshop, and conferencing to an art form—and who is deeply loved by the students for whom she opens doors every day of her life (Thank you, Judy, for just letting me be there); to Barbara Andrews, whose tireless and ingenious spirit brings the traits to life every day for her middle school writers, and who never runs out of new ways to teach; to my cherished friend and mentor Donna Flood, whose intelligence guides me like a light in the dark, and who continues to share her vast knowledge, wisdom, sensitivity, and gentle humor with all students and teachers lucky enough to know her; to the inimitable Barry Lane, the finest teacher of revision skills I've yet to encounter, and unquestionably the wittiest, who always seems to make me laugh just when I need it most (and who gets workshop participants to perform interpretive poetry in ways they never imagined themselves doing in public); to all my teacher friends in Hawaii—Monica Mann, Gail Lee, Sean Doi, Sandra Haynes, Donna Nakamura, Dori Anne Saito, Cindy Otsu, Laurie Meyer, Stanley Kayatani, Gail Sakata, and others—who opened so many, many doors for me; especially to the incredible (and hilarious) Leila Naka, who embodies the best of what education should be, who has helped countless teachers see the traits as a vision and not a program (and who plays a mean game of Wii bowling); to Richard (aka Rick) Stiggins, the guru of classroom assessment (and fly fishing), whose vision of quality assessment guides every facet of my educational life (and may yet influence my fishing as well); to the comical, inspirational Rosey Dorsey (aka Rosey Comfort), who never found a formula she couldn't outwit and who, as a force of nature, coaxes the kind of writing from her students that rocks the world; to Andrea Dabbs, whose creativity and compassion give children who have never spoken English the courage to write in English; to the extraordinary Sally Shorr, whose understanding of writing process is unsurpassed, and who has so often been for me the person Mem Fox calls "the watcher," the heart to whom you write; to the phenomenally talented Lois Burdett, who let me watch as she coached her second graders through *Macbeth*, and who taught me to "take the lid off" because there are no limits to what children of any age can do; to Sneed B. Collard, my writer-teacher friend, who writes so prolifically I had to add a new shelf to my library just for him—and so well that I didn't mind; to my colleagues and long-time friends Darle Fearl, Jeff Hicks (best co-author of all time) and Fred Wolff, who have unerringly guided me to books "you're gonna love," and who have continued to share those little "behind-the scenes" tips that make writing instruction work; and to my many colleagues in Weber School District, particularly Jeff Stephens, Rebecca Okey, and Sue Porter, who became not just writing buddies and mentors but lifelong friends.

My continued appreciation to those who started the ball rolling so long ago. In particular, thanks to my dear friend Carol Meyer, former assessment and evaluation specialist for Beaverton (Oregon) School District #48, and to those 17 teachers who made up the Analytical Writing Assessment Model Committee. Thank you all for hanging in there through mountains of student essays and countless early drafts. Thank you for making history and letting me be there.

No book comes together without extensive behind-the-scenes effort. I wish to thank my editor, Maria Aurora Martínez Ramos, who has encouraged me to make this book the extension of myself I always wanted it to be. I am also deeply indebted to Barbara Andrews, Rosey Dorsey, Judy Mazur and all the participating student writers for their time and skill in providing (from their own classrooms) the photos for this book that illustrate six-trait writing workshop in action. My sincere thanks also to the reviewers of this edition: Elizabeth Belcher, Lakeview Elementary School, Colonial Heights, VA, and Virginia Commonwealth University; Tamara Doehring; Kristina J. Doubet, James Madison University; Jane Feber; Gayla LaBreck, Thomas College; Judy Mazur, Buena Vista Elementary School, Walnut Creek, CA; David Salyer, Loras College; and Lanette Waddell, Lehigh University.

Ongoing thanks to my family, whom I hardly ever see. It takes more than a year to build a book (This is edition 6—and that's only *this* book). Thank you, Jerry—my lifelong love, for cooking, listening, encouraging me, remaining calm through all computer crises, reloading the printer continuously, putting up with three work stations filled with "manuscript," and continuing to plan that trip we are (definitely) going to take someday. Thanks to my remarkable, loving, and disarmingly humorous children, Nikki and Michael, my terrific son-in-law Chris—and my grandson and future writer Jack (now 7), who is teaching me to love Arnold Lobel, Roald Dahl, and Maurice Sendak all over again.

In each edition, I close with a special note of thanks to Margery Stricker Durham, the university teacher who taught me to write. She was a thinker who dared to say what was in her mind and heart—and expected no less of us, her students. We, on the other hand, had been academically suppressed (most of us), taught to please, and becoming independent and outspoken did not come naturally. The oddest part of it all was that Margery was not a writing teacher in the conventional sense. She didn't do mini lessons or correct *anything*. She did something far more important: She read every word we wrote, and wrote back. She didn't comment on semicolons or participles; she commented on our thinking—or lack thereof. It didn't occur to me at the time that she was modeling the best way—the only way—to teach writing well. Dear Margery, thank you from my heart. It took a while, but I really do *get* it.

Vicki Spandel
www.sixtraitgurus.com

CourseSmart eBook and other eBook Options Available

CourseSmart is an exciting new choice for purchasing this book. As an alternative to purchasing the printed book, you may purchase an electronic version of the same content via CourseSmart for reading on PC, Mac, as well as Android devices, iPad, iPhone, and iPod Touch with CourseSmart Apps. With a CourseSmart eBook, readers can search the text, make notes online, and bookmark important passages for later review. For more information or to purchase access to the CourseSmart eBook, visit www.coursesmart.com. Also look for availability of this book on a number of other eBook devices and platforms.

Website Resources for *Creating Writers: 6 Traits, Process, Workshop, and Literature*

www.pearsonhighered.com/spandel6e

The free website for *Creating Writers: 6 Traits, Process, Workshop, and Literature* features a wealth of printable resources selected from Vicki Spandel's best-selling text.

The following resources are available:

- Practice papers, tables, and figures designed for use in classroom assessment.
- The "Write Connection" tips and activities from the author.

CHAPTER 1

Getting Acquainted with the 6 Traits

We teach students how to read books, but not how to read their own writing. Unless we show children how to read their own writing, their work will not improve.

DONALD H. GRAVES
Writing: Teachers and Children at Work, 2003, xvi

Six-trait writing is not a program, curriculum, or formula. It's a vision. A way of thinking and talking about writing that helps teachers, and most important, helps *students* answer the question all writers must ask: *What makes writing work?* What makes such a tiny question so powerful? Just this: In answering it, students learn to revise with purpose and take charge of their own writing process.

How important is that? Try vital. Writers are thinkers. They're not *just* poets and story tellers. They are analysts. Writers work their way through mountains of information and make sense of it. Writers educate us—and educate themselves in the bargain. The act of writing, thinking on paper, takes our students inside math, history, science, and technology. Moreover, writing, like reading, holds one critical key to lifelong success. In *Because Writing Matters,* Carl Nagin and the National Writing Project (2006, 105) underscore how essential writing skills are for our students, both in the classroom and beyond:

> Writing helps students become better readers and thinkers. It can help students reflect critically about the information and ideas they must understand and make use of both in academia and in the world outside its doors. It can improve achievement in schools and in the professions students aspire to. It supports their growth as adult independent thinkers. Writing is a gateway to students' emerging role in our nation's future as participants and decision makers in a democratic society.

Enter the Traits . . .

Where do the six traits fit into this picture? In a word . . . *everywhere.* For one thing, they make the teaching of writing easier by breaking it into manageable components—ideas, organization, voice, and the rest.

Second, the traits offer us a language for talking about writing in meaningful, productive ways. "That was great!" is a positive comment—but it's virtually useless to a writer. Writers need to know *precisely* what is working and why. A helpful comment sounds more like this: "Your lead—'*I knew I shouldn't have gone in*'—pulled me right in. It created tension." Conferences turn into meaningful writer-to-writer conversations when students feel comfortable with words like *lead, pacing, message, conclusion, detail, voice, strong verbs, sentence variety, dialogue,* and so on.

The biggest difference, however, lies in the impact traits have upon writing process. We have known for a long time that writing is a process—or a combination of processes. It takes planning, drafting, and revising. But somehow this insight has not dramatically simplified the teaching of writing. Why not? Much of the answer rests within one word: *revision.* Teachers are relatively comfortable teaching planning or prewriting. And drafting is fairly painless from the teacher's perspective because most—not all, but *most*—of the work falls to the writer. But what do writers *do* when they revise? How do we teach this? How do we model it for our students? This has been the challenge. This is where, for many writers (and teachers), process comes unraveled. And this is precisely where the traits shine—because a good rubric is *so much more* than a list of criteria.

Look carefully at Figure 1.1. What do you see? Perhaps you see a tall, elegant vase. But if you look at the picture another way, you'll see two people looking at each other. A good writing rubric should be just like that: Look at it one way, and it's a guide to assessment, but look at it in another way, and it's a guide to *revision.* As you read through the criteria, you should find yourself saying, "These are the *very things* writers do when they revise." They add detail. They cut clutter. They unleash the voice. They write leads that hook readers, conclusions that leave you thinking. . . . This means that when you teach

FIGURE 1.1

Two-Way Picture

the traits, you literally unlock the door to revision for your writers. You teach them to think by asking them to continually analyze writing—their own and that of others. This puts *students* in charge of their own writing process, so that you do not need to choreograph every tiny revision line by line. What a relief for you. What a gift to them. (Figure 1.2 offers six reasons for teaching the traits as part of your writing curriculum.)

And finally, keep in mind that this book isn't *just* about success in grade school or high school or college, or even improving scores on state tests. It is about students becoming strong and confident writers for *life*—in any context, for any purpose.

The College Board's National Commission on Writing issued a report in 2003 (*The Neglected "R": The Need for a Writing Revolution*) that cites several critical writing skills students need to work successfully in a twenty-first-century environment. Among them are "first-rate organization" (16), ability to generate "convincing and elaborate" text, the use of "rich, evocative and compelling language" (17), knowledge of "mechanics of grammar and punctuation" and a "'voice' and . . . feel for the audience" (20). Do these traits sound familiar? We should not be surprised. The six traits are, after all, the very foundation of good writing—not some superficial extension, but the essence of writing itself.

This same report points out that many Americans "would not be able to hold their positions if they were not excellent writers" (10). But this is only the beginning. "At its best," the report continues, "writing has helped transform the world. Revolutions have been started by it. Oppression has been toppled by it. And it has enlightened the human condition. American life has been richer because people like Rachel Carson, Cesar Chavez, Thomas Jefferson, and Martin Luther King, Jr., have given voice to the aspirations of the nation and its people. And it has become fuller because writers like James Baldwin, William Faulkner, Toni Morrison, and Edith Wharton have explored the range of human misery and joy" (10).

Our student writers will soon add their voices to the mix. What sorts of things will they write about? With each year, we view our solar system and indeed our whole universe differently. New moons and planets appear, while others, like Pluto, retire. Through DNA research, we track the genetic history of the human adventure, discovering ancestors, cultures, and landscapes we never imagined. Facebook changes the very definition of "friend," while blogs and tweets topple regimes and reshape our world. We uncover life forms we didn't know existed, conduct heroic rescues, predict natural disasters and cope with the aftermath, create customized "super" foods to sustain life, design cars that anticipate accidents, and develop virtual relationships with computers that read *us*.

What will help us to understand, recall, or connect these events to our own lives? Writing. In their capacity as writers, our students will document the human story through film and television scripts, dramas, speeches, textbooks, greeting cards, cartoons, journals, poems, advertisements, picture books, novels, editorials, song lyrics, blogs, wikis, podcasts, and more. We will all, through most of our working lives, be

---

FIGURE 1.2

6 Reasons for Teaching the 6 Traits

1. **Building students' understanding** of concepts like "voice"
2. **Providing language** for thinking and talking about writing
3. **Giving students options** for revising
4. **Teaching students to think**—by making them evaluators
5. **Connecting reading and writing** through mentor texts
6. **Putting students in charge** of their own writing process

© 2012 Vicki Spandel

You write in order to change the world . . .

—James Baldwin
In Mary Pipher, *Writing to Change the World,* 2006, Introduction

---

In the past 30 years, researchers and theorists have come to know that teaching writing entails teaching thinking.

—George Hillocks Jr.
The Testing Trap: How State Writing Assessments Control Learning, 2002, 6

writing to inform, record, define, and explain; to condense, summarize, and interpret; to teach, persuade, amuse, or inspire. And because, as Mem Fox (1993, 38) tells us, "No one writes for no one to read," knowing how to touch a reader's soul can only help us to do it better.

Who Invented the 6 Traits?

Author's Note

The term *rubric* has a certain connotation that I happen to not like very much. Rubrics are descriptions, not sets of rules or laws. They are living, breathing documents that need to be flexible enough to change as our thinking about writing expands and deepens. I prefer the term *writing guide* because it suggests just what this document should do: serve as a *guide to revision*.

No one. Though the number of persons who take credit for having "invented" or "developed" the six traits seems to grow geometrically each year, the truth is that the traits themselves are not *anyone's* invention. Like stars or planets awaiting discovery, the traits have been around as long as writing itself and are an inherent part of what makes writing work. It is impossible to write without ideas, words, sentences, or conventions of *some* kind, without organizing information or giving voice to the message. What *is* new (within the past three decades) is a written description of what the traits *look like* at different levels of performance. In other words, a *rubric,* or *writing guide*—a term I prefer.

The original six-trait guide for assessing and teaching writing came *not* from a publisher, governmental agency, or national laboratory, but *from teachers.* It was developed in 1984 by the Analytical Writing Assessment Committee, a group of seventeen teachers from the Beaverton, Oregon school district with whom I was privileged to work. These teachers wanted a better way of assessing and teaching writing. They wanted to be able to talk to their writers in conferences, to encourage them about what was going well and help them figure out problems they couldn't solve on their own. They invited me to help.

We understood from the beginning that to meet the district's goals we had to identify the qualities that make writing work. So we read and read—and read some more. In all, we read more than 15,000 student papers, grades 3 through 12, and took

endless notes, identifying those things that separated the truly successful papers from those that were "just making a beginning" or "about halfway home." And when we compared notes, we found that we were all, every single one of us, influenced by the same six qualities that became known as the six traits. The notes we made were combined and revised multiple times, and gradually they evolved into a six-trait rubric or writing guide. See Figure 1.3 for an in-process draft of the original with my handwritten notes. (For more information on the history of the six-trait model—including the pioneering work of Paul Diederich—please see Appendix 1.)

FIGURE 1.3

In-Process Draft of the Original Six-Trait Rubric

Spandel, 1985—Beaverton edition.

IDEAS AND CONTENT (Development)

an understanding of life—a knack for picking out what is significant.

5: This paper is clear, focused ~~and interesting~~. *and* It holds the reader's attention. Relevant anecdotes and details enrich the central theme or story line. Ideas are fresh and original.

- The writer seems to be writing from *knowledge or* experiences and shows insight: ~~a good sense of how events unfold, how people respond to life and to each other.~~

- ~~Supporting,~~ *Relevant,* telling details give the reader important information that ~~he or she could not personally bring to the text.~~ *goes beyond what's obvious or predictable.*

- ~~The writing balance. Main ideas stand out.~~

Every piece adds something to the whole.

- The writer seems in control and develops the topic in an enlightening, ~~entertaining~~ *purposeful* way, *that makes a point or tells a story.*

- ~~The writer works with and shapes ideas, making connections and sharing insights.~~

3: The paper is clear and focused. *coming into focus* ~~The topic shows promise,~~ even though development is still ~~limited, sketchy~~ or general. *basic*

- The writer is beginning to define the topic, ~~but is not there yet.~~ It is pretty easy to see where the writer is headed, though more information is needed to "fill in the blanks."

- The writer does seem to be ~~writing from~~ *using his or her knowledge or* experience, but has some trouble going from general observations to specifics.

- Ideas are reasonably clear ~~and purposeful,~~ even though they may not be ~~explicit,~~ detailed, personalized, or expanded to show indepth understanding, *or a strong sense of purpose.*

- Support is attempted, but doesn't go far enough yet in ~~expanding, clarifying, or~~ *fleshing out the main point or storyline.* ~~adding new insights.~~

- ~~Themes or main points seem a blend of the original and the predictable.~~ *Details often ... with ...*

1: As yet, the paper has no clear sense of purpose or central theme. To extract meaning from the text, the reader must make inferences based on sketchy details. ~~More than one of the following problems is likely to be evident.~~ *The writing reflects more than one of these problems:*

- Information is very limited or unclear.

- The text ~~is very~~ *may be* repetitive, or reads *may* like a collection of random thoughts from which no central theme emerges.

- Everything seems as important as everything else; the reader has a hard time sifting out what's critical.

- The writer has not yet begun to define the topic in a meaningful or personal way.

- The writer ~~may still be~~ *is* in search of a real topic or ~~sense of direction to guide development.~~

A Quick Overview

Following are definitions of each trait, together with examples that show the traits in action.

IDEAS . . .

The heart of it all, the writer's main message together with all the details that support or expand that message.

Example

Detail is the sine qua non of all good description—as in this passage where Roald Dahl (*Boy*, 2009, 108) helps us picture Captain Hardcastle:

On the football field he wore white running shorts and white gymshoes and short white socks. His legs were as hard and thin as a ram's legs and the skin around his calves was almost exactly the color of mutton fat. The hair on his head was not ginger. It was a brilliant dark vermilion, like a ripe orange. . . . The parting in his hair was a white line straight down the middle of the scalp, so straight it could only have been made with a ruler. On either side of the parting you could see the comb tracks running back through the greasy orange hair like little tramlines.

ORGANIZATION . . .

The internal structure or design that guides a reader through a story, explanation, or discussion.

Example

Good organization involves creative and logical design, connections between ideas, and a conclusion that leaves us thinking—and often, wanting more. It all begins, however, with a strong lead, words that pull us in and won't let go, like these words that open Gus Lee's riveting novel *China Boy* (1991, 1):

The sky collapsed like an old roof in an avalanche of rock and boulder, cracking me on the noggin and crushing me to the pavement. Through a fog of hot tears and slick blood I heard words that at once sounded distant and entirely too close. It was the Voice of Doom.

"China Boy," said Big Willie Mack in his deep and easy slum basso, "I be from Fist City. Gimme yo' lunch money, ratface."

VOICE

The writer's fingerprints on the page, that special something that keeps readers reading.

Examples

Voice can chill the blood or warm the heart. It can have comic overtones—as in this passage from *The Wednesday Wars* by Gary D. Schmidt (2007, 119). Middle schooler Holling Hoodhood has marched through a blizzard to take a standardized achievement test. Expecting the room to be frigid, he is amazed (and dismayed) to discover the radiators are working overtime:

The room was now downright tropical. And I had on thermal underwear—thermal underwear that was supposed to keep me warm in minus-ten-degree temperatures. I was starting to sweat everywhere—even my fingernails—and I think that I was probably turning the color of the rusted radiators.

Voice can also be intensely serious, as in the closing chapter from *Sugar Changed the World* by Marc Aronson and Marina Budhos (2010, 125):

Sugar turned human beings into property, yet sugar led people to reject the idea that any person could be owned by another. Sugar murdered millions, and yet it gave the voiceless a way to speak.

WORD CHOICE . . .

Words or phrases that clarify meaning or create an image or impression in the reader's mind.

Examples

In *Brave Irene* (2011, unpaginated), author William Steig uses strong verbs to show how the wind, like a persistent thief, tries to snatch a valuable bundle from the hands of the plucky Irene:

The wind wrestled her for the package—walloped it, twisted it, shook it, snatched at it.

In informational writing, precise word choice defines a concept—like *terminal velocity*—as in this passage from "The Cats That Fly by Themselves" by David Quammen (*The Boilerplate Rhino*, 2000, 118):

Terminal velocity is the speed at which a body falling through air stops accelerating. The force of gravity (which corresponds to body weight) reaches equilibrium with the force of air resistance (which corresponds to the size, shape, and posture of the falling body), and at that point of equilibrium, the speed of descent remains constant . . . A plummeting human will reach terminal velocity at about 120 miles per hour. For a plummeting cat . . . the figure is just forty miles per hour.

SENTENCE FLUENCY . . .

Rhythm and flow, the music and poetry of language—how it all plays to the ear.

Example

The name Sandra Cisneros is virtually synonymous with fluency—and this writer shows us definitively how breaking the rules can be every bit as effective as following them. In *The House on Mango Street* (1989, 74), her prose dances over the page with such grace that we forget all about sentence variety and celebrate the beauty of rhetorical echoes sounding their notes in all the right places:

Four skinny trees with skinny necks and pointy elbows like mine. Four who do not belong here but are here. Four raggedy excuses planted by the city. . . . Their strength is secret. They send ferocious roots beneath the ground. They grow up and they grow down and grab the earth between their hairy toes and bite the sky with violent teeth and never quit their anger.

CONVENTIONS & PRESENTATION . . .

Skill in using an editor's tools (punctuation, spelling, grammar, capitalization, paragraphing, and design) to enhance readability and meaning, while giving readers access to information.

An Example of Conventions at Work

Conventions are about editorial correctness—and so much more. Consider how conventions help you to read the following passage from *Lousy, Rotten, Stinkin' Grapes* by Margie Palatini (2009, unpaginated) in precisely the way the author intended:

"Excellent! Look and listen. Here's the plan," explained Fox. "You stand—here. I will stand on your head—there. On the count of three—you give a bit of a boost—and voila! Grapes!"

Author's Note

The trait of *Conventions & Presentation* was originally known simply as *Conventions*. *Presentation* has a far more meaningful role to play than it did in 1984 when most student pieces were handwritten. In this technological age, most writers have computer access and much more control over document design than ever before—even when working at home. *Presentation*, as we think of it, now includes such factors as font selection, use of color or white (empty) space, use and placement of illustrations, charts, or graphs—and a myriad of related issues. *Conventions & Presentation* work together to ensure that a document is ready for publication.

As for Presentation . . .

Take a moment to leaf quickly through the book you are reading right now. Pay attention to the overall look of the pages, the placement of illustrations and figures. You will notice variations in font style and size, some purely for aesthetics and some done to draw your eye to certain parts of the text. You will also notice features such as boxes, shading, or bulleted lists, designed to help you, the reader, find or scan information easily and quickly. Are there other books and documents around you right now? Take a moment to notice covers or illustrations. Think about where your eye is drawn, or where you linger longest. Color and design are used to package a message so that number one, you'll notice it, and two, you'll remember it.

Responding to Student Writing

To really understand the traits, to get right inside them, you need to work with them personally by responding to samples of writing. In introducing the traits, I like to use "The Redwoods" and "Mouse Alert" (see Figures 1.4 and 1.5).

Reading and responding to these papers right now will help define the traits in your own mind. You can also use them when introducing the traits to students or to adults (colleagues, parents). Begin by

- reading each paper aloud,
- having participants talk about the paper with partners or in small groups, and finally,
- identifying those traits that you think are especially strong or weak in each paper.

Reading aloud is important. We are very visual in our response to writing, and hearing a piece causes us to assess with our ears—not just our eyes. Your ears will tell you far more about voice or fluency than your eyes alone ever could.

Note: Don't use a writing guide (or rubric) right now. Use your own judgment about what is strong or weak in each paper. If possible, print copies of the papers so you can make notes or underline moments that stand out.

Questions to Ask about "The Redwoods"

Here are four interesting questions to ask about the paper titled "The Redwoods":

1. What are the strongest—and weakest—traits, in your opinion?
2. Is the writer male or female?
3. How old is the writer?
4. What writing assignment prompted this piece?

What are the strongest— and weakest—traits?

Most readers (teachers and students alike) see conventions as the strength of the piece. (That's sad in a way because no one ever says, "You've *got* to read this book—remarkable conventions.")

FIGURE 1.4

The Redwoods

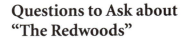

Last year, we went on a vacation and we had a wonderful time. The weather was sunny and warm and there was lots to do, so we were never bored.

My parents visited friends and took pictures for their friends back home. My brother and I swam and also hiked in the woods. When we got tired of that, we just ate and had a wonderful time.

It was exciting and fun to be together as a family and to do things together. I love my family, and this is a time that I will remember for a long time. I hope we will go back again next year for more fun and an even better time than we had this year.

Occasionally someone mentions organization as a relative strength. The weakest trait, for most readers, is voice. But close seconds are ideas (no detail) and word choice (everything was just so *wonderful*). Here are a few recurring comments:

- *Boring—it put me right to sleep.*
- *Safe.*
- *The person was writing just to get it done.*
- *It doesn't say anything.*
- *What Redwoods? The title doesn't go with the paper.*

Is the writer male or female?

Readers are divided about whether this writer is male or female (*female* is correct). This is an interesting question to ask because it's a good lead-in to teaching voice. Voice, after all, is the person behind the words. So—what sort of person do you picture or hear? The first things most of us try to identify in a writer are sex and age. Which brings us to the next question . . .

How old is the writer?

Many people initially hear this as a first or second grade piece, but the strength of the conventions gives them pause. The most popular answers are third and fourth grade. But middle school teachers often say, "I have kids who write *just* like this. I *know* it's a middle school student." All these guesses, however, are wrong. Actually, the writer is an eleventh grader.

Knowing the grade level leads to some intriguing discussions about assumptions we routinely make as we read. Teachers often say, "Well, for *eleventh* grade I expected more, you know? If you'd told me it was third grade, I would have felt different." But would they really? Would *you*?

I agree that the conventions would be excellent if this were a third grade paper. But would it *say* more? Or would we say, "Well, for grade 3, this is a powerhouse in voice." No. When the voice is missing, it is just missing.

Still, as one teacher pointed out, "Look, she's in eleventh grade, and she wants to go vacationing with her family. I'd like to give her a couple points for that." Me, too. There's a likable tone to this piece that makes me want to say, "Come out of hiding. I know you have more to share."

What was the assignment?

You might be thinking that the assignment was some offshoot of the cliché "My Summer Vacation"—or "A Time with My Family"—but you would be mistaken. You could guess for a year and not come up with it, so let me end the suspense: The assignment was to *describe an experience in which the five senses play an important part.* If you've been to the Redwoods in California, felt the mist on your face, felt the bark, stared up at gigantic trees that provide a built-in ecosystem for hundreds of animals and plants, trees so big they make their own rain, then you can appreciate what a stellar topic choice this was. Perfect. But it's never *just* the topic—it's what you do with it.

Questions to Ask about "Mouse Alert"

Ask the same four questions about this paper—plus one more:

1. What are the strongest—and weakest—traits, in your opinion?
2. Is the writer male or female?
3. How old is the writer?

FIGURE 1.5

Mouse Alert

As soon as school was out, we left on vacation. Nothing went the way it was supposed to. Dad backed into a tree on the way out of the driveway, pushing the bike rack through the rear window and nearly scaring my sister to death. She was cranky the rest of the trip. We had to take our other car, which is smaller and you can't hook the bike rack up to it. Now my sister and me were crowded together so much she kept complaining about me breathing on her and taking up all her air and foot room. Plus now Dad knew a big bill would be waiting for him when we got home. It put everyone in a lovely trip starting mood.

We were supposed to go to Yellowstone Park. Well, actually, we did but just barely. I think we hold the world's record for shortest time spent in the park. This was all due to my mother's new attitude toward animals. The night before yellowstone we stayed in a cabin on the edge of the park. It had a lot of mice, but most of them had the good sense to stay hidden in the walls. One poor furry guy had a death wish and showed himself. The whole family went into action. My father got a broom, which looked like an oversized weapon for a mouse. My mother hugged her pink flanel nightgown around her knees, jumped up on a wood chair and started shrieking "Kill him! Kill him!" Her eyes were as big as her fists. I had never seen her quite so blood thirsty.

My sister spent the whole time dancing on the bed crying her eyes out and yelling, "Don't kill it Dad! Don't kill it!" It was up to Dad and me to trap it. We got it in a pickle jar and took it down to the lake and let it go. It seemed really happy to get away from us. I thought I knew how it felt.

The next day we raced through Yellowstone and then headed home. My Mother said she had enough of animals. For weeks afterwards, this was the big story she told everyone who asked about our vacation. You'd have thought the whole point of our trip was to go on a mouse hunt. Dad said all the money we saved by not staying at Yellowstone could go to pay for the broken car window, so for him the trip worked out perfect. As for me, I'm still planning to get back to Yellowstone one day. I want to see something bigger than a mouse.

4. What was the writing assignment that prompted this piece?
5. Could you make a movie of this?

What are the strongest—and weakest—traits?

Students love this paper—so do teachers. True, there are minor problems with conventions, many more than in "The Redwoods," but the text is also more complex.

Most readers identify voice and ideas as the strongest traits. My litmus test for voice is always whether I would read the piece aloud to a friend. In this case, yes, I would. I would not read "The Redwoods" aloud for fun—and am assuming you would not, either.

The weakest trait, most people agree, is conventions. Interestingly, however, many a veteran teacher reads through this piece barely noticing the errors. This is understandable. We tend to be forgiving of conventional errors when we are having a good time. If the writer of "The Redwoods" made this many errors, we might be downright annoyed.

Teachers' comments on "Mouse Alert" typically include these:

- *I can just see it. I feel like I'm in that car. (Actually, I was once.)*
- *I love this piece because I identify with it—I feel as if I'm reading about my own family.*
- *I love the line "Her eyes were as big as her fists."*
- *This writer is having a good time.*
- *This is a story teller—can I get him next year?*
- *It comes full circle—great organization.*
- *I love how this writer doesn't try to tell us everything.*
- *You get every point of view—even the mouse's!*

Is the writer male or female?

Readers nearly always hear this writer as male, perhaps because the writer helps Dad rescue and release the mouse. But—that might be a stereotype. This writer is female. Does that surprise you?

How old is the writer?

Almost always, readers hear this as a middle school voice, and this time, they're right. It's a seventh grader.

What was the assignment?

The assignment for this paper was very general and open—"An experience you still remember." That can be just about anything, and a writer with imagination (like this one) will sift through memories and come upon the one that feels just right. Make no mistake, though: Identifying the moment that will make a fine story is a skill. (More about this in Chapter 3.)

Could you make a movie of this?

To test the strength of ideas (in any piece of writing—not just this one), I often ask students, "Could you make a movie of it?" I cannot imagine—nor can they—a film of "The Redwoods." But they immediately get excited about a film version of "Mouse Alert." Why? Maybe because it's already a video in our heads. We see Dad backing into the tree. We see Mom in her pink nightgown and hear the sister shrieking as she bounces on the bed. We smell the juice in that pickle jar, and cheer as the terrified but relieved mouse makes his escape. Students even cast the movie, putting Chevy Chase or Steve Martin in the role of Dad.

What Teachers Value in Writing

We have seen how teachers responded to "The Redwoods" and to "Mouse Alert." Take additional teacher comments, based on responses to *many* pieces of writing, group them together by trait, and the result is Figure 1.6: *What Teachers Value in Writing*.

Most likely you see many things on this list that *you* value as well. Understand, though: A list, however complete, is not yet a writing guide. Why not? Because it does not yet define performance at multiple levels. Put these same qualities along a performance continuum that ranges from a beginning level (score of 1) to strong or proficient (5 or 6), and you have a guide or rubric.

The writing guide in this chapter (see Figure 1.7) is intended to cover virtually *any* type of prose writing that is not research-based: narrative, expository, persuasive,

FIGURE 1.6

What Teachers Value in Writing

IDEAS

Clear—makes sense
Topic narrowed to manageable size
Has a key message (or messages)
Teaches me something
Holds my attention
Fresh, original perspective
Important, telling details
Details go beyond common knowledge
Minimal filler (unneeded information)
Insight
Authenticity
New information

WORD CHOICE

"Just right" words
Memorable words—worth highlighting, quoting
Creates word pictures, movies in the mind
Accurate, precise
Enlightening—helps me "get it"
Strong verbs
Easy on the modifiers (adjectives, adverbs)
Simple, everyday language used well
Repeats as necessary—or for effect
Concise and to the point
Uses language to teach, not impress
Uses terminology well (as needed)

ORGANIZATION

Inviting lead that draws me in
Starts somewhere, goes somewhere
Compelling sense of direction
Provides connections—detail to detail,
   thought to thought, paragraph to paragraph
Well-paced, spending time where it matters
Easy to follow—like a good road map
Satisfying conclusion—sense of resolution
An occasional surprise
Not formulaic or too predictable
Organization supports the message or story

SENTENCE FLUENCY

Easy to read on the first try
Has rhythm, flow, cadence
Easy to read with voice, expression
Carefully crafted sentences
Variety in length, structure . . . OR
Repetition of patterns for effect
Concise, direct sentences in informational or technical writing
Fragments used only for effect
Run-ons used only for effect (as in dialogue)
Authentic dialogue
Consistency in tense (past, present, future)

VOICE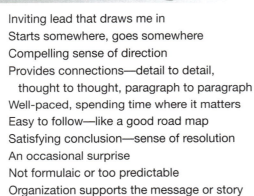

Sounds like this writer and no other
Writer is "at home" in the writing
Writer seems engaged by the topic
Brings topic to life for me, the reader
Shows concern for me as a reader
Individual, distinctive—unlike others
Makes me cry, laugh, get chills
Confident—the writer knows his/her stuff
Lively, energetic, passionate
Writing I want to reread or share

CONVENTIONS & PRESENTATION

Clean, carefully edited text
No distracting errors
No "mental editing" needed
Conventions guide reader
Conventions support meaning and voice
Design draws reader's eye to key points
Design makes information easy to find
Free of distracting visuals, hard-to-read fonts
Uses graphics as needed to enhance text
Makes good use of white (open) space

FIGURE 1.7

Teacher Six-Point Writing Guide

IDEAS

6
- Clear, focused, compelling, holds reader's attention
- Strong main point, idea, story line
- Striking insight, in-depth knowledge of topic
- Takes reader on journey of understanding
- Significant, intriguing details paint a vivid picture

5
- Clear and focused
- Evident main point, idea, story line
- Reflects thorough knowledge of topic
- Authentic, intriguing information
- Important, helpful, well-chosen details

4
- Clear and focused more often than not
- Main point, story line easily inferred
- Sufficient knowledge for broad overview
- Some new info, some common knowledge
- Quality details outweigh generalities

3
- Some undeveloped text—or a list
- Reader must work to get the message
- Gaps in writer's knowledge of topic
- Mostly common knowledge, best guesses
- Generalities, broad brush strokes

2
- Writer still defining, shaping message
- Main idea or message hard to infer
- Writer struggles to fill space
- Broad, unsupported generalities
- Repetition, filler, minimal support

1
- Minimal text
- Topic not defined yet in writer's mind
- Reader left with many questions
- Notes, first thoughts
- Writer needs help choosing/defining topic

ORGANIZATION

6
- Thoughtful structure guides reader through text
- Provocative opening, satisfying conclusion
- Well-crafted transitions create coherence
- Balanced pacing—slows or speeds up as needed
- Easy to follow—may have a surprise or two

5
- Purposeful organization, sense of direction
- Strong lead, conclusion provides closure
- Thoughtful transitions connect ideas
- Good pacing—time spent on what matters
- Easy to follow—stays on track

4
- Organization supports message/story
- Functional lead and conclusion
- Helpful transitions keep ideas flowing
- Balanced—most time spent on key points
- Easy to follow—sometimes predictable

3
- Organization somewhat loose—or formulaic
- Lead and/or conclusion need work
- Transitions sometimes needed—or overdone
- Too much time spent on trivia
- Not always easy to follow without work

2
- Order more random than purposeful
- Lead/conclusion missing or formulaic
- Transitions unclear or missing
- Hard to tell what points matter most
- Requires rereading to follow writer's thinking

1
- No clear sense of direction
- Starts right in (no lead)— just stops (no ending)
- A challenge to follow the writer's thinking
- Everything is as important as everything else
- Writer needs help sorting/organizing ideas

VOICE

6
- As individual as fingerprints
- Writer AND reader love sharing this aloud
- Mirrors writer's innermost thoughts, feelings
- Passionate, vibrant, electric, compelling
- Pulls reader right into the piece

5
- Original, distinctive
- A good read-aloud candidate
- Reveals writer's thoughts, feelings
- Spontaneous, lively, enthusiastic
- Shows sensitivity to readers

4
- Stands out from many others
- Share-aloud moments
- Writer seems "present" in the piece
- Earnest, sincere
- Shows awareness of readers

3
- Sporadic—voice comes and goes
- Not quite ready to share, but getting there
- Needs more voice—or a different voice
- Restrained, quiet, cautious
- Reader awareness? Sometimes, perhaps . . .

2
- Writer not really "at home" in this writing
- Hint of voice—or we could be reading in
- Reader cannot tell who writer is
- Distant, encyclopedic—or wrong for the purpose
- Not yet "writing to be read"

1
- No sense of person behind the words—yet
- Writer is not ready to share this piece
- Writer's thoughts/feelings do not come through
- Something (topic choice?) is stifling the voice
- Writer needs help with topic—or voice

© 2012. *Creating Writers: 6 Traits, Process, Workshop, and Literature* 6/e by Vicki Spandel. Allyn & Bacon, an imprint of Pearson Education, Inc. All rights reserved. Used with permission.

What Teachers Value in Writing

13

FIGURE 1.7

Teacher Six-Point Writing Guide

WORD CHOICE

6
- ☐ Clear, fresh, original language adds voice
- ☐ Quotable—the right word at the right moment
- ☐ Every word counts—any repetition is purposeful
- ☐ Powerful verbs, unique phrasing, memorable moments
- ☐ Words create vivid message, striking images/impressions

5
- ☐ Natural language used well, confidently
- ☐ Engaging—moments to remember or highlight
- ☐ Concise yet expressive—a good balance
- ☐ Strong verbs, striking expressions
- ☐ Words create a clear message, image, impression

4
- ☐ Functional, clear language used correctly
- ☐ Understandable—sometimes noteworthy
- ☐ Minimal wordiness or unintended repetition
- ☐ Strong moments—few clichés, overwritten text
- ☐ Words help reader get the "big picture"

3
- ☐ Vague words (*special, great*)—OR thesaurus overload
- ☐ An occasional stand-out moment
- ☐ Moments may need pruning—or expansion
- ☐ Writer rarely stretches for individual expression
- ☐ Images/impressions still coming into focus

2
- ☐ Words may be unclear, vague, or overused
- ☐ Writer settles for first words that come to mind
- ☐ Fuzziness, wordiness, unintended repetition
- ☐ Words lack energy, life, vitality
- ☐ Reader must work to "see" and "feel" the message

1
- ☐ Getting words on paper seems a struggle
- ☐ Word choice feels random—not a real "choice"
- ☐ Writer says very little—or repeats a lot
- ☐ Overworked words—*nice, good, fun*—flatten voice
- ☐ Writer needs help with message or wording

SENTENCE FLUENCY

6
- ☐ Easy to read with inflection that brings out voice
- ☐ Rhythm you want to imitate—poetic, musical
- ☐ Striking variety in sentence style, structure, length
- ☐ Fragments or repetition rhetorically effective
- ☐ Strong sentences make meaning instantly clear

5
- ☐ Readable even on the first try
- ☐ Easy-on-the-ear rhythm, cadence, flow
- ☐ Variety in sentence style, structure, length
- ☐ Fragments or repetition add emphasis
- ☐ Readily understandable

4
- ☐ Readable with minimal rehearsal
- ☐ Pleasant, rhythmic flow dominates
- ☐ Some sentence variety
- ☐ Fragments or repetition are not a problem
- ☐ Sentences are clear and connected

3
- ☐ Readable with rehearsal and close attention
- ☐ Sentence-to-sentence flow needs work
- ☐ More sentence variety needed
- ☐ A few moments cry out for revision
- ☐ Sentences not always clear at first

2
- ☐ Hard to read in spots, even with rehearsal
- ☐ Many sentences need rewording
- ☐ Minimal variety in length or structure
- ☐ Problems (choppiness, run-ons) disrupt the flow
- ☐ Reader must pause or reread to get meaning

1
- ☐ Reader must pause or fill in to read this aloud
- ☐ Many sentences need rewording
- ☐ Hard to tell where sentences begin or end
- ☐ Sentence problems may block meaning
- ☐ Writer needs help revising sentences

CONVENTIONS & PRESENTATION

6
- ☐ Only the pickiest editors will spot problems
- ☐ Creative use of conventions enhances meaning, voice
- ☐ Complex text shows off writer's editorial control
- ☐ Enticing, eye-catching presentation
- ☐ Virtually ready to publish

5
- ☐ Minor errors that are easily overlooked
- ☐ Correct conventions support meaning, voice
- ☐ Shows writer's control over numerous conventions
- ☐ Pleasing, effective presentation
- ☐ Ready to publish with light touch-ups

4
- ☐ Errors are noticeable but not troublesome
- ☐ Errors do not interfere with the message
- ☐ Shows control over basics (most spelling, punctuation)
- ☐ Acceptable presentation
- ☐ Good once-over needed prior to publication

3
- ☐ Noticeable errors may slow reader
- ☐ Reader may pause to mentally "correct" text
- ☐ Some problems even on basics
- ☐ More attention to presentation needed
- ☐ Thorough editing required prior to publication

2
- ☐ Distracting or repeated errors
- ☐ Errors may interfere with writer's message
- ☐ Shaky control over basics—reads like a hasty first draft
- ☐ Immediately noticeable problems with presentation
- ☐ Line-by-line editing needed prior to publication

1
- ☐ Serious, frequent errors make reading a challenge
- ☐ Reader must "decode" before focusing on message
- ☐ Writer not yet in control of basic conventions
- ☐ Writing not yet ready for final design or presentation
- ☐ Writer needs help with editing

descriptive, and so on. It is formatted here as a "One-Pager," which many teachers find handy because, as the name suggests, everything is right there on one page (front and back). Please note that if a piece requires research (that is, the writer cannot pull the information out of his or her head, but must consult an outside source), you should use the Informational Writing Guide (Figure 9.1, Chapter 9).

What Happened to the Five-Point Scale?

The original six-trait rubric was based on a five-point scale defined at three levels: 5, 3, and 1. This came about because as the Beaverton team was reading and making notes, we also *ranked* the writing samples, sorting them into three piles: strong, midlevel, and beginning. It was logical to move from these rankings to a five-point scale, with a score of 5 representing strong performance; a score of 3, midlevel; and a score of 1, the beginning level. Scores of 4 and 2 were seen as "compromises." Only a few people use the five-point scale these days, and so, for purposes of simplification, it does not appear in this chapter. However, some people do like it because of the richness of the language. You can find a copy in Appendix 2.

Leaping the River with the Six-Point Scale

The six-point scale was developed partly to provide a way of responding to those papers that exceeded expectations—the 5+ papers, we might say. Such papers could be considered exemplars, or papers you could teach from: *"This is what I mean by strong word choice."*

In addition, the six-point scale eliminated a big problem—namely, assigning too many 3s. When raters (or classroom teachers) get tired, they tend to see *everything* as a 3 (lunch, the weather, you name it). But on a five-point scale, a score of 3—maddeningly right there in the middle—doesn't tell us whether strengths outweigh problems or vice versa, and for assessment purposes, this is troublesome. The six-point scale requires a rater to make a choice: A 3 is a midlevel score tending *down*. A 4 is a midlevel score tending *up*.

I nicknamed the six-point scale the "Leaping the River" model because as you cross from 3 to 4, it's like leaping into the "land of proficiency." Remember jumping a creek as a child? Maybe you barely got to the other side, pulling yourself up by a tree branch— that's a 4, a "just made it." Or maybe your feet found no purchase, and you slipped down the muddy bank and into the water—that's a 3, an "almost." The scale is designed to separate the *just-made-its* from the *almosts* with this fundamental question: *Does it leap the river?*

Remember: It's the Discussion That Matters—*Not* the Scores

When you teach the traits to students, use scoring as a basis for generating discussion. If some students think a piece is a 5 or 6, while others think it's a 3 or 4, you have an outstanding basis for conversation about what constitutes good writing. The scores themselves are just stepping stones into that conversation.

Many years ago, psychologists found that there is a limit to what we can hold in short-term memory and the number of criteria we can use in making absolute judgments. George A. Miller (1956) called it "the magic number 7, plus or minus 2."

—George Hillocks Jr.
The Testing Trap: How State Writing Assessments Control Learning, 2002, 6

Author's Note

Don't stop with scoring! Highlight strong passages and talk about what the writer did that worked. If the piece has problems, discuss what you would do to revise it—or better yet, *do* the revision. You don't necessarily have to revise a whole piece. Focus on the lead or conclusion. Spark up the verbs. Add two or three details. Practicing revision on someone else's work is one of the BEST ways of learning to write well. Every problematic paper you come across—"The Redwoods" included—is a lesson or series of lessons waiting to happen.

For other writing guides . . .

What about a "leap-the-river" version of the One-Pager writing guide?
See Chapters 3 through 8 for the same writing guide, in trait by trait, leap-the-river format.

What about a student-friendly version of this writing guide?
Ready to go. Check Chapters 3 through 8 for trait by trait student versions.

What if I prefer a five-point scale?
In the Appendix you will find three-level scales for both teachers (Appendix 2) and students (Appendix 3). I have modified them so that they can be used as five- or six-point scales—your choice. These scales have the advantage of richer language because performance is defined only at three levels: beginning (1 or 1–2 split), developing (3 or 3–4 split), and strong (5 or 5–6 split).

Where will I find a Spanish translation?
See Appendix 4 for a Student Writing Guide in Spanish. See Appendix 5 for a Student Checklist in Spanish.

FIGURE 1.8

Basking in Entertainment
A Personal Essay by Kaylee (Grade 5)

The idea of going on vacation with your family might make you fall asleep. It might make you scream. It might make your lunch squirm around in your stomach. At least at one point in your life, you probably thought exactly this: Why do my parents make such a big deal about taking me on vacation? Well, I can think of lots of reasons why they'd make a big deal out of it. And I think you should too.

It's important to go on vacation with your family, because you get good food.

"I'm starved!" I moaned, "I'm dying of hungriness!"

"Don't worry. We'll get food soon," my dad said calmly.

I couldn't believe he wasn't hungry. We'd been strolling down the streets of Monterey ALL DAY.

"Does soon mean now?" my sister, Emily, asked.

"No – wait! Yes!" my mom replied.

Everyone cheered. My mom pointed to a crepe place down the street. We tore off down the road, pushing past people, our stomachs growling the whole way. We didn't care if we looked like crazy chickens. Our minds were set on one thing: FOOD. Even my mom was running. My dad wasn't, though, so we had to wait even longer while he caught up to us. Finally, we got the crepes. Food had never tasted this good. My teeth sank into the thin, creamy pancake full of strawberries. Maybe I can be a magician when I grow up, I was thinking, because my crepe disappeared like magic. It's REALLY important to go on vacation with your family, because you get good food.

Another reason going on vacation with your family is important is because you don't have to worry about your house burning down. (All your stuff's with you!) One day, my friend Kira was sitting in front of her fireplace, when SNAP! The fire turned into Rice Krispies. CRACKLE! POP! Kira's heart was beating fast. She was breathing so hard, she almost ran out of air. Kira's eyes were fixed on the fire. Sparks were flying. She thought about peering up the chimney, but decided not to. She didn't want to watch her house catch on fire. Because sparks are so bouncy, she was sure they'd jump up there and land on the roof. Her brain was telling her to frantically run around the house and grab everything she could, but apparently Kira's legs weren't listening. They stayed right where they were. Lucky for her, she didn't need to run around screaming. The house didn't catch on fire. But if she'd been on vacation, she wouldn't have even known there were giant sparks in her fireplace.

Perhaps the most important reason to go on vacation with your family is because, even if it's in your own backyard, it's special. One time, my friend Kari and I were making a tropical resort for my mom to "Stay at for a week" in my backyard. We tried to make it as real as possible. We tacked dolphin photos on trees, wrote room numbers on cards, and set out tiny cups of milk. When my mom came, we'd tell her it was coconut milk. After two hours of preparing magic tricks for entertainment, and food in case mom wanted room service, we were ready. Kari and I made a grand entrance into the house.

"Would you like to stay in our 5 star resort and bask in entertainment?" we asked.

Of course my mom had to say yes.

I let out a quick "Yippee!" then went back to being an owner of a fancy resort. We led my mom to the refreshment table.

"Would you like some coconut milk?"

My mom picked up a cup and took a sip. "Blech!"

Because we were kids, we immediately wanted to find out how horrible it tasted. It definitely was a 0 on the great beverage scale. Because my mom hated coconut milk in the first place, she really believed that it was coconut milk. Or at least she pretended to believe it. I will never forget that "coconut milk." Yep. Even if it's in your own backyard, it's special.

This makes me realize that vacationing with your family isn't just for fun. It's for making memories to last a lifetime.

Warming Up with the One-Pager

Our earlier assessment of "The Redwoods" and "Mouse Alert" focused on personal responses—but likely you have an idea about how you would score both papers. To give you more of a challenge, let's look at a new piece, also on the vacation theme. It's "Basking in Entertainment" by fifth grader Kaylee (Figure 1.8). Read it once, thinking about your first impressions; then read it again and score it, using the six-point One-Pager writing guide (Figure 1.7). If you are working with a group, allow time for discussion. Note that you can score the piece for just one trait—or all six. Your choice. My suggested scores and comments appear at the end of the chapter.

9 Tips for Scoring Well

You will have an opportunity to score many more papers, trait by trait, in upcoming chapters. Here are some tips for making your assessment of these papers—and *your own students' papers*—more consistent, efficient, and fair.

1. Remember—there is no "right" score.

All the student papers in this book have been scored by experienced teachers/raters, but their suggested scores should not be considered the "correct" scores. There is no such thing. They are *suggestions* and cannot be more. The goal is to come up with a *defensible* score, one based on thorough reading of the paper and analysis of the rubric.

If you and your partner or your group disagree by only one point on a given score, you can still consider that agreement. On a continuum, remember, a high 3 and a low 4 would actually be quite close.

2. Refer to the writing guide often.

Print a copy so you can write on it, and highlight phrases that help you distinguish among scoring levels. Make it your own, but don't try to memorize it. You'll be surprised how quickly it will feel comfortable and familiar. You may want to revise the guide as you and your students think of other important features that should influence assessment.

3. Remember that a score of 1 indicates *beginning* performance, not failure.

When you give a score of 1, you are saying to the student, in effect, "You have made a beginning. Now let's try to build on those first thoughts."

4. Remember that a score of 5 or 6 represents strength, not perfection.

Papers that receive 5s and 6s are not all alike. Some are hilarious, and some are profoundly moving or well researched. If you feel that a paper has strength, go for the gusto; don't wait for that mythical "better" paper that is waiting around the bend. You can give another 5 or 6 tomorrow.

5. Spend your time *reading the paper.*

Sometimes people ask whether, since there are six traits, they must read a paper six times. Thankfully, no. Reading one time will do the trick—provided you take your time and concentrate on the writer's message. This is why scoring holistically (just one overall score for the paper as a whole) isn't really the time saver it's often cracked up to be. No matter how you score the paper, you still have to *read* it.

6. Consider grade level—but don't make it *the* factor.

Grade level does not count as much as performance per se—but it still counts. That's why we are surprised to learn that the author of "The Redwoods" is a young adult.

Nevertheless, we can—and should—have high expectations at *all grade levels*. We should not assume, for example, that students in second or third grade will have only minimal voice. It does not work that way. What changes, with experience and sophistication, is a writer's control over a trait. An eleventh grader might have more consistent voice throughout a piece of writing, but a third or even a first grader could have moments of voice that would rival that of any writer—even an adult.

7. Watch out for rater bias.

Many little things get in the way of scoring fairly or appropriately. Here are the most common sources of bias, in both large-scale assessment and the classroom:

- **Having a "high/low" tendency**
  Some teachers have a tendency to be too hard (or too easy) on *everyone* as a matter of principle. We've all known the teacher who cannot bear to give anything but an A—and the one who is holding an A in reserve for that special student he or she hopes to meet one day.

- **Reacting to appearance**
  We may find ourselves irritated by messy or tiny handwriting, especially when we're tired. But poor handwriting, while often annoying, is not the same thing as weak voice, unsupported ideas, or faulty conventions, and it should not influence trait-based scores. (Note: If you are scoring a published piece for *Conventions & Presentation*, *do* consider appearance—but go beyond neatness to include such features as overall design, use of illustrations or color, fonts, and so on.)

- **Assuming longer is better**
  Is it? We might like to think so. In fact, though, many students who write well for one or two pages have enormous difficulty sustaining the flow. They just run out of juice. Furthermore, ability to condense is often a virtue; it may give voice just the boot it needs.

- **Loving—or hating—the topic**
  Do you love football? Hate cats? Vice versa? These little quirks and preferences can and *do* get in the way of fair scoring. Assess the writing, not the topic (it's not as simple as it sounds).

- **Letting preconceptions influence you**
  Researcher and writer Paul Diederich (1974) discovered that raters actually scored the *very same* essays higher when told they had been written by honors English students. If I told you The "Redwoods" had been written by Hemingway, would you see its simplicity as ingenious?

- **Skimming**
  Some readers think that they can tell after the first few lines whether a paper will be strong. Rarely is this true. A strong lead may disintegrate into generalities; a slow start may explode into a burst of inspiration.

- **Self-Scoring**
  Are you a perceptive reader? If so, be careful that you score the *work of the writer* and not your own talent in deciphering the "hidden message."

- **Personal response to violence or vulgarity**
  How do you respond to vulgar language in student writing? To profanity? To extreme violence? Some people have a very ho-hum attitude; others are readily offended. Take a position, and let your students know what it is.

  Profanity is part of the landscape in a narrative on war; but it may seem jolting, cumbersome, or self-conscious in a persuasive essay on school locker searches. The question (for me) is not really about violence or profanity per se, but about whether the writing works and whether the language is appropriate for the context and intended audience.

8. Be aware of pet peeves.

Everyone has a pet peeve. Some of us have many. The trick is to know what they are so that they will not trap you into assessing unfairly by *over*reacting. See Figure 1.9 for a list—and as you read through them, ask yourself whether any of these might influence you.

Keep a list of your own pet peeves, and share it openly with your students. It can teach us all a little about the way we respond to writing.

9. Remember that no writing guide tells all.

Writing guides are by nature simple documents, intended to capture the essence of what we are *likely to see* at various levels. They cannot capture *everything* because the variety in writing samples is infinite.

Author's Note

When scoring, make the best match you can, asking, "Which level comes *closest* to the way I see this paper?" Every bullet may not apply. You may wish the writing guide said *engaging* instead of *exciting or electric*. Fine. Be flexible. And feel free to modify the wording—so long as you consider *actual student performance* when doing so. That way, your words will reflect what you actually see in the writing—not just what you think you might like to see.

FIGURE 1.9

Pet Peeves

- Big, loopy writing
- **Teeny-tiny writing**
- No margins!
- Commas or periods outside the quotation marks
- Shifting tenses with no reason
- Writing in ALL CAPITAL LETTERS
- Mixing *it's* and *its*
- Mixing *are* and *our*—Do they even sound alike?
- Mixing *their, there,* and *they're*—when we just finished a unit on it
- *Goes* for *said,* as in *So he goes, "Let's dance," and I go, "Yeah, cool."*
- Endless connectives: *and, but then, because, and so, so then, so*
- The words and phrases *yuck, awesome, dude, radical, rad, in the zone, humongous, pushing the envelope, I mean, like, as if, cool* (I use cool, but hate it in print)
- Missing words—Didn't the writer notice?
- Sudden endings
- Writing just to fill the page—nothing goes with anything else
- Empty words used to snow the reader: *His unobstructed prejudice presupposed the obliteration of his potential. Just say, His prejudice held him back.*
- *The End* (as if I would look for more)
- The phrase *You know what I mean?* (I can't tell if it's more annoying when I do or when I don't)
- *Alot* (If you can have alot, what's wrong with *alittle*?)
- No punctuation at all—like driving without traffic signs
- No title—Take a minute and think of one
- A title that doesn't seem to go at all with the paper
- A lead that repeats the prompt or assignment—If I can't tell what the topic is, there's a problem with the writing
- Exclamation points after every breathless line!!!!!!!!!!!!!!!!!!!!!!!!!
- *Between you and I* (versus *me*)
- *Me and my friend . . .* (as a sentence subject)
- *Her and me . . .* (as a sentence subject)
- Cliché adjectives: *crashing waves, blue skies, fluffy clouds*
- Tired words: *nice, good, great, wonderful, special, exciting . . .*
- No paragraphs!
- Paragraphs for every single sentence
- Cliché leads: *In this paper . . . Hi, my name is . . .*
- The ending *That's all for now . . .*
- Fifteen *different* **fonts** on **one** page

In *The 9 Rights of Every Writer* (2005, 93–95), I tell the story of a student paper titled *Ginweed* that I have carried with me since 1987. That's a long while to care about a piece of writing. Each time I read the story of a young boy and his 4-H calf, I am moved all over again. I laugh, I get tears in my eyes, and the unexpected ending still gives me chills. The county fair judge in the piece still reminds me of actor Melvyn Douglas in the classic film *Hud*—especially when he remarks, "When you got a Jersey like this, it almost makes me want to change breeds." But of course, we cannot very well incorporate such personal responses into a writing guide:

- Causes the reader to tear up
- Compels the reader to carry it around for twenty years or more
- Reminds the reader of famous actors

Personal responses cannot and *should not* be transformed into expectations. These are things we must convey in conferences and through our comments. A score, no matter how accurate, can never take the place of words from your heart. You need both.

In addition, a writing guide is more than words on paper. It has three parts: the written document (like the One-Pager you have been using in this chapter); samples of performance that help us understand the criteria (like "The Redwoods" and "Mouse Alert"); and your own teacher judgment, the result of experience, insight, intuition, and your own skill in using a writing guide (or any assessment tool) wisely and well. See Figure 1.10 for a summary.

FIGURE 1.10

3 Parts to a Writing Guide

Any good writing guide comprises 3 parts . . .

1. The actual written criteria

2. Samples that illustrate those criteria

3. YOU . . . the interpreter, using your best judgment

Connecting the 6 Traits to Research

In 2007, Steve Graham and Dolores Perin prepared a report for the Carnegie Corporation of New York titled *Writing Next* (Alliance for Excellent Education, 4–5). In that report, they identified eleven instructional strategies that (according to the extensive research cited) appear to have a significant impact on student writing performance. Although the report targets middle and high school students, it is not much of a stretch to infer that many of these strategies—perhaps all—could make a measurable difference even for our youngest writers.

It is not my intention to summarize the report here (to access a copy, type in "Writing Next" online); however, I wish to point out five *very* strong connections to trait-based instruction:

1. Specific Writing Strategies

First, the report cites the importance of teaching **specific "writing strategies"** that improve students' skills in planning, drafting, and revising their writing. Trait-based instruction emphasizes such strategies, through the sharing of literature, assessment of writing samples, and presentation of focus lessons. Many such strategies are detailed, trait by trait, in Chapters 3 through 8.

2. Collaborative Writing

Second, the report notes **the value of "collaborative writing,"** which encourages students to work together in designing and carrying out writing tasks. In a trait-based writing classroom, students work together continuously. They discuss writing samples, assess them together, and design revision. They plan their own writing together, brainstorming and discussing possibilities. They also share their writing—both during drafting and as part of revision.

3. Specific, Reachable Goals

Third, the report notes how critical it is to **provide students with "specific, reachable goals"** so that they have no confusion about what success looks like or what they must do to achieve it. Making goals clear is precisely what a good writing guide does. Further, in trait-based writing, students have a voice in setting those goals.

4. Analyzing the Writing of Others

Fourth, the report cites how helpful it can be for students to "read, analyze, and emulate" **carefully selected models of good writing.** This occurs every time students look at and discuss samples of other students' work, or use literary mentors to discover the power of strong details, powerful leads and conclusions, honest voice, original phrasing, and more. Trait-based instruction emphasizes the use of both student writing models and good literature.

5. Focusing on Process

Fifth, the report emphasizes the importance of **a process-based approach to writing instruction.** In any successful trait-based writing approach, process is foundational. As Chapter 2 shows, the traits are interwoven throughout the cycle of writing process, but are particularly critical to purposeful revision.

I encourage you to read the report in its entirety. And if you teach the traits now, I am confident that you will feel validated.

Connecting the 6 Traits to the Common Core Standards for Writing

INTRODUCTION

The Common Core State Standards represent an initiative to—

- Lay out a clear vision for what is expected of students for success in college and work.
- Give students, parents, and teachers a clear vision for success in every school.
- Create consistency in expectations from state to state.

The Standards are a collaborative effort of the Council of Chief State School Officers (CCSSO) and the National Governors Association (NGA), with input from professional educators, scholars, assessment developers, parents, students, and other members of the public. They are intended to be rigorous, to build upon existing state standards, to increase clarity and continuity among those standards, to align well with the expectations of colleges and universities, and to reflect requirements from other top-performing countries in order to prepare U.S. students to compete in a global economy. In short, developers say, "the Standards lay out a vision of what it means to be a literate person in the twenty-first century" (www.corestandards.org).

SETTING UP YOUR OWN REVIEW

Distinct standards have been developed for mathematics and for English language arts, and the language arts standards are intended to cross over into other content areas, such as science, history, and social studies. The consistency from grade to grade makes the Standards fairly easy to review. If you have not already done so, I urge you to check the website (www.corestandards.org), and to begin by reviewing the Anchor Standards, those that lay out general guidelines for college and career readiness.

Once you have done that, go on to the individual grade-level standards, where you will find additional detail on writing (or other) expectations for each grade. The grade-level standards are direct derivatives of the Anchor Standards, demonstrating a kind of stairway to success that begins in kindergarten and grows increasingly complex and demanding up through grade 12.

You will notice that conventions and vocabulary development have their own strand, under Language Arts Standards. The reason for this is that while both are integral to writing, they are also critical to reading, speaking, and listening, and so the developers did not want to link them exclusively to writing. The Language Arts Standards include components for Conventions and Standard English, Knowledge of Language, and Vocabulary Acquisition and Use.

To facilitate your review, I recommend printing out copies of—

1. The Anchor Standards that define college and career readiness
2. A copy of the Writing Standards that pertain specifically *to the grade level you teach*
3. A copy of the Language Arts Standards *for the grade level that you teach*
4. A copy of "Key Points in Language Arts," which will highlight some things to look for

THE ANCHOR STANDARDS

The Anchor Standards for Writing define expectations for college or career readiness. You may be thinking, "Why would I begin *here* if I am teaching younger writers?" Two reasons: First, all other standards are derivatives of this list. And second, it is easier to get where we are going if we know what the end goal is. The Anchor Standards are divided into four broad sections:

1. Text Types and Purposes (genre and related skills)
2. Production and Distribution of Writing (process and use of technology)
3. Research to Build and Present Knowledge (research, quoting and paraphrasing, citing of sources, and use of technology)
4. Range of Writing (writing for a wide range of purposes and audiences, and writing both over time and on-demand)

See Figure 1.11 for a quick summary of how these four sections connect directly to the six traits of writing. (All bold-faced trait connections in Figure 1.11 are mine.)

Section 1: Text Types and Purposes (Standards 1–3)

The first section, Text Types and Purposes, focuses on three umbrella genres:

- Opinion pieces or arguments
- Informative/explanatory texts
- Narrative texts

FIGURE 1.11

Connection Between College and Career Readiness Anchor Standards for Writing and the Six Traits of Writing

TEXT TYPES AND PURPOSES (GENRE AND RELATED SKILLS)

1. Write arguments to support claims in an analysis of substantive texts, using valid reasoning and relevant and sufficient evidence. (Trait connection: **Ideas**)

2. Write informative/explanatory texts to examine and convey complex ideas and information clearly and accurately through the effective selection, organization, and analysis of content. (**Ideas, Organization**)

3. Write narratives to develop real or imagined experiences or events using effective technique, well-chosen details, and well-structured event sequences. (**Ideas, Organization, Voice**)

PRODUCTION/DISTRIBUTION OF WRITING (PROCESS & TECHNOLOGY)

4. Produce clear and coherent writing in which the development, organization and style are appropriate to task, purpose and audience. (**All Traits, notably Ideas, Organization, Voice**)

5. Develop and strengthen writing as needed by planning, revising, editing, rewriting, or trying a new approach. (**All Traits**)

6. Use technology, including the Internet, to produce and publish writing and to interact and collaborate with others. (**All Traits, notably Conventions & Presentation**)

RESEARCH TO BUILD & PRESENT KNOWLEDGE (RESEARCH & TECHNOLOGY)

7. Conduct short as well as more sustained research projects based on focused questions, demonstrating understanding of the subject under investigation. (**Ideas**)

8. Gather relevant information from multiple print and digital sources, assess the credibility and accuracy of each source, and integrate the information while avoiding plagiarism. (**All Traits, notably Ideas and Conventions & Presentation**)

9. Draw evidence from literary or informational texts to support analysis, reflection, and research. (**All Traits, notably Ideas and Conventions & Presentation**)

RANGE OF WRITING (PURPOSE, GENRE, AUDIENCE, TIME)

10. Write routinely over extended time frames (time for research, reflection, and revision) and shorter time frames (a single sitting or a day or two) for a range of tasks, purposes, and audiences. (**All Traits**)

NOTE

The Career- and College-Readiness Standards for Language include additional writing standards connected specifically to conventions and word choice.

Source:

http://www.corestandards.org/the-standards/english-language-arts-standards/anchor-standards/
college-and-career-readiness-anchor-standards-for-writing/

I call these "umbrella" genres because obviously these categories are extremely broad and comprise many subgenres of writing—as the developers note in their Appendix A. For example, informational writing could include textbooks, encyclopedias, signage for a museum, histories, journalistic articles, lab reports, police reports, and hundreds of other things. Narratives might include memoirs, biographies and autobiographies, journals, news stories, picture books, film scripts, and other types of stories. Persuasive

Author's Note

At the end of Appendix A of the Common Core Standards, you will find expansive definitions of narrative, informational/explanatory writing, and argument. These definitions are extremely helpful not only in distinguishing among these broad genres, but also in understanding the fundamental requirements of each one. Look also for an important statement about how much of our best writing blends genres, as well as a section titled "The Special Place of Argument in the Standards." The Standards writers make a fine distinction between argument and persuasion, noting that despite similarities, the former depends more on logic and the merit of the evidence presented, while the latter may rest partly on emotion or what the reader perceives as a decision beneficial to him or her. Note the emphasis on the power of argument to help readers make a good decision.

Author's Note

As you review the Common Core State Standards, look for a grade-to-grade parallel organization. What is required at one grade level will usually appear in some form at other grade levels, but the demands will be more or less exacting, as appropriate. Note that certain standards do not take effect until grade 3 or 4.

pieces might include film or book reviews, editorials, speeches, position papers, proposals, advertisements, and so on. The expectations or skills related to each genre begin at a very basic level in kindergarten, growing in complexity and difficulty through grades 11 and 12.

Informational writing and research. For example, tasks connected to informational writing range from naming a topic and providing information on that topic (kindergarten or grade 1) to presenting a complex topic supported by research, expanding that topic through examples and graphics, and tying all elements together with organizational elements such as subheads and transitional language (grade 12). Research requirements also grow more rigorous with each grade level. Primary students are asked to engage in teacher-supported research (W.K.2), perhaps responding to a text and related questions shared by the instructor. By grade 12, students are expected to pose an important informational question and research it independently, over time (W.11-12.2).

Narrative writing. Students from kindergarten through grade 12 are expected to write narratives, but again, the range of expectations is very great. Kindergarteners are asked to use a combination of "drawing, dictating, and writing" to tell about an event or several related events (W.K.3). By grade 8, students are asked to include such elements as dialogue, pacing, description, and character development, and to develop real or imagined experiences or events using "effective technique, well-chosen details, and well-structured event sequences" (W.8.3). By grade 12, students are asked to create sophisticated and engaging stories that may include "multiple points of view" or even "multiple plot lines." They are also asked to use rhetorical techniques (such as pacing, description, dialogue, or reflection) not only to develop the plot and characters, but also to create a particular tone, mood, or voice within the piece: "a sense of mystery, suspense, growth, or resolution" (W.11-12.3)

Argument. Argument, often considered a challenging genre, is emphasized at all levels as well, beginning with kindergarten. Very young writers may be asked to "name a topic" or "tell the name of a book" they are writing about and to state an opinion about that topic or book (W.K.1). By grade 12, students are expected to explore and analyze a complex topic, setting forth a well-supported opinion backed by research, acknowledging and refuting counterarguments, and organizing all information (claims, counterclaims, reasons, evidence) in a rhetorically effective manner (W.11-12.1).

Connection to traits. The connection to the traits is very strong in Standards 1 through 3 because all three major genres require trait-based skills. Throughout these first three standards, emphasis is on development of central *ideas*, effective use of detail or support (also relating to the trait of *ideas*), and strong *organization* of information—particularly in terms of a strong lead and conclusion, as well as transitions to link ideas.

Interestingly, "words, phrases, clauses" and "varied syntax" (what we will subsequently call *word choice* and *sentence fluency*) are seen as *primarily* fulfilling a transitional purpose, although word choice is also implicitly connected to expectations regarding clarity or use of sensory detail. The word *voice* is not used directly—but voice is a definite presence, both in references to *tone* and in the recurring emphasis on addressing the needs of the audience (or what we might call the reader-writer connection).

Section 2: Production and Distribution of Writing (Standards 4–6)

The second section, Production and Distribution of Writing, focuses on all steps of the writing process, particularly emphasizing development and revision. It also covers publication—which may involve the use of technology.

Younger writers are encouraged to work with peers and to receive support. For example, a kindergarten or first-grade student might share writing with a group and use feedback to add one detail to her piece (W.K.6). By grade 12, students are expected to match "development, organization, and style" to "task, purpose, and audience" (W.11-12.4). In addition, secondary writers are expected to use technology proficiently "including the Internet, to produce, publish, and update individual or shared writing products in response to ongoing feedback, including new arguments or information" (W.11-12.6). This means that by their senior year, students must not only conduct research online, but also draft and revise using technology, as well as create multi-voiced documents, such as wikis—and publish online as well (more on this in Chapter 8).

Again, the connection to the traits is very strong. "Clear and coherent writing," emphasized in Standard 4, is writing in which ideas, organization, and word choice shine. Standard 5 focuses on writing process. As Chapter 2 makes clear, each step of writing process is linked inexorably to the traits, but revision in particular is strengthened dramatically by knowledge of the traits. Knowing how to read and revise one's own work is the key to independence. Standard 6 calls for the use of technology to publish writing. This standard connects most closely to the trait of conventions & presentation.

Section 3: Research to Build and Present Knowledge (Standards 7–9)

The third section, Research to Build and Present Knowledge, covers integration of information from multiple sources, summarizing or paraphrasing information, and identifying passages within written works that will support a particular point of view, as well as quoting and citing such passages and works correctly.

The youngest writers engage in "shared research" (W.K.7) under the direction and guidance of a teacher, who may present a book or film to the whole class, for example, or assist writers in recalling the details of a personal experience (W.K.8). By grade 4, students are expected to also begin exploring informational texts independently (W.4.9). Older writers take responsibility for coordinating their own research, and are expected to use multiple and diverse sources to conduct "advanced searches" while "avoiding plagiarism" or "overreliance on any one source" (W.11-12.8). They are also required to document sources appropriately.

Because research is primarily about the gathering and sorting of information, Standards 7 through 9 connect most strongly to the traits of ideas and organization. However, appropriate citing of sources is an important element of conventions & presentation.

Section 4: Range of Writing (Standard 10)

The fourth section, Range of Writing, distinguishes between writing that occurs over an extended period and requires ongoing research and continual revision, and writing that may take place in one sitting (such as on-demand writing for an assessment). This standard also emphasizes writing for a wide range of purposes and audiences—and hence connects directly to all traits.

Conclusions About the Writing Standards and Language Arts Standards

In summary, as you look through the Writing Standards for your grade level, you will notice a particularly strong emphasis on the traits of ideas and organization. As you review the Language Arts Standards, you will find more emphasis on the traits of word choice, sentence fluency, and conventions & presentation.

In addition, though, notice the recurring references to *style* and the importance of ensuring that any document is appropriate not only for the task and purpose, but for the audience as well. Matching style to audience is a hallmark of voice, and *style* embraces three traits that always work in harmony: voice, word choice, and sentence fluency.

Overall, keep in mind that *all six traits* are important in *every piece of writing*. Nevertheless, many people are more comfortable when they can identify specific words or phrases that directly connect to each trait. See Figure 1.12 for a guide to help you do just that.

FIGURE 1.12

Trait Language in the Core Standards

Use this guide as you review grade-specific standards for the grade level you teach.

The trait of . . .	is referenced in words or phrases like . . .
Ideas	*analysis, content, message, thesis, theme, details, information, development, purpose, research, support, thoughtfulness, insight, focus, clarity, meaning, reasoning, synthesis, integrating information from multiple sources*
Organization	*design, order, structure, coherence, cohesiveness, pattern, purpose, intent, focus, connections, unity, lead, conclusion, transitions, linking ideas, sequence*
Voice	*style, tone, effective stylistic techniques, textual interest, presence on the page, person behind the words, confidence, connection to the reader or audience, style that suits the needs of the audience*
Word Choice	*words, wording, language, phrasing, expression, terminology, turn of phrase, style, meaning, idioms, expressing meaning, precise words, figurative language*
Sentence Fluency	*style, language patterning, sentence structure, sentence style, phrasing, readability, sentence sense, using clauses to show transition*
Conventions & Presentation	*spelling, punctuation, grammar and usage, editing, formatting, mechanics, correctness, design, appearance, format, layout, appeal, eye appeal, look of the document, text features, using technology to create effective presentation, documenting sources*

As you will notice in your own review, the Common Core Standards for Writing repeatedly reference writing process, from planning through publishing. This is where the link to the traits becomes perhaps the most powerful because in teaching traits to students, we help them to become independent planners, drafters, revisers, and editors. Planning and drafting may link most closely to the traits of ideas and organization, but revision links to *all* traits, and editing depends heavily on conventions & presentation. In short, the connection between the traits and the Standards is very strong.

Developers of the Common Core Standards are quick to point out that this is a work in progress. They welcome input. Write to them. Be heard.

Some Closing Thoughts

Isn't assessment an odd place from which to begin writing instruction? Actually, no. It's the very best place, once we understand what assessment is.

When we think *assessment*, we usually think *grading* or *testing*. This is a very limited view. Assessment is looking within. It means getting an insider's perspective. Isn't this what we want for our students? To be insiders? We can list dozens of strategies and create hundreds of standards, but nothing meaningful happens until students themselves can look at their own work and figure out the next step—without help.

In the quotation that opens this chapter, Donald Graves reminds us that we must teach children to "read their own work." That doesn't mean looking it over or checking the spelling. It means teaching them to read the way *we* read—with insight and understanding, looking for strengths and problems, noticing what's working and what isn't there yet. If we don't show them how to assess on this very personal level—not with numbers or grades, but with *language*—their writing will not improve. But if we *do* show them, their skills will soar. The very core of this book rests on one foundational belief: *What you can assess, you can revise.* And if you can revise with purpose, the world of writing is yours.

Interactive Questions and Activities

1. **Discussion.** Which term do you prefer—*rubric* or *writing guide*? In your mind, do they have different connotations?

2. **Activity and Discussion.** Discuss your scores for Kaylee's paper titled "Basking in Entertainment" (Figure 1.8). Your scores need not match mine (see below), but be sure you can back your scores with sound reasons, just as if you were conferring directly with Kaylee. For additional practice, choose a piece of student writing from one of your own classes to score on all six traits. Go for something that is not immediately obvious, that is, neither clearly strong nor problematic. Jot scores down individually—then open up the discussion. Notice the kinds of questions and issues that emerge when scores *do not* agree.

3. **Activity and Discussion.** Make a group list of your pet peeves. Compare it with the list in Figure 1.10. Did you include anything that is not on that list?

4. **Activity and Discussion.** Expand your scoring skills by looking at writing *not generated by students*. Consider a blog, short story or essay, news story, excerpt from a textbook, letter to the editor, or any writing that is part of your life. Score it on any trait using the One-Pager guide. Then, consider how you might create lessons in which students assess and discuss similar kinds of writing.

5. **Activity and Discussion.** Consider keeping a writer's notebook as you read this text. As one of your first entries, create your own vision of writing success,

focusing on writing within your classroom (now or in the future). Ask yourself this question: *What would successful performance look like in my classroom?* List things you feel are important in terms of product (actual student writing), classroom atmosphere (the general philosophy that guides how you teach), and writing workshop and process (how students behave as writers). Don't try for an exhaustive list. Think of this as a rough draft that you will revise as you go through the rest of the book. When you finish (days or weeks from now), compare your vision with those of your colleagues. Continue to revise that vision, not only during the time you are reading this book, but throughout the time you are teaching.

6. **Activity and Discussion.** Get a copy of *Writing Next* by Steve Graham and Dolores Perin (available online). Read and discuss it with your group, seeing how many connections you can make to trait-based instruction.

7. **Activity and Discussion.** Check out the Common Core State Standards online (www.corestandards.org) and print out relevant copies for yourself and other members of your group. (Be sure to include Appendix A of the Common Core State Standards in your discussion.) Go through them with a highlighter and pencil, marking your own connections to the traits. What are the strongest connections? Is there anything you feel is missing and should be included? Consider writing a response to the Standards from your own point of view.

8. **Activity and Discussion.** This chapter talks about the traits of successful writing. What about the traits of successful *writers*? List the qualities you think a successful writer would need (you may wish to include this in your notebook). Then compare your list with qualities listed by your colleagues—and with those in Figure 1.13. Why is it important to focus on the *writer*, and not just on the *writing*?

FIGURE 1.13

The 6 Traits* of Successful Writers

1. PERSEVERANCE

   Successful writers never give up. It isn't an option for them. When the writing isn't working, they know to leave it alone for a time and come back, or get more information and come back. But they *keep coming back* until they are satisfied.

2. WATCHFULNESS

   Writers notice what others overlook. They have a knack for identifying what matters. And they think like writers all the time, with their senses on high alert.

3. COURAGE

   Successful writers are daring—and bold. Because they're willing to take risks, they rip the limits off what they can achieve. They also know how to sift through criticism *thoughtfully*, making use of what's helpful, and quieting voices that only get in the way.

4. INSIGHT

   Successful writers are thinkers. They're good at analyzing human nature, solving problems, anticipating outcomes, and making connections. When they write, we tune in—because they help us to think more clearly, too.

5. CURIOSITY

   By nature, writers are people who always want to know more—about everything. They're nosy. They ask questions. They *enjoy* research. And they use the best of what they learn to teach and entertain the rest of us.

6. HONESTY

   The most successful writers are unflinching. They look life right in the eye and share what they see. The result can be stirring, disarming, or intensely comical in its truth.

There are undoubtedly more than six! Please add your own thoughts to this list.

© 2012 Vicki Spandel

Coming Up

The traits cannot be taught in a vacuum. Classroom environment is everything. In the next chapter, we'll consider ways of "setting the stage" for teaching the traits, with writing process and writing workshop. In Chapters 3 through 8, we'll look at each of the six traits, one by one—introducing individual writing guides, sample papers to assess, teaching ideas, and suggested literature connected to each trait.

Suggested Scores and Comments for "Basking in Entertainment" by Kaylee

Comments

Three things stand out for me in this piece: First, the writer's ability to notice and capture small details, like biting into the strawberry crepes, Kira's brain being unable to make her legs move, or Mom spitting out the "coconut milk." The idea that vacationing can be special even in your own back yard gives sudden depth to a paper that up to that point was fairly light. Second, the voice—this writer loves to write and it shows. She has thought about this topic—and wants to convince us to think as she does. And finally, the original organizational structure—three small episodes to make a point about vacationing with families. That's clever, and it works. The word choice, fluency, and conventions are all strong, but as we'll see shortly, ideas, organization, and voice are the building blocks without which writing cannot stand.

Scores

Ideas: 6 (It's the details!)
Organization: 6 (An original approach makes this work.)
Voice: 6 (Continual enthusiasm—beginning to end.)
Word choice: 5 (Though some moments are routine, many are stellar—use a yellow highlighter.)
Fluency: 6 (Variety galore, plus skill with dialogue and fragments.)
Conventions & Presentation: 6 (An editor has almost nothing to do.)

I've often had these prompts in my Lit classes that ask, "Do you like to write?" It is like asking me if I like to breathe, if I like my heart beating. Writing just is. It is a part of me, and I love every part of it. I enjoy researching, contemplating, screwing up, draft writing, revising, and printing out the crisp, white, finished piece. I love the smell of ink on paper.

—Simona Patange, student writer

Who's Teaching Whom?
Written in Response to Kaylee's personal essay, Basking in Entertainment

We always think top-down when we consider learning. Adults are the know-it-alls and kids are the empty vessels. But really smart people know they're always learning. And really smart adults know they have a lot to learn from kids.

I am privileged to know a 5th grader named Kaylee. Although I'm five times her age, she has a lot to teach me. And it's not just because Kaylee is smart . . . she teaches me to delight in the ordinary events of life. She gave a speech about her little brother, Joey. While we howled at his antics, I learned that Kaylee is enchanted by her sibling. She wrote a personal essay about spending time with her parents. Now that is a topic of potential deadly boredom, but Kaylee showed us how she turned her backyard into a 5-star resort in order to make her mom spit coconut milk. With style and grace, Kaylee reminds me daily that there is joy hiding in every moment. Kids inspire adults.

—Judy Mazur, fifth grade teacher

CHAPTER 2

Setting the Stage

with Writing Process and Writing Workshop

The writing process is an untidy business. In the years since Writing: Teachers and Children at Work was published, I've found that some teachers have misunderstood the writing process. They deliberately take children through phases of making a choice, rehearsing, composing, and then rewriting. Of course, these processes do exist, but each child uses them differently. We simply cannot legislate their precise timing.

DONALD H. GRAVES
A Fresh Look at Writing, 1994, 82

Every aspect of [writing] workshop is set up to support children learning to do what writers really do. The teaching is challenging because what writers really do is engage in a complex, multi-layered, slippery process to produce texts.

KATIE WOOD RAY
The Writing Workshop, 2001, xii

If you have ever grown a lawn from seed, you know how much love and effort you have to put into it. If you simply scatter seeds across a barren patch of earth, you're likely to be disappointed in the results. But if you prepare the earth first, enrich it with compost, dig deep to create a bed in which even fragile plants can take root, the result is a blanket of green shoots sturdy enough to choke out the most persistent weeds.

Teaching traits works very much this way. True enough, traits have power. As young writers recognize the impact of phrasing and detail, or feel themselves under the spell of a writer's voice, they discover things they can try as writers, too. But the traits do not and *cannot* exist in a vacuum. They work *only* in the context of writing workshop and writing process. Process offers us a means for creating writing in the first place—through planning, drafting, and revising. Workshop provides an environment in which young writers learn to manage their own writing process by doing the kinds of things real writers do: making choices, identifying their own needs, managing time, seeking information, giving and receiving feedback, deciding how to begin, knowing when a piece is finished, and much more.

If you begin not with the traits themselves, but instead by creating an environment in which the traits can flourish, you will feel their power. Instead of some short-lived novelty, a tack-on gimmick that gives you but one more thing to try, the traits become a way for writers to think and talk about writing, writer to writer. You will be stunned at the difference writers' language (trait language) makes in the way your students compose, revise, coach you or one another, and receive and discuss literature. The lessons you teach about detail, leads, transitions, voice, verbs, and fluency will then fall on fertile soil because your writers will see how to apply those lessons in the drafting and revising that are part of their everyday lives.

Setting the Stage with Writing Process

When I first became a teacher, I did not *teach* writing at all. I assigned it. That's because the assigning of writing, followed by the collecting and correcting of writing, is what had been modeled for me. I did not see a single one of my teachers write—and certainly never saw them revise. I knew precious little about choosing writing topics, warming up to write, reading my own work aloud to listen for voice or rhythm, revising for purpose, or connecting with an audience other than the teacher.

I did not learn these things by teaching, either. I learned them by *writing*—and then taking my own process apart so I could share it with students and with other teachers.

Of course, today's writing instruction is very different, thanks to the research of people like Janet Emig, Donald Murray, Donald Graves, and Lucy Calkins, who revolutionized the teaching of writing by observing and documenting what real writers do. They taught us that, as Donald Murray puts it, "meaning is not thought up and put down" (2004, p. 3). Writing evolves as we write—and think. Putting words on the page allows us to have a dialogue with ourselves, to say, "No—that's not quite it. *Let me try it this way . . .* "

Writing process is foundational to writing instruction. A process-based approach, however, is strengthened—*dramatically*—by the inclusion of traits. *Process* provides a *context for the traits*. Process makes the traits *make sense*.

This comes clear at once when we think about what writing is at the core: the processes of planning, writing, revising—all in a never-ending, recursive cycle. For most people, the most difficult part of writing to teach is revision. Traits make it easier.

Teachers should write so they understand the process of writing from within. They should know the territory intellectually and emotionally: how you have to think to write, how you feel when writing. Teachers of writing do not have to be great writers, but they should have frequent and recent experience in writing.

—Donald M. Murray
A Writer Teaches Writing, 2004, 74

Instead of *traits,* think *strategies.* Then picture yourself saying to students, "I am going to show you some strategies for making your revision more powerful than you ever thought it could be. I am going to share a way of thinking—a way of 'reading' your own work—that will help you make your writing soar."

First, consider how various processes within writing connect to the traits. Figure 2.1 may help you get a "big picture" view. In considering these various processes, keep in mind that writers don't proceed through them as if they were steps along a path. Although a writer may very well *begin* by getting an idea and may very well *end* by publishing, almost everything that happens in the middle—planning, drafting, sharing, revising—can happen *at any time* during writing, and tends to happen in a recursive cycle, rather than all at once.

Research by Janet Emig in 1971 concluded that "writing is a complex, recursive process, one that involves going back and forth in the text while composing" (Samway, 2006, 7). In other words, a writer may begin by choosing a topic, but later change his or her mind. And while planning is helpful, it's almost never final; the writer continues to plan all the while he or she writes—and revises. Writers usually do some revising and editing once a draft is done, but many don't wait until then. They revise as they write—and even revise in their heads as they plan. Writing is not really *a* process so much as a group of interwoven *processes,* working together in ways that are as complex as the mind of the writer. Let's take a closer look at some of the smaller processes that make up the larger writing cycle.

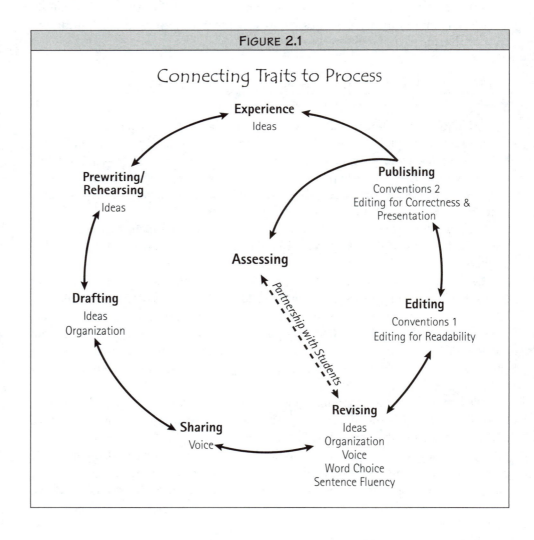

FIGURE 2.1

Connecting Traits to Process

Experience
Ideas

**Prewriting/
Rehearsing**
Ideas

Publishing
Conventions 2
Editing for Correctness &
Presentation

Drafting
Ideas
Organization

Assessing

Partnership with Students

Editing
Conventions 1
Editing for Readability

Sharing
Voice

Revising
Ideas
Organization
Voice
Word Choice
Sentence Fluency

EXPERIENCE: THE WELL WE DRAW FROM

Trait Connection: Ideas

Writing does not really begin with prewriting, as many diagrams suggest. It begins with life, our personal experience, our sense of what is important and what is worth sharing. In *Winterdance* (1994), Gary Paulsen writes of the Iditarod, the stillness of the Alaskan northlands, the beauty of the aurora borealis, and his near-death experiences from freezing and being attacked by an enraged moose.

Sy Montgomery's insatiable curiosity has led her, as a science and nature writer, to explore falconry, to help rescue orphaned hummingbirds, to adopt a scrawny orphan pig (named Christopher Hogwood), and to hike into cloud forests hoping for one small glimpse of the elusive tree kangaroo. Her "writing process" has been anything but ordinary. She describes having her interview tapes eaten by an orangutan, and losing her notebook, only to have an elephant retrieve it with her trunk and hand it back (2006, *Author's Note*).

In *At Home* (2010, 5), author Bill Bryson tells how buying a Victorian parsonage in England sparked his curiosity about the things of everyday life—and how his efforts to answer his own questions turned into a fascinating account of wars, famines, discoveries, and revolutions: "So the history of household life isn't just a history of beds and sofas and kitchen stoves, as I had vaguely supposed it would be, but of scurvy and guano and the Eiffel Tower and bedbugs and body-snatching and just about everything else that has ever happened. Houses aren't refuges from history. They are where history ends up."

Occasionally, we take the task of finding writing topics out of students' hands. This is all right *sometimes*. Part of writing is learning to deal effectively with writing tasks required by someone else, including employers. If we write ourselves, though, we also know how important it is for writers to identify the topics that are important in their own lives. "Children who are fed topics, story starters, lead sentences, even opening paragraphs as a steady diet for three or four years," says Donald Graves (2003, 21), "rightfully panic when topics have to come from them. The anxiety is not unlike that of the child whose mother has just turned off the television set. 'Now what do I do?' bellows the child." Writers must learn to sense the moment when writing begins. In *What You Know by Heart*, Katie Wood Ray (2002, 4) notes how an experience as simple as visiting Wal-Mart influenced author Billie Letts:

> When we hear Billie Letts say, "I walked in a Wal-Mart and looked around and I thought, 'You could live here. There's everything you need. You could exist in this place.'" "This happening, this walking-into-Wal-Mart, was the beginning that led Letts to write the novel *Where the Heart Is* (1995). So we hear her say this and then we know: writers get ideas for writing when they are away from their desks. Writers can get ideas at Wal-Mart.

Identifying topics requires sifting through the sands of your experience, looking for what is writing worthy, and listening for moments that speak to you. In order to teach this, you must find the treasures buried in the sands of your own life and share what you find with your students.

My personal writing comes largely from family memories and childhood experiences. Among my most vivid recollections is the sight of my mother, an air pistol tucked neatly beneath her apron, preparing to protect my five-year-old friend Gail from an attacking dog. She shot the dog unflinchingly, without one regret (he was stunned and frightened but not injured), and returned to her baking.

More than thirty years later, I was wheeling my mother—who by then had lost her sense of time and place—through the corridors of a nursing facility, trying to hold back

I like to tell my as-yet-unrealized philosophers at the start of our journey together that everyone has a philosopher inside and that kids always impress me with their seemingly endless ability to wonder. How high does the sky go? Why are there so many different languages? Does the world look the same to a frog as it does to me? Why do people hurt one another? Does my dog know how much I love him?

—Marietta McCarty
Little Big Minds, 2006, 2

I came from a background that was filled with sin, guilt, and threats of Hell and damnation. I was brought up with a grandmother who was paralyzed when I was young, and it was my job when I woke up early in the morning to see if she was still alive.

—Donald M. Murray
A Writer Teaches Writing, 2004, 11

my tears, and she was asking me if I had lost my mind and, if not, why in God's name I had selected this particular hotel as the place to spend our holidays. I have written about both episodes.

I also have written extensively of my grandmother, who taught a K–12 class in a single room in North Dakota and who could slice the head off a rattlesnake as cleanly and swiftly as Emeril dices celery. Her kitchen, with its uniquely rustic linoleum-covered table, smelling of vanilla, bread, chocolate, and coffee, was my place of refuge, where I listened to stories of her legendary feral cat, Snooky, who chased everything that dared to invade her territory.

When you model topic selection, help your students to see how writing topics grow out of humble adventures—dealing with your neighbor's biting dog, watching your grandmother bake bread. The best topics, Donald Graves suggests, come from an "everyday reading of the world." If we don't teach children how to seek out what matters, they will think that *only* trips to Disneyland or emergency appendectomies make good copy. They will feel compelled to "draw only on the experiences of others, which they do not necessarily understand" (*A Fresh Look at Writing*, 1994, 58).

REHEARSING AND PREWRITING: GIVING SHAPE TO THE IDEAS WE'VE CHOSEN

Trait Connection: Ideas

In prewriting or rehearsing, we give shape and focus to the ideas that come from experience. I think of rehearsing as playing with an idea in my head, the sort of thinking a person might do while taking a walk or gardening. Prewriting involves actual planning—putting something on paper or talking it through. Rehearsing is internal, whereas prewriting makes a topic visible, perhaps through webbing, sketching, or listing.

We often think of prewriting as tiny. Drafting is the big kahuna of writing. In reality, though, it often is—and should be—just the other way around. Prewriting is the time for exploring—searching, thinking, investigating, and reshaping our thoughts. And exploration is potentially limitless. What's more, prewriting approaches are as varied as the writers who use them, so we do well to give our students a wide range of strategies. Here are just a few.

Talking. Talking is especially helpful to young children—or to any writers who struggle to get words on paper. We often say that "writing is thinking," and that is true, but if you have to stretch for every word, that can slow the thinking process to an agonizing crawl. Sometimes talking feels more natural—and more comfortable.

As teachers Martha Horn and Mary Ellen Giacobbe point out (*Talking, Drawing, Writing*, 2007, 16), talking is a way for young writers to "'unfold' their thinking for an audience that needs to understand, and in doing so, they come to understand it better themselves." Talk spurs questions from listeners—and that lets a writer know where the informational "holes" are. In addition, it's an opportunity for writers to rehearse organization in their minds, and this makes the physical act of writing much easier.

Horn and Giacobbe (2007) also emphasize the importance of discovering what listeners think—how they respond to a piece. Positive reinforcement can build a writer's confidence. In addition, by learning to "read" listeners' body language and facial expressions, writers grow increasingly skilled at judging the impact of their writing on an audience.

FIGURE 2.2

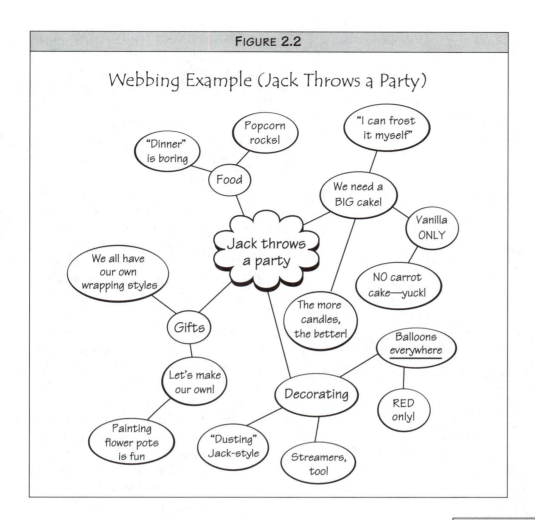

Webbing Example (Jack Throws a Party)

The whole act of talking through a piece before writing emphasizes this underlying truth: that writing is done *for* someone—and that our chosen details, order, words, and voice must reach that someone.

Webbing. Many writers like webbing, and although it does not work as well for me as talking or making a list, I think it's important to teach it and model it because it does work well for many writers. See Figure 2.2 for a sample of webbing I did for a story about my grandson called "Jack Throws a Party."

Listing. I love lists of potential readers' questions and often will elicit these from a class of students (see Figure 2.3) by presenting them with a one-liner, e.g., *I was attacked by jellyfish*. Then I simply ask, "What would you like to know?" Questions work well for many writers, especially those who struggle with organization, because the draft flows right out of answering the questions. A good list provides all the structural sturdiness of an outline without any of the cumbersome complexity.

Drawing. Prewriting can also include drawing. Through drawing, writers not only get in touch with topics that are important in their lives, but also extend detail—sometimes beyond what they can express in words alone. In Figure 2.4, you'll see Jamila's charming portrait of Mr. and Mrs. "Woody" (Woodfield) dancing. Jamila, a kindergartener, used drawing

FIGURE 2.3

Readers' Questions

✓ Where were you?
✓ How big was the jellyfish?
✓ Was there more than one?
✓ How long did the "attack" last?
✓ What made them attack you?
✓ Was anyone with you?
✓ What did you do?
✓ Was it painful?
✓ Were you frightened?
✓ Did you bleed?
✓ Could you get out of the water?
✓ How long did it take to get better?
✓ Did the stings leave any marks?
✓ Are you afraid of jellyfish now?
✓ Do you still go swimming?
✓ Does the jellyfish die after it attacks?
✓ Do jellyfish sting one another?

FIGURE 2.4

Jamila's Portrait of Mr. and Mrs. Woody

Name: Jamila A Woody

Mrs Woody A Mr woody
areHAVing a rmaicTim
DNASing At
the bol.
"I Love you Mrs
Woody" sed Mr
Woody.

Jamila you make me laugh!
Mr Woody an d I love to dance together.

to jumpstart her writing—and notice her "revision." Originally, she placed the figures farther right, but wanted to have Mr. Woody speak, so she needed to move them. This is the sort of thinking that lets us say, "I love how you noticed you'd need more space, and then rearranged your drawing. That's just the kind of revision good writers make." Mr. Woody seems to be giving Mrs. Woody a rather smart kick, but as we learn from Jamila's text (and the happy expressions on both faces), it's actually a tender moment: "Mrs. Woody and Mr. Woody are having a romantic time dancing at the ball. 'I love you Mrs. Woody,' said Mr. Woody." It doesn't get better than that.

For Jamila, the drawing is an integral part of the writing; words and drawing complement and expand each other. But with older writers, drawing is more often a way in—a precursor to writing. See Figure 2.5 for an example of a life map, courtesy of my teacher friend and colleague Sally Shorr. This sketch captures some main events in Sally's life, any of which could provide fuel for a story, poem, or essay. In creating this life map, Sally must reflect on what memories are most vivid or what events have helped define who she is. A student's life map might just explore the past year or so to capture moments that stand out.

Drawing has enormous benefits in developing a writer's voice and eye for detail. Horn and Giacobbe remind us that drawing helps children learn to use their eyes more "intensely." Drawing demands paying attention—and ultimately, that lays the foundation for good writing, too.

Writing itself—just diving in. Many writers find that the *act of writing* is their most helpful form of prewriting. They may not come to the heart of the message in the first few sentences—or even (for older writers) the first few pages. But that's not the point. The act of writing feels good; it awakens the mind.

I recall Don Graves (in a writing workshop) recounting a time he shared his writing with treasured friend and colleague Donald Murray. "He just kept leafing through it," Graves told us, imitating Murray as he flipped the pages solemnly, eyes trained on the page. "And he'd say 'Mm-hm. Mm-hm.' Then finally, on about page four, [Murray] pointed to a paragraph midway down and said, 'Here. Your writing begins *here.*'" Sometimes we have to write our way through several warm-up pages to get to the real beginning.

FIGURE 2.5

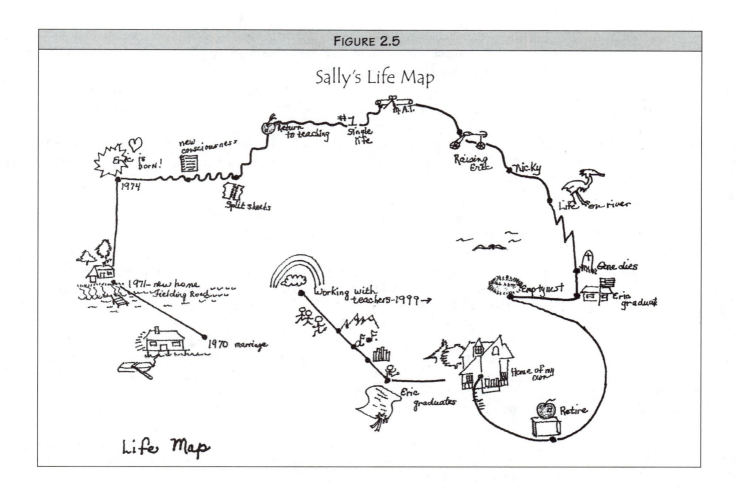

Sally's Life Map

Life Map

DRAFTING: GOING FROM BEGINNING TO END

Trait Connections: Ideas and Organization

Drafting provides writers substance with which to work. The key to drafting, there-fore, is to *keep writing* so that later there will be *something to revise*. Moreover, writing is generative. You discover what you want to say *not* so much during prewriting (as nonwriters often suppose) but during the act of writing itself. Writing creates mental connections. The first full draft requires some sort of beginning and ending—hence the connection to organization.

As teachers, we often think drafting means extending ideas. True—with a caveat. Trying to tell everything about everything can stretch detail so thin it all but disappears. As writers, we soon learn that before we can expand, we must focus. *Tell more about less* is a good mantra. As Barry Lane says, "Write small." Don't write that the "Holocaust was inhuman"; describe a "mountain of children's shoes." Don't write about how messy your brother is; tell the reader how you hate finding hair on the soap (*Reviser's Toolbox,* 1999, 52–53).

Drafting also depends on information—a wealth of it. When students write in generalities, we often say, "Be specific." *Sometimes* this is helpful—if the topic is per-sonal, something the student knows well. But often, the student's writing style is not at fault; rather, it's a lack of information that leads to detail-free writing. Instead of "Be specific," we should say, "Read. Investigate. Do *all* you need to do to answer your read-ers' questions."

Write a first draft as though you were thinking aloud, not carving a monument.

—Patricia T. O'Conner
Words Fail Me, 1999, 38

There is no substitute for really knowing what you are talking about.

—Wallace Stegner
On Teaching and Writing Fiction,
2002, 45

When Sebastian Junger wrote *The Perfect Storm* (1998, 129), he didn't lull us to sleep with generalities: "Hurricanes are powerful storms. They do enormous damage." He waited until he had enough information to write this:

> During the Labor Day hurricane of 1935, winds surpassed 200 miles an hour and people caught outside were sandblasted to death. Rescue workers found nothing but their shoes and belt buckles.

In writing about Brian's battle with north woods mosquitoes in *Hatchet* (2007), Gary Paulsen drew on his own experience, recounted in *Guts* (2001, 60), a nonfiction book on real-life research:

> I must have attracted every mosquito in the county. The cloud swarmed over me, filled my nostrils and my eyes, flooded my mouth when I breathed. They blinded me, choked me and, worst of all, tore into me like eight or nine thousand starving vampires.

A critical part of drafting is getting everything down on paper so that we have a sense of the "whole." Later we can see where the informational gaps are and add detail. Have students skip lines and leave big margins so there is plenty of room to fill in missing details down the road.

Drafting also requires continuity. First drafts aren't always finished in a day, and if writers don't return to their work for several days, the train of thought can be hard to recapture. We can encourage this sense of continuity by asking questions like, "How far did you get today?" Or "Where will you pick up tomorrow?" We should also suggest that writers jot notes (at the bottom of a draft) about what they plan to do next. As Donald Graves tells us, people who write all the time carry their writing in their heads, testing ideas, rehearsing lines. They enter what Graves calls "a constant state of composition" (1994, 104). When children enter this state, they truly become writers, for they are then seeing the world through a writer's eyes.

SHARING WITH AN AUDIENCE

Trait Connection: Voice

I never insist that any child *must* speak, and I make this known at the beginning of the first class. Shy children can be paralyzed by the fear of being called on and forced to answer before they're ready.

—Marietta McCarty
Little Big Minds, 2006, 14

If we believe the words of Donald Graves, that "writing is the making of reading," then we realize that mostly—*mostly*—we write to be read. That makes sharing—with a partner, a small writing circle of three or four, or even with a larger group—very important. Through sharing, we learn to read an audience. We learn where the voice is—and isn't.

For many writers, though, sharing is the most difficult part of the whole process. If you have writers who are shy, ease them into sharing by having them read aloud to themselves first (or even make a recording). Then move on to sharing with a trusted friend, then a small group. You (or another student) can also help with the actual reading, if that makes the student more comfortable.

When [my students] saw me, the vulnerable, egotistical writer, offering up my work to their questions, it gave them an incentive to do the same.

—Roy Peter Clark
Free to Write, 1987, 41

Your students can learn a lot about sharing by watching you model it. Read your writing aloud, with confidence, but with an open mind. Read the way you would like your students to read. Don't be afraid to love your writing. That lets students know it's OK for them to love their writing, too. Don't be afraid to laugh at yourself, either—to say, "I can't believe I *wrote* that!" if that's how you feel. You don't need to be perfect. You just need to be real.

When it's your turn to be a listener, focus on two things. First, really listen. Listen for content. Listen for voice. Form a circle (even if there are only three or four of you);

this gives a sense of community to the group and support to the writer. Let your whole demeanor, including your body language, show how tuned in to the writer you are. Truly taking in a writer's message is a profound means of showing respect, and is a way for the very shyest students to participate in the process, even when they do not speak. (For more about sharing, see Chapter 11, *Communicating about Students' Writing*.)

REVISING: LETTING THE TRAITS SHINE

Trait Connections: Ideas, Organization, Voice, Word Choice, Sentence Fluency

What exactly are we teaching when we teach revision? In a nutshell, we are *teaching the traits*. Scan across levels 5 and 6 from the One-Pager writing guide (Figure 1.7, pages 13 and 14) and you will see a whole menu of things writers do when they revise: add detail, take out filler, craft a new lead or conclusion, make transitions stronger, change the order of things, write from the heart to add voice, make the verbs stronger, re-craft sentences, and so forth. When students know the traits, the whole world of revision opens up for them. This is the most important reason for teaching students the traits.

And this is why it is so important for students to have their own student-friendly versions of these writing guides (see chapters 3 through 8 for copies). They don't need to *score* their writing, nor should they. Numbers aren't the point. We want them to identify strengths in their work—and moments that need revision

It is also important for students to understand the fine line between revision and editing. Professional writers do these tasks together, usually. But if students do not make the distinction, they may think editing *is* revising, and they may never go beyond tinkering with spelling and punctuation.

You might tell them, "Revision is structural. If you were revising a house, you'd push out walls, add a room, raise the ceiling, or put in skylights. Editing is more like tidying up or beautifying: moving the furniture, dusting, dimming the lights or setting out flowers. Revision changes a space *structurally*, while editing changes *the look*."

Don't just talk about it, though; model it. Show students how it looks to add detail—or take out information you don't need, reshape a sentence, boost a tired lead or title. Your examples can be small and focused. Revise one sentence, one phrase, one word. But do it—often. And talk through your revision as you write. A three-minute modeling lesson is worth more than a half-hour lecture. Help students understand various revision possibilities:

- Taking information out
- Putting new information in
- Changing wording
- Moving things around
- Changing the point of view (writing from the perspective of someone else)
- Starting over (a legitimate form of revision when things are not working)

For an example of focused revision, let's consider a piece by Kaylee, a fifth-grade student. Kaylee had written a memoir she felt very good about—except for the ending. It just wouldn't

Author's Note

So often when I emphasize how important it is for students to *assess* their own writing, teachers interpret my comment to mean that students should score their work: *5 in ideas, 4 in organization,* and so on. That is not what I mean *at all*. I mean for students to *read* their own writing in the sense that Donald Graves describes it: to look deeply within their writing and identify what is strong and what needs work, what is reaching the audience—and what isn't.

Author's Note

What is particularly striking about Kaylee's revision is that her new endings are all very different from her original—and different from one another. She thought hard about this piece of writing, and the result shows what can happen when the desire to revise comes from within the student, rather than being a requirement imposed from without.

FIGURE 2.6

Kaylee's 4 Endings (Grade 5)

Alternate Ending 1

Even though that was the worst night ever, some good came out of it. I now knew that you can't trust anyone—even things, but you can always trust that if you get hurt and you cry loud enough, your parents will always be there for you. And you can trust me that you should never, EVER touch a vaporizer.

Alternate Ending 2

Photosynthesis is a plant's way of making food to fuel itself all day. My way is Parentsynthesis. My parents always help me get through each day. Plants may have the world's biggest food making factory, but I think parents are way better. Parentsynthesis.

Alternate Ending 3

The vaporizer really hurt, but the thing that could hurt me most in the world would be having no one to help me when I need it. This time, my parents were there to help, and when other people need it, this is why I try my best to help too.

Alternate Ending 4

When I woke up the next morning, I was full of hate. I glared at the vaporizer. I really wanted to hit it, but I knew that wouldn't turn out too good.

come together. Her paper about a bad experience (getting burned when she touched a vaporizer) ended this way:

> That night I went to sleep thinking about how lucky I was. Whatever happens, I know my parents will always be there for me. Even though my eyes were red from crying, all I could see were happy colors like pink and bright orange.

In a conference, Kaylee's teacher talked with her about the reflective aspect of a memoir's conclusion. That discussion prompted Kaylee to write four *new* possible endings (see Figure 2.6). Choose a favorite before reading the whole paper (Figure 2.7) to see which one Kaylee wound up using.

Reading aloud is essential to good revision. Through reading aloud we discover whether the message makes sense, whether the sentences are fluent as written on the page, and whether the voice is true. Author and teacher Mem Fox (1993, 114) puts it this way: "As I write this chapter, I hear every cadence, listen to every pause, and check every beat. I'm hoping that if you enjoy the rhythm of my words, you might be inclined to like my content as well."

My colleague Judy Mazur teaches and reinforces the concept of revision through her students' own examples. Her writers share their rough drafts and revisions aloud as classmates listen and take notes. Then together, listeners brainstorm a list of differences they hear, before and after. This activity not only encourages attentive listening, but awakens writers to possibilities others have tried that they might not have yet considered. See Figure 2.8 for brainstormed lists based on just three writing samples from Judy's own class. (Each bullet is a student's comment on that revision.)

Author's Note

Technology has changed the look and feel of revision forever. Just a few years ago, we had distinctive "drafts" of writing. We could keep them in folders, look through them, and see the changes. This is still possible in classrooms where handwriting prevails. Composing on the computer, however, is different. By tinkering continually, we lose the sense of individual drafts. At the same time, word processing has made revision *infinitely* easier and less tedious. Therefore, whenever possible, encourage writers—especially those challenged by adding or changing information—to compose and revise on the computer.

FIGURE 2.7

Parentsynthesis by Kaylee (Grade 5)

Not everything you do is going to end up being good. I learned that the hard way.

I shot my eyes open. It was the middle of the night, and I was more tempted to do something than I ever had been.

A vaporizer was on in my room. Unfortunately, my brain wasn't. I thought that the vaporizer was as calm as a grown up drinking morning coffee. What I didn't know was that if vaporizers were alive, their hearts would be as cold and hard as a rock in the fiercest blizzard ever. And their eyes would be fiery red.

I just HAD to touch it. What could happen? Slowly, I reached out my fingers. It was 2:00 in the morning, and I was 3 years old.

A loud, shrill scream bombed the night. It was followed by crying. My mom jumped into action. She ran to my room and burst through the door.

"What happened?" she asked me. I kept on crying. My mom had no idea what had happened.

I felt lonely. I was the only person in the whole entire world that knew I had touched the vaporizer. My mom thought my hand was asleep, so she rubbed it. I kept right on sobbing. Water streamed out of my eyes like dew rolling down a leaf. My mom's eyes looked this way and that. Then they landed on the vaporizer.

At that moment, my dad thundered down the hall. I must have been crying REALLY loudly, because my dad almost NEVER wakes up in the middle of the night.

"I think she got burned by the vaporizer!" my mom shouted over the sound of my wailing.

"Oh boy!" Dad yelled back. He picked me up and carried me to the kitchen. Dad set me on the counter.

I hate that vaporizer, I thought.

My mom turned on the kitchen faucet and ran my hand under the cool water. My crying got slower and slower, and softer and softer, until it finally stopped like a room that gets dimmer and dimmer, and then it suddenly goes pitch black.

Photosynthesis is a plant's way of making food to fuel itself all day. My way is Parentsynthesis. My parents always help me get through each day. Plants may have the world's biggest food making factory, but I think parents are way better. Parentsynthesis.

EDITING: MAKING THE READER FEEL "AT HOME" IN YOUR TEXT

Trait Connection: Conventions & Presentation

Every single piece of writing gets edited, one way or another. The question is, *Who will do the work—the writer or the reader?* When *the reader* must do it, it can be difficult to concentrate on anything else. When *the writer* does it, the reader can relax and focus on the message.

Editing involves correcting spelling, punctuation, and grammar; deciding issues of formality (contractions or not?); considering usage and idioms; and ensuring that sentences are complete and grammatical, that parentheses come in pairs, that colons do not follow verbs, and that paragraphs begin where they should. Editing is not just about

FIGURE 2.8

Judy's Revision Chart

I Stink!
- The tone got tougher—not so nice!
- There were pictures in the final draft.
- The writer combined all early drafts in the final.
- It got longer.
- She kept the lights and the sound effects.
- There was more rhyming in the final.
- Added in the line, "Did I wake you? Too bad!"
- Revised the time order.
- All from a truck's point of view!
- It changed from a poem into a story.
- Lots of big words added!

What a Party!
- Change of feeling.
- More poetry.
- Onomatopoeia.
- In the rough draft, Froggie didn't want to sing alone—but in the final, he did.
- There was more dialogue.
- Fewer repetitive lines.
- Pictures helped us understand the book.

The Secret Project Notebook
- A different title.
- More talking.
- Changes from third to first person.
- More showing—less telling!
- A name change!
- It has mystery now.
- The final pulls the reader in more.
- There are more questions for the reader.
- You really feel something is going to happen—it's spooky!

correctness, however. To view editing this way suggests that conventions are little more than a rigid set of rules—when nothing could be further from the truth. Conventions exist to make meaning clear and voice expressive. They literally guide readers through the text—offering little clues that show a reader just how to read the copy:

- Let's eat, Grandma.
- Let's eat. *Grandma?*
- Let's eat Grandma.

The best editors—

- Use excellent handbooks and check what is *currently* correct
- Use every tool available, including personal dictionaries and spell check programs
- Ask for help if another qualified editor is available
- Read text both silently and aloud to check for errors
- Put writing away for a time prior to editing in order to gain mental distance
- Double space and allow wide margins so that there is room for corrections *or* (if editing on a word processor) so that reading/proofing is easier

Editing can occur at two levels, as I indicated in Figure 2.1. At the first level, we edit text for readability so that we can process it with ease. This level focuses on conventions.

If we publish something formally, whether through a school publishing house or a professional publishing house, editing at a second level is required. This level focuses on presentation, the look of the document. Presentation, as its name implies, involves laying out the document in a way that makes information both accessible and appealing.

PUBLISHING: HONORING AND PRESERVING WRITING

Trait Connections: Conventions & Presentation

Publishing—going public with writing—can take many forms. Sometimes it involves making a book or even submitting work to a publishing house. Other times it may be more informal—reading from an author's chair or posting work on a wall. Informal publishing does not, in my view, demand the attention to conventions that more formal publishing requires.

Publication honors the writer's work, but it should not be mandatory. Consider the wisdom of Mem Fox (1993, 39), who declares, "It depresses me utterly to see children being forced to finish a piece of writing when they're sick of it, lacking in inspiration, and getting negative feedback in writing conferences. No one forces me to finish my writing, and I'm a published writer, so why should any writer be ruled in such a manner by someone who doesn't own the writing anyway?" You do not need to publish every piece students write—or assess every piece for that matter. Freeing yourself from this responsibility will encourage more frequent writing. And frequent writing, after all, is one of our primary goals.

Formal publication is easier than ever these days. For one thing, writers have more access to computers, which makes document design much easier. In addition, many agencies will publish student work without the usual hoops of submission and editorial acceptance (or rejection!). Simply search online under "Student Publishing" for a list of current resources. If you go this route, use formal publication as an opportunity to ask students to edit with special care, having another "pair of eyes" (you, another student, a qualified parent volunteer, an older student from another class) review the document.

Give due attention to presentation as well. In designing documents (from brochures to posters to picture books), students can make their own decisions about such things as—

- Font style and choice
- Use of color
- Use of charts, drawings, photos, cartoons, or other graphics
- General layout—placement of text, photos, and other graphics
- Inclusion of table of contents, foreword, glossary, or other additions
- Cover design

. . . and much more. (See Chapter 8 for more on presentation.)

Published documents almost always include work by more than one person. So remember to provide credit to everyone who has worked on a given piece (see Figure 2.9).

FIGURE 2.9
Sample Credit Page
Credits Written by Jeff Hicks Illustrated by Fred Wolff & Billie Lamkin Edited by Sally Shorr © 2004 Hicks, Wolff, Lamkin & Shorr

ASSESSING: FOR STUDENTS, THE FIRST STEP IN *REVISING*

Trait Connection: All Traits

Assessment typically comes at the end of the writing process, and is typically teacher directed and grade connected. All of this is fine so far as it goes. Teachers, not students, should be responsible for assigning grades (so long as we remain convinced we need grades). However, as Figure 2.1 suggests, what we really need is a partnership, one in which *the most important assessor* is the student.

Students assess their own work *not* to assign a grade but to see what needs to be revised. Self-assessment is the most important assessment of any piece of writing that can occur—*ever*. That's because this is the *only* assessment to occur during the process of revision, while there is still time for the writing to grow and change. It is also the only assessment (media hoopla notwithstanding) to have major impact upon students' thinking, and hence, upon their writing performance.

Once a grade falls on the paper, the writing is finished—usually. But when a student assesses to say, "How can I make this stronger?" it is time for the real writing to begin.

WHAT ABOUT GENRE?

You may be wondering where genre fits into this picture. I long believed it made the most sense to teach forms of writing last, *after process* and *after traits*—mostly because the traits shift slightly from one genre to another. The voice in a mystery story is very different from that in a business letter. The conventions in a dramatic script or poem will be quite different from those in a lab report or legal contract, and so on.

I now believe, however, that genre needs to be addressed *in conjunction with* the traits, so that as you teach ideas, for example, you might talk about how detail in a report differs from detail in, say, a poem. As you teach organization, you can explore the limitless designs that emerge in various genres: a journal, cookbook, signage for a museum, script for a play, voice-over for a video documentary—or a book such as this one. As you teach voice, invite students to listen for the contrasting voices we hear in song lyrics, letters, resumes, histories, nonfiction books, blogs, picture books, and more. You may also touch upon those genres in which voice is deliberately suppressed because the message matters more than the messenger: technical reports, police reports, medical journals, or contracts. I have also come to see genre as particularly closely aligned with the trait of organization because genre helps us envision the shape and internal mapping of the final document.

Setting the Stage with Writing Workshop

Writing workshop is an extension of *you*. It's the atmosphere—the feeling—you create within your classroom, together with the day-to-day logistics that determine how you and your writers work, and what happens when.

WHAT HAPPENS IN WRITING WORKSHOP?

Although writing workshop probably looks a little different in every classroom, there are some commonalities. First, workshop fosters independence. This means that the writers themselves make numerous decisions, such as what to write about, what genre to choose, when and how much to revise, how to spend time on a given day, and so forth. Within parameters set by the teacher and the group, writers govern themselves—just as writers in the real world do.

Second, workshop, as its name implies, is all about getting the business of writing done. Students are busy—at *something*—all the time.

Third, the process of writing is honored. By that I mean not just that writers plan, draft, and revise, but that they continually seek better and more efficient ways to do these things. And they share their discoveries with one another so that, potentially, any member of the workshop community can be an in-house expert.

And fourth, the focus is on process more than product. This doesn't mean that writers are not serious about producing good copy. They most certainly are. But they are even more serious about learning to *be writers*.

FOLLOWING A ROUTINE

Writing workshop also tends to follow a routine—which is a good thing. Routine allows writers to know when they will write and how much time they will have. Ask anyone who has carried writing over day to day, and they will tell you how enormously helpful such predictability can be. Allowing for differences, that routine usually has three core parts:

An Introduction
The teacher might kick off workshop by (1) teaching a mini-lesson on any relevant topic, (2) sharing a sample of literature (or giving students a chance to do that within writing circles), (3) modeling some part of writing process, or (4) giving writers an opportunity to share insights or suggestions that could benefit the group.

Writing Time
During this time, writers plan, begin, or continue drafts (often rereading what they wrote during the last session), confer with one another, revise and edit, or plan publication. The teacher may use this time to confer with individual students or small groups who share common questions or concerns.

Sharing Time
This part of workshop offers writers a chance to share what they have written—with a partner, within a small group, or with the class as a whole.

ON DAY 1

On the very first day of writing workshop, the teacher might begin by modeling topic selection—just going through a list of four or five possible topics and choosing one to write on, then asking students to do the same. The teacher may also talk a little about writing process—and perhaps model one or two forms of prewriting. At this point, students need time to write. And on Day 1, this may be a very different experience for various students. Some will plunge right in while others may feel stuck after the first sentence. That's OK. One of the main benefits of workshop is its capacity to increase students' comfort with writing—as well as their capacity to keep going.

During actual work time, there's often a soft, steady hum as people seek and share advice or read their writing aloud. Some might be going over the writing they began in a previous session, some might be drawing, researching, drafting or revising, or putting finishing touches on posters, essays, reports, books, blogs, or photo-journals. As students work on their writing, *you* might be—

> "Establishing a community of writers" is a phrase that has been overused, but I still promote the concept. I believe that in the most productive writing environments, the teacher and learner are one.
>
> —Jennifer Jacobson
> *No More "I'm Done,"* 2010, 2

- Roaming and conferring with individual students at their desks
- Conferring with students in a quiet corner
- Coaching small groups
- Writing a piece of your own
- Sharing your own writing in a small group—or listening to students as they share

ARE SOME WRITERS TOO YOUNG?

Can workshop function well with even the youngest writers? Absolutely. Second-grade teacher Megan Sloan offers some simple advice: "Begin at the Beginning. Find out what your students know and can do, and start there" (2009, 16). On the first day of her workshop, Megan hands her students paper and asks them to draw a picture, then write about it. This very simple strategy has several benefits:

1. With this gesture, Megan has initiated workshop in her classroom, and begun to show her students what to expect.
2. She gains an overview of the range of skills her students bring to workshop.
3. She affirms her strong belief that every child is a writer, regardless of whether he or she knows it yet.
4. Megan also discovers who is already comfortable as a writer and who will need some encouragement and coaching.
5. She learns a little about individual students—who they are and what interests them. Who loves race cars or ballet, dogs or football? Who is curious about spiders or stars? Who wants to be an athlete or scientist, dancer or artist? Who's a journalist—and who's a poet? Knowing students well is infinitely helpful in guiding them as they choose topics.

ENSURING SAFETY

One salient no-compromise feature of writing workshop is that it must feel safe. Safe for the shy student, the non-writer, the writer who doesn't like to share, the beginner, the second-language student—everyone. As Katie Wood Ray tells us, "writing workshop teachers have to make a place in their classrooms where it is okay for everyone to write, where it is safe for everyone to write, no matter what that looks like when a student does it. It needs to be okay for even the most struggling student to do what he or she is capable of with writing" (*Writing Workshop*, 2001, 14).

ALLOTTING TIME

Author's Note

Be flexible in designing your writing workshop time, too. While you might often want to follow an *introduction–writing time–sharing time* design, you don't want to be rigid about it. There could be times when your writers need additional time for research—or for sharing. Don't let a schedule dictate how you spend your writing time.

Most teachers like to devote the majority of workshop time to writing (often as much as half or more of the whole workshop); however, the precise schedule is—and should be—flexible. If you are new to writing workshop, you might start with the simplest of schedules: half an hour total, with about ten minutes, give or take, for each of the three parts. Then extend each part, or just the writing portion, as you become comfortable (which you will), and as your students feel ready to write more (which they will). Ultimately, you want writing time to consume at least half of your total workshop time. How will you do this?

Work on increasing your writers' stamina so that ten minutes no longer feels like a long time to write. It should feel like *nothing*. Poof, and it's gone. This takes practice—especially with beginning writers. Follow Megan Sloan's lead (even if you work with older students), and begin with a definition of stamina: *the energy and strength to keep doing something—sometimes for a long while.* Then ask students themselves to offer suggestions for extending their own writing stamina. See Figure 2.10 for a list of things various students have suggested. Practice these strategies, and increase your students' writing time gradually—say by two minutes at a time—until you reach your goal, whatever that may be. For primary teacher Megan Sloan, it is about a half hour. Older students may want—and need—to write longer. Increased writing time favors strong idea development—and hence voice.

FIGURE 2.10

Students' Suggestions for Increasing Stamina

1. Choose a topic you know well.
2. Choose a topic you really like.
3. Pick the quietest place you can to write.
4. If you need help, ask quietly.
5. If you get stuck, reread what you've written so far.
6. Close your eyes for a minute to get a picture in your mind.
7. Push yourself hard even when you feel like stopping.
8. Try to write just *one more sentence.*

TWO MYTHS

Here are two myths about writing workshop:

- *Myth 1: Workshop has no structure.* Nothing could be further from the truth, actually. Workshop cannot even function without structure. Students need to know what time it will begin and end, where to look for supplies, what behaviors are acceptable, when and how conferences can occur, where to go for help, and so on. As Katie Wood Ray (2001, 15) tells us, "For the writing workshop to be successful, it must be highly structured and must work the same way basically every day so that it could almost run itself independent of directed activity."

- *Myth 2: Workshop should be quiet—or nothing important is happening.* Just the opposite is true. There are limits, of course. There's a big difference between the quiet buzz of writers at work and the cacophony of an unruly group. As Donald Graves (1994, 117) emphasizes, "Responsibility is the key to classroom organization. Children need to have a clear sense of what is expected of them during writing time." Post some rules you develop *as a group*—guidelines about noise, for example. At the same time, respect your writers' very real *need to talk.* This is what writers do. And one of the most important things we teach writers is to seek responses about their work. Writers need listeners who will applaud, laugh—or sometimes say, "You lost me. I didn't quite understand that part." Audience response can feed revision.

Author's Note

You may be wondering whether students should do all their writing in class. For most older students, especially those doing research, this is not usually practical. Nevertheless, you do want as much in-class workshop time as your schedule will allow because this is your writers' chance to learn from one another and to confer with you. The energy of workshop is hard to capture elsewhere.

Following are five examples chosen to help you picture what writing workshop *can* look like. These are not intended as models. Think of them as "classroom visits" with teachers who have enjoyed great success in teaching writing. And keep in mind, too, that workshop in your classroom should reflect *you*.

In Judy's Third-Grade Writing Workshop

THE ATMOSPHERE

One step into Judy Mazur's classroom and it's apparent that *everything* is set up to support trait-based instruction. On the walls are trait posters—not purchased, but written and designed by Judy's own students. Sentence strips throughout the room capture students' spontaneous comments on what it means to have strong ideas or personal voice, or to use words that move readers. (Any time a student offers a comment about what makes writing work, Judy says, "Wait—let me get that," and writes it down on the spot.) Near the posters are displays of student writing that show strengths in various traits—writing chosen by the students.

ROOM ARRANGEMENT

Books are everywhere, and organized by topic: the solar system, insects, mammals, volcanoes, dinosaurs, U.S. history, etc. Open tables are designated for reading and note-taking.

Students are seated in small groups of four, so they can readily confer with one another. They store their writing in three-ring binders so they can continually add or move pieces to create an ever-fluctuating portfolio. Personal student writing guides are tucked into the front inside pockets. All work is dated so that students can track their growth.

Judy rarely sits down—but when she does, it is usually (1) to read aloud to students, (2) to participate in sharing, or (3) to confer with a student—often at her computer, where she can help students with last-minute editing or capture a dictated rough draft from a second-language learner.

WORKSHOP SCHEDULE

Judy's workshop runs four times a week for one hour: 10–15 minutes for a focus lesson, 30–35 minutes to write, and 15 minutes for sharing.

Judy always addresses her students as "writers," and (inspired by Lucy Calkins) opens each workshop with the words "Writers, today I want to teach you . . ." She draws on both writing process and the six traits for her organizational structure. Content might be as simple as one convention or something more complex—explaining paragraphing, modeling ways to write a strong lead, or sharing a picture book focusing on a particular trait. She ends her focus lesson with "Go write, writers!"

Students scramble to pick up their writing binders from the shelf, and almost everyone begins by reading over his or her writing from the last session. Then students move quickly into finishing drafts, revising, editing, formatting, or beginning a new piece—depending on personal priorities. Nearly every student is working on something slightly different. Students work for 30 to 35 minutes on personally selected topics while Judy holds individual conferences of about 5 minutes each. These students are writers, no doubt about it. They love what they do, they are fully engaged, and they don't want workshop to end.

CONFERENCES

During writing time, up to four students can sign up (on the board) for conferences with Judy. They sign up because they have a specific concern or question—and you can hear writers' language (trait language) in their concerns and questions:

- *Remember that example on basketball from the encyclopedia? I don't want my writing to sound like that!*
- *I think I have two topics. Can that work, or do I need to pick just one?*
- *I want this lead to be really scary. Does it work better to start with some creepy sounds— creak, creak, creak. Or maybe just say, "I heard a noise"? Which one is scarier?*
- *I just called this "My Best Friend." I think that title is boring. What else could I call it?*

"I listen carefully to what each child is saying," Judy comments, "and consider his work with respect. I begin each conference by asking, 'How can I help you today?' Students know they need to come to the conference ready to answer that question. I always end the conference by asking, 'What are you going to do now?'" This gives the child a chance to reflect on what he or she has learned and provides a transition into the act of writing.

SHARING

Judy saves 15 minutes of the writer's workshop for sharing, a process that, she says, "never ceases to amaze me." Writers know that the point is not just to read their work aloud but to get help from the class. Judy explains, "Sharers MUST begin by stating (something like) 'I'm sharing because I need help with a title/I can't figure out how to move through time/I'm wondering if I need more details to make the middle more clear/I think I might have too much dialog. . . .'

"You will be amazed," she adds, "by the quality of student comments and suggestions and how quickly the kids pick up writerly talk."

Writing is noisy business, Judy has discovered: "My workshop is not a silent place. . . . I want us to be a community of learners who are (as James Britton described it) 'floating on a sea of talk.'" The talk pays off. Judy was delighted one day when one of her third graders echoed a lesson from earlier in the year during a sharing session: "Remember when we said we don't want to get to the end of the piece and then say, 'Huh?'" These third graders are thinking and working like writers.

I want each child to feel safe and comfortable and important and valued because only then can we learn. I want students to be proud of their writing, and to share their work with the confidence that classmates will ask respectful questions and offer caring, thoughtful advice.

—Judy Mazur
Instructor, Grades 3 and 5

In Billie's Seventh-Grade Writing Workshop

Billie Lamkin teaches middle school in a district where classes tend to be large— usually over 40 students. Her seventh graders use rubrics and posters, and they are used to assessing writing samples and discussing literature using trait language. For a number of students in Billie's class, English is a second language, and Billie uses many

Author's Note

Billie, like the other teachers whose classes are profiled here, follows a general workshop format that includes an introductory lesson, writing time, and sharing. Rather than repeat that each time, I will focus on features that make each classroom unique.

creative strategies to help them gain comfort with the writing process. Billie's writing workshop runs about 45 minutes, with 10 minutes for a focus lesson or literature, about 20–25 minutes for writing, and a final 10 minutes for sharing, much of which happens in pairs or small groups. Billie enriches her instruction with modeling, lots of reading aloud—and "brain breaks," which allow students to get up and move. Following are some key features of her instruction.

TRAIT AEROBICS

"We take brain breaks during class," she explains. "This consists of standing next to our desks and participating in the six-traits aerobics (Lamkin, 2004). It's a total physical response (TPR) activity, which is one way of teaching English language or second-language learners, as well as all students who are kinesthetic learners. They work like this . . .

"For ideas, we stand with our hands made into fists just above our heads, then reach upward, one hand at a time. As each hand moves up, it opens up just like our ideas spring out of our minds and open themselves up to the world. I ask students to think about a topic they could write about, and I call on a few to share their ideas.

"Then I ask 'What do we need to do with our ideas as we write?' They call out, 'Organize.' Then we move to the motion for organization, which is stacking our hands (with a little space between) right in front of our bodies—put the left hand near your stomach, right hand about six inches above, then continue this pattern till we can't reach anymore—and reverse the process. As we do this, I ask students to call out organizational techniques . . . 'a catchy lead . . . pattern of ideas . . . good transitions . . . smooth ending.'

"Next I ask, 'What do we need to do to make sure the reader believes us?' and they respond, 'Tell the truth.' I add that in telling the truth, we reveal confidence in our organized ideas, and these must come from our heart—which is where the voice lies. I show the motion for voice by having my hands spring forth from just above my heart. Then I call on a few students to share a comment about something they are confident about in their writing.

"On to word choice. I ask 'If I am going to confidently organize my ideas, what do I need to choose to get my message out?' They respond, 'Words!' I tell them we need to choose our words wisely. For this trait, we reach and grab at the air in all directions. I bend and stretch, to show students I want them to reach for the *best* way to say something. I ask a few students to share favorite words.

"As they are still reaching, I ask, 'What do we call it when we put a bunch of words together to convey one meaning?' They respond, 'A sentence!' I explain that we need to create rhythm with our sentences. We imitate this rhythmic motion by intertwining the fingers of both hands and making a wave with our arms, right to left, then left to right, swaying as we move. Waves of the ocean are different lengths and crash against the shore with different force. How do we create this variety in our sentences? 'Begin with different words . . . have different sentence lengths,' they say.

"Finally we come to the last trait. I ask, 'What do we do to hold our clear, organized, voice-filled ideas together?' And they respond, 'We use periods, commas, and other punctuation!' I say yes, as I untangle my fingers, wrap both arms around my body, and give myself a big squeeze. I explain that conventions hold our thoughts together just the way a good hug holds us together.

"We then have silent peer conferences where the students read each other's writing pieces and are *only* allowed to use hand signals to point out positive trait usage. They will give a 'thumbs up' and then act out the trait that was very strong in the paper."

Author's Note

Billie has generously allowed me to use her "Trait Aerobics" activity in classrooms and in teacher workshops. It has been a favorite activity for both students—of all ages—and teachers. We don't always get to "write on our feet." Thanks to Billie, sometimes we can.

THE MAGIC OF MODELING

"Modeling my own writing with students is very effective," Billie says. "Students look at, critique, and score my writing—then assess their own writing. Sometimes they offer suggestions for revision—or they tell me what's working well or what they might try. Every assignment I ask students to do is presented to them with *my* writing example for that assignment. They know that if I ask them to do it, I will do it too."

BACKWARDS PLANNING

"My students are asked to have three writing pieces of their choice completed per quarter," Billie explains. "When a writing piece is assigned, they are also given a blank calendar that shows only a three-week time period. They are also given a list of possible writing stages they may choose to use (brainstorming, drafting, self-conference, revision, peer conference, editing, proofreading, publishing, reflection, scoring, etc.). They first decide what date they are going to complete the writing piece and then work *backwards* through the writing stages, allowing a few days for revision or just letting the paper sit and marinate for a few days to give it a fresh perspective until they reach the day that it was assigned. The student chooses all of his or her dates and can make appointments for a conference with me based on those choices. It not only teaches students goal setting but also the responsibility of following a plan."

In Barbara's Middle School Writing Workshop

At the beginning of the school year, Barbara asks her sixth-, seventh-, and eighth-grade students to purchase a spiral notebook (about 120 pages) for all writing notes, brainstorms, prewrites, etc. Students create a section for each trait. Like Billie, Barbara devotes the majority of her 45-minute classes to writing, with short focus lessons and a brief sharing time—that sometimes spills over into another session.

Focus lessons often include modeling (beginning with topic choice) or literature. In addition, Barbara's students become proficient assessors of writing, using student writing guides. They often open class by scoring and discussing a writing sample, then applying what they have learned to their own writing. Here, in her own words, are some distinctive features of Barbara's classroom.

CHOOSING TOPICS

"My sixth-grade class includes about twenty challenged writers. I begin by generating a list of things on the white board that *I* want to write about and I talk through this process out loud for all students to hear my thinking. Next, students go to their writer's notebooks and they generate their own lists of what Nancie Atwell calls 'writing territories.' From that list, the students pick what they want to write about and then they're ready to begin planning."

MODELING

"To give students a context for what works or doesn't, I write a weak paragraph and have students break into groups of four and rewrite a much stronger paragraph, using my weak one as a springboard. This gives them a chance to get more 'touchy-feely'

What's the secret to good writing instruction? Modeling, modeling, modeling . . . oh, and humor, humor, humor. You need to laugh a lot, at yourself and with your students. I tell my students that I have the best job in the world because I get paid to act like a 13-year-old all over again. There isn't a job out there that is as rewarding as hanging around middle school students for six hours a day.

—Billie Lamkin
Middle School Teacher

with ideas. They feel comfortable because they are not working alone, and they're not pressured to write for a grade. I want students to *love* to write and nothing is more fun than doing a lesson with your friends and having the teacher tell you what a great job you have done."

ASSESSING WRITING AS A CLASS

"Here's a process I use all of the time with *all students*—ELL, challenged, gifted, you name it. After we have written a piece, I share a one-paragraph sample and students use a student rubric to assess it. We read the piece out loud, and using the language of the rubric, each group rates the paragraph. As we discuss the paragraph, groups defend their position and we get into some spirited debates. This is how they learn to really get inside the writing and think like writers.

"I also use this process with pre-scored papers from *Creating Writers* (2009) and from the *Write Traits Kits* (2010, Vicki Spandel and Jeff Hicks, Great Source Education). For sixth graders, we begin with ideas and slowly add organization. By the end of the school year, the students are comfortable with all six traits and it is not unusual to score a piece of writing for three or four traits at a time."

PICK YOUR CORNER!

"I mark corners of the room: all the 4's go here [indicating the corner], the 5's over there, and so on. Then students have to go to the appropriate corner to indicate their scores. They *love* actually getting up and moving to record their votes. In September my sixth graders are all over the place, but as the year moves on, students begin to agree more. Once students have moved to an area, they *must* use the language of the rubric to defend their position. This is all done orally so that everyone can hear and participate. If some students are shy (maybe because of language issues) I call on them *after* they have heard discussion from others.

"Once we have discussed a paper, students are given a chance to re-vote. Of course we always end with the big finish, 'And the *raters* say. . . .' Then I read out of *Creating Writers* or one of the kits to share what teachers have said about the same piece. My students really get into the game show atmosphere! The important part is, they're learning to think."

REVIEWING INDIVIDUAL STUDENTS' WORK

"Each student knows that at some point his or her work will be sampled for the entire class to read. I like this approach for a couple of reasons.

Author's Note

Barbara also, of course, confers with students individually. In the case of Sophia, for example, she says, "I started the students brainstorming via categories. Students had also interviewed parents, grandparents, and if available, great grandparents—about favorite toys, foods, and memories." Working from those interviews, Sophia brainstormed the list in Figure 2.11. With coaching from Barbara, she wrote the rough draft in Figure 2.12. Using *who/what/where/when* questions, Barbara encouraged Sophia to extend her writing: e.g., "Do they hold their heads high in an arrogant way—or are they proud people, coping with adversity?" This question prompted Sophia to add the phrase "even if the sun does not shine" that appears in her final draft, Figure 2.13 (see page 54).

FIGURE 2.11	FIGURE 2.12
Sophia's Brainstormed List	Sophia's Rough Draft

Sophia's Brainstormed List

Where I'm From

Toys	Sports
• Dolls	• Swimming
• dress up	• tennis
• board games	• gymnastics
• puzzles	• running
• crafts	

Games	Food
• handball	• Glop
• 4 square	• Celery + cream cheese •
• hide and seek (at night)	peprica
• green light - red light	• chicken, rice, carrots
• Okami	• gum
	• jelly beans
	• rice candy
Shows/Plays	• salmon
• Kimba the white lion	• lobster
• Sonic X	• meatballs
• Yu-gi-oh	
• tmnt	
• sky hawks	
• inuyasha	
• Lion King (movie & play)	
• Repo man (rock opera)	
• Jurassic Park	
• Pokemon	

Sophia's Rough Draft

I'm from my Great Grand mother's sewing shop that she ran when she arrived in America. brought up when she arrived

I'm from independent women who hold their head's high even if the sun dose not shine. From taking walks at dusk after a long days work, from working in the garden or in the house. I'm from hearts that have been broken and repaired, from sitting by the fire, and old stories mythical tales.

I'm from purple potatoes, butter-nut-squash, the Irish dish called glop and seafood that makes your mouth into a river. I'm from freshly made lemonade and smoothies. From gooey and crunchy smores, and gold rush gum.

I'm from the green lands of Inland and scottland and from the spices and treats of Italy. I'm from staring up at the night sky to the blissful and cool caress of mist in the morning.

I'm from corsets, boddests, blouses, ripped jeans, long and short flowing skirts, and funny t-shirts. I'm from tall to short to dark and light. I'm from different sights, smells, sounds, and smiles. And I may be from all of these but I am me and that sits just right on my family tree.

"First, students see that their writing is not just for the teacher's eyes only—it is for the entire classroom community. Yes, we learn as individuals but we also need to lean on each other to become stronger writers.

"Second, it shows each student that his or her writing is truly valued and important no matter how weak or strong. Even if a piece is very weak, I always find something of value and share that with the class. Maybe it's a phrase that stands out or some emerging idea. I'll take that opportunity to encourage that student in front of the entire class with a compliment then add something like, "I really want to hear more about that event. Can you write more about it for the class?"

LEARNING TO "READ" EACH OTHER'S WRITING

"Let's say it is September and the class is working on personal narrative. After a number of mini-lessons on beginning writing, I rearrange my classroom into groups of four. Students take their writers' notebooks and pass them to the person on their left. Each student reads the piece, writes comments in the student's notebook, and signs his or her name—then passes the notebook on until everyone in the small group has commented. At the beginning of the year, typical comments sound like this:

- *This is good.*
- *I like this.*
- *Good idea.*
- *Good organization.*

FIGURE 2.13

Where I'm From
by Sophia

I'm from independent women
who hold their heads high even if the sun doesn't shine.
I'm from the stitches from my Great Grandmother's sewing shop
that she brought up when she arrived in America.
From taking walks at dusk after a long day's work in the garden and house.
I'm from hearts that have been broken
and repaired,
from sitting by the fire,
and old mythical tales.

I'm from purple potatoes, smooth butter-nut-squash,
the Irish dish called glop,
and seafood that turns your mouth into a river of warm saliva!
I'm from freshly made lemonade
and smoothies on hot summer days.
From gooey and crunchy s'mores
that stick to your fingers as the joy of sharing a treat with people you love,
and gold rush gum shared and loved by my mother and her siblings.

I'm from the green rolling lands of Ireland and Scotland,
from the spices of Italy and the sweet treats from Germany.
I'm from staring up at the night sky
and the blissful and cool caressing
touch of mist in the morning.

I'm from corsets, bodices, and blouses, to funny t-shirts,
From ripped jeans, and long to short flowing skirts.
I'm from different sights, sounds, and smells to short, tall, dark, and light.
From strange and creative personalities
and headstrong opinions.

And I may be from all of these things
But I am me
And that sits just right on my
Family tree.

"Not very helpful! But to become good trait raters, students need to see me do it first, so I choose a group and join in, modeling the reading and writing of comments. Typically, I can "hit" three groups. As each group reads my comments, various group members slowly get the idea of using what *you* know as a writer to help someone else. As the school year goes on, I begin to get comments more like these:

- *Your words need more life. Don't use* nice *and* good.
- *This reads like a laundry list! You need more voice here! Don't be afraid to say what you mean.*
- *This idea is really good, but it would be even better if you explained it more.*
- *I think this idea would stand out more if you put it at the beginning of the paragraph.*
- *I don't see any internal dialogue here. Get me inside your character's head.*

Learning to be a strong writer takes lots of instruction, modeling, demonstration, partner sharing, revising—and more revising.

—Barbara Andrews
Middle School Teacher

In Andrea's Multiage Second-Language Classroom

Andrea is a specialist in working with second-language students, and her secret is a magical combination of deep respect for students' skills and creative adaptation of the six traits to fit the learning style of someone who is just learning to speak English. *Keep it simple* is rule one. Workshop in Andrea's classroom is similar structurally to that of Judy, Billie, or Barbara—but there are a few special adaptations she has made for her struggling writers.

KEY WORDS

"My way of adapting the rubrics for non-English or beginning English speakers is to identify the 'key words.' For example, I identify *details* and *main idea* for ideas and development. At first, students look at those two concepts *only*. We read sample papers and look at the quality of detail and assess how well the story or essay sticks to the main point. As the language becomes more familiar, other features of the trait come in to play."

LEARNING KINESTHETICALLY

Andrea is also sensitive to the kinesthetic learning style of many students. "I use many, *many* physical activities. We go on 'digs' around campus, meaning we walk around, collecting words, phrases, and mental pictures of what we see. We put them on index cards, and these cards are later incorporated into dialogue or descriptions or made into found poetry. We listen to music and discuss fluency. We take pictures with disposable cameras and talk about details and 'focus.' We cook to learn new words and to discuss following directions as a way of organizing information. Just about any snack that can be made in the microwave or on a burner has been made in my classroom."

EVERYONE WRITES

In addition, Andrea is a whole-hearted believer in the maxim that to become a proficient writer, you must write. "My ELL students write. And write. And write. They write from the first day they arrive. If they have no English skills, they copy a paragraph that introduces me and my classroom. If they have some English skills, they practice the act of writing during our writing time. They practice writing their vocabulary words, they practice writing their names in English, if they are not familiar with the alphabet. They never have an excuse not to write. I don't grade these pieces, of course, but they are turned in and commented on. My philosophy is: If they can write letters, they can learn to write words. If they can write words, they can learn to write sentences, and if they can write sentences, they can write *anything*. ELL students *can* produce written work. They just need some support to get there. Not speaking English is a reason they struggle, but it isn't an excuse not to provide opportunities to stretch them as learners and writers. I look on them as writers, and I provide opportunities to write every day."

> Although newcomers may not be as fluent when writing English as they are in their native languages, and their writing may not be as fluent or as standardized as that of their fluent English-speaking peers, they are clearly able to use writing to express their thoughts and emotions. When working with ELLs whose writing is filled with unconventional uses of English, it is important to keep in mind that writing is a developmental process, whether writing in the native or nonnative language.
> —Katharine Davies Samway
> *When English Language Learners Write*, 2006, 58

Author's Note

You may be thinking, "I can't cook in my classroom!" But remember, it's the *kinesthetic experience* that counts. The scent of spices, the textures of cloth or natural materials, the sounds of music or musical instruments—any or all could be part of the classroom experience you create.

Author's Note

Andrea's very positive approach is confirmed by research. In her book *When English Language Learners Write*, author Katharine Davies Samway (2006, 151–152) writes of a classroom in upstate New York where nonnative-English speaking children met two to three times per week with ESOL teacher Jean Olsen. Olsen shunned worksheets and drills in favor of a print-rich environment where children read constantly—and listened to her read, too: "Instead of focusing on their limitations, such as their nonstandard oral and written English, she focused on their accomplishments and development, such as their writing of a compelling draft or thoughtful response to a peer's writing. The classroom was invitingly filled with books, children's work, and objects from around the world, and it often seemed that this ESOL class was the only time in the school day that the children were seen as having expertise."

USING TECHNOLOGY

"In grades 3 through 5, my ESL students produce commercials and movies . . . and follow the same process for essay writing. We pick a topic, narrow it down to one main idea, pick out our best details and then write a rough draft (the storyboard), write a final draft (the script) and then revise while we are filming. (See Figures 2.14a and 2.14b for storyboard and accompanying script by one of Andrea's students who made a film on being careful with pencil sharpeners.)

"It's such a huge developmental leap for my 5th graders. . . . They get the whole writing process as a *real* process now. The homeroom teachers are telling me that the ESL students are transferring this knowledge in their regularly scheduled writing time. When the kids see their published piece (the actual commercial or short movie), they understand how the process is related to the product. It's an *ah-ha* moment I can't produce any other way.

"The greatest thing is that I can incorporate all my favorite things about teaching writing into an activity that has real meaning for students. They aren't producing a piece of writing for me . . . they are producing something that has a 'real' audience. One student told me she loves that people 'see her writing' now. And talk about being motivated to use correct grammar and vocabulary. I hear second-language learners arguing over which preposition is correct, if a word is really a noun or a verb in a certain sentence, and how word endings are pronounced.

"I use the record feature on PowerPoint to have students tell their story. A computer, headphones with a microphone and a story in their head is all I need. It's a great pre-writing center. We focus on one thing at a time . . . sometimes it's transition words,

FIGURE 2.14a

Storyboarding Example

CHAPTER 2 Setting the Stage

FIGURE 2.14b

Script for Pencil Sharpener Video
by Nayeli

Characters
- Pencil Kid (PK)
- Super Safe Hero (SSH)
- Narrator (N)

Opening
The boy is standing at the pencil sharpener. He is confused.

Intro
N: It looks like the boy has a problem. His pencil is dull. He needs to do something.
PK: I need to sharpen my pencil!

Scene 1
PK: What would happen if I put my finger in the pencil sharpener?
N: Oh no! This looks like a job for Super Safe Hero!

Scene 2
N: Da ta da da!
(SSH jumps into the scene.)
SSH: Don't put your finger in the pencil sharpener. That's not safe!
PK: Why?
SSH: Because it can cut you. Only pencils go in there.
N: That's right! Pencils are the only things we put in the pencil sharpener.

Scene 3
(SSH shows PK how to use the pencil sharpener.)
SSH: That's how you sharpen a pencil.
(SSH and PK high-five and yell "Whoo-hoo!")

Closing
PK: Thank you, Super Safe Hero!
SSH: You're welcome. It's my job to make sure you're safe.
(SSH flies off.)
N: It's important for everyone to be safe at school. Remember, being safe at WCE is everyone's responsibility.

I like the pacing of the six traits. I know that eventually we will focus on transitions, for example, so I don't need to race to get there. Without the traits, I think that I would feel pressured to teach everything about writing every time we wrote. I'd be afraid of forgetting something important. Students are often overwhelmed when writing for school—and a lot of that comes from the pressure to learn too many complex things at once. With the traits, we can focus on one component until my students understand. They don't feel overwhelmed, and neither do I.

—Andrea Dabbs
ELL Specialist and Teacher
www.writewiseconsulting.com

main idea, three good details. The goal for the listener is to have one thing to say to the storyteller.

"My first and second graders are natural storytellers. Little people remind me that we have to be able to *tell* our story before we can write it. My more advanced students transcribe their stories onto paper. I have also made CDs for parents. What a great way to share the stories their children have told."

In Rosey's High School Writing Workshop

In a paper titled "Reflections on Writing" (*Creating Writers*, 5th edition, pp. 100–101) high school senior Maisha wrote this about her first encounter with a truly remarkable teacher:

The teacher breezed into the first class of the semester late, clutching a coffee mug and an overflowing purse, and sporting a baseball cap pulled low in an attempt to contain her bad hair day. "Put the desks in a circle, my darlings," she said, accidentally dropping her mug and spilling half the contents of her purse onto a table. One of my

I must believe in each student every day—in their integrity, creativity, and effort. I must believe in it genuinely, from the heart, or they know right away. We need to teach students from the outset how to talk to each other intelligently about the written word. I am serious about this. State it, expect it, and it will happen.

—Rosey Dorsey
High School Teacher

friends had warned me about this earlier, in just three words: "Dorsey is awesome." She was right.

Rosey continues to inspire and mesmerize students, many of whom sign up for more than one of her popular writing classes—*if* they can get in. Rumor has it these classes will be active, demanding, unpredictable, and *totally* student-centered. High school writers cannot get enough.

Rosey begins the year with free writing (mostly in journals)—and opens most classes the same way. Through writing or discussion, students are expected to discover their own story or essay topics. Sharing is vital—and students are eager to share, knowing Rosey honors that most intimate part of workshop: "There is nothing, absolutely nothing, more important than a student sharing a poem or excerpt from a story or free write. That student is sharing a snippet from her interior world, and that is a sacred moment. It creates indescribable community—and community makes everything possible."

As much as the writing itself, community is the center of Rosey's workshop. As she says, "Creating community at the beginning of the year is the best use of time ever. I model how it *is*, how it *feels*, to be a writer, and this sets the tone immediately. Even 40 kids in a classroom can and will embrace community if the teacher becomes an integral part of it. Everything, absolutely everything, springs from this."

Modeling comes naturally to Rosey—but as she freely admits, making time for it takes effort. Sometimes, hard as it is, other things have to be nudged aside. "I am a writer," she says. "I carry my Moleskine notebook all the time. I pull it out, and write almost *all the time* the students write. Is it hard? YOU BET. Are there grades to be done and failing students and papers to assess? YOU BET. But I want an authentic classroom and in order for that to happen I must read and write with my students. Share their agony when the writing doesn't live up to my expectations and the joy when I nail it."

There's an underlying structure to all this. But it's embedded, not obvious. Rosey cites the following five elements as the "philosophical underpinnings" of her class:

1. Tony Wagner's 7 Survival Skills: "We memorize them and use them daily. It doesn't seem ethical on any level if we don't teach these to our students."

2. Leveled questioning based on Bloom's taxonomy: "It's all in the questions we ask!"

3. Socratic Seminars: "The Socrates Café is my source."

4. *Creating Writers:* "Of course!"

5. The poetry of William Stafford and Kim Stafford

As important as any embedded structure, however, is a natural flow and flexibility, all centered around the needs of the students. Rosey says, "I am intentionally vague about giving writing, reading, or discussion instructions—with the underlying hope that students will carve out their own prompts and topics, and have a vested interest in the quality of their work because they have a voice." There's plenty of room for spontaneity, too. If a student shows up with a piece of music he's composed (this happened recently), his song lyrics (performed, of course) can become the focus of the lesson—after all, composers are among our most creative writers. "A well-structured lesson plan is the perfect venue for diversion," Rosey claims. "Like Opus, in "Good night Opus," a perfect time to depart the text. The teachable moment is alive, very alive. If students destroy a lesson plan because they have a more relevant one, then I am doing my job."

And speaking of creativity . . . Rosey's students are encouraged to stretch their skills across a wide range of genres, including informational writing, argument, story, poetry, and more (even song lyrics). But creativity, from Rosey's perspective, isn't a *type* of writing at all; it's an inherent quality in all good writing. "There is within us," she explains, "a unique, creative language that is one of the greatest human gifts. It is available to every one of us. Even a research paper invites creativity, and it is my job—my oath—to keep that passion alive in every student. Our creativity—whether in words, images, art, or movement—is what gives our life meaning."

Recently, Rosey asked her students for their take on what made the class special. Following are just a few of their many responses:

- *In this classroom we are heard.*
- *It's based on Level 5 and Level 6 questions [from Bloom's taxonomy]. We rarely ask Level 1 questions.*
- *You turn haters of writing into lovers of writing by taking away that cage we had to stay in before.*
- *You die laughing at your own jokes.*
- *This classroom is safe. We can talk about anything.*
- *In this class you, and we, are shaping the thinkers of tomorrow.*

So often, our best teachers are the ones who can see the world through young eyes. Rosey says of herself, "I look forward to the journey every day. I am an open-minded student too. I make mistakes and laugh at them. I don't know the definition of every word in the dictionary and my commas are sometimes out of place. And, if I am truly honest, I have a really hard time with passive voice."

Recently, Rosey and her students (using the Blurb publishing service, blurb.com) self-published *See the Beauty,* a compilation of students' prose and poetry, complete with photos and bios.

On the last day of a writing workshop in Arizona, each of us wrote a list of what he or she wanted to leave behind in that room: shame, lack of time, fear that I'll hurt someone with the truth, fear of failure, fear that no one will really listen to me. . . . Next we wrote what we wanted to take with us, what we needed for the writing journey: the voices of other struggling writers, the courage to write the truth, more time, the belief that what I write will make a difference.

—Georgia Heard
Writing Toward Home, 1995, 137

Interactive Questions and Activities

1. **Activity and Discussion.** Draw your own diagram or sketch of the writing process as *you* see it. (It doesn't have to look like a wheel. Think divergently!) Base your sketch on how you teach writing or how you write, or both. Compare your personal "vision" with those of your colleagues and also with the diagram shown in Figure 2.1.

2. **Activity and Discussion.** As a writer, which of the following strategies do *you* use to prewrite? Which might you teach to students? Discuss your responses with colleagues.
   ____ Talking
   ____ Sketching
   ____ Just starting right in
   ____ Webbing
   ____ Making a list of questions or key points
   ____ Finding a literary model
   ____ Other _____

3. **Activity and Discussion.** As a writer, which of the following strategies do *you* use to revise? Which might you teach to students? Discuss your responses with colleagues.
   ____ Putting a draft away for two or more days (to gain perspective)
   ____ Reading my writing aloud to myself
   ____ Sharing my writing with a colleague or group
   ____ Using a writing guide or checklist
   ____ Other _____

Author's Note

In my all-time favorite depiction of writing process the writer began (during prewriting) as a stick figure, but by publication time had grown into a quite "well-rounded" character—albeit a very smiley one. Along the way, during "thinking" times, the writer enjoyed a number of nosh-y treats, from doughnuts to pizza, showing that writing sometimes involves more than just getting words on paper.

4. **Activity and Discussion.** Put an X by each of the following statements with which you agree. Then compare responses with your colleagues.

___ The traits are much more powerful and meaningful when taught in the context of writing process and writing workshop.

___ Writing process is different for every writer.

___ The main thing that makes workshop successful is students' opportunity to learn from and coach one another.

___ Students should write every day (or nearly every day).

___ Some writing should be revised—and some should not.

___ Most student writing should be assessed in some way.

___ It is essential for teachers of writing to write.

5. **Activity and Discussion.** With your group, brainstorm a list of features you consider essential to writing workshop. If you teach currently, would you describe your writing instruction as "writing workshop," based on the way workshop is defined in this chapter? If you are preparing to teach, do you envision your classroom as a writing workshop? Why or why not?

6. **Discussion.** Katie Wood Ray, who is quoted in this chapter, is a firm advocate of writing workshop. However, she views it as very different from writing process—rather than complementary to process, as presented here. Ray says, "In writing workshops, teachers invite children to do all the things a writer really does: research, explore, collect, interview, talk, read, stare off into space, co-author, and yes, prewrite, draft, revise, edit, and publish." (*The Writing Workshop: Working Through the Hard Parts*, 2001, 5). Do you agree with Ray's perspective that workshop gives a much

"bigger picture" of the world of writing? Is there more to writing than process? What *do* writers actually do?

7. **Activity and Discussion.** As a group, arrange to visit a classroom in which writing workshop is ongoing. Observe for more than one class period, if you can. Notice how the teacher opens workshop, and how writers spend their time. Notice how independent they are, and the extent to which they support one another as writers. Also observe how the teacher brings workshop to a close. Make notes for a discussion with your group later. What did you see that you would like to replicate in your own classroom?

8. **Activity and Discussion.** Do you work with ELL/ESL students? If so, what strategies do you use to get them engaged in writing and to help them find success? Are any of the strategies suggested by Andrea Dabbs (pages 55–57) familiar to you? With your group, make a list of things you have tried and found helpful. Expand your discussion by sharing Chapter 3 of Katharine Davies Samway's book (*When English Language Learners Write*) titled "Sketches of English Language Learners Becoming Writers." How were the ELL students described in that book influenced by such factors as environment, literature, topic choice, reading aloud, and willingness to take a risk?

9. **Activity and Discussion.** In the closing quotation from this chapter, poet and teacher Georgia Heard talks about closing a writing workshop by identifying things to let go of, such as fear or lack of support—and things to hang on to, such as writers' voices and courage. Try that with your study group or with students in your classroom. Talk about those things that, as a writer and teacher, you would most like to hold on to—or walk away from.

Coming Up

Now that the stage is set, we will spend the next six chapters exploring the traits, one by one, beginning with the trait of ideas. Each chapter includes a definition of the trait, writing guides (for teachers and students) in "leap-the-river" format, and suggestions for teaching that trait to students using focus lessons, modeling, and favorite literature. In this edition, you will find most information pertaining to any given trait within one chapter.

Being a writer has changed my life. It's something I can feel proud about. When I'm trying to think of a story, I will think of different settings and problems, and suddenly one will appeal to me. I'll think of a piece and it will start to grow in my head.

At my old school we had VOCP: vocabulary, openings, connectors, punctuation. That's how we thought about writing. Here at Buena Vista, in third grade writer's workshop, it's very different. Now I'm working on different traits, including word choice, ideas, and organization, as well as genres like fiction and poetry.

When I write fiction, I can do the impossible. I can make my enemies lose the state championship. The bottom line is this: Writing has opened up a whole new door for me . . . a door I didn't know existed.

—Lily, Grade 3

In my portfolio is some of the best work I've done in the past two years. The projects I've chosen to include show I'm a creative person with good ideas. This is my main strength. I have trouble with spelling and I don't have access to a spell checker outside of school. The hardest thing I did all year was write reports. I don't know how to take good notes. I can never figure out what is important enough to write down. I hope my portfolio shows I am a strong enough writer to make it in an accelerated class. The thing is, in accelerated classes, the discussions are different. They don't talk down to kids. All classes should be like that—then kids would like school more.

—Nikki, Grade 7

CHAPTER **3**

Making Meaning with IDEAS

An effective piece of writing says one dominant thing.

DONALD M. MURRAY
A Writer Teaches Writing, 2004, 18

This business of writing—of sentence length and sound, of verbs and adverbs, of creating pictures and hitting the senses, of getting rid of clutter—is never just about the words we use and how they look and sound on the page. Bound up with those language concerns is meaning. Meaning is the right bower. Meaning trumps everything.

TOM ROMANO
Crafting Authentic Voice, 2004, 174

Ideas are everything you think, remember, notice, believe, wish for, or dream up. They come from memory, from experience, and from imagination. The hallmark of strong ideas—originality—is the ability to see what others miss, to make connections others might not think of.

We begin with this trait because ideas are the heart of the matter. They influence—and are influenced by—every other trait. How we organize information, the voice with which we express ourselves, the words we choose, the way sentences flow, even the formality or playfulness of conventions: all, *all* are deeply, profoundly affected by the message.

This chapter has several purposes:

1. To introduce the trait of ideas through definitions, writing guides, and examples.

2. To share samples of student writing you and your students can discuss or assess together.

3. To suggest additional strategies for teaching this trait.

4. To lay some logistical groundwork that will guide you through the teaching of ALL the traits.

How Do I Begin?

Before introducing ideas—or any trait—begin by giving students the big picture: the whole spectrum of traits. You can do this by sharing "The Redwoods" and "Mouse Alert," or any writing samples you think will generate discussion. After talking about them, brainstorm a list of things that *make writing work*. Only instead of writing them down randomly, create a chart in which you frame six spaces, and arrange the comments by trait. Don't label the traits—*yet*. Just number the spaces within your chart, 1 through 6, and as your writers call out suggestions, write each comment in the space where *you* think it fits: ideas, organization, voice, word choice, sentence fluency, or conventions & presentation. (Yes, you *do* need to keep track of which space is which since you have no labels yet.)

The result will look *something* like Figure 3.1—only with *your* students' comments. You may notice something interesting about these comments (all of which I have received from students or teachers over the past several years). Even though they correspond to the traits, the language is personal. It doesn't match exactly what you will see on any rubric. And that's good. You want students to begin with a personal definition of each trait—and then to expand on this definition using the language within each writing guide.

Once you have finished your brainstorm list, you can say, "Guess what? You have just identified the six traits of writing—in your *own words*. Let me show you what teachers call these different traits." Then add labels, trait by trait:

- 1 = Ideas
- 2 = Organization
- 3 = Voice
- 4 = Word Choice
- 5 = Sentence Fluency
- 6 = Conventions & Presentation

Author's Note

Hold on to these personal responses. They're important. As you and your students work through the traits, you may want to use some of this language to modify the writing guides for your own class—or simply to refine your thinking about what makes writing work. Remember that when you teach traits, you are not teaching rubrics. You are teaching the *concepts* of ideas, organization, voice, and so on.

FIGURE 3.1

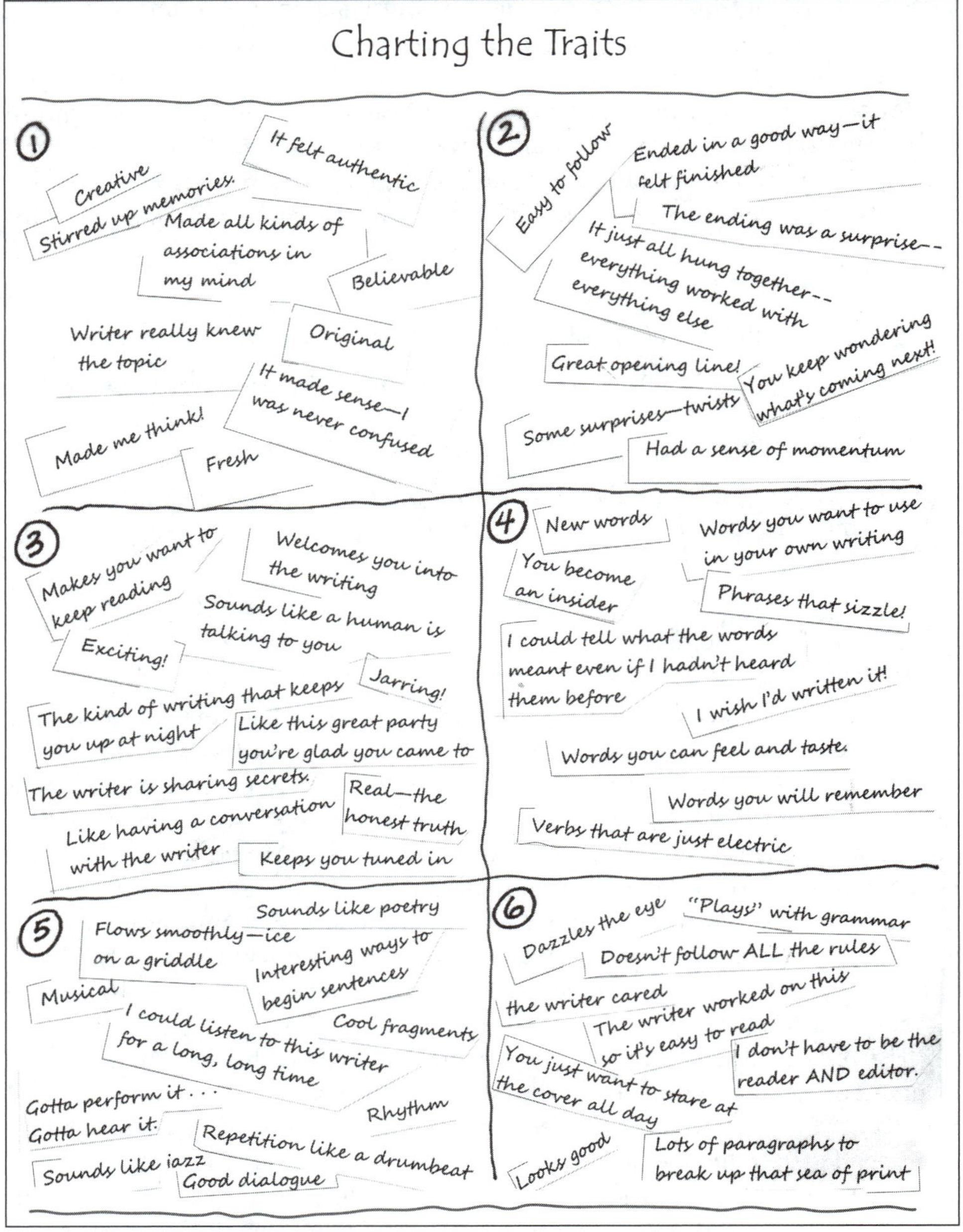

Charting the Traits

① Creative
Stirred up memories.
It felt authentic
Made all kinds of associations in my mind
Believable
Writer really knew the topic
Original
It made sense—I was never confused
Made me think!
Fresh

② Easy to follow
Ended in a good way—it felt finished
The ending was a surprise--
It just all hung together-- everything worked with everything else
Great opening line!
You keep wondering what's coming next!
Some surprises—twists
Had a sense of momentum

③ Makes you want to keep reading
Welcomes you into the writing
Sounds like a human is talking to you
Exciting!
Jarring!
The kind of writing that keeps you up at night
Like this great party you're glad you came to
The writer is sharing secrets.
Real—the honest truth
Like having a conversation with the writer
Keeps you tuned in

④ New words
Words you want to use in your own writing
You become an insider
Phrases that sizzle!
I could tell what the words meant even if I hadn't heard them before
I wish I'd written it!
Words you can feel and taste.
Words you will remember
Verbs that are just electric

⑤ Sounds like poetry
Flows smoothly—ice on a griddle
Interesting ways to begin sentences
Musical
Cool fragments
I could listen to this writer for a long, long time
Gotta perform it . . . Gotta hear it.
Rhythm
Repetition like a drumbeat
Sounds like jazz
Good dialogue

⑥ Dazzles the eye
"Plays" with grammar
Doesn't follow ALL the rules
the writer cared
The writer worked on this so it's easy to read
You just want to stare at the cover all day
I don't have to be the reader AND editor.
Looks good
Lots of paragraphs to break up that sea of print

Author's Note

As you share this writing guide, be sure you also take time to explain the "leap the river" concept. You can explain it this way: Scores of 1, 2, and 3 indicate writing in need of serious revision, with the only question being *how much*. Then we leap into the land of "proficiency," with scores of 4, 5, and 6. These are papers in which strengths outweigh problems— again, the only question being *by how much*. Asking "Does it leap the river?" *first* makes scoring easier. When discussing writing with students, sometimes this is the ONLY question you need to ask. You don't always have to assign scores. The real issue is strengths and problems.

Ask who has heard these terms before, and find out whether they are meaningful to your writers. Then ask if they would like to see what language teachers have used to describe performance on the first trait—ideas—from beginning level through strong. At this point, share the Student Writing Guide for Ideas, Figure 3.2, and compare the language of that guide to what you entered in the first space on your chart.

Explain to students that you will spend a week or two on each trait, and that by the time you have looked at all six, they will have a vast repertoire of skills they can use in planning, drafting, and revising.

The teacher version of this writing guide, for your use in assessing writing, appears in Figure 3.3. This is the same writing guide you used in Chapter 1 (Figure 1.7, the One-Pager), only formatted differently to emphasize that "leaping the river" concept.

FIGURE 3.2

Student Writing Guide for
IDEAS

6
- ❑ My writing will grab and hold your attention.
- ❑ The main idea or message really jumps out at you.
- ❑ I know this topic inside and out.
- ❑ This writing will make you think—and remember.
- ❑ The details I chose will intrigue you—and perhaps make a picture or movie in your mind.

5
- ❑ My writing makes sense and stays "on message."
- ❑ You can tell right away what the main point is.
- ❑ I know a lot about this topic.
- ❑ I share important, interesting information.
- ❑ My details are helpful and important.

4
- ❑ *Most of the time* I stick with the message.
- ❑ You can figure out my main point.
- ❑ I know enough to give you an overview.
- ❑ I share *some* new information—and some things you've heard before.
- ❑ You'll get the general idea.

3
- ❑ I listed some ideas—I didn't develop all of them.
- ❑ You might figure out my message or you might not.
- ❑ I wish I knew more about this topic.
- ❑ If I got stuck, I made things up—or just guessed.
- ❑ I *think* you'll get the general idea.

2
- ❑ I'm still figuring out what I want to say.
- ❑ It might be hard to figure out my message.
- ❑ Writing about this topic was hard.
- ❑ I said some things I could not prove or support.
- ❑ I ran out of things to say and had to repeat or write about something else.

1
- ❑ I don't have much to say yet.
- ❑ I'm still searching for a clear topic.
- ❑ I'm sure I left readers with a LOT of questions.
- ❑ These are my first thoughts—I just wrote to fill up the page.
- ❑ I need help choosing or understanding my topic.

© 2012. Vicki Spandel. Designed for use in classroom assessment.

IDEAS: Meaning & Message

A Definition

Ideas are the heart of the writer's message—the main thing the writer has to say—plus all the details (facts, explanations, anecdotes, observations) that clarify or expand that message. The strength of the writer's ideas depends on knowledge of the topic, observation skills (especially the ability to notice what others miss), and a knack for choosing details that make the message both clear and interesting. Hallmarks of good ideas include clarity, focus, thoroughness, insight, authenticity, and originality.

Share my definition—but feel free to add your own interpretation or insights. Give students time to look over the writing guide, and to ask any questions about the language or about how to use the guide in scoring writing. Remind students that they can use this guide to score writing samples of all kinds. You might begin with student papers, but you will enrich your discussion enormously if you also assess and discuss passages from textbooks, newspapers or journals, promotional pieces, business writing—or a host of other things. As you do so, your students will be teaching themselves and one another countless lessons about what to do—or *not* do—as writers.

FIGURE 3.3

Teacher Writing Guide for
IDEAS

6
- ❏ Clear, focused, compelling—holds reader's attention
- ❏ Strong main point, idea, story line
- ❏ Striking insight, in-depth knowledge of topic
- ❏ Takes reader on journey of understanding
- ❏ Significant, telling details paint a vivid picture

5
- ❏ Clear and focused
- ❏ Evident main point, idea, story line
- ❏ Reflects thorough knowledge of topic
- ❏ Authentic, intriguing information
- ❏ Important, helpful details expand main points

4
- ❏ Clear and focused more often than not
- ❏ Main point, story line easily inferred
- ❏ Sufficient knowledge for a broad overview
- ❏ Some new info, some common knowledge
- ❏ Details provide development on general level

3
- ❏ *Some* undeveloped text—or a list of general ideas
- ❏ Reader must work to get the message
- ❏ Some gaps in writer's knowledge of topic
- ❏ Mostly common knowledge, best guesses
- ❏ Generalities, broad brushstrokes

2
- ❏ Writer still defining, shaping message
- ❏ Main idea or message hard to infer
- ❏ Writer struggles to fill space
- ❏ Broad, unsupported generalities
- ❏ Repetition, filler, minimal support

1
- ❏ Minimal text
- ❏ Topic not yet defined in writer's mind
- ❏ Reader left with many questions
- ❏ Notes, first thoughts
- ❏ Writer needs help choosing/defining topic

© 2012. Vicki Spandel. Designed for use in classroom assessment.

Author's Note

Adopt a strategy used by teacher Judy Mazur (See "In Judy's Classroom," Chapter 2), and as your students think of other important features of strong ideas, write them on sentence strips and add them to your Trait Shortie poster.

Author's Note

Literature is a terrific way to introduce ideas—or any trait. Share several examples. Then have students look for their own passages the whole time you are working with each trait.

Along with the writing guide, you may wish to share the "trait shortie"—a summary of the key features within each trait. (See Figure 3.4.) These features remind students of some important things to look for in writing—or to think about as they are writing themselves. Key features for each trait also provide the *focus for your instruction.* Enlarge this and make a poster of it, if you wish.

WARMING UP WITH LITERATURE

Once you have reviewed a definition of the trait and have shared writing guides and the trait shortie (perhaps putting it on the wall in poster form), get warmed up with some samples from literature that illustrate specific features of the trait at hand. Choose passages from *any* books (or other written materials) you love. Or in some cases, use the whole book. In choosing literature to illustrate ideas, you are looking for—

- A strong central message
- Exceptional detail
- Vivid imagery
- Striking clarity

JUST A TASTE . . .

SAMPLE

A good writer never tells everything, but seeks those details that put us right at the scene. The scene becomes real, and we dissolve into it effortlessly. Consider this passage from Walter Dean Myers's book *Slam* (1996, 2), in which the main character describes the sounds of the city:

> When it's late night you hear the sound of car doors and people talking and boom boxes spilling out the latest tunes. When it rains the tires hiss on the street and when there's a real rain with the wind blowing sometimes you can hear it against the tin sign over Billy's bicycle shop. If there's a fight you hear the voices rising and catching each other up. The sound of broken glass can cut through other noises, even if it's just a bottle of wine somebody dropped. And behind all the other sounds there's always the sirens, bringing their bad news from far off and making you hold your breath until they pass so you know it ain't any of your people who's getting arrested or being taken to the hospital.

This example is especially striking because although it relies on sensory detail, Myers doesn't try to cover all the senses; instead, he focuses just on sounds. Yes, we picture the scene. But *mostly* we hear . . . the boom boxes, hiss of tires, rain pelting the tin sign, angry voices, and the ominous sounds of glass breaking.

USING A WHOLE BOOK

Sometimes, you may want to use the whole text, in which case your discussion may overlap several class periods. Here are two examples that show some of the ways you might use a longer piece of literature to prompt discussion or independent writing.

Sample 1

Extreme Animals: The Toughest Creatures on Earth by Nicola Davies. 2006.
Ages: Upper elementary through early middle school
Genre: Nonfiction

Summary

In this charming overview of Earth's most durable life forms, writer and zoologist Nicola Davies treats us to some unusual insights about what helps certain creatures survive—especially where people could not. We discover, for example, that penguins can go more than 100 days without food, that some birds can fly for eight

---

Author's Note

Don't be afraid to use picture books with older writers. They're engaging—and short enough to share within a single class period, allowing you to make a point quickly. The publication of picture books has become enormously competitive, ensuring that some of the world's best literature falls within this genre. Use the art in picture books (equally magnificent) to teach detail, voice, and presentation. You may have noticed also that there's a new subgenre on the scene: picture books for older readers (up to and including adults). Examples include Albert Marrin's *Years of Dust* (2009) and Patricia Polacco's *January's Sparrow* (2009).

hours nonstop (the equivalent of a human running 1,200 four-minute miles), and that some frogs turn into "frogsicles" to survive freezing temperatures (20, 34).

Suggestions for Discussion and Writing

1. Begin by sharing the title and subtitle. Which creatures do your students imagine made the list? As you read, check to see which of your guesses are correct.

2. This book has a strong central idea. What is it? You can make a good guess from the title—but your decision might change slightly as you read.

3. Davies opens her book with a striking lead. Take a moment to enjoy it. Do the same with the book's conclusion.

4. Share the whole book aloud—or as many sections as you wish. Have students keep notes on a few of the details they find most striking. What stands out? What captures their imagination?

5. Compare Davies's book with any passage from an encyclopedia about the polar bear, Arctic musk ox, penguin, sponge, or any creature Davies describes. How do the passages differ?

6. Notice how the book is divided into small chapters so that, as readers, we only need to digest one "chunk" of information at a time. Is this helpful? How?

7. Also notice the glossary and index, pages 60 and 61. Are these features your students might use in an informational piece?

8. The illustrations by Neal Layton have a comical, almost irreverent flavor. Suppose Davies had decided to use photographs instead. Would that have worked as well? Why?

9. Use Davies' descriptions as a springboard to write longer informational pieces about any creature described here.

10. Imagine that the tardigrades (pages 56 ff.) really *do* colonize another planet. What might that be like? Describe it—perhaps from the tardigrade's point of view.

11. How do other animals view humans? If they could put their thoughts into words, what might they say? Create a multi-voiced journal.

12. Humans clearly lack the stamina and resilience to withstand extremes of temperature or other difficult conditions. Yet human life thrives on Earth. What's our secret? Will we continue to be successful? Write an opinion piece on this.

13. Create a review of this book, either on paper or online.

Sample 2

The Surrender Tree: Poems of Cuba's Struggle for Freedom by Margarita Engle. 2008.
Ages: Young Adult
Genre: Poetry/Journal/History

Summary

In haunting free verse, Margarita Engle details Cuba's struggle for freedom from Spain, spanning the years from 1850 through 1899, including the Spanish American War. The book is a marvelous blend of genres: poetry, history, and personal journal, told in several voices. Central to the story is the legendary Rosa, a freed slave and self-taught healer. Other voices include those of Jose, her husband and devoted friend; and the dreaded Teniente Muerta, Lieutenant Death, who first knows Rosa as a child but, in an ugly twist of fate, grows up vowing to kill her for reward. The imagery of the book is powerful—and sometimes disturbing. Yet beneath these brutal images we sense Engle's love for Cuba, its beautiful landscapes, and the heart of a people who will not give up their soul.

I thought of the read aloud as being like candy—the kids loved it, but it seemed not so good for them—like time away from what we *should* have been doing. I still think of the read aloud as something deliciously edible, only now I see it as a wonderful vegetable—something so good for us as a class that we need several helpings of it each day.

—Katie Wood Ray
Wondrous Words, 1999, 65

Suggestions for Discussion and Writing

1. Take time to discuss Cuban history. What do your students know of the period from the mid-1800s until the turn of the century? Who has heard of the Spanish-American War or knows why it was fought?

2. How many cultures throughout the world rely on herbal medicines and other natural cures? Do your students know anyone who practices naturopathic medicine? Talk or write about this approach to healing in contrast to Western medicine as we think of it in a technological age.

3. Read all or part of the book aloud, and encourage students to read the whole book, beginning to end. Discuss events or images that stand out.

4. This is a book rich with sensory detail. Discuss the feelings and sounds that make the setting for the book especially vivid. What is it like to be in the cave where Rosa treats the sick or wounded? Write a descriptive piece from a patient's viewpoint.

5. Genres are often defined as if they are distinctive: narrative, expository, persuasive, and so on. Yet this book clearly blends several genres. Talk about that. Do your writers find this unusual—or more typical—in the real world of writing?

6. Read portions of the book aloud, having each reader assume one of the voices. Why is it important to include multiple voices in a book like this?

7. Imagine that this book were to become the basis for a film or documentary. Which scenes would you film and why? What would you want the world to know about Cuba's fight for independence?

OTHER WONDERFUL BOOKS FOR TEACHING IDEAS

***Animal Farm* by George Orwell. Centennial edition. 2003. New York: Plume. Allegorical novel.**

Although most classics are well suited to teaching ideas, this one truly stands out. Page by page, life is ever changing at Manor Farm—raising questions that provoke thinking about change, justice, equality, and "human" rights. The centennial edition is gorgeously illustrated by Ralph Steadman. Middle school and beyond.

***The Book Thief* by Markus Zusak. 2005. New York: Alfred A. Knopf. Novel.**

The highly original and compelling story of Liesel, who steals a book from her brother's grave—and is soon stealing books from Nazi book burnings—at great peril. A mesmerizing tale for sophisticated readers, told by an unexpected narrator. High school and adult.

***Boy* by Roald Dahl. 1984. New York: Penguin. Memoir.**

The story of Roald Dahl's younger years helps us understand where he got all those terrific writing ideas. Vivid details. All ages.

***Charlotte's Web* by E. B. White. 1980. New York: HarperCollins. Fiction.**

A classic with many elements vital in teaching strong ideas: compelling central theme, detail, imagery, fascinating characters. Primary and elementary.

***Guts* by Gary Paulsen. 2001. New York: Random House. Memoir.**

The extraordinary and often hair-raising real-life stories behind *Hatchet* and other Brian Robeson books. Upper elementary to adult.

January's Sparrow **by Patricia Polacco. 2009. New York: Philomel Books. Fact-based narrative.**

True story of a slave left for dead and the brave family that never gave up hope. Graphic details and illustrations. Middle school and up.

Matilda **by Roald Dahl. 1988. New York: Puffin. Chapter book.**

Watch out . . . the Trunchbull is coming! For imagery and detail that's a perfect blend of alarming and comical, this one is hard to beat. A page turner for young readers. Primary and elementary.

More Than Meets the Eye **by Bob Raczka. 2003. Minneapolis: Millbrook Press. Nonfiction/collection of art.**

Smell old shoes or a stack of wheat, pat a tortilla or stroke an ermine. Bob Raczka uses the five senses to take us on a guided tour of some famous paintings, one sensation at a time. All ages.

Puppies, DOGS, and Blue Northers **by Gary Paulsen. 1996. New York: Houghton Mifflin Harcourt. Nonfiction.**

True stories—hilarious to heartbreaking—about raising sled dogs to run the Alaskan Iditarod. All ages for selected passages.

The Relatives Came **by Cynthia Rylant. 1993. New York: Aladdin Paperbacks.**

The relatives come up from Virginia in their overloaded car, making their way through tall mountains over a precarious road. Their visit is recounted through sensory detail so brilliant and vivid we feel they are visiting us. Primary and elementary.

Sahara Special **by Esme Raji Codell. 2003. New York: Hyperion. Fiction.**

Sahara is just entering fifth grade—and she's about to meet one of the most unusual teachers ever. Extraordinary detail and rich imagery. Don't miss the creative use of conventions. Elementary, middle school.

The Story of Salt **by Mark Kurlansky. 2006. New York: G. P. Putnam's Sons. Nonfiction.**

Captivating history of the discovery and uses for salt, together with its impact on civilization throughout the world. Upper elementary through middle school.

Where in the Wild? **by David M. Schwartz and Yael Schy. Photos by Dwight Kuhn. 2007. Berkeley: Tricycle Press. Nonfiction.**

Stunning photos show some of nature's most intriguing creatures cleverly camouflaged. The premise is compelling: Imagine yourself a predator trying to spot your prey. If you cannot do it, lift the flap to reveal the location. Outstanding poetry and short informational essays provide details. All ages.

Assessing Writing Samples for IDEAS

By the time you have shared several samples of literature that show clarity and detail in action, your students will have developed a good sense of what to look and listen for in relation to this trait. This is the perfect time to give them practice in assessing writing samples such as those that follow. You will want to go through these samples yourself before sharing them with students. That way, you will be familiar with them, feel prepared to read them aloud with expression, have a sense of how *you* would assess them, and have some discussion questions in mind.

To get started . . .

- Choose the paper(s) you want to assess.
- Make copies so students can highlight, underline, or write in margins.

- Review the Write Connection to see if the suggested activity is something you would like to do with your students.

If you want to score papers, also . . .

- Print a copy of the Teacher Writing Guide for yourself—and copies of the Student Writing Guide for your writers.
- Read each paper aloud prior to scoring.
- Give students time to discuss the paper with a partner—or in a small writing circle of three or four peers.
- Begin by asking whether the paper "leaps the river" in ideas. Then . . .
- Ask writers to score the paper for the trait of ideas, from 1 (very beginning level) to 6 (strong enough to use as an example), OR
- Simply identify strengths and problems requiring revision.

Paper 1

Making Decisions (Expository, Grade 8)

When making a decision, take your time and not rush into a hasty conclusion. Clarify the decision you are making. Be sure you understand all aspects of your decision, without confusion. Reason out the consequences your decision will effect. Question whether the concluding effects will be positive or negative.

Before proceeding ahead with any decision making process, devise other alternatives, if any, noticing who and what may be effected. Be sure to ask others for their opinion on the subject. Keep in mind, however, that their opinion may not be correct or even helpful. Quality decision making depends on facts, not opinions. Eventually, your decision will have an impact on other things. These impacts cannot always be foreseen. Take your time in determining which impacts are most effected, and be careful in the end.

Suggested Score for IDEAS: 2

Lessons Learned from "Making Decisions"

- Generalities weaken ideas.
- Specific examples (in this case, a decision with good or bad results) are a must.

Comments

This paper *seems* to say something. The problem is, it's a compilation of generalizations and platitudes. What's more, no people populate this paper. It is sterile. The strengths of the piece are fluency and conventions. While it says virtually nothing, it flows smoothly enough to come across as authoritative. The language is sophisticated but imprecise: "Take your time in determining which impacts are most effected." This *probably* means "Take time to figure out how your decision will affect your life." That revision is clear—but still general. Compare this: "A bad decision can have unforeseen—and disastrous—consequences." Think how different this paper would be if the writer had chosen *one* difficult decision (say, leaving home or giving up drugs) and given us possible outcomes: The writer might have gotten more involved, and so might we.

The Write Connection

Making Decisions

This is the first of many expository/informational pieces in this book. In addition to asking how strong the ideas are, think about genre. Check Appendix 6 for a list of Common Core Standards requirements by genre. Go through the list for expository/informational writing point by point. How does this piece measure up? What *very specific* revisions would make it stronger?

Suggested Scores for Other Traits

Organization: **2**

Voice: **2**

Word choice: **2**

Sentence fluency: **4**

Conventions & presentation: **4**

Paper 2

The Best Gift (Memoir, Grade 6)

The best gift I ever got was time—and it's a gift I got from my grandmother, who was never too busy for me. I remember calling her up, hoping she would be happy to hear from me, and thinking she probably would. But then, what if she wasn't? What if she had something better to do than hang out with a kid who wanted to learn to bake? She never did. She always said the same magical words: "I can't wait to see you. How soon can you get here?"

She didn't live far away. I rode my bike, and the whole way, I'd be thinking of what we'd make that day. It might be a triple layer white cake with lemon filling (one of her secret recipes) or a meringue pie that rose so high we had to scrape it off the top of the oven. Sometimes, she'd already be making caramel rolls when I called, and by the time I got within three blocks, I could smell them baking.

One thing that made my time with Delia so special was that she never worried about how many dishes got dirty—or if one got broken. My parents always worried about those things. They would start cleaning up before you could finish making the mess. Delia always said, "Things are meant to be used and enjoyed. Otherwise, why do we have them?" I always thought that would be my philosophy when I grew up.

Over the years, Delia taught me to make about a hundred gourmet desserts. But we didn't only make desserts. We made scalloped potatoes, Swiss steak, deviled eggs, cabbage rolls stuffed with rice, fried chicken, sautéed string beans, and the most amazing bread. One thing was better than the other. I loved it that Delia didn't have a single recipe written down. They were all in her head. "Watch me," she'd laugh. "I don't share this with just anyone, you know." I did watch—and I remembered. I couldn't write any of those recipes down to this day. But I know them well. They live in my hands—and my heart.

If you're ever wondering what you can give to someone you love, give them your time. Just be together. Talk and laugh and make memories. That's what Delia did for me. I lost her last year, and I thought I would never stop crying. I thought I wouldn't bake again either. How could I? It just didn't feel the same without her. But then something funny happened. I wound up making a cake for my brother's birthday and—you guessed it. No recipe. I just had Delia talking me through it the whole time. "Do you think I can do this?" That was me, talking out loud to her. Well, it came out perfect. I was so proud of it. I felt like it was my birthday, not my brother's. He opened about a dozen gifts and I guess they were great. I don't remember. What I do remember is the best gift that day belonged to me. Thank you, Delia.

Whenever I smell molasses, I remember my grandmother baking molasses cookies in her kitchen in New Hampshire, the click of her high heels on the linoleum floor, my grandfather's clocks ticking and chiming on the hour, a whippoorwill calling at dusk from the deep woods, as if it were happening right now.

—Georgia Heard
Writing Toward Home, 1995, 74

CHAPTER 3   Making Meaning with IDEAS

Suggested Scores for IDEAS: 6

Lessons Learned from "The Best Gift"

- Close-up details make us feel as if we know the writer.
- Readers like to picture what's happening: e.g., "a meringue pie that rose so high we had to scrape it off the top of the oven."
- When writers share personal information—such as the parents "cleaning up before you could finish making the mess," we, as readers, feel like insiders.
- Rich detail strengthens voice.

Comments

This paper speaks to anyone who has had a close relationship with a grandparent (or another relative). It is filled with vivid memories that come from a deep friendship. "The Best Gift" is an almost perfect contrast with "Making Decisions" in that it avoids all generalities. Instead, we feel as if we're watching a video: *The writer is pedaling her bike to Delia's, hoping she will be happy for company . . . they're cooking up some magnificent concoction . . . they're making a mess and it doesn't matter . . .* This piece has a strong central theme: in giving our time, we create memories that last forever. (Note: The word choice is very good, although some readers were surprised not to find more moments they would highlight. That dropped this score to a 5—still very high.)

Suggested Scores for Other Traits

Organization: **6**

Voice: **6**

Word choice: **5**

Sentence fluency: **6**

Conventions & presentation: **6**

The Write Connection

The Best Gift

Write your own memoir, connected to an event, place, or person. In planning, envision the piece as a video, and imagine yourself with a camera, shooting just the right scene for the moment. The final piece might have one to five scenes, each with a detail that makes it stick in memory.

Author's Note

It may seem to you that there is a natural and logical connection between ideas and informational writing. You're right! Ideas are all about information, after all. To explore this connection in much more detail, please see Chapter 9, which includes many informational writing samples, as well as discussions of how the trait of ideas looks in that particular genre.

Paper 3

The Baseball (Narrative/Descriptive, Grade 5)

I remember the day I got it well. It was an everyday type day until the doorbell rang. I got up to awnser it. But my sister beat me to it, as usual. It was dad's friend Tom. He got back from a New York yankees baseball fantasy camp a couple weeks ago. I said hi to him and he asked me if I knew who Micky Mantel was. I said of corse I do. At that point I was a little confused. Then he haded me a baseball. It wasen't the kind of baseball we use in little luege. It was nicer than that. Made of real leather. It even smelled like leather. Like the smell of a new leather jacket. And the seems were hand stitched too. I turned it around in my hand then I saw it. I saw a Micky Mantel aughtograph. I coulden't believe it. I had an aughtograph in ink of one of the greatest baseball players of all time. Wow. I teushered it ever since that everyday type day that changed at the ring of a doorbell.

Suggested Scores for IDEAS: 6

Lessons Learned from "The Baseball"

- The lead and conclusion really do frame the writing.

• Stretching out the moment by focusing in (the smell of the leather, the stitches) gives the writing authenticity—the reader feels part of the scene.

The Write Connection

The Baseball

Edit "The Baseball" by correcting all conventional errors. Were there more than you thought when you first read it? Why don't we notice them more? Notice how much this writer appreciates the gift of the baseball, noticing the seams and the smell of the leather. Write a short descriptive paragraph on a gift you have given or received that was deeply appreciated in this detailed way. As you write, think about why descriptive pieces are often called *sketches*.

Comments

Small moments make the best stories, as this writer shows us so well in his tale of the "everyday type day that changed at the ring of a doorbell." Notice how the story comes full circle, beginning with the doorbell and returning to it at the end—when it's even more powerful because now we know its importance. Throughout, ideas drive the organization, which is why the piece works so well. You have to respect a writer who, even as a fifth grader, is so careful with his details. There is a reason behind everything. Consider the question about Mickey Mantle. It's not a throw-away detail; it matters. The writer did not understand why the question was important when it was first asked; later, he knows—and so do we. This writer is especially good at stretching out the moment: Time slows as he turns the baseball over and over in his hand, smelling the leather, noticing the stitches—and finally, noticing the autograph: "Wow." Imagine filming this moment and you can appreciate its power.

Suggested Scores for Other Traits

Organization: **6**

Voice: **6**

Word choice: **4**

Sentence fluency: **5**

Conventions & presentation: **2**

Paper 4

Metamorphosis (Narrative, Grade 9)

Out of all the terrible things that can happen to you on Halloween, like getting your candy ripped off, tearing your store bought but precious Halloween costume on your crabby neighbor's deceased rose bushes or being plagued by people with heavier artillery than you (such as shaving cream or Silly String), the absolute worst thing that could ever happen to you on Halloween has got to be someone else choosing a costume for you. Now I'm not talking about someone making a suggestion to you. I'm talking about them totally choosing an identity for you.

I can remember such a Halloween when I was about eight or nine years old. It was the first year I really had my costume figured out and I was to be a gypsy. I had necklaces, bandanas, and the ultimate loop earrings.

It was then the witch entered my life. My Uncle Gus saw the witch face first. Its hue was that of a green olive gone bad. The warts on its grotesque face had little hairs protruding from the midst of the blood red rubber. But not even that was the worst thing about the witch. The dilapidated witch's nose was the most horrid, twisted protrusion I had ever seen in my life. It hung down a good two or three inches and was covered in those whiskered warts. I hated it. My uncle thought it was too good to pass up. I still hated it. How he could ever possibly like such a detestable vizard I will never know. From the minute he saw that mask, I could see the wheels turning in his head and I saw his thoughts come to words

(continued on following page)

as he mumbled more to himself than to me, "My niece is going to be the best darn witch the world has ever seen."

You know, something very strange happens to adults around the time of Halloween. They get a nostalgic look in their eyes. I was seeing that look in my uncle's eyes and right then I could tell we were not going home without that mask.

I pleaded for him not to get the witch face but he wouldn't listen. I told him that I didn't want to be a witch and I was going to be a gypsy. But when I heard the words, "Here's your receipt, sir," I knew I had lost the battle.

We drove home in silence. I still had a fighting chance to be a gypsy if my mother protested, and I really thought she might . . . boy, was I wrong . . .

"That is the most spectacularly grotesque witch mask I have ever seen!" were her first words. I could feel the walls caving in around me.

Halloween night came. My gypsy costume had been long forgotten, lost in the farthest reaches of my closet. I stood like a mannequin in front of the mirror. Nothing in the mirror reflected my personality at all. "It's so hot in here! Can't I take this thing off for a few minutes??"

"What, honey?" my mother replied. "I can't hear you through the mask."

Ding-dong. "Trick or treat!"

"Gotta go, mom!"

My friends were waiting for me outside. The candy to come would help make up for not being a gypsy. We jogged down the first street, the cold air helping me feel better. Heck, it was Halloween. It couldn't be too bad.

After an hour, though, I was really beginning to sweat. I could feel my face clinging to the inside of the mask. Sweat dribbled down my face and clung to my eyelashes.

The last house we approached was big and white. We lugged our now enormous bags of candy up to the front door, rang the bell, and waited. A woman opened the door. "What a wonderful witch!" she exclaimed and squeezed my long nose, spraying the salty sweat that had been collecting there all over my face. Right then, no amount of candy could compensate for my discomfort and humiliation. I grabbed my candy, and ran for home.

Once upstairs, I tore my mask off, and crammed it into the darkest hole of my closet, where no one but moths would find it again. My mother has searched for it in vain—but she won't find it. One time as a witch is enough.

Suggested Scores for IDEAS: 6

Lessons Learned from "Metamorphosis"

- A high point—most important moment—really makes the story.
- Conflict is an important element in any good narrative.
- It's good to wrap things up—but also leave a little room for the reader to wonder what will happen.

Comments

This story deftly blends nostalgia with a loving but deeply felt tension between generations. The central message? You must find your own identity. Notice how the adults in

---

The Write Connection

Metamorphosis

This piece is one of several narratives in the book. Notice that it is more than a *list of events*; it's a true *story*. What is the difference? Talk about this. Then check the list of requirements for narrative writing from the Common Core Standards in Appendix 6. How does "Metamorphosis" measure up? Be sure to check other narratives against this list as well.

this story never listen to the narrator; they are busy fulfilling their own fantasies. This is the heart of the story on one level, and the writer handles it well. This is also, of course, a Halloween adventure, which culminates in that wonderfully humiliating moment when the writer is drenched in her own sweat—by yet another adult who will only see the world through her own eyes. The story has depth, vivid imagery, wonderful detail, and striking word choice: *dilapidated witch's nose, twisted protrusion, saw his thoughts come to words, heavier artillery, green olive gone bad, stood like a mannequin.* In case you're wondering, *vizard* is not, to my knowledge, a word; perhaps it's a hybrid of *visage* and *buzzard*. The lead sets up the story well; the conclusion is brief but effective. Some readers have suggested that paragraphs 1 and 2 could be combined—and paragraphs 3, 4, and 5 condensed. If you agree, give it a try.

Suggested Scores for Other Traits

Organization: **5** (Faster pacing early on would have resulted in a 6.)

Voice: **6**

Word choice: **6**

Sentence fluency: **6** (Some people loved the long first sentence; some didn't. But overall, fluency is extremely strong in this piece.)

Conventions and presentation: **6** (Even if "vizard" isn't a word, that's one tiny problem, weighed against many strengths.)

Paper 5

Going Veggie (Argument, Grade 4)

If you have ever thought of becoming a vegatarian, now might be a good time to DO IT. There are several benafits. Let me show you.

First of all, you might be trying to lose weight. Who isn't, right? Meat has a LOT of calories and a LOT of fat. If you cut meat out of your diet, you will most likely lose weight. My aunt did this and lost 20 pounds in less than one month. How does that sound? You might be thinking, well, I'll only eat a LITTLE meat. But trust me, if you cut it out completely, you will lose weight a lot faster. You think you will miss it, but you won't! (And no more stinky garbage either! Did you ever smell meat scraps after a couple days? Yikes.)

Second, we need to use the land for cattle and other animals to grow other crops. Most people in the world do not eat meat and not because they are vegatarians, but because they can't afford it or it is just too hard to get it to where they live. We can not raise enough cattle or pigs to feed the whole world but we could take the land we use for cattle or pigs and use it to grow beans, rice, corn or other things that we could use to feed hungry people. They are cheaper to ship and use up a lot less of our resources. They are also healthier to eat and the cows and pigs will thank you, too.

Last of all, it is good for the planet. When we raise cattle or pigs or other animals in huge, huge amounts, it creates a lot of waste. That waste has to go somewhere, and guess what? It goes into our water supply. It pollutes our rivers and evenchually our oceans. This means fish and shrimp or oyesters or other

(continued on following page)

things you might eat could be bad for you. It could even make you sick. Run-off water from rice or beans will NOT make you sick, so that is a healthier choice.

If you become a vegetarian, get ready to be made fun of! People will say things like "Is THAT all your having for lunch!?" They will also ask you how in the world you can get any protean without meat in your diet. They don't understand yet how it works. You will need to explain it. Beans have a lot of protean. Also, explain that you can be a vegetarian and still drink milk or eat yogourt and eggs, and these have a lot of protean too. Meat isn't the only thing.

So enjoy a big salad for lunch or dinner, knowing you are helping the planet and getting skinny at the same time. Plus getting all your vitamins and cutting down on pollution. Wow. That is a lot to do while you are just having lunch!

©2012. Vicki Spandel.

Suggested Score for IDEAS: 4/5

Lessons Learned from "Going Veggie"

- Strong conventions can help you make your case.
- Having more than one reason to back your argument makes it stronger.
- It's helpful to anticipate a reader's objections (e.g., *I'll need more protein*).

Comments

This is the beginning of a fine persuasive argument. The writer sets up the discussion clearly and provides multiple reasons for her position—expanding each one to help us understand her thinking. She also prepares the reader to deal with friends who may poke fun at a vegetarian diet—or not understand the protein issue. Her conclusion wraps up key points without being too obvious about it, and paragraphs open with clear transitional phrases that make the piece easy to follow. In addition, her unbridled enthusiasm creates voice. On the other hand, she could use more support for her points. Just how much pollution do cows and pigs generate? And is there an expert opinion to support the idea that land used for animals would be better used to raise crops like corn or rice? Not all sentences (especially in the third paragraph) are clear the first time through—and some pronouns (*it, that*) could use clearer antecedents. Conventions need a closer look, though many things are done well and those capitals enhance the voice. Over all, a good persuasive effort from a fourth-grade writer.

Suggested Scores for Other Traits

Organization: **5**

Voice: **6**

Word choice: **4**

Sentence fluency: **4**

Conventions & presentation: **4**

The Write Connection

Going Veggie

Use this paper to talk about how personal perspectives and opinions influence our reading. How many of your students are vegetarian—or have friends or relatives who are? How many are committed omnivores who disagree with the writer's point of view? Discuss which of the writer's points appeal to either side, what she left out (if anything), and what she could say that would make her argument more convincing to those who eat meat—or those who do not. Does she need to win over both sides? Why? *Note:* You may also wish to check out the Common Core Standards requirements for argument in Appendix 6—for this or other persuasive pieces that follow.

Writing Is Important

Give this paper more focus by trying three things: (1) open with the final paragraph; (2) create a stronger transition from this new opening paragraph to the three key tips for writing well; (3) ask yourself whether you need the writer's existing first paragraph—and if not, get rid of it. Opening paragraphs in rough drafts are often like exercise warm-ups. Once you're warmed up, they've served their purpose.

Paper 6

Writing Is Important (Expository, Grade 11)

Writeing is important. It allows you to express your thoughts but also your feelings. through writeing you provide entertainment and information which is useful to others. Writeing is both useful and enjoyable. it helps you explore ideas and issues you might not think of otherwise. If you are going to write, you will need plenty of information.

Writing well means knowing what you are talking about. This takes research and information. If you do not know enough about your topic, your reader will not be convinced. It also means putting feelings into your paper. no one wants to read something where the writer sounds bored and like they wish they were doing something else. it can take courage to say what you really think and feel but it is worth it. You will get your audiences attention.

third, keep your writing simple if you want it to be affective. Trying to impress people with big long super complicated sentenes and five dollar words does not work. They might just decide reading your writing is not worth the time and trouble it takes. So keep it simple if you want to have an audience.

the most important advice of all is to write about what you know about the best. If you are a good auto mechanic for instence maybe you should write about cars or if you have a summer job at the veteranian's office, you could write stories about the animals you treat. If you try to write what you do not know it will be obvous to your audience and they will not believe in you. Use what you know and use your experiences from everyday life

writeing is important in all occupations. Today, it is more true than ever before. If you do not believe it just ask around. Everyone from doctors and dentists to garage mechanics and salesmen have to write as part of their job. But the most important reason is because writeing is a way of sharing the ideas that belong to you. If you work on your writeing skills, It just might help you in ways you have not even throught of.

Suggested Score for IDEAS: 4

Lessons Learned from "Writing Is Important"

- Writing about two things at once can make your thinking hard to follow.
- A good ending sometimes makes the best beginning.
- If you shift focus, toss the reader a transition.
- Don't just make a point and leave the reader hanging. Offer examples.
- Careful editing (like it or not) causes many readers to take you more seriously.

Comments

Despite some banal truisms, this writer makes some insightful points, but they need to be ordered, expanded, and set up better. They also need to be backed by examples. The writer is trying to tell us two things, really: (1) Everyone writes, making it an important skill (see the final paragraph), and (2) there are several keys (knowing your topic, keeping it simple, having the courage to say what you think) to writing well. These ideas could easily be connected with thoughtful transitions, but that hasn't happened yet. The lead is stiff (the writer is still warming up); the conclusion is far stronger and could be bumped right up front. It sets the stage for why writing well is important in the first place. The voice comes and goes, and word choice is fairly routine. Many sentences are short and choppy, which breaks the flow and creates the impression that the thinking is simplistic, too—which it is not. Careful reading could correct many small problems with conventions.

Suggested Scores for Other Traits

Organization: **3**

Voice: **4**

Word choice: **4**

Sentence fluency: **4**

Conventions & presentation: **3**

Paper 7

Harder Than You Think (Expository, Grade 10)

I walk up the hill with my friends, turn into our cul-de-sac, go to the front door, put the key in the lock, turn, and step in. The house breathes a kind of spooky hello as I set my books down and go to the kitchen where the inevitable note is waiting: "Have a snack. Be home soon. I love you." As I'm munching cookies, I think how I'd like to go out and shoot a few hoops if I had someone to do it with. You can play Nintendo by yourself, but it isn't the same. So I forget that for now. I should be doing my Spanish homework anyway. Too bad I don't have an older brother or sister to help conjugate all those dumb verbs. I could call a friend, sure, but if I had a brother or sister, I'd have a built-in friend.

While I'm feeling so sorry for myself, I hear my friends Kelly and Kyle across the street. She's screaming bloody murder because he is throwing leaves in her hair and threatening to put a beetle in her backpack. She has just stepped on his new Nikes. I do not have these squabbles. I guess the big advantage, if you call it that, to being an only child is my room is my own. Nobody "borrows" my CDs or my books or clothes. I also get a bigger allowance than I probably would if I had siblings. My parents take me everywhere, from the mall to the East Coast. Maybe they wouldn't if they had other kids. (On the other hand, it would be more fun going if I had someone my own age.)

All these great advantages are overshadowed by one big disadvantage, though, and it's the main reason I would change things if I could. When you are an only child, your parents depend on you to be the big success all the time. You are their big hope, so you cannot fail. You have to be good at sports, popular, and have good grades. You need a career goal. You have to have neat hair and clothes that look pressed. You have to have good grammar, clean socks, good breath, and table manners. If you've ever felt jealous of somebody who is an only child, don't. It's a lot of pressure. I often wish for a little screw-up brother my parents could worry about for a while.

So—while having a neat room with nothing disturbed is great, I'd take a brother or sister in a minute if I could. The big irony is, if I had that mythical brother or sister, I would probably be wishing myself an only child again the first time my baseball shirt didn't come back or my stereo got broken. Life is like that. What you don't have always seems to be the thing you want.

Suggested Score for IDEAS: 6

Lessons Learned from "Harder Than You Think"

- Beginning with an anecdote can be a good way to set up a discussion.
- Multiple examples make an argument convincing.
- Honesty makes voice sing.

Comments

I like the authenticity of this piece. The writer uses two contrasting examples—the neighbor children squabbling and his own home life—to make some key points about how peaceful yet lonely life as an only child can be. The examples are realistic, and the writer seems to have thought through what he has to say. The opening paints a clear picture of the writer's feelings of isolation, although some readers feel it could be condensed. That's a killer ending, and it makes an important point without being redundant. The voice, a definite presence in paragraphs 1 and 2, springs to life in paragraph 3, bolstered by precise, original ideas—and by the writer's unwavering honesty about life with his hovering parents. Overall, a fluent, well-edited, readable piece.

Suggested Scores for Other Traits

Organization: **5**

Voice: **6**

Word choice: **5**

Sentence fluency: **5**

Conventions & presentation: **6**

Paper 8

Why Writing Matters (Expository, Grade 6)

Writing is like sculpting. We get this vision in our own mind, and we want to share it. We scramble to find the words that will work, that will bring our ideas to life. Sometimes they just flow onto the page. Other times, we find ourselves scratching through the dictionary (or worse, the thesaurus), going, "No—that's not it. That's not what I meant."

This brings me to my point. This is why writing matters. It makes us think. It pushes us to get rid of the clutter in our minds and make sense of things. Did you ever have someone say to you, "What do you mean? What are you *talking* about?" That person probably didn't ask you to write a note. But maybe they should have. See, here's the thing. Your first words, your first thoughts, on paper give you something real to look at. They help you reflect. You can add to what you wrote, take a little away, move this piece over here—or there. Like sculpting clay.

Something else happens when you write, too. You start out saying one thing, and you wind up saying something completely different. Something about seeing words on paper changes your view of life. You start out sculpting a cat and wind up with a tiger. This is why you can never follow an outline precisely. You should

(continued on following page)

still make one, though. It's your first vision of what your writing will be. Respect it. Treasure it. Then—blow it to pieces with your new thinking!

And there's another reason writing matters. It matters because we love to read! As you sit there by the fire, all cozy with your blanket and hot chocolate, think about the person who sat at a desk somewhere, wanting to be out hiking or golfing and thinking, "No, no—I'm going to finish this book. Someone, somewhere, will want to read it." And sure enough, someone does. It's you! That writer taught himself (or herself) to think—and is now teaching you, too. You become part of the artistic vision.

©2012. Vicki Spandel.

The Write Connection
Why Writing Matters

The author of Paper 6 (Writing Is Important) writes on a similar topic—but there is a noticeable difference in conventions between these two papers. Talk about this. To what extent do conventions influence our responses to these two writings—or to any writing we encounter? Suppose Paper 6 had flawless conventions. Could this influence the scores in other traits? Should it?

Suggested Score for IDEAS: 6

Lessons Learned from "Why Writing Matters"

- Believing what you say makes ideas stronger.
- When you are writing from experience, it shows—and lends credibility to ideas.
- Talking right to the reader increases voice.
- Have a good time when you write. That creates voice, too!

Comments

Here's a thoughtful essay, emphasizing the importance of writing as thinking—creating something physical we can "sculpt" as our thinking changes. That's not all, though. The writer goes on to argue that outlines, while important, shouldn't define how writing turns out. We should make them, treasure them, then "blow [them] to pieces"! The essay closes with what is perhaps the best point of all: As we read, we should remember the writer who gave up time and fun to speak just to us. This writer makes her points clearly—and in an interesting way. She really believes what she's saying. I like the idea of setting out to sculpt a cat and winding up with a tiger. It's also refreshing to see how the writer doesn't devalue outlines; she just puts them in their place. Notice the opening sentences in paragraphs 2, 3, and 4; these openers make the discussion easy to follow. The conversational tone, strong conventions, and highly varied fluency also make it easy to read.

Suggested Scores for Other Traits

Organization: **6**

Voice: **6**

Word choice: **5–6**

Sentence fluency: **6**

Conventions & presentation: **6**

Author's Note

You're probably thinking: *I need more papers, more samples of writing.* Where will they come from? From *you.* And your colleagues. Right today, begin collecting. Be thoughtful about it. Choose each sample because it has a lesson to teach: something to do or not do as a writer. Think about questions you might ask your students or things you want them to see in the writing. Choose interesting pieces that are difficult to assess—or those where writers "break the rules," yet create something wonderful. Get a signed release (from the student's parents) for each piece you choose to use in your instruction, and make sure that the student is comfortable with this use of his/her work. Also consider removing names for writers who prefer that.

Over and over in the first weeks of school, I model, thinking aloud my process for choosing a topic. [Students] see the choices I make: the everyday, ordinary, real-life topics. . . . These demonstrations encourage students to see the significance of their own lives . . .

—Megan S. Sloan
Into Writing, 2009, 29

Lessons and Strategies for Teaching IDEAS

The main things you want to teach . . .

- *Having a strong main message*
- *Keeping that message focused enough to be manageable*
- *Choosing vivid, memorable details*
- *Writing clearly*

Here are some suggested strategies.

1. MODEL TOPIC CHOICE.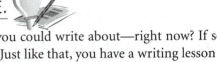

Can you think of three to five things you could write about—right now? If so, grab a piece of scratch paper and make a list. Just like that, you have a writing lesson in hand. Now all you need do is share those topics with students and talk about why you chose each one. Here are mine:

1. Jellyfish attack
2. Jack learning to ride his bike
3. Buying a pedometer
4. Invasion of the dreaded voles

Here, briefly, are my reasons for choosing these topics: (1) Being stung by jellyfish was an unforgettable experience. I'll always recall wondering what was making my arms and legs feel numb as I slowly snorkeled my way to shore, then stepping out of the ocean with red welts covering my body, neck to toes. I recall dashing for the shower, then hearing later, "That's the worst thing you can do!" (2) Our grandson Jack just learned to ride a bike, and he lives for speed. Unfortunately, he has not figured out how to stop without crashing. This makes observers (like me) very nervous. (3) I love Dr. Oz. When he said we should walk 10,000 steps a day, I dutifully bought a pedometer and started to do just that. Then I discovered myself getting competitive, trying to walk more and *more*, finding creative, even sneaky, ways to add steps ("Need something from the fridge? Let me get that for you . . .") (4) Voles are ugly, clever little varmints. They destroy landscaping, and as a result, make few friends among humans. I hate them unabashedly, and passion always makes for good writing.

Share the reasons behind *your* choices in just this way—only orally, with your students. Do this more than once because the topics that are important to you today will be different a month from now or six months from now. In addition, students need to see this reasoning modeled often. It helps them understand how writers think.

Having trouble coming up with your own topics? In *Shoptalk* (1990, 79–80), Donald M. Murray describes himself as a great observer of life, but confesses that sometimes even he does not "feel the muse" perched on his shoulder, and so he uses questions such as these to uncover possible topics:

- *What surprised me recently?*
- *What's bugging me?*
- *What is changing?*
- *What did I expect to happen that didn't?*
- *Why did something make me so mad?*

- *What do I keep remembering?*
- *What have I learned?*

And if you can only come up with two or three topics at a time, that's fine. Begin with those—and share more later. Don't give yourself an excuse not to model because nothing—absolutely *nothing*—you do in teaching writing will take the place of modeling. As Katie Wood Ray tells us, "Everything we do in our writing workshops, every move we make, teaches students. Either we can be walking, breathing, talking examples of all we advocate for our students, or we can have them sitting around wondering why we are trying to get them into something that we are obviously not into ourselves" (2001, 98).

2. NOTICE THE LITTLE THINGS.

Becoming a good observer is essential to writing well. You can help students practice this by focusing on anything of interest in your classroom (or on a short field trip around the campus). Good objects for observation include:

- A plant
- An ant farm
- An animal of any kind
- A pair of old shoes
- A seashell, rock, or piece of driftwood
- A photograph
- A sculpture or painting
- A collection of random objects from a backpack or desk drawer

Have students look at the object—touch it, sniff it, watch it over time. Ask them to make notes about what they notice. You may wish to have them work in pairs so that they can talk and coach each other. See which team can list the most details—and the most *unusual* details, things others overlook.

In *Little Big Minds* (2006, 116), teacher and educational consultant Marietta McCarty recommends asking students to spend up to 10 minutes focused on a single object, such as a blade of grass, a flower, the bark of a tree, or an apple, taking it in through as many senses as possible.

You might also try a lesson called "One Small Square," developed by Georgia Heard and Jennifer McDonough (2009, 37). They invite students to look at the world through a small square, a "window" cut into a sheet of paper. McDonough uses the book *One Small Square: Backyard* (1993), part of a series by Donald M. Silver, to introduce this activity. As she explains, "The book points out how there's more to be seen if you look closely at the world around you. The author describes one small square in a backyard, a forest, a seashore, and so on, and invites children to smell, to listen, and to look at the world around them closely."

3. MODEL REVISING FOR DETAIL.

After sharing writing topics with students, I ask *them* to pick one, and I turn it into a piece of writing that I can revise with their help (see Figure 3.5). I create this draft

Detail is electric . . . Be exhaustive in your detailing of something ordinary, like a teaspoon, in front of you; use at least twenty details. Go back over what you have written and pick out the electric ones.

—Bonni Goldberg
Room to Write, 1996, 67

FIGURE 3.5

Voles (Rough Draft)

Voles are a nuisance. They are very

destructive. What's more, they're ugly.

Not that you ever see them up close.

They live underground, and seldom

poke their heads out. Unfortunately,

they are hard to get rid of. Almost

nothing stops them.

quickly, and I don't try to make it striking and memorable (even though no matter *how good* I make it, students will find something to revise), but I don't try to write really badly either, because they'll think that's phony. I usually triple space it and make the print large, even with older students. That way, it's easy to read the original draft once it gets messy, and the triple spacing gives me plenty of room in which to write revisions.

I read the draft aloud, and ask students to assess it. They might give it a score or just tell me if they think it is very strong, so-so, or in need of work. The answer (if I've been hasty enough in creating my draft) is always "in need of work." Good, I tell them. You get to help me. Ask me questions that will get me to think and remember details I've left out. Help me make this vivid, so the reader can picture and feel what's going on. Here are some of the typical questions students ask during this revision:

- *What ARE voles?*
- *What do they do that's so destructive?*
- *You say they're ugly. What do they look like?*
- *How big are they?*
- *Are they dangerous? Do they bite?*
- *How can you get rid of them?*

I don't try to answer all these questions at once (and some may not get answered at all, even in the revision). I go through the draft line by line, asking students what I need to do to make each sentence stronger and more detailed:

- *"Voles are a nuisance." Do you like the sound of that? Is it strong enough?*
- *"They are very destructive." How could I make that more clear?*
- *"What's more, they're ugly." Can you picture them? What else do I need to say?*

When I finish, I read the revised draft aloud and ask them how much it has improved. You can judge for yourself with the revised example in Figure 3.6. Each time I do this lesson, it turns out a little bit differently, but the revised draft is *always* an improvement. And it always provides a chance to model several different revision strategies, such as:

- Use of a caret (^) to insert information
- Use of arrows and loops to show what goes where
- Willingness to get rid of any word or sentence that's not working
- Continual effort to create images (*scruffy, beady-eyed miniature weasels, mutilating the yard with their tunnels*)
- Changing an adjective (*destructive*) into a verb (*destroy*) to give a sentence more punch
- Writing with a little "attitude" (clearly, I dislike these creatures) to create drama.

4. KEEP THE MESSAGE SMALL AND FOCUSED.

Of course, if you're writing "The History of France"—or something similar—that's one thing. But even the largest structures are built brick by brick.

And when the final piece will run, say, half a page to five pages in length, focus is critical. The writer of "Mouse Alert" knew this instinctively; the writer of "The Redwoods" did not. Think how much more interesting the latter might have been if the writer had told us "four things we might not believe about Redwood trees," or "two ways to make vacationing with your family bearable." Focus keeps *readers* interested—and keeps *writers* on track. Have students work with you to narrow big topics until they get very good at it. They don't have to write about these topics; this is just practice in gaining focus. Here's a short list with a couple of suggestions. With your students, fill in the blanks for the others—then expand the list yourself to create more narrowing opportunities:

Too Big	Narrowed and manageable
Baseball	Two great hitters and their secrets
Animals	Migration of the Monarch butterfly
Music	Who had more influence: The Beatles or Elvis?
Clothing	_____
Architecture	_____
Plants	_____
Games	_____

FIGURE 3.6

Stop the
∧ Voles! (Revised)

Voles are a ~~nuisance.~~ nightmare ~~They are very~~ Using their sharp rodent teeth, ⟨destroy every plant in their path.⟩

∧ ~~destructive.~~ What's more, they're ugly. Scrawny, scruffy, and beady-eyed, they look like miniature weasels.

Not that you ever see them up close.

They live underground, ∧ and ~~seldom~~ ONLY (constantly excavating and mutilating the yard with their tunnels,)

poke their heads out ⟨to sneer at humans.⟩ Unfortunately,

they are hard to get rid of. ~~Almost~~ (You need a steel trap—

~~nothing stops them.~~ or a quick cat with a BIG appetite.)

5. CHOOSE DETAILS THAT MATTER.

Everyone (well, nearly everyone) knows that those special sponges we use in the bath, the ones that really soak up the water, once lived in the sea. You probably also know that sponges are animals, not plants—but that they do not have brains, and cannot think. They cannot even move on their own. They just rest quietly, growing, enjoying their spongey lives—until a diver comes along to harvest them. If I am writing about sponges, I may include some of this information, but I'll skip over it quickly to get to the good parts: the things you *don't* know.

For example, you might not know that sponges can be tiny and flat or huge and cone shaped. So when I tell you that, I give you a reason to keep reading (*This writer knows her sponges*). But I'm not out of fabulous details yet. A sponge can do something NO other animal on earth can do. Do you know what it is? If you don't, this is a gotcha

FIGURE 3.7

How to Be a Sponge

Sit there.
Sit there some more.
Just be and be . . .
Don't dream, think, or imagine.
Don't worry.
Grow tiny and flat, like a dime—
Or huge, like a traffic cone.
Let the tide wash over you, feeding you.
If fate tears you to pieces, don't despair.
Get yourself together.
Once you leave the ocean,
Dry up.
Feel at home in a tub.
Caress humans, pets, windows, and hubcaps.
Outperform artificial imitators.
Stay in shape.
Be flexible.
Soak up life.
Spit it back.

© 2012, Vicki Spandel

moment for me, the writer, for I get to surprise you with this tidbit: If you put a sponge into a blender and chopped it into a bazillion tiny pieces, you could pour it back into the ocean and it would reassemble itself, bit by bit (Davies, 2006, 49). Nifty trick. And nifty writing, too (on the part of Nicola Davies, who first taught me this) because readers love what is new or unusual.

Barry Lane (*Reviser's Toolbox*, 1999) calls these elusive, less-than-obvious details "potatoes"—because you have to dig for them. And you can use them to write a "how-to" poem, which is essentially a set of directions on how to be a particular person, thing, or concept. See Figure 3.7 for my how-to poem on sponges. See Figure 3.8 for a ninth grader's delightfully diabolical example of how to be a water bug.

> When I wrote reports in school I used a dump truck. I'd take my dump truck to the library, fill it up with facts, and then backload it onto the paper . . . I didn't know that facts were fun, that facts were funny. Did you know, for example, that a hummingbird's heart is half the size of its body? That the Roman legions used urine as laundry detergent?
>
> —Barry Lane
> *51 Wacky We-Search Reports,* 2003, 13

FIGURE 3.8

How to Be a Water Bug

Boring Facts

- One of the largest insects
- Survives in water—even under ice
- Short breathing tubes stick out as they hunt
- Active in late summer
- Wings overlap abdomen
- Exoskeleton
- Sharp teeth
- Known as boatmen

How to Be a Water Bug

Swim fast below every stream of water.

Breathe out of small tubes.

Don't let your prey suspect you exist.

Row with oar-like hind legs, as a boatman would do.

Attack other insects, small fish, frogs, tadpoles—even birds.

Inject your toxin.

Dine on fresh meat.

When winter comes,

Slip under water.

Hide beneath the ice.

Wait for summer.

Come back to life.

6. PUT YOUR SENSES TO WORK.

Sensory details—sights, sounds, smells, tastes, and feelings (tactile or of the heart)—bring a writer's world to life. Sensory details put us right at the scene, and sometimes make us remember experiences of our own, so powerful are the associations we have with the sound of a doorbell, the aroma of bread baking, the feel of snow on the tongue.

In *How the Irish Saved Civilization* (1995, 16), Thomas Cahill writes of the barbarian hordes who plan to attack the apparently invincible Romans: "A crone in a filthy blanket stirs a cauldron, slicing roots and bits of rancid meat into the concoction from time to time. She slices a carrot crosswise up its shaft, so that the circular pieces she cuts off float like foolish yellow eyes on the surface of her brew." With rancid meat and carrot eyes, Cahill captures the look, feel, and smell of the scene. We are right there.

To help students develop an appreciation for sensory detail, begin with any sensory-rich passage from literature. Share it aloud with students, and (if possible) give them a hard copy on which to make notes. Ask them, in pairs, to make a sensory chart of the sights, sounds, smells, etc., they notice. One I have used for this purpose is from Kate DiCamillo's classic *The Tale of Despereaux* (2003). This passage comes from Chapter 2, in which Despereaux's sister Merlot tries very hard to teach her odd little brother to eat books, as all normal mice do. Despereaux, however, has something quite different in mind, as he begins to discover that books are meant for reading, not eating.

Check Figure 3.9 for a sensory chart made by a group of fifth graders with whom I shared this passage (check pages 21–22 of DiCamillo's book). As you can see, they went well beyond the literal, letting themselves surmise how it might feel, smell, look, or sound to actually be in that library. The next step is to have students create their own sensory details chart (as a form of planning) in preparation for writing a descriptive piece or story with a vivid setting.

> Writing from the heart is not just about writing from the heart. It's also about writing from and for all the senses. Readers want to feel, they want to taste, they want to smell.
>
> —Nancy Slonim Aronie
> *Writing from the Heart*, 1998, 143

FIGURE 3.9

Sensory Details Chart by Grade 5 Students

Sensory Details Based on

The Tale of Despereaux
by Kate DiCamillo

Sights	Sounds	Tastes & Smells	Feelings
Sunlight	Mice scurrying	Glue	Warmth of the sun
Yellow patches on the floor	Paper crunching	Paper	Smooth surface of the table
Table	Talking	That "library" smell	Roughness of paper
Books	The words "Once" upon a time"	Old furniture	Glue on your tongue
Mice		Carpeting	Paper in your mouth
Squiggles		Mouse fur	The chills—when Despereaux begins to read
Words			
Wooden floors			

---

7. REVISE FUZZY WRITING.

So-called "fuzzy" writing is vague, unclear, confusing. In *The Reviser's Toolbox*, writer and teacher Barry Lane talks about "turning the knob" on the binoculars by asking ourselves questions: *How did it look, feel, smell? What was I doing? Was anyone else there? What were they doing? What just happened—or was about to happen? What do I recall best? How did I feel? Why do I remember this?* In answering these and similar questions, we fine tune our binoculars, focusing in on the little details that make writing interesting.

Barry begins with this "blurry sentence":

I walked into the McDonald's and there were people everywhere.

Then he revises it. Try it. You've been to McDonald's—or at least peeked in the window or seen it on television. Put yourself at the scene. Fine tune your binoculars until your description explodes with detail. If you're currently teaching, you might have your students do this. Then compare your revision with Barry's (from *The Reviser's Toolbox* by Barry Lane, ©1999 Discover Writing, www.discoverwriting.com. Used with permission):

The workmen leaned on the stainless steel counters, bellies bursting out of stained tee shirts. An old man in the corner held an aluminum cane in one hand and a rolled-up newspaper in the other. He swatted at flies as the workers scurried behind the counters, stuffing bags with greasy burgers, rushing to the beeping fryolaters to scoop the golden greasy potato sticks, slinging steaming robot food into cardboard trays and paper bags. The smell of sizzling fat hung in the air and I could taste, swallow, and digest that hamburger before the young girl could say, "Have a nice day" (42).

8. PUT IT TO THE TEST.

You can tell in a heartbeat whether an informational piece actually is teaching you something because you can write a multiple-choice quiz based on it. Take this example from one of my favorite nonfiction books, Sneed Collard's *Lizards* (2012, 34):

After people settled on the island of Tonga about three thousand years ago, they quickly hunted the island's giant iguana species to extinction. Today, common iguanas are eaten in Central America and have disappeared from many regions. Each year people slaughter millions of monitor lizards and South American teiid lizards for their skins, which are turned into lizard-skin boots for wealthy Americans and Europeans. In many parts of the world, people kill lizards because they mistakenly believe the reptiles are venomous or because they look like snakes—a poor excuse to kill anything.

Collards's book, filled with detail, readily lends itself to creation of multiple-choice (or other) quiz questions, such as these:

1. Which of the following is a particularly common reason for killing lizards?
   a. People find hunting lizards challenging and exciting.
   b. People make expensive clothing from the lizard's skins.
   c. Lizards are extremely venomous and threaten people's lives.
   d. Lizards destroy many crops throughout Central America.

2. Which of the following is a widely held misconception about lizards?
   a. Nearly all are venomous.
   b. They can resemble snakes.
   c. Humans have hunted some species to extinction.
   d. Some types of lizards are edible.

Writing your own multiple-choice items, by the way, is a good strategy for remembering what you have read and guessing (often quite accurately) what might be on *someone else's* test. Writing items based on your own work is one way of testing whether you have written something of substance, or only written in generalities. It's hard to base a good test on generalities. (By the way, the answer to Question 1 is b; the answer to Question 2 is a.)

9. Help students collect information.

In Judy Mazur's third-grade class, students do *a lot* of informational writing. But they do not try to pull the information out of their heads—nor does Judy leave them adrift, hoping they will bump into the details they need. She reads to them, and they read on their own. One whole section of her in-class library is devoted to the current research focus. Students do firsthand research on many topics through observation or field trips. They watch films. They talk and ask questions. *Then*, they write.

In Figures 3.10, "Tarantulas," and 3.11, "The Funnel Web Spider," you can see the detail and confidence that comes from having time to explore a topic before trying to write about it yourself.

FIGURE 3.10
Tarantulas

The insect world is the tarantula's paradise.

Tarantulas are a type of hunting spider, so they don't build webs. Even some of the largest spiders cannot eat their whole food at once. First, they have to paralyze their prey, its victim, with poison called venom. Now, they drink the prey's blood.

North American tarantulas are easily found in the United States of America, Mexico, and in central South America. Tarantulas live in a burrow, which they call home. Tarantulas are nocturnal hunters like bats.

Can you imagine that some tarantulas eat animals like frogs and snakes? Yikes! But tarantulas aren't that dangerous to humans. Tarantulas attack by biting, but it won't hurt as you think it will.

From the amazing world of spiders, tarantulas are the most interesting creatures.

FIGURE 3.11
The Funnel Web Spider

Have you ever wondered what crawls underground in Australia? Well, it's called a Funnel Web Spider.

It looks like a tiny ball of hair with legs.

Funnel Webs gorge on tasty insects that get too close. Funnel Webs are the most poisonous spiders in the world. They can kill a human. Luckily, scientists developed a medicine to treat these kinds of bites.

You should be happy that spiders exist because they eat the nasty little creatures we don't like. Enjoy having them in the world.

Author's Note

Although informational writing is important (it is emphasized in the Common Core Standards), it is not necessarily the best place to begin for a beginning or struggling student—unless that student has personal knowledge of a topic from which to draw in his/her writing. "Write what you know" is still a good beginning rule of thumb. Writers need practice identifying personally important topics and writing from the world of experience first—as José Garcia does in Figure 3.12 on the following page. Then they can take that base and add the important—but sophisticated and challenging—skills of seeking, narrowing, summarizing, and translating outside information for a reader.

FIGURE 3.12

"Problems,"
by José Garcia

Cars cost too much
My dad can't drive.
My mom, dad, sister and me
Walk on hot days, cold days
Windy days, and foggy days,
But
We have fun
When I go to summer school
We take the bus when we go to
Summer school
We go on the bridge
When we go home.
I can't stand the sun.
I take water,
We take a break
At the park.
When I get
Home, I rest a lot.

For struggling writers . . .

10. BEGIN WITH WHAT'S TANGIBLE.

If you've ever held a photograph, postcard or artifact that takes you to another time or place, you know the power of physical objects to call up emotions and memories. Put this to work in your classroom, asking students to bring in any object they can hold in their hands that has significance for them—and to use it as a starting point for writing. They do not need to write about the object itself. They can use it as the basis for conversation with a partner—a conversation that helps them to recall a time, place, experience, or person they might wish to write about. (An excellent text to kick this off is Mem Fox's *Wilfred Gordon McDonald Partridge*, 1989.)

Author's Note

Struggling writers benefit from direct experience: touring the campus of the school, for example, or cooking, line dancing, singing, watching a baby, holding an animal. Direct experience fixes details in memory and generates the need for language. Common writing tasks such as "Write about an object that has meaning for you" become much easier when the writer holds the object in his or her hand. Similarly, "Write about a person who has been important in your life" is easier when looking at a photo—or even better, a collection of photos.

For procrastinators . . .

11. TAKE 10.

An inordinate amount of difficulty with writing comes from sheer procrastination. Try this strategy, which is loosely based on an idea from Barry Lane ("The 9 Minute Research Paper," *The Reviser's Toolbox*, 1999, 125).

Gather around you all the notes (if any) from which you will draw your information. Or use your imagination. Write the very best lead you can. Then set a timer for 10 minutes, and within that time, write the most complete report your knowledge of the topic allows. Beginning to end: you *must finish*. Here's the trick, though: Write on *every other line* (or better yet, every third line).

Once you've finished, go back and use questions to identify gaps where you will need to expand your thinking or add detail. (Write them in the blank lines you remembered to leave.) Now you've done two things: finished a rough draft (that feels good!), and made a plan for research or revision, using your questions. Not bad for 10 minutes.

For writers who need a visual connection . . .

12. DO SOME FORMATIVE ASSESSMENT.

Formative assessment—the kind that happens while performance is still in process, and while there is still time to influence the final product—is vital to success. But teachers do not always have time to visit every student during the writing process, so put students in charge of their own formative assessment.

This is easy to do when you have rubrics or writing guides. In the Student Writing Guide for IDEAS, you'll notice some very specific things students can look for in their own writing. Under Level 6, for example, they might underline the words "main idea or message really jumps out" or "details I chose will intrigue you." Then they can look for those things in their own writing, perhaps underlining a sentence that captures the main message and highlighting any intriguing details they find. If this task is easy, that tells them the writing is working; if it is difficult, they have work to do.

Author's Note

You will want to have students do this kind of formative assessment with each of the traits—not just IDEAS. And as a group, you and your students may decide to look for additional things that do not as yet appear in a writing guide. Scan the guide together first, asking students to identify what is most important—what they should be looking for in their own work. Then, as you explore other writing, including literary examples, see if you can identify other critical features to look for.

Something for every content area . . .

13. SUMMARIZE.

Nothing teaches the concept of "main idea" better than writing a summary. This practice teaches students to read for the core, the heart, of the writing—and to pay attention to moments when the writer wanders. It also helps them become more conscious of main idea and focus in their own writing. In addition, summarizing is one kind of writing they can do in *any* content area—history, math, or whatever.

Author's Note

An outstanding text for introducing the art of condensing (or summarizing) is Geoffrey Kloske's witty take on well-known fairy tales and nursery rhymes, *Once upon a time, the End (asleep in 60 seconds)*, 2005. In this book, a frustrated father makes bed-time stories shorter and shorter until he has truly trimmed them down to the very basics—with hilarious results.

Some Quick Trait Logistics

In the five chapters that follow, we'll look at each of the other six traits, from organization through conventions & presentation. For each one, you will see writing guides, samples of writing to score and discuss, suggested focus lessons, and so on. But this is a good time to take a step back and get a larger view. Here are some answers to questions many teachers ask.

HOW LONG SHOULD I SPEND TEACHING A SINGLE TRAIT?

This is really up to you—and your students. If you teach primary writers, you may focus on just one or two features of a trait. For example, with ideas, you might focus on main message and detail; with organization, you might focus on leads and conclusions. This approach allows you to go fairly quickly, perhaps spending *up to* a week on each trait.

If you work with older writers, however, you may wish to do more. Instead of thinking how long it takes to teach a trait, picture exactly what you will be doing:

- Introducing the trait
- Sharing and discussing writing samples that are strong or weak in ideas
- Reading passages that illustrate clear writing, a strong main idea, or good detail
- Inviting students to find similar passages of their own and share them in writing circles
- Asking students to write an original piece and revise it, using what they have learned about ideas

It is difficult to imagine doing all this in less than a week or two, but this is merely a guideline. You should be flexible. You don't want to spend much more than two weeks introducing a trait, or students will lose the larger picture of how traits work together to create good writing.

IS IT IMPORTANT TO TEACH THE TRAITS IN A PARTICULAR ORDER?

I think so, yes. Ideas are about message. It makes sense to begin there. The early stages of writing—finding a topic, planning, prewriting, talking, thinking—are all about ideas.

It makes sense to teach organization second because order supports ideas by giving us a roadmap for the writer's thinking. Think of all the items in your living room as *ideas*. The way you arranged them is your *organization*.

I have usually taught voice next, as the third of the "deep text" traits—those that most strongly influence message and are most powerfully affected by revision. Voice is in many respects a compilation of other traits, and is affected by detail, word choice, fluency, and more. (We'll discuss this further in Chapter 5.) It is perhaps the most complex of the traits, and certainly the most elusive. It's also the trait where many writers who struggle with conventions find success. This means that the earlier you introduce voice, the earlier those students will feel like successful writers. Word choice and sentence fluency are first cousins of voice; each enhances voice tremendously. Therefore, as you teach each of them you, in effect, expand your discussion of voice.

Conventions & presentation should be taught, I believe, right from the start, and in conjunction with *all other traits*. Both influence and support other traits in a number of ways. Correct spelling, for example, makes word choice clear. Paragraphing enhances organization. Punctuation influences voice. It also guides readers in interpreting sentences and reading them with expression. Graphic features of presentation such as boxes, bulleted lists, formatted subheadings, or bold print support ideas by identifying what's important, and also support organization by making information easy to find. As you think about the conventions you teach (and the presentation features, too), consider the ways in which they support the writer's message.

Do I—Should I—Teach Every Feature of Every Trait?

Balance is the key here. You do not need to teach every last thing you know about every trait, and you'll go a little crazy if you try. At the same time, don't think that just because your students studied leads or details in grade 3, those are now taboo subjects in grade 4. Remember, there are countless ways to write leads or handle detail. These are big topics—things you continue to learn for as long as you write. They're worth revisiting.

At each new grade level, you and your students will be studying new literature—and looking at different writing samples. Each time you look at the work of a new author, you'll discover nuances of craft that you hadn't even thought of before, and those will become part of your teaching. To help put together a general plan for teaching a given trait, see the chart in Figure 3.13. This chart is not a lesson planner by any means. It is simply meant to give you a general sense of the *kinds* of lessons you could use to teach features of a trait. For example, the trait of organization could be divided into these features:

- Leads
- Overall design or structure
- Conclusions
- Transitions
- Pacing (where the writer spends time)

As a teacher, you will probably not have time or inclination to cover all of these features in depth. So perhaps you'll choose three. Then for each of the three, you have choices about the *kinds* of lessons or strategies you might use to teach them:

- Modeling
- Reading aloud
- Having students revise a weak example
- Having students do original writing of their own
- Presenting a focus lesson concentrating on a particular skill (such as using transitions)

My decision to include three features is totally arbitrary. I picked that number because I think it allows for a good look at a given trait without requiring undue amounts of time.

> **Author's Note**
>
> One thing you do not want to do—ever—is teach one trait per grade level: ideas at grade 1, organization at grade 2, and so on. This would be tantamount to breaking up writing process into distinct steps and teaching prewriting at one grade level, drafting at another, and revising at a third. This kind of disjointed approach causes students to lose sight of what writing is all about. Remember that you are ONLY teaching traits individually so that you can focus on particular strategies, such as use of action verbs, that make drafting and revising easier—and better. Real-world math isn't a series of disconnected processes, either. But if we tried to teach addition, subtraction, multiplication, geometry, and algebra all together, we could rightly expect to confuse beginners.

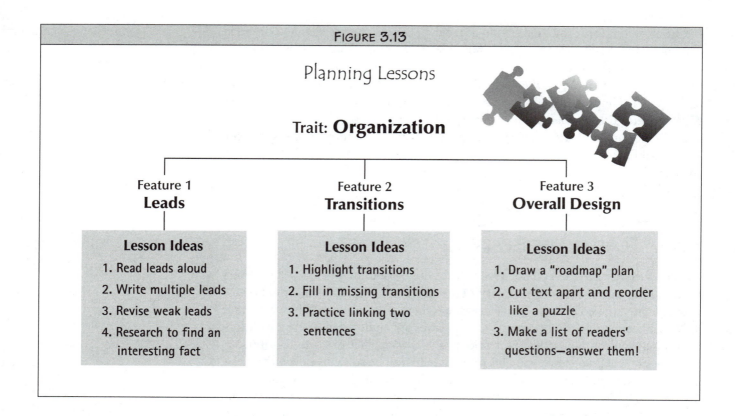

FIGURE 3.13

Planning Lessons

Trait: **Organization**

Feature 1 **Leads**	Feature 2 **Transitions**	Feature 3 **Overall Design**
Lesson Ideas 1. Read leads aloud 2. Write multiple leads 3. Revise weak leads 4. Research to find an interesting fact	**Lesson Ideas** 1. Highlight transitions 2. Fill in missing transitions 3. Practice linking two sentences	**Lesson Ideas** 1. Draw a "roadmap" plan 2. Cut text apart and reorder like a puzzle 3. Make a list of readers' questions—answer them!

WHAT HAPPENS ONCE I FINISH TEACHING ALL THE TRAITS?

Author's Note

For additional lessons on revising for ideas, see the complementary series *Creating Revisers and Editors* (by Vicki Spandel, Pearson Education). Grade-specific lessons address such things as adding information, deleting filler, revising for focus or clarity, revising with the 5 W's, revising a character sketch, revising by showing, going beyond listing, and more.

You cycle back so you can continue reinforcing what you have taught. Let's say you teach ideas in October. Along about February, you might say, "Remember when we talked about detail? Back then, we were writing memoirs, personal pieces. Right now we're doing research papers. Let's take another look at detail in informational writing to see how that looks and sounds." Other features you might cycle back to—because they are especially significant—include these:

- Clarity
- Leads
- Transitions
- Conclusions
- Strong verbs
- Precise phrasing
- Sentence variety
- Dialogue
- Use of conventions to strengthen meaning or voice

No doubt you can think of other things to add to this list. The beauty of teaching the traits is that it gives you and your writers a common language for talking about writing in any context. And that's forever.

Interactive Questions and Activities

1. **Activity and Discussion.** Put an X by each of the following statements with which you agree. Then discuss your responses with your team or class.

   ___ No rubric or scoring guide can cover everything that is important in a piece of writing.

   ___ It makes sense to teach the trait of ideas first since it is foundational.

   ___ It is important to teach conventions & presentation as you go along—not wait to have a unit on this trait down the road.

   ___ In choosing sample papers to share with students, it's more important to focus on the lessons each paper teaches rather than on grade level.

   ___ Identifying strengths and weaknesses within a piece of writing is more important than assigning a score.

   ___ Every writing trait influences every other trait in some way.

   ___ You could easily teach the traits without using a rubric or writing guide at all.

2. **Activity and Discussion.** Review any paper from this chapter (or one from your own students) with a partner. Make two copies so you can work independently. Use a highlighter to mark specific words or phrases that influence you, and ask your partner to do the same.

   Then compare your notes. Were you influenced by the same things? Talk about how this strategy could be helpful in setting up a conference with a student writer.

3. **Activity and Discussion.** As a group, choose any three papers from this chapter, and without reviewing scores or my comments, write (individually) the comment you would make to each student if you were his or her teacher. When everyone is finished writing, compare comments. Talk about the information scores provide versus the information comments provide.

4. **Activity.** Using Figure 3.13, "Planning Lessons," as a model, identify three features of the trait of ideas on which you would likely focus your teaching. Then, identify at least three instructional strategies you could use to teach each feature. Work with your group on this.

5. **Activity and Discussion.** Ask everyone in your group to bring in one favorite picture or chapter book. Look for short passages you could use to illustrate strengths in the trait of ideas, and share them aloud. Talk about how you knew when you had found the "right" passage. If possible, have a volunteer keep a running list of book recommendations that everyone can refer to when teaching. (Note: Expect to have similar discussions relating to books used in teaching other traits.)

Coming Up

In Chapter 4, we'll look at the trait of organization: writing guides, writing samples, literature, and lesson ideas. In subsequent chapters, we'll look at the other traits, beginning with voice in Chapter 5, up through conventions & presentation in Chapter 8. Please keep in mind the recommendation to teach conventions & presentation as you go along. You may want to at least *preview* that chapter at this time.

I write because the day is over and the night is young and someone had a baby and someone or something just died—and whatever it is, I must write about it.
                                                                    —Kirsten Ray, student writer

Everything I see and hear I am thinking of how I can use it in a story, painting a parallel world where florid strokes of life and death sashay across the canvas. This would surprise most people who know me, because on the outside I am quiet, calm, collected, rational, and all those other good words that mean you are grounded here in this reality called life. But I am never fully here.
                                                                    —Simona Patange, student writer

CHAPTER 4

Showcasing the Message with ORGANIZATION

Good work has parts: beginning, middle, and ending. Even writers who achieve a seamless tapestry can point out the invisible stitching.

ROY PETER CLARK
Writing Tools, 2006, 119

Readers need a sense of structure. It is, after all, the artist's job to make meaning of chaos. The shape of the writing is satisfying and important to the readers, for shape or form is in a very real sense meaning.

DONALD M. MURRAY
A Writer Teaches Writing, 2004, 141

Ernest Hemingway once said that "prose is architecture, not interior decoration." That is a very good way to think about organization—it is the architecture that frames the writing. Organization is both flexible and evolutionary. It adapts to the message, growing or changing throughout the writing process. Lead, sequence, transitions, conclusion: *everything* can—and *must*—adjust to reflect the writer's thinking, making both message and purpose clear and easy to navigate. The best organization is quiet and unobtrusive. Without drawing attention to itself, it makes sure that the writer's ideas get center stage.

ORGANIZATION: Structure and Design

A Definition

Good writing is writing by design. It has "good bones," we might say—an underlying structure that holds things together so well we don't even have to think about it. We don't want to be hit over the head (*"My first point . . . My second point . . ."*); our attention should be on the message. But we want the comfort of knowing that the writer has a clear direction and is guiding us through the discussion or story in a purposeful way. Look for an inviting lead that sets up the piece and pulls you in; also look for an insightful conclusion that shows the writer made some discoveries, and is hoping you did, too. In between, the writing should be easy to follow, thanks to strong transitions and a design that fits the message: step by step, visual description, chronological order, comparison-contrast, main idea and support, problem-solution—or just the irresistible flow of clear thinking. We can't always put a name to the design, but like travelers on a guided tour, we have the feeling of being in good hands. Effective organization is flexible, not formulaic, allowing for surprises. In addition, it's often complex. Especially in larger pieces, writers need the freedom to organize information in multiple ways.

Share my definition—or define organization in your own words. This is a good time to introduce the Student Writing Guide for Organization, Figure 4.1 on page 98. Give students time to look over the writing guide, and to ask you any questions they may have. The teacher version, for your use in assessing writing, appears in Figure 4.2 on page 99. Remind students that, as with the trait of ideas, you can use this writing guide to assess any piece of writing (with the exception of research-based writing, which has its own scoring guides, presented in Chapter 9).

Along with the writing guide, you may wish to share the "trait shortie" (see Figure 4.3 on page 100)—a summary of key features to look for in writing, or to focus on through lessons and modeling.

Author's Note

As you score writing for organization, continue to focus on ideas, discussing that trait as well. Help writers understand how organization supports ideas (not the reverse), making meaning clear and information accessible.

Warming Up with Literature

In sharing literature to illustrate strong organization, you might start with just one feature—such as leads—or consider the overall structure of the piece. You are looking for—

- A captivating lead
- Effective design or informational flow that is easy to follow
- Originality—an unusual but effective way to order details
- Good pacing that slows or speeds up time to fit the moment
- An effective ending that creates a sense of resolution or discovery

FIGURE 4.1

Student Writing Guide for
ORGANIZATION

6
- ❏ My organization leads you through the piece like a light in the dark.
- ❏ My lead will hook you—my conclusion will leave you thinking.
- ❏ I connect ideas so you never feel lost.
- ❏ I spend time where it counts—on important points.
- ❏ I might have a few surprises, but this is easy to follow.

3
- ❏ Parts are predictable—or else confusing!
- ❏ My lead and conclusion could use work.
- ❏ You can't always tell how I got from point to point.
- ❏ I spent too much time on some things—not enough on others.
- ❏ Sometimes you have to pay attention to follow this!

5
- ❏ I "know where I'm going" in this writing.
- ❏ I have a strong lead, and a conclusion that wraps things up.
- ❏ It's clear how I got from one idea to the next.
- ❏ I spend most of my time on the important things.
- ❏ I stay on track so you can follow my thinking.

2
- ❏ I didn't worry about order—I just wrote!
- ❏ I don't have a lead or conclusion—or else they're ones you've heard a million times.
- ❏ I wasn't sure how to connect ideas.
- ❏ Which are the "important" parts? I'm not sure . . .
- ❏ This is hard to follow even when you pay attention.

4
- ❏ My organization helps make the message clear.
- ❏ My lead and conclusion work pretty well.
- ❏ I try to lead the reader from point to point.
- ❏ The important ideas stand out—most of the time.
- ❏ You can follow it—but you might know what's coming!

1
- ❏ I don't know how to organize this information.
- ❏ It just starts and stops—there's no lead or conclusion.
- ❏ I don't think these ideas are connected.
- ❏ I don't have a real message yet, so it's hard to tell what matters the most.
- ❏ I need help revising my organization.

© 2012. Vicki Spandel. Designed for use in classroom assessment.

JUST A TASTE . . .

Following are just a handful of my favorite leads. Add your own favorites to this list; then use a similar collection to illustrate good endings. When you have finished sharing *your* examples, put students to work tracking down leads or conclusions they find effective.

Author's Note

A lead is the writer's opportunity to reveal the voice of a piece. Just ask yourself how many times you have stood in a library or book store, reading leads from various books to see which struck the right chord—and you will know at once how important this is.

Sample 1

It's hard not to be hooked by this very first line of Sy Montgomery's fascinating nonfiction biography of a pig that changed lives (*The Good, Good Pig*, 2007, 3):

> Christopher Hogwood came home on my lap in a shoe box.

Sample 2

Zoologist turned author Nicola Davies opens her nonfiction book *Just the Right Size* (2009, 7) by dispelling some myths:

> In comics and movies, superheroes zoom across the sky, run up walls, lift things as big as buses, and use their powers to fight giant monsters! It's all very exciting, but it's a complete load of nonsense.

FIGURE 4.2

Teacher Writing Guide for
ORGANIZATION

6
❑ Thoughtful structure guides reader through text
❑ Provocative opening—satisfying, "just right" conclusion
❑ Smooth, well-crafted transitions create coherence
❑ Balanced pacing—slows or speeds up to fit the moment
❑ Easy to follow throughout—may have a surprise or two

5
❑ Purposeful organization, sense of direction
❑ Strong lead, conclusion that provides closure
❑ Thoughtful transitions connect ideas
❑ Good pacing—time spent on what matters
❑ Easy to follow—stays on track

4
❑ Organization supports message/story
❑ Functional lead and conclusion
❑ Helpful transitions keep ideas flowing
❑ Balanced—*most* time spent on key points
❑ Easy to follow—sometimes predictable

3
❑ Organization somewhat loose—or formulaic
❑ Lead and/or conclusion needs work
❑ Transitions sometimes needed—or overdone
❑ Too much time spent on trivia, too little on key points
❑ Not always easy to follow without work

2
❑ Order more random than purposeful
❑ Lead and/or conclusion missing or formulaic
❑ Transitions unclear or missing
❑ Hard to tell what points matter most
❑ Requires rereading to follow writer's thinking

1
❑ No clear sense of direction
❑ Starts right in (no lead); just stops (no conclusion)
❑ A challenge to follow the writer's thinking
❑ Everything is as important as everything else
❑ Writer needs help sorting/organizing ideas

Sample 3

Many readers consider this lead from *Charlotte's Web* by E. B. White among the best ever (1952, 1980, p. 1):

"Where's Papa going with that ax?" said Fern to her mother as they were setting the table for breakfast.

USING A WHOLE BOOK

Following are several examples that go beyond the standard organizational "molds" we usually think of: step by step, comparison-contrast, and so on. It is extremely useful to teach such forms to students as an introduction to structure. But we have to be careful. We don't want students thinking that they are limited to these forms, any more than they are limited to five-paragraph essays. The world of organization is as diverse as the world of architecture, and you must build your house to suit yourself.

FIGURE 4.3

Trait "Shortie" for ORGANIZATION
Use this summary as a poster—and have students add to it!

Keys to . . . ORGANIZATION
The Design

 The whole piece has a strong sense of direction and purpose.

 An enticing lead pulls readers in.

 Good structure and/or clear thinking guides readers through the piece.

 Strong transitions clearly connect ideas.

 The writer paces things well, slowing down or speeding up at just the right moments.

 A satisfying ending wraps things up and leaves readers thinking.

© 2012. Vicki Spandel.

Author's Note

We often teach organization as if writers chose ONE WAY to organize a book or other text. The truth is, writers are often employing *several* organizational strategies simultaneously. Encourage students to identify as many as possible with each piece you share.

Sample 1
Surprising Sharks by Nicola Davies. 2003.
Ages: Elementary
Genre: Nonfiction picture book (CD available)

Summary

Nicola Davies doesn't try to tell *everything* about sharks; by being selective, she makes both her writing task and our reading task easier. Davies opens with a dramatic lead, then plays on our natural fear of sharks to show us, one by one, many things that may come as a surprise: sharks have unusual qualities (some can blow up like balloons or disguise themselves by looking "like a scrap of old carpet"); sharks are not all killers (some eat plankton); and we humans kill 100 million sharks annually, using them for everything from fertilizer to fish and chips.

Suggestions for Discussion and Writing

1. Find out what your students already know about sharks. Have any of them seen a shark close up—or even been swimming with sharks of any kind?

2. Part of the secret to good organization is having a strong, clear message to which all details can connect—like spokes to the hub of a wheel. What is this author's central message?

3. Davies opens her book with a lead that is both dramatic and fun to read. Share it aloud, and also talk about the conventions on pages 6 and 7. How does the print on this page help readers know how to interpret the writing?

4. As you share the book, keep track of details that really DO surprise you. You might want to make a list. Have you or your students learned anything new about sharks?

5. Ask students to notice the strategies (visual and verbal) that this author uses to organize information. They may notice use of big and little print, use of text that wraps around illustrations, use of diagrams—and more.

6. Talk about how the lead connects to the ending. Is this a good strategy?

7. What other creatures might surprise us if we knew more about them? Make a class list. Then have students (in writing circles of 3 or 4) choose one animal to research and write about.

Sample 2

Down, Down, Down: A Journey to the Bottom of the Sea by Steve Jenkins. 2009.
Ages: Upper elementary and above
Genre: Nonfiction picture book

Summary

In a book that is basically organized visually, author Steve Jenkins takes us on a guided tour from the surface of the ocean to the bottom of the sea, nearly seven miles down. At each level, we get a glimpse of the sea creatures that dwell in that environment. Like Nicola Davies' book *Surprising Sharks*, this book is filled with details new to many readers. We learn, for example, that "more humans have walked on the moon than have visited the deepest spot in the sea."

Suggestions for Discussion and Writing

1. Ask how many students have read other books by Steve Jenkins. What is he known for? (Collage art, clear and focused writing, strong research—among other things.)

2. Respond to just the title first: *Down, Down, Down.* What does it make your writers think the book will be about? If they guess it is about a journey to the ocean floor, see if they can guess how deep that is.

3. Talk about who has visited the ocean—been to a beach, ridden on a boat, or gone swimming, snorkeling, or diving. What creatures do they recall seeing? List a few. What creatures—if any—do your writers predict would live at the *very bottom* of the ocean floor?

4. Have students tell you how this book is organized. If they do not notice it, draw their attention to the scale on the far right of each two-page spread. What information is contained there? Also think about color. What do the changing colors throughout the book tell us?

5. Jenkins uses subheads to begin each new section. Is this a device your writers have used in their work? Take time to notice the wording of these subheads. Are they creative?

6. If this book were to become the basis for a documentary film, what would your writers want to show in the opening scene? What would they want to show in the final scene?

7. Create your own pieces with visual organization. For example, writers might explore the flora or fauna they would encounter traveling north to south in your state, in a region of the country, or in another part of the world.

> ### Author's Note
>
> Explore other books by this author for additional ideas on organizing factual information. For example, the book *What Do You Do With a Tail Like This?* (2003, Houghton Mifflin Harcourt) and *What Do You Do When Something Wants to Eat You?* (2001, Sandpiper) show a highly effective yet simple organizational structure in which the writer poses a general question, then shows many different ways to answer it.

Sample 3

Ubiquitous: Celebrating Nature's Survivors by Joyce Sidman. 2010.
Ages: Middle school and up (younger if shared aloud)
Genre: Nonfiction picture book/poetry

Summary

This creative book uses two structures for organizing information. The first is a timeline, cleverly portrayed by artist Beckie Prange in the form of a curved string (see inside cover two-page displays, front and back). The string itself is 46 meters long, color coded to represent major periods in Earth's history: Archaen and Proterozoic, Precambrian, Cambrian, Triassic, Jurassic, and so forth. The second is genre. Each of fourteen creatures—from bacteria to humans—is the subject of both an informational essay and a poem by writer Joyce Sidman. This combination shows how *everything*—voice, word choice, fluency—shifts with genre.

Suggestions for Discussion or Writing

1. Ask who knows what the word *ubiquitous* means. Be sure your writers can define this term, and have them speculate how it might be used in this title.

2. Before you begin to read, have writers notice the subtitle: *Celebrating Nature's Survivors*. Explain that this is a book about creatures that have been highly successful on Earth. Some have been around an extraordinarily long time, whereas most species on the planet have gone extinct (99 percent, in fact). Which creatures do your writers guess have been around the longest? Make a list—then compare your list to the subjects of each essay/poem.

3. Before showing the timeline, ask if students have any ideas about solving the problem this illustrator faced: showing a time span of 4.6 billion years. After discussing this, show the timeline and read Beckie Prange's Illustrator's Note (end of book).

4. Talk about this two-genre way of sharing information. How are the genres different? How do things like voice or detail change as the genre shifts?

5. How long might it take to research a book like this? After speculating, check out the Author's Note at the end of the book.

6. Share a few definitions from the glossary. Why is a glossary especially helpful in an informational book like this?

7. Choose subjects of your own and explore them in two ways: through poetry *and* through a short informational paragraph. How does exploring a subject through multiple genres deepen a writer's understanding?

OTHER BOOKS WITH INTERESTING ORGANIZATIONAL STRUCTURE

The Arrival **by Shaun Tan. 2006. New York: Arthur A. Levine Books. Wordless historical fiction.**

This jarring and challenging book relies totally on visual organization to examine the difficulties, achievements, joys, and terrors of the immigrant experience. Middle school through adult.

Falling Down the Page, **edited by Georgia Heard. 2009. New York: Roaring Book Press. Poetry.**

A collection of poems organized around a common theme: using lists to explore the wonder of everyday things. Middle school and up.

Flotsam by David Wiesner. 2006. New York: Houghton Mifflin Harcourt. Wordless picture book.

A day of beachcombing leads to the discovery of an underwater camera—one that will take its finder on an amazing journey for which students must find their own interpretations and words. All ages.

If the World Were a Village by David J. Smith. 2011. 2nd edition. New York: Kids Can Press. Nonfiction.

What if the world were a village of only 100 people? That question forms the central point for this collection of essays on timely topics: nationalities, languages, schooling, access to air, food, and water, economies, and much more. Upper elementary and up.

Love That Dog by Sharon Creech. 2001. New York: HarperCollins. Poetic novel in the form of a journal.

A dated personal journal provides one organizational structure to guide us through the story of Jack—but underlying this is the understructure of problem-solution: How does Jack cope with the loss of his dog Sky, and also discover the power of poetry? Upper elementary and middle school.

Mirror, Mirror by Marilyn Singer. 2010. New York: Dutton. Poetry.

What if you stood a poem on its head? That's the organizational premise of an intriguing collection of twin poems presented as visual and verbal opposites. Are their meanings opposites as well? Upper elementary and middle school.

Never Smile at a Monkey by Steve Jenkins. 2009. New York: Houghton Mifflin Harcourt. Nonfiction.

This series of alliterative warnings ("Never harass a hippopotamus" . . . "Never jostle a jellyfish") explores a central theme: the unusual ways in which creatures protect themselves (and things NEVER to do around them). Early elementary and up.

Rain by Manja Stojic. 2000. New York: Crown Publishers. Fictional narrative based on real events.

Animals of the African savannah use their senses to track the coming of rain, the beginning of a new cycle of life; that cycle is the organizational structure of the book. Primary and early elementary.

Seedfolks by Paul Fleischman. 2004. New York: HarperTrophy. Fictional multi-voiced narrative.

Author Paul Fleischman uses multiple voices from diverse ages and cultures to explore life in an inner city Cleveland neighborhood. Middle school and up.

To Kill a Mockingbird by Harper Lee. 2010. 50th anniversary edition. New York: Harper. Novel.

Harper Lee's beloved classic is filled with passion and voice—and raises countless questions about culture, courage, and prejudice as attorney Atticus Finch defies convention to defend an innocent black man for whom the town of Maycomb has little sympathy. Don't miss the timeless lead and conclusion, or Lee's skill in weaving together multiple plots—and deftly playing with time. Middle school and up.

Zoom by Istvan Banyai. 1995. New York: Viking. Wordless visual narrative.

We begin by looking at a close-up of a rooster's comb—then zoom back and back . . . and back. In this wordless book of continually shifting perspectives, the challenge is to find the transitions. All ages.

Assessing Writing Samples for ORGANIZATION

Choose several (or all) of the following papers to share with students. As before, be prepared to read them aloud with expression, and have a list of questions ready to prompt students' thinking.

Paper 1

Some Cartoons Are Violent! (Argument, Grade 3)

Some cartoons are violent. And sometimes ther not! Some ar just funny like Tinny Tunes but some aren't. Take loony Tunes wich is violent but ther not all violent. They could be both. I wach cartoons alot and some are violent. Thers boms that get thrown down in som cartoons. and blows them up. But me I like cartoons some of the time. never will I stop waching but well more are violent than the loony toons. but if I were to mak a cartoon myself I would have well mabe just 1 mane violent thing and then just keep the rest funny OK?

Suggested Score for ORGANIZATION: 2

Lessons Learned from "Some Cartoons Are Violent!"

- It's important to choose a side before trying to persuade others.
- It's difficult to organize writing when the message is not clear.

Comments

The question of how much violence is too much continues to plague television and film executives, so we should not be too surprised that it proved challenging to a third grader. Nevertheless, this young writer takes an exuberant stab at the prompt she is dealt. She sticks with the main theme—violence—but has a hard time choosing sides. Her thinking goes something like this: A little violence in cartoons is entertaining; too much could be a bad thing (for reasons not fully explored)—but it won't hurt me because I know it's phony! What this piece lacks in persuasive logic and organization (it's almost humorously random), it makes up for in voice. The writer is clearly speaking to an audience. By the end of the essay she is negotiating for position: How about just one violent episode per cartoon and keep the rest funny—what do you say?

Suggested Scores for Other Traits

Ideas: **2**

Voice: **4/5**

Word choice: **3**

Sentence fluency: **4**

Conventions & presentation: **2**

Paper 2

A Great Book (Literary Analysis, Grade 8)

There are many themes in <u>To Kill a Mockingbird</u>. Three of the themes that stand out are fairness, justice and courage. These themes are widely spread throughout the book. Harper Lee helps explain these themes through her characters and the way she writes about them.

Fairness is one of the many interesting themes in this great book. The main character Atticus shows the importance of fairness by the way he tries to treat others. Other characters demonstrate fairness as well.

Respect is another important theme of the book, though not as frequent as some of the other themes. Atticus shows respect for his community and for Tom Robinson, and they respect him as well. This is one of the main themes throughout the book.

Courage is a very important theme in this book. Jem shows courage in several parts of the book. Atticus shows courage by defending Tom in the trial.

These three themes of courage, fairness and justice are important parts of this book just as they are important to our society.

Suggested Score for ORGANIZATION: 3

Lessons Learned from This Paper

- When organization is too predictable, the reader's mind wanders.

- Without content, organization serves no real purpose—it's like empty shelving.

- Literary analysis demands specifics. We need quotations, scenes, images. We want to see and hear characters in action.

Comments

Here's a cheery but lightweight analysis of Harper Lee's novel, *To Kill a Mockingbird.* The paper is fluent, pleasant, and noncontroversial. It says virtually nothing except that, apparently, there are some "themes in this great book." This is a handy approach because this report can now be used for other books, too—*Moby-Dick, The Great Gatsby,* or really, any book having themes.

Oddly enough, the organization is stronger than the content only because the writer presents points in an orderly fashion, plodding right along, never reflecting or enlightening us for a moment. Where are the examples, the quotations? We want to picture Atticus thundering away in the courtroom or see Scout reaching out to Boo Radley. This is a fill-in-the-blank paper—one of the best arguments ever for *not teaching formula.* After all, *this* is the result. The voice is not daring, revealing, or personal. It's distant, almost a dust-jacket voice, except that we're tempted to ask (don't say you didn't think of it), "Did you actually *read* the book?" Did you notice that the "great themes" started out as fairness, justice, and courage but shifted to fairness, *respect,* and courage? (If you didn't notice, what does that tell you?)

 The Write Connection

A Great Book

If you happen to be reading *To Kill a Mockingbird* in your classroom, explore *one* of the four themes this writer mentions: fairness, justice, respect, and courage. First, express the theme as a sentence, not a word: e.g., *Courage sometimes means doing the unpopular thing.* Then look for evidence of how the theme plays out in the book: (1) an image or scene, (2) a character's response to a situation, or (3) a quotation to back your statement. With these specific details in hand, write one paragraph exploring one theme. *Note:* Apply these same steps in analyzing themes within *any* book you are currently reading.

Suggested Scores for Other Traits

Ideas: **2**

Voice: **2**

Word choice: **3**

Sentence fluency: **4**

Conventions & presentation: **4**

Paper 3

Movies and Books:
A Comparison (Analysis, Grade 8)

One of the hardest challenges for a movie producer is to make a book as great as To Kill a Mockingbird into a two-hour movie. The director is forced to cut scenes and take out characters so that the movie is not too long. There is also not enough time for description of the town or characters because a movie is based more on action than is a novel.

In the movie version of To Kill a Mockingbird, many of the characters such as Scout's Uncle Jack were taken out. The book contains a long discussion of Maycomb's history and of Atticus, his career, and his family; these were omitted from the movie, along with many scenes showing Jem and Scout at school—scenes that help us understand who these characters are. When Scout's teacher demands that her father stop teaching her to read, we get a glimpse into Scout's mind: "Until I feared I would lose it, I never loved to read. One does not love breathing" (p. 20).

Some description can be handled in a film (as it was in the film version of "To Kill a Mockingbird") through what directors call "voice-overs," in which a narrator speaks to the audience. "Scout," as an adult, speaks to the movie audience about Maycomb in the very first scene of the film—and off and on, throughout the film. Her speeches make smooth transitions between film segments and also establish the setting—the "quiet old town" of Maycomb, where it was so hot that "men's stiff collars wilted by nine in the morning" and ladies turned into "soft teacakes with frostings of sweat and sweet talcum" (p. 6). In the book, she also has time to go into great detail about the history of Maycomb, her feelings about Jem and Dill, and her relationship with Atticus—from whom she develops most of her philosophy about life.

The main difference between books and movies is that movies are more visual so they depend more on action. Directors and script writers take the main idea or concept from a book and put it into a movie, but when they do this, they have to sacrifice some dialogue and scenes. A director has to think about what will play well dramatically, such as the trial scene in which Atticus shows that Tom is left-handed (and so is very unlikely to be the person who struck Mayella), or the scene where Scout reaches out to take Boo's hand. Much of the final conversation between Atticus Finch and Sheriff Tate—in which Atticus slowly realizes

(continued on following page)

the roles played by Jem and Boo Radley in Bob Ewell's death—is preserved in the film. That scene is essential to the closure of the story, and so the director gave it quite a lot of screen time.

Sometimes when making a movie, they have to cut so much that the plot thins and the characters are hard to understand. In "To Kill a Mockingbird," however, I think they did an excellent job of trying to preserve as much as they could. Atticus Finch comes across in both the film and the book as a dignified, thoughtful man—strong, courageous, and filled with conviction. He defends Tom even though he knows it will turn much of the town against him. Scout is curious, brave, and intelligent. She is always trying to figure things out. Boo is mysterious and unexpectedly gentle. Bob Ewell is evil and plotting.

It takes a strong book to make a strong movie. <u>To Kill a Mockingbird</u> is an excellent example of a book-to-movie translation. It hit all the major and important points of the book: the encounters with Boo, the relationship between Atticus and Scout, and most of all, Tom's trial. Sometimes you need the movie and the book to get the whole picture.

Suggested Score for ORGANIZATION: 6

Lessons Learned from This Paper

- Specific examples help the reader follow the conversation.
- Having a main point to make—*it's a challenge to make a great book into a two-hour movie*—gives writing focus.

Comments

This is a thoughtful comparison that uses examples effectively to show how the film reflects the "best" of the book—and suffers minimally from what must be cut. The writer helps us to understand the challenges a director might face—long sections of narrative (that become voice-overs) or numerous characters, not all of whom can make a stage appearance in a film of limited duration. It's an intriguing premise, and the writer puts us continually in the position of the director, deciding what stays and what goes. The writer's examples also show a familiarity with both the book and the film that gives us confidence. The voice is straightforward but somewhat restrained—hence the slightly lower scores. Both voice and ideas would be strengthened by additional quotations to support the excellent points this writer makes.

Suggested Scores for Other Traits

Ideas: **5**

Voice: **5**

Word choice: **6**

Sentence fluency: **6**

Conventions & presentation: **6**

 The Write Connection

Movies and Books: A Comparison

Although this is a much stronger piece than Paper 2, it could benefit from a few more quotations that would show Atticus as courageous, Boo Radley as surprisingly gentle, or Bob Ewell as plotting. Insert a caret (^) at each point where you think a quotation is needed to support the writer's thinking. If you are familiar with the book, identify one or two specific quotations that would work in this paper.

Are Films Too Violent? (Argument, Grade 5)

The easy answer to this question is yes, absolutely. This is a simple position to defend. Just show a movie clip from "Gladiator," "Braveheart," "The Dark Knight," or almost any blockbuster film from the last decade and you can make a convincing case. Films today are filled with brutality and blood spilling. People die every few minutes—or are horribly maimed or tortured. Violence is not just tolerated. It is worshipped. What would a modern film be without multi-wreck car chases, explosions, and flying body parts?

So the real question is, "When do films go too far?" Again, I could take the easy way out. I could say, "It's a matter of opinion" or "Everyone has to decide this for themselves." But is it really just a matter of what we can put up with? Films have already gone too far. Here's why I think so.

First of all, the violence in many films is disturbing. If you have ever seen an old TV show from the 60s or 70s, you know that back then, when people got shot, they just fell over. You didn't see any blood at all. That wasn't too realistic, maybe, but at least it didn't give people nightmares. Today, people have to look away during some movie scenes. They can't bear to watch. And I am talking about adults who have watched violent movies their whole lives. Film makers want to sell tickets, so they make movies more and more violent until now they are psychologically disturbing—to both children and adults.

Second, movie violence does not reflect real life. If you watch the evening news, you will see people shot or injured or swept away by tsunami waves or floods just about every night. They don't pop back up. When a child loses a limb, she or he bleeds. Real people suffer. They get bruises and scars. They cry or pass out. They don't bounce around like robots on trampolines. Watching films encourages young people to think that violence is a game. It's not.

Finally, constant violence on television and in movies (not to mention video games—we won't even go there!) encourages people to think that taking part in violent acts makes you a hero. It isn't brave to carry a knife or gun, but that's how it looks in movies. How many movie heroes go around unarmed, just trying to talk sensibly to villains? It sounds ridiculous to even say it. But if you are laughing, you have already bought in to how movie people want you to think. You can't expect teenagers to think it's wrong to be part of a gang that beats people up for fun when films make it look as if it _is_ fun and natural and "cool." No one wants to be left out.

We show our values by the films we make and the ones we honor with Oscars and other awards. Looking at films is like looking in a mirror of our society. We have to ask ourselves if we like what we see, and if we don't, we need to do something about it.

Violence is a real part of our world. We shouldn't eliminate it from films completely. People have to know what is happening in the world. But we shouldn't make every violent act heroic. We should show the real consequences of violent action—heartache and suffering. Making violence exciting is dishonest. Having movie heroes walk away from car crashes and brutal fights is dishonest. We should also make an effort to show the good side of human nature. Not everyone responds to hard times by killing or injuring every person in sight. What's wrong with having a quiet hero for a change? The real answer to having better films is not simply making them less violent but also showing the rewards of a nonviolent life.

Suggested Score for ORGANIZATION: 6

Lessons Learned from This Paper

- Organization flows smoothly when the writer takes a strong position and sticks with it.
- Voice—in the form of conviction—enhances persuasive writing.
- Precise language—e.g., "the violence in many films is disturbing," "When a child loses a limb, she or he bleeds"—enhances voice and makes the writer's message much stronger.

Comments

This writer takes a clear position and sticks with it throughout the piece: *Yes, films are too violent—by far.* Furthermore, she has specific reasons for this position, and details them effectively in paragraphs 3, 4, and 5. The only thing missing—and it's probably picky even to bring it up with a piece this well written—are references to specific films or scenes (beyond what is included in the lead paragraph). On the other hand, the writer does include general examples—good ones. She reminds us, for instance, that once upon a time, shootouts didn't involve blood, and that people in films often appear to be bouncing on trampolines (in fact, the actors often are). The piece rings with voice, and that's because the writer clearly knows what she is talking about and believes it.

Suggested Scores for Other Traits

Ideas: **5/6**

Voice: **6**

Word choice: **6**

Sentence fluency: **6**

Conventions & presentation: **6**

The Write Connection

Are Films Too Violent?

This is an excellent paper with good examples—on a general level. However, the writer doesn't mention specific films after the opening paragraph. Should she? See if you can brainstorm specific examples (both the film and the scene) that would support the writer's position in paragraphs 3, 4, and/or 5. Use a caret (^) to mark places that need more specificity.

Paper 5

How to Be a Good Driver (Expository, Grade 12)

Being a good driver is not a big fat secret. I have been driving for just over two years and I know what it takes: caution, the alertness of a cat on the hunt, and knowledge of your car. It takes a little luck, too—but that part will always be beyond your control.

If you want a clean driving record like mine—no tickets, no pull-overs—you must be cautious. That's number one. I don't tailgate, and I don't barrel into intersections without looking. I don't back up till I'm sure there's no one behind me, either. Also—fussy people will appreciate this one—I don't park so close to the car next to me you need a can opener to separate us. I know banging a car door into the next guy isn't like a head-on collision—but it still causes damage, both to your car and to your mental health. Courtesy and common sense are important components of caution, you see.

Right up there with caution is a sense of alertness. I don't mean gripping the wheel with everything you've got (like I see some drivers do) and staring straight ahead like your neck won't move. Alertness means being aware of all the other

(continued on following page)

Paper 5 (continued)

vehicles around you at all times, and that includes those way, way out there in the distance (as well as those behind and to the sides). There could be an accident or stalled vehicle a half mile out, so anticipate. Assume the guy next to you will cut you off, pull right in front of you barely missing your front fender, and then slow down—for reasons known only to him and his therapist. This kind of irritating maneuver is all too common. That guy behind you? The one following too close? He doesn't know you're going to need to stop for some kid or dog that's about to run into the road. If you didn't know he was even there, that means you're not looking in your rear-view mirror enough. You should also assume that people approaching a yellow light at an intersection will storm on through. Heck—at least one guy is going to sneak through on the red. Be ready. That's what it means to be alert. It could save your life.

Finally, you need to know something about how your car works. Could you change a tire if you had to? If not, stay out of remote areas and at least have a cell phone. (Or drive with a buddy who can change tires!) Watch that gas gauge; boy, nothing ruins a good time like hiking down the road for gas. Also, don't allow people to make a lot of noise in the car. Make them wear seat belts. Keep the radio to a level where you might hear a police or fire siren a block away. Occasionally, turn the radio off so you can see if your car is making unusual noises, like the sound of a muffler scraping on pavement.

See how much of this is common sense? Yet, how much of it is included in the typical driver's test? That's right! Almost none! Know what that means? See those people out there on the highway? That's right! They're not ready to drive—but they're driving anyway! So, be defensive. Be alert, cautious, and knowledgeable, and with some luck thrown in, you'll have a chance.

✎ The Write Connection

How to Be a Good Driver

Many readers find this paper highly humorous—but some object to the informal, conversational tone. Suppose you are an editor preparing this piece for publication in a journal that doesn't approve of informalities. With a partner, go through the paper carefully, highlighting any words or expressions you might need to revise. Then see if you can express the writer's ideas in slightly more formal language—without losing the meaning or voice. Can you do it? Do you like the revision better than, or at least as much as the original? Or does your revision tamper too much with voice?

Suggested Score for ORGANIZATION: 6

Lessons Learned from "How to Be a Good Driver"

- The five-paragraph organizational structure *can* work—IF you are writing an expository essay, IF you *really do have* three legitimate points to make, and IF you handle transitions creatively and smoothly.
- Similarly, a summary ending can work if you take a fresh perspective and avoid word-for-word restatement.
- Humor and understatement are as effective in expository writing as in narrative.

Comments

This paper is fun to read and easy to follow. The already convincing arguments could be strengthened by statistical support: e.g., the number of traffic accidents triggered by tailgating. Still, the writer is direct, confident, and not afraid to weave in humor, though he does not rely on it; he has specific points to make and delivers them clearly and forcefully. What could have dissolved into formula works this time because the writer really has three clear points to make: the need for caution, alertness, and knowledge of one's car. In this case, the structure enhances the message instead of fighting it, and that's what good organization should do. Some readers believe the language is too casual (*some kid, one guy*), but it can be argued that this conversational tone adds to the voice. Expressions like *irritating maneuver* and *storm on through* push me to a 6 in word choice. Notice the extraordinary variety in sentences, and the careful and creative use of conventions to enhance readability.

Suggested Scores for Other Traits

Ideas: **5/6**

Voice: **6**

Word choice: **6**

Sentence fluency: **6**

Conventions & presentation: **6**

Paper 6

Computing Batting Averages (Expository, Grade 6)

Math is all around us in almost everything we do. Math is involved in banking, shopping, the weather, the national economy and just about everything we do. It is hard to think of even one thing that doesn't use math in one way or another.

You wouldn't think math would be such a big part of sports but it is. Take baseball for example. In baseball people use math for many things. One example is figuring out batting averages. This is important because when players see how well they are doing, they have a way to improve. How would players improve if they didn't know how well they are doing.

A batting average is really like a percentage. To find out your batting average, all you need are two numbers: how many times you are up and how many times you hit safely (meaning that you get at least to first base on a hit). Then you need to divide the number of times you hit safely by the total number of times you are up to bat.

Here is an example of a batting average. Lets say you are up 50 times and hit safely 25 of those times. Your batting average would look like this: 25/50. You would have a batting average of .500, which is pretty good. Suppose you hit safely every time you were up. Your batting average would then be 50/50, or 1.000—which is pronounced "one thousand." This were we get the famous saying "batting a thousand." Of course, nobody could ever bat this well in real life.

With the use of batting averages it is easy to set goals for yourself and see how well you are doing. A good batting average for a pro ball player is somewhere between .300 and .400. The all time record is held by Ted Williams, who batted .410.

My best batting average was in the summer of 1998, when I averaged .370. Maybe it was me, or maybe it was the pitching!

Think about your own life for a minute and you'll be surprised what a big role math plays.

Suggested Score for ORGANIZATION: 4

Lessons Learned from "Computing Batting Averages"

- Sometimes the paper really takes off with the second paragraph.
- You may not need that last line.

Comments

The lead in this paper works, but feels a little forced. Similarly, the conclusion feels unnecessary. Both are distractions to an otherwise good discussion of how to compute batting averages. The discussion itself is clear and easy to follow. The voice is pleasant and reasonably engaging, although the piece is not quite a read-aloud yet. Or *is it?* Cut the beginning and ending, and what's left has more voice. Excellent conventions (including the math conventions). (And I'm told that the true average for Ted Williams is .406 for his final year, .344 for his lifetime.)

Suggested Scores for Other Traits

Ideas: **4/5**

Voice: **4**

Word choice: **4**

Sentence fluency: **4**

Conventions & presentation: **6**

Paper 7

Cats or Dogs (Argument, Grade 6)

Cats or dogs, that is the question. My opinion is I like both. Cats are one of the most groomed animals in the world. Dogs are one of the most loyal. There are just some problems about both.

I really like cats because they are so clean. They always like to clean there selve's a lot. Most cats are very well mannered and they love people. They are also very fast. I have a cat, kind of. They really like string.

I also like dogs. They can run real fast to. I really like dogs because they can jump real high and catch a Frisbee. They can also do a lot of tricks like swimming.

There are some problems with both. I wish I could have both but it can't happen. Dogs just like to chase cats. Cats cough up fur balls. Dogs bark and eat lots of weird stuff. Now you see the reasons I like both. I really like cats. Dogs I really like to but there are some problems. I just can't decide.

Suggested Score for ORGANIZATION: 2

Lessons Learned from "Cats or Dogs"

- Comparison papers need to be set up carefully. Choose the bases for comparison (e.g., loyalty, cleanliness) and explore each one through examples.
- "I just can't decide" is an ineffective ending. Either make a clear choice or explain what has to happen before a good choice can be made.

Comments

This paper has some good points to make: Cats are clean and well groomed; they are well mannered and love people. Dogs can run, jump, and catch things (so they are fun to play with), and make loyal pets. Each pet has problems: Cats "cough up fur balls," whereas dogs "eat lots of weird stuff." Two things keep ideas and organization from working well. First, the writer refers to problems in paragraph 1, but does not get back to them until much later. Second, both good qualities and problems are presented essentially as lists, with minimal development. Cats "really love string." Why is this important? The sentence "I have a cat, kind of" is bewildering: It isn't really mine? Or it isn't really a cat? Overall, the jump from dogs to cats and back again makes the discussion hard to follow. Questions could help: *What kind of person gets along best with cats (or dogs)? If you could only have one pet, what would you pick?* Smaller issues: The conventions are fairly clean (despite "thereselves" and "to" for "too"). Frisbee is capitalized and the paragraphing is quite good. The word choice, by contrast, is quite simple, and the sentences are short and sometimes choppy, disrupting the fluency.

Suggested Scores for Other Traits

Ideas: **3/4**

Voice: **3**

Word choice: **3**

Sentence fluency: **3**

Conventions & presentation: **5**

The Write Connection

Cats or Dogs

Organization—particularly in persuasive writing and opinion pieces—is always easier when the writer has a clear sense of direction. Imagine yourself writing a brochure for the local pet shelter. The purpose is to help people who are considering adopting a pet decide which one—cat or dog—is right for them. Hint: Maybe the secret to organizing this well is to focus on the characteristics of a prospective *pet owner* that make that person better suited to life with a cat or dog. Try it from this perspective!

Paper 8

Sand Dollar (Narrative, Grade 8)

In yester your, when Moby Dick was a tadpole and the seas rolled and thundered over the jettys and onto the shore, I searched for my first sand doller still hidden somewhere in the ever stretching Silver Beach peninsula.

I'd been going there since a little toddler not finding much more than sea wead and empty crab shells, wich were plucked clean by the screeching sea gulls, nature's best garbage man. Now I was five, I could run and search on my own, no more holding hands with mom and dad. I could run with the big kids down the beach with the wind roaring in my ears like huge jet engines. I was in search of the still fashionable sand doller, that naturally perfect round disc with a dotted star on top and a hole in the center of its flat bottom. While in town the first evening of beachcoming, I spotted just the box I needed for my collection of valuables-to-be. It was not just a box, but a red ceder chest approximately 6 by 8 inches and designed like a treasure chest. Mom and dad thought it was just what I needed.

I couldn't wait for morning to come and the night went slow. I could hear the waves beckoning me through the partially open window in my room. Like counting sheep the waves took there toll.

Clam digging started early before light and my parents went clam digging while the tide was still out and I looked for shells. I found different kinds of shells,

(continued on following page)

Paper 8 (continued)

broken crabs, empty clams because the sea gulls got to them first, but still no sand dollers.

After lunch, mom and dad decided to help me find some sand dollars, but first dad had to stop at a store in Silver Beach.

Dad left me to go ahead and look for sand dollars with mom. When dad got back he helped me too. I was looking up and down, around rocks and in tide pools. Then I spotted it, partially sticking out of the sand. I found it, my first sand doller, it was probably the only one on the beach for 50 miles. I put it in my treasure box with sand still softly seeping through the hole in the bottom. This shell is in my box besides years of awards, pins and buttons from athletics and scouting. A shark's tooth from Australia that my Grandpa got for me, and a swiss army knife I found in the woods where I used to live.

These things keep a warm link to my past.

Silver Beach, I found out later didn't have sand dollars, but the local souviner shop kept them In reserve for when Moms and dads would help build up a memory.

Suggested Score for ORGANIZATION: 5

Lessons Learned from "Sand Dollar"

- The lead and conclusion are vital to the success of any piece.
- A good story involves a few surprises.
- While editing isn't *everything*, errors in spelling and punctuation can be distracting.
- Sometimes, it's good to read a piece more than once.

Comments

This is a masterpiece of sensory detail: the screeching gulls, the wind sounding in your ears like jet engines—the feel of the sand. The original version contained a number of cross-outs; the writer worked hard, but ran out of editing time, and so was not able to correct all the errors. To appreciate the voice, have a friend read it aloud—someone who reads with expression and can dance around faulty punctuation and spelling. This is the work of a natural storyteller who knows how to set the scene and recreate the way it feels to be five. The piece opens with a lead almost poetic in its rhythm, and closes with a thought so poignant and understated that it touches me each time I read it. Many readers feel the writer goes off track when Dad heads to town—but the significance of that journey comes clear at the end. A stronger transitional sequence would have boosted organization to a 6. But give the writer credit: he made *us* figure it out. The word choice is wonderful: *rolled and thundered over the jetties, plucked clean, nature's best garbage man, roaring in my ears like huge jet engines* . . . Someone invariably points out that Moby Dick did not begin life as a tadpole. I confess I'm just not as troubled by this bit of poetic license as a lot of people would like me to be. This paper has lived in my head since the very first time I read it. That must say something.

The Write Connection

Sand Dollar

Consider that moment when Dad slips into town to visit the souvenir shop (see paragraph 5). Could a good transitional sentence here (perhaps showing what the writer was thinking or wondering at that moment) help us connect Dad's disappearance to the hunt for sand dollars? See if you can smooth the link between paragraphs 5 and 6.

Suggested Scores for Other Traits

Ideas: **6**

Voice: **6**

Word choice: **6**

Sentence fluency: **5**

Conventions & presentation: **3**

Lessons and Strategies for Teaching ORGANIZATION

The main things you want to teach . . .

- *Writing a strong lead*
- *Making genre and design work to showcase the message*
- *Ordering information to make it easy to follow*
- *Connecting thoughts to help readers follow the story or discussion*
- *Slowing the pace or speeding up at the right time*
- *Ending with a conclusion that leaves the reader something to think about*

Following are some lesson ideas and strategies that will help.

1. MODEL THE WRITING OF A LEAD.

Remember those writing topics I chose for myself in Chapter 3? (See pages 82–83, Lesson Idea 1.) When you create a list like that, keep it handy, and at some point, ask students, "Which topic would you like to see me write about right now?" Then as they watch, create several possible leads for a piece on that topic. Let's say that from my list students choose whale watching for my writing topic. Fine. My leads might look like this:

Lead 1

> *"There she is!" the captain shouts. On a chilly (for Hawaii) day, 75 drizzly degrees, we head out over a steel gray ocean, dotted with threatening whitecaps, in search of 40-ton whales that cruise just below the surface, and are mighty enough to pop our little catamaran about like a ping pong ball.*

Lead 2

> *Almost 50 of us are crammed onto this small catamaran in the middle of the bay, and it's a wonder it doesn't tilt as we scramble to one side or the other, cameras in hand, vying for position to snap the best picture, to get the flukes, the spray—or best shot of all, that moment when the whale breaches and collectively, we catch our breath.*

Lead 3

> *They've all gone to the other side of the boat to see the whale, but . . . she isn't there. She's here—right below me. We are alone in this moment, just the two of us, and she slips above the surface of the sea, water streaming down over her rough blue-gray skin, her enormous black eye staring right into me with an expression that is startlingly gentle and curious.*

Remember a lead can be more than a sentence. It can be a paragraph or two or even a few pages.

—Barry Lane
The Reviser's Toolbox, 1999, 28

One thing that will make it easier to get started is to write three leads to your paper instead of agonizing over one that must be perfect.

—Bruce Ballenger
The Curious Researcher, 2004, 168

When I finish, I have writers choose their favorite and tell me what they like about it—or if they don't like any of them, they can offer suggestions. Often—not always—I wind up liking the third lead best, and it's often the one students choose, too. This gives me a chance to tell them that writing more than one lead is a good idea because we warm up as we work.

For students who struggle with leads . . .

2. LIST "TIRED" LEADS TO AVOID.

With students' help, list leads that are overused and print them on a poster for all to see. That way, students are less likely to resort to such time-worn beginnings as

- *Hi, my name is Sean and I want to tell you . . .*
- *This will be a report about . . .*
- *In this paper . . .*
- *Do you like California? I do. Let me tell you why . . .*

For students who need something more concrete . . .

3. GET SPECIFIC ABOUT HOW TO BEGIN.

Use your exploration of literature to create a list of effective ways to begin. Then encourage students to write more than one lead for a given piece—and to take different approaches, such as one of these:

- An anecdote
- A startling fact
- A scene that sets the stage
- An intriguing quotation
- Action, action, action!!!
- Dialogue
- A promise to readers, e.g., "You'll be a cook within one week!"
- A striking image
- A summary of a problem—to which the paper offers a solution

Some students may enjoy creating a new lead for an old favorite. See Figure 4.4 for kindergartener Caleb's take on "Jack and the Beanstalk." It's even more suspenseful than the original.

FIGURE 4.4

Caleb's New Lead for
"Jack and the Beanstalk" (Kindergarten)

Jack and the Beanstalk. HOLY BEANSTALK! Jack wants to clime a big big big big BIG beanstalk! What will be up there? and what will happen? Oh the suspense! But what about the Real story? how about I Just tell it to you?

For students who enjoy playing with writing . . .

4. WRITE BADLY ON PURPOSE.

Whether writing leads, conclusions, or something in between, writing badly on purpose is great fun—and highly instructive because you have to think about what *not* to do. Here are a few spoofs of leads you might recognize:

- *Hi, I'm E. B. White, and I want to tell you the story of Charlotte the spider and her friend Wilbur.*

- *Do you like chocolate? In this story you'll learn about a determined boy named Charlie and the way chocolate changed his life.*

- *It was a dark and stormy night. Ahab paced the deck, smoking his pipe. Somewhere out there lurked Moby. Moby Dick.*

Host a "Bad Leads" award ceremony, where you can have some fun reading bad revisions aloud and voting for the worst of the lot: "Lead Least Likely to Get a Reader's Attention," "Most Action-Free Lead," "Most Obnoxiously Perky Lead," and so on.

5. "ENVISION" WRITING BY EXPLORING GENRE.

In *Wondrous Words* (1999), Katie Wood Ray suggests that envisioning should be part of writing process as we teach and practice it. *Envisioning* in this sense means imagining or picturing what the writing will become.

We can help students see how big the world of writing really is by sharing a wide range of documents (think beyond books)—and by encouraging them to write in many genres for many purposes. It's easy to suppose that narrative, informational, and persuasive writing are the only forms we need worry about, and that stories and essays will give our students the range of writing experience they need. But those three genres are very broad, and include thousands of sub-genres that do not even occur to many students until they begin looking for them consciously. See Figure 4.5 for a list of genres to expand your reading—and writing.

Reread what you've written. Listen to what it is telling you. What does it want to be? a poem? a story? a memoir? an essay? What other images and thoughts occur to you? It might seem frightening to allow the writing to guide you but try to relax, and don't panic if it wants to take you into strange and uncharted water.

~Georgia Heard
Writing Toward Home, 1995, 41

6. DESCRIBE *A FEW* DESIGN POSSIBILITIES.

Although the number of organizational designs is infinite, you can help your writers understand the *concept* of design by acquainting them with a few possibilities—

- Step by step
- Visual design (description)
- Comparison-contrast
- Problem-solution
- Main point and support
- Chronological order

. . . or any others you feel are important. The best way to do this is through example. Look for written materials that illustrate these or other designs. A recipe, for example, or instructions for playing a board game shows how step-by-step organization can look.

Hint: Don't be too quick to identify the design. You don't want to say, "Here's a good example of step-by-step organization." Instead, show students a sample and ask,

FIGURE 4.5

Possible Writing Genres

- ❑ Adventure story
- ❑ Advertisement
- ❑ Advice column
- ❑ Analysis
- ❑ Autobiography
- ❑ Biography
- ❑ Blog
- ❑ Board game
- ❑ Book jacket
- ❑ Brochure
- ❑ Bumper sticker
- ❑ Cartoon
- ❑ Comic strip
- ❑ Commercial
- ❑ Concrete poem
- ❑ Directions
- ❑ Drama
- ❑ Encyclopedia entry
- ❑ E-mail
- ❑ Fairy tale
- ❑ Folk tale

- ❑ Graphic novel
- ❑ Greeting card
- ❑ Historical fiction
- ❑ How-to manual
- ❑ Instructions
- ❑ Invitation
- ❑ Journal
- ❑ Lab report
- ❑ Label
- ❑ Legend
- ❑ Lesson plan
- ❑ Letter
- ❑ Magazine article
- ❑ Memoir
- ❑ Mystery
- ❑ Newscast
- ❑ Newsletter
- ❑ Newspaper column
- ❑ Persuasive argument
- ❑ Picture book
- ❑ Poem

- ❑ Podcast
- ❑ Poster
- ❑ Proposal
- ❑ Radio script
- ❑ Recipe
- ❑ Report
- ❑ Résumé
- ❑ Review
- ❑ Science fiction
- ❑ Script for TV, film
- ❑ Signage
- ❑ Song lyrics
- ❑ Speech
- ❑ Summary
- ❑ Textbook
- ❑ Travel guide
- ❑ Travelogue
- ❑ Weather forecast
- ❑ Web page
- ❑ Webcast
- ❑ Wiki

Remember . . . organizational design varies with genre.

"How is this organized?" You also want them to think about whether the organizational structure was a good choice. For variety, begin with a hypothetical topic and ask, "What would be one good way to organize information for this piece?" Here are some possibilities:

- A piece on how to adopt a dog
- The history of your town
- The story of a bank robbery for the nightly news
- A weather forecast
- An introduction for a math textbook
- Signage for a local aquarium exhibit
- A menu

Talking through such examples will help students understand how organization and document design work hand in hand. Keep in mind too that many (if not most) documents involve multiple designs.

7. ORDER THE DETAILS.

Practice in tracking a writer's thinking makes us more thoughtful about putting together an informational path for another reader to follow. It helps us appreciate good transitions, clear beginning and ending points, and a logical flow of details. You can give your students this practice with a simple activity they will love.

Choose a sample of text that is *well organized,* with good sequencing and clear transitions. It should not be too long—perhaps three lines for younger students, up to ten or twelve lines for older students, but not much more. (As an alternative, use whole paragraphs, rather than sentences, as the basic "chunks" of text.) If the piece has a clear beginning and ending, so much the better.

Copy it, line by line (or paragraph by paragraph). Cut the copy into strips so that students can play with it like a puzzle. If possible, laminate the strips so that you can use them over and over.

For practice, try the sample (see Figure 4.6) from Sneed Collard's extraordinary book, *The Deep-Sea Floor* (2003). I chose this text because informational writing is slightly more challenging than narrative; yet Collard's writing is always characterized by clear organization and thoughtfully embedded transitions. (*Hint:* There are two paragraphs. The answer is in Figure 4.10 at the end of this chapter.)

Stories work well for beginners because they usually have a clear event-to-event flow. Informational writing (like the Collard example) is harder; you have to connect each supporting detail to a main idea. Persuasive writing is harder yet because it has many parts: thesis, support, counterargument(s), closing argument, and conclusion. Consider, though: If you try various genres, you can talk about how organization shifts with form. Here are some suggestions:

> **Author's Note**
>
> This activity cannot be done without careful reading. Students go back again and again to read the piece *as they put it together* in order to figure out what goes where. This emphasizes the importance of reading everything we write—from a reader's perspective—asking, "Does this make sense? Is this easy to follow? What is the reader expecting will come next?"

> **Author's Note**
>
> You can do this activity using students' own writing, but they need to format it so that it can be cut into pieces, either single sentences or short paragraphs. Then a partner can try to reassemble it. A word of caution: Writers *must* be able to reassemble their own copy. One teacher found, to her dismay, that many of her writers could not do this—and regretted she had not made copies.

Easy	Challenging
• Recipe	• Blog
• Directions	• Poem
• Fable	• Encyclopedia entry
• Advertisement	• Documentary script
• Book or film review	• Picture book
• Cartoon	• Podcast

> **Author's Note**
>
> You may be thinking that you'd like to give your students practice in organizing a whole book—but how would you ever do it? It's simple, really. Instead of sentences or paragraphs, copy the table of contents—and scramble it. This provides wonderful practice in thinking about how to organize subtopics within a larger piece of writing—good practice for writers who need a challenge.

FIGURE 4.6

Out-of-Order Lines from Sneed B. Collard's
The Deep-Sea Floor

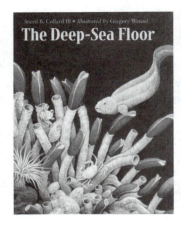

> The sonar made loud noises that bounced off the sea bottom.

> As recently as the mid-nineteenth century, many people believed that the ocean was bottomless or that no life existed in the deep.

> During World War I, they began mapping the ocean bottom with a new invention called **sonar.**

> In the 1870s, though, scientists began a serious search for deep-sea animals by lowering nets and other collection devices far below the surface.

> Photosynthesis, the production of food using light energy from the sun, cannot take place on the deep-sea floor.

> The echoes from these noises gave people a detailed outline of what the deep-sea floor looked like.

> Others felt sure that the deep sea was filled with terrifying sea serpents or animals that had disappeared from shallower waters millions of years before.

> For most of history, the geography and animal life of the deep-sea floor have remained a total mystery.

*For young students and any writers
who have trouble with the big picture . . .*

8. TALK BEFORE YOU WRITE.

Talking is an excellent organizational strategy because it's quick and the speaker can see at once whether listeners are puzzled or are following along with ease. Talking helps us organize information in our own minds before writing, and gives listeners a chance to help fill in holes by asking questions when something doesn't make sense.

You can model this. Think of something unusual, frightening, funny, or otherwise significant that has happened to you in the past year. Tell the story to your students. Here's a story of mine as I would *tell* it:

> En route to New York, I got delayed in Chicago. Around 1 a.m., airport people bused us to a hotel, where it took forever to check in. We were exhausted—and starving. But all they gave us was the standard "kit" with a tiny toothbrush, one ounce of toothpaste, a razor, and a plastic shower cap. When I checked into my room, I discovered only one light worked, the one right by the bed. There was no light in the bathroom at all, so I showered in the dark. I assumed the only small container in the shower would be shampoo. Ha! It was hand lotion. Have you ever seen what happens to your hair when you wash it with lotion? I looked like an extra on the Star Trek set. And that is how I flew home the next day. People on the plane tried to avoid looking at me—that was definitely a bad hair day for me!

After telling your story, list the events (see Figure 4.7), possibly including a few details you *don't* need (what time you got up, what you had for breakfast). Your list may be ordered somewhat randomly, and may omit one or two important details. Now ask for students' help. Have them—

- Read through the list with you
- Help you cross out what you don't need
- Remind you to add anything you forgot
- Re-order the rest

With their help, your revised list will look something like Figure 4.8. Note that while a story is an easy place to begin, you can use this activity with any genre.

9. PLAY WITH TIME.

Everyone is familiar with movie moments where time slows to a crawl as the lovers run toward each other over the meadow—or the villain creeps up the dark stairs. Or other times the screen dissolves into a message: "*Five years later . . .*" and we know that apparently nothing central to the writer's message has occurred during that time.

As Barry Lane is fond of saying, in writing we don't have to live in real time—we can play

FIGURE 4.7

Re-Ordering Random Story Events

- What can be cut?
- What should be added?
- Is anything out of order?

1. I was flying to New York.
2. I got up early to head to the airport.
3. I was excited!
4. In Chicago, I missed my connection.
5. They bused us to an old, old hotel.
6. We waited a long time to check in.
7. They gave us some toiletry kits.
8. My room was very dark and dingy.
9. The only light that worked was right by the bed.
10. I wound up shampooing my hair with hand lotion!
11. It looked really, really bad!
12. The rest of the trip, I kept wishing for shampoo and fresh clothes!

FIGURE 4.8

Re-Ordering Random Story Events

- What can be cut?
- What should be added?
- Is anything out of order?

1. I was flying to New York. — *Combine with #4.*
2. I got up early to head to the airport.
3. I was excited!
4. In Chicago, I missed my connection. — *Talk about how long you had to wait.*
5. They bused us to an (old, old) hotel. — *Good! More description!*
6. We waited a long time to check in. — *How long? Talk about how tired and hungry you were.*
7. They gave us some (toiletry kits.) — *Tell what's inside!*
8. My room was very dark and dingy.
9. The only light that worked was right by the bed. — *Combine 8 & 9. How?! Explain!!*
10. I wound up shampooing my hair with hand lotion!
11. It looked (really, really bad!) — *Too vague! Put in the Star Trek part – how people didn't want to look at you.*
12. The rest of the trip, I kept wishing for shampoo and fresh clothes! — *Ending is too weak! Write about checking in in NY with Star Trek hair.*

You need to add more about the shampoo. How did it feel? Was it hard to comb your hair?

FIGURE 4.9

"My Grandpa," by Emma (Grade 3)

I never met my grandpa. He died before I was born. He fought for my country in World War II. He signed up illegally to be a soldier when he was fifteen. He lived.

Years passed, and he had his first child, my dad. More years passed, and he had my four aunts and two uncles.

My dad tells stories about him. My favorite one is when he and his family were camping when it was raining. My grandpa was drinking coffee on a hill looking one direction while his family floated away in the water, going the other direction. Even though I have heard that story so many times, it makes me laugh so hard. I bet my grandpa would laugh, too.

Even though I have never met my grandpa, I feel like I have known him forever. I know I have.

with it. In Figure 4.9, third grader Emma writes about her grandfather, introducing him with some essentials in paragraph one, speeding along through the family history in paragraph two, then slowing down to recap Grandpa's memorable coffee break, and coming full circle in paragraph four to echo her lead. This young writer already has a strong sense of how to achieve good pacing.

For an outstanding literary example of how to slow time down and focus on the moment, see "A Visit to the Doctor" from Roald Dahl's autobiography *Boy* (1984, 69) In that chapter, Dahl tells about having his adenoids out at the age of eight. He and his mother walk to the doctor's in-house office, where little Roald is seated in a chair and covered with a large red rubber apron—facing the dentist:

> The doctor was bending over me. In his hand he held that long shiny steel instrument. He held it right in front of my face and to this day I can still describe it perfectly. It was about the thickness and length of a pencil, and like most pencils it had a lot of sides to it. Toward the end, the metal became much thinner, and at the very end of the thin bit of metal there was a tiny blade set at an angle. The blade wasn't more than a centimetre long, very small, very sharp and very shiny.

Everything at the beginning and end of Dahl's story happens very quickly; the majority of our reading time is spent right there in the chair, watching that blade come closer and closer. Remind students to think carefully about those "movie moments" in their own writing where time should speed up or slow down. And remember that it's also good to slow down in informational writing when the subject is complicated.

10. Use questions to create a "middle."

We often tell students that their writing needs a beginning, middle, and end. Most understand what a lead is because the term defines itself. Similarly, they grasp that a good ending wraps things up. But what the heck is a *middle?*

Until we define this for students, we cannot teach them the most difficult part of organizing because the middle takes up most of the writing. Tell them this: *The middle is the writer's opportunity to answer all the readers' questions.* Here's one brief example.

Let's say I am writing about cockroaches. I might ask students to help me brainstorm a list of interesting questions they think my writing should answer:

1. What *is* a cockroach—and what does it look like?
2. How long have cockroaches been around?
3. Where are they found?
4. How large do they get?
5. Are they intelligent?
6. What do they eat?
7. Do people ever eat *them?*
8. Do people ever keep cockroaches as pets?
9. Why are they so difficult to kill?
10. Can we do *anything* to control them?

All that remains is to put these questions in the best order—then answer them.

11. Explore transitions.

Transitions are words, phrases, sentences, or related ideas that show readers how one thought is connected to another. To see how transitions work, consider the difference between these two passages:

- Ted sat for a long time in the waiting room. He opened the door.
- Ted sat for a long time in the waiting room. Finally, he could stand the suspense no longer. With a sigh of exasperation, he leaped up and opened the door.

Now we can picture the scene. We know what's motivating Ted—and we begin to anticipate what might happen next. You can create examples just like this and have students create transitions—links—that explain how two thoughts connect:

- Jack ran three miles. He stopped and looked around.
- Mom announced they were having squash for dinner. Judy went to her friend Rosa's house.
- Raul loved Facebook. He did not have a Facebook page.
- The weather report called for a storm. A million stars were visible in the night sky.

Look for Transitions in Literature.

Choose a passage with strong transitions; then omit a few and see if your students can fill in the blanks. Here's one example from author Sneed Collard's nonfiction slice of history, *The World Famous Miles City Bucking Horse Sale* (2010, 5). Here, Collard—a master at transitions—describes the battle between bronc and rider, a battle that will help rodeo managers decide if a horse is wild and cantankerous enough to be worth bidding on. Some transitional words *and phrases* have been omitted. See if you can fill in the blanks. (The original passage appears in Figure 4.11 at the close of this chapter.) Don't try to guess precisely what the author wrote—that's often hard. Just revise the passage to make sense (Notice that some blanks are longer—indicating multiple words):

> The bucking horse bursts out of its holding pen, hooves flying, and catapults into the air. The rider's boots fling skyward _____ his torso slams back like a feedsack onto the horse's rump. _____ , the young rider hangs on, grunting with determination—or desperation—as the horse lands with a stiff-legged jolt.
>
> _____ the horse is just getting started. _____ , the bronc twists to the left and kicks its back legs almost vertically. ___ , _____ , it launches like a NASA booster rocket, arching gracefully into the air before its front legs stab back into the earth. _____ , the rider sticks with the explosive twelve-hundred-pound beast beneath him. _____ , the cowboy thinks, the buzzer will sound at any moment, giving him a good riding score.
>
> (Reprinted by permission: www.buckinghorsebooks.com)

Sneed Collard's transitions are especially strong because (1) he often uses words or expressions the reader isn't expecting, and (2) he seldom repeats a transitional phrase within a given passage.

Create a List of Transitional Words or Phrases.

You don't need an exhaustive list. Just a few examples help students understand what transitions are and how they work:

after a while	*to put it another way*
next	*despite all this*
because of that	*for example*
nonetheless	*on the other hand*
after the money ran out	*moreover*
however	*just as the rain stopped*

12. PRACTICE WRITING KILLER ENDINGS.

The students with whom I shared my bad hair day story (Figure 4.7) were clearly disappointed with the ending on my "story events" list, so that's a good one for me to model. They knew what they wanted: a vivid image and plenty of feeling. No generalities.

It is important for me to write the draft first. Otherwise, I can't know what ending sounds and feels right. I won't share the whole draft here—just the last sentence before the conclusion:

> . . . I looked like a refugee from the Star Trek set.

That ending sounds very abrupt. Here are three possible sentences I could add:

- To this day, I am careful not to allow any hand lotion in the shower.
- People stared—probably wanting to know what I had done so they could avoid doing the same thing.
- Bad hair days come and go, but once you have had hand lotion hair, nothing much can frighten you.

My best advice about endings is this: Keep it simple. Endings shouldn't be mini-novels or lectures. Share a thought and then go away.

Interactive Questions and Activities

1. **Activity and Discussion.** This chapter suggests broadening students' exposure to multiple genres. Which genres do your students typically experience as readers or writers in your classroom? Make a group list. Discuss the advantages of giving students opportunities to create more real world writing—such as copy for a newscast, a website, a proposal, a resume, blog, wiki, podcast, and so forth.

2. **Activity and Discussion.** Ask everyone in your group to bring in a favorite picture or chapter book. Take turns reading leads and conclusions aloud. (If you have chapter books, read leads or conclusions from several chapters.) Talk about which ones you like best and why. Also notice each book's organizational design. How would you describe it? How many involve more than one type of design?

3. **Activity and Discussion.** Put an X by each of the following statements with which you agree. Discuss your responses with your group.

___ The five-paragraph essay should never be taught.

___ To teach organization effectively, we must have students write in more genres.

___ The most important parts of any writing are the lead and conclusion.

___ Organization should be subtle, not obvious.

___ Most good writing is a blend of several organizational designs.

___ If you can follow a piece, it's well-organized, regardless of whether you can identify the design.

___ The best design or structure is determined by the writer's message and purpose.

4. **Activity and Discussion.** View any short video and talk about how organization works in this medium. What are the video equivalents of such organizational features as lead, conclusion, transition, or pacing?

FIGURE 4.10 (see Figure 4.6, page 120)

Answers to Sneed Collard Scramble Game Activity

Paragraph 1:

- For most of history, the geography and animal life of the deep-sea floor have remained a total mystery.
- As recently as the mid-nineteenth century, many people believed that the ocean was bottomless or that no life existed in the deep.
- Others felt sure that the deep sea was filled with terrifying sea serpents or animals that had disappeared from shallower waters millions of years before.

Paragraph 2:

- In the 1870s, though, scientists began a serious search for deep-sea animals by lowering nets and other collection devices far below the surface.
- During World War I, they began mapping the ocean bottom with a new invention called **sonar**.
- The sonar made loud noises that bounced off the sea bottom.
- The echoes from these noises gave people a detailed outline of what the deep-sea floor looked like.

Note: The line—

> Photosynthesis, the production of food using light energy from the sun, cannot take place on the deep-sea floor—

is not part of the original text! If you deleted it, that was a good instinct. Organization is partly about ensuring strong connections among ideas, and discarding what does not fit.

FIGURE 4.11 *(see page 124)*

Answers to Transitions Activity (underlining added)

The bucking horse bursts out of its holding pen, hooves flying, and catapults into the air. The rider's boots fling skyward while his torso slams back like a feedsack onto the horse's rump. <u>Remarkably</u>, the young rider hangs on, grunting with determination—or desperation—as the horse lands with a stiff-legged jolt.

   <u>But</u> the horse is just getting started. <u>Having failed to dislodge the annoying pest on its back</u>, the bronc twists to the left and kicks its back legs almost vertically. <u>Then</u>, <u>without pause</u>, it launches like a NASA booster rocket, arching gracefully into the air before its front legs stab back into the earth. <u>Still</u>, the rider sticks with the explosive twelve-hundred-pound beast beneath him. <u>Even better</u>, the cowboy thinks, the buzzer will sound at any moment, giving him a good riding score.

(From *The World Famous Miles City Bucking Horse Sale* by Sneed B. Collard III. 2010. Missoula, MT: Bucking Horse Books, page 5. Reprinted by permission: www.buckinghorsebooks.com)

Coming Up

In Chapter 5, we'll consider voice—the trait many consider the most elusive to define and most difficult to teach.

> I write because I am a visual learner. Seeing something in text makes me learn it. I also write because I like to read. I can go back to something I wrote months or even years ago and have a great time reading what I wrote myself!
>
> —Sammy Geiger, student writer

> I wish I could write essays in a way that would let me create my own structure, a structure that would fit my purpose and aid the reader. Not so much writing like I talk, but writing the way I think. The idea sounds a lot more appealing than a five-paragraph structure. Those are easy and thoughtless, and putting any creativity into them is too difficult. If the writer is bored, won't the reader be? Who cares where the thesis is placed? Who decided one quotation per paragraph is the right number? If a quotation fits, it fits. Why fight it? Doesn't that make it worse? Perhaps I care more about the message than the form.
>
> —Meghan Eremeyeff, student writer

Making the Heart Beat with VOICE

Writing with voice is writing into which someone has breathed. . . . Writing with real voice has the power to make you pay attention and understand. The words go deep.

PETER ELBOW
Writing with Power, 1998, 299

Voice is everything that we are, all that we have observed, the emotional chords that are uniquely ours—all our flaws and all of our strengths, expressed in the words that best reflect us. Voice is like a snowflake—complicated, beautiful, and individual.

MARY PIPHER
Writing to Change the World, 2006, 42

In 1985, a group of us—teachers, writers, lovers of literature—shared the enviable task of assessing the writing of Oregon's eighth graders. We loved our work. Our writing assessment was *nothing* like the large-scale assessment of today. We pored over every sentence, and paused often to read aloud from students' work, appreciating the fluency, detail, wording, and of course, the voice. One moment stands out for me. Early one morning, my friend and colleague Darle Fearl, a veteran teacher, broke the silence, saying, "You *have* to hear this." We put down our pencils and listened for the first time to the opening words from an eighth grade paper that would become legendary:

> I don't get along with people too good, and when I am alone, I like to walk to Forests and places where only me and the animals are. My best friend is God, but when I don't believe He's around sometimes, my dog stands in. (*Oregon Statewide Assessment Final Report*, 1985, 24)

No one moved. We sat spellbound as Darle continued the story of a boy and his dog ("My dog's name is Fox 'cause he looks like an Arctic Fox"), who "patrolled" the pond in back of their house, catching frogs, sailing their raft, keeping watch from a bridge shaded by willows, and building a friendship like no other. To this day, when I think of voice, I think of Fox—and the story that let an eighth grade student hold 40 teachers in the palm of his hand. Voice is many things—passion, flavor, personality, individuality, engagement with the topic, enthusiasm, and audience sensitivity. But as much as anything, voice is power. It calls to us from the page, and says, "Listen. Listen to me. I have something to say."

VOICE: The Heartbeat

A Definition

Voice is the imprint of the writer on the page. It is the pulse of the writing, our sense of a person behind the words—the feeling that a living, breathing soul is there, speaking to us. Voice connects writer to reader. It does far more than dress up the message. It is the human touch that makes readers tune in and believe what is said. Voice comes in many guises and shifts with writer, audience, and purpose. Just as we use different speaking voices when talking with a soulmate or cheering a favorite football team, so our writing voices can (and must) shift to suit the occasion. But always we are there in our writing, each of us, defined by the voice that is uniquely ours.

Share my definition—or define voice in your own words. You may also wish to ask your writers what they think of when they hear the word *voice*—and brainstorm a list of responses, like those in Figure 5.1.

Next, share the Student Writing Guide for Voice, Figure 5.2. Give students time to look over the writing guide, and to compare the language of the guide to some of the connections they have made with voice. The teacher version, for your use in assessing writing, appears in Figure 5.3 on page 130. As you assess and discuss writing and look for voice in the literature you share, you may find your definition expanding—and you may wish to revise the writing guides accordingly.

Author's Note

As before, continue to consider the traits you have already discussed—ideas and organization—as you assess writing for voice. In addition, think about how other traits affect voice. For example, although detail contributes to ideas, does it also contribute to the voice of a piece? We'll explore other connections in conjunction with the upcoming traits of word choice and sentence fluency.

FIGURE 5.1

What Is VOICE?

- The heartbeat of the writer
- Fingerprints on the page
- Everything the writer truly thinks and feels
- Imagination
- Vision
- Connection with the reader
- The writer's love for the topic coming through the words
- The something that keeps you reading

- The pulse
- Daring, courage
- Just letting go
- The writer totally being him- or herself
- Individuality
- Honesty
- Insight
- A fierce drive to write
- Power

- The writer's own way of saying things
- The writer's wish to be heard
- A need to connect
- Spirit
- The joy of writing
- Personality
- The self on the page
- An extension of the writer
- Humanity

FIGURE 5.2

Student Writing Guide for
VOICE

6
- ❑ This writing is as individual as my fingerprints.
- ❑ Trust me—you will want to share this aloud.
- ❑ This is *me*: what I think, how I feel.
- ❑ Hear the excitement in my voice? I want you to love this topic!!
- ❑ When you start reading this, you won't want to stop.

5
- ❑ This is original and distinctive. It's definitely *me*.
- ❑ I think you'll want to read this aloud.
- ❑ My personal thoughts and feelings come through.
- ❑ My voice is lively and enthusiastic.
- ❑ You can tell I am thinking about the reader.

4
- ❑ It's different from MOST things you'll read.
- ❑ You might share a line or two aloud.
- ❑ I think my own voice comes through.
- ❑ My writing is sincere. I mean what I say.
- ❑ I want people to read this.

3
- ❑ My voice comes and goes. You hear it in spots.
- ❑ This isn't ready to share—but it's getting there!
- ❑ I need more voice—or a *different* voice.
- ❑ I was quiet in this paper—I held back.
- ❑ I didn't honestly think about my readers that much.

2
- ❑ This doesn't really sound like me.
- ❑ It has a hint of voice—but it's not ready to share.
- ❑ The writing doesn't show anything about me.
- ❑ I sound bored—or maybe like an encyclopedia.
- ❑ I wasn't ready to think about readers yet.

1
- ❑ I'm not "at home" in this paper. I can't hear one whisper of my real voice.
- ❑ I definitely would NOT share this aloud.
- ❑ This is an "anybody" voice. It's not me.
- ❑ I just could not get excited about this topic.
- ❑ I need help choosing a topic or revising for voice.

FIGURE 5.3

Teacher Writing Guide for VOICE

6
- ❏ As individual as fingerprints
- ❏ Writer AND reader love sharing this aloud
- ❏ Mirrors writer's innermost thoughts and feelings
- ❏ Passionate, vibrant, electric, compelling
- ❏ Pulls reader right into the piece

5
- ❏ Original, distinctive
- ❏ A good read-aloud candidate
- ❏ Reveals writer's thoughts, feelings
- ❏ Spontaneous, lively, enthusiastic
- ❏ Shows sensitivity to readers

4
- ❏ Stands out from many others
- ❏ Share-aloud moments
- ❏ Writer is present in the piece
- ❏ Earnest, sincere
- ❏ Shows awareness of readers

3
- ❏ Sporadic—voice comes and goes
- ❏ Not quite ready to share—but getting there
- ❏ Needs *more* voice—or a *different* voice
- ❏ Restrained, quiet, cautious
- ❏ Reader awareness? Sometimes, perhaps . . .

2
- ❏ Writer not really "at home" in this writing
- ❏ Hint of voice—or we could be reading in
- ❏ Reader cannot tell who writer is
- ❏ Distant, disengaged—or wrong for the purpose
- ❏ Not yet "writing to be read"

1
- ❏ No sense of person behind the words
- ❏ Writer is not ready to share this piece
- ❏ Writer's own thoughts/feelings do not come through
- ❏ Something (topic choice?) is stifling the voice
- ❏ Writer needs help with topic—or voice

© 2012. Vicki Spandel. Designed for use in classroom assessment.

The "trait shortie" for voice summarizes key features to look for—or teach. (See Figure 5.4.) Remember to leave space at the bottom to add additional features you or your students think of as you study voice.

Warming Up with Literature

We don't all fall in love with the same person (thank goodness) and we don't all respond to the same written passages—so I cannot list the things that should move you. *You* must do that. But here are things that to my mind and heart say, "This has voice."

- Words I want to read—or hear—again and again
- A passage I might quote
- Something I want to share aloud with a friend
- Writing that makes me pay attention, tune in, want more
- A piece that triggers an undeniable emotional response
- Words I simply cannot get out of my head
- Writing that causes me to admire the writer's honesty or courage

Just a Taste . . .

Pick samples like these to read aloud in opening or closing workshop. And encourage your writers to look for samples of their own.

Sample 1

J. D. Salinger plunges right into an intimate conversation, creating an immediate and vivid impression (*The Catcher in the Rye*, 1951, 1):

> If you really want to hear about it, the first thing you'll probably want to know is where I was born, and what my lousy childhood was like, and how my parents were occupied and all before they had me, and all that David Copperfield kind of crap, but I don't feel like going into it if you want to know the truth.

Sample 2

In her riveting memoir *My Thirteenth Winter* (2003, 13), writer Samantha Abeel talks of her struggle with a learning disorder called *dyscalculia*, affecting her ability to learn anything involving sequence—including math, grammar, spelling, or even telling time. Here, as she rushes through a math test, she realizes that unlike the students around her, she has no way to tell how much time remains:

> My eyes shift from my paper up to the big, black-rimmed, circular face of the clock that looms over the classroom from its perch above the door. It tells me nothing. I can name the numbers I see, and I know the hands that stretch out from its center are supposed to give me the answer I am looking for, but for me the direction that they point to doesn't mean anything. Panic and helplessness surge through me. I know I am running out of time, but I am unable to tell when the end will come and how much time I have left until it does. I feel completely disoriented, like I am falling through space without any beginning or end.

FIGURE 5.4

Trait "Shortie" for VOICE

Use this summary as a poster—and have students add to it!

Keys to . . . VOICE
The Writer's "Presence" on the Page

 The writing is individual and distinctive.

 You might recognize this writer's voice in another piece.

You enjoy sharing the writing aloud.

 The writer seems passionate about the topic.

 This writing "speaks" to readers—they feel part of the conversation.

 The writer knows the topic well enough to write with confidence.

 Readers trust this writer to tell what is true and important.

Readers feel they "know" the person behind the words.

Readers don't want the piece to end.

© 2012. Vicki Spandel.

Using a Whole Book

Some books are too long to be practical for classroom discussion. But you might choose several chapters, passages, or sections of a longer text that you feel effectively represent a particular writer's voice. Choose diverse samples so your writers hear both fiction and nonfiction (perhaps poetry or drama, as well), along with voices from multiple cultures.

Author's Note

When choosing books (or other materials) to share for voice, pick what moves you, what you love—or are just struck by. Writing that makes you pause, reflect, feel something. You should be saying to yourself, "I'm glad I read this. I wouldn't have missed it for anything."

Individual voices can be quiet or noisy, wry or schmaltzy, self-disclosing or guarded, kind or angry. Voice comes from genetics, gender, relationships, place; from ethnic background and educational experience. Voice resonates with our sorrows and fears, but also our joys, and it sings out all of who we are.

—Mary Pipher
Writing to Change the World, 2006, 42

Sample 1

Knucklehead by Jon Scieszka. 2008.
Ages: Upper elementary and older.
Genre: Memoir

Summary

Fans of Jon Scieszka's books—*The True Story of the 3 Little Pigs, The Stinky Cheese Man*, and others—will love hearing tales of the author's wildly rambunctious childhood, growing up as one of six brothers. Not even their father—an elementary school principal—could keep the names straight, and so he simply referred to the children (affectionately) as the "knuckleheads," as in, "All you knuckleheads just get in the car" (p. 30). Students will thoroughly enjoy the humor-filled stories of "growing up Scieszka."

Suggestions for Discussion and Writing

1. How many of your students have read other books by author Jon Scieszka? Given what they know—and the book's title—what sort of book would they expect this to be?

2. Talk about memoir as a genre. What should such a book include? Is it similar to an autobiography? How do these genres differ?

3. Jon Scieszka grew up with five brothers—and that simple fact dictated much of what his early life was like. What is it like to grow up in a large family? Have you or your writers had this experience? What are some details of daily life that stand out?

4. Share selected chapters aloud. You do not *necessarily* need to read the whole book. You might choose three (or more) favorite chapters and share one a day. If you have a document projector, be sure to share the family photos and other illustrations.

5. Talk about the voice in this book. How would your writers describe it? What does the voice teach us about Jon Scieszka the person?

6. The author couldn't include everything in a book of just over 100 pages; he had to be selective. Have writers imagine they are going to write autobiographies or memoirs of their own. What events—or family photos—might they include?

7. Have writers create short memoirs (a half page or more). They may wish to illustrate the writing with photos or sketches.

Sample 2

Sing a Song of Tunafish: A Memoir of My Fifth-Grade Year by Esmé Raji Codell. 2004.
Ages: Elementary through middle school
Genre: Memoir

Summary

This book—which comes to life when read aloud—is Codell's collection of memories of her fifth grade year in Chicago. The real-life stories—egging an illegally parked car, stealing a matzoh from under the rabbi's chair in order to win a prize—put most fictional narratives to shame. Codell writes with unabashed honesty and a virtually matchless eye for detail (see her description of Woolworth's, pages 17–19).

CHAPTER 5 *Making the Heart Beat with VOICE*

Suggestions for Discussion and Writing

1. How many of your students have read books by Esmé Raji Codell (*Vive la Paris, Sahara Special, Diary of a Fairy Godmother*)? If they are familiar with this author, talk about her voice. Do they find it distinctive?

2. You might begin by sharing the Introduction, pages 3–4. There, Codell compares her brain to an attic, talking about blowing away the dust to go *all the way back* to 1979. Do your writers like this "attic" comparison? How far back can they go in their own attic of memories?

3. Every chapter in this book opens with the line "Let me tell you something about _____ ." Often, we tell writers to avoid repetition—but sometimes repetition can be powerful. Is that the case here?

4. This book is set in Chicago. How many of your students have lived or visited there? Have you? Talk about what you remember—or picture. If you have photos of Chicago, you might share them, using your document projector. To get inside Codell's memories of the city, share Chapter 2, "My Neighborhood," pages 15–34. What details from this chapter stick in your writers' minds as they listen? How does detail enrich voice?

5. Take the next step and create some "Let me tell you about _____" pieces of your own. Students might write about school, family traditions, transportation, communication, entertainment, pets, your local neighborhood—anything they know well from living it. Have them picture a reader, say, 30 to 40 years from now, reading this memoir. What would they want that reader to know about life in their town, school, neighborhood, family?

Author's Note

Sing a Song of Tunafish has been difficult to find in the paperback edition in recent years (and prohibitively expensive, as well). Ironically, the hardcover edition is not only *far* less expensive, but also easy to obtain from online vendors. It is also a staple in many school and public libraries. Don't give up. It's well worth the search.

Sample 3

How Fast Is It? by Ben Hillman. 2008.
Ages: Middle school and up (younger if shared aloud)
Genre: Nonfiction short essay picture book

Summary

This delightful collection of short essays centers on one theme: speed. It's an outstanding example of thematic organization, spanning a wide range of subtopics, from the ostrich, cheetah, sailfish, sloth, and peregrine falcon to the train, computer, bicycle, whip, sneeze, and Voyager. Twenty-two essays in all. Author Ben Hillman shows how to put zip and pizzazz into informational writing—by digging for accurate, fascinating details and by addressing the reader in a conversational tone that is both engaging and enlightening: "In the summer you mow the grass and, if you don't like mowing, you might think it's annoying that the grass grows so fast . . . Well, consider yourself lucky, because if your lawn was covered in bamboo instead of regular grass, you might have to mow it *once an hour*!" (15)

Suggestions for Discussion or Writing

1. As you share the title, ask how many writers know what is pictured on the cover (It's a car—a Thrust SSC, to be exact—see page 13).

2. Talk about the thematic organization of the book. Is this a common organizational structure? What else have your students read that is organized around a central theme (such as speed)?

3. Share the table of contents. That way, your students can choose several essays they would like to hear aloud. They are sufficiently short that you can share several within a class period.

4. Talk about how the voice of this book differs from, say, the voice of an encyclopedia entry. To emphasize the difference, look up any of the subtopics in an encyclopedia and read all or part of the entry aloud. You may wish to have two students read, one doing the encyclopedia and one Hillman's complementary piece. How do they compare? Which one says to readers, "Keep reading"? Why are these voices so different? (Think about the writer's purpose.)

5. How much research is required to support this writing? What drives an author like Hillman to do this much research? Is that intensity and drive part of what creates voice?

6. Part of Hillman's voice comes from his strategy of addressing the reader directly. Have your writers try this with a short informational piece on any topic. Writers should think first about what readers might most like to know, gathering at least 3 or 4 particularly intriguing details. Then, have them write the piece in the form of an informational letter. Read the results aloud.

OTHER BOOKS WITH STRIKING (READ-ALOUD) VOICE

Afghan Dreams: Young Voices of Afghanistan **by Tony O'Brien and Mike Sullivan. Photographs by Mike Sullivan. 2008. New York: Bloomsbury Children's Books. Nonfiction multi-voiced biography.**

The faces of Afghanistan's young people—beautiful, hopeful, defiant, determined, resigned—grace the pages of this extraordinary book. Hear each one, in his or her own voice, talk of life as a street worker, student, pickpocket, family member—or future professional. Many have lost family members and friends; none have lost hope. Najamudin, 13, says, "I hope to be a teacher, to bring the light to other children. I want to be a teacher of teachers." Middle school and up.

Author: A True Story **by Helen Lester. 1997. New York: Houghton Mifflin Harcourt. Autobiographical picture book.**

Lester's humble and hilarious account of how she went from mirror writer to successful published author—with numerous stumbling blocks in between. All ages.

China Boy **by Gus Lee. 1991. New York: Penguin. Novel.**

The unforgettable story of Kai Ting, American-born son of an aristocratic Mandarin family, who grows up in San Francisco's ghetto, battling street gangs, a cold-hearted stepmother, and his own fears. Young adult and adult.

Claudette Colvin: Twice Toward Justice **by Phillip Hoose. 2009. New York: Farrar Straus Giroux. Biography, nonfiction historical narrative, and interview.**

A fascinating and detailed look at the life and impact of Claudette Colvin, the little-known Civil Rights figure who, at age 15 (nine months before Rosa Parks would make her stand) refused to yield her seat on an Alabama bus—and began a lifelong fight for justice. Colvin's frank and courageous words, together with striking black and white photos, lend powerful voice to a well-researched account. Middle and high school.

Countdown **by Deborah Wiles. 2010. New York: Scholastic. Documentary novel.**

Franny Chapman's life is in upheaval—and so is the world in which she lives. While Russia is sending nuclear missiles to Cuba, Franny tries to cope with a "perfect" younger brother, an impossibly beautiful older sister, strict parents, and the very interesting boy across the street. Photos, song lyrics, poetry, and news reports from the 1960s make the setting vivid and real. Upper elementary and middle school.

Children who had been denied school for so many years had a burning desire for education and peace. Mukhtar, our translator, explained that education is truly their dream, although for many it is out of their reach.

—Tony O'Brien and Mike Sullivan
Authors of *Afghan Dreams*
Santa Fe, 2008

Creepy Creatures **by Sneed B. Collard. 1992. Watertown, MA: Charlesbridge. Nonfiction picture book.**

The world is filled with creatures that can scare us—tarantulas, sharks, hyenas, bats, pythons, and piranhas, just to name a few. But each, as it turns out, serves a purpose—and some might not be as frightening as we first thought. Primary and early elementary.

The Good, Good Pig **by Sy Montgomery. 2006. New York: Random House. Nonfiction biography.**

Naturalist Sy Montgomery brings a runt pig, Christopher Hogwood, home in a shoebox, and he transforms the lives of everyone who knows him. Middle school through high school (All ages for selected read-aloud passages).

Guys Read Funny Business **edited by Jon Scieszka. 2010. New York: Walden Pond Press. Anthology of original stories.**

Humorous, often poignant, coming of age tales by writers such as Eoin Colfer, Jon Scieszka, Jack Gantos, David Yoo, and others. Middle school.

Interrupting Chicken **by David Ezra Stein. 2010. Somerville, MA: Candlewick Press. Children's picture book.**

Hilarious account of a father's failed attempts to put the little red chicken to bed with a story. She can't help interrupting—she has to save her favorite characters from impending doom. Primary and early elementary (but adults will laugh, too).

Oh, Rats! **by Albert Marrin. 2006. New York: Dutton Children's Books. Nonfiction picture book with woodcut illustrations.**

In a voice that is consistently lively and engaging, Marrin tells us all we need to know about rats: where they came from, how they live, what they eat, how they interact with humans—even how they've been tried for crimes and how they help humans detect land mines. All ages.

Matilda **by Roald Dahl. 1988. Illustrated by Quentin Blake. New York: Puffin Books. Imaginative fiction.**

The master of fictional voice was never better than in this tale of outrageous bullying and sweet comeuppance. Combine with Dahl's nonfiction autobiography *Boy* (1984, Puffin)—and discuss Dahl's real-life experiences that likely gave rise to incidents and characters in *Matilda*. Elementary.

Mockingbird **by Kathryn Erskine. 2010. New York: Philomel Books. First-person fictional narrative.**

From the perspective of 10-year-old Caitlin, who has Asperger's syndrome, life is filled with continual challenges, requiring her to Look At the Person—and Get It. All connects to the Day Our Life Fell Apart, when she and her dad lost Caitlin's brother Devon. Now, she seeks something called Closure. Whatever that means. Upper elementary and middle school.

No More Dead Dogs **by Gordon Korman. 2000. New York: Hyperion. Young adult novel.**

One of the all-time great read-aloud books. The tale of Wallace Wallace, who cannot tell a lie, and the transformation of a sappy dog story into a rollicking rock and roll musical—the ultimate tribute to the power of revision. Upper elementary through middle school.

Pictures of Hollis Woods **by Patricia Reilly Giff. 2002. New York: Random House. Novel.**

Hollis Woods drifts from one foster home to another—and then winds up with Josie, an elderly woman who is losing her memory. Social Services will have a thing or two to say if they find out. Middle school.

Scaredy Squirrel by Melanie Watt. 2008. Tonawanda, NY: Kids Can Press. **Picture book.**

Scaredy Squirrel leads a dull but terribly organized life, never venturing into The Unknown. Then one day . . . things go differently, and he must re-organize. Primary and elementary.

Something Permanent. **Photographs by Walker Evans. Poetry by Cynthia Rylant. 1994. New York: Harcourt Brace and Company. Poetry and photography representing the Great Depression.**

Behind every photo is a story, a life. This book makes the point with the award-winning photos of Walker Evans—and striking contemporary interpretations by poet Cynthia Rylant. Middle school and up.

Sugar Changed the World: A Story of Magic, Spice, Slavery, Freedom, and Science **by Marc Aronson and Marina Budhos. 2010. Boston: Houghton Mifflin Harcourt. Nonfictional history.**

An eye-opening look at the history of sugar and its impact upon world economies. We discover that the Atlantic slave trade was not driven mainly by cotton or tobacco, but by humans' insatiable desire for sugar. This craving would cost the lives of countless Africans, not only in North America, but (to a far greater degree) in Central and South America and the islands of the Caribbean. Middle school and up.

Those Darn Squirrels! **by Adam Rubin. Illustrated by Daniel Salmieri. 2008. New York: Houghton Mifflin Harcourt. Fictional picture book.**

Hilarious account of Old Man Fookwire, bird lover, and his attempt to outwit the hungry, mischievous, scheming squirrels. Primary and elementary.

War Horse **by Michael Morpurgo. 2010. New York: Scholastic. Historic fiction.**

A moving story of World War I told through the voice of a horse, Joey, who is conscripted for battle duty on the Western Front—and must leave his owner Albert, who is too young to be a soldier. Basis for the Tony Award-winning play and Oscar-nominated film of the same name. Upper elementary through middle school.

The Wednesday Wars **by Gary D. Schmidt. 2007. New York: Houghton Mifflin Harcourt. Young adult novel.**

The hilarious story of seventh grader Holling Hoodhood, whose teacher Mrs. Baker insists that he read Shakespeare. Unbelievably, he finds countless parallels with the zany mishaps and adventures of his own life. Middle school and up.

Assessing Writing Samples for VOICE

It is particularly important when scoring papers for voice to read each piece aloud, asking whether and when the piece "speaks" to you. Also ask, *Where does the voice come from? Is it from honesty, an attitude, the words, the details—or something else?* Identifying the source of the voice is one good way to teach ourselves what voice is about, and learn how to achieve it in our own writing.

Paper 1

Why You Need a Job (Argument, Grade 9)

Young adults in our country need to learn more responsibility, and having a job while you are going to school is one way to get there.

Many times, young kids take their lives and theyre parents for granit. Parents have been around to care for them as long as they can remember. But it doesnt last forever. Sooner or later you will be out on your own without one clue of your life or responsibility. A job teaches kids to care for themselves without help from their parents. To buy things like clothes and insurance. Jobs are not just about money though. A job shows you how to get a long with people out side your family. A job is good for your future. It introduces you to new skills and new people. This paper gives solid reasons for getting a job while you are in school. Do it. You will not be sorry.

Author's Note

Personal comments are always important—but never more than when teaching or encouraging voice. So as you go through these papers, I invite you, especially if you are working with a group, to think of the comments you would make *to each writer.* You might begin by thinking of how the paper affects you—and which moments seem to have the strongest voice.

Suggested Score for VOICE: 3

Lessons Learned from "Why You Need a Job"

- Generalities weaken voice.
- Persuasive writing requires persuasive examples.
- Faulty conventions can weaken an argument—fairly or not.

Comments

Good persuasive writing should lead readers toward an insider's understanding of what's at stake. But instead of crafting an argument, this writer simply states an opinion, and generalities squeeze the life right out of it: A job gives you experience, teaches you new skills, and is good for your future. In place of insight and personal experience, we get platitudes. Readers want more. The beginning is fairly forceful, and if the writer had sustained this level of voice, the paper could have become truly persuasive. Notice that voice emerges in spurts—*"you will be out on your own without one clue of your life"*—but quickly retreats. It picks up the tempo in the conclusion: *"Do it."* But by then it is too late to get real momentum going. Faulty conventions make the writer appear (whether it's true or not) uninvolved.

Suggested Scores for Other Traits

Ideas: **3**
Organization: **2**
Word choice: **4**
Sentence fluency: **4**
Conventions & presentation: **3**

The Write Connection

Why You Need a Job

Tom Romano (author of *Crafting Authentic Voice,* 2004, p. 49) tells us that voice is mostly about telling the truth—"Not THE truth," he emphasizes, but "your truth." So do that. Think about how YOU feel about the importance of getting a job. What does having a job really teach a person? It isn't the perfect experience, is it? What is it *really* like to work while you are going to school? Now see if you can make "Why You Need a Job" a little edgier by saying very honestly how you really feel. Hold nothing back. When you read your revision aloud, do you hear the difference?

Paper 2
Zeena and the Marshmellows (Narrative/Argument, Grade 5)

Zeena, I know just how you feel. I love chocolate covered marshmellows too! But let me tell you what happened to me.

My mom came home from the store one day and let me have a chocolate covered marshmellow. It was love at first bite. So lite, fluffy, chewy and slipped down my throat like a small piece of heaven. Just thinking about it makes me want to have another one until I recall what happened when I finished my last bag of those squishy delights.

My mom told me I can help myself to a few and before I knew it the whole bag was gone. My mom called me to dinner, and you know, the last thing I wanted or even cared about was dinner, but you know how mothers are, I had to sit down and take one bite of everything. And after that, I had diaria, diaria, diaria. But I was convinced it wasn't the marshmellows.

Last fall my mom bought me all of these cute clothes for my birthday, shorts, jeans, skirts, so when the weather got warm, and I went to put on my new clothes, they didn't fit to my amazement and not because I had grown too tall, just because I couldn't even zip them up. But it couldn't be the marshmellows, their too lite and fluffy; infact a whole bag of marshmellows doesn't weight as much as one orange.

One day, when I put the tight clothes out of my mind, I grabbed myself some chocolate covered marshmellows, when I was biting down on one, a sharp stabbing pain went up my tooth and the side of my head. And when ever I ate, my teeth hurt. So my mom took me to the dentist, and let me tell you it was not a pretty picture. I had seven expensive, painful cavities.

So Zeena, you can keep popping those marshmellows into your mouth, but before you do, remember not everything about chocolate covered marshmellows is sweet.

Suggested Score for VOICE: 6

Lessons Learned from "Zeena and the Marshmellows"

- Anecdotes enhance voice and clarity—and make persuasion stronger.
- Willingness to laugh at yourself—the tight clothes, the diarrhea—nearly always produces voice.
- Most good writing is a blend of genres; in this case, narrative is used for a persuasive purpose—and purpose ultimately defines genre.

Comments

"Zeena and the Marshmellows" is a knockout in voice. This young writer speaks right to her audience, and the main thing I always want to say is, "Thanks for helping me understand why diets don't work." It's that dieter's logic: "A whole bag of marshmellows doesn't weigh as much as one orange." Strong imagery and sensory detail enhance the voice—*"slipped down my throat like a small piece of heaven . . . I had to sit down and take one bite . . . couldn't even zip them up . . . a sharp, stabbing pain went up my tooth."*

The Write Connection

Zeena and the Marshmellows

"Zeena and the Marshmellows" is a favorite with readers everywhere—especially when it's read aloud. There are a number of little editorial problems—which usually go overlooked by readers enjoying the humor. See how many you can find. Edit "Zeena" so it's ready to go to press.

Readers love the way this writer pokes fun at herself, along with the dieting world. Although basically persuasive, this paper (contrast with Paper 1) uses three humorous anecdotes to make the point. It's a good technique. Many of us can identify with the bingeing, the tight clothes—even the trip to the dentist. In addition, the writer chose to write her essay as a letter. Letters, by nature, encourage voice.

Suggested Scores for Other Traits

Ideas: **6**

Organization: **5**

Word choice: **4**

Sentence fluency: **5**

Conventions & presentation: **4**

Paper 3

A Sunflower Seed (Expository/Reflective, Grade 5)

Now most people I know would think something like a football is most important but this sunflower seed ment a lot to me. It helped me understand the struggles and needs to stay alive in this world. How the seed needed water to live, and that water to me represented the thirst to stay alive. How it needed the sun to grow, and that sun is like our need to be with others.

I thought the sunflower seed died because it had been more than week since I had planted it. The next morning, a clot of dirt was being held midair by the sunflower, so I choped up the dirt to make it softer so the sunflower could grow easyer. In life you have to eas up on other people so they can relax in growing up and don't have to push or force their way up. In life there will be people that will hold you back from what you want (just like the dirt) and you have to break free from them if you want to live your own life.

Just like the seed you must prosper or life will pass you by.

Suggested Score for VOICE: 6

Lessons Learned from "A Sunflower Seed"

- Go for the unique topic—the sunflower seed, not the football.
- Strong voice doesn't have to be emotional (or humorous), just heartfelt.

Comments

The philosophical message and tone of this piece are very strong. The sunflower seed metaphor works well. It's visual but kinesthetic, too; we can actually *feel* ourselves pushing up through the earth. Few papers are so well centered around one strong main theme: Life is a struggle, but with luck, perseverance, and the help of sensitive friends, you can make it. Organization (along with voice) is a real strength here. Here's a writer speaking from reflective experience. The paper forces us to think and makes us want to "[ease] up on other people" and encourage them to do the same for us. Words are simple but carry weight. The writer uses fragments, but they work. Conventions need some attention.

 The Write Connection

A Sunflower Seed

This writer is responding to a prompt asking him to consider an important object in his life. He knows many students will write about footballs, teddy bears, or watches. Hence the reference (*. . . most people I know would think something like a football is most important . . .*) in the lead. If a reader did not know about the prompt, could the lead be confusing? Revise it so a reader coming to this paper with no knowledge of the writing prompt would still feel drawn in.

Suggested Scores for Other Traits

Ideas: **6**

Organization: **6**

Word choice: **5**

Sentence fluency: **5**

Conventions & presentation: **4**

Paper 4

Fishing (Expository, Grade 11)

"I'm jumping out," I yelled frantically to my father. It was in response to the flopping northern Pike that was near my feet in our boat. I was six and on my first trip to Canada to fish. It was a totally different fishing experience than I was accustomed to in Pennsylvania. It was not like catching Bluegills in Leaser Lake. Surely I had a right to be scared. The Northern Pike is an extremely mean looking fish with sharp teeth which it uses to kill its prey. Being six, I thought I was on its list of prey. My father responded to my plea by saying, "Go ahead and jump, but there are a hundred more in that water."

Most of my knowledge and love of fishing came from that same man who told me to "Go ahead and jump." Since I can remember, I have always fished. My father probably taught me to fish before I could walk. At first he taught me the basics: tying a swivel to a line, threading the line through the pole, removing hooks from any part of the body that they may enter, how to get a lure out of a tree, why to check the inside of hip boots that have been sitting in the garage all year before putting them on, if the sign says "No Fishing—Violators will be prosecuted," it usually means it, and probably most important, if you have to go to the bathroom while on the boat what to do. Occasionally, he also revealed a hot tip while fishing, such as, "See this lure, son? This one is going to catch the big one. It's only legal in two states and this isn't one of them."

The key to fishing, I was taught, is patience. Obviously, my father has a little of that if he could teach me to fish. There were numerous occasions when I crossed my line with his and caused a "rat's nest," or the several times that I used a lure and forgot to close the tackle box, and when he picked it up, all the lures fell out. One time he really showed his patience when I reached back in the boat to cast, but accidentally hooked onto his hat and threw it into the water. My brother and I laughed hysterically while I reeled it in through the water. Eventually, my father joined in.

Since I was young, there was one aspect of fishing my father heavily emphasized. Fishing is not about the amount of fish you catch, but the amount of fun you have. There were times when we wouldn't catch one fish but would still have a great time. I learned fishing is a time to just be with nature and your thoughts, a time to relax and share good times with friends. Anyone who only cares about catching fish all the time is missing the true meaning. Fishing is like an education. It is a lifelong experience. After high school, you could go to college and get a Bachelor's degree. In fishing, if you graduate from regular fishing, you could go on to ice fishing or maybe deep sea fishing. Then, if you move on to get your Master's degree, maybe you could start fly fishing.

One day, I will be teaching my kids to fish and will probably hear them complain about not catching any fish. I will think for a minute what Pop would say: "The worst day of fishing is better than the best day of work."

Suggested Score for VOICE: 6

Lessons Learned from "Fishing"

- Beginning right in the middle of things creates energy.
- Tell the truth because in the end we want Dad to be human—not perfect.

Comments

There is so much to love about this paper, from Dad giving the wonderful tip about the illegal lure to the son's recognition of a parent's patience when he spills the contents of the tackle box or uses Dad's hat for casting practice. The voice seems to echo the reverence this writer feels for his father and for the magic of fishing. The beginning and ending are trophy winners. Notice the small details that make a difference in almost every line. Nothing is really wrong with word choice; it just does not shine quite so much as other traits (but then, that's asking a lot). Your score for that trait may be higher. Fly fishing as a graduate degree? That's ingenious.

Suggested Scores for Other Traits

Ideas: **6**

Organization: **6**

Word choice: **5**

Sentence fluency: **6**

Conventions & presentation: **6**

The Write Connection

Fishing

Overall the voice in this piece is strong, yes. But where *specifically* does it emerge? In the righthand margin, put a letter "V" (for voice) beside each moment where you really hear the voice come through. Put a "V" in the lefthand margin each time the voice falls a bit. Then compare with partners or in small groups. Did you mark the same spots? What creates each moment of voice? Where do you suppose the writer felt the voice was strongest?

Paper 5

You Whant to Be My Friend? (Personal Essay, Grade 3)

You whant to be my friend? Well a good friend for me would be a female tomboy. She would like nature, animals and stones. She would like burping and burping the ABCs. If she couldn't & didn't like it she couldn't be my friend. If you don't like Star Wars you are not my friend. I love Star Wars. Oh & viva pinyatas, legos, bionicals. The things I like. You problebly can guse one of my favorite video games. Lego Star wars! Its kind of easy to be my friend just a few minuts or secons & We are friends. But if you don't like drumming thers a big chance you aren't my friend. I am a rocker. I am also very disgusting. Even boys thik so. No matter what age. But be carful. Warning. No vegitarians. I am mostly a carnivore. And last of all exploring & climbin trees are OK. Remember if you do everything you are my best friend.

Suggested Score for VOICE: 6

Lessons Learned from "You Whant to Be My Friend?"

- Burping the ABCs makes a great example—chances are, no one else will use that one.
- Reading aloud can help you catch small problems with fluency.
- Writing the way we speak can be effective—but sometimes it gets us into trouble, too!

The Write Connection

You Whant to Be My Friend?

This piece—unlike many friendship papers—relies on specifics (burping the ABCs) rather than trite generalities ("always being there for me"). Use it as an inspiration to create some reflective friendship pieces of your own. Encourage students to make the pluses and minuses as specific as they can. Just what would this hypothetical friend need to do—or not do? Share results aloud and discuss how both detail and topic choice influence voice.

Comments

This piece is hilarious. I *do* want to be this writer's friend—and I do like *most* of the same things. Voice is the standout trait here. You have to admire the way this writer just lays the friend qualifications on the line. The ideas are entertaining because they're highly individual. They are shared a bit randomly, but would we really want the writer to list all the qualifications followed by all the roadblocks? In this case, random works because it's conversational (you might disagree). The lead and conclusion aren't bad either. Moments of word choice jump out: *I am also very disgusting . . . Warning. No vegetarians. I am mostly a carnivore.* Some fragments work, but some do not: *The things I like.* Conventions need work, but do not impair the message. I would read anything this writer wrote; that says a lot. And yes, this is a girl.

Suggested Scores for Other Traits

> *Ideas:* **6**
>
> *Organization:* **5**
>
> *Word choice:* **4**
>
> *Sentence fluency:* **4**
>
> *Conventions & presentation:* **3**

Paper 6

Unscripted Television: Enjoy It While You Can
(Persuasive, Middle School)

After several decades of sitcoms, news shows, detective and adventure shows, most Americans feel they can predict the outcome of just about anything on television after five minutes. You can't always predict who gets voted off "Survivor" or who the American Idol will be, though. Sometimes it's refreshing not to know the ending. Reality TV should really be called "unscripted" TV since this is the factor that makes it different and (for now, anyway) appealing. Will it have a lasting impact? That's doubtful. Does anything on television?

For now, the only thing we can say for sure is that unscripted television reflects our culture. Reality TV tends to show a lot of gossip and intrigue. We see people scheming to outdo or outwit one another for money. This isn't very attractive, but it's a little naïve to say reality TV is a bad influence when in fact, it only shows who we really are. Reality shows often feature hosts who push people into dangerous or humiliating situations (which frankly, most of them seem to enjoy—or else they enjoy whining about it). And sometimes people on the shows are very rude, too. Will this teach Americans to be rude? Get real. We're already rude. Have you driven on a freeway lately?

(continued on following page)

Unscripted TV is mostly about entertainment—not character building or enlightenment. People watching "Survivor" don't necessarily think they are like the person on the show—or that they should be like that person. Rather, they wonder what they would do in the same situation: Would I be that low? Would I betray my friend? Would I dare do that stunt? This is no different from watching "Jeopardy" and asking yourself the questions contestants try to answer. (By the way, people on "Jeopardy" are trying to bump each other off just like contestants on "Survivor"—they just use their knowledge instead of winning challenges or telling lies, but they're equally money hungry.)

Reality shows (unscripted shows) are entertaining because they let us ask ourselves what we would do in similar situations. When it comes to entertainment, however, Americans are very unpredictable. Nothing lasts forever, even "Seinfeld." So when it comes to reality TV, there might be one "survivor," and the rest will disappear. Being the last survivor does not necessarily make you the best, however. Look at the cockroach.

Suggested Scores for VOICE: 6

Lessons Learned from "Unscripted Television"

- It *is* possible to have more than one key point—but keep your main argument in the spotlight.
- A strong ending gives both ideas and voice a boost.
- Opinions that are well stated help make a convincing argument, but you need more: facts, quotations from those involved, results of research, specific examples.

Comments

The main point of this paper is that reality television is unlikely to have any lasting impact on American culture. As part of this discussion, however, the writer has other things to say as well: Reality television is actually unscripted television; it's appealing because we do not know what will happen next; it's a reflection of our culture; and it isn't bad for us because we're already rude. These are interesting points, but they do take attention away from the main argument—hence the slightly lower organization score. Virtually everyone likes the ending, and by the last paragraph, voice is in full swing. The main thing missing from this piece is strong evidence. The writer needs to dig deeper to show the reality behind reality programming: Are those contestants motivated only by money, or is there more to it? Are they as evil and scheming as portrayed on television, or is that just clever editing? Quotations or other research-backed support would strengthen the piece dramatically.

Suggested Scores for Other Traits

Ideas: **4/5**

Organization: **4/5**

Word choice: **5**

Sentence fluency: **6**

Conventions & presentation: **6**

✎ **The Write Connection**

Unscripted Television: Enjoy It While You Can

Don Graves once remarked that in any strong piece of writing, you would be able to put your finger right on the sentence that comes closest to expressing the writer's main idea. Try that. Can you do it with this piece? Then, take the next step and highlight each sentence that supports the writer's position. How many do you find? Does this writer stay focused—or wander from her main point? Does a strong sense of conviction influence voice?

The Perfect Tree (Descriptive/Narrative, Grade 7)

My favorite family tradition is hunting for the right holiday tree. Not trimming the tree (I usually try to get out of that if I can). No, for me, it's all about the hunt.

It begins with the ceremonial loading of the car. Dad gets the saw, the hatchet (which we never use), an old rug to kneel on while he cuts, and snacks to eat on the way (we never eat these, but it's good to be prepared). Then my sister and I pile into the back seat, my parents get in front, and off we go to the tree lot. It's a long way from our house. We could go closer, but it is part of the tradition to drive as far as possible. And in addition, Mom reminds us that this tree lot serves hot chocolate—which no one but me drinks. I never get any, though, because Dad always says, "Let's do that later," and once we have the tree, everyone is in the mood to leave. But—I'm getting ahead of myself.

As soon as we pull in, Dad spots it: the perfect tree. It isn't really perfect. It's just close to the parking lot. Mom gets this look on her face like she just ate a bad sardine. Dad groans in recognition of the fact that we will have to walk miles in search of our tree—but this drama is all part of the tradition.

We get out and begin hunting, going, of course, in all different directions. Soon we're miles from the car and miles from one another. Periodically, we shout to each other, "I found it! This is the one! Come and see it!" But of course, no one goes to see anyone else's tree because that means leaving their own, and once you leave a tree in a forest of trees that all look more or less alike, it's incredibly hard to find again. Finally, Mom finds a tree she loves. We reluctantly leave our choices and gravitate to hers. It really IS the perfect tree. The shape is gorgeous, the color is deep green. It's bushy on all sides—no bad side that has to "face the corner." It is also too big to fit on the roof of the car, and much too wide for our living room. Dad frowns and shakes his head. He gestures dramatically with his arms to emphasize the width and height. Mom shrugs and laughs. She lays a hand on his shoulder and gives him a quick kiss on the cheek. He squints as if bracing for an injection. In the end, he caves in, sighs, and plunks himself down on the old rug to begin sawing as we all look on. "Too late now," he says, as he makes a deep cut. Dad won't leave a tree half cut down. We're in it now and we know it.

We wrestle our tree out through the woods and the people up front help us rope it into a bundle and put it on the roof. They offer us hot chocolate, but Dad says, "Thanks—but we'd better be getting home." My sister is pouting because we didn't choose her tree. Mom says, "You can pick the tree next year," but we all know this is not true. My sister will get to choose the tree once she is old enough to have a house of her own.

It is hard to drive because the tree is tall and hangs over the back window, blocking Dad's view. He comments on this as many times as possible, shaking his head when Mom says it looked so much smaller in the woods. Later, it's hard to get it through the door because it's so wide. Getting it into the tree stand takes almost more strength than we have combined, but we manage. The trunk

(continued on following page)

barely fits. It leans, of course. We straighten it by propping cardboard here and there until Mom says, "That's it! It's straight!"

Finally, we stand back to admire it. It IS too wide for our tiny living room. Dad was right about that part. It overlaps the couch on one side and our big over-stuffed chair on the other. It almost brushes the ceiling. But somehow it looks just right there in the corner. It looks as if it grew right out of the floor. Even my sister loves it. Mom explains that Dad actually saw the tree first, but waited to show it to her. He nods. "Well," he says, "you have to admit, it's perfect."

Suggested Score for VOICE: 6

Lessons Learned from "The Perfect Tree"

- Small details add to voice.
- It's OK for the tree to be perfect—but we love it when the family isn't.
- Good writers tend to be good observers.
- Everyday life is filled with terrific writing topics.

Comments

"The Perfect Tree" is a delightful anecdotal look into one family's life. By the end of the piece, we *know* these people. The father protests every inch of the way, but in the end, Mom gets the tree she wants—and through some brilliant verbal sleight of hand, lets Dad take the credit. It's the little details that make this piece work: Dad packing up the tools, the brother quietly wishing he could have hot chocolate and knowing it won't happen, family members spreading out to search and then finding it hard to reconnect, the sister pouting when the family doesn't go with her choice. Like the writer of "Mouse Alert," this writer takes a small slice of life and makes us want more.

Suggested Scores for Other Traits

Ideas: **6**

Organization: **6**

Word choice: **6**

Sentence fluency: **6**

Conventions & presentation: **6**

> ### The Write Connection
>
> The Perfect Tree
>
> Highlight the details this writer shares to make the people in this family seem like real people. Then imagine this piece written by the writer of "The Redwoods." Have fun seeing who can come up with the best "Redwoods" version (Don't forget to revise the title!)—and use the results to spark further discussion on the kinds of details that contribute most to voice.

Lessons and Strategies for Teaching VOICE

Can we really teach voice? The answer depends on what we mean by *teach*. Some elements of voice—writing with detail, knowing your audience, choosing words that say precisely what you mean, reading aloud to see if your writing really does sound like you—*can* be taught through modeling and sharing of carefully selected literature. But much of voice comes from within. Things like honesty, individuality, or courage must be invited, applauded, valued, and nurtured. Following are important things to teach—*or* encourage—in connection with voice:

- *Choosing a topic that matters to you as a writer*
- *Knowing the topic well—or finding information you need*
- *Having a point to make or story to tell*
- *Thinking about the reader as you write*
- *Writing honestly—saying what you mean*
- *Including small details that leave an impression*
- *Writing with confidence*

Following are some lesson ideas and strategies to help you draw out your students' voices.

1. PROVIDE A SAFETY NET.

Putting voice into writing is an act of courage. It only occurs in an environment where students feel safe writing the truth and sharing it aloud—even if the topic or position is not popular. When you share your own writing and ensure that all writing is received respectfully, you set the stage for this.

2. RESPOND TO STUDENTS' WORK WITH UNABASHED ENTHUSIASM.

Of all the gifts we can give our young writers, none is so sweet as full-out appreciation: "Your piece moved me," "Your writing had me laughing aloud," "You seemed so caught up in this story—and so was I." Never underestimate the power of a simple comment; it is the most powerful teaching tool you have, better than anything you will learn from any book or seminar. Nothing in all the world of writing is so compelling as the image of an excited reader waiting for your words.

3. REWARD RISK.

Nothing happens with voice when writers play it safe. They need to play with fire. Remember the lead from the "Fox" paper at the beginning of this chapter? That writer took risks. He admitted to not getting along with people. Most writers would never reveal something so personal—and it's his *opening line*. He talks of God not being around all the time, and his dog taking God's place; some readers might be offended by that. In choosing a "favorite place" about which to write, he didn't discuss Disneyland or the family picnic. Instead, he wrote about a place of personal importance—the pond behind his house. Toward the end of the paper, we learn that the writer has moved—but he carries with him deeply embedded memories of his days at the pond with Fox. The paper closes with these lines:

> Another year passed, and this would be our last year by the pond. I admired and respected that pond more than I ever did that year. But at long last, all good things must come to an end, we moved to another town. Fox and I still visit the pond, but it'll never be like them 3 years when she was mine. (*Oregon Statewide Assessment Final Report*, 1985, 24)

To my ear, that closing line hits just the right note—but I can imagine some readers hesitating, not quite ready to place high scores (even in voice) on a piece with faulty

Writing with real honesty takes tremendous courage. Such writing should never be taken for granted.

—Ralph Fletcher
What a Writer Needs, 1993, 25

When teachers give up their role as corrector and become genuine readers, students begin responding in their own voices and not some stilted cross between expectation and assignment.

—Barry Lane
After THE END, 1993, 162

grammar. (Never mind that the writer could be—probably *is*—playing with dialect.) A paper like this one forces us to make choices. We must decide what we value, treasure, appreciate. If students never feel safe stepping outside the boundaries of approved topics, attitudes, conventional rules, and—yes—rubrics, we're going to get a lot more clones of "The Redwoods." And we deserve them.

4. REMIND STUDENTS TO TELL THE TRUTH.

Take to heart the words of Anne Lamott (1995, 3): "The very first thing I tell my new students on the first day of a workshop is that good writing is about telling the truth."

Truth, of course, is not about literal facts. Truth is the world as you see it—what horrifies or amuses you, what you know to be true, what you know to be right or wrong, what makes you laugh or cry deep inside where no one can see the tears.

Sometimes, telling the truth is just being frank. It's the writer of "The Perfect Tree" (Paper 6) revealing that "My sister will get to choose the tree once she is old enough to have a house of her own." It's 5th grader Andrew writing about his favorite camp experience and offering this confession: "At Environmental Camp, we did at least 40 activities, but my favorite was the bus ride home. Call me crazy, but that's my favorite." Or 5th grader Nikki, who was asked to reflect on her South America project, and had a thing or two to say about the difficulties of finding information on Paraguay (See Figure 5.5).

> Risk being unliked. Tell the truth as you understand it. If you're a writer, you have a moral obligation to do this. And it is a revolutionary act—truth is always subversive.
>
> —Anne Lamott
> *Bird by Bird*, 1994, 226

5. LOOK TO THE TOPIC.

Writer Mary Pipher suggests that when writers' work sounds hollow to them, the topic is often to blame. I agree. Without topic choice, we are unlikely ever to see the strongest voices our writers have within them. Pipher suggests (2006, p. 44) finding your voice by posing questions of self-exploration, such as these:

- *"What makes you laugh, cry, and open your heart?"*
- *"What do you know to be true?"*
- *"What is beautiful to you?"*
- *"What do you want to accomplish before you die?"*

These are not questions we can ask of students. They're not prompts. These are philosophical questions students ask *themselves*, as they look for topics that matter.

Do some exploring of your own: inside your heart, outside in your neighborhood. Then remember the power of modeling topic choice. I mentioned this in connection with the trait of ideas (see pages 82–83), so you may have done this once already with your students. Good. Do it again. Because now your topics will be different, fresh, new. If you keep a writing notebook, share a passage or two—maybe you have a section where you jot down things that capture your imagination. Here are two of my new writing topics—and what I would say to students about each one:

FIGURE 5.5

Nikki's Social Studies Reflection (Grade 5)

The most important thing I learned was about the vast diversity of people living in South America. At the end, we had a big fiesta in the gym and everybody displayed his or her project. We had music going all the time and we dressed in Latin American clothing and danced. I loved it. I think I did a pretty good job on my project considering that compared to the guy that got Brazil, the library had squat on my country. Same with the bookstore. They had about 10-15 books on Brazil, but I could only find one that worked for me. Apparently no one visits Paraguay. How come? They should. Joel actually wanted Paraguay, but that was only because his sister had it two years ago.

Author's Note

The primary reason to assign a topic is that the *content* of the writing matters as much as (or sometimes more than) the writing itself. For example, you might want writers to complete a science lab report or explain a math process. The writing is still important for the sake of clarity, but it's primarily subject matter on which you're focusing. When it's the *writing itself* that matters most, however, let students choose their own topics—if you want to hear their voices.

Packaging

Everything now is packaged in a way that requires breaking and entering. "Tear here" is a euphemism for "Just *try* to get in. We dare you." Modern plastic cannot be cut, ripped, smashed, or punctured—though it does make the contents look shiny and appealing. There's a bright side, however: Things that annoy us make *wonderful* writing topics.

New Friend

Our friends lost their little dog, Molly. She was a sweetheart, and is now remembered with a commemorative stone that reads "Molly—our dearest friend." John and Marty now have a new dog, Mochy—but here's the interesting part: Mochy was trained as a "hearing companion" dog, but she didn't pass the course. I want to write about a dog that fails a class—but winds up healing hearts.

6. MAKE SURE WRITERS KNOW THE TOPIC.

Knowledge produces confidence—and confidence produces voice. Writers who do not know a topic well do two things that kill voice. First, they write in generalities:

Energy conservation is critical to our future.

Second, they qualify, qualify, qualify. You know those little words that politicians or other speakers use to conceal their true opinions: *sometimes, usually, often, nearly, almost, coming close to, somewhat,* and their many cousins. Cutting these from writing makes the text sound sure-footed, instead of uncertain. Compare these two versions:

- *We're rapidly approaching the point where many people may wish to rethink their position on the nuclear arms treaty.*

- *We must support the nuclear arms treaty—now.*

In *Zero: The Biography of a Dangerous Idea* (2000, 6), author Charles Seife writes with authority. He clearly trusts his research—and as a result, so do I. This is the voice of a writer who knows his topic inside and out:

A key clue to the nature of Stone Age mathematics was unearthed in the late 1930s when archaeologist Karl Absolom, sifting through Czechoslovakian dirt, uncovered a 30,000-year-old wolf bone with a series of notches carved into it. Nobody knows whether Gog the caveman had used the bone to count the deer he killed, the paintings he drew, or the days he had gone without a bath, but it is pretty clear that early humans were counting something.

Here are five things you can do to help writers write with that kind of confidence:

- Explain that confidence comes from knowledge—and that confidence increases the likelihood that readers will trust the writer.

- Share examples (like Seife's) of well-researched writing that demonstrate confidence.

- Encourage writers to choose topics they know well—through reading, interviews, or personal experience.

- Help writers locate the informational sources they need to expand their knowledge.

- Encourage writers to write with a tone of authority. It helps to imagine yourself an expert on your topic even when you don't quite believe it—yet. With a bit more research, after all, you may *become* the expert your readers want you to be.

7. MAKE SURE STUDENTS KNOW THEIR AUDIENCE, TOO.

The concept of "audience awareness" is less meaningful for students who write consistently for an audience of one: you. So teaching students to think consciously and sensitively about readers demands some stretching. Here are some things you can do:

- Have students really write to other audiences: younger students, parents, local businesses, a government agency, the local school board, a favorite author, and so on. Talk about how they adjust their voice to suit this audience. (See strategy 11 for related suggestions on this.)
- Share some of your own real-life writing, and have students try to identify the intended audience. Talk about the clues that help them.
- Share any real-world writing (an ad, encyclopedia entry, paragraph from a picture book, clause from a contract) that is clearly intended for a specific audience, but do not reveal the source of the writing at first. Have students try to identify the audience and again, tell you how they know this.

Take it to the next step and have students write pieces for different audiences and purposes to see how the voice shifts. In Figure 5.6, you'll see a list of facts on Golden Toads, shared courtesy of biologist and author Sneed B. Collard. Distribute copies of this to students in small groups, and have them choose the facts they would use to write (1) a 30-second report for the five o'clock local news, and (2) the first page or two of a young children's picture book. Spend about 10 minutes writing each one. Share results aloud and discuss how the voice shifts from one version to the other.

8. READ ALOUD—AND PLAY THE VOICE GAME.

When you read aloud, let your enthusiasm show. Encourage students to listen for the voice and to describe it in their own words. Is it timid, bold, funny, irreverent, brazen, accusatory—or what? Each voice is different, and each carries traces of the person who created it. Read the three voices in Figure 5.7. One is Jerry Seinfeld, one is Dr. Phil McGraw, and one is Ernest Hemingway. Can you identify each? What word(s) would you use to describe each voice?

Let's make the game a little more challenging. This time, I won't tell you any names; you'll have to guess. Read each of the four voices in Figure 5.8 aloud, more than once. Even if you cannot identify the writer, see what words you can use to describe the voice. Ask yourself whether each voice is male or female. Is it a contemporary voice, or one from another

---

FIGURE 5.6

Facts on Golden Toads

- Golden toads are amphibians.
- Many amphibian populations were harmed in 1988.
- Global warming may have hurt the Golden toads.
- Golden toads are orange.
- Golden toads have brilliant golden eyes.
- Golden toads stay hidden for most of the year.
- They like a moist environment.
- Golden toads live only in the Costa Rican cloud forest.
- Pesticides may have hurt the Golden toads.
- The last living Golden toad was seen in 1989.
- No one knows what happened to the Golden toads.
- Some may still be alive.
- Scientists discovered Golden toads in 1963.
- Golden toads are about as long as your thumb.
- Golden toads only come out of hiding to mate and lay eggs.

© 2010. Sneed B. Collard III. Missoula, MT: www.buckinghorsebooks.com Used with permission.

Three Voices

Seinfeld, Dr. Phil, Hemingway
Which Is Which?

Voice 1

I have no plants in my house. They won't live for me. Some of them don't even wait to die, they commit suicide. I once came home and found one hanging from a macramé noose, the pot kicked out from underneath. The note said, "I hate you and your albums."

Voice 2

Then he began to pity the great fish that he had hooked. He is wonderful and strange and who knows how old he is, he thought. Never have I had such a strong fish or one who acted so strangely. Perhaps he is too wise to jump.

Voice 3

You are sold "self-improvement" the same way you're sold everything else: it's easy; five simple steps; you can't help succeeding, because you're so wonderful; your results will be fast, fast, fast. But we're paying dearly—in more ways than one—for this polluting flood of psychobabble.

Voice 1: Jerry Seinfeld. 1993. *SeinLanguage.* New York: Bantam Books. 143.
Voice 2: Ernest Hemingway. 1980. *The Old Man and the Sea.* New York: Scribner. 48.
Voice 3: Phillip C. McGraw, PhD. 1999. *Strategies.* New York: Hyperion. 23.

Author's Note

Encourage *students* to find their own "mystery" voices to share. If each writer finds just one voice to share aloud, you can join the rest of the class in trying to guess who it might be. Also vary the game by using voices from students' everyday lives: the school principal, someone from the class, another teacher—or you. Can they tell which is which?

time? Which of these voices sounds the most like you? Which, if any, would you like to imitate? (The voices are identified at the end of this chapter, in Figure 5.17.)

9. THINK BEYOND BOOKS.

We all want to share favorite books we love. But voice is everywhere—and once you begin looking for it, you'll be surprised where it turns up. On a package of Sticky Fingers scone mix (very good, by the way), I found this message—personal as any note written right to me:

> Sure, you may be holding the best scone mix on the planet, but does that really mean you must be subjected to some braggadocious copy about how we make the world a better place to live? And who uses words like braggadocious anyway? (2007, stickyfingersbakeries.com, Spokane, Washington)

Recently, a do-not-disturb tag left hanging on the doorknob of my Embassy Suites hotel room read "There are days when I wish I could wear this around my neck!" (2008, Hilton Hospitality Inc.) That *did* help me start my day with a smile.

10. GO FOR CONTRAST.

Contrast is invaluable in teaching voice. A primary teacher I knew once used to give her students two foods to compare: rice cakes and chocolate chip cookies. Then she asked them which had more "voice." They got the idea immediately.

FIGURE 5.8

Four More Voices

Voice 1

You climbed a ladder to the hayloft. Then, holding the rope, you stood at the edge and looked down, and were scared and dizzy. Then you straddled the knot, so that it acted as a seat. Then you got up all your nerve, took a deep breath, and jumped. For a second you seemed to be falling to the barn floor far below, but then suddenly the rope would begin to catch you, and you would sail through the barn door going a mile a minute, with the wind whistling in your eyes and ears and hair.

Voice 2

Nothing compares with the paperweight as a bad gift. To me, there's no better way than a paperweight to express to someone, "I refused to put any thought into this at all." And where are these people working that the papers are just blowing right off their desks anyway? Is their office screwed to the back of a flatbed truck going down the highway or something?

Voice 3

You can never have too much sky. You can fall asleep and wake up drunk on sky, and sky can keep you safe when you are sad. Here there is too much sadness and not enough sky. Butterflies too are few and so are flowers and most things that are beautiful. Still, we take what we can get and make the best of it.

Voice 4

The thousand injuries of Fortunato I had borne as I best could, but when he ventured upon insult I vowed revenge. You, who so well know the nature of my soul, will not suppose, however, that I gave utterance to a threat. At length I would be avenged; this was a point definitely settled—but the very definitiveness with which it was resolved, precluded the idea of risk. I must not only punish, but punish with impunity.

(Answers appear at the end of Chapter 5, in Figure 5.17.)

Read the following passage from naturalist Craig Childs (*The Animal Dialogues*, 2007, 231):

> It looks like a mop, a bundle of ponderosa pine needles, a mobile hairstyle. It takes a while to find the front end, the side with the two dark eyes. Teddy bear eyes and a short snout . . . Peter Blue Cloud wrote, "When the porcupine goes night walking, he doesn't look behind himself and say, 'Ah, yes, I got my quills with me,' he knows what he's got."

Now look up *porcupine* in any encyclopedia, and read the passage aloud. Chances are, you will hear a marked contrast in voice. That's not to say that encyclopedias should be conversational—or passionate. Their purpose is to provide factual information in a condensed manner, not to entertain. But this lesson is a reminder that informational writing *can* be vibrant and engaging when the writer cares deeply about the topic and wants us to care, too. (If you have a copy of *The Animal Dialogues* available, read the full chapter titled "Porcupine," pages 229-235.)

> Writing with no voice is dead, mechanical, faceless. It lacks any sound. Writing with no voice may be saying something true, important or new; it may be logically organized. It may even be a work of genius. But it is as though the words came through some kind of mixer rather than being uttered by a person.
>
> —Peter Elbow
> *Writing with Power*, 1998, 287–288

11. HAVE STUDENTS READ ALOUD, TOO.

Reading with inflection and writing with inflection are mirror images of the same skill, so give students as many opportunities as possible to read aloud. Have them bring passages from favorite writers to class, and share them within writing circles or with the whole group.

12. WRITE LETTERS.

Author's Note

As of this writing, the Web sites Kidsreads.com or authortracker.com provide lists of authors to whom students can write. But you can also look up "Letters to Authors" for a host of email address sites as well as tips for writing letters that get responses. Many authors DO write back. I've received responses from Larry McMurtry (author of *Lonesome Dove*), Laura Hillenbrand (author of *Seabiscuit*), and others.

One biology teacher tells his students, "Don't just write about photosynthesis. Describe it the way you would explain it to Miss Piggy." Letters elicit voice because the audience is built in.

Figure 5.9 shows several letters written by elementary students to American armed forces personnel. When my mentor Ronda Woodruff first began teaching traits to fourth graders, she used letters to bring out voice. Ronda believed in writing to real people, so she asked her students to write to their favorite authors. One of her student's letters, written several years ago to author Roald Dahl, appears in Figure 5.10 (page 154). Writing notes to favorite writers is a simple matter these days. Just look up "authors' addresses" on the Web for a long list of sources.

Regardless of whether or not you are writing a letter, follow this sage advice from my good friend and colleague Sally Shorr: Think of your *very* best listener, the person in whom you would confide your most important secrets. Write as if you were writing *just to that person.*

13. TRY ROLE PLAYING.

From Cedar Park Middle School in Beaverton, Oregon, comes a knockout idea that combines writing, drama, historical research, and practice in developing a three-dimensional character. A seventh grader studying the Holocaust assumes the identity of "Isaac Stein," a prisoner who first creates a picture titled "Visions of Hope" (see photograph, Figure 5.11 on page 154), then writes about it (Figure 5.12 on page 155)—at apparent risk to his life. This is a case in which art inspires writing. Each element of the picture has meaning, and the physical creation of that picture has clearly influenced the writer's essay.

You may be thinking that role playing, while inspirational, is too difficult for young students—but you would be wrong. For examples that will thrill and amuse you, check out any of Lois Burdett's books from the *ShakespeareCanBeFun* series, beginning with *A Child's Portrait of Shakespeare.* In these remarkable books you will find children as young as second graders writing as characters from Shakespeare's plays—or sometimes as the bard himself, or his wife Anne. In one such letter, seven-year-old Marijke Altenburg, posing as a young Shakespeare, writes to Anne about the tragic burning of the beloved Globe Theater:

> My life is rooind. I won't be home tonight dear.
> I'm too sad hunny! (2009, 56)

14. TRY SOME "IMPROV."

Improv (improvisation) is a theatrical extension of role playing—and offers a chance to expand voice through reading, talking, writing—and a bit of drama. You will need to choose a sample of literature that includes *multiple characters* and a *sense of conflict.*

FIGURE 5.9

Letters to Soldiers

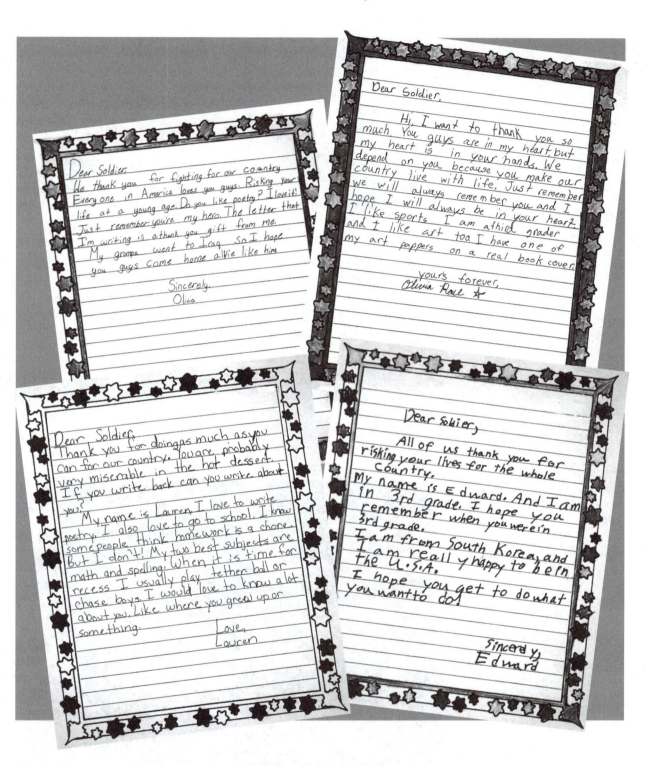

Dear Soldier,
We thank you for fighting for our country. Everyone in America loves you guys. Risking your life at a young age. Do you like poetry? I love it! Just remember you're my hero. The letter that I'm writing is a thank you gift from me. My grampa went to Iraq. So I hope you guys come home alive like him.

Sincerely,
Olivia

Dear Soldier,
Hi, I want to thank you so much. You guys are in my heart but my heart is in your hands. We depend on you because you make our country live with life. Just remember we will always remember you and I hope I will always be in your heart. I like sports. I am a third grader and I like art too. I have one of my art papers on a real book cover.

Yours forever,
Olivia Rose A.

Dear Soldier,
Thank you for doing as much as you can for our country. You are probably very miserable in the hot dessert. If you write back can you write about you?
My name is Lauren. I love to write poetry. I also love to go to school. I know some people think homework is a chore. But I don't! My two best subjects are math and spelling. When it is time for recess I usually play tether ball or chase boys. I would love to know a lot about you. Like where you grew up or something.

Love,
Lauren

Dear soldier,
All of us thank you for risking your lives for the whole country.
My name is Edward. And I am in 3rd grade. I hope you remember when you were in 3rd grade.
I am from South Korea, and I am really happy to be in the U.S.A.
I hope you get to do what you want to do!

Sincerely,
Edward

FIGURE 5.10

Letter to Roald Dahl

Roald Dahl
c/o Bantam Books
666 Fifth Avenue
New York, New York 10013

Dear Roald Dahl:

I'm nine years old. My purpose of writing is to tell you I know all of your books by heart.

I think you should write more books, and make them come out all around the globe. I'm talking about books with voice, like Matilda. Maybe even some sequels. Like Matilda II or Twits II and III.

I've always wondered how you get such creative ideas, and I am hoping if you send back a letter, you will send some tips for putting in just the right amount of information.

When you do send your letter, I would like it hand written and signed in pen. I hope you can come to our school.

I better sign off now. My time is limited.

FIGURE 5.11

Visions of Hope

FIGURE 5.12

Visions of Hope by "Isaac Stein"

I call my picture "Visions of Hope." If I'm caught with this picture, I'll be killed. But it's worth it if people outside see it. I want them to know what life was like in the camp and how we kept our hopes up.

You may be wondering how I got the materials used in this picture. It wasn't easy. I got the material for the prisoner figures from old pieces of uniforms that had been torn off. This was one of the easier things to get. Uniforms get torn all the time from hard work. All the people look alike because to the Nazis it doesn't matter what you look like—only what you can do. To the Nazis we are all just numbers, without faces, without names.

The buildings in the picture are black to represent evil and death. Most of the buildings, aside from the barracks, you would enter but never come out again alive. I got this cloth from an old blanket worn thin from overuse. The Nazis didn't care if we were cold or uncomfortable, so they didn't make any real effort to mend things. Everything in our world needs mending, including our spirits.

Inside the smoke of death from the smokestack you will see the Star of David. This star represents hope. Hope for life and for living. We will never totally die as long as our hope lives on.

My picture has two borders. One is barbed wire. It symbolizes tyranny, oppression, and total loss of freedom. The other border, outside the barbed wire, represents hope and dreams outside the camp. The flowers, sun, moon, and bright colors were all things we took for granted in our old world.

Even though we see sun through the clouds and smoke, we can't enjoy it anymore. The feathers represent the birds we barely see or hear inside the camp. We miss the cheeriness of their voices. The tiny brown twigs are as close as we come to the trees we remember.

I got the bright cloth from a dress. When prisoners come to the camp, they must take off their own clothes and put on the hated prison outfits. All the nice clothes are sent to Germans outside the camps. My job is to sort through the clothes and pick out things that will be sent away. When I saw this beautiful cloth, I tore off a piece and saved it for my picture.

I hope someone finds this and remembers that even when they took away everything else, they could never take our hope.

Fairy tales and fables work well. And young adult literature abounds with scenes in which characters find themselves on various sides of a situation.

My all-time favorite piece to use for this (and it's one that spans many grade levels) is Sandra Cisneros's classic story "Eleven." In this story, Cisneros writes in the voice of Rachel, who is just turning eleven. She is confronted by Mrs. Price, her domineering teacher, who insists that a ratty old red sweater found in the coat closet *must* belong to Rachel—and forces her to put it on despite Rachel's feeble protests. Humiliated and alienated from friends, Rachel's spirit is crushed. And in her mind, we see a flash of her mother at home, baking a cake for this "special" day.

For dramatic results, follow these steps:

1. Group students into teams of 3 to 5. You need a minimum of 3 to make the activity work; more than 5 will make later reading cumbersome. Have them sit in a circle.

2. Read "Eleven" (or your chosen selection) aloud to students—or have them read it to themselves.

3. Resist the urge to discuss the piece—just yet. You will want to. So will students. But improv works best if students write from their own thinking.

4. Ask students, within their groups, to choose characters whose identity they will assume. Give them a minute or two to discuss this. It is important that *within each group*, every person chooses a *different* character. Possibilities for "Eleven" include—

   - Rachel, the narrator of the piece
   - Mrs. Price, the teacher
   - Phyllis or Sylvia (classmates of Rachel's)
   - The red sweater (a marvelous role!)
   - Rachel's mother (home, innocently baking cake)

5. Once students have chosen roles, have them write journal entries for about 10 minutes *in character*. They should imagine it is the end of the day, and they are reflecting on what has happened. Have them begin with the words "Dear Journal . . ." (See Figure 5.13 for an example written in the voice of Mrs. Price.)

FIGURE 5.13

Improv Journal Example: Mrs. Price

Dear Journal,

What a day! First I have to deal with a new student teacher who wants to teach something called "traits." Oh, as if! Then the principal stops by to observe me. On this of all days. Fortunately, I showed how good I am at dealing with a crisis.

Rachel, the drama queen, did her BEST to ruin my math lesson. She literally burst into tears just because I tried to give her a gift—a lovely red sweater I retrieved from the coat room. You'd think she'd be grateful, but no! She dripped and slurped all over that beautiful sweater until it looked like some raggedy remnant no one would want./

After that, of course, I had to make the sweater hers—who else would have a soggy red rag like that? As soon as she put it on, and I could make my voice heard over her insufferable sniveling, our lesson went on as if nothing had happened. I'm sure the principal noticed how smoothly I handled things.

Ah, Dear Journal, only 43 more days, and then the joy of summer—and FREEDOM! Sometimes I wonder if I'll make it, but thank heavens I'm a strong person. These children just don't appreciate how lucky they are to be eleven. What a wonderful, carefree age!

© 2012, Vicki Spandel

---

6. Let them know when they have about a minute of writing time remaining, so they can finish smoothly. Then ask them to mark their text with a slash mark (/) at *any point* where they could divide it into two parts. Writing sometimes feels as if it's turning a corner—the sort of feeling a reader gets when a new paragraph starts. That's the place to put the slash. The point of this is to divide the writing into Parts 1 and 2—allowing each reader *two opportunities* to share aloud.

7. Now, let the fun begin! In groups, have writers read their journal entries aloud to one another, going round the circle. Each reader should read *just* Part 1 the first time around; then have them immediately cycle around again so everyone can read his or her Part 2. That way, every voice is heard twice, and this enriches the theatrical feel of the performance.

8. Once everyone is finished, ask how they liked the mini-play they created. Responses are nearly always extremely positive. And this activity teaches an indelible lesson about how voice emerges from *who we are*.

15. ENCOURAGE WRITERS TO WRITE THE WAY THEY SPEAK.

Peter Elbow suggests that we stifle voice by trying to make our "onpage" voices sound different—more formal, perhaps—when in fact, we should be doing all we can to make them sound more like the way we speak. "Force yourself to write as if you were writing to friends," Elbow advises. "Explain what's on your mind as though your readers—is it possible?—are just itching for a chance to understand and enjoy what you are saying" (1998, 189–190).

16. MODEL THE POWER OF DETAIL.

Details, of course, make ideas spring to life. But they boost voice, as well. And the best way to show students the power of detail is by modeling the revision of your own writing. Write a short rough draft about any topic you know well—expository or narrative. See Figure 5.14 for a fairly detail-free sample of my writing. You will notice that in addition to making the print big and the spacing wide, I also put each "section" into its own paragraph. This gives me ample room to add details.

First, I read the piece aloud to students—without showing it to them. This is important so they can focus on the voice, not the handwriting, conventions, or appearance. I ask

---

FIGURE 5.14

Detail-Free Draft

Today's packaging is frustrating. It's designed to keep

people from stealing or tampering with products.

The plastic is tough, so to open your purchase,

you need tools.

You also need patience.

With enough time and effort, you can open any

package successfully.

FIGURE 5.15

Detail-Free Draft

Today's packaging is frustrating. It's designed to keep *(for the same reasons it's helpful.)*

people from stealing or tampering with products. *Unfortunately, it also keeps consumers from "breaking in" to their purchases.*

The plastic is ~~tough~~, so to open your purchase, *(impossible to rip or puncture with your bare hands)*

you need tools: *a knife and strong scissors (a machete is helpful).*

You also need patience. *It could take hours – even days – to actually get inside.*

With enough time and ~~effort~~, you can open any package *sheer strength   almost*

successfully. *One caution, though: Even if you survive your battle with space-age plastic, your purchase might not: Ironic, isn't it?*

them, Does it *have* any voice? A hint even? Where? Do you *like* the voice? Would you keep reading? Then I tell them that basically I'm going to do *one thing* to boost the voice: add detail. And we'll see, together, whether that one change makes a difference. Then I talk through it, something like this, as I revise:

- *I say here that packaging is frustrating, but I don't explain why. I'm going to put that in.*

- *I also say the plastic is "tough," but that's vague. What I mean is that it's impossible to tear, so I'm going to say that—and also add the kinds of tools you need for this job. I might exaggerate just a little because that adds to the voice . . .*

- *OK—so I mentioned that you need to be "patient." But I could add to that. The truth is, almost no one is patient enough for this task.*

- *I wrap up by saying you can open your package successfully—but what I do NOT mention is that the product inside could be destroyed if you aren't careful. I think that could make a good ending.*

In Figure 5.15, you will see my revised draft. It's not screamingly hilarious or profoundly moving—but that isn't my goal. I want to achieve a level of detail and voice that will make writers say, "I could do that. I could write like that."

17. TAKE THE VOICE OUT.

It sounds crazy—but it works. That's because as you're getting rid of voice, you have to think to yourself, "What needs to go? What is contributing to the voice?" And the likely "culprits" are detail, strong word choice, and any hint of emotion.

For this exercise, begin with a piece that is strong in voice. Choose a favorite paper from this book—or one written by one of your students (with their approval, of course). I like to use Paper 2 from this chapter, "Zeena and the Marshmellows." Because "Zeena" is so neatly divided into paragraphed sections, you can divide your writers into groups and have each group work on just one section. This makes the revision itself go much faster, and lets students hear several approaches.

Urge students to work until *no shred* of voice remains. See Figure 5.16 for a revision that is virtually voice-free. That's not the end of this lesson, however.

First, read your revisions aloud. Have students listen for the faintest echoes of voice. If any part is still too strong, further voice annihilation is required. Then—this is the most important step—list the kinds of revisions students have made:

1. Removing descriptive language: *light, fluffy, chewy, squishy delights*

2. Removing language that shows the writer is talking right to the reader: *Zeena, I know just how you feel.*

3. Deleting imagery: *slipped down my throat like a small piece of heaven.*

4. Removing all strong verbs or original phrasing: *slipped, grabbed, popping, a whole bag of marshmallows doesn't weigh as much as one orange, not everything about chocolate covered marshmallows is sweet.*

5. Taking out personal feelings: *The last thing I cared about was dinner.*

6. Deleting all trace of humor: *Diarrhea, diarrhea, diarrhea!*

7. Taking out any honest revelation: *I couldn't even zip them up!*

8. Omitting the rationalization that takes us right inside the mind of the writer: *It couldn't be the marshmallows!*

9. Deleting all sensory detail: *sharp stabbing pain.*

10. Taking out all hints of energy, excitement, or enthusiasm.

As you make such a list, you are identifying the very things that contribute to voice—in this writing or *any* writing.

FIGURE 5.16

De-Voiced Zeena and the Marchmellows

Some people like junk food. Me, too.

My mom gave me chocolate covered marshmallows. Eating them made me remember some things.

First, when I ate too many, I didn't feel well.

Second, I gained weight.

Third, I got some cavities.

Junk food is not that great.

18. WRITE DIALOGUE.

Dialogue is a tremendous boost to voice because, of course, it is *made up* of voices. Speech energizes writing in a way almost nothing else can. It grabs our attention immediately and gives us a welcome reprieve from the intensity of straight prose.

There is one caveat. The dialogue has to be good. It can't sound stiff or forced:

"Let's go to the movies," said Lily.
"What a grand idea," answered Brad.

Compare this example from *The Twits* (1980, 16) by Roald Dahl. In this passage, Mrs. Twit is getting back at Mr. Twit for putting a frog in her bed by serving him spaghetti that is actually composed of worms—*live* worms. And notice how much more we enjoy the following conversation when we know Mrs. Twit's culinary secret:

"It's not as good as the ordinary kind," he said, talking with his mouth full. "It's too squishy."

"I find it very tasty," Mrs. Twit said. She was watching him from the other end of the table. It gave her great pleasure to watch him eating worms.

"I find it rather bitter," Mr. Twit said. "It's got a distinctly bitter flavor. Buy the other kind next time."

19. SHOW WRITERS HOW TO PERSONALIZE A TOPIC.

Choice of topic nearly always produces more voice. But sometimes you're handed a topic and you have no options. How do you take *someone else's* topic and make it your own? Let's look at some samples from this chapter:

- The writer of "Zeena and the Marshmellows" was asked to write a persuasive piece about why people should or shouldn't eat junk food. She wrote a letter to a friend about her own experience with *one specific* food—chocolate covered marshmallows. Those were all choices: *I'll write a letter, I'll write to a friend, I'll focus on one food, I'll write as if it were my experience.*

- The writer of "A Sunflower Seed" was asked to write about a favorite object. He knew that most of his friends were writing about things they owned—a football, a watch from a grandfather, and so on. He, too, made choices: *I'll choose something (a sunflower seed) that no one else will write about, I'll stretch the definition a bit since a sunflower seed isn't an* object *as most people think of it, I'll write about how the sunflower teaches me about life—instead of why I treasure a possession.*

Once we know how it feels to read something we cannot put down, we want our readers to feel that way, too. All it takes is to write with voice.

STUDY GROUP

Interactive Questions and Activities

1. **Activity and Discussion.** Define the trait of voice in your own words. *Do not look at a writing guide or anyone else's definition as you do this.* Make the words your own. When you finish, share definitions in your group and discuss different ways people think about voice.

2. **Activity and Discussion.** On a flip chart or white board, create a T-chart, with "Things we can teach directly" on one side, and "Things we need to encourage" on the other. Then, with your group, discuss those elements of voice that are important to teach or nurture—and decide in which column each should go. What things can we teach directly? And what things can we model, support, or encourage?

3. **Activity and Discussion.** Share a sample of writing from your own class (or that of a colleague). Have each person write a brief comment, specifically about voice, to this student. Share what you have written—and talk about the power of comments to support or increase voice.

4. **Activity and Discussion.** Choose any sample from literature (or everyday writing) to share with your group. Talk about the nature of the voice and how the writer achieves it. What is it about each passage that could broaden your students' understanding of voice?

5. **Activity and Discussion.** Write one to two paragraphs on any topic you care about deeply. Write on every other line to leave room for revision. Then leave the writing alone for at least one week before returning to read it cold. Share it aloud with yourself—and make any small revisions that occur to you. As you revise, coach yourself with these words: "Write like you mean it." Later, reflect on the kinds of changes you made: changing wording, adding detail, rewriting the lead, adding dialogue, and so forth. Share your revised writing with your group and talk about the nature of your revision. Which changes made the most difference in voice? Use this personal example—or one like it—to model revision for your students.

6. **Activity and Discussion.** Check each of the following statements you believe to be true. Then discuss your responses with your colleagues.

___ Some writing should not have voice.

___ Writing with voice is more interesting to read.

___ Some aspects of voice cannot be taught.

___ All writers have voice of some kind.

___ The comments we make as teachers have a lot to do with how much voice students put into their writing.

___ Prompts lead to voiceless writing—and there's nothing we can do about it.

___ It is important to emphasize voice in writing instruction.

___ Most writing that gets published has voice.

FIGURE 5.17

Answers to "Four More Voices" (Figure 5.8)

Voice 1

Charlotte's Web by E. B. White. 1980. New York: HarperCollins. Page 69.

Voice 2

SeinLanguage by Jerry Seinfeld. 1993. New York: Bantam. Page 61.

Voice 3

The House on Mango Street by Sandra Cisneros. 1991. New York: Vintage. Page 33.

Voice 4

"The Cask of Amontillado" by Edgar Allan Poe, in *Tales of Mystery and Imagination.* 1996. Harcourt. Page 8.

Coming Up

In Chapter 6, we'll consider the ways in which strong word choice supports both meaning (ideas) and voice.

> I write because it is a way to give someone the gift of love.
>
> —Katie Miller, student writer

> If you open my veins, you will find ink instead of blood.
>
> —Simona Patange, student writer

> In a movie called "Freedom Writers," students had a journal to write in . . . They wrote to express how they feel, what troubles them in the real world. That's what I think writing should be about, a way to show emotion, to share your personal thoughts on what happens in the real world.
>
> —Marcus Arellano, student writer

CHAPTER **6**

Enhancing Meaning & Voice with WORD CHOICE

A good soup attracts chairs. This is an African proverb. I can hear the shuffling and squeaking on the wood floor, the gathering 'round. This, from just five well-chosen words.

AMY KROUSE ROSENTHAL
Encyclopedia of an Ordinary Life, 2005, 183

Fish gotta swim, birds gotta fly, writers will go to stupefying lengths to get the infernal roar of words out of their skulls and onto paper.

BARBARA KINGSOLVER
Small Wonder, 2002, 38

Notice the decisions that other writers make in their choice of words and be finicky about the ones you select from the vast supply. The race in writing is not to the swift but to the original.

WILLIAM ZINSSER
On Writing Well, 2006, 34

Choose the *just right* word, and a simple image creates a world of meaning—and feeling. The precision in Jane Leavy's reverent description of Sandy Koufax helps us anticipate the unhittable pitch we know is coming (*Sandy Koufax: A Lefty's Legacy*, 2002, 12):

> The right knee, as it rose, seemed to touch his elbow. His toe extended like a dancer on point. For an instant he seemed in equipoise, his back leg a pedestal. It was his only point of contact with the earth. Every other part of his body was flying.

Words like these separate *functional* from *memorable* language. With well over a quarter of a million words in English, there is nearly always another way to say it. But choices can be tricky.

Take a word like *small*. It has numerous possible meanings—*tiny, minor, slight, trivial, petite, undersized, miniature, diminutive, trifling, insignificant*, and so on. These words are not interchangeable. We might add a *tiny* amount of cayenne pepper to the soup—but not a *miniature* amount. The ballerina might be described as *petite*, but not *trifling*. A raise might be considered *trivial*, but not *miniature*. Well . . . probably not.

Words also create mood. Rain drops dancing across the window pane are cheery, while fistfuls of rain hurled from an inky sky make us duck our heads.

Like voice, words are an extension of ourselves. Our words define us, reflecting not only what we think, but *how* we think. Tom Romano puts it this way: "That's you there in the words, my friends. You are responsible for how you appear. Your words are part of your identity" (2004, 213).

WORD CHOICE:
Phrasing and Terminology

A Definition

Word choice defines itself. It is the words, phrases, or expressions writers use to convey ideas, create images, or explain concepts. Good word choice may be poetic or technical, casual or formal. Like voice, it varies with audience and purpose. Word choice is more than individual words: this word versus that one. It's phrasing, or the use of words in patterns—together with the overall "sound" of a document. Careful word choice creates clarity, ensuring understanding, and also makes pictures in a reader's mind. No wonder we love precise detail—and feel cheated when we don't get it. We applaud when writers reach for new ways to say things, but sometimes young writers try *too* hard, slinging words at us faster than we can catch them. Good writers never write to impress. They write to teach, amuse—or touch us. They use ordinary words in extraordinary ways, as when Bill Bryson writes of Australia, "This is a country where even the fluffiest of caterpillars can lay you out with a toxic nip . . ." (*In a Sunburned Country*, 2001, 6). Word choice not only influences voice, but is an inherent *part* of voice. Through words, a writer puts his or her own stamp on the writing—or deliberately retreats into the background. It is quite possible, in a legal or technical document, to have precise word choice with virtually no personal voice whatsoever. But the reverse, voice without strong word choice, is difficult to achieve. Words are powerful.

Share my definition—and define word choice in your own words as well. Ask students what they look for in strong word choice, and what kinds of word choice problems annoy or confuse them. Make a T-chart, listing strengths on one side and problems on the other. With this simple step you take a big step in teaching this trait.

Next, share the Student Writing Guide for Word Choice, Figure 6.1. Give students time to look over the guide, comparing the language of the guide to some of the

All of us possess a reading vocabulary as big as a lake but draw from a writing vocabulary as small as a pond. The good news is that the acts of searching and gathering always expand the number of usable words. The writer sees and hears and records. The seeing leads to language.

—Roy Peter Clark
Writing Tools, 2008, 70

FIGURE 6.1

Student Writing Guide for
WORD CHOICE

6
❑ My word choice is clear and creative.
❑ I stretched for the word or phrase that was just right.
❑ Every word counts. If I repeated, I meant to do it.
❑ I used many strong verbs—and found my own way to say things. Look for stand-out moments.
❑ My words make pictures in your mind, touch your senses, or take you right inside my thinking.

5
❑ I wrote to make meaning clear—not to impress you.
❑ There are moments you'll notice or remember.
❑ My writing is concise. If I repeated, it works.
❑ Look for strong verbs—and some read-aloud moments.
❑ My words create meaning or help you picture things.

4
❑ My writing makes sense. I used words correctly.
❑ You'll spot a moment or two to highlight.
❑ Not much repetition. Not many wordy moments.
❑ In spots I tried too hard—or not hard enough!
❑ You will get the main idea.

3
❑ I have too many vague words: *nice, good, fun.*
❑ There's at least *one* part I like, however.
❑ Parts are wordy—or else I didn't say enough.
❑ I need more verbs—and more *precise* words.
❑ I'm still finding the "right" words to say what I mean.

2
❑ Some words seem unclear—or maybe incorrect.
❑ I wrote down the first words I thought of.
❑ Caution: Repetition! Fuzzy language! Wordiness!
❑ Strong verbs? No way! It's all *is, are, was, were.*
❑ The reader will need to work to "get the message."

1
❑ I struggled just to get words on the page.
❑ I wasn't sure what to say—or how to say it.
❑ I didn't say enough—or I just repeated things.
❑ I used the same old words I *always* use.
❑ I need help with word choice—or the whole message.

© 2012. Vicki Spandel. Designed for use in classroom assessment.

---

characteristics they associate with strong or ineffective word choice. The teacher version, for your use in assessing writing, appears in Figure 6.2.

Consider making a poster of the "trait shortie"—a summary of the key features within word choice (see Figure 6.3). Remember to leave space at the bottom to add additional features you or your students think of as you study this trait.

Warming Up with Literature

Just a chapter ago, you were looking for passages with strong voice. Now that you're on the hunt for powerful word choice, it may feel like déjà vu. That's because nearly every passage that's strong in word choice will ring with voice; technical writing, where the writer steps out of the spotlight to let you focus on the message, is an exception. Here are a few things to look and listen for as you track down examples of words used well:

- Words used not only correctly, but precisely
- Words that are new to you—but ones you can decipher from context
- Phrases you would highlight, share, recall, or save in a journal
- A piece that makes you say, "I wish I'd written that"

FIGURE 6.2

Teacher Writing Guide for
WORD CHOICE

6
❑ Clear, fresh, original language adds voice
❑ Quotable—the right word at the right moment
❑ Every word counts—any repetition is purposeful
❑ Powerful verbs, unique phrasing, memorable moments
❑ Words create vivid message, striking images

5
❑ Natural language used well and confidently
❑ Engaging—moments to remember or highlight
❑ Concise yet expressive—a good balance
❑ Strong verbs, striking expressions
❑ Words create clear message, image, impression

4
❑ Functional, clear language used correctly
❑ Understandable—sometimes noteworthy
❑ Minimal wordiness or unintended repetition
❑ Strong moments—few clichés or overwritten text
❑ Words help reader get the "big picture"

3
❑ Vague words (*special, great*)—OR thesaurus overload
❑ An occasional stand-out moment
❑ Moments need pruning—or expansion
❑ Writer rarely stretches for individual expression
❑ Images/impressions still coming into focus

2
❑ Words may be unclear, vague, or overused
❑ Writer settles for first words that come to mind
❑ Fuzziness, wordiness, unintended repetition
❑ Words lack energy, life, vitality
❑ Reader must work to "see" and "feel" the message

1
❑ Getting words on paper seems a struggle
❑ Word choice feels random—not a real "choice"
❑ Writer says very little—or repeats a lot
❑ Overworked words—*nice, good, great, fun*—flatten voice
❑ Writer needs help with message or wording

© 2012. Vicki Spandel. Designed for use in classroom assessment.

- Wording that "turns lights on" when you need information
- A writer's ability to use terminology (the "language of the territory") with skill
- Phrasing that moves you, touches you
- A word or words that seem "just right" for the occasion
- Concise writing
- Strong verbs that get things moving
- Everyday language used well

JUST A TASTE . . .

Following are just a few examples of words used effectively. Encourage your writers to look for samples of their own—and remind them to read passages aloud in order to hear the full force of the language.

Sample 1

Consider the elegance and measured grace of naturalist Sy Montgomery in *Birdology*. In this passage, she is describing a Southern cassowary, an inhabitant of the Australian rainforest, whom the natives call "Truly Big Man" or "Truly Important One" (2010, 73). And no wonder. The cassowary is one of the few birds that can—and occasionally does—kill humans. Enjoy the alliteration in this descriptive piece (2010, 74–75):

> Balletically, the cassowary moves forward with breathtaking grace. The tall, scaly legs seem to bend backward, and the clawed toes rise, curl, and open and fall as softly as a pianist playing legato. . . . The bird bends down to delicately lift an orangish fruit—the seed of a cycad?—from the ground with his beak. When he stands upright, I watch the seed slide, slowly and sumptuously, down the length of the naked, wrinkled neck.

Sample 2

Bill Bryson has a particular talent for combining everyday language (*blob, brainless, wallop*) with elegance verging on the technical (*translucent, lethality, toxicity*)—as in this description of the box jellyfish from *In a Sunburned Country* (2001, 232):

> It was remarkably unprepossessing—a translucent box-shaped blob, six or eight inches high, with threadlike tentacles several feet long trailing off beneath it. Like all jellyfish, it is all but brainless, but its lethality is unbelievable. The tentacles of a box jellyfish carry enough wallop to kill a roomful of people, yet they live exclusively on tiny krill-like shrimp—creatures that hardly require a great deal of subduing.

FIGURE 6.3

Trait "Shortie" for WORD CHOICE
Use this summary as a poster—and have students add to it!

Keys to . . . WORD CHOICE
Phrasing and Terminology

- The wording is clear and helps the reader understand the message.
- Phrasing is original—it reflects the writer's unique way of saying things.
- The wording is concise—it has punch.
- The words sound natural—the writer isn't straining to impress the reader.
- Strong verbs give the writing energy.
- The writer defines new or technical words—or makes the meaning clear from how they are used.
- Modifiers aren't overdone—nouns and verbs carry the weight.
- The words paint a clear picture in the reader's mind.
- The reader finds many moments to quote or highlight.

© 2012. Vicki Spandel.

Author's Note

Remember that what you share with students is what you encourage. If you read passages literally erupting with modifiers, your students will think adjectives and adverbs are the key to fine writing. If nouns and energetic verbs are the backbone of your selections, your students will want to write with that same strength. Think "poetry." Not just literally—but in spirit. You're looking for the writer who can say a lot in a few words. Remember the value of subtlety, as well. You wouldn't highlight "It was a dark and stormy night." When you find a passage that lets you know how dark and stormy it is without coming right out and saying it, *that's* the piece to share.

USING A WHOLE BOOK

To write is to create music. The words you write make sounds, and when those sounds are in harmony, the writing will work.

—Gary Provost
100 Ways to Improve Your Writing,
1985, 58

Following are several books to share in their entirety—or from which you might choose multiple passages. You want a mix of fiction and nonfiction, including some informational and technical samples, some business writing, some poetry. As you share various samples, have students search for their own, linking word choice to genre as well as to purpose and audience.

Sample 1

The Dreamer by Pam Muñoz Ryan. Illustrations by Peter Sìs. 2010. New York: Scholastic.

Ages: Upper elementary and older

Genre: Fictional biography

Summary

Young Neftalì's heart is pulled by two voices: One is that of his authoritarian father, who spurns the young boy's daydreaming, calling him absent-minded and suggesting he will amount to nothing. The other is the voice of his imagination, haunting him with persistent questions: "Neftalì? Who spoons the water from the cloud to the snowcap to the river and feeds it to the hungry ocean?" (9) Neftali is in fact the young Pablo Neruda, and through this book, Ryan chooses words to help us visualize the world through a poet's eyes.

Suggestions for Discussion and Writing

1. Ask how many of your students know the work of poet Pablo Neruda. Share some of his poems aloud. (Several are included at the end of the book, and sources for others are listed.) Ask writers what this poet's word choice and phrasing reveal about him.

2. Explain that this work—*The Dreamer*—is a fictional biography. How do your writers imagine that those two genres would blend? What obligations does the writer have to stick with literal history when writing in this blended genre?

3. Share all of the book—or a few chapters. You may wish to have some readers finish the book on their own. Talk about the two voices that tug at young Neftalì. How do they differ? Does it feel as if one voice will triumph?

4. Take time to linger over selected passages—like this description of the way Neftalì hears the storm outside his tiny house: "Raindrops strummed across the zinc roof. Water mysteriously trilled above him, worming its way indoors" (5). What words here are unusual—or enticing?

5. Imagine that Ryan's book is made into a film. How would it open? Why is that first scene so important? Consider transitions, too. In a book, a writer can use phrases, poetic questions, illustrations, or new chapters to transition from one scene to the next. How would this sort of transition be achieved on film?

Sample 2

The Tale of Despereaux. 2003. Kate DiCamillo. Illustrations by Timothy Basil Ering. Cambridge, MA: Candlewick Press.

Ages: Elementary through early middle school

Genre: Fairytale

Summary

In this tale, a tiny mouse with enormous ears defies tradition in virtually every way, disdaining food, loving language, and falling in love with a human princess. DiCamillo is a master at making word meaning clear from context, and, in addition, her text sings with sensory detail. She never writes condescendingly to children, and as a result, this unlikely tale of love and heroism and villainy can be enjoyed by readers of all ages.

Suggestions for Discussion and Writing

1. Share the book cover and title. How many of your students have read other books by Kate DiCamillo (*The Magician's Elephant, The Tiger Rising, Because*

> Everything exists in the word.
> —Pablo Neruda
> in Georgia Heard,
> *Writing Toward Home*, 1995, 48

Author's Note

Look carefully at the illustrations by writer and artist Peter Sìs. Do they capture the voice and mood of the book? Are they a good complement to the author's poetic language? What do they show about the way in which Neftalì sees the world?

of *Winn Dixie, The Miraculous Journey of Edward Tulane*)? What, if anything, have they noticed about DiCamillo's word choice prior to this?

2. This book was the basis for a film (in 2009) with voices by Matthew Broderick and Emma Watson. How many of your students have seen that film? Why, in their opinion, might this book have been chosen as the basis for a film?

3. Share the first few chapters (it's hard to stop)—or the whole book, if you wish. Pause to savor favorite passages, reading them more than once and encouraging students to record favorite words or expressions in their writing journals.

4. Talk about how the word choice contributes to voice. For example, just after Despereaux is born, the sun shines on him through the window. But DiCamillo doesn't use those words. Instead, she writes this: "The April sun, weak but determined, shone through a castle window and from there squeezed itself through a small hole in the wall and placed one golden finger on the little mouse" (13). How is this different from "The sun shone"?

5. Once you finish the book, watch all or part of the film. Then have writers work in pairs to create podcast reviews comparing the two. Which has more voice? Why? Which would they more strongly recommend?

Sample 3

Red Sings from the Treetops. 2009. Joyce Sidman. Illustrated by Pamela Zagarenski. New York: Houghton Mifflin Harcourt.

Ages: All ages
Genre: Poetry

Summary

What if colors came alive? What if we could feel, hear, taste, or smell them? This delightful and whimsical collection of poems looks at colors across the seasons, capturing them in ways that are simultaneously unexpected and delightfully familiar. Sidman has an eye for detail—and an ear for voice and verbs. Her hummingbirds "dart, jag, and hover," her ladybird beetles "whisper" along a finger. Every passage becomes a favorite—so pick a color you love and dive in.

Suggestions for Discussion or Writing

1. How many of your writers have a favorite color? Without naming the colors, have writers reflect for a moment on where they see each color—indoors or out. Make some quick-write lists (these can later become the basis for poetry of their own). Share your favorite color, too, and make a list of your own (but don't share the list just yet).

2. Talk about how colors change through the seasons. If you live in a tropical or semi-tropical climate, the changes may be subtle—fruits or vegetables coming into season, stormy versus sunny weather, various flowers blooming. If you live in a land of seasons, you may sometimes paint the landscape gray or brown in your mind. But is it really? And what colors show themselves indoors even when they disappear from the garden?

3. Share just the cover to begin. Talk about Pamela Zagarenski's illustration. What sort of voice comes through in her art? Talk about the title, too. How can a color "sing"? What is the word for this kind of language? (personification) How does this way of looking at the world open up a whole new way of using words?

4. Read through the book, noticing the sensory details—and the poet's use of unusual verbs. Most are words we've heard many times, but Sidman slips them into unexpected moments.

5. Use your earlier notes to create some color poems of your own. They could be four lines long—or forty. With each line, though, ask students to reach for an unusual detail or a verb that captures the power each color has over our human imagination. Colors may or may not be connected to seasons. Share your poems aloud, and/or create an online anthology.

Author's Note

For an example of color-based poetry, see "Purple" by Elizabeth, Figure 7.4, page 211.

OTHER BOOKS IN WHICH WORD CHOICE SINGS

***Amos and Boris* by William Steig. 2009 (reissue edition). New York: Square Fish. Picture book.**

Steig's timeless tale of friendship and undying loyalty sparkles with sophisticated phrasing children love. Steig never, ever settles for someone else's words. All ages, though directed at primary.

***The Bad Beginning* by Lemony Snicket. 2007. New York: HarperCollins. First novel in a series.**

The Baudelaire children may have been charming, intelligent, and resourceful, " . . . but they were extremely unlucky, and most everything that happened to them was rife with misfortune, misery, and despair" (1). So begins this tale of "unfortunate events," in which author Lemony Snicket has a rollicking good time infusing his text with expressive words and then defining them for readers. Darkly comic, easy reading. Elementary and beyond.

***Chains* by Laurie Halse Anderson. 2008. New York: Puffin Books. Historical novel.**

Set at the outbreak of the Revolutionary War, this book tells the story of thirteen-year-old Isabel and her young sister Ruth, who become the property of British sympathizers, the unscrupulous Locktons. The author's meticulous research shows itself in countless details—as well as in language that echoes the 1700s. Each chapter opens with an intriguing excerpt from a document of the time (letters, newspapers, bulletins, quotations), adding to the book's authenticity. Middle school and beyond.

***Crickwing* by Janell Cannon. 2000. New York: Harcourt Children's Books. Picture book.**

Prose that is virtually alive with strong verbs dramatizes the story of an artistic cockroach who wants to be left alone to create sculptures from his food—but finds himself in the midst of a raging battle between the none-too-friendly ants and the lethal anteater. Art and text alike will keep students captivated through multiple readings. Intended for primary and early elementary, but appealing to readers of all ages.

***Escape! The Story of the Great Houdini* by Sid Fleischman. 2006. New York: Greenwillow Books. Biography.**

Ambitious author Sid Fleischman sifts through a mountain of research to scavenge for us the best photos, anecdotes, and bits of history surrounding the life of Ehrich Weiss, aka Harry Houdini. The language of Fleischman's book is concise, witty, and deeply engaging. Expect young readers to expand vocabulary with this one. Upper elementary through middle school (high interest for older readers).

***Gentle Giant Octopus* by Karen Wallace. Illustrated by Mike Bostock. 2002. Cambridge, MA: Candlewick Press. Nonfiction picture book.**

Through vivid verbs and creative similes ("sinks like a huge rubber flower," p. 10), Wallace effectively takes us through the life cycle of one of the sea's most fascinating and intelligent inhabitants. Gorgeous illustrations expand the detail. Primary and early elementary.

Heart of a Samurai **by Margi Preus. 2006. New York: HarperCollins. Fictionalized history.**

This book, based on true events, tells the story of fourteen-year-old Manjiro, who is stranded with friends on isolated Bird Island and rescued by an American whaling ship—thus launching a truly remarkable series of adventures. Well written and filled with Japanese expressions and whaling terminology, all detailed in an excellent glossary. Middle school and beyond.

I, Crocodile **by Fred Marcellino. 1999. New York: Simon and Schuster. Picture book.**

A lively tongue-in-cheek look at life through the eyes of a crocodile—one who's not too fond of Napoleon. Playful, sassy word choice with plenty of voice. Primary through elementary.

M Is for Music **by Kathleen Krull. Illustrated by Stacy Innerst. 2003. New York: Houghton Mifflin Harcourt. Alphabet book.**

You could easily use this book to teach organization for, after all, alphabet books are one clear way to organize information on any topic. But what is especially delightful about this book are the original, unusual words the writer finds to represent each letter. For "o," how about octet, overture, oboe, opera, and one-man band? Students will be drawn to the contemporary folk art—and may want to try alphabet books of their own. Elementary and up.

Our Solar System **by Seymour Simon. 2007 (revised edition). New York: HarperCollins. Nonfiction picture book, illustrated with photographs.**

Simon's nonfiction books are wonderfully readable. This one shows off his skill in making complex ideas accessible through clear language, as well as making meaning clear from context. It's not the sort of book you would normally read cover to cover because there's too much information for that. Break it apart and share selected passages, taking time to discuss facts and photos. Upper elementary and beyond (younger with coaching). Other recommended books by Seymour Simon: *Guts, Gorillas, The Brain, The Heart, The Human Body, Sharks, Whales, Hurricanes, Earthquakes, Volcanoes, The Universe.*

Pride and Prejudice **by Jane Austen. Elebron Classics edition. 2011 (originally published 1813). New York: Michael O'Mara. Novel.**

Austen's witty social satire combines style, characterization, and outstanding dialogue. Middle school and up.

Sailing Alone Around the Room **by Billy Collins. 2001. New York: Random House. Poetry.**

Billy Collins' poetry is eminently readable. The words glide off the tongue. But underlying the simplicity is a depth of meaning that sneaks up on you. Many poems in this collection have special appeal for writers, readers, teachers—and those who love them. Don't miss "Schoolsville." Young adult and adult.

The Schwa Was Here **by Neal Schusterman. 2006. New York: Puffin. Young adult chapter book.**

Compassion meets humor in this riveting novel about a young man so hard to notice or recall that he is nicknamed "The Schwa." A dare and prank (stealing a dog dish) turns into commitment as the Schwa and his pal Antsy become unlikely companions for an elderly man's blind granddaughter, and everyone learns lessons they hadn't bargained for. Sophisticated language blends with some playful Brooklynese in this sensitive, page-turning tale. Grades 7 and up.

Seabiscuit **by Laura Hillenbrand. 2001. New York: Ballantine Books. Historical nonfiction narrative.**

You would be hard-pressed to find a text with verbs used more effectively. Hillenbrand has a clear, clean style that is highly readable whether she is explaining the dangers of life as a jockey or the economic realities of the Depression. Adult. (All ages for selected passages read aloud.)

***Small Wonder* by Barbara Kingsolver. 2002. New York: HarperCollins. Collection of essays.**

Filled with brilliance and undeniable beauty, Kingsolver's prose makes you fall in love with words all over again. Just try to find a lifeless passage. Adult. (All ages for selected passages read aloud.)

***Water Hole Waiting* by Jane Kurtz. Illustrated by Lee Christiansen. 2002. New York: Greenwillow Books. Fact-based picture book.**

"Morning slinks onto the savanna and licks up the night shadows one by one." So begins Kurtz's colorful, action-filled recounting of a day at the water hole. Primary and elementary.

***Wild Thoughts from Wild Places* by David Quammen. 1998. New York: Simon and Schuster. Informational essays with a persuasive edge.**

Multi-award-winning science author David Quammen shows how to put voice into informational writing. He knows his topics (different in each of the 23 essays) well—through reading, interviews, and first-hand investigation of countries and cities worldwide. Two favorites: "The White Tigers of Cincinnati" and "To Live and Die in L.A." Impressive bibliography and index. Middle school to adult.

Author's Note

Explore as many of the books on this list as you can—adding your own recommendations and expanding your class blog (if you have one) on books not to be missed. Remember to consider audience (age, interest, appropriateness) when recommending a book for word choice.

Assessing Writing Samples for WORD CHOICE

When assessing writing for word choice, it helps to have—or just imagine—a yellow highlighter in your hand. Then ask yourself, "How many words or expressions in this passage would I mark?" And if you really do some underlining or highlighting, you can compare your responses with those of your students—or other teachers.

Paper 1

Chad (Descriptive, Grade 3)

My friend is great because likes the same things I do. His name is Chad.

If theres nothing to do around the house, we get together and do stuff. I phone him up or he phones me. He's a real neat person. He's fun to do stuff with because we mostly like the same games and TV shows. He comes to my house or I go to his house. He has brown hair and is tall, about five feet! It is cool having a friend who is alot like you and likes the stuff you like. Chad is my friend.

Suggested Score for WORD CHOICE: 3

Lessons Learned from "Chad"

- Words like "stuff" and "things" block meaning and voice because they don't make us, as readers, see or feel anything.
- Details about hair color or height aren't really what readers crave. We want to know characters from the inside out—what makes them laugh or cry, what scares or delights or motivates them.
- We love words that create pictures.

Author's Note

With a paper like this one, it can be a challenge to provide the encouragement a writer needs. Have the student read it aloud, and be a note taker. When the writer says, "My friend is great," ask, "What is the very *best* thing about him, if you could only choose one?" When the writer says, ". . . we get together and do stuff," say, "Paint me a picture. What's one thing you *love* doing together?" Make notes as the writer speaks. List details. When you finish, share your notes and say, "Look at all your terrific words and ideas. Use them to have a conversation with me on paper." Students won't always follow up—but some will. And this exchange helps a struggling writer understand what we mean by *detail*.

Comments

This paper has the beginnings of a character sketch, but Chad has not become a person yet. We know that he's "neat," "great," and "fun" to be with and that it's "cool" having him for a friend, but we need the clarity of a good close-up to help us see Chad as an individual. Imagine this paper with just one vivid action scene showing Chad playing a video game, hitting a ball, throwing a Frisbee for the dog. We get to know literary figures the same way we get to know our real friends—by being with them.

Suggested Scores for Other Traits

> *Ideas:* **3**
>
> *Organization:* **2**
>
> *Voice:* **3**
>
> *Sentence fluency:* **3**
>
> *Conventions & presentation:* **4**

The Write Connection

Chad

"Chad" is an excellent candidate for revision. Begin by deleting all vague words—such as *cool* or *neat*. But instead of just replacing those words, invent details to show Chad "in action," being his cool, neat self. Imagine Chad in a short film clip, and describe how he walks, laughs, eats, talks. Show him being goofy or sneaky or kind. Have him speak. Think carefully about how much physical description you need—or don't need. *Hint:* Base Chad on someone you know.

Paper 2

Pets Are Forever: An Investigative Report

(Expository, Grade 8)

Many pet owners worry about that difficult day when they must say goodbye for the last time. A new method of preservation could make that day a whole lot easier. It's a sort of mummification of the 90s, minus the fuss of wrapping and the mess of embalming fluid. The new method, believe it or not, involves freeze drying your pet. It's clean, relatively affordable (compared to the cost of a live pet), produces authentic results, and enables you to keep Fluffy beside you on the couch forever, if you wish.

Freeze drying is really a simple procedure. First, highly trained technicians remove all the pet's internal organs. They do leave muscle tissue and bones intact, however, so there will be something to freeze dry. They replace the eyes with lifelike glass marbles in the color of choice. A special procedure temporarily reverses the effects of rigor mortis, allowing the owner to pose the pet as he or she wishes—sitting, lying down, curled by the fire, about to pounce, and so on. It is important to work quickly before the effects of rigor mortis resume. As a finishing touch, the technician uses special blow dryers with a fine nozzle to make the pet look more lifelike. One client posed her cat in the litterbox; apparently, that was her most striking memory of "Tiger."

Freeze drying costs from $500 to $1,000, depending on the size of the pet and the complexity of the final pose. "About to strike" is more expensive than, say, "napping by the woodstove." The entire procedure takes about six months, but satisfied clients claim the wait is worth it. After all, once the pet is returned, you have him or her forever—maintenance-free except for occasional re-fluffing of the fur. Technicians report that freeze-dried pets hold up best in a relatively low-humidity, dust-free environment.

Experts also offer one final piece of advice: It is NOT recommended that pet owners try freeze drying their own pets. Proper equipment and experience are essential if you wish your pet to bear a true resemblance to his or her old self.

The Write Connection

Pets Are Forever

Play with the language this writer puts at our fingertips by writing an advertisement for a company that provides freeze drying services for family pets. (Yes, they do exist.)

Suggested Score for WORD CHOICE: 6

Lessons Learned from "Pets Are Forever"

- Playful phrases like "about to strike" or "napping by the woodstove" create vivid images—and voice.
- If you enjoy writing it, the reader will enjoy reading it.
- Restraint is one key to strong voice.

Comments

One secret to putting voice into expository writing is to like the topic. Clearly, this writer does. We get the idea that she is mildly horrified by the idea of freeze-drying and stuffing a pet, yet also intrigued. The humor in this piece is ironic, extremely under-stated, and highly controlled for a writer this age. Who can help recoiling but snicker-ing at the image of Tiger posed in the litter box? Notice that her language is technically correct yet totally natural: *"mummification of the 90s,"* *"A special procedure temporarily reverses the effects of rigor mortis."* Best of all, she doesn't overdo it; she trusts us to get the humor. Awareness of audience is very strong, adding to voice. Each word and phrase seems chosen for impact. The prose is direct, forceful, and crisp, appropriate for expository writing with flair.

Suggested Scores for Other Traits

Ideas: **6**

Organization: **6**

Voice: **6**

Sentence fluency: **6**

Conventions & presentation: **6**

Paper 3

Fishing Lessons (Memoir, Grade 7)

It was a cool, crisp morning, about the time when the dew begins to form on the grassy banks of the stream. I had been anticipating this moment for some time and now it was here. Grandpa and I were going fishing at an ideal spot, swarming with fish. We had left at about 4, but by the time we got there and unpacked, the sun was just creeping over the horizon.

Grandpa pulled the rod back and let it fly, right down stream, farther than I could see. Then, I lowered my toy fishing line down until it was just under the surface. Right away, Grandpa got a tug on his line, but it wasn't a fish—it was a baby alligator. The alligator was semi-small, but it still put up a fight. Grandpa would gently reel it in, give it some line, then reel it some more. Just then, I realized he had gotten the scissors and was trying to cut the jumping line. Before I could blink, he cut the line and the alligator swam into a drain pipe. That really surprised me because that was his favorite hook.

I pondered over this while I doodled around with my plastic hook in the water. About when the sun got all the way over the horizon, and it was slowly starting to get hot, we headed home with a puny guppy I had caught in my plastic net. On the way to the house, I asked Grandpa why he hadn't just caught the alligator or at least reeled it in. He replied with a question—"Why cause the little fella any more pain than what life dishes out?" I learned that day that all things have a right to life and that life has a reason to be had.

Most readers like this paper very much. Are there moments you like particularly well? See how many you can identify. Some readers would like the very last sentence to be worded differently. First, think about what this writer is trying to say. Then see if you can come up with another way to express the same thought. Can you improve on the writer's wording in that one sentence?

Suggested Score for WORD CHOICE: 5

Lessons Learned from "Fishing Lessons"

- Readers respond to everyday language used well.
- You don't need to send readers scrambling for the dictionary to have strong word choice.
- By sharing just a few carefully chosen moments, the writer helps us to know his grandfather.

Comments

There's so much to like about this paper: the reflective voice, the wonderful character sketch of the writer's grandfather, the vivid imagery—and certainly the phrasing: *swarming with fish, before I could blink, puny guppy, what life dishes out.* Can you see these two fishermen just at dawn, with the *sun creeping over the horizon*? Do you see Grandpa casting, then later alternately reeling the alligator in (*gently*) and letting out line, taking care not to hurt this *semi-small* creature? I especially like the opening to paragraph 3: *I pondered over this while I doodled around with my plastic hook in the water.* Like the grandfather in this piece, the word choice is gentle and efficient; it gets the job done. It is only the wording of the final sentence that kept some readers from giving this piece a 6 in word choice—but you may disagree. Overall, the writing is fluent and conventions are excellent.

Suggested Scores for Other Traits

Ideas: **6**

Organization: **6**

Voice: **4**

Sentence fluency: **6**

Conventions & presentation: **6**

Paper 4

Elephants (Expository, Grade 5)

If someone asked you which animals are the most like us, you would probably pick monkeys or chimpanzes, or maybe gorillas. And you would be right! OK, whales, maybe, too! Or parrots because they talk. But there is another animal you might not think of right away. That is the elephant.

Elephants are very much like us. They are social animals, for one thing. They live and travel in groups. Yes, elephants travel—just like humans. It is called migrating, though, not vacationing. (Humans are the only creatures who take vacations.) Unlike us, elephants do not travel to have a good time. They travel to find water. Without water they die, and the savanna where they live goes through drought each year. They must migrate to find water until the monsoon rains return. Just think if we had to do that!

There's another way elephants are like us. They live a long time. Many animals might only live three or four years. Or maybe a decade. Elephants can live for many decades, just like humans. During their lives, they learn many things, like

(continued on following page)

where to find water, which plants to eat, and which animals to avoid, such as lions. Because they are so big, elephants do not have many enemies, but lions will kill young elephants if the mother is not around. Humans are also enemies of elephants because we kill them for their ivory tusks. We also kill some of them because they trample crops during their migrations. The older, wiser elephants pass all there information along to the young ones, just the way humans do. Elephants do not have any way to record their knoweldge. Young elephants have to learn by watching the older ones and remembering what they learn. The old saying about elephants never forgetting is actually true.

Elephants communicate with one another and show feelings, just like humans. In a documentary once I saw a baby elephant cry for its mother who had been killed by a poacher. The other elephants tried to comfort the little one over her loss. They carressed her with their trunks and stayed close to her so she would not feel so alone. At the zoo I watched an elephant who had been in the hospital return to the compound. The other elephants got excited. They greeted her with a low murmering sound and looped their trunks around hers. It was kind of like when friends hug each other. If we apreciated how much elephants are like us and how sensative they are, maybe we would stop killing them.

If we don't stop, they won't be around, and we will never uncover all of their mysteries.

© 2012, Vicki Spandel

Suggested Score for WORD CHOICE: 4/5

Lessons Learned from "Elephants"

- Vivid images (elephants looping trunks) catch readers' attention and enhance voice.
- Bringing in information from your own experience (elephants at the zoo) gives writing authenticity.
- A strong title and lead set the stage—they're worth spending time on.

Comments

Although not every line is a read-aloud moment, this is a refreshing piece of writing: clear and virtually free from vague words, generalities, and tired expressions. The word choice sounds natural, and many phrases stand out: *very much like us; social animals; migrating, not vacationing; older, wiser elephants; caressed; greeted her with a low murmuring sound; looped their trunks around hers; how sensitive they are; all of their mysteries.* The piece as a whole has wonderful unity; all examples work to enhance the writer's central message that elephants are remarkably like humans. The lead is creative conceptually; the writer makes a good point about how we might identify with other animals before thinking of elephants. But some readers feel this could be stated more concisely. And the title does not do the piece justice. The writer's enthusiasm makes the voice strong. Sentences flow well and show a good deal of variety in structure. There are minor spelling errors, and you may notice that there is no citation for the documentary the writer mentions—but this is, after all, an expository piece (written from memory), not a true research paper.

The Write Connection

Elephants

This is a strong paper, but some readers have pointed out that it takes the writer a little time to get rolling. Do you agree? Could the lead be more forceful? Try rewriting just that part—and when you finish, brainstorm some possible titles to more closely reflect the writer's message.

Suggested Scores for Other Traits

Ideas: **6**

Organization: **5**

Voice: **5**

Sentence fluency: **6**

Conventions & presentation: **4**

Paper 5

A Strange Visitor (Narrative/Imaginative, Grade 5)

The doors flew open, the wind whipped around the room. The startled men looked up. Standing in the door was a man. His royal purple cloak rippled in the draft. The room was silent. There was a sudden noise as the men put down their wine goblets. Tink, tink, tink. The room grew hot and sweaty. Some men tried to speak but nothing came out. The gleam of the strange visiters eyes had frightened the knights who had slain many dragons, and fought bravley for the King. The errieness was unbearable. The visitor's gray beard sparkled in the candlelight giving it an errie glow. The windows let the dark seap in. The large room decorated with banners seemed to get smaller and smaller. The heavy aroma of wine hung in the air like fog on a dull morning. Their dinner bubbled in their stomachs. Their rough fingers grasped their sowrds stowed under their seats. The round table again fell silent. Then slowly the man spoke: "The King has come." The End

---

A Suggested Score for WORD CHOICE: 6

Lessons Learned from "A Strange Visitor"

- Disturb the silence with the clink of wine glasses and the reader will hear it.
- Tension and mystery heighten voice—and spark readers' interest.
- Writing "The End" can be anticlimactic after an already fine conclusion.

Comments

The problems in this piece are minor compared with the strengths. Although the paper does need some work in conventions, many things are done correctly (including spelling of difficult words). "The End" can be scrapped—it dulls the edge of an effective, punchline ending. Sentences tend toward the short side (with the exception of sentence 10, which stretches to 22 words). A little sentence combining and more variety (fewer *the*'s and *their*'s) would raise these scores significantly. On the other hand, there is extraordinary attention to detail—mood, tension, colors, sounds. I feel that I'm right there in the castle. Who is the mysterious visitor in royal purple? Why, the very man you've risked your life for—the *king*. Why don't they know? Remember, this takes place in medieval times, when you might not know what the king looked like unless you had met him. This is a great touch. The language has a simple elegance: *"The aroma of wine hung in the air like fog on a dull morning."* The writer uses mostly one-syllable words, giving the piece strength. A minor suggestion: Replace either *eerie* or *eeriness* to get rid of that echo in the reader's head.

The Write Connection

Strange Visitor

It's easy to fall into the habit of beginning almost every sentence with the same word. Try some sentence combining and vary sentence beginnings so that no more than two sentences begin with "The." Read the result aloud. You might want to finish by editing the piece for publication.

Suggested Scores for Other Traits

Ideas: **6**

Organization: **6**

Voice: **5**

Sentence fluency: **4**

Conventions & presentation: **4**

Paper 6

The Pirate Ship (Descriptive, Grade 5)

Up above the waters are rippling, but in the watery depths of the ocean floor a sunken pirate ship lies nestled in the golden sand. Its skeleton is battered and broken. Its tall pine mast lay on its side like a soldier fallen in battle. The once deadly ship's cargo of gold is forever lost in its spooky grave.

Hovering above the ship a whale is patrolling the waters of the Caribbean Sea. Like a vacuum, the giant mammal sucks up its scaly meal of krill and small fish until it rises to the surface to take a breath of salty air. The giant sea mammal casts a huge shadow that paints the sea floor a shade of misty gray.

A hammerhead shark lurks in the shadows. It's waiting for any unsuspecting prey to swim by its home in the deep. It blends in with its surroundings, making it nearly invisible in the depths of the ocean.

The jellyfish floats by waiting to catch a fish to feed its simple body. Its elongated tentacles lay limp below its body. Its transparent exterior makes it hard to notice as the jellyfish leaves the scene without a trace of its meaningless presence.

Suggested Score for WORD CHOICE: 6

Lessons Learned from "The Pirate Ship"

- Strong verbs really *do* make a difference.
- Careful word choice creates both pictures and mood.
- Effective adjectives (*simple* body, *transparent* exterior, *meaningless* presence) come as a bit of a surprise—they're not the first ones we might think of.
- Writing your title last ensures it will reflect what the piece becomes as you write.

Comments

This is an exceptionally vivid description, with the details painted on the canvas in layers. Clearly word choice is the standout trait: *battered and broken, soldier fallen in battle, patrolling the waters, its scaly meal, unsuspecting prey, elongated tentacles, its meaningless presence.* The high score in voice reflects the fact that this writer thoughtfully chose words that would create an ominous, dark mood, and this is consistent throughout the piece. There is drama and suspense in each paragraph. Slightly lower scores in sentence fluency reflect the fact that many sentences begin the same way and tend to follow a subject-verb structure. We'd like to see more of the variety that makes paragraph 2 especially graceful. Overall, conventions are strong. The writer uses *lay* for *lie* or *lies.*

 The Write Connection

The Pirate Ship

Do you agree that this piece needs a different ending? See if you can come up with a conclusion that wraps up this description with one last thought about the pirate ship. Consider revising the title, too. Could changing the title resolve the problem of not returning to a discussion of the ship?

But you can applaud the incredible spelling, correct use of *its* and *it's*, and excellent punctuation. Some readers find the title misleading because after the wonderful opening, the writer never returns to the ship itself (I confess I did not give this a thought until others pointed it out). The ending, while beautiful, does not seem to wrap up the larger message.

Suggested Scores for Other Traits

> *Ideas:* **6**
>
> *Organization:* **5** (because the ending feels abrupt)
>
> *Voice:* **6**
>
> *Sentence fluency:* **5/6**
>
> *Conventions & presentation:* **5/6**

Paper 7

Kill Measure 34—Now! (Argument, Grade 8)

I strongly oppose Ballot Measure 34. No good can come from passing a cruel, unfair law that allows hunters to hunt cougars with dogs or set out bait to attract bears. Hunters can simply sit in a truck enjoying a burger and wait for a bear to sniff out the bait. This is not hunting. There is no sportsmanship in shooting an unsuspecting bear with its head stuck in a barrel.

Similarly, hound hunting is unsporting. Hunters send out dogs with radio collars, then follow them to the place where a cougar is treed and kill it. Before the hunters can catch up, the cougar usually defends itself against the dogs, resulting in death or injury to many hunting dogs—as well as inhumane wounds to the cougar.

Proponents of the measure argue that the bear and cougar populations are threatening to campers and ranchers. Records of attacks do not support the former. Both bears and cougars tend to avoid people unless threatened. Cougar attacks on humans are rare, and sport hunting does not reduce the risk because most of it occurs far from populated areas. Furthermore, trophy hunters only want large, adult lions—the ones least likely to cause trouble. Such lions easily bring down deer or other small game, and are not tempted to seek food from backpackers or by raiding campsites.

Cougars occasionally kill livestock—but it is very rare. There are documented cases of cougars killing llamas, but it is so infrequent most llama ranchers have never experienced it. Such killings are usually made by juvenile cougars seeking territory, and as noted already, these cougars are not the target of trophy hunters. Further, ranchers lose far more money from prey species, such as rabbits, elk, and deer, than from cougars. Ironically, cougars help control these crop-devouring species, thereby doing ranchers more good than harm.

There is more at stake than preventing cruelty, though. If Measure 34 passes, it will hand all wildlife management authority over to the State Fish and Wildlife Commission. This group will then have all the power to say when, where, and how everyone can hunt, fish, and trap. It is never wise to put ALL the power in the hands of one group, no matter who they are. This measure was already voted down once—and should not even be up for reconsideration. It is opposed by the Humane Society, local Audubon chapters, and responsible ranchers—even sportsmen. The current law allows the hunting of bear and cougar using fair methods—and the taking of any rogue individuals that pose a specific threat. We do not need to "fix" a law that is serving us well. The only thing that should be killed—and now—is Measure 34.

CHAPTER 6   Enhancing Meaning & Voice with WORD CHOICE

Suggested Score for WORD CHOICE: 6

Lessons Learned from "Kill Measure 34—Now!"

- No matter how strong your argument, you need data plus the opinions of experts to back up that argument.
- Addressing the perspective of the other side makes any argument stronger.
- A confident, professional voice (not an angry voice) sets the right tone for a persuasive argument.

Comments

This writer does *almost* everything right. The argument is clear, and stated right up front. She returns to it in the end and restates it with even more force. Her reasons (as far as they go) are convincing, and she addresses counterarguments head-on and well. Word choice is clear and nonrepetitive—even striking at times: *an unsuspecting bear, hound hunting is unsporting, seeking territory, crop-devouring species, more at stake than preventing cruelty.* What's more, the word choice is laced with passion, designed to get our attention and win us over. The voice borders on caustic in the opening paragraph (*simply sit in a truck enjoying a burger*), but for the most part, is compelling, confident, and authoritative. To make her argument harder to refute, however, the writer needs to cite statistics from the Fish and Wildlife Commission or Humane Society, and quote experts on this issue. Because she writes clearly, fluently, and conventionally (not to mention passionately), it is easy to agree with her. But in the end, even strong rhetoric like this benefits from statistical backup.

Suggested Scores for Other Traits

Ideas: **5**

Organization: **6**

Voice: **6**

Sentence fluency: **6**

Conventions & presentation: **6**

The Write Connection

Kill Measure 34— Now!

First, read through the paper carefully, and put a star in the *right margin* every time the writer makes a compelling point that strengthens her argument. Put a check in the *left margin* each time you feel she needs further evidence or a quotation to support her claims. Discuss the results. Then, without taking time to actually track down the information, list some sources this writer could use to discover facts or anecdotal evidence or obtain quotations that would support her position.

Lessons and Strategies for Teaching WORD CHOICE

It would be terrific if there were a shortcut for teaching word choice. Don't count on it. Exposing students to new words through lists certainly cannot hurt, but expecting it to revolutionize the way they write and speak is probably as realistic as passing out dictionaries to toddlers.

Owning words takes time. For the most part, we learn language by experiencing it—through reading, listening, conversing, and writing. And while we can't really rush experience, we can intensify it—by reading aloud frequently, for example, and choosing books that make students want more. Here are the main things you want to emphasize in your teaching of word choice:

- Using words accurately and precisely
- Counting on strong verbs for heavy lifting
- Finding fresh, original ways to express ideas

- Creating word pictures in the reader's mind
- Daring to use new words—or use familiar words in an unexpected way
- Avoiding redundancy
- Writing concisely

Following are some lesson ideas and strategies to help you achieve these goals.

1. READ, READ, READ.

Reading isn't a quick fix. It's a lifestyle. And it works because it fills the well. If we expect writers to make good word choices, we need to continually give them more words to choose from. Read aloud as often as you can, and don't be afraid to share a passage more than once; that's one way to make language familiar.

Here's a familiar excerpt from Harper Lee's *To Kill a Mockingbird* (1960, 1988, 5–6) that I could hear a thousand times (and nearly have):

> Maycomb was an old town, but it was a tired old town when I first knew it. In rainy weather the streets turned to red slop; grass grew on the sidewalks, the courthouse sagged in the square . . . Men's stiff collars wilted by nine in the morning. Ladies bathed before noon, after their three o'clock naps, and by nightfall were soft teacakes with frostings of sweat and sweet talcum.

This "tired old town" with its sagging courthouse, wilting collars and "teacake" ladies lives in America's consciousness—in part because of language that is simultaneously simple and elegant.

2. READ SHORT PASSAGES *ABOVE* GRADE LEVEL.

I would not enjoy being cut off in the bookstore by a clerk who said, "Sorry—you're not ready for that book just yet." *That* would be the one I wanted. Students learn long, long before every word or sentence makes sense. New or unusual words make reading fun.

Many students would be hard pressed to define *all* of the following words in isolation: *imprison, individual, invader, renew, elastic, cascade, canvas, harbor.* In context, though, the words reveal their identity in a way that no vocabulary list can duplicate:

> Our skin is what stands between us and the world. If you think about it, no other part of us makes contact with something not us but the skin. It imprisons us, but also gives us individual shape, protects us from invaders, cools us down or heats us up as need be, produces vitamin D, holds in our body fluids. Most amazing, perhaps, is that it can mend itself when necessary, and it is constantly renewing itself. . . . Skin can take a startling variety of shapes: claws, spines, hooves, feathers, scales, hair. It's waterproof, washable, and elastic. Although it may cascade or roam as we grow older, it lasts surprisingly well. For most cultures, it's the ideal canvas to decorate with paints, tattoos, and jewelry. But most of all, it harbors the sense of touch.

This selection is from Diane Ackerman's *A Natural History of the Senses* (1995, 68), a book most would classify as secondary or adult level. I am not suggesting reading this book in its entirety to younger students—or *any* students. I am suggesting harvesting short passages with rich language from *many* sources to share with students of *any* age. Will they recall every word? Perhaps not. So what? They'll recall some, and they'll get a *sense* of the deeper meaning. Language in context is infinitely more powerful than language by list.

3. ENCOURAGE STUDENTS TO READ *PROACTIVELY*.

Having someone hand you (or read to you) passages he or she finds impressive *is* helpful. But finding your own is better. When *you* are the one on the hunt, pencil or highlighter in hand, you must think about the language, read it aloud, get the sound of it. You must be the one to choose the words that wind up in your writing journal. Maybe you can guess which words and phrases I marked in this passage by Craig Childs (*The Animal Dialogues*, 2007, 48–49):

> Five feet in front of me. The cat was in the air before I could jerk in any direction. In a quarter second it was all color and shape, moving fast, and my blood locked onto my organs as if I were flash frozen. I couldn't tell which way it was moving. The tail was out. It unraveled before my face for a third of a second. That is when I felt certain it was a lion. I was fixed on the tail, and it was fat like a jungle snake, its tip black.

4. MAKE SURE STUDENTS ARE COMFORTABLE USING RESOURCES.

No doubt your students have access to a dictionary and a thesaurus. But do they know how to use these resources effectively? Even if you work with older writers, don't assume they are skilled at looking words up and using the information they find. Model the use of both resources, and call on students frequently during discussions to check word meanings or track down synonyms for the class. Some writers who work on computers may not be aware of how many different language aids are available to them online. Some may not know what etymology is, or may have limited understanding of how words originate. Consider devoting one class period to the topic of resources. To look up word origins, check one of the following—

Oxford English Dictionary: http://www.oed.com/tour/

Etymological dictionary: http://www.etymonline.com/

Sources of common phrases in English: http://www.phrases.org.uk/bulletin_board/

5. PRACTICE PULLING MEANING FROM CONTEXT.

Readers have different responses when encountering a word they do not know. You might ask your students what they do: look it up, underline it and come back later, make a guess, ask someone—or just ignore it? While it is not *always* possible to decipher meaning from context, it helps to practice because good writers, deliberately or not, create small clues that help a careful reader figure out a word's meaning—which might not be clear if we saw the same word in isolation.

In *Zero: The Biography of a Dangerous Idea* (2000, 25), author Charles Seife explores the reluctance of Western civilization to accept the concept of "zero." What clues embedded within the following passage help us work out the meaning of the word *dire*?

In [the Greek] universe there is no such thing as nothing. There is no zero. Because of this, the West could not accept zero for nearly two millennia. The consequences were dire. Zero's absence would stunt the growth of mathematics, stifle innovation in science, and, incidentally, make a mess of the calendar.

6. HARNESS THE POWER OF VERBS.

Verbs give energy to writing. No passage in recent memory brings this concept home more clearly than Laura Hillenbrand's description of the stirring horse race between runty underdog Seabiscuit and the legendary thoroughbred War Admiral, winner of the Triple Crown (*Seabiscuit*, 2001, 272–273):

> They ripped out of the backstretch and leaned together into the final turn, their strides still rising and falling together . . . War Admiral was slashing at the air, reaching deeper and deeper into himself . . . Woolf saw Seabiscuit's ears flatten to his head and knew that the moment Fitzsimmons had spoken of was near: One horse was going to crack.

Imagine that Hillenbrand had written "War Admiral was *touching* the air, *going* deeper and deeper into himself. Woolf saw Seabiscuit's ears *move closer* to his head and knew that one horse was going to *give up*." Hear the difference? What happened to War Admiral's desperation and Seabiscuit's cunning?

7. MODEL REVISING FOR WORD CHOICE.

Little changes can make a big difference. Show this to students by modeling a revision of your own writing. Start with a short sample like that in Figure 6.4. Write quickly without thinking too deeply about word choice. Then follow these steps:

- Read the whole piece aloud to students.
- Give them a minute to reflect on the word choice, perhaps talking with a partner, or marking words and phrases *they* would revise.
- Go through the piece, line by line, highlighting weak verbs—or any other words or phrases you wish to work on. Ask for students' suggestions as you work.
- Talk through your revision—explaining why you make each change.
- Read your revised piece aloud and talk about which changes made the greatest difference.

The result will look something like the piece in Figure 6.5. As with all modeling, this is an activity you want to repeat often. But—this is the secret, really—you will only do that if you *keep the writing sample short.*

FIGURE 6.4

Cross-Country? (Rough Draft)

I was moving right along over the fresh

powder. Then I saw it: a hill. I called to my

friend to slow down, but she just went on

down as if she didn't hear me! As if hills

didn't matter! What choice did I have? I got

a good grip on my ski poles, pushed off, and

sailed down that hill with snow flying into

my eyes and the wind nearly blowing my

poor hat clean off my head.

In Figure 6.6 you'll see how a third grader revised a short passage from *Creating Revisers and Editors,* a companion book to this one.

8. MAKE THAT THESAURUS WORK FOR YOU.

Many students are reluctant to revise because it feels so BIG and OVERWHELMING. Help them to see that changing even a single word can often make a difference to meaning, imagery, and mood. Begin with a simple sentence like this one:

- Tom *walked* down the road.

Then suggest a few revisions for the very bland verb *walked*—

- Tom *raced* down the road.
- Tom *strode* down the road.
- Tom *inched* down the road.

For each example, ask your writers: What do you see in your mind with this new word? How does Tom look *now?* What does the way Tom moves tell us about him? Hint: Have students act out some of these verbs. They will love doing it—and the kinesthetic experience will help imprint meaning in their minds.

FIGURE 6.5

Cross-Country? (Revised Draft)

I was ~~moving right along~~ *gliding* over the fresh

powder. Then I saw it: ~~a hill.~~ *the hill of death.* I called to my

friend to slow down, but she just ~~went on~~ *raced down that hill*

~~down~~ as if she didn't hear me! As if ~~hills~~ *she'd never even*

~~didn't matter!~~ *noticed a hill was there!* What choice did I have? I ~~got~~ *clenched*

~~a good grip on~~ my ski poles, pushed off, and

sailed down that hill with snow ~~flying into~~ *stinging*

my eyes and the wind nearly ~~blowing~~ *whipping* my

poor hat clean off my head.

FIGURE 6.6

Sample Revision from
Creating Revisers and Editors, Grade 3, by Vicki Spandel
(Pearson Education, Inc., 2009). Lesson 10: *Word Choice.*

Sample D: Revision With Partners

The weather was ~~bad.~~ *terrible.* In fact, it was ~~really~~ *worse than terrible.*

~~bad.~~ Rain ~~fell everywhere.~~ *pelted the sidewalks.* The wind was

whipping the branches of the old willow tree I stood next to. ~~blowing.~~ If this kept up, we might ~~not be able~~ *have to cancel*

~~to hold~~ our soccer ~~game.~~ *match.*

Author's Note

After thinking up some alternatives on your own, check out *walked* in the thesaurus—online or otherwise. It may yield some synonyms that didn't immediately come to mind: *paced, toddled, sauntered, promenaded, staggered, trudged, slogged, trekked, zigzagged, tramped, journeyed.* This gives you a chance to talk about nuance of meaning. A *racing* Tom is different from a *marching* Tom—or a *trudging* Tom. But . . . *how?* Why aren't these words interchangeable?

9. RANK WORDS FOR INTENSITY.

This quick lesson (borrowed from my friend and colleague Jeff Hicks) pairs well with strategy 6. Imagine a person who's upset. Perhaps she has purchased a CD. She wasn't going to buy another one—*ever*—but she did, and now she can't seem to remove the wrapping. Imagine various words that could be used to describe her mood and see if you can put them in order, based on intensity. And as you do this, watch the person's face change in your mind:

- Cross
- Furious
- Annoyed
- Fuming
- Incensed
- Hopping mad
- Frustrated
- Concerned

- Bothered
- Irritated
- Enraged
- Beside herself
- Irate
- Distracted
- Seeing red
- Livid

Use all these words—or a handful. Have students line up in front of the class, each holding a card with one of the words printed on it. Have other students arrange and rearrange the line, left to right, from least to most intense. This will generate an excellent discussion of subtle differences in words that may seem to mean the same thing, but in truth have meanings that are distinct.

10. GIVE "TIRED" WORDS A REST.

With your students, brainstorm a list of words we could all stand to shelve for a while:

fun (as an adjective)	*good*
awesome	*great*
nice	*downer*
bad (meaning *good*)	*bummer*
special	*whatever*
cool	*make it pop*
grand	*give me a break*
great	*you know*
super	*really*

. . . and any others you can think of. From this list, choose just *four or five* (no more)—the ones you are most tired of hearing. Write each word or expression in colorful letters at the top of a large sheet of chart paper. Then group students into teams of three to five, and give one member of each team a colored marker pen. Ask students to do a gallery walk, circling through the room from one tired word poster to the next, writing as many other "ways to say it" as they can think of in just under a minute. The brainstorming grows more challenging as they go along and the chart paper fills up—but often the options become more creative, too. Once each team has visited each "word stop," ask teams to select their four favorite alternatives and read them aloud.

Zachary's Word Cache for "The Movie House" (Grade 5)

Motion words	Smells	Feelings	Sounds
tucking into line	fresh popcorn	cushy, velvet seats	crackling wrappers
blinking in the dark	stale air	darkness enveloping me	whispers everywhere
slumping into my seat	oil and grease	clutching my ticket	the announcer's droney voice
straining to see around the annoying TALL people!!!!	mud and grime	sticky fingers	endless chewing
shifting restlessly	body odor	cramped legs—I need to stretch!	muffled coughs
racing for the best seat in the back corner		stomach tightening	scuffling feet
grinning when I get it!		stubbing my toe	OVER-LOUD audio
			Shhhhh! From the lady behind me

Note: Zachary's categories are only examples. Writers should choose their own word categories. Keep in mind that Zachary will probably not use all these words and phrases—he can pick and choose.

11. CREATE A WORD CACHE.

A word cache—a collection of words, phrases, sensory impressions, or general ideas—can be enormously helpful in jumpstarting writing. This is an especially useful strategy for ELL students—or any writers who have difficulty getting started. Encourage them to work with partners, or in small groups.

If all students are writing on similar topics, such as kinds of sea life, you can work as a class, creating subtopics that will work for everyone: names of sea creatures, ocean colors, motion words, and so on. When you finish, post the lists where they are readily visible.

Writers with specific subtopics sometimes prefer to work individually (or with partners). Zachary's class was writing on the theme of "memorable place" and he chose the local movie theater. See Figure 6.7 for a word cache he created based on sensory details.

12. CUT THE CLUTTER.

Wordy writing usually comes about because the writer rambles, unsure of what to say—or because the writer doesn't take time to read a rough draft aloud. Simply revising a single wordy sentence provides good practice in shaking this habit:

- *Tuesday was my birthday and when I woke up, I remembered it was my birthday.*
- *Sam, our dog, is a really protective dog and he would protect us no matter what.*
- *If you need current information, the Internet is a good place to find it.*

FIGURE 6.8

Suggested Revisions of Wordy Sentences

- Tuesday I woke up remembering it was my birthday.

- Our dog Sam would protect us no matter what.

- The Internet keeps us informed.

- Tease a snake at your own risk.

- One glance outside and I grabbed my umbrella.

- *If you tease a snake it could be dangerous because they will bite when they are teased.*
- *When I looked out the window and saw it was rainy and stormy, I quickly grabbed my umbrella.*

See Figure 6.8 for suggested revisions.

13. EXPLORE NEW WORDS.

Someone has to come up with a word that first time—then it has to get the attention of people who create or revise dictionaries. Dictionaries employ usage panels, which include teachers, writers, editors, and journalists, who meet regularly to discuss what words should or should not be included in their lists. As William Zinsser tells us, "Today's spoken garbage may be tomorrow's written gold" (2006, p. 42). Words like *nutrient, psychology, presidential, Americanize, checkers, chore, chowder, energize, flytrap, folder, immigrant, notice, penmanship, skunk, surf,* and *snowshoe* were all once considered "new" and had to win approval.

See Figure 6.9 for a list of recent additions to many American dictionaries. How many of these words are already a part of your vocabulary—or that of your students? (See how many you can define as a class, working together; have volunteers look up any you do not know.) For an even longer list to consider, simply use your search engine to track "new words." This makes an interesting and simple research project for students and can lead to lively discussions of how language does, and should, change.

Stick to the standard, [E. B.] White decreed, because 'by the time this paragraph sees print, *uptight, ripoff, rap, dude, vibes, copout,* and *funky* will be the words of yesteryear.' That was some thirty years ago—and dude, those words are still very much around.

—Arthur Plotnik
Spunk & Bite, 2007, 5

FIGURE 6.9

New Words

agritourism	manga
aquascape	microgreen
big-box	mouse potato
biodiesel	perfect storm
Bollywood	ringtone
crunk	sandwich generation
drama queen	smackdown
DVR	snowboardcross
flex-cuff	spyware
gastric bypass	sudoku
gray literature	supersize
ginormous	telenovela
hardscape	viewshed

How many of these words are already part of your vocabulary?

Author's Note

One site, www.merriam-webster.com, will lead to several intriguing listings, including both new words (including slang like *staycation* and *Webhead*) and those that were considered new more than a century ago. Some words have more staying power than others. Of those in Figure 6.9, which do your students believe will still be with us 100 years from now?

14. Revise for clarity.

Good word choice isn't *just* about beautiful phrasing—though that's important, to be sure. Above all, it's about making meaning clear. A few years ago when I worked for an educational agency, we were forever "facilitating the implementation of viable alternatives among stakeholders." Actually, we were helping dedicated educators make good choices—but no one wanted to say it that way. Jargon is habit forming.

Dig through junk mail, memos, notices, directions for games, or recipes, and you will find an abundance of fuzzy writing. To revise such writing, you need to—

1. Read the piece carefully.

2. Figure out what the writer is trying to say.

3. Rewrite it in simple, straightforward language.

4. Test your revision by sharing it with someone who will tell you the truth.

I found the following paragraph in a book called *An English Grammar for Public Schools*, part of the *Nova Scotia Series*. Don't be surprised if you are not familiar with it; it was first published in 1883—which is one of the things that makes the writing somewhat tedious to decipher (or as the writer of that book might have put it, "The proclivity of the text toward obscurity generates substantial and sustained tedium for the modern reader"). Here's a small piece (from "Suggestions to Teachers," vi) that you might work on (Pour a cup of strong tea first):

> The Lessons are submitted as a general guide to teachers, who, it is assumed, are capable of clothing the outlines furnished with appropriate explanations and illustrations of their own. No class exercise should be begun by placing before the children a bald statement of the principle to be established. The latter should be educed by proper questioning from knowledge already possessed by the pupils in connection with illustrative sentences on the black-board. The greatest care should be taken to unfold and impress by repeated practice in sentence-building the relations which the various elements of language sustain to one another. (*Suggestions to Teachers*)

Even if you do nothing more than revise "be begun" (sentence 2), you will have achieved something worthwhile. A passage such as this one makes a person infinitely grateful that language is evolving—and even eager to give it a push. To see my revision, check Figure 6.12 at the end of this chapter (after writing your own revision, of course).

If your students read Shakespeare—or any text from another century—translating the text into modern vernacular provides helpful practice in making meaning from words that are not immediately clear. See Figure 6.10 for an excerpt from an eighth grader's pop translation of Act IV, Scene iii, from *Hamlet*.

FIGURE 6.10

Pop Culture Translation of Shakespeare, Grade 8

CLAUDIUS: Hamlet! What's up? Where's Polonius?

HAMLET: He's at supper.

CLAUDIUS: At supper? You're kidding! Where?

HAMLET: Well, not any of the usual places, that's for sure. He's the main course! The worms are after him like a bunch of angry politicians. That's how it works—we fatten up the animals so we can eat them to fatten up ourselves. See what I'm saying? But in the end, all we are is food to fatten up the worms.

CLAUDIUS: Sure is depressing talking to you, Hamlet.

HAMLET: No—just think about it! A guy is fishing with a worm and maybe that worm has eaten part of a king. You follow me?

CLAUDIUS: No. What on earth is your point?

HAMLET: No big deal. I'm just trying to say that kings think they're some great shakes, but in the end, they wind up as worm food like everybody else.

FIGURE 6.11

WOW Poster

15. WOW YOUR STUDENTS.

If you've ever felt discouraged by the number of students who forget all or most of the weekly vocabulary list within seconds of completing the quiz, this idea is for you. *Word of the Week* posters (WOWs) are an idea borrowed from middle school teacher Susan Doyle. In creating WOWs, students each celebrate *one* word (chosen by luck of the draw from a basket) by defining it; giving pronunciation, part of speech, and etymology; using it in a sentence; and illustrating it (see Figure 6.11).

Author's Note

What makes the WOW approach so effective is its focus: Each student works on only *one word*. But of course, when the posters go up, students learn much more. It isn't the words or definitions themselves—it's the art. Pictures create an impression that's hard to shake. Many teachers like to use words from current literature or other texts students are studying. You can also have students themselves identify the words; that way, each writer looks to see how his or her chosen word is defined by someone else.

16. GO EASY ON THE MODIFIERS.

One of my students once wrote a piece about a sensory-overload deli where the pickles were *tart, juicy,* and *crisp;* the corned beef *succulent* and *delectable;* the mustard *tangy* and *refreshing;* and the bread *fluffy* and *fragrant.* Even the clerk was *gracious* and *accommodating.* Enough. Adjectives don't always have to come in pairs—the sweeping, breathtaking landscape; the boisterous, bouncy children. Often we don't need them at all. We don't need to talk about congested traffic—that's the nature of traffic. Or rushing rivers. Unless the river is sluggish, there's no need to comment.

Similarly, while adverbs can be useful, an adverb often implies that the verb it modifies needs more force—as in these examples:

Author's Note

I was surprised (and mildly amused) recently to read a "summary" of my comments mistakenly suggesting I had virtually declared war on adjectives. So let me be clear (oops, adjective alert): There is *nothing whatsoever* wrong with thoughtfully chosen modifiers. When I read (in "The Pirate Ship," paper 6) about the "scaly meal" of fish and krill, the "transparent exterior" of the jellyfish or its "meaningless presence," I am applauding along with (probably) most teachers. But when adjectives hit me like a barrage of darts, I feel overwhelmed. Used sparingly, and chosen specifically to inform or surprise the reader, modifiers command more respect.

- *He shut the door forcefully* <u>versus</u> *He slammed the door.*
- *She talked loudly and shrilly* <u>versus</u> *She screeched.*
- *Her voice spoke to us alluringly* <u>versus</u> *Her voice seduced us.*
- *He left hastily* <u>versus</u> *He vanished.*

Never let an adverb steal work that should go to a worthy verb.

Interactive Questions and Activities

1. **Activity and Discussion.** What is the primary goal in teaching word choice? Is it to help students write clearly? To build vocabulary? To offer options? Write down your thoughts—then share them with the group.

2. **Activity and Discussion.** Many people believe that word choice not only supports voice, but is actually an integral part of voice. Do you agree? Find one or two passages with strong word choice (from any source) to share aloud with your group. Discuss the voice in these samples. Is it separate from or intertwined with word choice? Or does this depend on the selection?

3. **Activity and Discussion.** For many years, word choice has been taught through vocabulary lists and similar approaches. But many educators feel this approach is ineffective. With your group, make a T-chart, and brainstorm the general strategies you feel are effective or ineffective for helping writers acquire a more expansive vocabulary.

4. **Activity and Discussion.** Choose any writing sample from this chapter (or a new sample, if you prefer) and, prior to discussing it with your group, have everyone highlight his or her favorite words and phrases and underline in pencil any that should be revised. Discuss the piece in light of your agreements and differences. Talk about how you might use this strategy in a conference with a student, comparing the student's responses with your own.

5. **Activity and Discussion.** The literature section of this chapter lists many books you might use to teach or illustrate word choice. Identify another sample of your own to share with the group. In addition to sharing it aloud, talk about why you chose it and what features of strong word choice you feel it illustrates.

6. **Activity and Discussion.** Look for examples of ineffective word choice, particularly samples your students might revise. Problems calling for revision: wordiness; language that's flat and uninteresting; writing that is overdone--jargon, too many adjectives or adverbs; writing that is unclear. Choose one example to revise with your group.

7. **Activity and Discussion.** With your group, search out examples of fine word choice in non-print sources: documentary films, television news, podcasts, and so forth. Talk about whether word choice is sometimes even more important when words are heard and not seen.

FIGURE 6.12

My Revision of "Suggestions to Teachers" from *English Grammar*

The lessons in this book are only meant as a guide; feel free to expand them with your own examples. For each lesson, consider beginning with an example rather than the rule itself; that way, students figure out the rule on their own and are more likely to remember it. Grammar is tricky business, so be prepared to offer many illustrations and opportunities for young writers to discuss how sentences work. *(Does my revision come close to your own?)*

> Every book you pick up has its own lesson or lessons, and quite often the bad books have more to teach than the good ones.
>
> —Stephen King
> *On Writing,* 2000, 145

Coming Up

In Chapter 7, we'll consider the ways in which another trait, sentence fluency, also supports both meaning and voice.

> I write because I love to write. The words flow from my hand as if I am in the story, as if I am the writing.... I write because I am addicted to writing. I get one idea flowing out of my head and my imagination goes crazy like a maniac in a lab.... I write because I feel free, like an eagle stretching its wings across the canyon.
>
> —Becca Zoller, student writer

CHAPTER **7**

Enhancing
Meaning & Voice with
SENTENCE FLUENCY

Often when we speak, our ideas fly out half formed, in scattered confessions and pronouncements, in tattered repartee. It is in writing that we have the time and place to shape our sentences and see what we really think, taking ourselves as well as our readers by surprise or storm.

CONSTANCE HALE
Sin and Syntax, 2001, Foreword

Powerful writing includes sparkling details, apt metaphors, surprises, and restraint. It has tones and rhythms that change like those of a symphony. The best writing causes readers' breathing to change.

MARY PIPHER
Writing to Change the World, 2006, 104

Fluent writing makes for easy reading. It's the writing we notice, remember, record, and recite.

Because fluency is all about rhythm and flow, reading aloud is essential to understanding and scoring this trait. You must *hear* the writing—put it in motion. Where does the reader's voice rise? Where do the beats fall? Is repetition purposeful and dramatic, or does it strike the ear like a wrong note? In most instances variety is the soul of fluency. Variety in length. Variety in beginnings. Variety in structure. Sometimes, though, as in the example I have just created, repetition reinforces a key word or idea. Listen. Your ear will tell you the difference: "It was the best of times, it was the worst of times, it was the age of wisdom, it was the age of foolishness, it was the epoch of disbelief, it was the epoch of incredulity, it was the season of light, it was the season of darkness, it was the spring of hope, it was the winter of despair . . ." (Charles Dickens, *A Tale of Two Cities*, 1859, 1).

Fluency is different from grammatical correctness, although a sense of syntax can definitely give fluency a boost. A piece may be quite correct, however, and have very little fluency at all: *It turned cloudy. Then it rained. We got soaked. We headed inside. The fire warmed us.* This is a very bumpy ride—but we can readily smooth it out with connecting phrases that carry us from thought to thought: *Suddenly, it turned cloudy and began to rain. The next thing we knew, we were soaked. Grabbing our things, we headed in to the warmth of the fire.*

Now we see that while the sentences in the first example are short, shortness is not their problem. The problem is their relentless, choppy, stuck-in-a-rut rhythm. Short *can* work. So can fragments. Even run-ons used with skill to echo human thought may sound like the familiar drifty musings in our own heads. We like that. Sometimes. That's why we need to listen attentively and judge fluency case by case.

How Can I Tell If the Real Problem Is with Conventions—or Fluency?

Think about how the two are connected. In the hands of a skilled writer, punctuation shows us where to pause and what to emphasize. Unfortunately, many students *hear* fluent sentences in their heads, but never put in the punctuation that could help us hear that fluency, too. So try this: When assessing fluency, read for rhythm and flow, and mentally *fill in* missing punctuation to see if that is the *only* problem. If that light mental editing puts everything in order, the real problem is with *conventions*. Capitals and periods alone will not solve problems caused by choppy sentences, repetitive structure,

Create a sound that pleases the reader's ear. Don't just write words. Write music.

—Gary Provost
100 Ways to Improve Your Writing,
1985, 61

or awkward construction, however. If rewriting is needed, there are problems with fluency *and* conventions.

SENTENCE FLUENCY: Rhythm and Readability

A Definition

Fluency makes writing dance. More than any other trait, sentence fluency separates readable writing from writing we must work to process. Writers achieve fluency in the same way we come to appreciate it—by reading aloud. Good writers will listen carefully to the beat, playing with wording to get the rhythm *just right.* Three things mark fluent writing. It's easy to read with expressiveness and voice. It's immediately understandable. And it's marked by variety in sentence length, style, and structure. Of course, there are countless exceptions. Fluency is as personal as voice itself, and the most fluent writers tend to bend the rules—occasionally. Little syntactical nuances, such as well-placed fragments, parallel structure, purposeful repetition, or alliteration may add significantly to fluency. And while these are not essentials—and you won't find them on most rubrics—they are most certainly worth pointing out as you and your students explore great literature. Like all traits, fluency varies with genre. In narrative or memoir, sentences may be long and languid, gradually unfolding meaning. Poetry may rely on fragments, phrases, even single words. In a technical piece, sentences are usually complete, but short and direct, carrying only one significant informational tidbit apiece. But readability and rhythm remain constant, from genre to genre.

Share my definition, and define sentence fluency in your own words as well. Ask students what *they* think makes sentences readable: length, word order, sensibility, rhythm, or other feature(s). Begin a search for fluent sentences—the most readable ones you can find. Collect them, read them, post them, and imitate them.

Share the Student Writing Guide for Sentence Fluency shown in Figure 7.1. Give students time to look over the guide, and ask them to think about sentences not just in terms of grammar, but also sound. The teacher version, for your use in assessing writing, appears in Figure 7.2. See the "trait shortie" for sentence fluency (Figure 7.3) for a quick summary of features to look for or teach.

Warming Up with Literature

As you look for fluent samples, keep an open mind. Don't discount a piece that contains fragments, or even run-on sentences. Think about context. Ask, *Does this work? How does it sound when read aloud?* Here are a few things to look and listen for as you assemble your collection:

- Phrasing so clear that meaning seems to pop, corklike, into view
- Writing so easy to read you don't have to think about it—or rehearse
- Writing that makes you "tune in"—like a good song on the radio
- Sentences that are clear on the first pass—no rereading required
- Writing that sounds rhythmic and graceful
- Writing that defies rules—and works
- Effective repetition, use of fragments or run-ons, or other stylistic strategy
- Writing you read aloud, remember, or quote

I let Gary Paulsen *show* my students about active verbs and short sentences. I let Patricia MacLachlan *show* my students how to make phrases tumble off the ends of their sentences.

—Jeff Anderson
Mechanically Inclined, 2005, 16

FIGURE 7.1

Student Writing Guide for
SENTENCE FLUENCY

6
- ❑ This is easy and fun to read aloud.
- ❑ Some sentences are almost poetic.
- ❑ Sentence variety adds voice to this piece.
- ❑ Repetition or fragments (if used) are effective.
- ❑ My sentences make meaning clear at once.

5
- ❑ You can read this easily even on the first try.
- ❑ I like the sound when I read it aloud.
- ❑ You will notice a lot of sentence variety.
- ❑ Repetition or fragments (if used) work.
- ❑ My sentences are clear and understandable.

4
- ❑ You can read this aloud without much practice.
- ❑ I like the sound in certain parts.
- ❑ I have *some* variety in my sentences.
- ❑ If I did use fragments or repeat words, it's not a problem.
- ❑ My sentences make sense.

3
- ❑ If you pay attention and practice, you can read this.
- ❑ Sometimes it's hard to see how I got from one sentence to another.
- ❑ Many sentences are the same length—or begin the same way.
- ❑ Some sentences could be combined or revised.
- ❑ My sentences are not *all* clear or logical.

2
- ❑ Even with practice, this could be hard to read aloud.
- ❑ I need to rewrite *many* of these sentences.
- ❑ Most of my sentences seem to all sound alike.
- ❑ Sentence problems interrupt the "flow."
- ❑ You might have to stop and think—or read things twice.

1
- ❑ You might need to fill in words—or revise as you read.
- ❑ *Most* sentences need work.
- ❑ It's hard to tell where my sentences begin and end.
- ❑ Sentence problems will make you pause or go back.
- ❑ Sometimes, you can't tell what a sentence means.
- ❑ I need help revising for fluency.

© 2012. Vicki Spandel. Designed for use in classroom assessment.

JUST A TASTE . . .

Following are just a few examples of fluent writing. Encourage your writers to look for their own favorite sentences or passages—and to add them to their writing journals.

Sample 1

In the classic *A Child's Christmas in Wales* (1993, unpaginated), poet Dylan Thomas shows us how to stretch a sentence out seemingly forever, making us wander through many subordinate clauses before arriving at the much-anticipated subject-verb punch at the very end:

> Years and years and years ago, when I was a boy, when there were wolves in Wales, and birds the colour of red-flannel petticoats whisked past the harp-shaped hills, when we sang and wallowed all night and day in caves that smelt like Sunday afternoons in damp front farmhouse parlours and we chased, with the jawbones of deacons, the English and the bears, before the motor-car, before the wheel, before the duchess-faced horse, when we rode the daft and happy hills bareback, it snowed and it snowed.

Author's Note

My friend and colleague Jeff Anderson—whose wonderful book *Mechanically Inclined* is quoted here—calls himself a "sentence stalker." He saves favorite sentences, not just to read, but to have his students imitate. His book contains many of his favorites. For some of mine, see page 217.

FIGURE 7.2

Teacher Writing Guide for
SENTENCE FLUENCY

6
- ❏ Easy to read with inflection that brings out voice
- ❏ Rhythm you want to imitate—poetic, musical
- ❏ Striking variety in sentence style, structure, length
- ❏ Fragments or repetition are rhetorically effective
- ❏ Strong sentences make meaning instantly clear

5
- ❏ Readable even on the first try
- ❏ Easy-on-the-ear rhythm, cadence, flow
- ❏ Variety in sentence style, structure, length
- ❏ Fragments or repetition add emphasis
- ❏ Readily understandable

4
- ❏ Readable with minimal rehearsal
- ❏ Pleasant, rhythmic flow dominates
- ❏ Some sentence variety
- ❏ Fragments or repetition are not a problem
- ❏ Sentences are clear and connected

3
- ❏ Readable with rehearsal and close attention
- ❏ Sentence-to-sentence flow needs work
- ❏ More sentence variety needed
- ❏ A few moments cry out for revision
- ❏ Sentences not always clear at first

2
- ❏ Hard to read in spots, even with rehearsal
- ❏ Many sentences need rewording
- ❏ Minimal variety in length or structure
- ❏ Problems (choppiness, run-ons) disrupt the flow
- ❏ Reader must pause or reread to get the meaning

1
- ❏ Reader must pause or fill in to read this aloud
- ❏ Many sentences need rewording
- ❏ Hard to tell where sentences begin or end
- ❏ Sentence problems may block meaning
- ❏ Writer needs help revising sentences

Sample 2

We often think of sentence fluency as supporting meaning and voice, but it supports organization as well—particularly the coherence within paragraphs. This only occurs, of course, when sentences are carefully connected with transitional words that build bridges from thought to thought. One writer who is particularly good at this—in fact, I'm not sure he can write *without* doing it—is Sneed Collard. The following example from the nonfiction book *Reign of the Sea Dragons* (2008, 38) is excellent for illustrating purposeful beginnings that make each sentence sound as if it glides right out of the one before:

> Today's fish, turtles, and marine mammals often exhibit countershading. Their top, or dorsal, surfaces are dark, while their bottom, or ventral, surfaces are pale. This camouflages these animals from above and below. When viewed from above, the top surface of a countershaded animal blends in with the darker waters around it. When seen from below, the pale ventral surface blends in with the bright light coming down from the water's surface.

Sample 3

Some authors, like Gary Paulsen or Sandra Cisneros, can make repetition work like a haunting echo. But most of the time, the mind craves variety. For excellent examples of varied length *and* structure, check any page of Avi's delightful novel *Ragweed*, the story of an intrepid country mouse who leaves home seeking adventure (1999, 23):

> All that night the freight train carrying Ragweed rumbled on. He was too excited to sleep. Instead, he remained by the open door and watched the passing scene. And pass it did. One rapid vision after another flashed before his eager eyes. No sooner did he see something of great interest—barely grasping what it was, than it vanished, to be replaced by something just as new, just as fascinating. The one constant was the moon, which remained in the night sky like an old friend.

Long sentences—I sometimes call them journey sentences—create a flow that carries the reader down a stream of understanding, an effect that Don Fry calls "steady advance." A short sentence slams on the brakes.

—Roy Peter Clark
Writing Tools, 2008, 88

FIGURE 7.3

Trait "Shortie" for SENTENCE FLUENCY

Use this summary as a poster—and have students add to it!

Keys to . . . SENTENCE FLUENCY
Rhythm and Flow

- Sentences are clear and make sense.
- They begin in different ways.
- The piece sounds rhythmic and fluent when read aloud.
- Purposeful beginnings create a sentence-to-sentence flow.
- Sentences range from short to long.
- Repetition, run-ons, or fragments—if used—work.
- The writing is easy to read—even on the first try.
- The writer may use any of these to add variety: questions, exclamations, monologue, dialogue.

© 2012. Vicki Spandel.

USING A WHOLE BOOK

Following are several books you might choose to share in their entirety, or from which you might choose multiple passages that show a writer's flexibility.

Sample 1

The House on Mango Street by Sandra Cisneros. 1991. New York: Vintage Books.
Ages: Upper elementary and older.
Genre: Fictional memoir

Summary

Cisneros—whose name is almost synonymous with fluency—assumes the voice of young Esperanza Cordero, relating in prose and verse the realities of coming of age in the Hispanic quarter of Chicago. Short chapters shift in mood from haunting to witty, comic, nostalgic, and thoughtful, as Cisneros explores issues of friendship, family, love, alienation, and more.

Suggestions for Discussion and Writing

1. Check www.sandracisneros.com for a short bio of this writer to share in its entirety or in part with your students.
2. After previewing *The House on Mango Street*, select chapters to share aloud. As you share, talk about the images the writing invokes—and the overall sound of the text. What makes this writing fluent?

Author's Note

The chapter "Hairs" from *The House on Mango Street* is available as a picture book: *Hairs/Pelitos* (1997, Dragonfly Books). Beautifully illustrated, this book (like the chapter on which it is based) provides a poetic exploration of the beauty of diversity.

3. Have volunteers choose favorite chapters or passages to share aloud with the class, or use writing circles in which each reader takes one paragraph. Be sure to allow time for rehearsal. The chapter called "A Smart Cookie" lends itself to sharing in two voices. "Four Skinny Trees" is especially good for multi-voiced choral reading.

4. Cisneros is known for her ability to capture human speech authentically. Have students try creating authentic speech of their own. Suggest they begin by listening to people talk: in the lunchroom, on the bus, at the park, on the street, in a shopping mall. Discuss how human speech sounds—it does not always occur in full sentences. Then have students write. Share the voices aloud and talk about the kinds of "sentences" used to create them.

Sample 2

Just the Right Size: Why Big Animals Are Big and Little Animals Are Little. 2009. Nicola Davies. Illustrations by Neal Layton. Cambridge, MA: Candlewick Press.
Ages: Elementary through middle school
Genre: Informational

Summary

In a comically illustrated, highly readable text, Nicola Davies explains why King Kong is a myth, why geckos can walk upside down across ceilings (while we cannot), why ants and rhinoceros beetles can lift things many times their own weight (while we cannot)—and much more based on the enlightening BTLT (Big Thing Little Thing) rule.

Suggestions for Discussion and Writing

1. How many of your students have read stories or seen films where animals grow to unimaginable, grotesque sizes? Have they ever thought this might be possible? Explain that this book explores this very issue.

2. Share the first few chapters—or the whole book. As you begin, notice the lead on page 7. Is it effective? Why?

3. Do your students agree that Davies writes in a clear manner? Talk about specific strategies she uses to make her writing clear.

4. Think about presentation. Notice that the book is divided so that most chapters (the second is an exception) only take up one or two pages. Is this effective? Why? Also pay attention to the illustrations. Do your students like them? What makes them appealing?

5. Have your students apply the BTLT (Big Thing, Little Thing) rule to explain the behaviors, habits, or limitations of any creature with which they are familiar.

Sample 3

Hatchet, 20th Anniversary Edition. 2007. Illustrated by Drew Willis. New York: Simon and Schuster.
Ages: Upper elementary through middle school
Genre: Fiction

Summary

Gary Paulsen's classic book gets a facelift in this anniversary edition that includes beautiful sketches by Drew Willis and journalistic notes (artistically rendered) by the author. These notes take readers behind the scenes, explaining the author's thinking or sources for information. And when it comes to sentence fluency, Paulsen can do it *all:* variety, long and short, effective fragments, dialogue, monologue, parallel construction—even effective run-ons.

Suggestions for Discussion or Writing

1. How many of your writers have read the original *Hatchet?* What do they remember about it? Some may also be familiar with Gary Paulsen's other books, including *Brian's Return, Woods Runner, Lawn Boy, Tracker, Guts, Woodsong, My Life in Dog Years, Notes from the Dog, The Winter Room, The Rifle, Harris and Me*, and many more.

2. You may or may not decide to share the whole book. It is an excellent read-aloud, and if you and your students love it, go for it. As you share, have a document camera available, if possible, so you can pause to enjoy the journal entries and illustrations.

3. Ask students to identify sentences they find particularly effective. What are some of the strategies Paulsen uses to make his writing so fluent?

4. Have students write a short piece on any topic—either narrative or expository—then include one brief journalistic note commenting on some aspect of the writing: where the idea came from, how they learned what they had to know to write the piece, or any interesting tidbit that didn't fit into the main copy. Talk about ways of "presenting" such notes to give them eye appeal.

The foolbirds. If I never eat another grouse—if I never SEE another grouse, I'll be glad. I ate so many when I was dead broke and living in the woods that I swear sometimes I still spit feathers.

—Gary Paulsen
Hatchet (Journal Entry on Foolbirds), 2007, 140

OTHER BOOKS WITH LYRICAL SENTENCE FLUENCY

The Adventures of Marco Polo by Russell Freedman. 2006. New York: Scholastic. Picture book history.

Lavish illustrations and parchment-like pages make this a book as beautiful to scan as it is to read. Freedman does wonders with long sentences, never sacrificing clarity, never creating a sense of wordiness: "With no trace of vegetation in sight, they built glowing campfires of dry camel dung at night and ate their evening meal under the stars as the hobbled camels, grunting and grumbling, grazed nearby" (19). An excellent book for stretching students' reading and writing abilities. Middle school and beyond (younger if read aloud in small sections).

Bat Loves the Night by Nicola Davies. 2004. Cambridge, MA: Candlewick Press. Picture book.

This is a terrific little book for teaching truly interesting sentence structures, such as opening with a participle: "Gliding and fluttering back and forth . . ." (15). Or opening with prepositional phrases: "Over bushes, under trees . . ." (12). Suddenly sentences are fascinating and filled with possibilities. All ages; directed at primary.

A Christmas Memory, One Christmas, & the Thanksgiving Visitor by Truman Capote. 1996. New York: The Modern Library. Memoir.

This book is a treasure trove of syntactical gems: "The one we pick is twice as tall as me. A brave handsome brute that survives thirty hatchet strokes before it keels with a creaking rending cry. Lugging it like a kill, we commence the long trek out" (20). Also look for incredible word choice, imagery, and voice. High school and adult (middle school for skilled readers).

The Curious Garden by Peter Brown. 2009. New York: Little, Brown and Company. Picture book.

Beautifully written story of a well-tended garden that grew to fill a city—and a boy's heart. This text has more sentence variety and complexity than you will find in most books directed at very young readers. Primary through early elementary.

We were not taught to learn to write from writers . . . No one ever said to us, "Hey, you could try and write *like* Robert Frost if you want." . . . . So learning how to write from writers is a fairly new concept in many classrooms. Not surprisingly, however, it isn't at all new to professional writers.

—Katie Wood Ray
Wondrous Words, 1999, 11

Author's Note

If you teach older writers, don't overlook books like *Bat Loves the Night* or *The Curious Garden.* Even though your students may be beyond the storylines or content, these books provide strikingly clear illustrations of sentence structures that older writers—even adults—will benefit from imitating.

Dark Emperor & Other Poems of the Night **by Joyce Sidman. Illustrated by Rick Allen. 2010. Boston: Houghton Mifflin Harcourt. Poetry combined with nonfiction prose.**

Welcome to the night! Again, Sidman shows her skill in spanning genres, this time writing about creatures of the night (bats, raccoons, snails, great-horned owls, crickets, and others) both in multi-form poetry and in her signature short informational essays. The unusual illustrations combine linoleum cuts (prints made from pre-cut blocks) with watercolor (gouache) painting. As beautiful as it is educational. All ages.

A Frog Thing **by Eric Drachman. Illustrated by James Muscarello. 2005. Los Angeles: Kidwick Books. Picture book.**

More than anything, Frank wants to fly. The problem is . . . he's a frog. And flying is not, well, a frog thing. Everyone is laughing, but Frank is determined—and brave. Sentence fluency in this book is inventive. See how it works with conventions (full capitals, ellipsis, quotation marks) to help us read with inflection. Excellent dialogue. Primary through early elementary.

Heartbeat **by Sharon Creech. 2004. New York: HarperCollins. Poetry in the form of a novel.**

Twelve-year-old Annie loves to run. And as she runs, she feels and hears her heart beat: thump-thump. She feels and hears her feet hit the ground: thump-thump. As she runs, she can think—about Moody Max, her running friend; about Grandpa, who seems to forget more and more; about her mother, who has a baby coming; about Mrs. Freely, who wants the class to draw the same apple EVERY DAY for 100 days! These are the rhythms of Annie's life, and the poetry of Sharon Creech weaves them all together, brilliantly. Upper elementary through middle school.

Hoops **by Robert Burleigh. 2001. Orlando, FL: Harcourt, Brace and Company. Poetic narrative.**

Many students fall in love with the catchy rhythm of this book and want to hear it again and again. It captures the very spirit of basketball—you will hear the ball hit the net, pound the court. You will feel the pivots and turns. After reading once or twice, let students move with the text as you read. You can feel this one in your bones. All ages. (Reading level is elementary.)

Jimi: Sounds Like a Rainbow (A Story of the Young Jimi Hendrix) **by Gary Golio. Illustrated by Javaka Steptoe. 2010. Boston: Houghton Mifflin Harcourt. Nonfiction narrative.**

"Electricity ripped through the air. A lightning flash lit up the room. Thunder rocked the house" (4). So begins a fluent, poetic, and compassionate tribute to a man many fans consider the greatest electric guitar player of all time. The author, a clinical social worker, focuses on the earliest years of Jimi's life, and the musical forces that influenced his artistic development. Brilliantly illustrated—the sentences dip and curve to show off their rhythm. All ages.

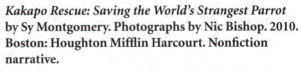

Kakapo Rescue: Saving the World's Strangest Parrot **by Sy Montgomery. Photographs by Nic Bishop. 2010. Boston: Houghton Mifflin Harcourt. Nonfiction narrative.**

As in all her books, Sy Montgomery's readable prose invites readers right into the conversation: "Imagine shaking the trunk of a sapling and finding giant parrots falling to the ground like apples!" (5). This is a captivating subject, clearly and entertainingly presented. Nic Bishop's remarkable photos show presentation at its finest. Middle school and up. (All ages if shared aloud.)

The Little Yellow Leaf **by Carin Berger. 2008. New York: Greenwillow Books. Free verse poetry.**

From award-winning illustrator and writer Carin Berger comes the story of one timid yellow leaf who cannot bear to leave the tree until he gets the right motivation. A terrific story for anyone who's had to drum up the courage to do something difficult. Beautiful illustrations include subtle suggestions that trees already hold words. All ages, though aimed at primary.

Looking Like Me **by Walter Dean Myers. Illustrated by Christopher Myers. 2009. New York: Egmont USA. Poetry.**

In playful, rhythmic verbal jazz, Walter Dean Myers spins out the identity of Jeremy, who is brother, son, writer, artist, dancer, dreamer—and more. This book invites imitation as students explore their own identities. All ages.

Maya Angelou: Poetry for Young People **edited by Edwin Graves Wilson, Ph.D. Illustrated by Jerome Lagarrigue. 2007. Toronto: Sterling Publishing. Poetry.**

Angelou's poems, some rhyming, some not, are filled with language and imagery that springs from her expansive knowledge of and passion for black history, as well as her own personal history as a singer, dancer, actor, writer, public speaker, and poet. Share one or two poems or the whole collection. Invite students to read aloud as well. These poems cry out to be read with all the passion the poet poured into them. Young adult and adult.

Author's Note

The *Poetry for Young People* series also includes collections by William Blake, Lewis Carroll, Emily Dickinson, Robert Frost, Langston Hughes, Carl Sandburg, William Shakespeare, Walt Whitman, William Carlos Williams, William Butler Yeats, and others.

My Man Blue **by Nikki Grimes. Pictures by Jerome Lagarrigue. 1999. New York: Dial Books. Narrative in poetic verse.**

Nikki Grimes' rhythmic verse tells the story of friendship between Blue, a man who has lost his son, and a young man Damon, whose father has left home. A story of the streets emerges as a tribute to friendship and trust. All ages.

Okay for Now **by Gary D. Schmidt. 2011. New York: Houghton Mifflin Harcourt. Young adult novel.**

Doug Swieteck (who first appeared in Newberry Honor book *The Wednesday Wars*) returns in rare form to juggle the challenges of life in the tiny town of Marysville: an abusive father, accusations of theft, a badly injured brother returning from Vietnam, a school filled with teachers and students who have little time for him, and the surprising discovery that he has a profound artistic gift. Schmidt uses stream-of-consciousness (with multiple run-ons) to create the feeling of thoughts piling atop one another in Doug's mind. Upper elementary to middle school.

The Old Man and the Sea **by Ernest Hemingway. [1952] 1980. New York: Scribner. Fiction.**

The timeless story of the old man who sets out to catch a great fish and winds up in the battle of his life. The first few pages provide countless lessons in how to express deep ideas in the most straightforward sentences—like this one: "The old man had taught the boy to fish and the boy loved him" (10). Notice the combined grace and simplicity; few words have more than one or two syllables. Hemingway writes striking dialogue—most of it in full sentences. It's edgy, but highly distinctive. Middle school and beyond.

Peter and the Starcatchers **by Dave Barry and Ridley Pearson. Illustrations by Greg Call. 2005. New York: Hyperion. Novel.**

This prequel to the classic Peter Pan story is filled with adventure, vivid imagery, a motley crew of pirates, and wonderfully crafted sentences—like this terrific example of parallel construction: "Molly saw it all, from under the palms: saw the pirates in trouble, saw Slank gloating in triumph; saw the trunk" (378). High interest. Expect to find numerous enticing sentences for writers to imitate. Upper elementary through middle school.

Author's Note

Add your own choices to this list, remembering to spend time reading aloud—and having students do the same—and looking for beautifully written or interesting sentences to imitate.

Assessing Writing Samples for SENTENCE FLUENCY

As you read the following pieces aloud, ask yourself if the writer makes reading easy for you—and if so, how. Listen to where your voice rises and falls. Notice sentence beginnings and endings—and the little words and phrases (*however, The next day, After a while*) that link one thought to another. Also listen for patterns—and any rule-breaking nuances you find irresistible. Nothing's off limits if it works.

Paper 1

The Closet Monster (Fiction, Grade 3)

Hi, I'm Michael. I'm looking for what I call the closet monster.

I'm looking for the closet monster because last night around midnight I woke up from a rattling sound coming from my closet. I went over to check out what it was. I opened the closet door and nothing was there. I thought to myself it must of just been the wind. When I went back to get into my bed I saw a gigantic shadow move swiftly across my room. Then I was mabey thinking I had someone or something in my room that wasn't supposed to be here, and I had to get out of my room and quick because it was giving me the creeps. I stayed up looking around for whatever was in my room. Just then there was another rattling sound coming from the closet again. I creeped over to the closet and nothing was there. CRASH! My lamp came down on the other side of the room. Right after the lamp came crashing down I caught a glimpse of something scurry under my bed. My knees were trembling as I slowly crept over and nelt down in front. I pulled up the bed skirt and looked underneath and there was something furry with big, black, round eyes. I jumped back in shock. My heart beat was going 10 times it's normal rate.

To be continued . . .

What was under Michael's bed? Will Michael ever get it out of his room? Tune in next time for The Closet Monster.

Suggested Score for SENTENCE FLUENCY: 4

Lessons Learned from "A Closet Monster"

- Though purposeful repetition can be effective, you don't want too many sentences to begin the same way (with "I," for instance).
- There's usually no need to introduce yourself in the first line. Get right into the story.
- A "to be continued" story can work if it stops at the right spot. (This one does.)

Comments

This writer loves mysteries—both reading and writing them. He does a good job of including details to provoke our curiosity and anxiety: rattling sounds and spooky shadows. He also builds very carefully to the high point: the "big, black, round eyes" under the

---

The Write Connection

The Closet Monster

Where does this piece really begin? Read carefully and slowly until you come to the strongest possible opening moment. (Does the writer need "Hi, I'm Michael"?) Notice how many sentences begin with "I"—or a phrase including "I." Highlight those and revise to keep the "I's" to a minimum. Consider recording the revision as a podcast. Mysteries are meant to be *heard.* (Don't forget the sound effects.)

bed. This shows real organizational skill. The fluency is far stronger in the second half of the paper. We're treated to some variety in length and sentence beginnings: *CRASH! My lamp came down. . . . Right after . . . My knees were trembling . . .* In terms of fluency, this is the strongest writing in the piece. The first part plays with our imagination a bit—is the monster real or is it just the wind? This is highly effective, although the whole first half could be condensed. Still, this is a third grade writer, not Edgar Allan Poe (yet).

Suggested Scores for Other Traits

Ideas: **5**

Organization: **5**

Voice: **5**

Word choice: 4

Conventions & presentation: **4**
(Although conventions are not troublesome in this piece, there are a few spelling errors, some missing commas, and a noticeable absence of paragraphs.)

Paper 2

The Big Road (Narrative, Grade 7)

From the moment my sister got her license, I knew there would be interesting and dangerous adventures ahead. Whenever there was anywhere to go, Jessica always volunteered for the job. She went here and there and everywhere. What a pro. She liked to go to the store and pick up dinner. She would do anything. She went to the gas station, the cleaners, the mall. Naturally, when it was time to go to my baseball game, Jessica volunteered without hesitation.

Obviously, after being driven everywhere by my parents my whole life, I was a little apprehensive about being driven to a big game by someone who was fairly inexperienced. I told my parents I wouldn't feel safe, but they didn't think anything of letting Jessica drive with me in the car. Was my life worth so little?

While I put my baseball uniform on, Jessica gathered all of the things that she likes to take with her whenever she drives: her coffee cup from Starbuck's, her sunglasses, and her favorite Beatles CDs. We both got into the car. I buckled up and pulled the thing snug, wondering if the airbags worked. Jessica started the car and jolted back out of the driveway. She seemed to drive well without speeding. As we pulled out of the neighborhood, Jessica popped in a CD and we headed toward the field. I began to relax.

After a few minutes I noticed that Jessica had picked up the habit of yelling at drivers who tailgated or drove too slow. It was pretty funny to hear her ask the other drivers if that piece of #@#$!! had a gas peddle.

We got to the field safely and I had a great game. I was a little nervous about the trip home even after being driven safely to the field. After all, it would be dark by the time the game was over. "What if she can't see in the dark?" I thought. "But what can I do? I don't want to walk home with all of my gear."

The game ended and she pulled up to the walk and I hopped in the car. The stars were bright in the cloudless sky. Jessica turned on the signal to pull out of the field parking lot. She started her turn and pulled out. "Oh God!", I yelled. A car was tearing right for us. Jessica hit the gas and we lurched to safety. "That was close," she said. "It sure was," I said back.

Read the first sentence of the last paragraph aloud. Do you hear too many *and's*? If so, rewrite this sentence (making more than one sentence if you wish) to make it smoother. Look for any other sentences that are not quite as fluent as your ear tells you they should be. Highlight those—and revise each one. Finally—think about that ending. If you feel it should be stronger, revise it to make the writer's attitude toward his sister and her driving more clear.

Suggested Score for SENTENCE FLUENCY: 5

Lessons Learned from "The Big Road"

- A sudden short sentence like "What a pro" adds punch.
- Transitional phrases—*Naturally, Obviously, While I put my baseball uniform on, After a few minutes*—provide connections between ideas and smooth the sentence-to-sentence flow.
- Good pacing (notice how fast we pass over the "great game" in paragraph 5) keeps writing focused.
- Titles are important. (This one works.)
- A subtle ending is risky—some readers may hear it as a sudden stop.

Comments

So many students feel they have nothing to write about; here's a perfect example of an everyday event turned into a delightful personal essay. It is easy to picture every part of this scenario, from Jessica gathering her traveling paraphernalia to the writer wondering whether the airbags will deploy. Personally, I like the ending very much, but some readers feel the piece stops abruptly. I read the writer's last comment as veiled sarcasm. I think he is saying, "I'm calm through it all." He's also implying (maybe I'm reading in) that this is but the first of many harrowing trips, and he must resign himself: It's either travel with Jessica or walk.

Suggested Scores for Other Traits

Ideas: **5**

Organization: **5**
  (I have no trouble with a 6—but it depends on how you read the ending.)

Voice: **6**

Word choice: **5**

Conventions & presentation: **4**
  (Some small errors—"peddle" and the double punctuation—may cause you to drop this score to a 5, but it's still a strong performance.)

Paper 3

Xeriscaping: A Plan for the Future (Argument, Grade 5)

Have you heard of xeriscaping? Don't worry. You will. It is a special way of planting. It is also a way of conserving water.

"Xeri" comes from a Greek word. The word is "xeros." It means dry. The x sounds like a z. Think of "zero". Like "zero water." (Not quite but just about.)

Xeriscaping is the best way of landscaping. You could call it essential. Everyone should do it. We are running out of potable water. Potable means you can drink it. We have to conserve. If we don't, even more people will not have water to drink.

There are many ways to save water. Maybe you do some of them. You can take showers instead of baths. You can also take short showers! Don't wash your car too often. Use appliances (like washing machines) that are easy on water.

(continued on following page)

It's good to do all these things. But they are not enough. Most of the water we use goes to watering our lawns or golf courses. If we didn't do that, we could save a LOT of water. We could save thousands of gallons a month for the average person. You're probably thinking, oh great. Now we have to have concrete yards. No!

We can still have plants. Just not any old plants. We need plants that don't get thirsty every five minutes. This is where xeriscaping comes in. It works like this.

First, think about a yard without grass. Grass takes more water than anything. You could have fake grass. You could also have gravel. You could have a big deck. Second, plan to have only a few shrubs. Choose shrubs that need only a little water. Examples are yucca, cactus, wild grass, wild flowers, and sage. Don't plant shrubs in the sun unless you know they can take it. If you do, they will need more water. Watch the light in your yard for a few days. You will find out where the sunny spots are. Third, decorate with other things. You could use rocks. You could also put in benches or pieces of art.

Xeriscaping has many benefits. You will save money on your water bill. But that's only one thing! Your yard will not need as much care. This means you can spend your time doing other things. You can leave town and not think your yard will die. That's a relief. You will also be helping the planet. Here's another thing you can do. If you have drain spouts, connect them to a rain barrel. When it rains, you can collect a lot of water. You could collect up to a thousand gallons a month. That might be all you need. Especially if you use xeriscaping!!

Some people say xeriscaping is not as beautiful as grass. That's because they are not used to it. It's artistic! We got used to grass. Now we can get used to something else. You can do it. Besides, xeriscaping or dying of thirst. Which do you choose? That's what I thought.

© 2012, Vicki Spandel

Suggested Score for SENTENCE FLUENCY: 4

Lessons Learned from "Xeriscaping: A Plan for the Future"

- Read what you write aloud so you can hear choppy moments and smooth them out.
- Specifics are important in persuasive writing, but you also need to back them up.

Comments

This writer is enthusiastic about his topic and makes many good points: xeriscaping is the most effective way to conserve water and it has benefits—low water bill, low maintenance, and the satisfying feeling of helping the planet. We also get tips for redesigning our yards to make them both attractive and carefree. But could we really save "thousands of gallons a month for the average person"? Without a reliable source, we're not sure. We also cannot be sure of collecting a thousand gallons a month in rain water. Won't this depend on where the reader lives? Will plants like the yucca or cactus grow in non-desert climates? Clearly, we have some unanswered questions. On the positive side, though, the writer offers multiple reasons for accepting his argument, and also addresses potential objections.

The Write Connection

Xeriscaping:
A Plan for the Future

Here's a piece that could benefit enormously from sentence combining. Divide it into 4 or 5 segments, and have students work (in teams of two) on just one of those parts to see if they can take the text from bumpy to smooth by (1) combining sentences, (2) varying beginnings, and (3) changing wording. Read the original and revised version aloud, side by side.

Suggested Scores for Other Traits

Ideas: **4**

Organization: **4**

Voice: **5**

Word choice: **4/5**

Conventions & presentation: **5**

Paper 4

The Ritual of Rocks and Sticks
(Imaginative/Narrative, Grade 6)

While visiting America I had the opportunity to attend a ritual called the baseball game. In this ritual, an enormous crowd of people gather around, sitting on multi-leveled seats, watching a crowd of people perform.

The performers of the ritual are dressed in striped clothes similar to a zebra. They have pieces of cowhide tied to one hand, and they beat the cowhide with their free hand and make loud grunting noises. Sometimes they spit, and everyone seems to enjoy this part. Their heads are covered in bright colored cloth, which they touch quite often, sometimes running their hands along the front part of the cloth, which hangs over their eyes. When one does this, other performers nod and slap the cowhide hard. Clearly, this is a significant part of the ritual.

The performer in the middle of the flat area is known as the pitcher. He stands on a small hill and throws a hard ball of string at another performer, who holds a long stick. The stick man, also known as a batter, tries to hit the ball of string. If he succeeds, he immediately drops his stick and runs in a huge circle, touching white squares as he passes. The people dressed in stripes run after the ball of string, and then go after the stick man, tossing the ball of string hard as they go. They rarely catch him, but if they do, he yanks the cloth from his head and whacks his leg with it, giving out a mighty yell. The crowd yells with him. This much I have figured out: Once the stick man hits the ball of string, he does not want it back. He is very unhappy if the other performers return it to him.

This hitting and running part of the ritual is performed many times until both the performers and the people in the multi-leveled seats grow tired. As they go, they make more grunting noises and hit one another on the back quite a lot. This means the ritual is over for that day. But they will hold it again. They always take their balls of string and their sticks with them to be ready for the next time.

The Write Connection

The Ritual of Rocks and Sticks

Imagine viewing something familiar for the very first time—the way this visitor to America views baseball. Create a one-paragraph description with vivid images, sensory details, and varying sentences, relaying how the event would look from a newcomer's perspective.

Suggested Score for SENTENCE FLUENCY: 6

Lessons Learned from "The Ritual of Rocks and Sticks"

- Understatement can be effective.
- Readers love figuring things out on their own; just be sure you provide good clues. (This writer does.)

- We know the baseballs are the "rocks" (see the title), but it would help to make this clear in the text itself (where the phrase "ball of string" is substituted). Consistency matters.
- Adopting the perspective of someone else can be a way of achieving strong voice.

Comments

How might the game of baseball look to someone seeing it for the first time? This is the premise of this understated but strong piece. You really must hear it to appreciate the fluency. Connecting words—*While visiting, Sometimes, When one does this, Clearly*—make ideas easy to follow. Notice the variety in both sentence length and structure. This writer does something else careful readers will appreciate; he begins with present tense and *sticks with it*. What's more, the piece has a terrific deadpan voice. Fans will identify with various parts of the ritual—spitting, slapping the cowhide hard, and the wonderful line about the runner not wanting the hard ball of string back. The pacing is good; the writer provides sharp imagery but does not take us play by play through a whole game. We shift effortlessly from players to fans and back again. The language includes a number of lively verbs—*beat, spit, yank, nod, whack, slap*. But even within his adopted persona, this writer recognizes the psychological as well as physical aspect of the game. The rocks mutate into hard balls of string, but this is a minor point.

Suggested Scores for Other Traits

Ideas: **6**

Organization: **6**

Voice: **6**

Word choice: **5**

Conventions & presentation: **6**

> The art of sentence making comes down to variety. Just because you can do the three-and-a-half somersault tuck off the high board doesn't mean you must ditch the gorgeous swan dive.
>
> —Constance Hale
> *Sin and Syntax,* 2001, 188

Paper 5

Why I Write (Expository, Grade 7)

I write for no reason. If I'm forced to write, my pencil is my enemy, but if I'm bored in my room or a teacher won't stop talking and there's a piece of paper in front of me, a pencil is my best friend because in my opinion, writing passes the time better than any conversation.

I write to make people cry and talk to make people laugh because it's easier to make people laugh when you're in the moment than to write it in a story. Sadness is the greatest thing to write about because everybody has a different sense of humor, everybody has their opinion on who's interesting, but everybody knows what's sad: change and death.

I write because everyone thinks writing pieces will never be perfect, so they don't expect my stories to be. If you do sports everybody wants you to be the best, but with writing, they accept the fact that you don't have writing talent. They think that if you're not good at a sport, you can practice and be good. The same is true with writing, except no matter how many workshops you take, you may never have that certain edge it takes.

(continued on following page)

Paper 5 (continued)

I write to make people use the dictionary. I think it's one of the greatest books ever written and if I use the dictionary it will create a chain of using it: I look up a few words in the dictionary and use them in my story, the person that reads it looks them up, then they will probably show off their improved vocabulary to their friends, and their friends will want to know what the word is. It's all a process of making the world less idiotic.

I write because writing is like a thousand piece puzzle. There are almost a million ways to arrange the giant thing, but you have to carefully arrange it piece-by-piece, step-by-step. It seems like a never-ending process, some people think it is, but once you have done all of your trial and errors, your mistakes, and slip ups, you find yourself looking at a masterpiece.

I write to teach someone ignorant a lesson. Whether it's something about my life, life in general, or that I'm not a moron, they will learn something. When you read my stories, you might love it, hate it, or just want to shoot me for trying, but when you see the story, you will learn a thing or two about a thing or two.

Suggested Score for SENTENCE FLUENCY: 4/5

Lessons Learned from "Why I Write"

- A key phrase—such as *I write . . .*—can connect thoughts that might otherwise seem random.
- Insight (*Everybody knows what's sad: change and death.*) is one secret to voice.

Comments

One good way to assess the fluency of a piece (other than reading aloud) is to ask, "If I were the writer, would I change the wording or overall structure of any of these sentences?" Try that with your students—and ask yourself the same question. This is an interesting piece because overall, it's *highly* readable—yet it's still tempting to play with sentence structure. For example, paragraph 1 might begin this way: *I write for no reason. If I'm forced to write, my pencil is my enemy. But if I'm bored or a teacher won't stop talking—and there's a piece of paper in front of me—a pencil is my best friend.* The voice shifts from funny to philosophical—but it's always there, a driving force behind the writing. Word choice is sometimes very strong (*when you're in the moment, that certain edge, thousand piece puzzle*) and sometimes more routine (*one of the greatest books ever written, or that I'm not a moron*). Paragraph 3 is a puzzle since this writer *does* have the talent and the edge. Strong ideas. This piece makes us think.

Suggested Scores for Other Traits

Ideas: **6**

Organization: **5**

Voice: **5**

Word choice: **4**

Conventions & presentation: **5**

The Write Connection

Why I Write

Have students experiment with the sentence fluency in this piece by just asking, sentence by sentence, "Would I say this differently?" To make the task manageable, divide the piece up, having each student (or group) work on just *one paragraph.* Encourage them to revise, read aloud, then revise again. They can make a number of revisions in just 10 minutes. Ask for volunteers to read their revised paragraphs aloud, in the original order; then compare fluency in the before and after versions.

Paper 6

A Rescue (Narrative, Grade 4)

Once a bunch of my friends and I went to this old hounted house and I'm not talking about some amusement park thing or something like that but but this was a for real hounted house, but we couln't go in because we were too scared and my friend Robert kept making these jokes that made us laugh so hard we couldn't walk so we just kept talking about should we do it or not?.

So the next day we went back and this time we followed Robert into the front door and I was right behind him and I could hear him breathing in this kind of panting way and I toled him to keep quiet or he would wake up he gosts. So just then I saw something real creepy move in the corner of the kitchen and robert said Shhhh its only a stray cat but I said ha I don't think so buddy in a million years so I took off like a rocket from the moon and waited outside in the fog that was nice and creepy and then I saw the thing again and this time I knew it was too big for a cat so I ran back to the house to save my freniends. I grabed Robert by the hair and he let out this inormous shreek but I had to get him out of the monster's claws and I pulled and pulled and finally got him out of the house and he said what in the heck are you doing?? I had yanked some of his hair clean out of his head and he didn't like it much. I gues he didn't apreschiate beging saved from the gost so I took off for home to have dinner. And then had dinner and went to bed and that is the last time we went to that house, but me and Robert are still best friends as long as I don't pull his hair.

Suggested Score for SENTENCE FLUENCY: 2

Lessons Learned from "A Rescue"

- A good ghost story needs a stronger ending than heading home for dinner.
- Too many connectives—*and, but, then*—weaken fluency and make ideas hard to follow.

Comments

Stream-of-consciousness writing requires a light touch. If well done, it echoes human thought and can create the impression that things are happening so rapidly the writer can barely sort them out. When it's overdone, however, it creates the illusion that ideas are connected even when they're not—and this can be confusing. On the positive side, the writer seems to love his topic, and writes with enthusiasm and energy, producing quite a lot of voice. The ending would be stronger without the interruptive reference to going home for dinner. In addition, the introduction could be stronger if the writer set up the story by telling us more about the urban "legend" behind this haunted house. Where is it? How did it come to have this reputation? More imagery and sensory detail would also add to the power of the piece.

Try some stream-of-conscious-ness pieces of your own. Students should choose their own topics, but encourage them to focus on something with strong emotional engage-ment—as this writer did with the haunted house. This keeps the flow of thoughts going. Remind them that this style does *not* demand full sen-tences. Fragments or run-ons sound spontaneous and natu-ral, taking readers inside the writer's head. For several out-standing read-aloud examples, scan Chapter 1, "The Arctic Tern," from Gary D. Schmidt's *Okay for Now* (Houghton Mifflin Harcourt, 2011).

Suggested Scores for Other Traits

Ideas: **3**

Organization: **2**

Voice: **4**

Word choice: **4**

Conventions & presentation: **2/3**

Paper 7

Marco Polo (Imaginative Journal, Grade 4)

Dear Diary,

I'm standing on the deck of our ship, memorizing the beautiful church of San Marco, the pillars and the pink and yellow buildings lining the canals of Venice. Good-bye to the gondoliers! Good-bye to the crowds on the docks, my family, my friends. My Venetian world looks smaller and paler as we sail farther out to the sea.

I'm seventeen years old. Will I be twenty when I return? Who knows? Uncle Maffeo says we might never get home. Papa says of course we will, but to our eyes Venice will never look quite the same. I don't have to say good-bye to our Venetian lion, though. He waves on our flag, red and gold, proud, high up on our masts. A little bit of Venice will always be with all of us.

Without our papa and Uncle Maffeo with me, I might not sound so brave. But, we are the Polo family, and we are strong together. I turn my head to the gray ocean and don't look back again.

Our journey has begun.

Suggested Score for SENTENCE FLUENCY: 6

Lessons Learned from "Marco Polo"

- A strong sentence can make a paragraph all by itself.
- Forceful, direct writing makes for strong fluency.
- An occasional question (or a goodbye) is an effective way of adding variety.

Comments

Within a few lines, this deceptively simple paper creates a vivid world—not only the visual world of Venice, but also the world inside the mind of a seventeen-year-old explorer off to a new land. What does he feel? Pride, anticipation, apprehension, home-sickness, love, courage. Notice that the voice of the persona is much older than the actual writer. Also notice how much information the writer offers us in only a few words: "I turn my head to the gray ocean and don't look back again. Our journey has begun." Worlds of meaning rest in these poetic lines—and of course, we're filled with questions too, notably, Does this young man survive the journey? The vocabulary is striking; words are simple, but eloquent: *memorizing the beautiful church, world looks smaller and paler, to our eyes Venice will never look quite the same, we are strong together.* Strong fluency gives the piece a sophisticated sound—as if it had been written by an adult. Virtually *every sentence* has its own tone, texture, and style.

Suggested Scores for Other Traits

Ideas: **6**

Organization: **6**

Voice: **6**

Word choice: **6**

Conventions & presentation: **6**

The Write Connection

Marco Polo

Count the number of different ways this writer finds to begin sentences. Then, have students try imitating her varied style by writing another journal entry in the same voice: that of the young explorer journeying with the Polo family. Can they attain the same level of variety?

Paper 8

Call Me When You Get There (Expository, Grade 7)

If my parents had a motto, this would be it. I don't want to say they're worry warts or anything. But they need to know where I am at all times. ALL TIMES. As in EVERY MOMENT OF EVERY DAY. I don't have to phone from the bathroom or the back yard, but if they think of it, I will. And leaving the house is a very big deal. The second I reach for my coat, it starts. "Where are you going?" The last thing my mom says as I am leaving is, "Call me when you get there." She means the very minute I get there. Not after I've said hello or taken off my coat. No. The MINUTE. It's like she has this ESP and she knows the very second my foot hits the doorstep. If I don't phone, she will call *me*. No one wants that.

Don't get me wrong. It's good to have people care about you. It really is. My parents are great and I know they just want me to be OK. But sometimes I feel like there's this giant parent helicopter hovering over my head. During the last year, it has gotten worse. For my birthday, I got a cell phone. At first, I thought it was the coolest gift ever. Then I started to resent it. It was actually a present my parents gave *themselves*. I had to call every morning when I got to school. Seriously. "Just say I'M HERE," my dad said, like this was no big deal. Like this was perfectly normal. Right. When my friends found out about this rule, they would pile around me—"Hey, Rob, did you call yet?" I seriously could not take this.

So now I text. My dad says no problem, he can read my shortcuts. He likes to be cool. So I text "HR. CU LTR." Does he know what this means? I have no idea. At least he knows I can move my thumbs, so I'm probably alive. As for me, I *love* texting. It's silent—and private.

About once a week I walk to Ben's house—about three blocks from our house. You can see me the whole way except for about 2.5 seconds when I disappear behind this giant old oak tree. I phoned my mom from there and told her not to worry, I'd be visible again in about one second. She did not find this funny for some reason, though Ben is still laughing about it.

This week we're supposed to write what we would want on our tombstones. Are you kidding me? That's an easy one: "I'll call you when I get there."

© 2012, Vicki Spandel

Suggested Score for SENTENCE FLUENCY: 6

Lessons Learned from "Call Me When You Get There"

- Sentence fluency definitely contributes to voice.
- Variety is about more than length or beginnings—it's also found in sentence style, structure, and type.

Try writing on this same topic—only in the voice of the writer's mom or dad—or friend Ben. It's not necessary to write four or five paragraphs—just one will do. The point is to see if you can achieve a similarly strong voice by varying sentences as much as this writer does. *Hint:* Warm up by reading Paper 8 aloud.

Comments

If you like this writer's voice, you have to love this piece. Voice is definitely the standout trait here—and it is supported throughout by fluency and word choice. The sentence variety is wonderful—statements, commands, questions, fragments, long and short, marked by a wide range of punctuation and flavored by many different beginnings, all making the paper great fun to read aloud. Though individual words may not be striking, the phrasing is individual and filled with attitude: *As in EVERY MOMENT . . . phone from the bathroom . . . she knows the very second my foot hits the doorstep . . . this giant parent helicopter . . . I can move my thumbs, so I'm probably alive.* The central message could hardly be more clear, and the organization is easy to follow: general set-up, the cell phone, texting, the Ben episode, the wrap-up. Notice how this writer also uses conventions to create voice.

Suggested Scores for Other Traits

Ideas: **6**

Organization: **6**

Voice: **6**

Word choice: **5**

Conventions & presentation: **6**

Lessons and Strategies for Teaching SENTENCE FLUENCY

Two sentences can say essentially the same thing, and yet one will be more pleasing to the ear. Why? To figure this out, we must be attentive as we read—and both daring and experimental as we write. Here are some things you'll want to emphasize as you teach sentence fluency:

- *Knowing what a sentence is*
- *Exploring the many forms sentences can take*
- *Creating easy-to-read sentences that make meaning clear*
- *Varying sentence length and structure*
- *Reading aloud to listen for fluency*
- *Using transitional words to connect sentences, thoughts, ideas*
- *Using fragments or repetition purposefully*

Following are some lesson ideas and strategies to help you achieve these goals.

1. WRITE POETRY.

Poetry is simultaneously challenging enough for the best writers, while offering an accessible form to beginners. Poets can be quite irreverent about sentence structure and punctuation, creating impressions through single words, fragments, or phrases. This makes poetry inviting and manageable for writers who struggle with complete sentences or punctuation. These writers have carte blanche to touch our hearts without fear of making a mistake. Notice how many ideas blossom in Elizabeth's poem "Purple" (Figure 7.4).

For a special lesson that combines sentence fluency and voice, try the "I Am Me" poem (see Figure 7.5) in three parts: *I am . . . I remember . . . I've learned . . .* The result is a poetic essay that is fun to share aloud—or perform in choral reading.

2. ENCOURAGE STUDENTS TO READ ALOUD.

Reading aloud with fluency is the flip side of writing with fluency. So you'll want to teach these together. Encourage students to—

- Hunt for selections (a sentence to a paragraph long) that they want to share aloud
- "Perform" chosen pieces for the whole class or just in a writing circle
- Participate in choral reading

Books for younger students that lend themselves to choral reading include these:

- *Dinothesaurus* by Douglas Florian (2009)
- *Dogteam* by Gary Paulsen (1993)
- *Hoops* by Robert Burleigh (1997)
- *Insectlopedia* by Douglas Florian (1998)
- *Is There Really a Human Race?* by Jamie Lee Curtis (2006)
- *Joyful Noise: Poems for Two Voices,* by Paul Fleischman (1992)
- *Life Doesn't Frighten Me* by Maya Angelou (1993)
- *Messing Around on the Monkey Bars* by Betsy Franco (2009)
- *Misery is a Smell in Your Backpack* by Harriet Ziefert (2005)
- *Moon Bear* by Brenda Z. Guiberson (2010)
- *Poetrees* by Douglas Florian (2010)
- *Red Sings from the Treetops* by Joyce Sidman (2009)
- *Zero Is the Leaves on the Tree* by Betsy Franco (2009)

For older students, try the following (choose one chapter, excerpt, or poem):

- *Falling Down the Page: A Book of List Poems* edited by Georgia Heard ((2009)
- *The House on Mango Street* by Sandra Cisneros (1989)
- *Looking Like Me* by Walter Dean Myers (2009)
- *Love That Dog* by Sharon Creech (2001)
- *Math Talk* by Theonni Pappas (2004)
- *Mirror Mirror* by Marilyn Singer (2010)
- *Poems from Homeroom: A Writer's Place to Start* by Kathi Appelt (2002)
- *Sailing Alone Around the Room* by Billy Collins (2001)
- *Seedfolks* by Paul Fleischman (1997)
- *Things I Have to Tell You: Poems and Writing by Teenage Girls* edited by Betsy Franco (2001)
- *Ubiquitous* by Joyce Sidman (2010)

FIGURE 7.4

"Purple"
by Elizabeth, Grade 3

Purple is the wave, lapping the beach.
Owls hoot at the sight of it.
Purple.
It feels smooth, soft, furry,
Like that blanket your mom gave you
Last winter.
Fresh picked lavender
Is purple.
Calm,
Peaceful,
Happy.
The pillow when you're sleeping.
The blanket when you're cold.
The comfort when you're sad.
Purple.
That relaxed feeling you get when you look up at the sky
Just before dark.
The scent of lavender comes
Through the deep color
The younger sister to blue.

Author's Note

In choral reading, students decide how to perform the text. A group of four, for example, may decide to do certain parts in one voice—and other parts in two, three, or four voices. Those who are not reading sometimes provide background music or sound effects. All these variations can be enhanced (particularly the addition of music) by doing choral reading as a podcast.

I read aloud, no matter how old the students are. The more behind students are, the more I need to read aloud from newspapers, novels, and poetry.

—Jeff Anderson
Mechanically Inclined, 2005, 17

FIGURE 7.5

"I Am Me"
by Katie, Grade 5

I am . . .
    The youngest child.
    The Precious Moment who speaks to you.
    The narrator of my own story.
    The stars in Van Gogh's painting.
    A friend a friend would like to have.
    The soaring tire swing on the tree.

I remember . . .
    The gentle sound on my violin.
    The towering oaks in my back yard.
    The pain in my cheek while saying cheese.
    Tears, slowly washing away the pain.
    The glide under my skate.

I've learned . . .
    No one can learn without mistakes.
    Tears are a sign of strength.
    Believing is not always seeing and seeing is not always practical.
    Falling is a sign of courage.
    The expert in anything was once a beginner.

- *What Have You Lost?* edited by Naomi Shihab Nye (2001)
- *You Hear Me? Poems and Writing by Teenage Boys* edited by Betsy Franco (2000)

3. REMIND STUDENTS TO READ EVERYTHING *THEY WRITE* ALOUD.

Reading our writing aloud is particularly important in achieving fluency because it's the *only* way to tell if the rhythm is working. Good writers often read aloud *as they work*, not just when the draft is finished. In addition, reading what you wrote the day before is one of the most painless ways to pick up unfinished writing.

4. TEACH STUDENTS WHAT A SENTENCE *IS*.

When students understand what a sentence *is*, they have opened the first and most important door in understanding how sentences work. You can teach this basic lesson by having students write simple sentences of their own. Have them work independently first—then check with a partner to make sure each example has a subject and verb:

- Rats scurry.
- Leaves fall.
- Mushrooms simmer.
- Alice screams.
- The teacher faints.

Everything students learn about sentences, from compound to complex, rests on this essential understanding: Simple sentences are made up of a subject and verb: Sean laughs. Who or what laughs? Sean, the subject. What does he do? Laughs, the verb.

—Jeff Anderson
Mechanically Inclined, 2005, 64

FIGURE 7.6

Sentence—or Not?

- Chickens.
- The chickens escaped.
- Blazed.
- Fire blazed.
- Trees fell.
- Falling.
- Lions!
- I hear lions.
- Heroes.
- They're heroes.
- A house.
- A house appeared.
- Writing.
- What are you writing?
- Silver icicles.
- Silver icicles dripped.
- The film.
- The film ended.
- Meandering.
- Meandering rivers.
- Rivers meandered.
- Slippery road.
- A slippery road.
- The long slippery road.
- The long slippery road turned.

> **Author's Note**
> Commands are an exception because the subject—*you*—is implied, but usually not expressed: *Line up, Stay together, Leave now, Make room, Please sit, Run!,* and so forth.

Then play a game: sentence—or not? Have students stand. Then, on your document projector (if you have one—or you can hold up sentence strips), show a series of sentences and fragments, like those in Figure 7.6. If the example is a sentence, students remain standing. If it's a fragment, they sit. Discuss any samples about which they disagree, stressing why an example is or is not a sentence. Your examples can be very simple and short at first because you're driving home the subject-verb concept. Following the next strategy—Build a Sentence—you can play this game again, but with more complex examples.

5. BUILD A SENTENCE.

This sentence game is also included in my companion book, *Creating Young Writers* (2011). Although it can certainly be used with primary writers, it is good for any students who need a stronger grasp of how the basic components of sentences work together. Take it as far as you want, just doing the first couple of steps with beginners, and working your way through more steps with writers who are ready. Write with your students. That way, they can use your writing as a model, but see their own sentences unfold in front of their eyes. This is grammar with a light touch—no drills.

> **Author's Note**
> You want students to write their own sentences, so reveal your copy *after* they finish writing. ELL students may work with partners, at your discretion. Please note that my subject (people) is only an example; *your subject* should be different. *Tip:* Create a sentence of your own on scratch paper *right now* as you go through this lesson, and you'll be more than ready to do it with students.

Step 1: Name the subject.
Name the thing you plan to write about. Print the word in big letters:

People

Step 2: Tell what the subject does.
This is where you add a verb. Call it a verb. Ask if this is now a complete sentence. (Yes, it is.) We've now come as far as we did with Strategy 3. (*Teach students what a sentence is.*) Note that you also need to add punctuation—most (if not all) of your writers will know this, but have them *tell you* anyway:

People rush.

[The] grammatical names for things are useful. They make it easier to talk about writing. "Adjective" is easier to say than "a word that describes a noun."

—Katie Wood Ray
Wondrous Words, 1999, 44

Step 3: Describe the subject.

This time you'll be adding an adjective. Call it that—and explain that adjectives are describing words. Ask students for suggestions, and use one of their words if possible—or two, perhaps:

<u>Crazy, excited</u> people rush.

Step 4: Tell HOW.

Here you're adding an adverb—something to show readers *how* the people rush. Use the word *adverb,* explaining that adverbs tell HOW. Again, ask for a suggestion from the class.

Crazy, excited people rush <u>frantically</u>.

Step 5: Tell WHERE.

Here the sentence begins to get interesting. This time we're adding a prepositional phrase—or perhaps more than one. Use this term, explaining that prepositional phrases often (not always) show WHERE. Even though I have added two, you can add just one if you like. But notice how two phrases make the sentence more visual . . .

Crazy, excited people rush frantically <u>over the pavement</u> and <u>through the doors</u>.

Step 6: Tell WHY.

This time we're adding a participle: an *–ing* form of a verb. Use the term. You can say, This time we're going to start the sentence with an *–ing word, a participle,* to show *why* these people are in such a hurry. Offer suggestions—*Looking for fun, Hoping for a front-row seat, Hunting for bargains*—and have students choose one. Ask them to notice how participles create pictures in the mind:

<u>Hunting for bargains</u>, crazy, excited people rush frantically over the pavement and through the doors.

6. MODEL WAYS TO DEAL WITH CHOPPY SENTENCES.

If you find a good example to work with, terrific. Otherwise, make one up. In Figure 7.7, you will see an example I wrote to illustrate how choppy sentences sound. I read my rough draft aloud, then do a little "think aloud" as I revise—like this:

- Let's combine the first two sentences.
- I also want to combine sentences 3 and 4.
- I'm going to combine sentences 5 and 6 into one thought, but rewrite it for a little variety and to get inside Samone's head.
- Let's take the sentence "She would not make it" and turn it into a question.
- I'm going to leave sentences 8 and 9 as is—short and punchy—for contrast.

FIGURE 7.7	**FIGURE 7.8**
## Short Choppy Sentences (Draft)	## Choppy Sentences (Revised)

FIGURE 7.7

Short Choppy Sentences (Draft)

Samone looked up. The sun beat down. She

felt hot. She felt tired. The race was long. It was

too long. She would not make it. Her legs were

cramping. Her face was flushed. Where was the

finish?

FIGURE 7.8

Choppy Sentences (Revised)

Samone looked up, ^as~~T~~he sun beat down.

She felt hot, ^and ~~She felt~~ tired. ~~The race was~~ *It felt as if she'd been*

running this race for days!

^ ~~long. It was too long,~~ (She) would ~~not~~ make

it^?~~.~~ Her legs were cramping. Her face was

flushed. Where ^*on earth* was the finish?~~?~~*!*

- In the final sentence, though, the rhythm feels wrong to me, so I'm going to insert the words "on earth."
- Let's read the whole thing to hear how it sounds—and you tell me if it's better.

The revision appears in Figure 7.8.

7. MODEL WAYS TO DEAL WITH REPETITIVE BEGINNINGS.

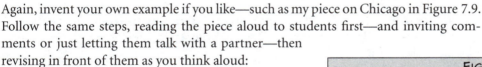

Again, invent your own example if you like—such as my piece on Chicago in Figure 7.9. Follow the same steps, reading the piece aloud to students first—and inviting comments or just letting them talk with a partner—then revising in front of them as you think aloud:

- I've said there are a million things to do [pointing to sentence 1] and you'll never get bored [pointing to sentence 4], so I think I can eliminate sentence 2.
- The last sentence is really strong, so I want to begin there [inserting the symbol for a new paragraph]— but I'm going to combine it with the first sentence.
- The words "In Chicago they have" sound weak to me. I need some verbs there—to advise a visitor what to do—verbs like "check out," "visit," or "take in." Let's add those and hear how it sounds now . . .

Author's Note

You can enrich modeling lessons by asking students to do their own revisions of your example first, *and then* watch as you revise the same piece. That way, you can compare notes and they have a basis for asking why you made particular changes—or for suggesting things you didn't think of.

FIGURE 7.9

Repetitive Beginnings (Draft)

In Chicago, there are a million things to

do. Chicago is a really interesting city. In

Chicago they have museums and a

wonderful aquarium, not to mention an art

gallery. Chicago is one place you will never

get bored.

FIGURE 7.10

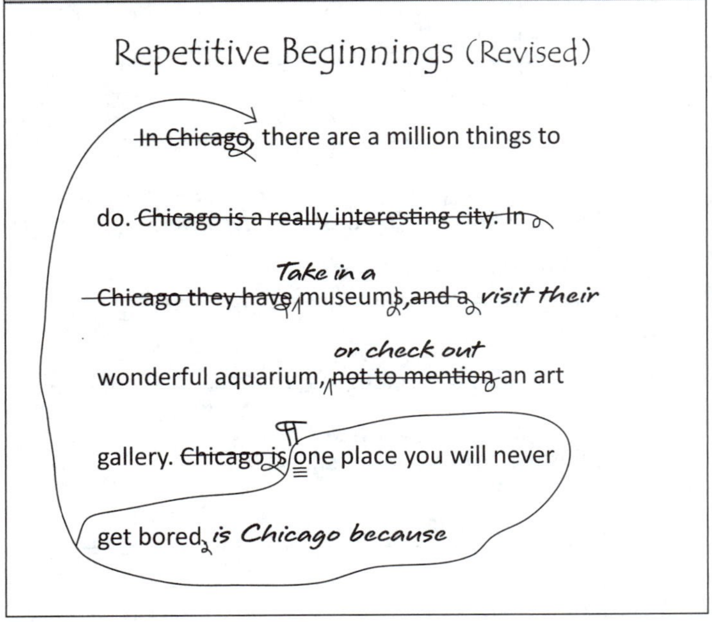

Repetitive Beginnings (Revised)

~~In Chicago,~~ there are a million things to

do. ~~Chicago is a really interesting city. In~~

Take in a
~~Chicago they have~~ museums, ~~and a~~ *visit their*

or check out
wonderful aquarium, ~~not to mention~~ an art

gallery. ~~Chicago is~~ one place you will never

get bored, *is Chicago because*

8. TRY SENTENCE AEROBICS.

Any sentence can be written many ways. A stellar example comes from E.B. White in Strunk and White's *The Elements of Style* (2008). The authors cite Thomas Paine's famous line "These are the times that try men's souls," then fashion four variations (67):

- *Times like these try men's souls.*
- *How trying it is to live in these times!*
- *These are trying times for men's souls.*
- *Soulwise, these are trying times.*

Try the same thing—writing as many versions of a given sentence as possible in two minutes. Following are two more versions of sentence aerobics—both of which build flexibility: Ask students to work in groups of four to six, and to begin with a half sheet of paper or a 3 × 5 card. Each student writes at every step, but except for the first step, they are revising someone else's writing. Ask them to follow these steps, writing one complete sentence each time:

- **Write one thing you know to be true:** Winter is terrific.
- *Pass your sentence to the LEFT.*
- Read the sentence in front of you and rewrite it—only this time, **begin the sentence a different way:** Of all the seasons, I love winter best.
- *Pass to the LEFT.*
- Read and rewrite the second sentence, this time **starting with a pronoun:** *One, He, She, I, They, We, Everyone*: Everyone has a favorite season, and for me it's winter.
- *Pass to the LEFT.*
- Read and rewrite the third sentence, **starting with the word *If*:** If I lived where there was no winter, I'd miss it.
- *Pass LEFT.*
- Read and rewrite the fourth sentence, this time **turning the sentence into a question:** How could anyone be happy without winter?

Return the five sentences to the original writer and read some aloud to hear the possibilities. For another version of sentence aerobics, see Figure 7.11.

9. COPY "MENTOR" SENTENCES.

Borrow an idea from one of the most creative writing teachers around, Jeff Anderson (*Mechanically Inclined*, 2005, 15–29), and collect sentences. Look for what is striking, inventive, or quotable, and use the sentences as models, showing students interesting word patterns, beginnings, and more.

Jeff always begins this lesson by asking students what *they* notice about a sentence. They might focus on imagery, word order, punctuation, grammatical construction, phrasing—just about anything. Following this discussion, they use the sentence as a

---

FIGURE 7.11

Alternate Sentence Aerobics

When a book is really good, you cannot put it down.

Write it as many ways as you can in 90 seconds.

Start with . . .

- You can't _____
- When you _____
- A really good _____
- If _____
- Who _____
- You know _____
- The only _____
- I want_____
- Wouldn't_____

© 2012. Vicki Spandel.

---

model for writing an original sentence of their own. Here are a handful of examples to illustrate the kinds of things you *might* model. What do *you* notice about each sentence?

1. *Imagine, if you will, having spent the whole of your life in a dungeon.* (DiCamillo, *The Tale of Despereaux*, 2003, 103)

2. *The brakes had failed, and the train slammed through the guardrail, jumped off the tracks, barreled across the floor of the station, rammed through two walls, and flew out the window, shattering the glass into a billion pieces.* (Selznick, *The Invention of Hugo Cabret*, 2007, 381)

3. *Never. Never in all the food, all the hamburgers and malts, all the fries or meals at home, never in all the candies or pies or cakes, never in all the roasts or steaks or pizzas, never in all the submarine sandwiches, never never never had he tasted anything as fine as that first bite.* (Paulsen, *Hatchet*, 2007, 146)

10. REMEMBER AN OLD FRIEND: SENTENCE COMBINING.

Check out Figure 7.12 for a lesson on sentence combining—this one involving sentences in pairs. I developed this lesson to be used by students at many ability levels. Beginners can start by combining just *one pair* of sentences—then, perhaps, another pair. More advanced students can do more than two sentences at a time—for example, combining all sentences in lines 1 and 2. For a real challenge, advanced writers can try combining all ten sentences (or as many as possible).

Sentence Combining

*Combine just the two—or keep adding new thoughts
to build a multi-detail sentence.*

1. I saw something. It was a bear.

2. The bear was coming down the trail. She was coming toward me.

3. The bear was huge. She had enormous black eyes.

4. It was early this morning. I was still in my pajamas.

5. The bear was staring at me. She had a hungry expression on her face.

_____

_____

_____

_____

_____

_____

© 2012. Vicki Spandel.

---

11. BREAK THE RULES (AT THE RIGHT MOMENT).

Fragments and run-ons can work like magic in the right spot. Author Gary D. Schmidt (*Okay for Now,* 2011, 30) breaks the "no run-ons" rule in this scene, where Lily is trying to teach Doug to drink a whole bottle of Coke without taking a breath:

> By the time the Coke was done coming out of both places, my eyes were all watered up like I was about to bawl—which I wasn't but it probably looked like I was—and there was this puddle of still fizzing Coked and snot on the steps, and what hadn't landed on the steps had landed on my sneakers, which, if they had been new, I would have been upset about, but since they had been my brother's, it didn't matter.

Schmidt achieves comic tension by letting the syntax roll on like a river, echoing the speaker's thinking. Students can play with run-ons, too, as in the excerpt from "The Advice of a Coach" in Figure 7.13, meant to capture the coach's voice as the players hear it.

12. TEACH STUDENTS TO "HIT THE END NOTE."

Where is the power of the sentence? At the end. Experienced writers learn to embed the most important word or thought right there—like a punch. After a while, this becomes automatic, but at first, you have to point it out. Which of these sentences has more power?

- Victor turned slowly, aimed the gun, and fired.
- Victor fired, after turning slowly and aiming the gun.

FIGURE 7.13

"The Advice of a Coach"
(Advice Poem, Grade 10)

Get in the game! Show up for practice and if you don't play, shut up but if you do play, don't rake the field. Winning is more fun than losing. You guys are KILLIN' ME!! If you ever get the chance to play, then you had better show me something and if you have any questions, always come to me first don't try to go over my head. Warm up if you have time don't play catch on the apron stay warm in case I need to put you in always be ready to play don't sit on the bench don't spit when I'm talking to you don't forget to warm up the pitcher keep your eye on the ball and remember to treat the equipment with respect. Try to remember all of the signs. If you are late, don't bother coming because homework always comes before sports but if you don't show up, you will not play in the next game but you probably wouldn't have played anyway, so you could have at least had good grades. Listen when I'm talking to you. You guys think you're good, but you're not. Don't stand directly behind me. At least look ready to play and don't leave your hat at home. Keep the locker room clean don't come to practice without your cleats and damn it, don't forget your sleeves. Don't talk back to the coach I have no conscience I can watch you run all day.

To a writer's ear, the second sentence simply sounds *wrong*, putting the emphasis on *aiming the gun*, not *firing*. It isn't just individual sentences that are guided by this organizational principle, either. Sentences, paragraphs, and whole pieces all drive relentlessly toward the rhythm, the force, the power of the end note. Remember this number: 231. It will remind you that the opening is the second most important spot, the middle is third, and the ending is number one.

13. Avoid weak beginnings.

An easy trick to teach students—one with huge rewards—is to avoid weak sentence beginnings:

- *There is*
- *There are*
- *I think*

Model this, using an example like the one in Figure 7.14. Read it aloud, and ask students how it sounds. Is it fluent? Does it have voice? Explain that beginnings such as "There is" or "There are" (though admittedly hard to avoid at times) weaken sentences. In some cases you can just cross them out, but often, you need to restructure the sentence so it begins differently.

Start by highlighting the weak beginnings. Then revise. The result will look *something* like Figure 7.15.

> The end of a sentence or paragraph is a powerful spot for placing information. End with something strong, and readers receive a payoff.
>
> —Tom Romano
> *Crafting Authentic Voice*, 2004, 166

FIGURE 7.14

Weak Beginnings (Draft)

There is one thing I love on pizza and

it's olives. There are no olives remaining in

the fridge, unfortunately. I think Rudy ate

every last one. There are no words to

express how furious this makes me! There is

not going to be any pizza here tonight.

FIGURE 7.15

Weak Beginnings (Revised)

olives

~~There is one thing~~ I love on pizza ~~and~~

~~it's olives~~ ~~There are~~ no olives remain~~ing~~ in

this huge, empty

~~the~~ fridge, unfortunately. ~~I think~~ Rudy ate

every ... last ... one. ~~There are no words to~~

!!

~~express how~~ furious this makes me ~~! There is~~

Well . . . no

~~not going to be any~~ pizza ~~here~~ tonight.

14. HELP STUDENTS MASTER PARALLEL STRUCTURE.

Parallel structure, or *patterning* in sentences adds the same kind of rhythm that percussion adds to music. Consider the following passage about lobster fishing from Elizabeth Gilbert's *Stern Men* (2009, 5):

> It is a mean business, and it makes for mean men. As humans, after all, we become that which we seek. Dairy farming makes men steady and reliable and temperate; deer hunting makes men quiet and fast and sensitive; lobster fishing makes men suspicious and wily and ruthless.

To give your writer practice with parallel structure, create samples that are *not* parallel, and have students revise them. Try these yourself (Hint: Don't be afraid to condense considerably and change the wording—as in the first example):

- *The food at the Old Mill Café cost a lot of money. However, it had little if any taste. Luckily, it was the kind of food that was easy to forget if it wasn't right in front of your nose.* (Revised: *The food at the Old Mill was expensive, tasteless, and—luckily—utterly forgettable.*)
- *Eloise was tenacious. In addition, her manners weren't very good. Besides that, she often scared the living daylights out of us.*
- *Some called the January weather in the mountains dangerous. One thing was certain: You couldn't predict it. In addition, it had the potential to be deadly at times.*
- *I arrived at the site, I took a careful look around, and then I made sure to win the battle.*

Author's Note

See the *Creating Revisers and Editors* series by Vicki Spandel (2008, Pearson Education) for grade-specific fluency lessons on such topics as writing with rhythm, applying parallel structure, using prepositions and participles effectively, disconnecting long sentences, writing dialogue, and making sentences forceful.

Interactive Questions and Activities

1. **Discussion.** Put a check by each of the following sentences with which you agree. Then discuss results with your colleagues.

   ___ Students should write in complete sentences, always.

   ___ Of all the traits, sentence fluency influences readability the most.

   ___ So-called rule breaking—use of fragments, run-ons, repetition, and so forth—often enhances fluency.

   ___ A piece can be fluent even if it is not punctuated correctly.

   ___ The kind of writing we regard as fluent today will not be considered fluent in 50 or 100 years.

   ___ It doesn't really matter whether students know any grammar. What matters is whether they can write.

2. **Activity and Discussion.** The literature section of this chapter lists many books you might use to teach or illustrate sentence fluency. Identify an additional sample of your own to share with the group, and plan to read it (or a selection) aloud. Talk about why you chose it as an example of fluency.

3. **Activity and Discussion.** On your own or with one partner, scan the preceding chapters (3 through 7) to find one to three samples of writing you would consider strong in sentence fluency. Present your choices to the group with a rationale for each selection.

4. **Activity and Discussion.** Look for a *short* example of *non-fluent* writing—from any source. (It need not be longer than a single sentence.) Share your example with the group, using a document projector. Have each person in your writing group attempt a revision, and read aloud as many examples as possible. Talk about how many different ways there are to revise a given sentence.

5. **Activity and Discussion.** The preceding chapter offers several examples of modeling with "think-aloud" text to show the kinds of things you might say to students as you revise. Using these examples as a guide, create a modeling lesson of your own and present it to the group—or to your students.

6. **Activity and Discussion.** Identify a favorite sentence from literature. Include it in your writing journal—and also share it with your group. As others share, add more sentences that you like. Talk about the value of being, like teacher and author Jeff Anderson, a "sentence stalker."

Coming Up

In Chapter 8, we'll consider conventions and presentation, the trait of publication.

> I don't stress about essays for school anymore. I use the same rhythm, the same words, the same wit as my stories. It's no fun quoting Sparknotes.
> —Simona Patange, student writer

> I write because I like hearing the river of words flow like the ocean, so smooth and graceful. I like to read it over and over until the words ask me to stop.
> —Ryan Sterner, student writer

CHAPTER **8**

Preparing to Publish with CONVENTIONS & PRESENTATION

Conventions belong to all of us. In acquiring them we gain the power to say new things, extend our meaning, and discover new relationships between ideas.

DONALD H. GRAVES
A Fresh Look at Writing, 1994, 210

We are dealing with a complicated system, and every element of that system, down to the conventional signs for pauses and nuances, has had a long testing. Its function is to help reproduce in cold print what was a human voice speaking for human ears.

WALLACE STEGNER
On Teaching and Writing Fiction, 2002, 63

We are preparing for a different kind of world—a world where [students] need to know how to tell compelling stories. And the types of stories that are compelling these days are not just print stories.

JOEL MALLEY
English Language Arts Teacher in *Teachers Are the Center of Education: Writing, Learning and Leading in the Digital Age* College Board, the National Writing Project, and Phi Delta Kappa International, 2010, 4

Conventions and presentation are intimately connected; both are vital in preparing a piece for publication. Going public means sharing ideas with people who come to the message from a different knowledge base, different values, different interests. Reaching them—and holding their attention—requires packaging ideas in a way that makes them both easy to understand and irresistibly appealing. And as we will see, in the digital age, the latter sometimes takes forms other than print.

Step 1: Editing (Textual Conventions)

Textual conventions cover anything a copyeditor would deal with: spelling, punctuation, grammar, and more. Such conventions clearly change over time, and so to assess or teach them well, we need to rely on up-to-date handbooks and dictionaries and use them often.

Textual conventions not only support meaning but also help readers to understand intended inflection and voice. In *Peter and the Starcatchers*, Peter and his friends are being held hostage by pirates aboard a ship called the *Never Land*. Famished, they are nevertheless cautious when served a pot of liquid full of slimy gray lumps (Barry and Pearson, 2004, 38). Tubby Ted, one of Peter's cohorts, ventures a taste—and has an immediate reaction:

> "IT'S ALIVE!" he screamed.

Imagine this same text all in lower case with no punctuation, and you can see at once how conventions give voice to what Wallace Stegner calls "cold print."

Everything that is read gets edited. The question is, Who will do the work: writer or reader? A few years ago, when a student wrote "Space: the finnel fruter," to open his writing assessment essay, readers had to pause, reflect, and mentally edit. *Writers* edit as a courtesy—a way of saying to readers, "Let me make reading this as easy for you as possible."

> Among the opinionated, the speed of language evolution is a lot like speed on the highway. George Carlin's observation comes to mind: "Why is it that anybody who drives slower than you is a moron, but anybody who drives faster than you is a maniac?"
>
> —Bill Walsh
> *The Elephants of Style*, 2004, xii–xiii

CONVENTIONS? ISN'T THAT THE *EASIEST* TRAIT TO ASSESS?

Not really. We do not all agree on what is conventionally correct, for one thing. How many commas go in a series? Which words should be capitalized? Which numbers should be spelled out? Is it ever all right to begin a sentence with *And*? Is *data* plural? What about *none*? Do you cringe at *firstly*? *And secondly*, is second person sometimes *alright*? Do you use it *alot*?

Little things get to us all, and we strike back: *Score of 1 for you!* Such things as failing to capitalize the pronoun *i* or writing *alot* as one word are not federal offenses and should not cause a drop in a student's score from, say, a 5 to a 1 or 2, but sometimes this is what happens.

Recognizing the purpose behind conventions—helping readers interpret text—frees us to assess and teach them differently. We put our red pens down for a moment and breathe, understanding that conventions create readability. Maybe we don't have to correct every mistake. Maybe we don't have to count errors—or figure out whether a paper that scores a 6 can have one error or two—or none at all. In place of all that calculating, we decide that strong papers are those in which conventions enhance meaning and voice.

Step 2: Packaging (Visual Conventions/Presentation)

Packaging written text (as a newspaper, letter, advertisement, script, book, or pamphlet) requires attention to visual conventions, so called because they visually organize and enhance text, guiding the reader's eye and making certain facts or features stand out.

Designers rely on such things as varied fonts, graphics (maps, charts, photographs) that support text or expand meaning, bulleted or numbered lists, titles and subheads to guide readers to the information they need. Anything that breaks up the monotony of print, whether visuals or white space, is relaxing and inviting. Figures 8.1a and 8.1b show two versions of the very same text, formatted quite differently. Suppose this excerpt opens a 300-page book. Which version would you prefer to read?

As you leaf through this edition of *Creating Writers*, you may notice the photos, various fonts, *Notes from the Author*, *Write Connections*, quotations, and other designed features. Each element affects the visual appeal and the accessibility of information for you, the reader. Each represents decisions about size, placement, and style made either by me, as the author, or by a design editor—a specialist in packaging information.

A multi-chapter book, of course, is more complex than most documents students normally create. But even a simple document such as a poster, poem, business letter, or résumé is influenced by design. It is important to note that decisions about design are much easier to make—and carry out—with the aid of a computer. In teaching and assessing presentation, we must be very careful to take into account our students' access to technology—and to push for greater access when possible.

Conventions & Presentation: Readiness for Publication

A Definition

Conventions, as the word implies, are a reflection of what is currently acceptable in print. Written conventions encompass spelling, punctuation, grammar, usage, capitalization, and paragraphing: *anything* about which a copyeditor might say, "This is acceptable—and this is not." It also includes little nuances such as use of italics, dashes, or ellipses—things that affect voice as well as meaning. Because conventions are forever changing, and because even editors do not always agree, we must rely on current handbooks and online resources to support our choices. We must also read, regularly, the writing of those contemporary authors we trust to show us what is correct, currently acceptable, and effective. **Presentation** is anything that affects the overall look of a document: artwork, font choice, color, arrangement of various elements on the page, shape of the text (as in a concrete poem), special features, graphics, and such structural elements as a table of contents, index, glossary, or appendix. Presentation is not about right or wrong—which is one reason it is difficult to assess. It is about stylistic preference. We know which fonts or book covers we like, but we cannot say one is "the *correct* choice." We can, however, identify fonts that are easily readable, maps that are simple to decipher, graphs and charts that are helpful, subheads that make location of data a breeze, or illustrations that complement or expand the meaning of text. And from these observations we can create, with our students' help, guidelines (not requirements) for making presentation effective.

> ### FIGURE 8.1a
>
> Rainforests
>
> Rainforests, as their name suggests, are characterized by exceptionally heavy rainfall, usually more than 100 inches per year. Visitors are amazed to discover that it is often possible to walk through a rainforest quite easily. The overhead canopy is so dense that most of the rain never reaches the ground, leaving that vegetation lighter. If the canopy is destroyed, the rain penetrates at once, turning the softly carpeted forest floor into a jungle through which no human can walk. Rainforests are ecologically vital. It is estimated, for example, that more than a quarter of the earth's natural medicines have been discovered there. In addition, rainforests are responsible for well over a fourth of the world's oxygen turnover, converting carbon dioxide into the oxygen that lets us breathe.
>
> Butler, R. A. (2005) *A Place Out of Time: Tropical Rainforests and the Perils They Face.* Published online: Rainforests.mongabay.com
> Richards, P. W. (1996). *The tropical rain forest.* 2nd ed. Cambridge University Press ISBN 0-521-42194-2

FIGURE 8.1b

Rainforests: Jewels of the Earth

Rainforests, as their name suggests, are characterized by exceptionally heavy rainfall, usually more than 100 inches per year. Visitors are amazed to discover that it is often possible to walk through a rainforest quite easily. The overhead canopy is so dense that most of the rain never reaches the ground, leaving that vegetation lighter. If the canopy is destroyed, the rain penetrates at once, turning the softly carpeted forest floor into a jungle through which no human can travel.

Rainforests are ecologically vital. It is estimated, for example, that more than a quarter of the earth's natural medicines have been discovered there.

In addition, rainforests are responsible for well over a fourth of the world's oxygen turnover, converting carbon dioxide into the oxygen that lets us breathe.

For additional information, check these sources:
Butler, R. A. (2005) *A Place Out of Time: Tropical Rainforests and the Perils They Face.* Published online: Rainforests.mongabay.com

Richards, P. W. (1996). *The tropical rain forest.* 2nd ed. Cambridge University Press ISBN 0-521-42194-2

FIGURE 8.2

Student Writing Guide for
CONVENTIONS & PRESENTATION

6
- ❑ I edited this *well*. I read it silently and aloud.
- ❑ My conventions make meaning clear and show readers how to read this piece with voice.
- ❑ I worked on the presentation. It will catch your eye.
- ❑ This piece is ready to publish.

3
- ❑ I have enough errors to slow a reader down.
- ❑ I can picture a reader mentally "editing" this.
- ❑ My presentation needs work.
- ❑ I need to read this silently and aloud, pen in hand.

5
- ❑ I might have a few *small* errors—I'll look again.
- ❑ My conventions make the writing easy to read and understand.
- ❑ I worked on the presentation. It looks good.
- ❑ This is *almost* ready to publish.

2
- ❑ Errors could be the first thing a reader notices.
- ❑ So many errors make it hard to think about the message.
- ❑ This presentation is definitely NOT working.
- ❑ I need to read line by line, pen in hand.

4
- ❑ I see a few errors I need to fix.
- ❑ I don't think my errors get in the way of the message.
- ❑ I worked on the presentation. It's OK, but I could do more.
- ❑ This will be ready to publish once I go through it again.

1
- ❑ Errors make this hard to read, even for me!
- ❑ I see errors even on easy things I should have caught.
- ❑ I'm not ready to think about presentation yet.
- ❑ I need help with my editing.

Share my definition—and define conventions and presentation in your own words as well. Have students name those elements of conventions and presentation that they consider critical—or perhaps challenging.

Share the Student Writing Guide for Conventions and Presentation, shown in Figure 8.2. The teacher version, for your use in assessing writing, appears in Figure 8.3. The "trait shortie" for conventions and presentation appears in Figure 8.4.

HOW IMPORTANT IS PRESENTATION IN THE OVERALL CONVENTIONS & PRESENTATION SCORE?

If your students are creating newsletter copy, business letters, posters, brochures, illustrated reports, picture books, videos, PowerPoint presentations or other writing in which layout and graphics play an important role, then presentation matters. For much of the writing we have looked at in this book—essays, stories, memoirs, and expository paragraphs—presentation (beyond general neatness and use of a readable font) is much less important than careful editing. That's not to say that these documents could not be reformatted to include illustrations, covers, and so on. But we need to be very clear with students about whether our emphasis is on the writing itself, the packaging,

FIGURE 8.3

Teacher Writing Guide for
CONVENTIONS & PRESENTATION

6
- ❑ Only the pickiest editors will spot problems
- ❑ Creative use of conventions enhances meaning, voice
- ❑ Complexity of text shows off writer's editorial control
- ❑ Enticing, eye-catching presentation (as needed)*
- ❑ Virtually ready to publish

5
- ❑ Minor errors that are easily overlooked
- ❑ Correct conventions support meaning, voice
- ❑ Shows writer's control over numerous conventions
- ❑ Pleasing, effective presentation
- ❑ Ready to publish with light touch-ups

4
- ❑ Errors are noticeable, but not troublesome
- ❑ Errors do not interfere with the message
- ❑ Shows control over basics (most spelling, punctuation)
- ❑ Acceptable presentation
- ❑ Good once-over needed prior to publication

3
- ❑ Noticeable errors may slow reader
- ❑ Reader may pause to mentally "correct" text
- ❑ Some problems even on basics
- ❑ More attention to presentation needed
- ❑ Thorough editing required prior to publication

2
- ❑ Distracting or repeated errors
- ❑ Errors may interfere with writer's message
- ❑ Shaky control over basics—reads like a hasty first draft
- ❑ Immediately noticeable problems with presentation
- ❑ Line-by-line editing needed prior to publication

1
- ❑ Serious, frequent errors make reading a challenge
- ❑ Reader must "decode" before focusing on message
- ❑ Writer not yet in control of basic conventions
- ❑ Writing not yet ready for final design/presentation
- ❑ Writer needs help with editing

*Note: Presentation should be weighted to reflect its importance given the purpose and audience for the document.

© 2012. Vicki Spandel. Designed for use in classroom assessment.

or both. That decision depends largely on who will see the document and how it will be used.

When scoring your own students' writing in the classroom, weight presentation in accordance with the purpose of the document. A report that no one but you and the writer will see is one thing. A newsletter that needs to attract a general audience is quite another.

Once you determine that presentation is important, you must also decide what, specifically, to look for; this will vary according to the assignment and genre. Here are some *general* suggestions, but your choices will (and should) vary from piece to piece:

- Appropriate and pleasing format that is a match with purpose (as in a business letter or résumé)
- Format that enhances the piece artistically (as for a poem)
- Coordination of text with illustrations (as in a picture book or informational report)
- Properly formatted citations
- Effective use of titles, headings, and subheads
- Effective use of graphics (charts, illustrations, maps, etc.)
- Font style and size that enhance readability (for example, nothing under 11 point)

> ### Author's Note
> If you are assessing an essay or story for which presentation is a secondary issue, base the Conventions & Presentation score mostly (or entirely) on the conventions.

- Sufficient margins to make text width comfortable for reading
- Use of bullets or numbers that make long lists easy to "digest"

As you and your students explore the world of presentation, you will identify numerous features that work in a given context (e.g., for PowerPoint or for picture books). But because every publication is different—considering genre, purpose, and the writer's unique style—we have to be cautious about turning a *suggestion* into a *requirement*.

Going Beyond Print

In a technological age, communication takes forms that go far beyond written documents, and our assessment and instruction must embrace these new forms and offer students opportunities to share ideas in new ways. In *The Digital Writing Workshop*, author Troy Hicks tells us that "a definition of writing as simply putting words on paper (or screen) is not sufficient in this age, and we need to carefully consider what it means to be a writer and a teacher of writing in relation to digital texts" (2009, 131). Troy credits Kathleen Blake Yancey with giving us what may be a far more appropriate term—*composition*—for broadening "our notions of what it means to write with text, images, sounds, and video" (4).

Indeed, students are now composing (to use Yancey's term) podcasts, webcasts, wikis, videos, blogs, digital stories, and much more. This does not mean that detail, organizational design, voice, and word choice no longer matter. They matter more than ever. But they will look very different. A "lead" may now be an image or an opening scene. Detail may be captured in a photo or a video. Word choice and sentence fluency may be heard through the voice of a narrator, but never seen because the words no longer appear in print (except in the narrator's personal notes or script). Voice may be the identity a composer creates for him- or herself through the visual impact of a program—and the style of narration that accompanies it. We will look more closely at technological possibilities for communicating under Lessons and Strategies, page 245.

Warming Up with Literature

Literature for teaching conventions and presentation? Absolutely! For years (it felt more like centuries) our teachers passed out rules and worksheets. What we needed were *examples*. Let's begin with conventions (and we'll get to the presentation part shortly).

Start by choosing a handbook that will be the "authority" for your classroom. Choose carefully. It should be easy to read and filled with useful illustrations of the concepts presented. On pages 255–256, I list a number of resources that you will find useful as a teacher, and you may wish to read aloud from some of them. They're filled with helpful conventional tips and written with voice.

Then, as you read poems, stories, or informational pieces, notice each writer's use of conventions. When you find an example that shows interesting or unusual use of capitals, italics, ellipsis, bold print, or any other convention that catches your eye, share it with students. As you do so, you are not just teaching the convention of the moment. You are teaching students to pay attention to text, so they can realize that conventions influence how we read and how we hear the writer's voice.

BOOKS WITH INTRIGUING CONVENTIONS

Following are a handful of books that use conventions in interesting ways; you may have looked at some of them when studying other traits. I have deliberately *not* separated them by grade level because even books written for primary students have much to teach older writers conventionally—and vice versa.

The BFG by Roald Dahl. 2007. New York: Puffin.

Dahl has a whiz-bang time inventing words to be spoken by the Big Friendly Giant. Because he doesn't eat humans, it's a "squelching tricky" problem coming up with something he *can* eat. He cannot bear *snozzcumbers*, he tells his new friend, the *human bean* Sophie. She is skeptical that such veggies even exist. But as the giant points out, "Just because we happen not to have *seen* something with our own two little winkles, we think it is not existing" (48).

Dogteam by Gary Paulsen. 1993. New York: Delacorte Press.

Take one more look at this lyrical book, this time noticing the extreme care with which Paulsen punctuates his sentences. The absence of punctuation in some sections pushes us to keep reading, the way the dogs keep moving over the snow. Ellipses, commas, and periods signal pauses—all different. Spend time on several examples to see how punctuation reinforces meaning.

The Dreamer by Pam Muñoz Ryan. 2010. New York: Scholastic.

There's much to love conventionally about this wonderful book. Notice how the author plays with phonics to create the sounds of footfalls (4) and dripping water (6–7). One sound is ominous, one soothing. Throughout the book, the voice of Neftalí's poetic imagination whispers to him in italics: "*What is the color of a minute? A month? A year?*" (75). Spanish words also appear in italics.

Fables by Arnold Lobel. 1980. New York: HarperTrophy.

This book is outstanding for showing how to punctuate and paragraph dialogue. The fables are written partially if not primarily through dialogue, providing numerous opportunities for illustrating the use of quotation marks, commas, periods, split quotations, separation of speakers, and the rest.

January's Sparrow by Patricia Polacco. 2009. New York: Philomel Books.

In a graphically illustrated picture book definitely for older readers, Polacco takes on a conventionally challenging task: the creation of dialect for her narrator and characters. Notice how spelling, punctuation, and grammar are manipulated with enormous skill to create a distinctive voice.

Knuffle Bunny: A Cautionary Tale by Mo Willems. 2004. New York: Hyperion.

Have your students ever tried to capture the actual sound of a toddler speaking? It's a challenge. But Willems (Emmy-winning writer for "Sesame Street") attempts it for his character Trixie—with very comical results.

Mirror Mirror by Marilyn Singer. 2010. New York: Penguin Group.

If you've explored this book already, you know it's verse in reverse. Clever idea—but how do you punctuate it? Do the capitals fall in the same places? What about punctuation? Review an entry or two to see how careful manipulation of conventions reinforces meaning.

Mockingbird by Kathryn Erskine. 2010. New York: Philomel.

Compare Erskine's use of capitals to signify important words and phrases with A. A. Milne's similar strategy in *Winnie the Pooh* (listed later in this section). What are the similarities? What are the differences? What do the capital letters signify about a person's thinking?

The Music of Dolphins by Karen Hesse. 1996. New York: Scholastic.

Small but very noticeable shifts in font are highly revealing in the story of a girl who grows up with dolphins and longs to return to them. If you know the story, talk about the shifts from italic to roman, and the changes in font size. What do these things signify?

Peter and the Starcatchers by Dave Barry and Ridley Pearson. 2004. New York: Hyperion.

Students will enjoy learning one easy way to separate action from internal monologue: just put the character's thoughts in italics.

A Prayer for Owen Meany by John Irving. 2002. New York: Ballantine Books.

Owen Meany is a character like no other. We meet him as a child—one who has an extraordinary and life-shattering experience—but though he grows emotionally and intellectually all through the book, he never gets bigger, nor does his voice change. In the final chapter, we learn why. To make him especially distinctive, Irving has Owen speak in capital letters. ALL THE TIME.

Silent Letters Loud and Clear by Robin Pulver. 2010. Guang Dong Province, China: Kwong Fat Offset Printing Company.

Robin Pulver strikes again—this time with a book about those pesky letters (like *k* in *knife*) for which we need to use our eyes, not just our ears. If some letters are silent, why do we need them, anyway? Have fun decoding the protest letter to the editor from Mr. Wright's class. Don't overlook the postscript: "Cat rot this." Pardon?

Silent Music: A Story of Baghdad by James Rumford. 2008. New York: Roaring Brook Press.

This elegantly illustrated book, dedicated to the art of Arabic calligraphy, can spark discussions about how conventions differ from language to language, culture to culture. Illustrations are done in a collage of art forms with a strong Middle Eastern flavor.

The dialect for this book is a modified dialect derived from entries in *Unchained Memories: Readings from the Slave Narratives,* an adaptation of the original HBO documentary of the same name, published in 2003 by Little, Brown & Company.

—Note from Patricia Lee Gauch,
Editor, *January's Sparrow*

Owen's voice *is* irritating, not only because of how it sounds but because of how right he is. People who are always right, and are given to reminding us of it, are irritating; prophets are irritating, and Owen Meany is decidedly a prophet.

—John Irving
Afterword, *A Prayer for Owen Meany*

Winnie the Pooh **by A. A. Milne. [1926] 1950. New York: E. P. Dutton Company, Inc.**

Author A. A. Milne has a veritable party with capital letters in the beloved Pooh series, using them (as someone might very well have told him once) to indicate the Important Words. Here's an example from the chapter "Piglet Meets a Heffalump," showing Piglet fretting over the possibilities: "Of course Pooh would be with him, and it was much more Friendly with two. But suppose Heffalumps were Very Fierce with Pigs *and* Bears? . . . And then he had a Clever Idea. He would go up very quietly to the Six Pine Trees now, peep very cautiously into the Trap, and see if there was a Heffalump there." (66)

Yo! Yes? **By Chris Raschka. 1993. New York: Scholastic.**

This delightful tale of friendship is told totally in dialogue (no quotation marks, however). Readers must think carefully about punctuation and print size in order to interpret the meaning—much of which can only be conveyed by reading the book aloud. Even older readers will enjoy trying this.

BOOKS WITH ARRESTING PRESENTATION

Sometimes presentation is subtle—a slight shift in font style or size, for example. Other times it's bold and inescapable, as in a book cover we can hardly stop staring at. Use this list as a guide in choosing samples you and your students can review in deciding which elements of presentation are most important.

Art & Max **by David Wiesner. 2010. Boston: Houghton Mifflin Harcourt.**

Art and Max, two lizards, are both artists—but they have totally different styles. Art is deliberate, thoughtful, reflective. Max is gung-ho, exuberant, confident. A series of misunderstandings shake things up in hilarious—and meaningful—ways, leaving Max to reassemble Art one detail and color splash at a time. Will Art be his old, gray, somber self—or emerge in a new guise?

Beautiful Oops! **by Barney Saltzberg. 2010. New York: Workman Publishing.**

Presentation *is* the book in this delightful, heartwarming homage to mistakes that turn inspirational. Spills, tears, holes, stains, and smudges: no mistake is too humble to celebrate.

Chester **by Melanie Watt. 2007. Tonawanda, NY: Kids Can Press.**

The presentation grows crazier with each page as Melanie Watt and her cat Chester vie to see who will be the controlling author/editor of this book. It's a fine *visual* alternative to a common literary device: a story told in two (or more) voices.

The Invention of Hugo Cabret **by Brian Selznick. 2007. New York: Scholastic.**

This extraordinary book, a combination mystery and graphic novel, contains 284 pages of original drawings. Those drawings, in stark black and white, tell the story of Hugo, who lives within the walls of a busy Paris train station, maintaining clocks—and secrets.

Jimi: Sounds Like a Rainbow, A Story of the Young Jimi Hendrix **by Gary Golio. Illustrated by Javaka Steptoe. 2010. Boston: Houghton Mifflin Harcourt.**

Just try to look away. Like the music of which it speaks, this book is rich, colorful, complex, jazzy, edgy. It has an artistic style all its own, with layers of collage paintings that seem to vibrate. You can hear the "buzzes and whistles, fuzzy hissing, and a raspy humming" (22).

The Lion and the Mouse by Jerry Pinkney. 2009. New York: Little, Brown and Company.

Maybe we don't buy books for their covers all the time—but this cover must have sold a few copies. *Stunning* doesn't capture it. And how often do we see a cover with NO print. Not a word. (Don't miss the back cover, either.) This almost-wordless (except for soft animal sounds) picture book retells through art, not words, the classic Aesop fable of the lion and the mouse. You must look carefully at each page (not that you won't want to) to get all the details. Note the facial expressions.

Math Talk: Mathematical Ideas in Poems for Two Voices by Theonni Pappas. 2004. San Carlos, CA: World Wide Publishing.

Pappas's unique book is filled with mathematical conventions. That makes for an intriguing discussion in itself. But in addition, notice the illustrations. What information do they add that we cannot get from the text alone?

The Other Side by Istvan Banyai. 2005. San Francisco: Chronicle Books.

When we see a window, we wonder what's on the other side. Same with a door, a large tree, a roadway, a wall . . . Here, we have only to turn the page to find out. But interpreting the message may take a moment or two. Banyai is also the author of *Zoom!* and *Re-Zoom!*

A River of Words: The Story of William Carlos Williams by Jen Bryant. Illustrated by Melissa Sweet. 2008. Grand Rapids, Michigan: Erdmans Books for Young Readers.

The presentation in this book is a feast for the eyes. We have the typewritten poems of William Carlos Williams—some of them on the prescription notepads where he first wrote them (Williams was both poet and physician). Combine these, a treasure in themselves, with handwritten text, artsy excerpts from the poet's writing, delightful depictions of the poet and his family, and a myriad of imaginative collages. You can page through it 50 times and find something new on each visit.

Scaredy Squirrel by Melanie Watts. 2008. Tonawanda, NY: Kids Can Press.

Has anyone come up with a more intriguing or comical way to use lists, diagrams, boxes, charts, maps, or schedules? Leaf through, enjoying every moment, and talk about how this writer's use of graphic organizers reveals her character, Scaredy Squirrel.

The Selected Works of T. S. Spivet by Reif Larsen. 2009. New York: Penguin.

T.S. Spivet is a 12-year-old genius who maps everything—not just geography. When he receives the prestigious Baird Award from the Smithsonian based on his "map" of the Bombardier Beetle (those bestowing the award believe him to be an adult), he must travel from the ranch in Montana where he lives to Washington, D.C., mapping lessons learned along the way. This docu-novel is decked out with marginalia. Prepare to read slowly and meticulously.

A Sick Day for Amos McGee by Philip C. Stead. Illustrated by Erin E. Stead. 2010. New York: Roaring Brook Press.

This Caldecott winner is a true visual treat. Zookeeper Amos has a tender spot in his heart for each of his animal friends—and understands their individual needs with remarkable intuition. Could it be he sees a bit of himself in each one? The facial expressions (those eyes!) and gestures reveal volumes in a text where illustrations are moderately detailed, but never busy.

***Technically, It's Not My Fault: Concrete Poems* by John Grandits. 2004. New York: Clarion Books.**

In concrete poems, after all, the shape *is* the message. Topics include pizza, new words, basketball, mowing, sleepovers, parents, pets, playing with food, thank-you letters, dinosaurs, the Australian Cane Toad—and much more. See also—

- *Blue Lipstick: Concrete Poems* by John Grandits (2007, Clarion)
- *A Poke in the I: A Collection of Concrete Poems* selected by Paul B. Janeczko, illustrated by Chris Raschka (2001, Candlewick Press)

***Wabi Sabi* by Mark Reibstein. Illustrated by Ed Young. 2008. New York: Little, Brown and Company.**

Everything about this book makes it a masterpiece of presentation. Notice how it opens: vertically. The early pages—like tea-stained parchment—are worn, yet beautiful. Each page is a delightful mix of narrative, papier-mâché collage, and haiku poetry, both in English and in the vertical Japanese. The Japanese haiku poems are written by Basho and Shiki, and appear translated into English in the back of the book. The original Japanese poetry honors a different system of conventions, and because they are so beautiful to look at, they serve to decorate the book as well as contribute to our understanding of what *wabi sabi* means.

***Years of Dust* by Albert Marrin. 2009. New York: Penguin Group.**

This brilliant, award-winning book creates the illusion of watching a documentary film. Marrin combines his insightful, carefully honed narrative with quotations, haunting song lyrics, newspaper clippings, posters, signs, shocking photographs, and more. Sepia tones emphasize the dust and darkness. We are transported to another time and place.

Assessing Writing Samples for CONVENTIONS

With the first few examples, we will focus on conventions. Then we will switch gears and consider presentation—but instead of scoring those pieces, we will consider features that make presentation work.

6 Keys to Scoring Conventions Well

As you look through the scoring guide for conventions & presentation, note the emphasis on *readability*: Do conventions *enhance, support,* or *block* the message? You do not need to mark papers or even count errors. But here are some important things to keep in mind:

1. *Look beyond spelling.* Many writers who struggle with spelling have other conventional strengths.
2. *Score conventions before scoring other traits.* If conventions are especially strong or weak, score that trait first and get it out of the way. Then you can focus on other things.
3. *Look for what is done well,* not just the mistakes.
4. *Do not overreact.* A mistake or two cannot spoil the whole performance. We go too far when we demand conventional perfection, for we cannot teach to such a standard or even meet it ourselves.

> ### Author's Note
>
> Although we're focusing on conventions for these first four samples, think about presentation in terms of how each document *could* look as a published piece. Imagine a cover. Or picture the piece done in multiple pages—as a picturebook, photo essay, or journal entry. Think how you would lay it out if you were a design editor: the fonts you would choose, the amount of white space you would allow, the texture of the paper, the borders. Imagine yourself as the illustrator and ask whether you would use photos, sketches, comics, watercolors, or paper-mâché collage. In discussing such things, you help your writers imagine presentation possibilities.

5. *Do not consider neatness or handwriting in scoring the conventions of your own students.* Such things may be important, but they are separate issues. Many people consider handwriting an artistic skill.

6. *Think of yourself as a copyeditor.* Ask, "How much work would I need to do to prepare this text for publication?"

   - Heavy editing? That's a 1 or 2.
   - Moderate? That's a 3 or 4.
   - Very light—touch-ups only? That's a 5 or 6.

Paper 1

Haircut from Hell (Narrative/Imaginative, Grade 7)

I failed to tell the new worker at "Haircroppers" how I wanted my hair cut. He swung my chair away from the mirror. The noises that fallowed sounded like chainswas, hedge trimmers, and helocopters. Then he swung my chair back to face the mirror. . . .

From the time he swung my chair around, I knew that would be my last visit to "Haircroppers."

My hair, or what was left of it, was tinted a brown olive green color. I felt my hair. A slimey sticky residue came off on my hand. I gave a quick smurk and vigorously rubbed the slime onto my pants.

Unbelievably enough, the quick smile I had given the nin-cum-poop barber was taken to be genuine and he quickly responded, "Glad you like it sir That's my best one yet!"

Disgusted, I turned back to my hair. Maybe a wig was the way to go. I felt some of the olive green goop dribbel down my neck.

I felt my hair again and was immediately stopped by a blur of barbers hands. With rage in his voice he yelled "What are you trying to do, ruin my masterpiece?!"

"Your masterpiece??!! More like your mess. What is this junk anyway? Some kind of axel greese?"

His voice was wavery, but refused to crack. "Its my own creation . . . face mud, hair spray, avacado dip . . ."

I let him get as far as turtle wax when I roared "Hold it!!"

My face was beginning to twist, my scalp to burn. "Hose this junk off, you incompitent moron. If my head doesn't just role to the floor, I'll have your hide!" I couldn't wait a moment longer. I grabed the hose and turned it on myself. Whew. The solution came out into a brown puddle on the floor, along with great chunks of my hair.

Fortunatly, I didn't have to pay for what I call today my hair's "mass suicide."

Suggested Score for CONVENTIONS: 4

Lessons Learned from "Haircut from Hell"

- Enough conventional errors—*even when other things are done well*—can cause us to overlook what's conventionally brilliant.
- Good dialogue adds voice.
- Voice will keep readers reading despite conventional problems.
- Difficulty with spelling should not deter the writer from using the words he or she wants.

Comments

Many of the conventional errors in this paper seem to be the result of hasty editing. Apostrophes are overlooked, and commas and capitals missed. There are too many paragraphs. A scrupulous reader will make corrections as he or she goes along, but this should be the *writer's* job. On the other hand—did you notice this?—many conventions are used with *great* skill. Notice the ellipses and the combined question marks/exclamation points, for example. And although a number of words are misspelled, the writer spells many difficult words correctly. Looking beyond conventions . . . she's enthusiastic. She throws herself into this story. The imagery is vivid, and voice is *very* strong. The phrasing is original and seems to come to her readily: *My face was beginning to twist, my scalp to burn.* Lead and conclusion are excellent, and dialogue is authentic. Read it aloud to appreciate the fluency. (By the way, this *is* a female writer, who chose to write in a male voice.)

Suggested Scores for Other Traits

Ideas: **6**

Organization: **6**

Voice: **6**

Word choice: **6**

Sentence fluency: **6**

The Write Connection

Haircut from Hell

Imagine designing this piece as a picture book. How many pages should it run? What might the cover look like? What illustrations would you like to see? As an alternative, divide the piece into four or five segments, and have students (in pairs or small groups) edit the piece for publication. Are you—and they—surprised by the actual number of errors?

Paper 2

Japan (Expository, Grade 3)

An interesting place to visit. That is my idea of Japan. It is my favrite place to visit I have been yet.

japanese people eat a lot of seafood and vegetables. most of their food they eat raw. they do not eat a lot of doughnuts and french fries. They do not have trouble with their weight!

In japan, you might walk or ride a bike. most people do not drive. If you see a while street blocked off it means do not drive here. Japan also has tranes. They are electric and travel about two times faster than our traines.

If you drive a car there is alot to remember. like do not drive on the right but on the left. Also a license is hard to get because the test is so, so hard to pass. You might have to take it two or three times and even then you might not pass because they make you drive in the very worst traffic for hours and if you get mad you do not pass. If you do not pass you might have to waite two years to try again and it is not good manners to complain about this.

The stores are small and even tiny but very crowded. You can buy every kind of fish you can think of. they have octopus and squid and many other things you might not even reckognize. I didn't! They have baskets too and dishes of all kinds. they have cloths of all kinds but most of them are small. it is best to be very skinny!

In your house if you hd a house you would find it crowded. The whole house might be the size of your living room in America and your whole family has to fit in no matter how big it is. You do not have a lot of privecy and you can't make alot of noise because it is bad manners.

At the end of the day you will fall asleep like anything because you are just stone tired. I am going back for shure! Want to come?

The Write Connection

Japan

Think "celebrationally"—as author and teacher Jeff Anderson reminds us to do. Go through the paper and highlight (or otherwise mark) moments where the writer does something right or creative with conventions. How does this balance out with the number of errors? Is there a lot to celebrate?

Suggested Score for CONVENTIONS: 3

Lessons Learned from "Japan"

- A mini-dictionary (on a sticky note) with just a few needed words—*Japan, a lot, privacy, sure, train, recognize*—can be a huge help to a young writer.
- Just because you can't spell a word, that does not mean you shouldn't use it (but check the spelling later).
- A wide range of visual and sensory details add interest and voice.
- Personal experience can be the best kind of research.

Comments

This is not a typical "all about Japan" paper. The writer is writing from experience, and that gives the piece authenticity. In addition, her details are decidedly refreshing. We learn that Japanese people like their food raw, that they enjoy a wide range of seafood, that they bike nearly everywhere, that small living quarters necessitate a respect for privacy, and that those with snarly dispositions may not get a license to drive. The writer maintains an "Imagine that!" sort of tone without ever making it seem artificial or forced. The organization is a bit random, but is never hard to follow—and the lead and conclusion are strong. Some readers are troubled that the writer opens with a fragment (always a risk); to my ear, it's just right. Despite many conventional strengths (paragraphing, end punctuation, many words spelled correctly), there are enough errors to slow most readers down a bit: spelling errors, missing capitals, missing commas. The errors do not interfere with the message, but they *do* interrupt us. Your decision to score it 3 or 4 depends on whether you think problems outweigh strengths—or vice versa.

Suggested Scores for Other Traits

Ideas: **5**

Organization: **5**

Voice: **5**

Word choice: **4**

Sentence fluency: **5**

Paper 3

The Joke (Memoir, Grade 7)

My grandma is 81. She has had rheumatoid arthritis for twelve years. When it was first diagnosed, her chief problem was constant, relentless pain. Now she can no longer walk, take herself to the bathroom, brush her own teeth or lift a fork to eat; forks and toothbrushes are too heavy for her to hold. To move from her bed to a chair she has to be lifted; sometimes, just the pressure of lifting under her arms causes her to shriek with pain. Despite her problems, though, she loves to sit up and talk with her family. "I'll start dinner in a minute," she tells us.

Unfortunately, pain and medication have dulled her memory, but they have never gotten the best of her imagination. She has many conversations with old friends and long-gone relatives. Sometimes she "goes shopping," then tells us of

(continued on following page)

---

the bargains she found or the clerks who gave her a hard time. My grandma is feisty, and tolerates no backtalk, even in her imagined world.

Last month, she had two molars pulled. Although she had dreaded it, she really liked the orthodontist, which made her experience a little better. She liked him so much she wanted everyone to benefit from his services. She told my brother and me—we're twelve and thirteen—that we should get our teeth pulled now because it would be so much harder if we waited till we were her age. "Just go now and get it over with," she said.

My brother nearly choked on his chicken. It was funny and sad at the same time. I remember my grandma's face. She was so happy to have made her grandson laugh, it made her laugh with us. It was her way of joining in the joke.

Suggested Score for CONVENTIONS: 5

Lessons Learned from "The Joke"

- Voice can be quiet sometimes—it's not always comical or exuberant.
- Occasionally we need to read between the lines to get the full meaning.
- When conventions are "clean," we barely notice them.

Comments

This portrait of the writer's grandmother is vivid, authentic, and loving. The writer notices little things—how the grandmother cannot lift a toothbrush or fork, or how she announces she's going to fix dinner, though she's obviously not up to it. The writer turns Grandma's imaginary shopping trips into a positive trait, hinting at the older woman's quirky, humorous stories. The most striking part of the piece comes at the end, but we must read carefully to understand what is going on. The suggestion that the writer and her brother have their teeth pulled now, while they're young, strikes the brother as outrageously comical. The grandmother is quite serious, however; but she's so delighted by her grandson's response that she cannot help laughing, too. The writer is flooded with mixed emotions: She sees the humor in the situation, but is overcome with sadness that her grandmother, whom she loves, no longer can. This writer, while not playful with conventions (contrast Papers 1 and 5), is a skilled editor.

The Write Connection

The Joke

Many readers feel that the conclusion of this paper, while intriguing, is a little confusing as written. Do you agree? Try revising just that last paragraph to make the situation more clear.

Suggested Scores for Other Traits

Ideas: **5**

Organization: **5** (A stronger conclusion would raise this to a 6.)

Voice: **4/5**

Word choice: **5**

Sentence fluency: **6**

Paper 4

Computer Blues (Narrative, Grade 12)

So there I was, my face aglow with the reflection of my computer screen, trying to conclude my essay. Writing it was akin to Chinese water torture. It dragged on and on, a never-ending babble about legumes, nutrients and soil degradation. I was tranquilizing myself with my own writing.

Suddenly, unexpectedly—I felt an ending coming on. Four or five punchy sentences would bring this baby to a close, and I'd be free of this dreadful assignment forever! Yes!

I had not saved yet, and decided I would do so now. I scooted the white mouse over the pad until the cursor hit the "File" menu—and had almost reached home when it happened. By accident, I clicked the mouse button just to the left of paragraph 66. The screen flashed briefly, and the next thing I knew, I was back to square one. Black. I stared at the blank screen for a moment in disbelief. Where was my essay? My ten-billion-page masterpiece? Gone?! No—that couldn't be! Not after all the work I had done! Would a computer be that unforgiving? That *unfeeling?* Didn't it care about me at all?

I decided not to give up hope just yet. The secret was to remain calm. After all, my file had to be somewhere—right? That's what all the manuals say—"It's in there somewhere." I went back to the "File" menu, much more carefully this time. First, I tried a friendly sounding category called "Find File." No luck there; I hadn't given my file a name.

Ah, then I had a brainstorm. I could simply go up to Undo. Yes, Undo would be my savior! A simple click of a button and my problem would be solved! Undo, however, looked a bit fuzzy. Not a good sign. "Fuzzy" means there's nothing to undo. Don't panic … don't panic …

I decided to try exiting the program, not really knowing what I would accomplish by this, but now feeling more than a little desperate. Next, I clicked on the icon that would allow me back in to word processing. A small sign appeared, telling me that my program was being used by "another user." Another user? What's it talking about? I'm the only user, you idiot! Or at least I'm trying to be a user! Give my paper back! Right now!

I clicked on the icon again and again—to no avail. Click . . . click . . . clickclickclickclick-CLICKCLICKCLICKCLICK!!!!! Without warning, a thin trickle of smoke began emanating from the back of the computer. I didn't know whether to laugh or cry. Sighing, I opened my desk drawer, and pulled out a tablet and pen. This was going to be a long day.

Student's Reflection

In this essay, I tried to capture the feelings of frustration that occur when human and machine do not communicate. The voice in this piece comes, I think, from the feeling that "We've all been there." Everyone who works with computers has had this experience—or something close to it. I also try to give the writer—me—some real personality so the sense of building tension comes through. A tiny writer's problem (not being able to find a good ending) turns into a major problem (losing a whole document). This makes the ideas clear, and also gives this little story some structure. I think the reader can picture this poor, frustrated writer at her computer, wanting, trying to communicate in a human way—but finding that in its own mechanical way, the computer is just as frustrated with her!

Suggested Score for CONVENTIONS: 6

Lessons Learned from "Computer Blues"

- Conventions are about much more than correctness.
- It is all but impossible to capture the sound of the human voice without conventions.
- Fragments can work—very well!

Comments

This piece reads like a mini-play. Anyone who's worked with an uncooperative computer will appreciate this writer's "conversation" with a machine that's clearly a control freak. The big difference, conventionally, between this paper and Paper 3 is that while the writer of "The Joke" is a skilled editor, this writer uses conventions creatively, to enhance voice. The writer's reflection is a bonus—but you should (if possible) score the piece before reading it. Then ask, *Does her thinking match my response?*

Suggested Scores for Other Traits

Ideas: **6**

Organization: **6**

Voice: **6**

Word choice: **6**

Sentence fluency: **6**

Considering PRESENTATION

Let's consider, briefly, several pieces for which presentation is important. We won't score them—just use them for discussion purposes. Review additional documents—posters, menus, pamphlets, and other publications—to broaden your perspective and your students' understanding of this concept.

POETRY

Have a look at Kira's poem (Figure 8.5). Notice how beautifully it is formatted to capture the rhythm and guide our reading. Format is important in poetry because it helps determine how we read and how we pick up specific images: "dark thundering thoughts" or "half-drenched ladybugs." Punctuation in poetry is important, but it does not follow the same rules as punctuation in prose. A writer who omits terminal punctuation, for example, creates the sense that thoughts are floating and continuous. In this poem, the short lines are punchlines, and sometimes serve the function of periods. You might ask yourself, however, where you would insert periods—if you were to add them.

The Write Connection

Computer Blues

The "Computer Blues" writer does a fine job of assessing her own writing—no scores, just an analysis of what stands out, where she got the idea, where the voice comes from. Try writing a similar reflection on a piece of your own work, focusing on what you think works, how you came to write the piece, and the effect you hope it has on readers.

FIGURE 8.5

"Rain and Ivy"
by Kira (Poetry, Grade 3)

Green, delicate, smooth, light green
Clumps of ivy
Shadows rain down with
Dark thundering thoughts
Rain
Rustling leaves whisper in your ears
It's silent, then it whispers
Soft, soothing
Mind-reading words
Rain pours down
You reach for your umbrella
Still keeping your eyes on those ivy leaves
You notice that ladybugs shelter under those leaves
Trying to keep dry
Rain thunders down
And your mother is calling you
To come
So you don't get drenched
You go
Leaving the ivy alone in the rain
Sheltering those poor half-drenched ladybugs
The next morning
You go to check on the ivy
After that you always look
At that ivy
With loving eyes.

A PUBLISHED PIECE: *COCO WRITES*

Figure 8.6 shows page 24 from the Big Book titled *Coco Writes*, part of *Write Traits Kindergarten: Bringing the Traits® to Kinderwriters* (2007, Great Source Education). For this book, my co-author Jeff Hicks and I created a series of stories featuring Coco the Crab.

Coco Writes is directed to two audiences: kindergarten students and their teachers. The visual takes up most of the page—because this is where the students' attention is directed. Along the left panel is what "Coco Says," an interactive adventure that the teacher reads aloud. At the bottom in very large print is a sample of Coco's *own* "writing."

Though a creative writer, Coco struggles with conventions, sometimes forgetting punctuation, omitting letters, and so on. Students help her edit, and the large print and extra spacing allow room for that. In her story, Coco tells how much she loves to "splash humans" on the beach because "they always squeal and I love that." When she tries to write about this, she cannot spell *splash* or *humans*, and so uses a letter-line strategy for these words. After figuring out what she is trying to say, the kindergartners help Coco fill in the missing letters.

The artist's rendition of each page in *Coco Writes* includes many decisions about design, color, fonts, and spacing. When I submitted the manuscript, it was mostly written in Tahoma 12-point on plain white 8½" × 11" paper. What a difference the designer's presentation has made.

FIGURE 8.6

Coco Writes, page 24

CHAPTER 8   Preparing to Publish with CONVENTIONS & PRESENTATION

FIGURE 8.7

Covers for *Thandi* (Grade 8)

 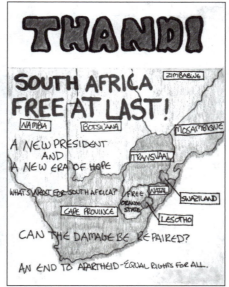

ORIGINAL ART FOR AN INFORMATIONAL REPORT: *THANDI*

Figure 8.7 shows two covers for Jamal's multipart report on Africa. He is studying the impact of apartheid and the devastating effects of AIDS on African children. The result is a series of reports, grouped in a "journal" Jamal has titled "Thandi" (which, he says, is African for "loved one"). He regretted not having access to a computer, which made design and layout (all done by hand) more challenging.

What if you were a designer for this document? You might very well keep this author's original art, but consider—with your students—which font or fonts you could use for the cover. Fonts have their own "voice," and while readability is one issue, a well-chosen font can also suggest genre, theme, and tone.

AN ORIGINAL PICTURE BOOK: *A GREAT JOURNEY*

Figure 8.8 shows four nonconsecutive key pages from a much longer picture book (titled *A Great Journey*), written by a seventh grader. Students were asked to write an illustrated story for primary readers. Each time something significant happened in the story, students were asked to capture it in an illustration. Envisioning their writing as a picture book, continually coordinating words and visuals, tremendously influenced the flow of the stories as well as the details and events the authors chose to include.

As you review this story, notice the strong correlation between visuals and words—and how each reveals something the other does not. In *A Great Journey*, a small but large-eared mouse named Blake is marooned during a hurricane and uses his ingenuity

> You must never illustrate exactly what is written. You must find a space in the text so that the pictures can do the work. Then you must let the words take over where words do it best. It's a funny kind of juggling act.
>
> —Maurice Sendak
> in *Artist to Artist*,
> edited by Eric Carle, 2009, 76

FIGURE 8.8

Four Pages from *A Great Journey* (Grade 7)

When hurricane Jerry blew past Hot Sandy Island one July day, it sank the U.S.S. Milford clear to the bottom of the sea. There was only one survivor: Blake, a small gray mouse with unusually large ears.

He was still wearing his orange life vest, but it was hanging from his body like limp rags. He almost tossed it away, but something stopped him. He remembered his mom saying, "Reuse! Recycle!" He decided he could use the vest for something. A pillow maybe. So he kept it.

Just before his trip, Blake had written to his parents telling them he was coming to visit. Now he didn't know what to do. He didn't think that he would ever see his parents again. He thought how worried they must feel wondering what had become of him. He knew then that he must get off the island. He had no idea how he was going to go about it.

FIGURE 8.8

Four Pages from *A Great Journey* (Grade 7)

All this work was making him very tired, and he lay down on top of his raft to rest. He had a wonderful dream that he was in a hammock on his own back porch with his mom on one side and his dad on the other, rocking him back and forth. When he woke up, fear seized him. His first thought was, "Where is my island?!" It took him a minute to figure out that while he had been asleep, the tide had come in and washed his raft out to sea. "What shall I do?" he thought, tugging on his ears the way he often did when he was nervous.

He thought of trying to get back to shore, but he did not know which way to go. The island was nowhere in sight. He had no water, but he did have a few bananas left. "I better ration them," he thought. He hoped he might drift toward the island, but it did not seem to happen. He floated the rest of the day and on into the night.

The night was scary to Blake, who had never slept outside his own bed. The waves seemed much bigger. He worried that a shark might eat him or his raft might come apart and strand him. Sudden raft failure. If he fell asleep he might roll off right into the sea, so he tried to stay awake, pinching his nose to keep himself alert.

By morning, he was nearly out of bananas and so tired he had to sit down to keep from falling. Just as he thought there was no hope, he saw a black dot in the distance. He thought he might be seeing things, but the dot kept growing larger and larger until he could make out the shapes of sails. It was a ship!

He flailed his arms frantically and squeaked with all his lung power.

"Help me! Help me!" he cried. Of course, they were too far away to hear anything, but yelling seemed like the right thing to do anyway.

Suddenly, he remembered his vest. He yanked it off and began waving it in the air like a flag.

to fashion a raft. In the second two-page spread, Blake has landed safely on the island, but his small boat is gone, and little remains but his life vest. In the third spread, he has fallen asleep on the raft he's built—and doesn't yet realize he's been washed back out to sea. In the final spread, he's about to be reunited with his family.

A COLLAGE OF COVERS: CREATING WRITERS

Since the first edition of this book came out in 1990, the covers have changed dramatically—color, art, size, everything. (See Figure 8.9 for a reminder.) Our first cover featured hieroglyphics. I loved it. The original mock-up also included an intruding red pen that had circled several of the symbols and added comments like "More detail!"

FIGURE 8.9

Collage of Covers from *Creating Writers*

or "Great voice!" I found this design hilariously inspired and fought to keep it, but it didn't pass editorial muster.

If cover designers could be said to have artistic "periods," like Picasso, then the second edition cover represents our "quiet period." Soft pastels, abstract art, forgettable fonts.

The third edition cover, bright and bold with its striking reds and blues, seemed to exude confidence. Readers loved it, and so did I. But many complained that student papers almost never fit totally on one page, so we changed the tearsheet size for the fourth edition. We also added a photograph, representing a much greater emphasis—with this edition—on instruction.

The fifth edition brought a new look. I loved what many teachers (notably Sue Adamson and Jane Kathol of Nebraska) were doing to connect the traits to art, and have always felt that voice can be expressed in countless ways, art being one. It was natural to use a cubist portrait, an expression of voice, done by a student, Sarena Anderson.

For the sixth edition, I wanted something to reflect the concept of a writer's (or teacher's) journey. Stephanie Brooks's "Four Season Tree" seemed just the thing.

Lessons and Strategies for Teaching CONVENTIONS

Traditionally, conventions have been corrected, not taught. Now we know better. We know that as we correct students' work, we teach *ourselves* to be very good editors indeed—for we're getting lots of practice. But we are teaching our writers to depend on us. To get comfortable as editors, students have to hold the pens.

Knowledge of and comfort with modern conventions of writing are important in virtually any set of standards you will encounter, including the Common Core Standards. This is not going to go away. Teachers editing *for* students will not prepare them to meet this challenge. They must be ready to edit any copy—their own or something you invent for practice—with skill and confidence. To prepare them, you want to emphasize these things:

- *Developing an editor's eye*
- *Knowing how to use helpful resources*
- *Reading everything you write both silently and aloud, pencil in hand*
- *Recognizing the value and purpose of conventions*

Following are some lesson ideas and strategies to help you achieve these goals.

1. HELP STUDENTS UNDERSTAND THE REASONS BEHIND CONVENTIONS.

Giv thm some unedted copie lik this thet let's their sea what happens? When, convintions is use incorrect. Porlie riten Koppey helpsthem seee the valeu; of Strong convenshons in Klewing. The reader?

Share the tongue-in-cheek "history" of conventions in Figure 8.10, "Intimegoneby." This can trigger a discussion of how and why conventions evolve. Why do we need commas, capitals, periods—any of it? Reading text without these little helpers makes it clear that conventions exist not just for writers—but for readers.

High-stakes testing increasingly relies on knowledge of grammar and mechanics. We have to teach more intentionally. Grammar and mechanics are not rules to be mastered as much as tools to serve a writer in creating a text readers will understand.

—Jeff Anderson
Mechanically Inclined, 2005, 5

FIGURE 8.10

Intimegoneby

therewerenospacesbetweenwordsandnopunctuation
markstosignalwhenasentencewasending then it occurred to some
clever writer that spacing would make a huge difference in
readability but of course it was still hard to tell where sentences
began or ended fortunately someone devised a clever little mark
called the period to signal a stop. could we ask questions too? we
could. if we wanted to shout there was a mark for that! And if we
could end sentences cleverly why not start them well? Along
came the capital letter. What an invention that was! Things were
getting easier. Before you could say presto, we were pausing with
commas . . . and taking longer pauses with ellipses—or getting
expressive with dashes! When someone spoke with *emphasis*, we
could capture that in *italics*. We could get **bold** with
important words. And if someone remarked, "How great
punctuation is!" we could surround that speech with
quotation marks and preserve it forever—well *almost*. (We could
make little side comments in parentheses, too. How sneaky.)
With a colon, we could introduce **important things**—
such as one of the greatest inventions of all time:
punctuation!!!
Ta-da! Whether at the end of a sentence or
tucked inside, conventions give us a way to imitate human speech.
Sorry to say, conventions are not equally popular; almost *no one*
loves the humble semicolon. People think it's hard to master; it isn't.
No matter, though. In the world of conventions . . .
NOTHING lasts forever ☺

© 2012. Vicki Spandel.

Author's Note

Check the complementary text, *Creating Young Writers* (K through 3), Pearson, 2011, for a much more elaborate discussion of teaching conventions and editing skills to younger writers.

2. TEACH COPYEDITORS' SYMBOLS.

Most young writers revise and edit on a word processing program these days. But teaching a few basic copyediting symbols does two important things: (1) it shows the *kinds* of changes editors make, and (2) it makes it simple for you to use these symbols in modeling, as you demonstrate editing for your class. For this edition, I have revised the list (Figure 8.11) to include those symbols I use frequently when modeling for students. Many dictionaries and handbooks include expanded lists of these symbols if you want more.

3. KEEP EDITING PRACTICE SHORT AND FOCUSED.

When you design an editing lesson of your own, make the print large, put *plenty* of room between lines and words for corrections, make margins generous, and be sure you keep the practice *simple* at first. The rule is this: *If you have to do it for your students, it's too hard.* When it counts, you won't be there (unless you plan to follow them on to college and then to the job site). Focus on one kind of problem at a time—at first. Later,

FIGURE 8.11

Copyeditors' Symbols

Symbol	Meaning	Example
	Delete the material.	There are ~~were~~ six traits.
∧	Insert a letter, word, phrase.	Jeff Anderson is ∧ a teacher. *an author and*
∧	Insert punctuation.	Good writing needs detail, voice, and strong verbs.
		Make your readers do three things: laugh, think, and remember.
		Who called voice the umbrella trait?
		Leads are important; endings matter too.
		That's my book you're shredding!
⊙	Insert a period.	That's my best lead ever ⊙
#/	Insert a space.	I can't think # of a better title.
∨'	Insert an apostrophe.	I love Garrison Keillor's humor.
≡	Capitalize a letter.	Lynne truss knows her commas.
/	Change to lower case.	We have a Math Test this Friday.
∿	Transpose words or letters.	We are there.
⌗	Start a new paragraph.	"What can a missing comma tell us?" queried Watson. ⌗ "You'd be surprised," replied Holmes.
❝ ❞	Insert quotation marks.	Elmore Leonard once said, "I try to leave out the parts people skip."
————	Put in italics.	Did you read *Mockingbird*?

FIGURE 8.12

Editing Practice

Goal: Fill in end punctuation and capitals for six sentences.

The Mount Rushmore National Monument located near Keystone, South Dakota, covers more than twelve hundred acres and sits on land considered sacred by the Lakota Sioux people the memorial, which is made of granite, has 60-foot sculptures of four presidents, including George Washington, Thomas Jefferson, Abraham Lincoln, and Theodore Roosevelt sculptors spent more than 25 years carving it though a few people were injured during the project, no one died more than two million tourists visit the monument annually it has appeared in many movies

Excerpt from *Creating Revisers and Editors, Grade 4,* by Vicki Spandel. 2009. Pearson Education, Inc. All rights reserved. Reprinted by permission.

FIGURE 8.13

Editing Practice, corrected

Goal: Fill in end punctuation and capitals for six sentences.

The Mount Rushmore National Monument located near Keystone, South Dakota, covers more than twelve hundred acres and sits on land considered sacred by the Lakota Sioux people. the memorial, which is made of granite, has 60-foot sculptures of four presidents, including George Washington, Thomas Jefferson, Abraham Lincoln, and Theodore Roosevelt. sculptors spent more than 25 years carving it. though a few people were injured during the project, no one died. more than two million tourists visit the monument annually. it has appeared in many movies.

Excerpt from *Creating Revisers and Editors, Grade 4,* by Vicki Spandel. 2009. Pearson Education, Inc. All rights reserved. Reprinted by permission.

combine various kinds of errors so that your now-experienced editors look for several things at once.

In Figure 8.12, students are asked *only* to fill in capitals and end punctuation for six sentences. Keeping the task focused like this dramatically increases a student's chances of success and reinforces a particular editorial skill.

4. DON'T CORRECT *EVERYTHING.*

In Figure 8.14, you'll see just the first two paragraphs from a much longer piece by an eighth grader writing about the love of his life, his fiancée Tammy. *Fiancée* was a difficult word for him, and he spelled it *feonsay*. He made a number of other conventional errors, as well. But one thing he got right: voice. As you can see from the teacher's marks, however, there is no personal response to the detail or heartfelt feelings embedded in the writing. I will leave it to you to imagine how the student responded.

Here's an alternative scenario. Suppose the teacher had said, "Your voice really touched me—I loved reading this. First, you chose a topic you care about deeply—and then you were so careful about choosing just the right details, like singing *Happy Birthday* to Tammy, or helping us understand she's a tiny person with a big heart. You put yourself into your writing, and that's a gift to your readers."

FIGURE 8.14

Eighth Grade Paper

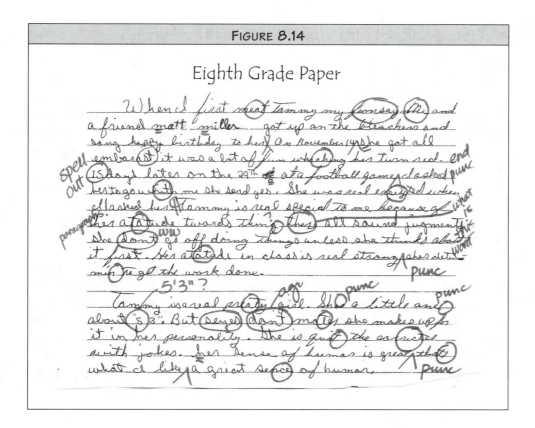

The teacher might also comment on conventions the writer handled well, such as paragraphing, end punctuation, or initial capitals. A mini-dictionary on a sticky note could be immensely helpful to a writer like this, who has so much to say but struggles to spell the words he needs. It would not need to include *every* misspelled word in the piece, just a few that are especially significant and difficult: *fiancée, excited, embarrassed, pretty, character.* Instead of telling this writer what he already knows (that he spelled some words incorrectly), a gesture like this says, "Here—let me give you something to make the writing easier." Of course, it is important to provide mini-dictionaries (or similar kinds of help) *during* the drafting process, not after the draft is finished.

5. LET STUDENTS GUIDE THE CURRICULUM.

The world of conventions is very big. If you try to teach everything, you'll make yourself *and* your students crazy. Be smart. Be selective. One evening or weekend when you think you might have 30–45 minutes to spare, go through a stack of student papers, not marking or grading, just listing conventional problems that come up frequently. Chances are, you'll notice things like faulty contractions, misplaced or unneeded commas, missing capitals, faulty subject-verb agreement, and problems with dialogue. There's your focus. Now, instead of relying on lessons from a textbook, you can invent your own lessons, tailored just to your class of writers and their needs of the moment.

In *Easy Writer*, 3rd edition (Bedford/St. Martin's, 2009), Andrea Lunsford, professor of English at Stanford University, has identified the 20 most common kinds of errors in English writing. Find a copy of the book if you can—it's worth the search. You can also find Lunsford's list online by simply searching under "20 most common errors in English." Compare her list to your own. And if you work with older writers, make the list available to them also. It will open their eyes about things to watch out for in their own writing.

> When I examine whole files of papers that have been marked and commented on by teachers, many of them look as though they have been trampled on by cleated boots.
>
> —Paul Diederich
> *Measuring Growth in English,* 1974, 20

6. Use worksheets to make airplanes.

Mem Fox once said that worksheets were best used to make paper airplanes. I agree. Research indicates that drills isolated from everyday reading and writing are not helpful. In fact, as George Hillocks Jr. points out in *Research on Written Composition: New Directions for Teaching* (1986, 248), an isolated skills emphasis combined with overcorrection actually may restrict students' growth as writers. Hillocks goes on to say that those "who impose the systematic study of traditional school grammar on students over lengthy periods of time in the name of teaching writing do them a gross disservice which should not be tolerated by anyone concerned with the effectiveness of teaching good writing."

7. Instead . . . look to literature.

Let's say I want to teach students about dashes. One good way to do this is with a literary example, like this one from *The Wednesday Wars* by Gary D. Schmidt (2007, 15). Holland Hoodhood has been cajoled into playing soccer against a team he knows can not only beat him—but literally crush him. As the forces of "destiny" head his way, he is determined to stand his ground. Notice how the dashes point like fingers right at those words the writer wants us to notice:

> Then I closed my eyes—nothing says you have to look at your destiny—and stepped out of the way.

I want the *students* to tell me why dashes work well here. This inductive thinking doesn't happen with worksheets.

8. Remember the 72-hour rule.

Ever tuck a "perfect" piece of writing into the file—only to have it sprout errors before you looked at it again two weeks later? Time is the editor's friend. If you encourage students to wait three days—or even more—between writing and editing, they'll edit much more efficiently. That mental break helps them see their writing more the way they would see someone else's work.

9. Encourage students to edit with their ears—not just their eyes.

Good editors read text more than once, and many read *aloud*. Reading aloud is important because—

- It slows the reader down
- It increases the odds of finding missing punctuation or words
- It increases the likelihood of finding faulty grammar (*We was on our way* doesn't look as bad as it sounds.)

Here are two simple tricks to help struggling editors:

- **Read from the bottom up.** This is a lifesaver for students who struggle with spelling because it's hard to skim when you read backwards. Students should then read again, aloud, from the beginning.
- **Use a ruler.** This helps readers focus on one line at a time. This is what is meant by the phrase "line by line editing" in the writing guide.

10. Become sleuths.

Errors are everywhere. Share mistakes you find in newspapers, memos, textbooks, or junk mail—online or on television. Have students identify the problem and show you how they would edit to correct it. Then share your perspective. Here's an example that came to me in a recent email:

> You are right we can tell the difference.

I want students to be able to edit a run-on like this. But I will not begin by saying, "Here's an example of a run-on." I ask them to tell *me* what the problem is.

> Here's a sentence from a recent television newscast:

> The outcome of events in Egypt, which will affect numerous people, are hard to predict. (Subject-verb agreement is tricky when subject and verb are this far apart.)

Here are two more:

> We need to eat good.

> Him and other members of Congress are no closer to agreement.

Good is probably on its way to becoming an adverb, but it's not quite there yet. Will *him* and *her* become acceptable sentence subjects? I hope not—but such usage is spreading.

11. Celebrate what students do correctly.

Once I was disappointed at a NCTE conference when I couldn't get a seat at Donald Murray's keynote presentation. Jammed into a crowded doorway, crushed by dozens of his ardent admirers, I heard him say something I'll recall forever: "We'd get farther, faster teaching conventions if we'd mark what students did *right*—instead of circling their mistakes."

We don't need to mark every tiny thing done correctly, of course. That would soon grow as tedious for students as reviewing their errors. But when you notice exceptionally good punctuation that helps you read a piece without pausing, or a student spells unusually challenging words correctly, don't be afraid to comment.

12. Use peer editing with caution.

Teaming for *practice* is an excellent instructional strategy; students can edit independently, then check with a partner to see if they approached problems in the same way. They can discuss samples and exchange ideas—as long as no grade hangs in the balance.

But when the editing is *for real*, partnering should be used with great caution. No one wants to edit herself into a lower grade than she would have received had she not asked for "help." Figure 8.15 shows a sample of peer editing gone awry.

What about peer review? That's a *whole* different game. Listening to a writer present her work, and then responding to detail or voice is vital. Responders/listeners don't take over the writer's text, look for errors, or mark up a paper. Usually, they don't look at the text at all; they listen, and respond to ideas and voice. This is a very good thing.

We learn to write primarily by building on our strengths, and it is important for the teacher to encourage the student to see what has potential, what has strength, and what can be developed.

Donald M. Murray
A Writer Teaches Writing, 2004, 157

Author's Note

Teacher and author Jeff Anderson introduces the concept of celebration to his students with Byrd Baylor's classic picture book *I'm in Charge of Celebrations* (1995). This book reminds us that the best celebrations are small and personal—as with students learning day by day to edit well.

Peer Editing Gone Awry

Driving Tests Should Be Harder

If drivers test were more rigorous, every one on the road would be safer.

About 50,000 people die in traffic accidents every year, and thousands more
are injured. The most common cause of accidents is drunk drivers but the
second most common cause is incompetent driving. Yet we grant driver's
licenses on the basis of a very simple test.

13. TEACH CONTENT AREA CONVENTIONS, TOO.

Math, music, business, and science all have their own conventions; they look a little different from commas or semicolons, but they serve much the same purpose, symbolizing meaning and guiding a reader. In math, for example, we use symbols to indicate division, square root, equality, and so forth. Exploring conventions in other fields helps students to better understand the broader nature of conventions and the way they influence us as readers.

14. CREATE A STYLE SHEET.

Think of your classroom as your own small publishing house. Design a style sheet (see Figure 8.16) that reflects your personal preferences—how you'd like graphics titled, where you want titles placed, how you want the writer's name (or yours) to appear, how many fonts you want to see per page, how you'd like references cited, how you'd like captions for graphics handled, and so on. You may want to three-hole-punch this sheet for inclusion in writing notebooks. Or enlarge it to post on the wall. Remember, mine is only a model; your style sheet should reflect what is important to you.

A Message for Parents and Guardians

Even adults who do not spell or punctuate well themselves often have high (sometimes unreasonable) expectations for the speed with which their children will develop conventional proficiency. They look to you to make it happen. You can assure them that it *will* happen, but

1. it will take time and patience because learning to be an editor is harder and takes longer than copying corrections, and
2. parents can help.

First, let parents know that their children will be taught to think and work like editors, and they will be largely responsible for *editing their own text*. You will provide instruction through modeling and multiple examples, but will not do the actual work for students. Because of this, their work may not come home corrected *at first* because

FIGURE 8.16

Sample Style Sheet

1. Use 12-point Times Roman (or similar font).

2. Make major headings 16-point, centered.

3. Make subheads 14-point, flush left.

4. **Boldface** all major headings and subheads.

5. Make all margins 1" wide.

6. Use endnotes, not footnotes.

7. In citing sources, refer to *Write Source 2000*, pages 231–232.

8. Use no more than two different fonts per page.

9. Double space all text (except long quotations—see #20).

10. You may use either bullets or numbers for lists.

11. Label illustrations or other graphics as Figure 1, Figure 2, etc. Refer to each one by number in your text.

12. If you prepare a title page (optional) please include the title of the piece, your name, and the date. Center *everything*.

13. Use *italics*, not underlining, to show emphasis.

14. Avoid **boldface** except for headings.

15. Avoid FULL CAPS except when quoting fully capitalized material.

16. Keep exclamation points to a minimum—no more than two per paper!!

17. Use contractions (*don't, can't, wouldn't, couldn't, we'll*, etc.) if you wish.

18. Number your pages, after the first page, in the upper right corner.

19. If you do not have a title page, include your name, my name, the class period, and the date in the upper right-hand corner of the first page, like this:

> Charles Naka
> Mr. Price
> Period 3
> March 1, 2012

20. Set off long (over 25 words) quotations by indenting five spaces on both right and left, and printing the quotation in single-spaced text, like this:

> *Always write with voice. If the voice fades, your reader*
> *will fade with it, and no one wants this to happen. Write like*
> *you mean it, and the reader will not only stay awake, but*
> *may actually purchase your next book.* (Marland, 2008, p. 10)

they may not (unless they're skilled high school editors) be up to editing every line they write—*yet*. They'll get there.

Next, invite parents in to observe editing lessons (and even to participate). Seeing students discuss and edit faulty text, and use copyediting symbols with skill will reassure parents that their children are truly *learning* conventions—and becoming independent editors. A note like the one in Figure 8.17 can help.

FIGURE 8.17

What to Tell Parents

Dear Parent,

This year, your child will be learning to both write and edit—and they are not quite the same thing! **As writers**, we will work on ideas, organization, voice, word choice, and fluency—the heart and soul of good writing. You can get a written copy of these traits any time. *Please ask.* You can also see them posted in our classroom.

As editors, we will work on spelling, punctuation, grammar, capital letters, paragraphs, and making copy look good on the page. As you can see, writing takes many skills!

Students will write and edit often. You can help by asking your child, "Are you working on writing or editing in this lesson? Or both?"

Except when we are *publishing* your child's work, I will not correct his or her writing. This may seem strange at first since many parents remember that their writing was always corrected by a teacher. The problem is, research shows that when the teacher does the correcting, the teacher also does all the learning. That is not what we want.

I will, however, be showing your child many ways to spot and correct editorial problems, and through the year, you will see your child's editing skills grow. Here are **eight things you can do as a parent to help:**

1. Ask your child to teach you the copy editor's symbols, one by one.
2. Ask your child to also teach you the traits of writing, one by one, as we work on them.
3. Remind your child to skip every other line when writing a rough draft so he or she will have plenty of room to revise and edit.
4. Give your child a pen or pencil he or she likes to work with to make editing more fun.
5. If possible, provide a good dictionary or handbook to use at home. I can give you suggestions if this is something you are able to do.
6. Practice together looking for mistakes in editing lessons I will send home.
7. Look for mistakes in newspapers or other print you and your child read together—and praise your child each time he or she spots an error.
8. When you write, ask for your child's help. Ask him or her to help you spell a word (even if you know it), or to show you where a comma, apostrophe, period, or question mark goes.

Finally, do not expect perfection right away. Editors need time and practice to gain skill. With enough of each, you will see your child's skills grow in ways that will amaze you. Please celebrate with me each step your child takes toward becoming an independent editor!

Sincerely,

Resource Books for You, Your Students, or Both

The following books deal partially or primarily with conventions, though many offer suggestions on writing with flair as well. I chose books written with voice. You might enter a given book thinking conventions are dry, and hoping to escape quickly; the writer will make you linger.

100 Ways to Improve Your Writing by Gary Provost. 1985. New York: Penguin.

This little, yet mighty book is short and to the point. You can read the whole thing in an evening, but it's a book you'll keep on a nearby shelf. Provost is sensible and opinionated, a good combination.

The Curious Researcher: A Guide to Writing Research Papers, MLA Update Edition (6th edition) by Bruce Ballenger. 2009. New York: Longman.

From notes to publication, one of the most readable books ever on conducting and presenting research. Written in a conversational style to make you feel you are getting one-on-one coaching.

Eats, Shoots & Leaves by Lynne Truss. Illustrated by Bonnie Timmons. 2006. New York: G.P. Putnam's Sons.

In this condensed version of her best-selling book for adults (by the same title), Truss makes the correct use of commas plain and simple—and the incorrect use hilarious.

The Elephants of Style: A Trunkload of Tips on the Big Issues and Gray Areas of Contemporary American English by Bill Walsh. 2004. New York: McGraw-Hill.

Bill Walsh is an editor for the Washington Post, and from the first sentence, you feel you're in good hands. His book is a delightful, enlightening compendium of what's current, off limits, ridiculous, and downright tacky.

Everyday Editing by Jeff Anderson. 2007. Portland, ME: Stenhouse.

Jeff Anderson scores another hit with this original take on editing: celebrating what students do well, and using mentor texts to teach conventional lessons of craft.

Mechanically Inclined by Jeff Anderson. 2005. Portland, ME: Stenhouse.

Since Jeff is a friend, it's hard to be objective. Were he not a friend, I would objectively state that this is hands down the best book ever written on teaching fundamental grammar and punctuation creatively, brilliantly, and within the context of writing process.

On Writing Well: The Classic Guide to Writing Nonfiction by William Zinsser. 30th Anniversary Edition. 2006. New York: HarperCollins.

When you're blessed with a 30th anniversary edition, it's a safe bet you had something worthwhile to say. This book is pointed, succinct, humorous, insightful—and seriously helpful. It's the book you wish you'd had in your college writing classes, written by the man you wish had taught them.

Origins of the Specious by Patricia T. O'Conner. 2010. New York: Random House.

If you ever wonder whether *none* is singular or plural, ponder the origin of *ain't*, or wish people would say *sneaked* instead of *snuck*, you'll love this book. With trademark humor and perception, O'Conner explores the etymology and validity of historical and contemporary usage and grammar, debunking myths and treating us to any number of entertaining anecdotes along the way.

People often ask me who decides what's right. The answer is we all do. Everybody has a vote. The "rules" are simply what educated speakers generally accept as right or wrong at a given time. When enough of us decide that "cool" can mean "hot," change happens.

—Patricia T. O'Conner
Origins of the Specious, 2010, xvii

Sin and Syntax: How to Craft Wickedly Effective Prose by Constance Hale. 2001. New York: Broadway Books.

Witty and fun to read, Hale's book contains countless tips for crafting strong sentences, as well as intelligent, in-depth discussions of various parts of speech. Examples will make you cringe—or laugh, depending on how much they remind you of yourself (or people you know).

Writing Tools: 50 Essential Strategies for Every Writer by Roy Peter Clark. 2006. New York: Little, Brown and Company.

Supremely conversational, readable, and practical. The book is filled with outstanding examples from classic and modern writing, and is a text from which you'll borrow and quote frequently. A special feature—"Workshop"—offers ideas to use in your own writing or teaching.

Woe Is I: The Grammarphobe's Guide to Better English in Plain English by Patricia T. O'Conner. 3rd edition. 2009. New York: Penguin.

The title says it all. O'Conner makes grammar understandable and entertaining. Her examples ensure you won't forget things five minutes later: "So don't assume that an exotic plural is more educated. Only *ignorami* would say they live in *condominia*." (32)

The Write Source Handbooks for Students, Second Generation, by Patrick Sebranek, Dave Kemper, and Verne Meyer. Burlington, WI: Write Source.

Comprehensive, authoritative, and user friendly. Kindergarten through college. These texts include references to the six traits, although their rubrics are different from mine.

The Chicago Manual of Style, 16th edition. 2010. Illinois: University of Chicago Press.

OK—this one doesn't have as much voice as some others, but it's still THE go-to guide for editorial questions of all kinds. Reviewers have been enthusiastic about this updated edition, and it has been reformatted for digital publishing.

Strategies for Introducing and Teaching PRESENTATION

Packaging a message effectively is about two primary things:

- Getting readers' attention
- Making information accessible

The first is accomplished primarily through art and color—as well as pleasing layout. The second is accomplished in a variety of ways. Writers use subheads to break copy into sections, for example, bullets to make lists easy to scan and recall, boxes or other devices to help readers locate information in a hurry.

This section offers suggestions for greatly broadening your students' understanding of how presentation works and why it is an important part of the publishing process.

1. Begin by collecting examples.

You might start with picture books because they're often particularly striking. Several memorable books are listed in the literature section, but have students search for additional books that are noteworthy because of the cover, illustrations, general layout, or all three.

As you examine your examples, make a list of features that enhance them. For example, the cover may suggest mystery or comedy, in keeping with the content of the book. The font may be funky or artistic. You may like the designer's use of color or the arrangement of features on the page. Add to this list as you examine more samples— and other types of documents, such as

- Advertisements
- Maps
- Textbook chapters
- Video or board game packaging
- Promotional materials, such as pamphlets
- Websites
- Signage in a museum, zoo, or other public display
- Theater (or other) posters
- Menus
- Product packaging

With each example, ask, *What does it take to package information effectively in this genre?*

2. GIVE STUDENTS OPPORTUNITIES TO WORK ON PIECES THAT *DEMAND STRONG PRESENTATION*.

Face it: Students will develop limited presentation skills if they are consistently writing short stories and essays that are seen only by you. They will think once the document is neat and bordered with wide margins, their job is done. Only when publishing for a broader audience do students have to think seriously about *document design*. As designers, students need to branch out, and they need computer access. That way, they can create such things as—

- Book covers
- Photo collages
- Websites
- Wikis
- Picture books
- PowerPoint presentations . . .

. . . and more. To do this, they will also need guidance from you, and that means some comfort with technology. (More about this in the next section.)

3. EXPLORE FONTS.

Fonts may seem like a small part of the presentation picture—but in fact, the right font can make the difference between a document that's easy or fatiguing to read. Fonts can be playful, crazy, serious, bold, exotic, formal, lazy, sleek, graceful, or commanding. Check out fonts on your computer. Print out a few and talk about which might be most appropriate for—

- A mystery novel
- A report on a medical discovery
- A ticker running across the bottom screen of a news program

- A humorous birthday greeting card
- The cover of a picture book for young children
- A pamphlet advertising a tropical getaway
- Directions for using a digital camera well
- Print on a map . . .

. . . and so on. A font that is perfect in one situation might be disastrous in another.

4. ENCOURAGE STUDENTS TO WORK IN GROUPS.

Projects involving presentation often require significant amounts of time, even with the help of technology. When students work in groups, they can designate specific responsibilities: One person may be a skilled editor, one a photographer, one a general document designer, one a copy writer.

5. PROVIDE ACCESS TO PUBLISHING RESOURCES.

Often, when we think of publishing, we think of students sharing from an author's chair, posting a document on the wall, or presenting their writing at a special gathering. But today, students have many opportunities to publish in the traditional sense: to have their copy and illustrations bound formally and made available to the public. This is enormously exciting—but it requires a major investment of time. You must be prepared to coach students through the steps of gathering information, prewriting, preparing and revising drafts, *and* putting together a final design. If you and your students are ready for publishing at that level, here are some resources that can help (or simply look up "student publishing" online):

www.publishingstudents.com

www.studenttreasures.com

www.amphi.com

http://college.holycross.edu

http://nces.ed.gov

http://niehs.nih.gov

http://pbskids.org

www.candlelightstories.com

www.veeceet.com

http://writekids.tripod.com

www.bookworm-mag.com

www.readwritethink.org
(see "stapleless book")

www.educationworld.com

www.showbeyond.com

www.tikatok.com/classroom

http://figment.com

Expanding Presentation through TECHNOLOGY

Technology has transformed the way we create documents. Thanks to word processing, revision and editing now happen so quickly that the whole concept of "first" and "second" drafts has all but disappeared. We write, revise, and edit in one fluid, continuous step. Only a few of us recall the days when we composed on an electric typewriter, holding our breath as we came to the end of a page—hoping that final footnote would fit.

Was it simply [Shakespeare's] destiny to arrive at *to be or not to be, that is the question* regardless of whether he wrote by hand, typewriter, or computer, or would there be distinct versions, different shades of that phrase, depending on which machine the initial thought had been ground through?

—Amy Krouse Rosenthal
Encyclopedia of an Ordinary Life,
2005, 214–215

In addition, technology has turned the whole way we communicate right on its head. Where once we had letters, stories, and reports, we now have blogs, tweets, digital stories, podcasts, videos, and wikis. We have imagery, sound, light, color. Our audience doesn't just read. They listen, view, and participate. The line between author—or composer—and reader/listener/viewer is no longer distinctive, or restrictive. We can, if we wish, play both parts.

Technology offers something more than ease, or even variety—something more precious. And that is a wider audience—world-wide, should we so desire. In addition, technology facilitates cooperation *during the composition process*. How big a deal is that, though? Aren't students working cooperatively all the time anyway? Yes—but not like this.

Now they can share information right *within the same document*. And because everyone wants to see what everyone else has written about the expanding/shrinking universe or the true size of the anaconda, there is reason to read, to check, to revise further. Technology offers motivation because it makes composition fun. Think about it. Given a choice, would you rather write an essay on an assigned topic, or be a videographer who could rock the world with a topic of your own choosing? The things we longed for—broad audience, motivation for writers—technology has plunked right in our laps. But we are, some of us, blooming terrified.

If you feel a little apprehensive about technology, know that you are not alone. As the report *Teachers Are the Center of Education* (College Board et al., 2010) reveals, many teachers feel nervous at first. Be fearless. It's easier than you think. Following are a few suggestions on getting started using technology to teach writing. And if you are proficient at this already, please coach others—inviting them into your classroom to see how it's done, so they can get comfortable too.

> The read/write web finally delivered the promise of having a real audience and varied purposes that writing teachers had so long looked to bring to their classrooms . . . We could write (and publish our writing) anytime, anywhere.
>
> —Troy Hicks
> *The Digital Writing Workshop*,
> 2010, 127

1. SHARE SOME BASIC LANGUAGE WITH STUDENTS.

Maybe you're the expert in the group. Or maybe—as often happens with technology—your students will wind up teaching you. That's fine. Either way, the whole learning process is easier, given a few basic terms—such as these:

Blog: Short for weblog. A blog is an online journal presented in reverse chronological order—with the most recent entries at the top. Blogs can be highly personal or primarily informational. Companies use them to keep in touch with customers. Individuals use them to promote products and services or just to share opinions. Readers may leave comments, making the blog interactive. Blog entries are archived, so they're available indefinitely. And blogs can be linked to other sites, creating a network of bloggers who share common interests in, say, Shakespeare—or the history of conventions (entirely feasible).

Ning: A ning is a social network that can be set up to reflect an individual's, group's, or organization's personal style, preferences, and interests. A ning is highly flexible, with numerous communication options, and can serve very large groups. Users can form small groups—to do a book chat, for example. They may also initiate blogs that any other user can access.

Podcast: A podcast is an audio broadcast converted into digital format. It can be played on a computer or on a digital music player. Podcasts are usually very short. A writer/composer with a lot to say will often create multiple podcasts, each covering one aspect of a broader topic. Think of them as audio paragraphs. They can be informational or editorial in nature. A podcast is a good medium for a book or film review, for instance—but it could also offer summaries, strategies, or updates on virtually any topic.

RSS: RSS stands for "really simple syndication." It's an online subscription service that allows a user to have information sent to an email inbox in much the way you would get a magazine in your regular mailbox. This is infinitely handy when you're doing research on a particular topic and want the computer to help you find things—versus tracking down every last relevant piece of info on your own. To get started with RSS, you need to (1) sign up for a news reader—a site to which the information will be sent; and (2) subscribe to any websites you want searched regularly. Subscription is free and easy; you just click on an icon (it will appear on your web menu) that tells you whether a website is available for subscription. And presto—you don't need to visit that website unless you want to. Anything new will come to you.

Webcast: A webcast is similar to a podcast, but with video. Essentially, a webcast is a media file distributed over the Internet in order to reach many listeners or viewers at the same time. It is sometimes distributed live (making it more spontaneous than the traditional video), but may also be available on demand. It is a little different from web conferencing, which involves interaction between a conference facilitator (or group) and the audience. A web conference may involve sharing of information through PowerPoint slides or a Smartboard. Web conferences may also provide opportunities for whole-group or one-on-one chats.

Wiki: A wiki is a special website created by numerous users who compile their research to create a more thorough and (it is hoped) more accurate information base than any of them could develop working alone. Wikis may be open for anyone to edit; no particular technological skill is required to participate, but often an editor must show that the information to be added comes from a reputable source. A wiki can be set up in such a way that someone monitors the editing, ensuring that additions to the information base are sound and useful for intended readers.

2. EXPAND YOUR KNOWLEDGE THROUGH ONLINE TUTORIALS.

Many are available. You and your students can view them together (and one day, make your own). I happen to particularly like the short, snappy, easy-to-follow videos available at www.commoncraft.com Their selections include—

- *Blogs in Plain English*
- *Cloud Computing in Plain English*
- *Podcasting in Plain English*
- *RSS in Plain English*
- *Social Networking in Plain English*
- *Wikis in Plain English*
- *Wikipedia—Explained by Common Craft*

3. SET UP A BLOG FOR DISCUSSION PURPOSES.

A class blog allows students to communicate about any issues important to the class—writing strategies, genres, books or other writing they are reading together, or whatever. It creates a sense of community, with students interested in one another's work. Students can post reviews of a book, for example—and hear what other students think. They can also establish links to heighten everyone's interest and understanding; a link to a video interview with an author would be one example.

Students may also post samples of their own work, either written or multi-media, for feedback. They can then use this feedback for future posts. They can also tag blogs with key words that make it easy to find entries in the future. A blog on Sandra Cisneros, for example, might be tagged with her name, but also the key words **author** and **poet**. Troy Hicks (*The Digital Writing Workshop*, 2009) likens the blog to "a natural extension of the writer's notebook" (29), suggesting that blogging in the digital workshop gives students a chance to write and revise in ways that the traditional notebook never did. (34).

He also cautions, however, that blog posts, once online, may be open to public scrutiny forever. It is critical for students to understand that, unlike a notebook, a blog is anything but private. It's best not to post anything a person does not want others to read. Hicks offers tutorials on his book's companion website (digitalwritingworkshop. ning.com) that provide suggestions on dealing with the privacy issue.

4. HAVE STUDENTS CREATE WIKIS.

A wiki is a special kind of website that can grow or be revised—even by multiple authors—over time. Students can create individual wikis—or a group might work on one wiki as a team. Writers can collaborate in different ways, too. For example, one group might create an anthology of poems. Another might create a collaborative report. The first represents a collage of voices, the second a synthesized voice.

A wiki is set up to change with the click of a button: *edit, save, link*. Contributors can click on "edit" to add information, then save the now-revised wiki page. They can also create links to other relevant websites. You can decide, within your own classroom, how and when such editing will be done. For example, do you want anyone from the class to edit anytime? Or do you want "specialists" in a particular content area to edit under your supervision so that you can observe the nature of the editing they do?

Note that because a wiki is constantly changing through revision, it provides an ideal stimulus for talking about the nature of revision itself. First wiki drafts may be significantly cropped or changed. It's important to discuss why and how this should happen because writers' feelings are involved. Balancing the feelings of contributing authors against the need to reach readers can teach students important lessons about revision.

5. GO MULTI-MEDIA.

Multi-media means combining, in some form, any of these elements—text, audio, still images, moving images, sound effects, and transitional or special effects—to create a coherent message for an audience. Podcasts, webcasts, videos, PowerPoint presentations, digital stories all apply.

Teacher David Brown works with second and fourth grade students at John H. Webster Elementary School in Philadelphia. He talks of getting hooked on technology when his students saw poems they had handwritten reproduced on the computer: [The] kids had a different feeling, a different look on their faces, when they saw their work typed up and printed out" (*Teachers Are the Center of Education*, 2010, 25).

Brown has since expanded his use of technology to include a program called iMovie, a form of video editing software. Students can now make films based on their poems, including music, audio, and visuals. (26)

Audio and video change everything. Writing is still the core. Videos need story boards. Audio presentations need scripts. But the published piece looks different. Instead of a written lead about Civil Rights activist Claudette Colvin, for example, a student might include a striking photo of Colvin, a video of Martin Luther King, Jr., speaking to a crowd, a photo collage of black students marching, singing, and entering universities,

> ### Author's Note
> A wiki is a little different from a blog in that it changes as it expands. A blog grows with new entries, but a wiki is continually *revised*. It may be updated to include new information, or writers may simply find other ways of saying things. And of course, as with a blog, they add new information too. You can find examples of wikis online just by searching under the word *wiki*. Seeing what other writers have done will give you a host of ideas.

with an audio voice-over by Phillip Hoose, author of *Claudette Colvin: Twice Toward Justice*. Suddenly, possibilities explode. Students need not publish in multi-media form every time, but they do need the options. They must know how to create—

- Podcasts on issues that are relevant (as one alternative to a persuasive paragraph)
- Digital photos and photo collages to illustrate writing in all genres
- Video to support narrative, memoir, informational writing, or other genres
- PowerPoint presentations
- Written material to support all multi-media productions

This is a new way of writing and demands new skills. Planning a video, for example, may require a student to create a storyboard, a planning graphic with video on one side and script for the voiceover on the other (see Figure 8.18). A PowerPoint presentation requires skillful transitions between slides—and these transitions cannot be accomplished through words alone. Students must learn to manipulate visuals, lighting, colors, and special effects like fading or folding slides or emerging print. Detail may come in the form of a photo or video—and that means gaining skill with things like lighting and angles, or just finding the right moment or image to shoot.

The results are worth the effort. As high school teacher Joe Malley tells us, students who produce an informational video learn far more about a given topic than they could hope to learn writing a traditional research paper (*Teachers Are the Center of Education*, 2010, 6). Imagine parents viewing videos—made by their children—about the history of their community. Imagine parents driving from work listening to podcasts their children have produced. Imagine your writers reaching people across the globe with memoirs and poetry. This is publication at its most powerful. Presentation has gone 3-D and iMax, and we can never put the genie in the bottle again.

6. THINK "TECH TRAITS."

With your students, explore multiple websites, podcasts, audio programs, and videos—as well as presentations that may combine these elements. As you do so, ask yourself how the following common trait features look in a multi-media world, and what makes each successful:

- Details
- Leads
- Conclusions
- Transitions
- Voice

- Fluency
- Variety
- Insight
- Main idea
- Word choice

7. ASSESS IN A NEW WAY.

If we're going to compose in a new way, maybe we need to assess in a new way also. What has made scoring guides work so well with writing samples is the fact that even though each sample is unique, they do share many commonalities. This makes it easy to identify features, such as a strong lead, that apply to all or most pieces.

But with multi-media work, we lose some of that commonality. This is exciting, but it also requires us to approach assessment in an open-minded way. That is to say, sans guides or rubrics—at least for now. Troy Hicks, whose book *The Digital Writing Workshop* I have quoted here, suggests that there may be a conceptual link between the traits and various forms of digital publishing (2009, Figure 6.2, 115–116). I agree with

FIGURE 8.18

Sample Storyboard

Video	Audio (Narrator's Voiceover)
Collage of videos: kangaroos, koala, aborigine people, sunset over Ayers Rock, beaches	What do most people think of when they hear the word "Australia"?
Zooming in over Sydney Harbor— opera house in distance	How about architecture? Australia is home to what some consider the most beautiful building in all the world: the famed Sydney opera house.
Close in-looking down on opera house from aerial view— shift to entry . . . dissolve	The Sydney Opera House, which covers more than four acres of land, was designed by Danish builder Jørn Utzon. In 2003, Utzon received the Pritzker Prize, architecture's highest award, for this accomplishment.
Open inside main hall—pan wide to rake in ceiling, then dissolve	The citation on the prize called the Opera House Utzon's "masterpiece."
Early footage of workers breaking ground—rapid time lapse to 1973 . . .	The building was originally budgeted at $7 million—and scheduled for completion in 1963. When it was finally finished, ten years late, the cost had risen to over $102 million.

this (particularly with respect to ideas, organization, and voice), but while acknowledging the value of Hicks's chart, let me suggest beginning in a slightly different place.

As you and your students explore the digital world, pause to review the work you have done and to record what you feel makes it successful. Maybe you'll move gradually from simple to complex. You may begin by taking digital photos to illustrate poems. Then perhaps you'll do podcasts. Then PowerPoints. And eventually digital stories or full-blown videos. With each new medium, take time to reflect. Maybe what emerges is a collection of thoughts, nothing more. Maybe it's a checklist of reminders—or a set of guidelines for publishing in a multi-media format. It won't be a rubric because it won't reflect degrees of success or levels of performance. It will simply celebrate what works.

And here's a thought: Perhaps your students will share that celebration through podcasts, webcasts, or videos about communicating and composing in the digital age.

STUDY GROUP

Interactive Questions and Activities

1. **Discussion.** Put a check by each of the following statements with which you agree. Then discuss results with your colleagues.

____ People in our society are judged by their conventions.

____ A student should have to write a flawless paper to get a score of 6 in this trait.

____ It is important to correct ALL errors in student work.

____ Conferring with students is more effective than correcting their work.

____ Students should do as much of their own editing as possible.

____ A hundred years from now, what we consider "correct" will be totally different.

____ A good writing program in the twenty-first century must include technology.

____ We cannot seriously teach presentation without computer access.

____ The traits are part of multi-media compositions, but reveal themselves in different ways.

2. **Activity and Discussion.** The lessons and strategies section of this chapter lists books you might use as handbooks or general resources for conventions. Do you have a favorite from that list—or a favorite of your own? Share it with the group and talk about why you find it useful.

3. **Activity and Discussion.** This chapter focuses heavily on modeling the correct or stylistic use of conventions. Create a lesson for doing this, based on a short sample of your own writing or an excerpt from any published piece. Present it to your group.

4. **Activity and Discussion.** With your group, brainstorm the 15–20 conventional problems you think are most troublesome for your young writers. (Don't be afraid to cross grade levels.) When you finish, look up Andrea Lunsford's list online, and compare. Are there similarities? Did you think of things her research did not identify?

5. **Discussion.** This chapter makes a strong case for students being the ones to wield the red pens. Do you agree with this philosophy? Should students take responsibility for their own editing? If you do agree, where do you draw the line between useful instruction or coaching and actually taking over the writing?

6. **Activity and Discussion.** This chapter suggests that in a digital age, students need new options for publishing—such as podcasts or videos. Do you agree with this? How prepared are you, and how prepared are your students, to enter a digital age? What obstacles, if any, stand in your path—and what could you do to eliminate or minimize them?

7. **Activity and Discussion.** Print out a copy of *Teachers Are the Center of Education: Writing, Learning and Leading in the Digital Age*, 2010, conceptualized and written by the College Board, the National Writing Project and Phi Delta Kappa International. The article is available online at this address: http://professionals. collegeboard.com/profdownload/2009-cb-advocacy-teachers-are-center.pdf.

In your group, do a "jigsaw" review of this article, with each member taking one chapter to read and summarize for the group. How do these teachers' experiences inform the way you plan to handle publication in a digital age?

Coming Up

In Chapter 9, we'll discuss informational writing that is research dependent, exploring ways this genre redefines quality performance trait by trait. Chapter 9 includes new scoring guides applicable to any writing based upon research, as well as suggestions for developing genre-specific checklists with your students.

> I write because I know that every bone in my body will appreciate my work, the long hours I put into it, and all the gears in my head working to their full capacity.
>
> —Ryan Sterner, student writer

> Writing is everything because it can be about everything. There are no limitations. Even grammar and correct spelling aren't barriers. How many times did Mark Twain spell something "wrong" when writing dialogue for Huckleberry? Here, with pen and paper, there is the possibility of freedom.
>
> —Elizabeth Kramer, student writer

CHAPTER 9

Going INFORMATIONAL

The purpose of research writing is not simply to show readers what you know. It is an effort to extend a conversation about a topic that is ongoing, a conversation that includes voices of people who have already spoken, often in different contexts and perhaps never together.

—BRUCE BALLENGER
The Curious Researcher, 2004, 15

Informational writing is different from creative writing in a number of ways. To honor these differences, the writing guides in this chapter have been adapted from the originals for use with text that a writer could not pull out of his or her own head—in other words, writing that requires research. Every trait in such writing looks a little different. To understand these nuances, think of the informational writer as a teacher who says to readers, "I know this topic well. And I'm going to teach the *best* of what I know to you. I'll make you an insider so you can love this topic as much as I do."

Trait by Trait: A Quick Review

Let's start with **ideas.** The purpose of research is to uncover what's new or interesting, to unveil the truth (especially unsuspected truth) about a topic. Accuracy matters. So does the writer's ability to synthesize information from multiple sources. The informational writer weaves details together to create meaning from chaos.

Donald Murray argues that readers have a "hunger for information" even when reading fiction or poetry (2004, 53). True. Detail *always* matters. Crime dramas written by police officers, courtroom dramas written by lawyers, adventure stories written by world travelers—all have the authenticity that only comes from firsthand experience.

With fiction, though, a writer has some freedom to be inventive with detail, as long as readers still buy into the message. In nonfiction, the writer must stay true to the facts. Nevertheless, good informational writing can be as compelling as any novel. The secret lies in the way that information is shared.

Nicola Davies gets readers' attention with her trademark conversational style, her skill in surprising us with things we didn't know, and her knack for linking the message to things that matter to us, as you can see in this passage from *What's Eating You?* (2007, 8)

> Almost every free-living animal on the planet is just a walking habitat—a "host" to many parasites—and that includes us humans.

Effective **organization** is critical to any informational piece because as readers, we only learn when we can follow what the writer is saying. Good informational writers create a base of knowledge, beginning with what's familiar before introducing something new. Consider this short passage from Seymour Simon's book *Our Solar System* (2007, unpaginated), in which he expands our knowledge with each sentence:

> Even if you look through a powerful telescope on Earth, Saturn appears to have just a few rings. But spacecraft photos . . . show that the large rings are made of thousands of smaller rings. If you were to get closer, you would see that the [smaller] rings are made of pieces of ice. Some are as small as a fingernail; others, as big as a house. The rings also contain dust and bits of rock. And all the materials in the rings spin around Saturn like millions of tiny moons.

Often, I am asked if it is possible to have **voice** in informational writing. Not only is it possible, it's vital—*if* you want readers. A strong informational voice is confident, inspiring, and knowledge driven. If Carl Sagan had written, "The Cosmos sure is a big place," no one would have paid attention. Instead, he wrote this:

> If we were randomly inserted into the Cosmos, the chance that we would find ourselves on or near a planet would be less than one in a billion trillion trillion (10^{33}, a one followed by 33 zeroes). In everyday life such odds are called compelling. Worlds are precious. (1980, 5)

In creative writing, when we think about **word choice,** we often think of imagery or sensory appeal. Informational writers also paint pictures for readers—like this one from *Pocket Babies* (2007, 36) by Sneed Collard:

One group of researchers tried to sort out the factors that helped third and fourth graders remember what they had been reading. They found that how interested the students were in the passage was thirty times more important than how "readable" the passage was.

—Alfie Kohn
Punished by Rewards, 1993, 145

Smart. Strong. Stubborn. Square. That pretty much sums up the wombat . . . . They look like furry tractors with legs.

Variety is always the soul of **sentence fluency**. But in most informational writing (especially if it's technical or contains numerous details) the tendency is toward shorter, more direct sentences that let the reader work through the topic one informational bite at a time—as in this tidbit from *Oh, Rats!* (2006, 13) by Albert Marrin:

> A rat is not finicky about its food; if necessary, it will eat anything that will not eat it first. This ability to get nourishment from many sources is a great survival advantage, especially when food is scarce. A rat can eat one-tenth of its body weight every day. If that held true for people, the average adult would need about sixteen pounds of food a day.

Informational **conventions** can be enormously helpful in making information clear. Notice how easy it is to navigate this passage from *The Story of Salt* (Kurlansky, 2006, 25)—thanks to italics and quotation marks:

> Many English words are based on the Roman word for salt, *sal*—even the word "salt" itself. *Sal* is the root of the words "salary" and "soldier" because Roman soldiers were often paid in salt. This is also the origin of the expressions "worth his salt" and "to earn his salt." "Salad," too, comes from *insalata*, a salt word because Romans ate their greens with a dressing based on salt water.

In *Our Planet: Change Is Possible*, the authors (2008, Myspace Community with Jeca Taudte) make extensive use of **presentation**, relying on color, boxes, logos, bulleted lists, and other devices to remind readers of the many ways to reduce their environmental impact: short showers, drought tolerant lawns, electronic greeting cards, locally grown produce, and more.

Because the traits take on a new look in informational writing, they call for new writing guides—summaries to help us recognize what writers are doing well and to suggest things we can teach to make informational writing strong. These guides are not intended for spontaneous expository paragraphs—writing that flows from a writer's personal knowledge and experience. Rather, they are intended for writing that relies on research. The following definition helps make this distinction.

Informational Writing

A Definition

Informational writing is defined *by purpose*: It is any writing (or other communication) that is intended primarily to teach or to summarize what's known or new about a given topic. The basis for this writing is research—which can take many forms. The writer may investigate a topic through reading, interviews, Internet searches, exploration of multi-media sources such as films or podcasts—or personal experience. The writing can take various forms, too, and often blends genres. A piece that is essentially informational in purpose may include photos, narrative, exposition, journalism, persuasion, definitions, memoir, data summaries, charts, and more. And of course, podcasts, webcasts, videos, and other multi-media forms of communication can enrich or extend written text. Good informational writing is marked by clarity, accuracy, a strong central message, credible support for that message, and surprising, intriguing, or unusual details that teach the reader something new—or cause the reader to see things in a new way. As we shall see later in this chapter, persuasive writing is a special form of informational writing—one in which the author uses examples, explanations, data, and passionate rhetoric to influence a reader's thinking or actions.

See Figure 9.1 for a one-pager version of the Informational Writing Guide for teachers. See Figures 9.2 through 9.7 for "leap the river" Informational Writing Guides designed for students.

FIGURE 9.1

One-Page Informational Writing Guide for Teachers

IDEAS	ORGANIZATION	VOICE
6	**6**	**6**
☐ Clear, focused, accurate, and thorough	☐ Thoughtful structure guides reader through text	☐ Individual, conversational—sparks reader's interest
☐ Writer has in-depth understanding/knowledge	☐ Engaging opening sets up the discussion	☐ Deeply passionate, committed to topic and message
☐ Has a well-defined thesis or answers a key question	☐ Well-crafted transitions make thinking crystal clear	☐ Rings with confidence from in-depth knowledge
☐ Writer pulls support from multiple credible sources	☐ Writer takes time to clarify complex sections	☐ Writer's curiosity/enthusiasm is contagious
☐ Significant details teach the reader something new	☐ The ending prompts reader to think/reflect/learn more	☐ Captures even readers with no prior interest in topic
5	**5**	**5**
☐ Clear, focused, and accurate	☐ Purposeful organization provides sense of direction	☐ A stand-out voice that makes the topic appealing
☐ Writer knows the topic well	☐ Strong lead pulls reader right into discussion	☐ Often passionate—many read-aloud moments
☐ Central question or thesis is clear	☐ Thoughtful transitions guide reader from point to point	☐ Confident and self-assured
☐ Writer draws from at least one excellent source	☐ Writer offers helpful examples as needed	☐ Writer's commitment keeps readers reading
☐ Important, helpful details expand the topic	☐ Satisfying ending wraps up the discussion	☐ Holds readers' attention throughout
4	**4**	**4**
☐ Message makes sense, covers main points	☐ Organization helps reader follow discussion	☐ A sincere voice that makes reading pleasant
☐ Writer has enough knowledge for a broad overview	☐ Functional lead introduces the topic	☐ Moments of excitement catch reader's attention
☐ Main concept, thesis, point can be inferred	☐ Helpful transitions keep ideas flowing	☐ Confident—but sometimes restrained
☐ Additional research would add strength	☐ Writer offers some examples—more would help	☐ Writer seems to find topic interesting
☐ Strong details mixed with guesses/generalities	☐ Functional ending closes the discussion	☐ Voice sometimes reaches out to readers
3	**3**	**3**
☐ Too skimpy—OR rambling/repetitious	☐ Following discussion takes some work	☐ Voice comes and goes
☐ Some gaps in writer's knowledge are evident	☐ Lead doesn't quite set up what follows	☐ Read-aloud moments are rare—but may exist
☐ Reader can make good guess at main concept/point	☐ Transitions missing—reader must connect the dots	☐ Writer often sounds uncertain, hesitant
☐ Research is thin—more info needed	☐ Writer dwells on trivia—or rushes through complex parts	☐ Writer doesn't seem "driven" to find answers
☐ Some questions remain unanswered	☐ Ending not completely satisfying	☐ Hints or echoes of voice hold promise
2	**2**	**2**
☐ Writer still defining, shaping message	☐ Reader often feels confused	☐ An "anybody" voice, encyclopedic, impersonal
☐ Writer seems uncomfortable with topic	☐ Lead missing or misleading	☐ Not a read-aloud piece as yet
☐ Main idea/concept still coming together	☐ Transitions missing—reads like a list	☐ Writer uncomfortable with topic—or indifferent
☐ Details limited	☐ Hard to tell what points matter most	☐ Reader has trouble staying engaged
☐ Reader is left with many questions	☐ Ending abrupt or confusing	☐ Voice is faint—no one is "at home" here
1	**1**	**1**
☐ Writer still searching for topic/concept	☐ Organization feels random	☐ No sense of commitment as yet
☐ No base of knowledge to work from as yet	☐ No lead or conclusion as yet	☐ Not enough detail to generate voice
☐ No clear direction or focus	☐ Ideas don't necessarily seem connected	☐ Writer not engaged—or has no topic yet
☐ Notes, first thoughts	☐ No "most important" points stand out	☐ This piece isn't ready to share with readers
☐ A topic conference could help	☐ Writer needs help finding/ordering details	☐ Writer needs help finding topic/research question

FIGURE 9.1

One-Page Informational Writing Guide for Teachers

Word Choice

6

- ❑ Explicit, precise words make message consistently clear
- ❑ Writer uses language of content area with ease and skill
- ❑ Writer helps reader feel at home with terms/concepts
- ❑ Language makes reader feel like an insider
- ❑ Quotable, memorable moments

5

- ❑ Carefully chosen words add to clarity
- ❑ Writer comfortable with language of the content area
- ❑ Writer clarifies most new words or concepts for reader
- ❑ Language supports reader's understanding
- ❑ Moments to highlight, read aloud

4

- ❑ Functional language makes message easy to interpret
- ❑ Writer seems familiar with basic terminology
- ❑ New terms, if used, are often defined, explained
- ❑ Reader can readily make sense of the message
- ❑ Moments a reader will notice, appreciate

3

- ❑ Occasional passages are unclear or ambiguous
- ❑ Writer tends to avoid "specialized language"
- ❑ Terminology avoided—or not explained
- ❑ Reader can still figure out the message
- ❑ Moments needing revision outnumber strong ones

2

- ❑ Imprecise or vague language creates confusion
- ❑ Terms may be used incorrectly—or just left out
- ❑ Language is general, unclear, wordy, or jargonistic
- ❑ Reader continually figuring out what writer *meant to say*
- ❑ Many moments need revision

1

- ❑ Word choice makes meaning unclear
- ❑ Writer struggles to come up with the right words
- ❑ Language vague, not right for the moment
- ❑ Hard to figure out what writer means
- ❑ Writer needs help with word choice

Sentence Fluency

6

- ❑ Sentences consistently clear, direct, to the point
- ❑ Graceful, varied phrasing creates meaning/voice
- ❑ Purposeful beginnings (*For example . . .*) make sentence-to-sentence connections clear
- ❑ Reading for meaning is easy and enjoyable

5

- ❑ Sentence structure consistently clear
- ❑ Smooth phrasing enhances readability
- ❑ Purposeful beginnings connect ideas
- ❑ Sentences help reader follow writer's thinking

4

- ❑ Sentences clear more often than not
- ❑ Smooth phrasing outweighs awkward moments
- ❑ Sentence-to-sentence flow is generally smooth
- ❑ Reader can follow the discussion

3

- ❑ Sentences aren't always clear the first time through
- ❑ A few revisions needed in length, wording, structure
- ❑ Sentence-to-sentence flow feels rough at times
- ❑ Reader must pay attention to follow discussion

2

- ❑ Many sentences require rereading
- ❑ Significant revision needed in length, wording, structure
- ❑ Sentence-to-sentence flow may feel disjointed
- ❑ Lack of fluency makes reader pause, reread

1

- ❑ Sentences don't always come clear, even with rereading
- ❑ Fluency problems block meaning and voice
- ❑ Sentences do not create a clear message
- ❑ Writer needs help with sentences, message, or both

Conventions & Presentation

6

- ❑ Thoroughly edited and proofed
- ❑ Conventions enhance the message
- ❑ All sources cited completely and correctly
- ❑ Striking presentation makes key info "jump out"
- ❑ Virtually ready to publish

5

- ❑ Edited well (minor errors are easily overlooked)
- ❑ Conventions support the message
- ❑ Citations essentially correct
- ❑ Strong presentation guides reader's eye to key points
- ❑ Ready to publish with light touch-ups

4

- ❑ Noticeable errors—but reader breezes right through
- ❑ Errors do not interfere with message
- ❑ Citations may need touch-ups, minor reformatting
- ❑ Presentation makes info accessible
- ❑ Good once-over needed prior to publication

3

- ❑ Errors create a distraction
- ❑ Errors may slow reader, interrupt message
- ❑ Citations need checking—some may be missing
- ❑ Small elements of presentation need work
- ❑ Thorough, careful editing needed prior to publication

2

- ❑ Frequent errors take attention from message
- ❑ Errors slow reader or interfere with clarity
- ❑ Citations missing, faulty
- ❑ Presentation needs significant work
- ❑ Line-by-line editing needed prior to publication

1

- ❑ Serious, frequent errors make reading a challenge
- ❑ Reader must slow down, fill in, decode
- ❑ Sources not cited (or not yet consulted)
- ❑ Document not ready for design/formatting
- ❑ Writer needs help with editing and/or research

© 2012. Vicki Spandel.

FIGURE 9.2

Informational Writing Guide for Students: IDEAS

6
- ❑ My writing is clear and focused. The information is accurate and covers the topic well.
- ❑ You can tell I did my research. I *know* this topic.
- ❑ My writing has a strong message or answers an important question for the reader.
- ❑ I pulled information from several good sources.
- ❑ My details will teach you something new and interesting.

5
- ❑ My writing is clear and accurate.
- ❑ I learned a lot from my research.
- ❑ The central message is clear.
- ❑ I had at least one good source for information.
- ❑ My writing is filled with helpful, relevant details.

4
- ❑ My writing makes sense.
- ❑ I knew enough to cover the most important things.
- ❑ You can figure out my main message.
- ❑ Some additional research would have helped me.
- ❑ It's a mix of really good details—and best guesses.

3
- ❑ I rambled—or else I didn't say enough!
- ❑ You'll spot a few "holes" in my information.
- ❑ You might have to guess at the main message.
- ❑ I definitely need to do more research.
- ❑ You may be left with a few questions about this topic.

2
- ❑ I'm still figuring out what I want to say.
- ❑ I'm not really comfortable with this topic.
- ❑ I'm working on a main message—or main question to answer.
- ❑ I don't have enough information to write—yet.
- ❑ My reader will be left with many questions.

1
- ❑ I'm still looking for a good topic.
- ❑ I need help with research.
- ❑ I don't have a clear message—or question to answer.
- ❑ I made a few notes to help me think.
- ❑ A conference could help me get started

© 2012. Vicki Spandel. Designed for use in classroom assessment.

FIGURE 9.3

Informational Writing Guide for Students: ORGANIZATION

6
- ❑ My organization guides you right through this discussion—like a light in the dark.
- ❑ My lead will hook you—and set up the conversation that follows.
- ❑ Transitions show exactly how each point leads to another.
- ❑ I spend time explaining or expanding key points.
- ❑ The ending ties up loose ends and makes you think.

5
- ❑ My organization gives the writing a strong sense of direction.
- ❑ My lead pulls you right into the discussion.
- ❑ Clear transitions help you move from point to point.
- ❑ I included helpful examples or explanations.
- ❑ A satisfying ending wraps things up.

4
- ❑ My organization helps you make sense of the discussion.
- ❑ My lead introduces the topic.
- ❑ I try to guide the reader from point to point.
- ❑ I could use more examples.
- ❑ The ending brings the discussion to a close.

3
- ❑ Sometimes you need to figure out where the discussion is headed.
- ❑ I have a lead—but it doesn't set up the discussion as well as it should.
- ❑ Ideas don't always seem connected clearly.
- ❑ I spent too much time on things that don't matter—or forgot examples when I needed them.
- ❑ I have an ending—but it doesn't fully wrap things up.

2
- ❑ You might feel lost or confused at times.
- ❑ My lead is confusing, misleading—or missing.
- ❑ I just listed ideas. I didn't try to connect things.
- ❑ It's hard to tell which points are really important.
- ❑ Either I don't have an ending—or it doesn't say anything important about my topic.

1
- ❑ There's no real order yet—I just wrote things down.
- ❑ I don't have a lead yet. Or an ending.
- ❑ I'm not sure these ideas are connected.
- ❑ I need to figure out my message before I can give the reader examples—or figure out what needs explaining.
- ❑ I need help finding and organizing information.

© 2012. Vicki Spandel. Designed for use in classroom assessment.

FIGURE 9.4

Informational Writing Guide for Students: VOICE

6
- ❏ My writing is individual, conversational, lively.
- ❏ I'm excited and passionate about this topic.
- ❏ I sound confident because I know what I'm talking about.
- ❏ I'm extremely curious about this topic—and my writing will make you want to learn more, too.
- ❏ Even if you weren't interested in this topic to begin with, I will change your mind.

5
- ❏ My voice is individual—it stands out from others.
- ❏ You'll find many moments to share aloud.
- ❏ I sound confident—sure of myself and my facts.
- ❏ You'll be curious enough to keep reading.
- ❏ My writing will get—and hold—your attention.

4
- ❏ There's enough voice to make reading fun.
- ❏ Here and there, my enthusiasm comes through.
- ❏ I sound confident—at least some of the time.
- ❏ I found this topic fairly interesting.
- ❏ I hope most readers will enjoy reading this.

3
- ❏ My voice comes and goes. You hear it in spots.
- ❏ I'm almost ready to share this aloud—not quite.
- ❏ I wasn't always sure of myself. More research would have boosted my confidence.
- ❏ I didn't really have a LOT of questions on this topic.
- ❏ I hear *some* voice, though—don't you?

2
- ❏ This isn't me! It sounds more like an encyclopedia.
- ❏ I'm a draft away from sharing any part of this aloud.
- ❏ I need a LOT more information to feel comfortable writing about this topic.
- ❏ I don't know enough to pose good research questions.
- ❏ Danger! Your mind could wander as you read!

1
- ❏ I'm not part of this writing.
- ❏ I don't have anything interesting to share—yet.
- ❏ I don't feel like I know anything about this topic.
- ❏ Maybe I need a NEW topic—or at least a question I'm curious about.
- ❏ I need help making a plan for research.

© 2012. Vicki Spandel. Designed for use in classroom assessment.

FIGURE 9.5

Informational Writing Guide for Students: WORD CHOICE

6
- ❏ My word choice makes every point clear and precise.
- ❏ I know the terminology that goes with this subject— and I can use it when I need it.
- ❏ I work hard to make the reader feel completely at home with this topic.
- ❏ Reading this will make you feel like an insider.
- ❏ You might find phrases to quote—or remember.

5
- ❏ My words are carefully chosen to make the message clear.
- ❏ I'm comfortable with the terminology for this content area.
- ❏ If I used new words or terms, I defined them.
- ❏ My word choice will help you understand the message.
- ❏ Look for phrases to highlight or read aloud.

4
- ❏ My words are easy to understand.
- ❏ I know some basic terms for this content area.
- ❏ If I used a new or unusual word, I defined it (I think).
- ❏ A careful reader can make sense of this message.
- ❏ You will notice a few strong moments.

3
- ❏ My words might not *always* be as clear as they should be.
- ❏ I tried to *avoid* terminology—or any hard words.
- ❏ I didn't worry about defining terms or new words.
- ❏ A reader can still figure out the message.
- ❏ I *could* revise a few words or phrases.

2
- ❏ In reading this over, I see many parts are unclear.
- ❏ I used terms incorrectly—or left important terms out.
- ❏ Parts are vague, wordy, or confusing.
- ❏ I know what I *meant* to say—I'm not sure you will.
- ❏ I see LOTS of moments to revise.

1
- ❏ My message doesn't come through.
- ❏ I could never seem to find the words I wanted.
- ❏ I used words incorrectly—or just used the first words that came to mind.
- ❏ I didn't always know what I was trying to say.
- ❏ I need help with wording—or with the topic.

© 2012. Vicki Spandel. Designed for use in classroom assessment.

FIGURE 9.6

Informational Writing Guide for Students: SENTENCE FLUENCY

6
- ❏ My sentences are clear and get right to the point.
- ❏ Variety makes reading easy—and creates voice.
- ❏ Beginnings (*For example, On the other hand, In contrast*) connect ideas sentence to sentence.
- ❏ Reading for meaning is easy and enjoyable.

5
- ❏ My sentences are consistently clear.
- ❏ Smooth phrasing makes this writing highly readable.
- ❏ Sentences work together to create meaning.
- ❏ It's easy to follow my thinking.

4
- ❏ Most sentences are clear. Some may carry too much information.
- ❏ The smooth parts outnumber the rough spots.
- ❏ Thoughts and ideas are usually connected.
- ❏ If you read carefully, you can follow my thinking.

3
- ❏ Some sentences may not be clear the first time through.
- ❏ I need to rewrite, combine, or shorten.
- ❏ The sentence-to-sentence flow is rough in spots; you have to read slowly to follow it.
- ❏ You'll need to slow down to get the meaning.

2
- ❏ You'll need to read many sentences more than once.
- ❏ I need to revise sentence length, structure, or wording.
- ❏ This is tough to read aloud, even for me.
- ❏ You may find yourself slowing down or going back to figure out the meaning.

1
- ❏ Even when you read more than once, you may not figure out what some sentences say.
- ❏ Many of these sentences are confusing or just hard to read.
- ❏ It's hard to figure out what I mean.
- ❏ I need help writing sentences that say what I mean.

© 2012. Vicki Spandel. Designed for use in classroom assessment.

FIGURE 9.7

Informational Writing Guide for Students: CONVENTIONS & PRESENTATION

6
- ❏ This copy is thoroughly edited and proofread.
- ❏ My conventions make meaning clear and show readers how to read this piece with voice.
- ❏ All sources are cited correctly with proper formatting.
- ❏ My presentation makes important information easy to spot—or find later.
- ❏ This piece is ready to publish.

5
- ❏ I might have a few *tiny* errors—I'll look again.
- ❏ My conventions bring out meaning and voice.
- ❏ The citations are correct.
- ❏ The presentation guides your eye to key points.
- ❏ This is *almost* ready to publish.

4
- ❏ I see a few errors I need to fix.
- ❏ I don't think my errors get in the way of the message.
- ❏ My citations could use a few touch-ups.
- ❏ My presentation makes the message clear and appealing.
- ❏ This will be ready to publish once I go through it again.

3
- ❏ My errors could take your mind off the message.
- ❏ They could also make you slow down to reread.
- ❏ I need to check my citations. I might have missed one.
- ❏ My presentation needs a little work.
- ❏ I need to read this silently and aloud, pen in hand.

2
- ❏ Errors really jump out at the reader—*not good!*
- ❏ They might also get in the way of my message.
- ❏ I think some citations are missing—or need rewriting.
- ❏ This presentation needs a LOT of work.
- ❏ I need to read this line by line, pen in hand.

1
- ❏ Errors make this hard to read, even for me!
- ❏ You'll probably need to "edit" this in your head.
- ❏ I did not cite any sources. (I might not have any yet.)
- ❏ I'm not ready to think about design or formatting.
- ❏ I need help with my editing and/or research.

© 2012. Vicki Spandel. Designed for use in classroom assessment.

Assessing INFORMATIONAL WRITING

The following papers were selected to represent a variety of topics, grade levels, writing approaches, and skills. For reasons of length, I have not included major research pieces such as might be typical in an AP high school or college freshman English class. Such writing can easily be assessed using the writing guides from this chapter, but that requires extensive time. If you regularly assign such writing to your students, though, include samples of their work in this practice.

Paper 1

Black Widows (Informational, Grade 3)

A small black spot moves slowly and silently across the ground. Her red patch glints in the sun. She climbs up her web.

She's a black widow.

A small fly collides with her well-made net. The spider approaches the thrashing insect. Soon, the fly is tightly wrapped up in strong, fine silk.

The spider has a nice, long meal. Its red hourglass stomach sparkles in the sun because no hairs get in the way.

This spider happens to live here in America. It could just as easily live in New Zealand, Australia, or countries surrounding the Mediterranean Sea, though.

She glides down from her web. Suddenly, the shadow of an unlucky person falls over the spider. A bare foot covers her. The black widow sinks her fangs into the skin. It is difficult for the person to breathe or move. Cramps find their way into the person's muscles. Thirty minutes later, the human is in great pain.

If you like breathing, don't step on a black widow spider!

The Write Connection

Black Widows

Of the nineteen sentences in this piece, twelve begin with one of these words: *A, She, The, It, This*. See if you can create more variety by combining sentences or rewriting them to begin in different ways. Can you tinker with fluency without compromising this writer's striking sense of drama? When you finish, see if you can come up with a title that doesn't give the subject away too quickly.

Suggested Scores for "Black Widows"

Ideas: **5**

Organization: **4**

Voice: **6**

Word choice: **6**

Sentence fluency: **5**

Conventions & presentation: **6** (Discounting missing citations)

Lessons Learned from "Black Widows"

- A little drama brings informational writing to life.
- Strong verbs give informational writing energy.
- Suspense makes a lead more interesting—but be careful not to give the game away in your title!

Comments

You can hear this writer's enthusiasm for her topic. She has singled out intriguing details—the strong silk, hourglass stomach, deadliness of the spider's bite—and focuses just on these features without trying to cover everything. We *are* left with some questions, notably: *Is the black widow's bite fatal? What happened to the person in the scenario?* Every image is clear and meaningful. The beginning is excellent; the ending is a little abrupt and leaves some things unresolved—hence the slightly lower score in organization. The word choice and voice seem just right for informational writing with a dark shadow. A bit more sentence variety would bump the fluency score to a 6.

Paper 2

Gorillas (Informational, Grade 4)

Gorillas are the coolest animals on earth. They are extremely large and strong. Yet they hardly ever hurt anyone or each other. The gorilla lives in the jungle and eats a wide variety of foods. It eats a lot, so it spends most of its time looking for food or eating. Gorillas are mainly vegetarians. Gorillas have one baby every five years. The baby stays close to its mother so it can learn what to eat. The whole group of gorillas will protect the baby from danger. Gorillas are highly intelligent. They live a very long time. They are one of the most popular animals at the zoo, but should they even be in zoos? Look on line to find more information about this fascinating animal.

© 2012, Vicki Spandel

Suggested Scores for "Gorillas"

Ideas: **4**

Organization: **3**

Voice: **4**

Word choice: **5**

Sentence fluency: **4**

Conventions & presentation: **5**

Lessons Learned from "Gorillas"

- Taking time to answer the reader's questions will make a "just made the leap" paper into something stellar.

- When a writer introduces a topic—such as gorillas "hardly ever" hurt anyone, or gorillas are "highly intelligent"—it makes the reader want to know more. *These* are moments for examples.

- Sometimes a writer comes to the main subject at the end of a piece: e.g., *Should gorillas even be in zoos?* This topic in itself could be worthy of another paragraph or two—or even a whole new piece.

- "Look on line for more information" is an easy way out. Readers like a memorable image, anecdote, or fact to close a discussion like this one.

Comments

This writer has made a strong beginning, raising many subtopics worthy of further exploration: gorillas' intelligence, eating habits, care of their young, protective character,

 The Write Connection

Gorillas

Imagine "Gorillas" as a documentary video. What would you like to see? Using information from the paper plus any outside source (e.g., *Gorillas* by Seymour Simon), construct a brief storyboard: narrative on one side, brief description of video on the other. Imagine that this storyboard will serve as the organizational plan for a documentary video.

longevity, and more. The piece is clearly written and very easy to understand. It just doesn't dig deep enough. We want images of the mother gorilla feeding her baby fruit for the first time. We want to see the old silverback crashing through the brush trying to frighten a potential attacker—and we want to know who or what would have the courage to approach the imposing gorilla. We want to know if gorillas are "mainly vegetarians" or omnivores. And just how intelligent are they? Are gorillas endangered? If so, what can we do about that? The organization is not confusing, but it is rather "listy." There are, however, a rudimentary lead and conclusion. And the writer seems sincere and engaged by her topic.

Paper 3

Our History: Strange but True (Informational, Grade 5)

Ten million years ago in a dull forest in Africa monkeys were already swooping back and forth in the trees. Everything seemed right but the sun started to beat down on the trees with renewed heat. This climate change destroyed the forests and replaced them with never ending fields of grass forcing the monkeys to spend more time on the ground. Some even learned the ability to walk on their hind legs which enabled them to see over the tall grass. When they lived on the ground they had to have cooperation, coordination, and increased intelligence. At this time they were considered australopithecines, animals with a human like body, but less hair than a modern monkey. The australopithecines had better teeth than the monkeys, and bigger brains. These early humans were the first step of human evolution.

Australopithecines had a very big diet which included plants (some which we call weeds), and animals. Even though they were very close to nature they had to live so they ate the plants and animals around them. Over thousands of years the australopithecines figured out what to, or not to, eat. Knowing what to eat was a very important factor to their survival. It also helped that they had their hands free because they could walk on two legs. This would help them in the future.

After hundreds of years one group of the australopithecines branched off into another group which was called Homo habilis (handy man). They were called this because they were the first early humans to make tools. Making tools included planning ahead, and coordination. Homo habilis had bigger brains than the group of australopithecines they came from. Making tools showed that they could adapt to their surroundings.

It may seem strange that we came from monkeys. But it's true, strange or not, it's true. We're all here because of evolution.

Suggested Scores for "Our History: Strange but True"

Ideas: **4**

Organization: **5**

Voice: **5**

Word choice: **5**

Sentence fluency: **6**

Conventions & presentation: **5**

Lessons Learned from "Our History: Strange but True"

- The little things—like commas—really do matter when it comes to readability.
- Never underestimate the importance of a good example (or two).
- Choosing a topic that fascinates you (as this writer did) boosts voice.

Comments

Here's a writer with a clear central message: We're the product of evolution. His enthusiasm for the subject produces a lively, energetic voice that is just right for an informational piece. He explains terms clearly: *australopithecines, animals with a human like body*. And there are additional fine moments of word choice: *swooping, renewed heat, destroyed, never ending, forcing*. The one moment that gives readers pause is "dull forest." Why dull? Dull as in a color—dry with heat? Or dull as in boring? Perhaps the greatest strength of the piece is sentence fluency. Notice the varied beginnings and how each sentence connects to the one before—and leads into the one that follows. The lead and conclusion also work well, and the piece is easy to follow. Even though the writing is extremely clear and focused, it needs more examples. We're left with many questions: Why does living on the ground demand more "cooperation, coordination, and increased intelligence"? What exactly was included in the australopithecines' menu? How did those better teeth evolve? This writer raises many good questions, but doesn't quite take time to answer them. The lower conventions score was a tough call because although the writer does many things well, he needs commas—a lot of them.

> **The Write Connection**
>
> Our History: Strange but True
>
> Go through the piece carefully, reading aloud, and thinking about questions that come to mind. Put a number (1, 2, 3, 4) by each spot where you wanted to know more, and make a corresponding list of questions you'd like this writer to answer. How many do you come up with? You might also look up *australopithecine* online to see if you uncover any interesting facts this writer could have included.

Paper 4

Mini Vampires (Informational, Grade 5)

A kid happily skips off to school, her lunch box in one hand, the other hand on her head, scratching away. The teacher stares as she rakes her fingers though her hair like a monkey all day long. Meanwhile, headlice are relaxing on her head sucking blood. They are big fat meanie vampires. The other kids in the lice infested girl's class better watch out. Lice spread VERY easily.

Lice are little bugs about 1/8 inch long. That's the size of a sesame seed! They eat blood for food. That's why they make your head REALLY itchy. They're busy biting into your skin to get all the red juice from your head. Head lice have to live on a human head to survive. If they aren't on a head for more than 2 days, they'll die. The scientific name for lice is *Pediculus Humanus Capitis*. But I think lice is MUCH easier to say than that. Lice have 3 stages of life. Nit, nymph, and adult. A nit is an egg. A nymph is like a kid, and an adult is when the bug is all grown up. Lice can normally live about a month. People have been getting lice for a long time! The person who sewed the first American flag, Betsy Ross, ironed her clothes all the time to keep lice away. Even Anne Frank had it!

Lice eggs are called nits. An adult bug can lay 150 of them in their lifetime! The bugs produce a glue-like substance to neatly stick the eggs to the hair. The nits stick to the hair SO tightly that they can only be removed by fingernails, a metal lice comb, or enzyme cleaners. In simpler words, enzyme cleaners are special shampoos with protein in them. It takes 7-10 days for nits to hatch. It has to be at least 82°F, and 70% humidity for the eggs to incubate. That means that if the temperature is less than 82°F, the eggs can't hatch! Hooray!

(continued on following page)

Lice spread VERY easily. That's why we should try to do all we can to prevent them. School is a zoo of lice. They are hiding around every corner. One minute they're on someone else's head, the next minute they're on yours. At least 10 MILLION children are infected EVERY year! But ... there IS a way to get revenge on the army of lice. They hate the smell of tea tree oil. You can put it on your head every morning to prevent yourself from getting lice. Also, you could have someone check your head once a month. Be careful! If you're checking someone's head and unluckily find lice, you have to pick through their hair and take it off. If you miss just ONE nit, they can have it again. Never share hairbrushes, jackets, or anything that touched someone else's head, because there could be lice on it. If you are a girl, it's a good idea to put your hair up. That can help keep them away. There is one more thing you should be careful of: MYTHS. Some people say that lice can fly and jump. Others think that you can get lice from animals, grass, and trees. Also, people think that the only way to get rid of head lice is to shave your head. None of those things are true. If you haven't had lice before, you are VERY lucky! Remember to try to prevent it as much as you can.

So next time you are playing a sport and someone is a ballhogger, don't think negative. Ball hoggers are a lot better than bloodhoggers.

And remember, YOU could be the bugs next victim!

The Write Connection

Mini Vampires

As noted earlier, one good way to judge the quality of an informational piece is to ask whether you could construct a multiple choice test based on the details. Try that. See if you can come up with three or four good multiple choice questions based on the information in "Mini Vampires."

Author's Note

Part of the presentation in this paper includes the author's choice of font: Chiller. Does this choice seem to echo her theme?

Suggested Scores for "Mini Vampires"

Ideas: **6**

Organization: **6**

Voice: **6**

Word choice: **6**

Sentence fluency: **6**

Conventions & presentation: **6**

Lessons Learned from "Mini Vampires"

- The right font can reinforce your theme.
- Good informational writing can include humor and drama.
- Make information relevant to a reader's own life, and you guarantee an engaged audience.

Comments

This piece has just about everything we could wish for in good informational writing: a good choice of topic (good in the sense that the writer is engaged), knowledge of that topic, interesting details (Who knew Betsy Ross ironed clothes to avoid lice?), easy-to-follow organization, a confident voice, excellent use of terminology, readability, and a knack for answering our pressing questions (such as "How do we avoid lice?"). The only thing missing is a list of sources. Perhaps most striking is the writer's skill in juggling an enormous amount of detail. Nearly every line teaches us something new. The word choice is consistently clear—and strong: "The teacher stares as she rakes her fingers though her hair like a monkey all day long." The writer allows herself some playfulness in both the lead and conclusion, reinforcing our impression that she enjoys sharing information on the sesame-seed-sized vampires. What will you remember from this piece? (That's one good indication of how strong it is.)

Stars (Informational, Grade 5)

Stars Are Born

A star is born in a huge cloud of hydrogen gas, and dust called a Nebula. After a while, the Nebula starts to break up into spinning balls. Inside, it gets so hot that nuclear reactions are triggered, and the core turns to helium. It's one huge ball of plasma!

> *Plasma is another form of matter similar to gas. Fire is a type of plasma.*

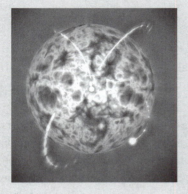

Star Size

Have you ever compared the sun to other stars? Your results would show that the sun is the biggest star of all. But it's not. The sun just looks big because it's the closest star to earth. The largest can grow to be up to 2000 times the size of the sun. They're called Super Giants because they're so huge. The next ones, the giants, can be up to 20-30 times bigger than the sun. Believe it or not, the sun is a medium sized star. The smallest are called white dwarfs.

Star Twins!

Twin stars are two separate stars born at the same time. They spend their whole life orbiting each other. However, they don't necessarily need to be identical. The 2 stars can have different size, shape, color, and brightness.

Star Dies

A super nova is an exploding star. It happens when, at the end of a star's life, it drains the rest of its nuclear fuel core, and it starts contracting. It keeps going until it can't be shrunk any longer. The light bounces back. The light can outshine an entire galaxy for a bit of time! After a few weeks or months, it dies. Until then it can radiate with about as much energy as the sun is expected to in its entire lifetime!

Not all stars die as supernovas. For example, some stars die as white dwarfs. The stars start running out of fuel, so it starts losing its outer layers, and the core shrinks until it's a small, glowing dense spot in space. Over billions of years, the star dies.

How do you think the sun will die?

Sources

http://www.kidsastronomy.com/stars.htm
http://en.wikipedia.org/wiki/Star
http:www.enchantedlearning.com/subjects/astronomy/stars/
http://en.wikipedia.org.wiki/Supernova
Black Holes and Other Space Phenomena, Philip Steele, Kingfisher.
Black Holes and Supernovae, Newton.

The Write Connection

Stars

This writer includes an extensive source list—and we have to applaud that. But—are all the items on that list formatted correctly? Compare one or more to the approved format for whatever handbook you use in your class. What about that title? Is it too broad? Can you think of a more focused one?

Suggested Scores for "Stars"

Ideas: **5**

Organization: **5**

Voice: **5**

Word choice: **6**

Sentence fluency: **6**

Conventions & presentation: **5**

Lessons Learned from "Stars"

- Research matters!
- Subheads are a good device for organizing information.
- Illustrations enhance both meaning and eye appeal.

Comments

What's particularly appealing to me about this piece is that even though the writer has clearly done extensive research, the paper is written in his own voice. He is doing what good researchers should do: filtering the information for us and sharing what he finds most important or interesting. As a result, the writing has that unique flavor that always comes from a personal perspective. His use of subheads is particularly effective; it helps both writer and reader keep things organized. The one problem with organization is the noticeable absence of an overview lead to set up the discussion. We begin with the birth of stars—that is a lead of sorts. But for the novice reader, the very notion that stars have a life cycle could be news, and it might provide a more encompassing opening. This writer is skilled at using terminology well, making meaning clear as he goes. He even includes a boxed definition of *plasma*. Outstanding sentence fluency, with meaningful beginnings that link ideas clearly and make reading easy for us.

Paper 6

The Middle Ages (Informational, Grade 7)

In the time of the Middle Ages many children drempt of being a knight. First they had to become a page. The next step to becoming a squire. Hard training and patience were required. A brave young squire could hardly wait to receive the accolade. During the period of being a squire you had to learn chivalry. Chivalry consisted of loyalty and devotion to the king or lord. Politeness and courtesy towards women was a very big part of being a knight. One also had to be brave and protect the defenseless.

A knight had to be wealthy in order to pay for the equipment. The equipment consists of a suit of armor, a shield, a sword, and of course a horse. The armor consists of many parts we won't name them all because it would take forever. However, we will name the helmet because it is the most important part of armor a knight could have because it protects the head from injury which could be fatal.

Tournaments took up what little free time a knight had. If a knight wasn't out on the battlefield he would be out jousting or sword fighting against another knight. The purpose of a tournament is to test one's strength. The object was not to kill a knight but to capture him.

Manors were the main ways of life during the middle age. They had farms, hunting grounds, people and castles. Castles were the main points of life in the middle ages. Castles were not built for comfort but for defense.

Well, after all that, there isn't much more to discuss, so for now, orevwa.

Source: Caselli, Giovanni. The middle Ages. New york, 1988, Peter Bedrick Books, pages 12–17.

Suggested Scores for "The Middle Ages"

Ideas: **3**

Organization: **2**

Voice: **3**

Word choice: **3**

Sentence fluency: **3**

Conventions & presentation: **3**

Lessons Learned from "The Middle Ages"

- Write your title last.
- A good ending should say goodbye metaphorically—but not literally.
- A little research never hurts.

Comments

If you already know a lot about the Middle Ages, you might sail right on through this essay. Otherwise, you are likely to find the information skimpy at best. There are many unanswered questions: Why did children dream of becoming knights? What was the accolade? Could anyone become a knight? Were the knights always at war? The writer seems to assume that the audience is right there in the social studies/history class and can therefore fill in the blanks. We need a better balance of details to give us a sense of history—and some little known information to spark the imagination. We're hungry for something new, something we've not heard before. The bibliography is short, but at least there is one. Is it formatted correctly?

The Write Connection

The Middle Ages

This writer leaves countless questions unanswered. Make a list as you read through the piece. Then have students—in teams of 3 or 4 or in pairs—track down answers to just one interesting question of their choice. Use the information you find to create a wiki on the Middle Ages. Working together, revise, add, change, expand. And—don't forget to cite sources.

Paper 7

Life in the Middle Ages (Informational, Grade 7)

Imagine yourself living in a time when the average man grew to a height of about 5'2", the average woman to about 4'10". And almost no one lived to be more than 45 years old. At 20 you would be middle aged, and probably would have lost many, if not most, of your teeth. Your skin would be pock marked from chicken pox or acne. At 13, you would either be married or (if you were a male), thinking about becoming a priest or knight. They were about the only people who were educated enough to read, write, or do simple math. This is just a small glimpse of what life was like in the Middle Ages in the part of the world we now call Great Britain. As we will see, life was very different then—in almost every possible way.

Society during the Middle Ages was organized in a somewhat military fashion. At the head of everything was the King, who had life and death control over all his subjects. He could conscript people for service in his "army," or confiscate their goods for use by the state. Not that there was much to confiscate. People during those times owned very little-a few clothes and dishes, some crude tools, some pigs or chickens, and perhaps a small shelter that passed for a house. Only the wealthy had dogs or horses, elaborate clothing, good leather shoes, weapons, jewelry or, in the cases of kings and lords, castles in which to live.

(continued on following page)

Of course, wealth is a relative thing. Today, we think little of owning things like automobiles, microwave ovens, computers, cameras and televisions, all of which would have seemed like magic to people of the 1300s. On the other hand, they dreamed of living in stone castles, for that was the height of elegance at the time. If we could go back in time and recapture the sights, sounds and smells of the Middle Ages, though, most of us would be horrified. Imagine no indoor sanitation, only crude buckets to dump human waste down the rock walls. Picture hogs, dogs, sheep, chickens and rats all sharing the larger space surrounding the inner castle where the King lived; the noise was deafening, the smell overpowering. Yet people looked on these surroundings as luxurious, for they knew nothing else.

Probably the worst thing to happen to anyone was to become ill or to be wounded. You might be bled into a bowl, or be given an herbal potion to drink, or a so-called doctor might stitch up your wounds with a filthy needle and some cat gut. Strangely enough, people then believed that washing actually pushed germs into your body, so no one washed if they could help it, not even the "doctors." Not only did they smell, but it was dangerous to be treated by one. Few people survived "surgery," which was more of a mutilation.

Entertainment in the Middle Ages was lively, to say the least. Knights practiced their jousting, trying to knock each other from horseback with a lance, in open tournaments. Some engaged in sword fights. They were not usually to the death, but sometimes accidents did occur. Executions were almost always public and were treated as a kind of entertainment. Many people would come to see someone hanged or beheaded. And of course there was almost always a wedding or funeral to attend if nothing else interesting was going on.

All in all, life was hard for people born in 1300. Maybe it's lucky they did only live to 45. Probably for them, that seemed like a long time!

Author's Note

Clearly there's a big contrast between papers 6 and 7. One has better detail, stronger voice, and more impressive word choice. But think beyond traits for a moment and see if you can, with your students, articulate the differences in terms of your personal response to the two pieces.

The Write Connection

Life in the Middle Ages

This piece is so vivid that we can almost imagine ourselves living during the Middle Ages. Try that. Have each student draft a short journal entry as one of the characters who might have lived in the manor. Begin by brainstorming a list of possible characters so students see how many choices there are. When everyone finishes writing, you might create a book—or make a podcast of oral readings.

Suggested Scores for "Life in the Middle Ages"

Ideas: **6**

Organization: **5**

Voice: **6**

Word choice: **6**

Sentence fluency: **6**

Conventions & presentation: **5**

Lessons Learned from "Life in the Middle Ages"

- Write about what you find interesting—and you'll interest readers too.
- When you know the topic well, you can be choosy about details.
- Once you've done the research, get credit for it: *Cite your sources.*

Comments

This writer has definitely done some research, and the result is an arresting, eye-opening, high on sensory detail walk through life in the 1300s. We learn how tall people were, how early they married, what they ate, how they lived, and how dangerous it could be to go to the doctor. The writer had us wincing as the doctor approached, holding our noses inside the castle, and shielding our eyes from the spectacle of "entertainment." Details are strong, language is vivid, and the voice is highly engaging. This writer—unlike many—does *not* run out of energy at the end. Refreshing—and impressive.

Paper 8

Humboldt Penguins (Informational, Grade 9)

Probably the most startling fact about the gentle Humboldt Penguin is that it is the most endangered penguin in the world. They have been hunted for years. Moreover, their main staple food, krill, are dwindling in numbers with the warming of the oceans, and the range of the Humboldt Penguin is not very big—and is not getting any bigger. Their habitat is unique, and they do not seem able to adapt. The only place it can be duplicated is in the zoo. Odds are, we have only a few decades left—maybe less—to enjoy these remarkable and friendly animals.

Environment

Humboldt Penguins live along the rocky coastline of South America, from Peru to Northern Chile. The warm currents of El Niño bring in plenty of fish and krill—for now—so the penguins do not migrate. They nest right in the rocks, making themselves comfortable along hard, unforgiving rock walls that most creatures would find less than inviting. The rocks and ocean are all they know their whole lives. Because they do not migrate, they know nothing of forests or sandy beaches or even pebbled coves.

Physical Description

Male and female Humboldts are similar in appearance. Both are about 26 inches tall and weigh about ten pounds. They have a black mask with touches of pink around a sharp, heavy beak, well suited to fishing. A black stripe runs like an inverted "U" up and around their sides and down their back. Their belly is mostly white, with scattered black speckles. Penguins have very short legs, perhaps only two inches long, but can nevertheless jump amazingly high, for the leg muscles are very powerful. Their webbed feet are black with pink spots, and they have three toes, with sharp, scaly claws at the end. A penguin's feet work like paddles, propelling the penguin through the water, and are very powerful.

Penguins are normally fairly clumsy on land, and waddle along at a slow pace—though they have been known to "launch" themselves at an enemy if attacked or provoked. They are built for underwater speed, however, and move like tiny torpedoes in the water. Their smooth, oval shape is reminiscent of a dolphin or trout, and they swim with the same ease.

Everyone knows that penguins do not fly. However, scientists believe that once they did. They are almost certainly descended from a flying bird, but so far, nobody has located the "missing link" that would prove this theory.

Food

The diet of the penguin is healthy, if a little monotonous. They dine primarily on fish and crustaceans, plus an occasional squid. They are especially fond of fish

(continued on following page)

Paper 8 (continued)

like anchovies which swim in large schools. Penguins have a lot of body fat to maintain in order to insulate themselves from the cold water, so they must eat a great deal and eat often to maintain their oval shapes.

The bill of the penguin is equipped with small spines which help hook and hold a fish. Once a penguin gets a grip on its meal, the fish rarely escapes.

Predators

Penguins are hunted by seals, killer whales and sharks. For this reason, they like to hunt close to shore and near the surface. If a penguin ventures too far out to sea, it may not have the endurance to outrun a hungry seal.

Land predators include gulls, jaegers, skuas and other large birds. These birds will not take on an adult penguin, which is a fierce fighter, but will prey on young chicks and eggs.

Behavior

A surprising fact about penguins is that they are quite territorial. They will attack others that come too close to their nesting site. Like humans, they sometimes resent neighbors who invade their privacy or become too nosy. If a penguin must walk through a crowded area, he will keep his head high and feathers sleeked down, as if trying to look invisible. Generally, though, penguins are very social. They swim together and hunt in groups for protection. They watch out for one another and are very affectionate with their young. Humboldts have not learned to fear humans, and will often allow people to come quite close.

Conclusion

The Humboldt Penguin is among the most intriguing of all penguin species. It is more social than most penguins, and remarkably like ourselves. With luck, it may survive long enough for us to study its curious ways further.

Sources

- Lynch, Wayne. 2001. <u>Penguins of the World</u>. Ontario: Firefly Books.
- Johnson, Russell. "Humboldt Penguins: An Endangered Species." In Penguin World. Vol. 4. No. 6. Spring 1992.
- Seattle Public Zoo. Site visit.

The Write Connection

Humboldt Penguins

This writer uses subheads to great advantage, neatly sectioning off information so we can follow the discussion—or later, find information easily. Have students try inserting subheads into any informational piece on which they are working. Doing so will help them identify sections that need more detail. Remind them that subheads benefit from careful, creative wording. Speaking of which …

This piece (Paper 8) has exceptional voice—except for the title and subheads. Brainstorm a few alternatives.

Suggested Scores for "Humboldt Penguins"

Ideas: **6**

Organization: **5**

Voice: **6**

Word choice: **6**

Sentence fluency: **6**

Conventions & presentation: **6**

Lessons Learned from "Humboldt Penguins"

- Take time to dig for unusual details. They make your writing stand out.
- Subheads are extremely useful—for both writer and reader.

- Personal research (such as a visit to the zoo) is helpful, and may deepen your understanding of a subject in a way that other research cannot.

Comments

This paper is a fine sample of informational writing at its best: informative, readable, and structured to help a reader find information quickly. It does not attempt to tell all there is to know about penguins, but focuses on significant, unusual details. It's interesting to learn, for instance, that penguins do not mind nesting in rocks, that they are affectionate with their young, that they bristle (like humans) when nosy neighbors come too close, and that (despite two-inch legs) they can launch themselves ferociously at a rude intruder. At the end we want to say, "Thanks for sharing so many intriguing tidbits—I learned a lot." Our only complaint (and it's minor) is that sections seem a little out of balance, with a lot of time spent on the penguins' appearance. The paper has fine conventions and a bibliography, too.

Paper 9

Method Acting (Informational, Grade 12)

The year is 1880. The theater is dark, except for one figure, illuminated on the stage. The figure, Prince Hamlet, begins his famous soliloquy:

To be, or not to be, that is the question—

The delivery of the lines is perfect, each word enunciated, clear from the rest. However, in the actor's face, there is no indication he feels the pain behind the words. While the character of Hamlet is clearly faced with a difficult decision, the actor is only considering what to have for dinner. The audience does not believe the actor *is* Hamlet. And the reason they do not believe is because the actor does not believe it himself.

The difference between reciting lines from memory and becoming the person characterized by those lines is the difference between acting *before* the Stanislavski Method and *after*. Prior to the twentieth century, when the influence of method acting was first felt in theater, it was up to the audience to figure out what emotions each character might be feeling. Because the lines had to carry all the meaning, one actor's Hamlet might be much like another's.

Enter Constantin Stanislavski, a Russian actor and director, who changed the role of the audience from that of casual observers or critics to that of engaged participants. Stanislavski wanted his audiences to cry and laugh—to feel life. So, in the late 1800s, he introduced the acting technique now widely known as "method acting" (also known as the Stanislavski System). With this method, emphasis on speech and clear delivery decreased, while emphasis on feelings and emotions increased perceptibly. As Foster Hirsch (1984, p. 18) explains, "The spectator ceased to watch the performance, and began to live it."

In method acting, the actor never stops evolving into the character he/she portrays. Actor and critic Sonia Moore points out that an actor must not only learn to "control his voice and body," but also to move across the stage as the character would do it—and to adopt the character's mannerisms and way of speaking, laughing, eating, or talking (1984, p. 13). Say the character is a

(continued on following page)

Paper 9 (continued)

police officer. The actor might then wear a police officer's uniform routinely—not just on the stage, but all day, even at home. He or she must learn to walk, run, sit, and look totally at home in that uniform so that it becomes an extension of who he or she is.

Method actors improvise. Stanislavski said that "mechanical memorization kills the imagination" (Moore, p. 58). He believed memorized words could never have the power of words that come from the heart—or cause an audience to think deeply about important moral issues. Actor Ellyn Burstyn has said that "to start with the words is to be too literal. Words are the last thing to come to" (Hirsch, p. 210). Many method actors believe they can "personalize" their lines so long as they project the writer's intended emotion and meaning.

Perhaps the most popular way for actors to find the right emotion is through a technique called "affective memory." It works like this: An actor recalls an incident that produced the desired emotion. Suppose she needs to call up anger. She recalls a time a careless driver cut her off in traffic, nearly causing an accident—or the time her mother broke her heart by ridiculing the way she dressed. The recollection triggers the anger, and the audience believes it because what they are seeing is real. With affective memory, actors feel emotions intensely, and the audience can sense the difference.

The influence of Constantin Stanislavski continues to this day. His method is used by many actors, including Al Pacino, Robert DeNiro, Jack Nicholson, Dustin Hoffman, and the late Marlon Brando—to name only a few. Some critics believe they can tell who is using method acting just by the intensity of emotion they project on stage or in films. Many people in today's audiences feel the same way . . .

It is 2006. The theater is dark except for one figure, illuminated on stage. Prince Hamlet breaks into his soliloquy. But this time, it is not the words on which the audience focuses, but the emotion behind them. We see pain on the actor's face, how he is experiencing the very real choice between life and death. Hamlet is no longer a shallow character, but a real human being. He is more. He is us. We have felt this pain, too. Art follows reality, and we get a glimpse of ourselves on the stage.

Sources Cited

Hirsch, Foster. 1984. *A Method to Their Madness: The History of the Actors Studio.* New York: Da Capo Press.

Moore, Sonia. 1984. *The Stanislavski System: The Professional Training of an Actor.* New York: Penguin Books.

Additional Sources Consulted

Stanislavski, Constantin. 1961. *Creating a Role.* Trans. Elizabeth Reynolds Hapgood. New York: Hill and Wang.

Stanislavski, Constantin. 1961. *Stanislavski on the Art of the Stage.* Trans. David Magershack. New York: Hill and Wang.

http://www.wisegeek.com/what-is-the-stanislavski-method-of-acting.htm

(continued on following page)

Reflection

This paper was easier for me to write than some—perhaps because I did not have trouble coming up with a solid thesis. This gave my writing focus. I think this paper is very easy to follow. It opens with a little drama and offers a bit of history on method acting without growing tedious. I give the reader several examples of how method acting works—enough to invite them to look for it themselves when they see a film or play. Then it comes full circle and ends back on stage. I read it aloud, and I feel it has voice. Al Pacino is my favorite actor, and I enjoyed discovering how he develops a character and makes the person so real. Also, I want to work in theater arts in college, so I had a personal stake in the whole method acting thing. I think that involvement comes through. It's fluent and readable—and it's not dry. The thing I'm working on the hardest right now is making sure an informational piece doesn't sound like a report—just a list of facts. If you don't want to just spit back an encyclopedia entry, you have to come up with a good topic and it has to be something you care about. This means you need time to think and plan. We never have enough time to really figure out what to write about or where to get good information. On the last assignment I wound up writing about Picasso, and it never came to life because I couldn't get into it and I ran out of time to switch topics. What I want to say is that the *writing itself* is the easy part. Conventions? No problem. It's the ideas and the voice you need to work to achieve. What we need is more time *before* we do the first draft, to gather information and to think. In spite of the fact I was trying to work on the spring break musical at the same time that I wrote this, it was a good project, and I loved the topic.

As you search for the right voice in doing your revision, look for a balance between flat, wooden prose, which sounds as if it were manufactured by a machine, and forced, flowery prose, which distracts the reader from what's most important: what you're trying to say.

—Bruce Ballenger
The Curious Researcher, 2004, 233

Suggested Scores for "Method Acting"

Ideas: **6**

Organization: **6**

Voice: **6**

Word choice: **6**

Sentence fluency: **6**

Conventions & presentation: **6**

Lessons Learned from "Method Acting"

- Taking time to research and plan pays off—so don't begin the actual draft until you feel ready.
- Research writing does not need to sound dull and dry.
- Write with confidence—and voice will soar.

Comments

Well written and supported with clear detail, this piece demonstrates that informational writing can be as engaging as any narrative piece. The writer's own assessment (in her reflection) sums it up: "It's fluent and readable—and it's not dry." One thing that tells me this is a good paper is the fact that I learned a good deal about method acting, and could easily describe it to someone else. And even though it's a relatively long piece (in

The Write Connection

Method Acting

Have students follow this writer's lead and create a short reflection for any informational piece they have finished. Like this writer, they should think about what they found exciting, challenging, or just plain frustrating. What advice would they offer other informational writers?

comparison to other examples here), I would have loved for it to go on; I thoroughly enjoyed the examples of "affective memory," and found myself picturing various actors using this technique. The sentence fluency is masterful. The variation is easy on the ear. But beyond that, this writer is very skilled at letting each sentence carry its weight in terms of detail. Sentences are never overloaded or stretched to the breaking point. The lead and conclusion, so carefully aligned, perfectly showcase the explanatory middle section. Outstanding conventions.

9 Strategies for Helping Students Create Powerful INFORMATIONAL WRITING

If you're bored by your research topic, your paper will almost certainly be boring as well, and you'll end up hating writing research papers as much as ever.

—Bruce Ballenger
The Curious Researcher, 2004, 25

Informational writing is special because it involves that extra step: research. And that step is, in and of itself, complex. Following are a few suggestions to help you and your students step comfortably and confidently into this exciting genre.

1. HELP STUDENTS CHOOSE A GOOD TOPIC.

Young writers all too often adopt a topic without investigating it first. This can be a big mistake. Bad topic choice gives birth to procrastination, hasty writing, limited research, and voiceless prose that no one wants to read. Help students explore topics in several ways:

Pay attention. Learn. Gather data . . . Then use your voice to write with zest, so readers quicken to the information you offer.

—Tom Romano
Crafting Authentic Voice, 2004, 28

- Read aloud from *your* favorite informational writers. What interested them may interest your students, too. (See my list of suggested titles, pages 296–300.)
- Read aloud from a good newspaper. Current events provide a rich resource for topics.
- Do some freewriting. Freewriting is a good way for writers to discover what they are thinking about, worrying over, curious about *right now*.
- Keep an ongoing topic list in your classroom, explaining that it is intended to stimulate ideas, not lock students in. Add to this list regularly. See Figure 9.8, *Informational Possibilities*, for some beginning ideas.
- Model. If you were to begin a research project today, what would *you* investigate?

2. REDEFINE THE CONCEPT OF "RESEARCH."

Research paper. Those are two of the heaviest words in the English language. Find a new way to think about it . . .

Research is investigation, exploration, poking around. It's a treasure hunt, an adventure, a journey—the search for booty in the sunken ship.

What's more, research can take many forms. Reading is one—but far from the only one. Encourage students to also—

Author's Note

In *The Curious Researcher* (2004, 230), author Bruce Ballenger recommends a website for "quick facts." It is www.refdesk.com. If you are not familiar with this site, have a look. You'll find the word of the day, quotation of the day, current news, biographical information, and a host of other tidbits right at your fingertips. Another site to check is www.ask.com

- **Check online,** looking for videos or podcasts that could hold relevant information
- **Interview people** they know (or can arrange to meet) who might have expertise in the field
- **Draw from personal experience**
- **Create a new experience**—through observation, a site visit, etc.

FIGURE 9.8

Informational Possibilities . . .

Explain (in a paper or on a blog, video, or wiki) . . .

- An invention that makes life harder, not easier
- How "old" is defined in the United States versus in other countries
- How women's rights have changed in the past 50 years
- What life will be like for the average person living in New York City (or anywhere) in the year 2050
- What it's like to be a child in any other country
- The kind of classroom environment in which students learn best
- How animal shelters cope with tight budgets
- How homeless people survive
- What it takes to train for a sport
- America's fascination with technology (or any specific medium or tool)

Describe (in a paper or on a blog, video, or wiki) . . .

- The oldest living creatures on earth
- The world's most hostile environments
- _____ 's life as a child
- Daily life in any other country
- A typical house in another country
- The life cycle of _____
- The environment on another planet
- Travel in outer space
- Travel to the deep sea floor

Combine research and imagination to create, write, or develop . . .

- A series of podcasts on any topic
- An introductory video, *Life on Earth*, written for intelligent beings visiting from another planet
- A job description likely to appear in your local paper 25 years from now
- A resume for a famous person, real or fictional
- A newspaper front page for any year in the past or future
- A "what if" paper or video on any of the following topics: What if—
  - *There were no national borders?*
  - *People had to purchase fresh air?*
  - *No one had children for the next 10 years?*
  - *Automobiles were made to decrease pollution?*
  - *Public education were no longer free?*
  - *Intelligent life was discovered on another planet?*
  - *People no longer required sleep?*
  - *We could read each other's minds?*

© 2012. Vicki Spandel.

3. MAKE INFORMATION ACCESSIBLE.

- Create a library of resources on topics students often explore. Put information at their fingertips.
- Teach students how to access information online. Many students may know this already, but those who do not may be timid about asking because technological

expertise is expected these days. Do you subscribe to an RSS (really simple syndication) feed? If not, consider doing so, and educate students about using the RSS to find the information they need.

- Take time to view films or listen to podcasts together. If students are working on a common topic, such as the solar system, time spent viewing a film can provide basic information that helps students zero in on a specific topic, and gets further exploration off to a good start.

- Make sure that each writer has at least one or two *potential* informational sources in mind before beginning. Otherwise, valuable time is lost just figuring out where to look. Aquariums, zoos, art galleries, museums, historical societies, libraries, and similar venues employ information specialists who are more than eager to map out a path for productive research.

- *Allow enough time.* This cannot be overstated. Students usually see prewriting as a small part of project—almost a step to skip if you're rushed—and drafting as huge. But research *is* prewriting, and if it's hurried, writing will be hard and unproductive.

4. PRACTICE NOTE TAKING.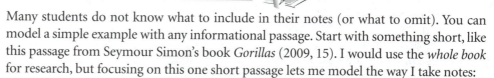

Many students do not know what to include in their notes (or what to omit). You can model a simple example with any informational passage. Start with something short, like this passage from Seymour Simon's book *Gorillas* (2009, 15). I would use the *whole book* for research, but focusing on this one short passage lets me model the way I take notes:

> A silverback is heavily built, weighing more than four hundred pounds and possibly as much as six hundred pounds. He stands five and a half feet tall or more and has an arm spread of eight feet, about the distance from the floor to the ceiling in a house. Despite his huge size, he is patient with the playful youngsters in his family. He allows them to cling to him and pull his hair.

Think about what stands out for *you* in this passage. Then, look at Figure 9.9 to see the same passage, only marked with the phrases I would highlight. See Figure 9.10 for my notes. Here I am very careful about using quotation marks to indicate Simon's exact words. If I summarize a concept in my own words, I don't need quotation marks. But *either way*, I must give credit to the author for his work, so I write down the author's name, the book title, year of publication, publisher, and page number.

FIGURE 9.9

Quotation from Seymour Simon for *Gorillas*

A silverback is heavily built, weighing more than four hundred pounds and possibly as much as six hundred pounds. He stands five and a half feet tall or more and has an arm spread of eight feet, about the distance from the floor to the ceiling in a house. Despite his huge size, he is patient with the playful youngsters in his family. He allows them to cling to him and pull his hair.

Source: Seymour Simon. 2009. *Gorillas.* New York: HarperCollins Publishers. Page 15. Used by permission.

FIGURE 9.10

My Notes Based on *Gorillas*

- Leader of the group called a "silverback"
- Weight: 400 to 600 pounds
- Height: stands "five and a half feet tall or more"
- "Arm spread of eight feet"
- "Patient" with baby gorillas. He "allows them to cling to him and pull his hair."

Each bullet would be transferred to a notecard—or would become one entry in my online notes.

Source: Seymour Simon. 2009. *Gorillas.* New York: HarperCollins Publishers. Page 15. Used by permission.

5. COACH WRITERS TO TEACH YOU *SOMETHING NEW.*

Young writers all too often write what they think we want or expect them to write, turning a research paper into an essay test. We have to make it clear that we want *new* information. *Teach me something worth knowing, something I'll remember—something not everyone knows,* should be the message.

Meleane (grade 5) is doing a research piece on owls (see Figure 9.11). She has made an excellent start, and is in a good place for a conference. Her paper shows terrific promise thanks to some striking details, and a small amount of additional research will take it over the top. Here are some *potential* comments/questions I might offer this young writer:

- I like the way you begin with the sound the owl makes. Do you think most people like that sound? Could some people find it scary?
- You mentioned that some owls build nests on the ground and some dig burrows. Do they ever have to worry about coyotes or other predators?
- I was shocked to hear owls eat deer! You taught me something new there. Are you saying owls are scavengers?
- So here you are with this intriguing beginning and the sound of the owl—then here at the end, you are talking more about your own writing process. I am thinking this could be the start of a really good *reflection*—a special addition to your paper. What if we made this a special section with a box around it—like this [drawing a box around Meleane's comments]. Then maybe you could write a *new* ending that includes one surprising fact—something you think I need to remember about owls.

FIGURE 9.11

"Owls" by Meleane (Grade 5)

Whoooo, have you ever heard of that noise? It's the sound of an owl and for some odd reason I like them. But owls can be more interesting than people tell it.

Some owls actually build nests on the ground; also some of them dig burrows. That's just the beginning.

Have you ever heard what owls eat? You would be surprised. Large owls eat rabbit, skunk, and rat, but small owls eat insects and mice. They even eat birds, fish, and even young deer. Not every day you hear that.

You probably already know that some owls have enemies such as birds that are bigger than them and crows. Well, they can be a real problem to owls; crows attack sleeping owls. Now and then, large owls attack small owls these days. Did you know young owls play dead when they get attacked?

I read a book about owls 1 day and had no idea how interesting they could be I hope you like owls just as much as I do.

6. GET CREATIVE ABOUT FORMAT.

Remember the two papers written on the Middle Ages (papers 6 and 7)? Here's a piece from a student who took a completely different approach. A seventh grader assumed the role of a page studying to be a knight in "Arthur's Diary" (see Figure 9.12). Notice how much detail about everyday medieval life this writer shares. The form is creative—but her research still shows through (the writer is female, writing in a male voice). The original diary is much longer, and is done in calligraphy on parchment paper, then bound in suede and tied together with a leather cord, giving it the hand-assembled look a publication might have had in the 1300s. (See the photo in Figure 9.13.) For this writer, presentation was part of the message.

Some people might not define Arthur's Diary as informational because of its format. I think that's a mistake. Although it is imaginative in format, the *primary* purpose of the diary is to share information gathered through research.

Student researchers can also incorporate sketches, collage art, photos, song lyrics, poetry, quotations, and more. Given access to technology, they can think about presenting information through podcasts, video interviews, or a documentary film. The traditional research paper still serves the purpose, but it is no longer the only option— or even the primary option.

7. SMOOOOOOTH OUT THOSE QUOTATIONS.

We want students to cite experts and to quote others who have interesting things to say. This makes the reading more exciting—and informative. But sometimes they stick quotations in as if they were pins on a corkboard.

FIGURE 9.12

Six Excerpts from Arthur's Diary (Grade 7)

May 3, 1385

My name is Arthur and I have decided to keep a diary. I am 14 and I am a squire, someone who is studying to be a knight. I have seen so many knights killed that I am not sure I really want to be a knight.

May 7, 1385

We just sent over 50 knights off to battle. I have been polishing armor till my shoulders ache. I also have to get the prize hunting dogs ready, and they're as big as I am. I feel sorry for the blacksmith, having to shoe all those horses. Yesterday he got bitten by a horse and they had to stitch it up with cat gut.

May 13, 1385

One of the Lord's old friends is coming up from the southern coast to visit Stonewall Castle. The cooks are preparing a special feast of cockentrice—a capon and a suckling pig cut in half, stuffed, and sewn back together—each with its head on the other's body. They are also going to cook a peacock with all its feathers on.

May 19, 1385

I really like my room because of its stained glass windows. It used to be the chapel before they built a larger one—and I'm lucky to have it. What I don't like is the person I have to share it with, a stuck up little beast of a squire named Edmond. He has perfect spelling, so the priest thinks he is wonderful. He steals the covers at night, puts boar grease in his hair, shoots birds with his sling shot, and lets them rot on the forest floor. He's going to make a rotten knight.

May 23, 1385

Today I got a haircut in town. The barber is also a dentist and surgeon. I saw him bleeding someone into a bowl. I hope I never get sick. He's a wretched barber. Next time I'll do it myself. We have a visitor from the East who claims to be an astronomer. He has been telling us of temples made from gold. Lord Charles says he wants gold walls in the new chapel. The visitor said people from the East believe the earth is round. Lord Charles says if he keeps on with such nonsense, he'll have him hanged. I think the earth might be round, but I'd better not let Lord Charles know.

May 26, 1385

Today I went exploring in the inner courtyard. I find it hard to believe how many servants can fit into those apartments. There are lots of smells and sounds, too. Dogs and cats running around and barking. At one wall it smells especially foul. It's where they dump waste down the wall. The noise is deafening because the peasants keep their cattle, sheep, pigs, and chickens right next to their sleeping quarters. Beats me how they get any sleep.

FIGURE 9.13

Photo of "Arthur's Diary"

Help students understand that quotations need a context. They need to be set up. Consider this passage from an eighth grader's paper explaining Jackie Robinson's positive influence on America's view of African-American baseball players:

> The African-American players who were up to the challenge had to fight for the right to represent; but for one player, Jackie Robinson, putting up with the prejudice paid off in overwhelming success in this game. "The 1947 Baseball season left Jackie Robinson not only the most celebrated black man in America but also one of the most respected men of any color" (Rampersad, 188). Jackie Robinson's success continued throughout his career and so did his fan base. "A nationwide contest placed him ahead in popularity of President Truman, General Eisenhower, General MacArthur, and comedian Bob Hope" (Rampersad, 189). Jackie Robinson helped to make baseball the gateway to help reduce racism in America. This was not a total solution to the racism problem, but the barrier to initial acceptance was broken and a glimpse of the future could be seen. [Quotations are from Arnold Rampersad, 1997. *Jackie Robinson: A Biography*. New York: Alfred A. Knopf.]

This writer has chosen some excellent quotations. With small changes in wording, he can set up these quotations so that they get our attention. Phrases like the following make good introductions:

- *As Rampersad tells us,*
- *For example,*
- *Rampersad indicates that . . .*

Here is the same paragraph split into three shorter paragraphs, with some smoother introductions (<u>underlined</u>) to set off those well-chosen quotations. Notice how placing the quotations at the *end* of each paragraph (remember 231?) provides added punch:

> The African-American players who were up to the challenge had to fight for the right to represent; but for one player, Jackie Robinson, putting up with the prejudice paid off in overwhelming success in this game. <u>Biographer Arnold Rampersad describes it this way</u>: "The 1947 Baseball season left Jackie Robinson not only the most celebrated black man in America but also one of the most respected men of any color" (188).
>
> Jackie Robinson's success continued throughout his career and <u>his fan base grew steadily. In fact, Arnold Rampersad offered this comparison between Robinson and some of the most popular figures of the day</u>: "A nationwide contest placed him ahead in popularity of President Truman, General Eisenhower, General MacArthur, and comedian Bob Hope" (189).
>
> Jackie Robinson helped to make baseball the gateway to help reduce racism in America. This was not a total solution to the racism problem, but the barrier to initial acceptance was broken and a glimpse of the future could be seen.

8. SHOW STUDENTS HOW TO CITE SOURCES.

The precise format for citations differs slightly from handbook to handbook, so begin by choosing a handbook you like and help students become familiar with it. Think about the kinds of sources they draw from most frequently (books, newspapers, websites, blogs), and be sure they are comfortable with end-of-paper citations and any information (publication date, page number) you want embedded in the text.

In addition, be sure students know what *plagiarism* is—and that they understand how to avoid it. Many students unintentionally plagiarize material when all they really mean to do is follow directions. After all, we tell them to "pull information from multiple sources"! Help them distinguish among these three terms:

- *Plagiarism* (quoting or paraphrasing without citing the source)
- *Paraphrasing* (borrowing an idea but expressing it in your own words)
- *Quoting* (reproducing the *precise words and punctuation* of someone else)

If you model note taking (as I did in strategy 4), you can show students how anything directly lifted from a publication must be quoted and referenced with correct citations. But—this is the tricky part—paraphrased ideas *must also be credited to the originator*. Most of the time, depending on wording, such ideas should be introduced as if they were quotations. For example, if I were writing about Jackie Robinson, I might say something like this:

> Biographer Arnold Rampersad compared the popularity of baseball great Jackie Robinson to that of famous celebrities like Bob Hope and statesmen like President Harry Truman. (*Jackie Robinson: A Biography*. 1997, 189)

No quotations are needed because I have not used Rampersad's words. But I *did* use his idea.

9. SHARE ALOUD FROM THE BEST INFORMATIONAL WRITING YOU CAN FIND.

When we read aloud, the first thing we reach for is often a story or a poem. There is nothing in the world wrong with this. But sometimes we need to reach for informational pieces. After all, this is often the writing we are asking students to produce. And students will write what they hear.

The following informational books make extraordinary read-alouds and contain striking visuals to share on a document projector. Some I have discussed earlier, but I'm listing them again here so you won't have to search them out in other chapters.

This list is only a beginning because books alone are not enough. Expand your repertoire to include podcasts and webcasts, documentary films, newspapers (online or otherwise), blogs, and more. Most of the world's writing is informational, so examples are everywhere.

Informational Favorites

The Animal Dialogues by Craig Childs. 2007. New York: Little, Brown and Company.

Naturalist and NPR contributor Craig Childs blends traditional with personal research to take readers face to face with wild creatures we only thought we knew. High school and adult. All ages for selected passages.

Animals in Translation by Temple Grandin. 2005. New York: Harcourt.

A fascinating book that will be hard for animal lovers to put down. Countless passages to intrigue and amaze readers—by an author with a unique perspective. All ages for selected passages.

At Home: A Short History of Private Life by Bill Bryson. 2010. New York: Doubleday.

Thanks to Bryson's extensive research, we learn the history of rooms themselves as well as the artifacts they hold. Who knew phones were first used for weather reports and fire alarms? (229) High school and adult. All ages for selected passages.

Birdology by Sy Montgomery. 2010. New York: Simon & Schuster. Nonfiction.

Naturalist and documentary scriptwriter Sy Montgomery takes us on adventure after adventure, soaring with falcons, saving orphaned hummingbirds, watching cockatoos dance on YouTube, cringing at cassowaries, and gasping in disbelief as parrots speak their minds. All ages for selected passages.

Bones by Steve Jenkins. 2010. New York: Scholastic.

Fold-out illustrations and revealing facts provide a fascinating overview of the hows and whys of skeletons—human and otherwise. Outstanding presentation. Grade 3 and up.

Case Closed? Nine Mysteries Unlocked by Modern Science by Susan Hughes. 2010. New York: Kids Can Press.

Fans of forensic science will dive right into this exploration of nine of history's most fascinating mysteries—including what became of Hatshepsut, the first female Egyptian pharaoh (was she murdered?); the city of Ubar, which seemingly vanished from the deserts of Saudi Arabia; George Mallory, who tried to scale Everest in 1924 and was never seen again—and six others. Middle school and up; all ages for segments shared aloud.

Cool Stuff and How It Works by Chris Woodford and Luke Collins, Clint Witchalls, Ben Morgan, and James Flint. 2005. New York: DK Publishing.

Captivating overviews of the toys and gadgets most of us find irresistible, from cell phones and MP3 players to satellites, pet translators, fireworks, robots, and much more. Middle school and up. All ages for segments shared aloud.

Disasters: Natural and Manmade Catastrophes through the Centuries by Brenda Guiberson. 2010. New York: Christy Ottaviano Books.

Each of the book's nineteen chapters describes a major disaster, from the smallpox that infected millions of Native Americans to the impact of Hurricane Katrina.

Guiberson's well-researched text examines factors that contributed to each disaster, its effect on civilizations of the time, and efforts to deal with the aftermath. Middle school and up; all ages for segments shared aloud.

***Down, Down, Down: A Journey to the Bottom of the Sea* by Steve Jenkins. 2009. Boston: Houghton Mifflin Harcourt.**

A revealing plunge through the upper levels of the sea and clear to the ocean floor, with a detailed and often surprising peek at the numerous and sometimes startling creatures who inhabit each level. Grade 3 and up.

***Extreme Animals: The Toughest Creatures on Earth* by Nicola Davies. Illustrated by Neal Layton. 2006. Cambridge, MA: Candlewick Press.**

An enthralling, fact-filled look at nature's toughies: the wood frog, polar bear, penguin, camel, lizard, spider, sponge, bacterium, and more. All ages.

***How Fast Is It?* by Ben Hillman. 2008. New York: Scholastic.**

Short, snappy essays reveal little-known statistics about ostriches, bamboo, comets, sailfish, cheetahs, light, peregrine falcons, computers, hummingbirds, and other icons of speed. All ages.

***How to Clean a Hippopotamus: A Look at Unusual Animal Partnerships* by Steve Jenkins and Robin Page. 2010. New York: Houghton Mifflin Harcourt.**

A detailed, expansive exploration of symbiosis, enriched with unusual detail and Jenkins' trademark collage art. Intended for young readers, but suitable for all ages as an illustration of how to use and define terminology well.

***If the World Were a Village* by David J. Smith. Illustrated by Shelagh Armstrong. 2011. Toronto: Kids Can Press.**

Ideal for showing how to make huge volumes of data manageable and understandable. Intriguing details that will surprise you. All ages.

***In a Sunburned Country* by Bill Bryson. 2001. New York: Random House.**

Humorous and well-researched blend of history, geography, science, travelogue, and memoir that offers a riveting and unique perspective on Australia, its history, and its culture. High school and adult. All ages for selected passages.

***Jellies: The Life of Jellyfish* by Twig C. George. 2000. Minneapolis: Millbrook Press. Nonfiction.**

Fascinating facts further illuminated by incredible photos that take us inside the world of this innocent (but sometimes lethal) creature. All ages, aimed at primary/early elementary.

***Just the Right Size: Why Big Animals Are Big and Little Animals Are Little* by Nicola Davies. Illustrated by Neal Layton. 2009. Cambridge: Candlewick Press.**

A witty, clear, and hilariously illustrated explanation of the relationships among size, weight, and strength. Grade 3 and up.

***Manfish: A Story of Jacques Cousteau* by Jennifer Berne. Illustrated by Eric Puybaret. 2008. New York: Chronicle Books.**

Outstanding, lyrical biography of Jacques Cousteau, beginning with the childhood curiosity that drew him into a lifelong love affair with the ocean. Gorgeously illustrated, and featuring striking word choice. Elementary and up.

***A Natural History of the Senses* by Diane Ackerman. 1990. New York: Random House.**

With striking voice and impeccable word choice, Ackerman blends anthropology, sociology, anatomy, and biology to show us how our senses put us in touch with the world. High school and adult. All ages for selected passages.

Neo Leo: The Ageless Ideas of Leonardo da Vinci **by Gene Barretta. 2008. New York: Henry Holt and Company.**

Barretta focuses on da Vinci's original sketches (comparing them to modern versions of the hang glider, contact lenses, robots, and other inventions) to show the visionary power of the Renaissance man who was author, artist, inventor, and more. Clear writing makes complex information highly accessible and appealing. Elementary and up.

Oh, Rats! The Story of Rats and People **by Albert Marrin. Illustrated by C. B. Mordan. 2006. New York: Penguin.**

Beautifully organized, filled with striking details, written with voice and fluency, and a masterpiece of design—this book has it all. A book to show "how it's done." Grade 5 and up.

Our Solar System **by Seymour Simon. 2007. New York: HarperCollins/Smithsonian Institution.**

Well-illustrated and easy-to-read overview that packs information into every sentence. Grade 3 and up.

Pocket Babies and Other Amazing Marsupials **by Sneed B. Collard III. 2007. Plain City, OH: Darby Creek Publishing.**

Outstanding photography and inviting design add to the readability of this mesmerizing glimpse into the life of marsupials—one of nature's most intriguing and adaptable specialties. All ages.

Quest for the Tree Kangaroo: An Expedition to the Cloud Forest of New Guinea **by Sy Montgomery. Photographs by Nic Bishop. 2006. Boston: Houghton Mifflin Company.**

Poetic description blends with scientific information as Montgomery recounts the challenging journey to find and photograph one of Earth's most elusive creatures. All ages.

Reign of the Sea Dragons **by Sneed B. Collard III. Illustrated by Andrew Plant. 2008. Cambridge, MA: Charlesbridge.**

An intriguing, informative, and sometimes downright scary journey into the oceans of long ago. Grade 5 and up. All ages for selected passages.

Remember: The Journey to School Integration **by Toni Morrison. 2004. New York: Houghton Mifflin Company.**

The inimitable Toni Morrison lends her voice to a book that brilliantly combines narrative, history, legal milestones, headlines, timelines, and unforgettable photos in tracing the fight to overturn school segregation—and change a nation's thinking. Middle school and up. All ages for selected passages.

Seabiscuit: An American Legend **by Laura Hillenbrand. 2001. New York: Ballantine Books.**

A meticulously researched history of life in 1930s America, as well as an informational tribute to the sport of horse racing. It's also a treasure trove of verb-energized sports writing at its finest. All ages for selected passages.

Seahorses **by Twig C. George. 2003. Brookfield, CT: The Millbrook Press.**

Lyrical and gorgeously illustrated with undersea photos, this little nonfiction gem is also perfect for showing how to stay focused by not telling everything: See the author's note at the end of the book. Early elementary and up.

Spiders and Their Websites **by Margery Facklam. Illustrated by Alan Male. 2001. New York: Little, Brown and Company.**

A cleverly organized book that opens with an overview of spiders, then gives us close-ups of twelve different kinds of spiders, each one expanding our expertise. Excellent glossary. Grade 4 and up.

So much of what is truly interesting and illuminating in history resides only in memory, which outlives events for only a brief time. In researching *Seabiscuit*, I wanted to capture as many of those memories as possible before they were lost forever.

—Laura Hillenbrand
Seabiscuit, 2001, "A Reader's Guide"

Whenever I write a book like *Seahorses* I read, research, talk to experts, and go to see whatever it is I am writing about as much as possible. Then I begin. As I write, many facts get left along the way, like film clips on a cutting room floor.

—Twig C. George
Seahorses, 2003, 32

The Story of Salt by Mark Kurlansky. Illustrated by S. D. Schindler. 2006. New York: G. P. Putnam's Sons.

Outstanding historical take on humans' attraction to salt—a commodity so prized it has been used for money. Grade 3 and up.

Surprising Sharks by Nicola Davies. Illustrated by James Croft. 2003. Cambridge, MA: Candlewick Press. (2008 edition includes CD.)

Remarkably detailed and entertaining introduction to sharks. Primary through early elementary.

Tracking Trash: Flotsam, Jetsam, and the Science of Ocean Motion by Loree Griffin Burns. 2007. Boston: Houghton Mifflin Company.

Ever wonder what happens to all that plastic we throw away? Dare to find out. Middle school and up.

Wild Thoughts from Wild Places by David Quammen. 1998. New York: Simon and Schuster.

Quammen is a master of the informational genre. His essays are by turns intriguing, humorous, and chilling. A multi-award winning author who knows how to make the complex accessible. High school and adult. All ages for selected passages.

Written in Bone: Buried Lives of Jamestown and Colonial Maryland by Sally M. Walker. 2009. Minneapolis: Carolrhoda Books.

Forensics is useful not only for solving crimes, but for unveiling long-forgotten truths about ancestry and lifestyle. Find out more than you could ever learn from television crime dramas. Remarkable photographs. Middle school and up.

Ubiquitous: Celebrating Nature's Survivors by Joyce Sidman. Illustrations by Beckie Prange. 2010. Boston: Houghton Mifflin Harcourt.

Combines poetry, illustrations, and informational text to offer in-depth portraits of creatures who have survived the longest on Earth. All ages.

The Watcher: Jane Goodall's Life with the Chimps by Jeanette Winter. 2011. New York: Random House Children's Books.

A simplified but well-written story of Goodall's landmark research (enhanced with numerous quotations) makes for a perfect introduction to the genre of biography. Elementary.

What's Eating You? by Nicola Davies. Illustrated by Neal Layton. 2007. Somerville, MA: Candlewick Press.

This is truly the most fun you can have learning about parasites. Davies manages (with help from Neal Layton) to make them both comical and fascinating. (Prepare to scratch a bit.) All ages.

World without Fish by Mark Kurlansky. Illustrated by Frank Stockton. 2011. New York: Workman Publishing.

Could it be true that the fish we most often eat—tuna, salmon, cod, and sword-fish—could be extinct within fifty years? And could the seas turn orange-red from algal blooms? Explore the potential effects of overfishing and global warming in an eleven-chapter persuasive argument. Each chapter builds on the one before. Notice the striking layout and unconventional use of fonts. Grade 6 to adult.

Years of Dust: The Story of the Dust Bowl by Albert Marrin. 2009. New York: Penguin.

Masterful blend of narrative, exposition, photography, song lyrics, quotations, and stunning photography that dramatically captures the impact of the Dust Bowl on American lives. (Often shelved with children's books, this text is clearly directed toward an older audience.) Grade 4 to adult.

Zero: The Biography of a Dangerous Idea **by Charles Seife. 2000. New York: Penguin Books. Nonfiction.**
Readable, voice-filled account of how the concept of zero reshaped cultures and shook world philosophies to their core. Middle school and up.

A Quick Look at PERSUASIVE ARGUMENT and Thoughts About "Trait Eight"

In this book, I make two general genre-based distinctions: writing that requires research and writing that the writer pulls from his or her own head, whether it takes the form of a narrative, an expository piece, a memoir, or something else. The two sets of writing guides we've looked at so far will cover most forms of writing very nicely. But still, there are times when, as a teacher, you may want to ask how well a particular piece of writing fulfills its intended purpose—to persuade, for example.

We could consider *genre* "trait eight." I say *eight* recognizing that many people see presentation as a seventh trait (hence "6+1"). I don't agree or disagree with this. Either perspective works. I simply prefer to consider conventions and presentation as a unified whole because they are inseparable in preparing a document for publication. Further, as noted earlier, presentation is a specialty that (in my view) is very difficult for anyone but an experienced designer to *assess* objectively. (This is not to say we shouldn't *teach* it.)

Genre, on the other hand, is not a specialty. It is an integral and essential part of writing. Moreover, students' understanding of what it means to write for a particular purpose (or a blend of several purposes) is a major contributor to their success as writers (and for that matter, as readers)—and is an integral component of the Common Core Standards.

Think of your own students for a moment. If you asked them to tell you the primary requirements of a good narrative, could they do it? Could they distinguish between a true narrative and a simple list of events? If not, they may list events and call it a narrative. But if they *do* know the difference, their narrative writing is more likely to include a setting, a lead that sets up the story or anticipates future events, characters we care about, a turning point, an ending that offers resolution, and (oh, happy day) a *point*—a reason for the telling. Understanding of genre matters because it defines how we write.

Wait a minute, though. If genre is "trait eight" (or if, at least, we think it's important), do we need more (and *more*) sets of writing guides? One per genre? I don't think so. Rather than develop a new set of writing guides for every genre on the planet, let me suggest a sane alternative. I want to show you how to develop a quick genre-specific writing guide in simple checklist form. This is something you can create right in your classroom with your own students, and the process will teach them more than any lecture you can deliver. I'm going to use persuasive argument as an example, but you can use narrative, memoir, drama, business writing, tech writing (think lab reports)—*anything*. You need—

- Samples of published work in the genre of focus (you don't need whole books—short paragraphs will usually do)
- A chart on which to record your impressions
- Copies of student work in the same genre

4 Simple Steps to Your Own Persuasive Checklist . . .

Step 1

I love to open a discussion of persuasive argument (no matter the grade level) with Phillip and Hannah Hoose's classic book *Hey, Little Ant* (1998, Tricycle Press). In this book, a young boy (pictured from the ant's point of view as a giant) has made up his mind to step on a small ant, who is just making his way home with a crumb or two for the family. Alternately, the ant pleads for his life and the boy offers reasons for going ahead with his plan. This is an outstanding example of persuasion—with the ant's very life at stake. One of the brilliant things about this book is that the authors do not resolve the dilemma; we the readers must make the final decision for ourselves. Try this:

- Rather than reading the book aloud, have students perform the parts. (Just two students can do this, or you can divide it up, giving each reader just a line or two.)
- When you finish reading the text, talk about the arguments put forth by each side. Which side has a stronger position? Why? Is there anything else either of them could have said?
- Vote: Should that foot come down on the ant—or not? Have students talk or write about this.

The greatest value of a rubric or checklist lies not in the document itself, but in its development. Coming to grips with what we value in writing (or reading, math, or science) teaches us to understand the content area we are exploring and challenges our accepted beliefs.

—Vicki Spandel,
The 9 Rights of Every Writer, 2005, 103

Step 2

At this point, your students already know quite a lot about persuasive writing. They know it involves making an argument, that some arguments are stronger than others, and that the point is to get your audience to see your side as valid—and perhaps to take some specific action (such as preventing the untimely end to a little ant's life).

There's more to it, of course, and this is why you need additional examples. Find as many as you can (have students search, too) because each example will have its own lessons to teach. Here are a few to get you started. (Gather *at least* four more.) As you share, record what you learn from each example on your checklist. As you go along, you're capturing what's "important" to persuasive writing. Later, you will narrow this list down to the "essentials."

Sample 1: Rachel Carson

In *Silent Spring*, Rachel Carson offers an eloquent argument against tampering with nature, whether it be in the form of dangerous chemicals and pollutants or by re-ordering the landscape. To strengthen her argument, she offers a number of examples. In this one, she suggests that replacing sagebrush with grass is a mistake—because sage has earned its place on the prairie through a long history of overcoming natural hardships. The take-away lesson? Use **clear, expansive examples** to support your position:

> The sage—low-growing and shrubby—could hold its place on the mountain slopes and on the plains, and within its small gray leaves it could hold moisture enough to defy the thieving winds. It was no accident, but rather the result of long ages of experimentation by nature, that the great plains of the West became the land of sage. . . .
>
> From Rachel Carson. 1962. "Earth's Green Mantle" in *Silent Spring*. New York: Houghton Mifflin Company, p. 65.

Sample 2: David Quammen

In his essay "To Live and Die in L.A.," writer David Quammen writes of an ongoing war between humans and the coyotes that have made themselves at home almost everywhere humans live—sometimes causing great destruction. Within this discussion, Quammen makes two important arguments: (1) the coyote is one of the most clever and adaptable creatures on the planet, and (2) efforts to eradicate the animal have ironically made things worse. We learn two things from this short passage. First, **explain** what you mean by words like "problematic." And second, **support your argument** by citing a source—like biologist Robert Crabtree:

> The fittest have survived, and doggone if the fittest aren't harder to trap, harder to poison, harder to fence out, harder to fool, harder to kill despite all the helicopters and leg-hold traps and high-powered rifles and cyanide booby traps that ADC can muster. "They've created their own worst nightmare," says [biologist Robert] Crabtree, not without sympathy for the many trappers and ranchers he has gotten to know. "They've created a coyote that's impervious to their means."
>
> From David Quammen. 1998. "To Live and Die in L.A." in *Wild Thoughts from Wild Places*. New York: Scribner, pp. 96–98.

Sample 3: Thomas L. Friedman

Following is a closing quotation from *Hot, Flat, and Crowded*, Friedman's argument for a greener America. With this ending, Friedman appeals to our adventurous spirit and courage (having us picture ourselves as Pilgrims on the *Mayflower*)—and uses **powerful rhetoric** (*We are all Pilgrims again*) to create the sense that we're already part of something vital and important. He is also creating drama, showing the consequences of not acting—versus taking steps to *redefine*, *revive*, and *regenerate*:

> We are all Pilgrims again. We are all sailing on the *Mayflower* anew. We have not been to this shore before. If we fail to recognize that, we will, indeed, become just one more endangered species. But if we rise to this challenge, and truly become the Re-generation—redefining green and rediscovering, reviving, and regenerating America—we, and the world, will not only survive but thrive in an age that is hot, flat, and crowded.
>
> From Thomas L. Friedman. 2008. *Hot, Flat, and Crowded*. New York: Farrar, Straus, and Giroux , p. 412.

Sample 4: MySpace and Jeca Taudte

By now, everyone has heard about "going green," and readers who are not already convinced might well tune out. To hold their attention, you need to be very eloquent, like Thomas Friedman—or you need to tell them simple **specific things they can do** to make a difference:

> The average American family generates more than 100 lbs. of trash a week. Bring your bathroom scale outside. See if you can cut down on the amount of garbage you create in one week by weighing your trash bag. Then see if you can keep those pounds off for a month.
>
> From MySpace with Jeca Taudte. 2008. *Our Planet: Change Is Possible*. New York: HarperCollins, p. 39.

Step 3

Let's say you have looked at eight to ten strong examples of persuasive argument. You and your students have recorded the lessons highlighted in my examples—plus those from your own examples. From that list, draw the six or seven you feel are *essential* to strong persuasive writing. The result will look something like Figure 9.14. This is only a model; your "critical points" may be different from mine.

You have now created a writing guide in the form of a checklist. You can use this simply as a set of reminders (a poster, let's say)—or you can use it to score writing, providing a point for each check on the list. This makes scoring extremely simple, and also

By the time they get to our classrooms, students are at best masters, or at the very least practitioners in the arts and crafts of persuasion. They have convinced their weary mothers to stay up late to watch that special show, they have talked their fathers into lending them the car . . . With a little tickling, students can articulate the truth about what persuasive techniques work for them.

—Barry Lane and Gretchen Barnabei
Why We Must Run with Scissors Sometimes, 2001, 1

guides revision. Why seven options if scores range from 1 through 6? Because first, your list should reflect what's important—not an effort to fill in six blanks (or any other number). And in addition, offering options gives your writing guide—and your writers—flexibility. Every persuasive piece is different, and writers will achieve success in varying ways. A writer who received 6 *or more* checks would receive a score of 6.

FIGURE 9.14

Checklist for Persuasive Writing

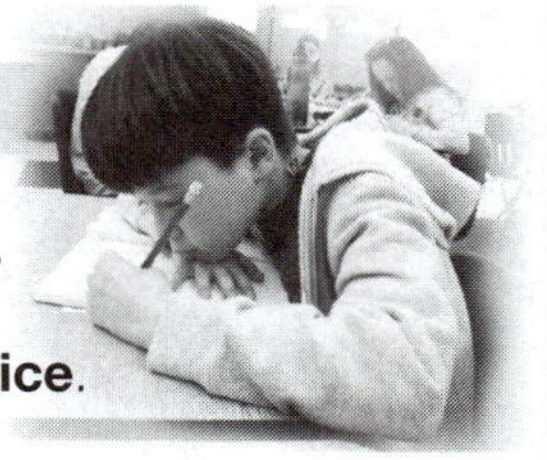

THE WRITER:

____ takes a **clear stand** and sticks with it.

____ writes in a **confident, passionate voice**.

____ **explains** his/her main points thoroughly.

____ offers **compelling evidence**: facts, examples, studies, quotations from experts, firsthand observations, etc.

____ acknowledges **other views**, and addresses them in a convincing, fair manner.

____ suggests **specific actions** the reader or others could take.

____ **convinces the reader**: makes the reader think, prompts some action, or causes the reader to see things in a new way.

Step 4

Once you have a checklist you're happy with, try it out on some actual samples of writing. In this chapter, we'll just consider two. But if your own writers are creating persuasive arguments, extend this practice to include what's typical in your own classroom.

Paper 10
Driving Tests Should Be Harder (Persuasive, Grade 7)

If driver's tests were more rigorous, everyone on the road would be safer. About 50,000 people die in traffic accidents each year, and thousands more are injured. Most of these fatal accidents involve 16-year-old drivers. Although one of the problems is driving under the influence of liquor, an even bigger problem is incompetent driving. We could do something about this, but we grant driver's licenses on the basis of a very simple test.

Did you know that the part of the test in which you actually get out in a car and drive is only about 20 minutes long? What's more, the test givers are not demanding at all. They only ask drivers to perform a few tasks, such as turning left, turning right, parking and stopping. It has only been in the last few years that they have added entering a freeway to the test requirements. How often does anyone have to parallel park compared to entering a freeway? Yet it took all this time to update this test.

(continued on following page)

Paper 10 (continued)

Tests are not conducted on the busiest streets or during heavy traffic hours. Anyone can pass this simple test in light traffic on a quiet street. It does not mean that driver is competent.

The true test is real-life driving. I mean things like driving in bad weather, such as on icy streets or in fog. Or coping with bad drivers, such as people who tailgate or honk for no good reason. Or learning to handle mechanical problems such as getting a flat tire. The current driver's test does not measure whether a person can handle any of these difficult but common situations.

Of course, a driver's test that had to cover all of these situations would be difficult to set up. It isn't easy to arrange for people to drive on icy roads, for instance. Plus it could be dangerous. Imagine if people got killed while taking their driver's test! Besides, a complicated test might cost more and there could be a long waiting line. Imagine if you were 16 and needed to drive to work and you could not get a license because the wait was so long. There is one solution. They could do part of the test as a computer simulation. That way, you would still need the skills, but you would not need to risk your life to show you were a competent driver.

There are several ways to make the current test better. First, make it longer, so people need to drive more. Second, use computer simulation to test skills under dangerous conditions. Third, make sure people really have to do the things they will do in everyday driving, like changing lanes on the freeway. Then, require a score of 90 to pass, not 70, which is too low. Right now, you can do a lot of things wrong and still pass.

Sure, it will cost a little to make the tests more rigorous. But lives are more important than keeping tests cheap. When was the last time you felt in danger because of an incompetent driver? Remember, almost every person in this country will have a driver's license at some time in his or her life. If even half of these people are not qualified, we are risking our lives every time we go out on the road. We need better driver's tests now!

Source: Oregon Department of Motor Vehicles.

Author's Note

Some readers may disagree about whether this writer offers "compelling evidence." On the plus side, he provides specific reasons for his position and examples of how the test could be improved. However, he provides no evidence that skill in driving in bad conditions or knowing how to change a flat tire would reduce traffic accidents—nor does he cite any sources for the facts cited in paragraphs one and two.

Suggested Score in Persuasive Writing: 6

   _×_ *Takes a clear stand*
   _×_ *Writes in a confident, passionate voice*
   _×_ *Explains things* (Yes—though we do need more info on the computerized test)
   _×_ *Offers compelling evidence* (facts, examples)
   _×_ *Acknowledges other views*
   _×_ *Suggests specific actions the reader or others could take*
   _×_ *Convinces the reader—or makes the reader think about the issue*

Lessons Learned from "Driving Tests Should Be Harder"

- When you raise an intriguing new concept, such as computerized driving tests, explore it fully.
- Stating your position in the opening line can be a good strategy.

Comments

The voice in this paper is strong and sustained, the writer is very aware of his audience, the language is clear and appropriate for the topic, and sentences are clear and readable. In addition, the writer makes many good points, explaining what is wrong with the current test and suggesting specific remedies. It would be helpful to have more information on the computer simulation; without this, the problem of how to make the tests more rigorous without incurring additional costs remains partially unresolved. Still, this writer puts forth a strong, compelling argument, accomplishing a lot in a short space. As a reader, I found myself either agreeing with him or at least considering new possibilities.

Paper 11

Smoking STINKS! (Persuasive, Grade 5)

Smoking will kill you. Smoking will—sniff sniff, ACK!

You probably heard that when you were 8, but then why do you still smoke? And why is it that smoking will kill you? Answer 1: The first time you smoke, your lungs and windpipe will protest and feel like they're burning on fire. This is because your lungs are trying to tell you something. If your lungs could talk, this is what they might say, "I'm choking! Please stop filling me with this disgusting gas!" Even from the very first time you smoke, nicotine is a chemical that addicts you.

Answer 2: OK. Down to what I like to call the Big Problem. Smoking has proved to be a hazard to all fun things in life. I mean, what's the point of living if you're slowly killing yourself? Smoking is the only product in the world that kills half of its buyers. OK, so you might think that you're safe from doom, but get this: everybody thinks that. Another thing is something totally gruesome, how you could die. One possible condition for smokers, is, Gum or Lung cancer. In gum cancer, it could start as something small, like a mouth sore. If it's not gum cancer, the sore eventually heals. But, if it is cancer, the sore will grow and spread, literally ripping your mouth apart and spreading to vital organs in the process. As for lung cancer, the tumor grows until it breaks apart spreading and slowly killing you.

Smokers don't usually have a lot of money. The reason for this is because smokers are spending all of their money on heavily addictive cigars, killing what they earned and leaving barely enough money for taxes and vacations. Eventually, heavy smokers will do stuff for gangsters and evil people that give them money to buy cigars. Basically, you're throwing away money to strangers just to get a feeling that lasts for only a couple minutes at a time.

Just because you don't care about your life and you want to exchange it to people for a pack of cigars, doesn't mean that other people don't care about theirs. Yes, you heard me, you're killing other people too when you put a smelly cigar in your mouth. You see, harmful emission, which you commonly see as a gray cloud of smoke and smells like sulfur, can be breathed in by other people which has the same effects as the smoke you inhale; eventually, in worst scenario cases, will kill some innocent souls. So smoking won't just hurt you, it hurts other people, even if they're not even born yet! In fact, over 19,000 babies die every year due to mothers smoking. Another large amount have birth defects. So quit smoking! It'll be good for you and your family!

Suggested Score in Persuasive Writing: 4

_×_ *Takes a clear stand*

_×_ *Writes in a confident, passionate voice*

_____ *Explains things* (We are, in fact, left with some questions)

_____ *Offers compelling evidence* (The assertions are compelling, but actual evidence is lacking)

_____ *Acknowledges other views* (Not yet—the writer acknowledges that others smoke, but never explains why smokers might make this choice)

_×_ *Suggests specific actions the reader or others could take*

_×_ *Convinces the reader—or makes the reader think about the issue*

Lessons Learned from "Smoking STINKS!"

- If you make specific assertions ("over 19,000 babies die every year due to mothers smoking"), then you must offer the reader evidence and cite a source.

- Passion is an important part of the persuasive puzzle, but it's not enough to carry an argument.

- Strong persuasion also considers the other side; acknowledge the reasons people *do* smoke; then, by comparison, reasons to quit may look more compelling.

Comments

This writer is extremely passionate in her campaign to get smokers to quit. We can almost hear this (with some editing) as a public service announcement. Some small problems keep the voice from reaching its full potential. For one thing, the piece is a little wordy; compressing it would add power—like coiling the spring. Second, some parts are hard to grasp—they're simply not logical: "Eventually, heavy smokers will do stuff for gangsters and evil people that give them money to buy cigars." Is the writer suggesting that profits from tobacco support criminal activity? Or that people will turn to criminal activity to support a smoking habit? Also, why the focus on cigars? Most smokers smoke cigarettes. And while cigarettes are surely expensive, that's not enough evidence to show that smokers "usually don't have a lot of money." There's a fine line between careful and documented observation and assertions. That's why, even though we might agree with this writer, we're not *fully* persuaded. She does make us think, though. She's just a little research and one draft away from a compelling argument.

Interactive Questions and Activities

1. **Activity and Discussion.** Carefully review the informational writing guides included in Chapter 9. Are there important features of informational or research-based writing that are not included in these writing guides? If so, revise, making each guide just what you need it to be.

2. **Activity and Discussion.** If your students routinely produce research-based writing that is five pages or longer, copy one paper for your group to review and assess. If you wish, modify the assessment by focusing on those traits (say, ideas, organization, and word choice) you feel are most important to the assignment at hand, keeping in mind that it is not necessary to assess *every* trait every time.

3. **Activity and Discussion.** This chapter suggests many informational books to share aloud—or to share visually, using a document projector. Bring in an additional favorite to share with your group. Or, as an alternative, bring in any informational piece, any genre (e.g., newspaper article, blog, short video). Talk about the features you would want your students to notice and imitate.

4. **Activity and Discussion.** Think about alternative formats for sharing information, particularly those incorporating technology. How realistic would this be in your classroom, given your current access to technology? How might writing or talking about a topic serve as a preliminary step in developing a podcast, webcast, wiki, video, or other multi-media production?

5. **Activity and Discussion.** With your group, develop a checklist for narrative, business, or technical writing. Use the persuasive checklist as a model. (Compare the persuasive checklist or any you develop yourself to the Common Core Standards' requirements listed in Appendix 6.)

6. **Activity and Discussion.** Check each of the following statements with which you agree. Then discuss your responses as a group.

____ Overall, informational writing is the most important writing students do.

____ The key to good informational writing is good research.

____ We should read aloud to students from more informational texts.

____ Informational writing does not need voice.

____ Most students are better at creative writing than at informational writing.

____ Research-based writing is mainly for secondary students.

____ Only students who are college bound need to worry about research-based writing.

____ The primary key to a good written argument is strong evidence.

Coming Up

Next, we'll teach ourselves to see the traits with new eyes, through the voices of our very youngest writers.

> Writing to me is like drinking a cup of hot coffee. At the beginning, it's hard to drink because it's so hot. If you drink, you'll burn yourself. That is like writing. You can't rush your ideas.
>
> —Ellie Oligmueller, student writer

> Sometimes writing can be like a mosquito. Pesky and annoying. Buzzing around you, as if it will never leave. Finally it bites you, and makes you itch.
>
> —Chelsey Santino, student writer

CHAPTER **10**

Exploring the World of
BEGINNING WRITERS

We need to think about creating primary classroom environments that give children the opportunity for wonder, mystery, and discovery; an environment that speaks to young children's inherent curiosity and innate yearning for exploration is a classroom where children are passionate about learning and love school.

GEORGIA HEARD & JENNIFER MCDONOUGH
A Place for Wonder, 2009, Introduction

You do not need to be writing fluent sentences yourself to know what fluency is. Your ears will tell you. You do not need to write stories filled with voice to know voice when you hear it. The smile on your face, the tears in your eyes, or the chill up your back will tell you.

VICKI SPANDEL
Creating Young Writers, 2012

At the primary level, writing is wondrous and magical. It comes to us in the form of sketches, scribbles, dictated stories, recordings, word play, "tadpole people" (mostly head, tiny arms and legs), pictographs—and conventional text as well. Sometimes text goes left to right on the page as we have been conditioned to expect, but primary writers, not yet bound by convention, find their own inventive ways to fill the page: right to left, bottom to top, around in a spiral—or clean off the page and on to adventure.

The writing of the very young combines their creative individuality with an uncanny ability to observe, recall, and use the conventions from the print that fills their world. At this age, there are no "errors" in the true sense, any more than beginning walkers make errors in foot placement. Rather, there are hundreds, thousands of experiments by beginning writers finding their own paths to learning and in the process, creating their own vision of the world.

> It's been a good thing that babies don't understand the concept of "clumsiness" or else they'd never learn to walk.
>
> —Alan Ziegler
> *The Writing Workshop,* 1981, 37

Focusing on Strengths

We know that primary writing looks very different from that of older writers. But like impatient parents imagining our children at that first book signing, we watch for paragraphs to emerge, for the first use of quotation marks, for complete sentences and correct spelling. We forget that there is much to get excited over long before these milestones of sophisticated writing ever appear. If we become too fixed on what is *not* yet present in the writing, we may fail to appreciate the many things our young writers have already learned to do well.

Consider Paper 1—by four-year-old Nikki. Although she isn't conveying ideas in words yet, her message is still remarkably expressive. Notice the look on the face of the bat: humorous, mischievous—that's *voice.* How many writer-artists of this age have noticed that spiders have eight legs and multiple eyes? Notice the toes of the bat, and the hollow ears. This young writer-artist takes more than a passing glance at the world around her. As a result, her work is brimming with details—and those are *ideas.*

Another sample of writing—by a slightly older writer, Mike—is shown in Paper 2. This piece is significant because it shows that wonderful moment of stand-alone

> Illustrators make meaning with pictures, and writers make meaning with words, but they both make meaning, and rich curriculum lies in understanding all the ways their decisions intersect.
>
> —Katie Wood Ray
> *In Pictures and in Words,* 2010, 72

Paper 1

Bat and Spider (by Nikki, Age 4)

Paper 2

Mike's Note

MOM ReMiDMe†iReD
MiBuk.

DiR Mike

writer-to-reader communication. We can say, "Mike, I read this without help, and it made perfect sense to me. You are an independent writer." Notice that Mike has created a complete sentence: "Mom, remind me to read my book." He signs his important message "Dear Mike" because when Mom writes to him, that's how she begins, so he now thinks of himself as "Dear Mike"—rather like "Sir Mike."

Consider conventions in this piece, too. Remember for a moment that all conventions, even the simplest and most taken-for-granted things, must be learned. What do you see? Left-to-right orientation on the page and the beginning of spaces between words. Even a period at the end that tells us, "This sentence is finished." These things seem so basic, but they are not automatic, nor are they necessarily simple to learn. This writer is also beginning to distinguish between capital and lowercase letters, although he does not yet use them correctly. Remember, though, discovery is worthy of celebration in its own right. Correct placement is a more sophisticated skill.

By using the language of the traits, we help our young writers see what is strong within their work so that they can build on those strengths. We want Nikki to keep noticing what others miss. We want her to let that sense of humor (that we see in the bat's mischievous face) continue to show in her writing. We want Mike to keep writing sentences, then paragraphs, feeling the confidence that comes from knowing readers can understand your message—even when you're not around to explain it.

Taking a Close Look at Primary Writing

When we sit beside our colleagues, student writing in hand, and read aloud their words and look at the stories in their pictures, we gain greater understanding of our students' strengths.

—Megan S. Sloan,
Into Writing, 2009, 223

The very best way to teach ourselves what to look for in primary students' writing is to spend time with examples—in the company of colleagues. That way, we can teach one another. We can slow down from our usual hurried pace and look beyond what is missing to observe what is there. We can read aloud and hear the words and the voice as the writer intended them. We can reflect on the tiny details embedded in the drawings and see how much meaning they offer.

Figure 10.1 provides a list of things you might look and listen for in young writers' work—and in their responses to literature, too.

Author's Note

If possible, go through the following writing samples with a colleague or a group so that you can talk to one another about what you see or hear. Look as carefully at the art as you do at the writing, viewing the whole piece as a composition. Don't be too influenced by my comments. You may see things in a piece that my colleagues and I have overlooked.

FIGURE 10.1

Things to Look for in Primary Writing

IDEAS

- Little close-up details: veins in leaves, wings and legs on insects, expressive faces
- Signs of movement (e.g., a person or animal running)
- Details of color, shape, size, sound, smell, taste, or texture
- Any message—no matter how delivered—that makes sense to you, the reader
- Ability to tell a personal story
- Ability to retell *someone else's* story (here, the child is reconstructing the meaning)
- Ability to recognize another writer's point or message
- Clear purpose: To entertain us, express ideas, persuade us, teach us, etc.

ORGANIZATION

- Balance on the page—good use of white space
- Use of a title (gives direction and focus to the writing)
- Ability to choose one title or lead over another
- Coordination of text with illustrations (an early form of coherence)
- Sequencing of events, details, or pictures
- Ability to predict what will happen next (when listening to a story)
- Ability to see how a picture and text go together (e.g., *What extra information does the picture give you?*)
- Ability to predict how a story (or any piece) will end
- Ability to choose one ending over another
- Ability to group "like" things (by shape, color, size, etc.)
- Use of "The End" or a closing sentence

VOICE

- Originality and expressiveness
- Emotion (Look at the characters' faces.)
- Individuality, ownership (You can tell it belongs to this child and no other.)
- Originality—the writer's/artist's own way of seeing the world
- An image, a moment, an idea that makes you feel something
- Love of life, love of writing/drawing
- Enthusiasm, exuberance, energy, excitement
- Passion for the topic
- A noticeable desire to communicate with readers
- Playfulness, humor
- Pleasure in hearing strong voice in the writing of others

WORD CHOICE

- Use of *words!* (They might be single letters, letter combinations, or letter strings at first, but in the young writer's mind, these are words.)
- Words that show action, energy, or movement (expressed orally or in writing)
- Words that describe
- Words that convey feelings
- A passion, a love, for new, unusual, or fun-to-say words
- Words that stretch *beyond* the child's spelling capabilities
- Words that help you see, feel, and understand
- Curiosity about new words

SENTENCE FLUENCY

- Letter strings that translate into sentences
- Word groupings that imitate sentence patterns
- Sentence sense (an ear for what a sentence is)
- That first whole, complete sentence
- Use of multiple sentences
- Patterns that reinforce meaning: "Cats sleep all day. Dogs sleep at night."
- A willingness to try new sentence forms—breaking out of patterns into variety (Compare *"I like my dog. I like my cat. I like school"* with *"I like cats and dogs. But I love my cat the most. Do you like school? Me too."*)

CONVENTIONS & PRESENTATION

- Left-to-right orientation
- Top-to-bottom orientation
- Spaces between words or lines
- Association of letters with sounds
- Letters that face the right direction
- *Readable* spelling
- Use of punctuation (whether placed correctly or not)
- Distinction between capital and lowercase letters (whether used correctly or not)
- Use of end punctuation
- Use of a title
- Awareness of margins
- Use of *I* (capitalized)
- Ability to spell own name
- Interest in environmental print
- Use of conventions (especially punctuation) to reinforce meaning or voice
- Layout that is pleasing to the eye, captures attention
- Creation of illustrations for any writing
- Creation of a cover, title page, author's bio, table of contents, or similar features
- Use of numbered or bulleted lists

FIGURE 10.2 (A)

Early Guide for IDEAS *

Check *each item* that is true of the writing.

____ Creates a message (decodable or not) on paper

____ Expresses a clear message or tells a story the reader can understand without help from the writer

____ Provides details through words and/or art

____ Appeals to senses: sight, sound, smell, taste, touch

____ Shares details that show knowledge of this topic

____ Provides details that are original, unusual, striking, or memorable

> * This scale is intended PRIMARILY for use with students who are writing or attempting sentences—and/or those whose art has a high level of complexity and detail.

© 2012. *Creating Young Writers* 3/e by Vicki Spandel. Published by Allyn & Bacon, an imprint of Pearson Education, Inc. May be reproduced only for classroom use. Other uses require permission from the publisher.

FIGURE 10.2 (B)

Early Guide for ORGANIZATION

____ Has unity: All parts (words, title, art) work together to form a message

____ Has "bones" or structure: an explanation, story over time, step-by-step process, solution of a problem, solving of a mystery, big idea with details or examples, etc.

____ Has a lead sentence and/or title

____ Has an ending sentence and/or *The End*

____ Easy-to-follow sequence (in words and/or art)

____ Clear connections, thought to thought, picture to picture, or sentence to sentence

© 2012. *Creating Young Writers* 3/e by Vicki Spandel. Published by Allyn & Bacon, an imprint of Pearson Education, Inc. May be reproduced only for classroom use. Other uses require permission from the publisher.

FIGURE 10.2 (C)

Early Guide for VOICE

____ Individual, personal, passionate—stands out from others

____ Can be read with expression—fun to share aloud

____ Shows engagement with topic, awareness of readers

____ Voice can be characterized: *funny, wistful, mischievous, courageous, angry, thoughtful*, etc.

____ Seems to express what the writer truly thinks and feels

____ Makes the reader feel something—*joy, amusement, wistfulness, anxiety, anger, empathy, nostalgia*, etc.

© 2012. *Creating Young Writers* 3/e by Vicki Spandel. Published by Allyn & Bacon, an imprint of Pearson Education, Inc. May be reproduced only for classroom use. Other uses require permission from the publisher.

FIGURE 10.2 (D)

Early Guide for WORD CHOICE

____ Words create a message

____ Words used correctly—message makes sense

____ Words create images or strong impressions

____ Strong verbs, precise nouns and modifiers

____ Sensory words or phrases appeal to the senses: sight, sound, smell, taste, touch

____ Phrasing colorful, striking, expressive, or memorable—*may* outpace writer's spelling ability*

> * Note: Do **not** assess spelling under this trait.

© 2012. *Creating Young Writers* 3/e by Vicki Spandel. Published by Allyn & Bacon, an imprint of Pearson Education, Inc. May be reproduced only for classroom use. Other uses require permission from the publisher.

Second, have a look at the Early Guides, writing guides (from *Creating Young Writers*, 3/e, 2011) developed specifically for use with younger writers (see Figure 10.2). Each guide focuses on the positive, on *what is working* within the writing. They are intended to capture the *essence* of what is contained in each Teacher Writing Guide, while recognizing the importance of art. Further, each Early Guide is designed to reflect performance goals that are achievable and realistic for young writers.

Feel free to decide for yourself which scale best suits your students' needs—and in some cases, you may wish to make adjustments on a student-by-student, or performance-by-performance, basis. Many writers at third-grade level (and even younger) are quite ready for assessment on the upper level writing guide. At the same time, a simpler scale may offer a good place to start for writers who are just beginning to write comfortably in English—regardless of age.

"Jack's Penguins" by Jack (1)

Jack is studying penguins in his first grade class, and using what he has learned to write a story (Paper 3). This is precisely how young writers begin to learn the value of research. Jack loves this topic (you can hear the voice in *Look, look! . . . see what I could see . . . freezing cold*) and manages to squeeze in details on leopard seals, king penguins, and Gentoo penguins. In fact, his story is quite extended; luckily, the teacher provides additional paper so Jack (and his classmates) can *keep writing*; this is a vital strategy for encouraging fluency. Notice the many conventions Jack is already getting under control: capital I, spacing between words, periods, use of hyphens, correct spelling on many small words and good phonetic guesses on others (*ice bergs, some dangerous animals, finally*). That sound-effects word in the second line is *Brrrrr!*

Jack's Penguins (by Jack, Grade 1)

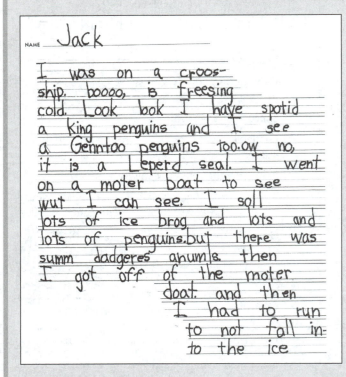

NAME Jack

I was on a croos-ship. boooo, is freesing cold. Look bok I have spotid a king penguins and I see a Genntoo penguins too. ow no, it is a Leperd seal. I went on a moter boat to see wut I can see. I soll lots of ice brog and lots and lots of penguins. but there was summ dadgeres ahumls. then I got off of the moter doat. and then I had to run to not fall into the ice

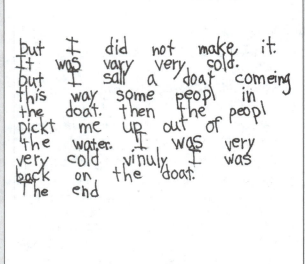

but I did not make it. It was vary very cold. but I sall a doat comeing this way some peopl in the doat. then the peopl pickt me up out of the water. I was very very cold vinuly I was back on the doat. The end

© Nikki Henningsen.

Sam Is My Friend (by Kean, Grade 1)

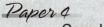

Sam is my friend we we're friends. Sins we were babys. I relly like Sam. And I ustu bit his finggers.

"Sam Is My Friend" by Kean (1)

Kean's piece (Paper 4) has a sincere, heartfelt tone ("*I relly like Sam*") and he writes right to us. Words like *very* and *really* are early ways of injecting voice. But even better is Kean's willingness to share a secret. Psst—come closer: "*I ustu bit his finggers.*" Direct connection to readers is the very foundation of voice. But we need to share this with Kean. We need to say, "I loved the part where you told about biting Sam's fingers. It was brave of you to admit that. I heard your voice in those words."

Author's Note

Much of what young writers learn about the traits, they learn from our comments. That's why it is so important to use words like *lead*, *detail*, *voice*, *verb*, or *ending*. As they learn writers' language, it becomes easier to talk with them about their writing—and to point out what's working well.

"My Favorite Brother Is Nick" by Lincoln (1)

Lincoln, also a first grader, writes very lovingly of his brother Nick (Paper 5). *"He plays a lot if hes not bisey."* We have to be delighted with this line, imagining Nick making time for Lincoln and noting how much Lincoln appreciates it. He generously refers to him as the "faveist" ("favorist," meaning *favorite*). But the last line is best of all: *"His kindnis gits biger avre day."* Wouldn't you love to have a friend say that about you? We need to tell Lincoln just that—and add, "When you write from the heart like that, you're writing with voice."

Some teachers get itchy when they see a line like the last one in Lincoln's piece. They want to write little red corrections right over it. I wouldn't do that, however, because it puts the focus in the wrong place. Instead, I might say to the whole class, "Writers come across great words when they write. One of the words Lincoln discovered for us today is *kindness*. What a terrific word. If we learn to spell it together, we can all use it in our writing when we want to. This word has eight letters, so I need eight volunteers to each hold a letter, and then we'll see if we can put you in the right order to spell out the word."

Paper 5

My Favorite Brother Is Nick
(by Lincoln, Grade 1)

My faverit brauther is nick   he hase bene the faveist in the famale. He plays a lot if hes not bisey. His kindnis gits biger avre day.

(See Author's Note above.)

"I Like My Library" by Nicholas (1)

Nicholas is a confident first-grade writer, and that confidence fills his writing (Paper 6) with voice. He uses his experience masterfully to fill his paper about the library with rich and personal details.

To appreciate the sophisticated sentence fluency of this piece, read it aloud. How many different ways does this writer find to begin? *"When I go . . . , First I'm greeted . . . , Then, it's up to me . . . , Luckily, she is patient."* This is beautiful writing—and quite remarkable from a first grader. Nicholas writes with some ease and has begun experimenting

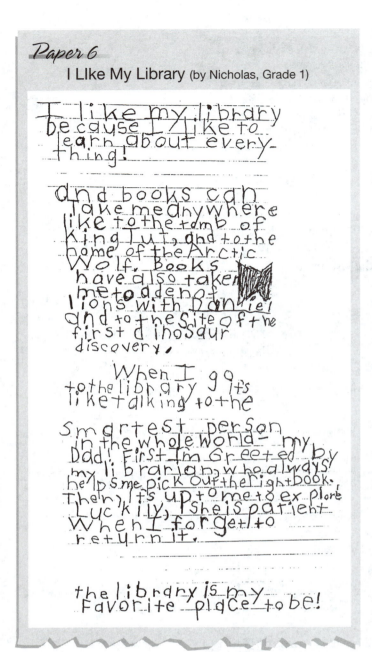

I like my library because I like to learn about everything!

and books can take me anywhere like to the tomb of King Tut, and to the home of the Arctic Wolf. Books have also taken me to dens of lions with Daniel and to the site of the first dinosaur discovery.

When I go to the library It's like talking to the smartest person in the whole world— my Dad! First Im Greeted by my librarian, who always helps me pick out the right book. Then, It's up to me to explore. Luckily, she is patient when I forget to return it.

the library is my Favorite place to be!

One day my cat and my dog were hungrey so they went to the cupbord to get somthing to eat but there was no cat or dog food in the cupbord and so they wint to the catdog shopping mall. They went to the grocry store and first they went to ial 8 and they looked at all the catfood and dogfood and they said 'this is disgusting!!!' so they went to ial 4 to get some sereil but all of the boxes of seriel were opened so they could not buy any seriel, and so they went to ial number 1 for ice cream sandwiches. they put the ice cream sandwiches in ther cart but the ice cream sandwiches melted and so they went back to ial 1 and got more ice cream sandwiches and they ate them in the store . . . then they called a taxi and on the way home they told jokes about ther mothrs and uncles and the dog laffed so hard he fell off the seat and then they were home and they went in the house.

with a wide range of conventions, including paragraphing, hyphens, dashes, commas, apostrophes, and exclamation points. Not all first graders have this repertoire of skills from which to draw, but when we enrich their worlds with samples of good writing, we might surprise ourselves with how far we can take them.

"Catdog Shopping" by Jocelyn (1)

The idea of a dog and cat who prefer ice cream sandwiches to their own "disgusting" food is comical and fresh. It's a vivid piece; I can picture the whole event in my mind—from the frenzied rush from aisle to aisle to the unbridled laughter as the friends head back. This is a home run in both ideas and voice. Jocelyn also shows wonderful fluency (fluency in the sense of "writing expansively") for a young writer. She hasn't quite learned to hear the endings of her sentences yet, or to punctuate them, but some modeling by the teacher could be helpful. Before we even think about corrections or revisions, I want Jocelyn to celebrate the sheer volume of her writing, the creative details, and the voice. I might say, "Look how *much* you wrote. Wow. This is a very detailed story. You made a whole movie in my mind. I can see the cat and dog shopping for their own food, then for cereal, and finally for *ice cream bars*. How did you think of that? I love the part where they laugh themselves silly. You made me laugh right along with them!"

This particular piece also shows remarkable control of many conventions and excellent experimenting with inventive (*temporary*) spelling. Notice the ellipses ("*ate them in the store . . . then they called a taxi*"), as well as the quotation marks and exclamation points ("*this is disgusting!!!*"). The inventive spelling shows a sharp ear for sound: *seriel, grocry* (this is how many of us actually pronounce it), *cupbord*, and *somthing*. In addition, many words are spelled with conventional accuracy: *taxi, disgusting, opened, melted, jokes, uncles,* and *shopping*—not to mention *ice cream sandwiches* (Did she look at the label?). The ending shows the cat and dog doing what most of us do at the end of a long shopping day—swapping stories until they grow punchy.

> When children can sit down and put their thoughts on paper quickly and easily, they are fluent writers even if they make errors. If the teacher is always correcting the students' spelling and punctuation errors, the children will stop guessing and trying. This will lead to dull writing with students afraid to use words they can't spell.
>
> —Bea Johnson
> *Never Too Early to Write*, 1999, 33

Mason's First Book (K)

Paper 8 shows Mason's first book, produced in kindergarten. Notice his organization. He has a cover page, plus two chapters. In Chapter 1 he's a good boy, but then, as so often happens as the plot unfolds, things go downhill in Chapter 2. I was struck by the fact that he could spell *naughty* correctly, but as his teacher explained, when Mason is acting up, his mom sometimes says, "Oh, Mason is being *n-a-u-g-h-t-y* again," and of course, Mason picked up that spelling at once. (Perhaps we should spell more "secret" words aloud.) As we look at his book together, I could tell Mason, "It's so clever of you to divide your book into two parts like this. Each part is like a new chapter. And I notice how the expression on your face changes with each picture. Those expressions really go with your writing."

Paper 8

Mason's First Book (Kindergarten)

"Old" by Megan (3)

What *does* it mean to be old—in the eyes of a young child? Perspective is everything. Megan (Paper 9) is quite mature in her thinking, but notice that as soon as she puts a number (60) with her definition, she is afraid she's hurt someone's feelings. At that point, her focus shifts from defining what it means to be old to reassuring the reader that it is okay, it is all right, you're a kid: "*Say it kid, kid. OK maybe not a kid but like a teenager.*" Whew. That's a relief. (Don't think I'll get another job *or* have more children, however.)

Paper 9

Old (by Megan, Grade 3)

OID

I think you get old when you are 60. If you are 60 it is ok because it is fine you are just like any body else and you should be happy about it. You will probadly get married and you will have grand kids. Or maybe even kids your self. Love your family and friends and grand kids. Don't think you are too old for any thing. Be happy and cheerful and go to church every Sunday. Take vacations and get a job probably. So don't be scared of being old. Well I'am not scared of being old but maybe you are. Like I was saying, old is not bad and it doesn't mean any thing bad either I'am 8 and I'am not scare of being 10 but kind of scared about being 60. I can't stop saying Old is not BAD! Actually you should be proud of being old. Think of your self as a kid. Say it kid, kid. Ok maybe not a kid but like a teenager. You're a teenager not old.

OID

By: Megan

Paper 10

Dear Tooth Fairy
(by Leah, Grade 2)

Dear Tooth Fairy,

I don't have a tooth right now because my dog ate my tooth.

So my point is, I lost my tooth, my dog ate it, so do I still get my money?

Your still beliver,

Leah

P.S. I don't know if my dog really ate it but I really lost it.

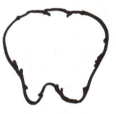

Read Megan's piece aloud to appreciate the voice. She is giving us one terrific pep talk—and she is definitely passionate about her topic. Listen to the sentence variety and her comfortable, natural use of fragments: *Or maybe even kids your self.* I want to tell this writer, "I love your energy. Your voice comes through in every line. You write as if you mean what you say."

"Dear Tooth Fairy" by Leah (2)

Letters, as noted earlier, are a powerful means for developing voice—as Leah's note to the tooth fairy (Paper 10) clearly illustrates. Like any good business letter, it comes right to the point: Do I get the money or not? Notice in particular the postscript; Leah seems to reflect that when writing to the tooth fairy, it may be best to come clean with the whole story.

"Jamey the Cat" by Veronica (2)

Perspective is the foundation for "Jamey The Cat" (Paper 11). Second grader Veronica has had some help with her editing but also has done much of it herself, via computer, and it is work to be proud of. Even more impressive, though, is her special point of view. Her teacher, an artist, has told the class how different the world can look, depending on who you are and where you are.

Veronica's understanding of this concept is quite profound: She adopts the role of a cat, and places herself in the window sill, right between "inside" and "outside." This division of Jamey's world is central to the theme: how Jamey's life has changed—thanks to Sarah. Notice the complexity. Jamey is loving yet a little resentful that her friend Sarah gets all the fun; revenge is afoot—a most sophisticated and subtle ending. I would like to tell Veronica, "I like the way you put yourself on the window sill, separating the inside world from the outside world. I can tell how much you want to go out. I can also tell how upset you are with Sarah. It seems to me you know that people and cats can feel more than one way at the same time. This paper makes readers think—about cats *and* feelings."

Take a moment to also notice how much of the meaning for this piece is carried in the illustration. Jamey the cat has a very human look about her, standing upright; she even has a belly button. She looks extraordinarily sad, with tears dripping from her eyes. And we can almost feel the pain in those little paws as we read the caption: "No nails." Consider words *and* drawings when assessing or commenting on ideas or voice.

Paper 11
Jamie the Cat (by Veronica, Grade 2)

My name is Jamey. I am a cat. I like this window sill. I can see a lot from here. Sarah is outside. She is having a picnic with a friend. I love Sarah. I love outside. But I can't go outside now. I've been fixed. That means I can't have kittens anymore. I didn't want kittens anyway. They are a lot of hard work. My nails were pulled too. If I go outside I will get clawed till I die. So I don't go outside. I'd like to, but I don't. I love Sarah, but I want to picnic too. When Sarah comes home I'm not letting her pet me!

by Veronica
Grade 2
St. Wilfrid

"Pyramid" by Brad (2)

Speaking of writing from a unique perspective . . . Brad (grade 2) combines art and text to create an impressive reflection on life and time in the voice of an ancient pyramid. Illustration 12*a* shows his collage art depiction of pyramids against an Egyptian sky. In his rough draft (12*b*), he does not allow spelling to interfere with his stretch for new, meaningful words (*protect, crumbling, officially, responsibility*). Compare his draft with the final (12*c*) to see how editing and formatting work together to create meaning for the reader. In deciding to format this piece as a poem, Brad had the opportunity to decide which words would go on each line. We could hear the poetry in the rough draft; now we can see it, too. Brad's writing is inspired by the research and teaching of Beth Olshansky (www.picturingwriting.org).

Three Short Pieces by Andrew (K)

In Paper 13, Andrew (a kindergartner) tries his hand at a full sentence: "Mr. Bear is loving." He gets just the first consonant of the last word and shows us a handy way for beginning writers to indicate a longer word they cannot quite spell yet. He'll be filling in the blanks in no time. He gets in some good practice with detail and spelling, first with his grocery list (Paper 14)—*peanut butter, bread,* and *honey*—and then his

Brad's Pyramid (Grade 2)

(a) Collage Art: The Pyramids; (b) Rough Draft; (c) Final Draft, Revised and Edited in Poetry Format

(a)

(b) I can pirteot véry preslsh thingslike the numy and the jewles but soon I will not be abelleto pirtect any thing for I am crumbling before my eyes. the heat wind and sand are beating awae at me my age is growing today i'm ofishaly fourthowsin years old. But at night when I gaze over all the stars I reamember wenI was being bilt geting a new reasponsebilite to portect a mumy. I am a pyramid.

(c)

I can protect very precious things
Like the mummy and the jewels.
But soon I will not be able to protect anything
For I am
Crumbling before my eyes.
The heat, wind, and sand are beating away at me.
My age is growing.
Today I am officially four thousand years old.
But at night
When I gaze over all the stars,
I remember when I was being built
And getting a new responsibility
To protect a mummy.
I am a pyramid.

Paper 13
Mr. Bear Is Loving! (by Andrew, Kindergarten)

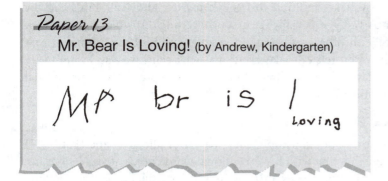

MR br is l
Loving

"To Do" list (Paper 15)—*eat, play, [watch] TV, [go to the] park, [ride my] bike, read,* and *draw.* He is bursting with ideas; a list gives him a simple, coordinated format for expressing them.

The list is a simple organizational structure, and one that even early beginners can handle with skill. This puts them in control.

"Love" by Kaden (1)

In Paper 16, first grader Kaden tackles a profound topic: love. Three things are striking about this piece. First, notice Kaden's fluency and ability to write multiple sentences on one topic. This is what we mean by "focus." Second, Kaden finds multiple ways to define love—it isn't just one thing, this paper seems to

Paper 14
My Grocery List (by Andrew, Kindergarten)

My Grocery List

PeKtBMtn
BroB
hune

Paper 15
My To Do List (by Andrew, Kindergarten)

My To Do List
1. et
2. PlA
3. TV
4. PrK
5. biK
6. red
7. bro
Name Andrew

Paper 16
Love (by Kaden, Grade 1)

Kaden

Love is Kyle thrwing me
on to the bed upside down.
Love looks like me going for
a walk with my babie brother.
Love is like hugs from mummy.
Love is family.

say, but many things. Love takes multiple forms in our lives. Above all, I'm struck by how unusual his examples are—especially the first two: getting thrown upside down on the bed by Kyle (his older brother) and going for a walk with his baby brother. It isn't every young writer who interprets everyday events in such a sensitive way. I want to say to Kaden, "You really show how many different ways people express love. Your unusual examples make your writing fun to read."

"My Friend" by Jane (1)

Friendship is an enormously popular topic with writers of all ages. Jane (Paper 17) gives it a fresh spin, though—first with her exceptional word choice: it was *marvelous*, and it was *fantastic*. It is satisfying to see this young writer stretch beyond her spelling ability for the word that is just right. Second, Jane personalizes her writing with carefully chosen details: She and Brooke both love to play outside, enjoy sleepovers, wear earrings, and have matching clogs. What more could you want in a friend? I would say

Paper 17

My Friend (by Jane, Grade 1)

Name Jane

I have a friend named Brooke she is oldr then me! I had a slep over at her home it was mrvlis with- her. We like to play ort side. We like to eat ice crem to gethr it is fantastick. She wers erings so do I! She has maching clogs. I love my best friend.

to Jane, "You found such interesting details to share. I enjoyed hearing about the ice cream, the earrings, and the matching clogs. I sense that you have even more to tell us about Brooke, and I bet you'll write about her again. In your drawing, you and Brooke seem to be wearing your clogs. I like that."

"Spiderman" by Wyatt (1)

Wyatt's unbridled enthusiasm (Paper 18) for Spiderman, birthdays, and life in general fills his paper with voice: *He klimd the wol I men rily climd the wol.* It's easy to read this piece with great expression—and that is one of the main things this young writer needs to know. Anyone who fears inventive (temporary) spelling should have a close look at Wyatt's piece. He never asked for help with his spelling. He's a very independent writer who sounded out the words for himself—*in-visubl.* That's a stellar attempt. I'd want to tell him, "Do you know how *close* you came? Wow! Check it out." As we keep congratulating his efforts, his spelling will get better and better. Notice too that Wyatt's class has been taught to use carets to make small insertions. He read his piece over, noticed he'd left out a word (*he*), and inserted it. Yes, the caret is upside down. One step at a time.

"My Winter Vacation" by Connor (2)

Notice how much information second grader Connor packs into his piece "My Winter Vacation" (Paper 19). The voice is strong yet very controlled and sophisticated for so young a writer: *"I had to have an IV; it was very annoying."* *Annoying!* The perfect word. Then there's good old Aunt Helen, who provides Connor with an exceptionally thorough history book.

In this piece, Connor's drawing adds both meaning and voice. We have a small patient laid out on a very large table—with tall legs. It's a long way to the floor. And you can't miss that expression. It could be worry—or even pain. I don't think so, though. I think it's rage. The implied title of this piece is "My *So-Called* Winter Vacation."

"Guess Why I Like School?" by Hollie

We must reward students who dare to speak with strong voices. Consider Hollie's tribute to her first-grade teacher (Paper 20). She writes directly from her heart about a special teacher who is a "sweety and a cupcake." She also tells us, "In my heart I love her," and "I wish she could be my 2nd grade teacher and all the way to high school." How many teachers would you have hung onto for twelve years?

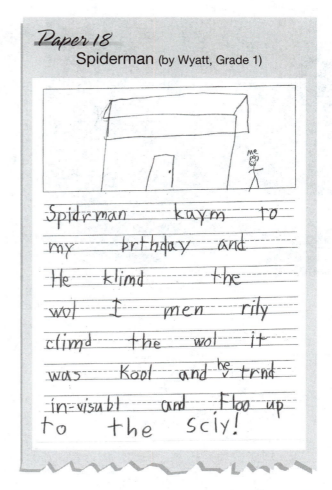

Paper 18
Spiderman (by Wyatt, Grade 1)

Spidrman kaym to my brthday and He klimd the wol I men rily climd the wol it was kool and he trnd in-visubl and floo up to the scíy!

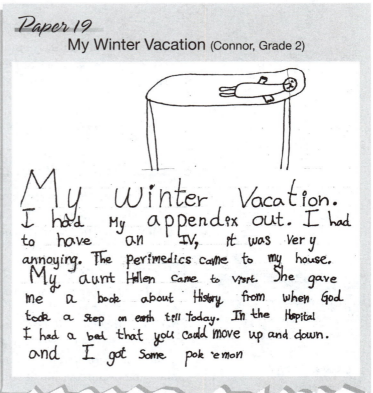

Paper 19
My Winter Vacation (Connor, Grade 2)

My Winter Vacation. I had My appendix out. I had to have an IV, it was very annoying. The perimedics came to my house. My aunt Hellen came to visrt. She gave me a book about History from when God took a step on earth till today. In the Hospital I had a bed that you could move up and down. and I got some pok'emon

Guess why I like school? I like school because I like my teacher. I like her because she is sweet and kind and also butteful. I wish she could be my 2nd grade teacher and all the way to high school. I also like her because she is thoughtful and relly nice. Shes a sweety and a cupcake. Shes a terrific friend In my heart I love her. Shes a loveable teacher. She teaches us good things like how to be friends and she wears nice, pretty, fashionable cloths. That's what I like about school.

I want to tell Hollie, "I read your paper several times, and even shared it with a friend. When you say what you really think and feel, your writing has voice. I can't wait to read your next piece."

Using the 6 Traits to Teach Primary Writing

At primary level, teaching with traits begins with noticing and commenting on what students are doing well. There is much more we can do, however. Following are eleven ideas for helping primary students reach their writing potential.

IDEA 1: CREATE AN ENVIRONMENT IN WHICH WRITING THRIVES.

Chapter 2 discusses the importance of teaching traits within the context of writing process and writing workshop. This is never more important than at primary level where so much of writing is about feeling excited, getting comfortable and confident, and having resources right at your fingertips. Here are just a few things to think about with respect to our youngest writers:

Author's Note

For numerous additional ideas, and more expansive discussion, please see the companion text to this one: *Creating Young Writers,* 3rd edition by Vicki Spandel, 2011, Pearson Education, Inc.

- *Seat writers to encourage interaction.* Chairs in a circle or chairs around a table create a sense of community. A simple thing like a good seating arrangement encourages teamwork, talking, and sharing—all the things we want to have happen in a writing workshop.
- *Provide a daily, consistent time for writing.* With experience, writers learn to "write" all the time—while riding in the car, taking a bath, sitting on the grass. They are routinely thinking about topics and words, anticipating a revision or the start of a new piece. You encourage this kind of thinking when you make the start-up time and the duration of workshop predictable, and when you begin workshop by asking questions like this: "Did anyone have an experience that made you think of a good writing topic?"
- *Fill your room with print and illustrations.* When young writers see what others have done, they find things they want to try. They need words, sentences, illustrations—all of it. Some of this fills the walls of the classroom. The rest can be shelved to make it easy for young writers and readers to find what they need.
- *Provide writing tools that are fun to use.* Do you have a favorite pen? Do you only compose on the keyboard? Would you rather paint or do a pencil sketch? Young writers have the same kinds of preferences, and having the freedom to make choices makes writing more fun.
- *Incorporate technology.* If you are not fully comfortable with technology, take a class or get a friend or colleague to support you as you learn. This is time well spent. Today's primary writers will be required to compose with audio and video in many forms. The sooner they begin, the more skilled and confident they will be.

> What very young children are doing with pictures and words when they are five and six and seven, they will no doubt one day be doing with interactive audio, video, simulated environments, and other technologies we can't even imagine at the moment.
>
> —Katie Wood Ray
> *In Pictures and in Words*, 2010, 17

IDEA 2: BE A WRITER (AND ILLUSTRATOR) YOURSELF.

This is essential. It is the *only* way to know how it feels to search for an idea, to figure out where and how to begin—or end, to get the right words to go with the picture in your mind, to put your heart on paper and hope someone will care.

You don't need to publish. But you do need to write. Write letters or emails. Start a blog. Keep a journal. And if your students are illustrators, you need to draw, too. Please don't say, "I can't draw." In the first place, yes you can. In your own way, with your own style, you *can*. And in the second place, if we're going to ask students to try new things, we must be brave, too.

IDEA 3: MODEL, MODEL, MODEL.

If you write, you will find this easy because you'll always be in the middle of something—even if it's only figuring out what to write about next. Modeling lets you show students how it looks when *you* do it—and gives them a beginning point. You are not setting the standard. You are demonstrating possibilities. You might say, for example, "This is something I do when I'm searching for a topic," or "Here's how I make sure my writing has the right voice for the reader."

Everything is new and mysterious to the person who has never done it. So imagine yourself taking young writers on a guided tour of the writing landscape, pointing out all the fabulous decision points along the way. Every decision offers a chance for modeling things such as—

- Choosing a topic
- Finding information on that topic
- Deciding what form (genre) the writing will take: story, picture book, greeting card, essay, journal, etc.

Author's Note

For tips on getting started with very easy drawings virtually anyone can do, check one of Ed Emberley's books: *Ed Emberley's Drawing Book of Animals* (2006); *Drawing Book of Faces* (2006); *Make a World* (2006); or *Picture Pie* (2006). The last deals specifically with collage art, and is excellent for beginners who aspire to (eventually) emulate such masters of this genre as Steve Jenkins. Also check out *Bruno Munari: Drawing a Tree* by Bruno Munari (2004).

> I always say if you do three things only when you teach writing to children, make sure it's these: Model, model, and model some more.
>
> —Megan S. Sloan
> *Into Writing*, 2009, 48

- Leaving big margins or skipping lines to allow room for later additions
- Choosing a pen or pencil or paper you love for your draft
- Deciding whether to begin with words or an illustration
- Deciding what your very first sentence will be
- Reading everything you write aloud to hear how it sounds
- Deciding to keep going even though you feel tired
- Putting your work away for a time, but returning to it later
- Checking to see what other authors have done
- Choosing one word or phrase over another
- Adding a detail you forgot the first time (in your text or illustration)
- Adding unusual sensory details, such as sounds or smells
- Revising wording to change the imagery, tone, or voice of a piece
- Choosing a title
- Using a thesaurus, dictionary, or handbook
- Inserting an example
- Adding an explaining sentence
- Combining two short sentences to make a longer, more graceful one
- Checking for initial capitals, end punctuation, or any other conventions
- Choosing a font or making other choices that affect presentation
- Designing a cover
- Sharing writing aloud with a partner or group
- Responding in a helpful way to another writer who shares

Modeling can be as simple as saying, "I'm remembering to double space this draft in case I want to add something later." In other words, it sometimes takes about five or ten seconds. Other times, though, you want to do something a little more elaborate—such as adding detail to a piece of writing. Following is one simple modeling lesson I do with primary writers based on an anonymous student paper entitled, "My Dog" (Paper 21). You could use this paper or any anonymous piece of student writing. If you don't have one you think will work, make one up. For this lesson—

- Choose a paper that does not belong to anyone in your class (so writers don't have to worry about hurting feelings).
- Share the piece in *large print*, using a Smartboard or document projector.
- Leave *lots* of space in margins and between lines for writing.
- Use carets, arrows, etc. to make additions.
- Talk aloud as you work.

Paper 21

My Dog

My dog is my friend and he plays with me when I come home from school. We do fun stuff. When my mom says to stop we stop. Then we go outside.

You can do one of two things: (1) Revise the piece all on your own, adding details as you go, and talking about your choices; or (2) Invite students to suggest details, and use *their* suggestions in your revision. I prefer the second option because it gets students more engaged. They are doing the actual revision (the thinking) and I am simply recording. When we finish, they are proud of what we created together. What I say as I work goes something like this:

FIGURE 10.3

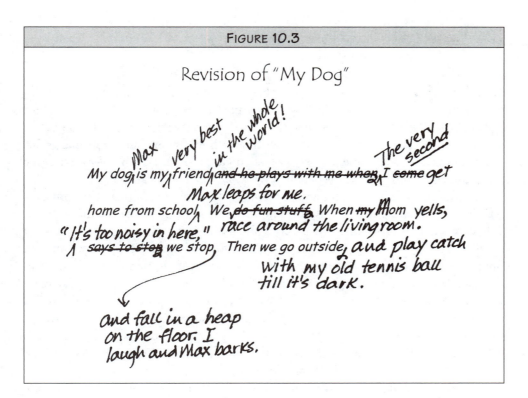

Revision of "My Dog"

This paper is called "My Dog." Do you think we should give this dog a name? Max? *OK, good . . .* Max is my friend—*but how good a friend? . . .Wow—yes, my* very best friend in the whole world. *Terrific. So he plays with me when I come home from school. How soon after I get home do we play? The* very second! *Excellent—I like that. It's specific. So,* The very second I get home, he plays with me. *What does he actually do, though? Can you see him? He* leaps for me? *Great—I can see that in my mind. OK, so—We do fun stuff. What kinds of things do we actually do, do you suppose? Play tag?* Race around the living room? *Can you see this? I can, too—much better than "fun stuff." When my mom says to stop—wait a second. What do you think Mom actually says? Let's hear her voice—right, good—*Mom yells, "It's too noisy in here!" *Then we stop—but what do you think Max and I actually do? Try to picture it—OK, we* fall in a heap on the floor. *And we laugh, right? Should I say that? OK—so* I laugh and Max barks. *All right, and then we go outside—what do you think we do?* Play catch—with my old tennis ball. *For how long?* Till it's dark. *Terrific. Now let's read the whole thing and see how it sounds . . .*

Figure 10.3 shows how it looks when we are finished.

I read the piece aloud with all revisions in place, and ask the students to help me illustrate it. Then I recopy it in its final form, and we give it a title (which we brainstorm together) and post the results. And though I have not requested it, it's likely that I'll see some playfulness with revision in students' own work. This lesson emphasizes reading aloud, adding little details, asking questions as you write, and using art to expand detail and voice.

Possible illustrations for "Wild and Wonderful Max" (previously "My Dog"):

- Max
- Max leaping for the writer
- Mom yelling, "It's too noisy in here!"
- The writer and Max racing through the living room
- The writer and Max falling in a heap on the floor
- Max and the writer playing catch in the "almost dark"

IDEA 4: TALK TRAITS— IN PRIMARY LANGUAGE.

How do we create criteria that primary or beginning writers can use? Simple. We begin with writers' questions, shown in the primary poster collection called "Thinking Like a Writer" (see Figure 10.4). These questions show young writers, in a simple but clear way, how to begin thinking about their writing without the pressure of formal evaluation. You will see that these posters contain language that is *even simpler* than in the Early Guides. That's because the Guides are *for you*. The posters are *for students*.

Introduce *one trait at a time* and *one question at a time*. Don't rush. Use your own writing as a model sometimes, asking yourself these same questions. In this way you will teach students to ask these questions of themselves as they write.

Use writers' vocabulary routinely to talk about students' writing. Never miss an opportunity to point out a moment of voice or a small indication of detail, however tiny. Remember Nikki's picture of the bat and spider in Paper 1? When you get a piece like that, it's a chance to say, "Nikki, you have really taken a close look at spiders! You noticed they have eight legs and multiple eyes. That's detail! And this bat—I love his toes and the hollow ears. Look at this smile on his face. He shows how he feels. That's what I call voice!" Then perhaps Nikki will think, "I'm a person who takes a close look at things. My writing has *detail*. My writing has *voice*."

With your comments, you plant a seed from which will blossom an amazing flower—*if* you nurture it. Don't paraphrase. Use terms like *details, organization, voice, leads* and *endings, word choice, conventions, presentation,* and *fluency*. Make these words and phrases part of your students' writing vocabulary, too. In this way you empower them to make purposeful choices about their writing.

IDEA 5: ENCOURAGE WRITERS TO CHOOSE THEIR OWN TOPICS.

When writers choose subjects they love, voice explodes from the page. Detail blossoms.

It isn't always easy. Far from it. But your writers have the support of writing workshop. They can talk with partners or table mates. They can gather ideas from what you read aloud. When you experience an adventure together, even if it's only a walk around the school grounds, you can encourage them to think like writers by saying, "Who noticed something to write about today?" And of course, they can watch and listen as you model topics *you* are considering writing about.

There's an art to modeling topic choice. If I say, "I think I'll write about my grandmother," I certainly suggest one writing possibility. But what I really want to model is not the topic per se ("Hey, let's all write about our grandmothers!"), but the thinking behind this particular choice: *Why is this a good topic for me and how did I come up with it?*

So instead, I might say something like this: "I was looking through an old photo album when I saw a picture of my grandmother. It reminded me of all the times we sat in her kitchen as she told me stories about growing up in Canada and teaching school. She taught all the grades at once—in one room! I think I'd love writing about that. When I think of her, I remember the good baking smells that filled her kitchen: chocolate and cinnamon, warm bread, vanilla for the cinnamon roll icing, and pecans toasting in the oven. I could put that in my writing. I can still hear the ticking clock and the screen door banging shut as people went in and out." Now I'm suggesting that it's

One of the real privileges of being a confident writer is the reward of seeing yourself do justice to a topic that matters to you.

—Katie Wood Ray and Matt Glover
Already Ready, 2008, 79

FIGURE 10.4 (B)

Thinking Like a Writer — Primary Poster

Organization

✏ How does my paper begin?

✏ Did I tell things in order?

✏ How does my paper end?

FIGURE 10.4 (A)

Thinking Like a Writer — Primary Poster

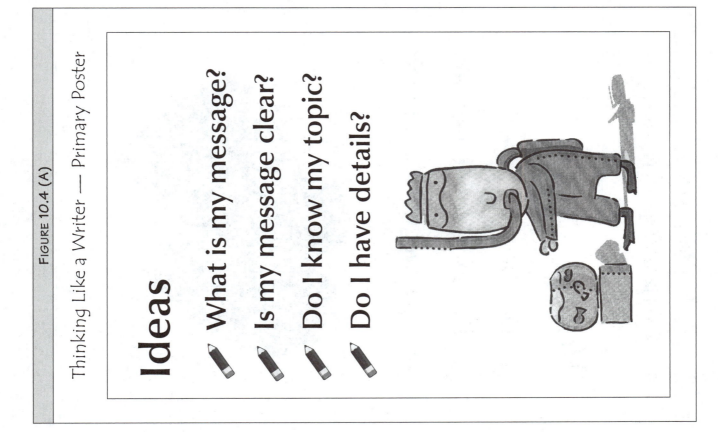

Ideas

✏ What is my message?

✏ Is my message clear?

✏ Do I know my topic?

✏ Do I have details?

FIGURE 10.4 (D)

Thinking Like a Writer — Primary Poster

Word Choice

✏ **Did I use words I LOVE?**

✏ **Did I use any NEW words?**

✏ **Do my words make sense?**

FIGURE 10.4 (C)

Thinking Like a Writer — Primary Poster

Voice

✏ **Do I like this paper?**

✏ **Does this sound like ME?**

✏ **How will my reader feel!**

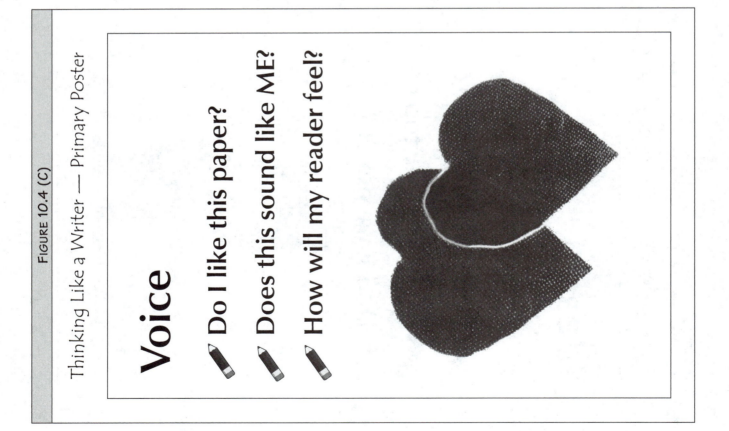

FIGURE 10.4 (F)

Thinking Like a Writer — Primary Poster

Conventions

✐ Left to right?

✐ Capitals?

✐ Periods and question marks?

✐ Spaces?

✐ My BEST spelling?

✐ Easy to read?

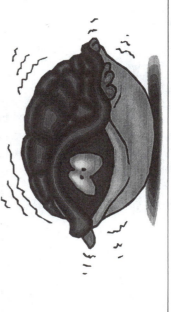

FIGURE 10.4 (E)

Thinking Like a Writer — Primary Poster

Sentence Fluency

✐ Did I use sentences?

✐ How many sentences?

✐ Are some long?

✐ Are some short?

✐ Do they start different ways?

helpful to look at photos to get ideas, that memories are a good source of writing topics, and that sensory details—the fragrant smells of my grandmother's kitchen or the banging of the old screen door—make writing interesting.

Idea 6: Create Experiences to Write About.

In *Talking, Drawing, Writing* (2007), authors Martha Horn and Mary Ellen Giacobbe acknowledge the fact that out-of-school experiences are, for some of our children, very limited. They suggest that some teachers might say, "My students . . . go to day care before and after school, and at night they watch TV, then go to bed. They don't go to the park. They don't ride bikes" (23). It is important for us to think of small ways to create experiences right in the classroom: watching fish in an aquarium, seeing tadpoles hatch or newborn chicks emerge from eggs, planting bulbs and watching the flowers sprout, then bloom, hearing new music, dancing, following the daily lives of ants in an ant farm. We can step outside the door and feel the rain (or sun) on our faces, experience snow falling on our tongues, watch the wind move through the leaves.

My teacher friend Arlene Moore (who has taught K-1 in Mt. Vernon, Washington for many years) consistently provides two experiences for her young writers. She has a friend with a small farm who brings in one animal visitor per month—a rabbit one time, a turkey another, a donkey another. She also does a little personal research to find out who has a new baby—and would be willing to make monthly classroom visits. Students weigh and measure the baby (it's almost impossible to describe how much fun they have doing this) and notice any new behaviors. Following this experience, they have no trouble coming up with writing topics.

Each year, Arlene has a mascot, a stuffed animal (Colors the Puffin or George the Monkey) who becomes very real to her children. On the weekends, this animal goes home for a sleepover with one of the students and his or her family. The child (with help from an adult at home) writes about this experience. See Figure 10.5 for one sample entry from George's Journal.

FIGURE 10.5

George's Journal

Thanks for taking me out of that backpack (whew! It's stinky and hot in there!). Where am I? Oh, right—Jeremy's house. Cool! I love Jeremy because he's quiet like me. Jeremy's mom loves to pick me up and hug me. Easy there—I'm small!

I'm not sure I want to go outside, but what choice do you have when people carry you everywhere? I wish I weighed more! I am afraid they might leave me to play with the neighbor's dog (the one with big teeth!). Thank goodness! Jeremy's mom is carrying me back inside to watch TV. Watching is one of my best things. Hey, salad for dinner. How did they know? Time for what? Baths? I don't need a bath. Just fluff my fur and I'm good to go!

Off to bed already? What story do we get tonight? "Curious George?" My favorite! I love this sleepover stuff.

© 2012. Vicki Spandel.

CHAPTER 10 Exploring the World of BEGINNING WRITERS

In *A Place for Wonder*, Georgia Heard and Jennifer McDonough describe the powerful effects of setting up a "wonder window," a place of observation through which children might watch seasons change, see people come and go, observe traffic or construction—perhaps watch someone plant a tree. "Creating an observation window," the authors suggest, "gives children the opportunity to look at their world outside the classroom window and to write about what they see, hear, and wonder about" (2009, 34). You can also create miniature windows by cutting 6x6-inch squares in sheets of paper, then having students see what they can observe through that small opening. Heard and McDonough did this with a group of primary students and were surprised by the number of tiny details the students noticed within a short time. They knew that learning to observe would strengthen the children's writing: "We realized that explicitly showing kids how to get up close and focus in on one thing would lead to writing with more detail" (40).

Many teachers love using jewelers' loupes, small magnifying glasses about the size of a large spool of thread, that allow children (or anyone) to observe objects in great detail. Good subjects to study include rocks, shells, leaves, lichen, fruits and vegetables of all kinds, insects, twigs, or just the palm of your hand.

IDEA 7: SPEND TIME TALKING—AND DRAWING.

Talking and drawing are two of the most important prewriting—and writing—techniques young children can possibly use. Talking is easy and fast in comparison to writing, and allows beginners to formulate thoughts in their minds, to expand and extend the message in a way that is natural to them, and to gauge the response of listeners as they talk.

A young writer who shares her story orally before writing can respond to questions from listeners, and those questions give her ideas about additional details she could add to her writing. As we all know from experience, talking also helps us organize our thoughts. As we remember things we should have said or need to add, the true organizational structure of our story or explanation reshapes itself inside our heads.

Drawing can be both an invaluable warm-up for writing and an integral part of that writing. In Paper 22, Andrew creates a highly detailed picture of the home he loves. Look carefully and you will be amazed at the detail: puffy clouds, birds flying high, an extraordinarily cheerful sun, smoke rising from the stone chimney, windows to peer out of—and a moving van with a very sad driver. There's just one word: *Move*. It's all we need. The picture tells us how Andrew feels. It is not just a precursor to his message; the drawing *is* the message.

Katie Wood Ray sees the picture book as "the perfect 'container' for the composition of beginning writers" (2010, 10). She points out that this is a familiar genre for children, who are (at least in their school environment) surrounded by picture books. The idea of creating meaning with both words and art is already familiar, and offers many ideas writers can try in their own work: "And when they see themselves as people who make picture books, people just like Mo Willems and Emily Gravett, for example, young children notice and pick up ideas for writing and illustrating from the books adults read to them" (13). Ray adds that picture books, because they are so much a part of students' everyday world, are especially helpful in making ELLs feel part of the classroom's literate community (13–14).

Many picture books run right around 32 pages in length. That is more by far than most primary writers will produce. But having that picture book vision in their minds

Author's Note

For information on purchasing jewelers' loupes, or lesson ideas involving the loupes, check out www.the-private-eye.com, or simply enter "jewelers' loupes" online.

And just as in my boyhood, making pictures is how I express my truest feelings, my truest self.
—Eric Carle
Artist to Artist, 2009, 26

Paper 22
Moving Day (by Andrew, Grade 1)

encourages young writers to expand their text beyond the traditional one-page design we suggest when we pass out pre-formatted pages that only allow a half page for drawing and a few lines for writing. What if we passed out multiple pages—and left them blank? Then we'd suggest to the writer, "Formatting is up to you. You decide what to put on each page, how big to make it, and how many pages you need."

IDEA 8: BE FLEXIBLE ABOUT FORMAT.

Primary students need a variety of ways in which to express themselves, including art and speech. Pictures, as we've seen, reflect the beginnings of ideas (details), voice (emotion, playfulness, individuality, and humor), and organization (format and balance). Children who are not quite ready to create extended text (they may not yet have the concentration, speed, ability to form words, or fine motor skills) can dictate stories or simply tell them to others. Through dictation they let loose the creative ideas, knowledge, and voice they cannot yet project through writing. See Paper 23, Griffin's charming and humorous dictated piece on "Milano Cookies." (Do you identify?)

IDEA 9: SHARE WRITERS' SECRETS.

Look again at Paper 7, Jocelyn's story of "Catdog Shopping." Detail, voice, organizational flow—it's all there. Right now, though, Jocelyn is following a sentence pattern many beginning writers use, connecting nearly all of her sentences with *and, so, and so,* or *so then.* These connecting phrases echo the way many people speak. But the result is an endless sentence that doesn't let the reader breathe.

A writer this fluent *may* be ready to move to the next step: disconnecting *some* of the clauses. I might say, "Jocelyn, do you know what is so great about this piece? You have idea after idea after idea. I can picture *everything!* I think you're ready for a little writer's secret. [*Conspiratorial whisper . . .*] Sometimes, if we hook *all* our little sentences together with words like *and* or *so* and make one BIG sentence, the reader gets out of breath. If you can find some places to put periods, and make *some* small sentences, your reader can pause to take a breath. Want to hear how one of your favorite writers does it?"

In his brilliant book *Mechanically Inclined* (2005), teacher-consultant Jeff Anderson talks about the importance of giving students mentor sentences as examples. Jocelyn is a *very* young writer, true, but she is also an avid reader who can understand the value of short sentences quite readily—*if* I come up with the right mentor text.

> The goal is not to point out what is wrong with [students'] writing, but to encourage students by showing them what they are ready for now.
>
> —Jeff Anderson
> *Mechanically Inclined*, 2005, 23

One writer who is gifted with the short sentence is E. B. White. He gives short sentences elegance so that they never sound choppy or fragmented. So I choose for my mentor text *Charlotte's Web*—and find the passage in which Mrs. Zuckerman is about to give Wilbur a buttermilk bath:

> Wilbur stood and closed his eyes. He could feel the buttermilk trickling down his sides. He opened his mouth and some buttermilk ran in. It was delicious. He felt radiant and happy. When Mrs. Zuckerman got through and rubbed him dry, he was the cleanest, prettiest pig you ever saw. (1980, 121)

As I share this example, reading aloud *slowly,* I'll ask Jocelyn to listen for pauses where the reader can take a breath. Then I'll ask if she would like to try this writer's strategy with just *one* of her sentences—and I will help. I might say, "Let's read your first sentence together and see if there is any place we could put in a period. You listen for a spot where you want the reader to take a breath, OK?"

I will read aloud very slowly (and deliberately—pausing where a period *might* go) so Jocelyn can listen. *She* will hold the pencil. *She* will put in the periods and capitals. And her first sentence may wind up looking and sounding something like this:

> One day my cat and my dog were hungrey. So they went to the cupboard to get something to eat, but there was no cat or dog food in the cupboard. ~~and~~ So they wint to the catdog shopping mall.

Jocelyn leaves the conference as a writer who has choices, and if she thinks, even once, "Should I write *and* here—or put in a period to make the reader pause to take a breath?" then this lesson has been a wild success. (And if this revision is beyond her, no harm, no foul. We'll just try again later.)

IDEA 10: TEACH PRIMARY WRITERS TO THINK LIKE EDITORS.

Anyone who works with primary writers for just one day will be struck by how much they notice and how quickly they begin to include in their writing exclamation points, quotation marks, ellipses, semicolons, and parentheses—not *always* placed correctly, but definitely present.

We can take advantage of young writers' curiosity by getting excited about conventions right along with them. We can fill their environment with plenty of print to borrow from and then start asking, "Have you noticed *this* convention in your reading? Can you find another one somewhere in this room? Why do you suppose writers use this? What does it show? When do you think *you* might use this?"

Paper 23

Cookies (by Griffin, Grade 2)

Cookies

Once when I was six years old I went to my pantry and stole the Milano cookies! I wasn't allowed to eat anymore cookies until lunch was over. So I ran and hid. I ate almost every Milano cookie. I said to myself I know this is wrong but I can't resist. Later on my mom was walking down the hall where the closet was. That's where I was hiding! I heard her walking down the hall making a click clack click clack sound with her high heels. So I ate the cookies as fast as the cookie monster could eat cookies. Right when I was about to eat my second to last Milano cookie, my mom opened the door right when the cookie monster made the sound crunch. She laughed and said no more cookies, you cookie monster.

> As a society, we allow children to learn to speak by trial and error. But when it comes to reading and writing, we expect them to be right the first time.
>
> —Donald H. Graves and Virginia Stuart
> *Write from the Start: Tapping Your Child's Natural Writing Ability,* 1987, 21

The Treasure Hunt

Start with a treasure hunt. You can use any text at all for this, or you can post bits of text around the room for a true treasure hunt format. Choose pieces that show a variety of conventions; it is *not* essential that students be able to read every word from these passages. Then invite them, with partners if you like, to find (and put their finger right on) each convention as you name it—for example:

- Capital letter
- Period, question mark, comma, semicolon, exclamation point
- Any proper name
- The word *I*
- Any simple word: *and, the, dog, like, see, we*
- Italics
- Ellipses
- Parentheses
- Quotation marks
- Margins (How many fingers fit in the margin?)
- A title (Is the print in the title bigger? How much bigger?)

Because a group of first graders were so exceptionally good at finding everything I could name, I told them I'd give them my conventions "challenge"—*ellipsis.* One girl in the front row put her finger immediately on the ellipsis and raised her hand. When I asked if she could explain how ellipses are used, she stood up before the group. "Ellipses," she explained, "are when you . . . [and her voice drifted off for a time, then resumed] pause in your thinking—like that." Not bad.

Simple Editing Tasks

You can also have students practice their editing skills with some very simple tasks, as shown in Figure 10.6, the "Simple Editing Checklist." Even very beginning writers can do these things, and they will feel like independent editors if you call it *editing.* What you are teaching, essentially, is the important habit of *taking another look.* Introduce tasks one at a time: Editors first look just to be sure they put their names on their papers, then they check for name and date, and so on. Later, as skills grow, you can create a more advanced editing checklist (see Figure 10.7).

Editing Practice

When students begin writing simple sentences, create simple editing practice that invites them to "track down" errors (see Figure 10.8). Notice that in this practice students are given the correct sentence first in big print. In this way you are not modeling errors—but rather helping them to find errors by matching other sentences against the correct one.

Each practice sentence (1) is short and complete and (2) contains *only one* error. The print is very large, and there is plenty of space for beginning editors to

Author's Note

A few picture books that are particularly fun to use for the treasure hunt activity include—

- *Stellaluna* by Janell Cannon
- *Surprising Sharks* by Nicola Davies
- *Knuffle Bunny* by Mo Willems
- *Muncha! Muncha! Muncha!* by Candace Fleming
- *Walter Was Worried* by Laura Vacarro Seeger
- *Chester* by Melanie Watt

FIGURE 10.6

Simple Editing Checklist for Primary Students

___ Name

___ Date

___ Capitals to start sentences

___ Capital "I"

___ Periods (.) to end sentences

___ Question marks (?) to end questions

___ Spaces between words

FIGURE 10.7

Advanced Editing Checklist for Primary Students

____ My name is on the paper.

____ The date is on the paper.

____ My title goes with the paper.

____ I used capitals to start sentences.

____ I used capital "I."

____ I used periods to end sentences.

____ I used question marks to end questions.

____ I used quotation marks to show talking: "Hello!"

____ I have one-inch margins all around.

____ I used my BEST spelling

____ You can read everything in my paper!

FIGURE 10.8

Primary Editing Practice

The cat ate my fish.

The ate my fish.

The cat ate my fish

the cat ate my fish.

The cat age my fish.

The Cat ate my fish.

The cat atemy fish.

Did the cat eat my fish.

---

work. Project the copy for everyone to see, and read sentences aloud, one by one, as you work together. Do just one sentence at a time—or more than one, depending on attention spans. Each time, though, you are looking for just *one* mistake.

When you do a lesson like this one, consider making copies for your students. (You can run two to four on a single page and then cut them.) In this way, you can let them correct the text *first,* using the copyediting symbols for beginning writers (see Figure 10.9). Don't worry if they cannot do all the editing at first. They will get there. Have them—

- Work independently the first time through.
- Check with a partner.
- Coach you in correcting the text OR
- Come up to make corrections in front of the class.

The process should be fast, lively, and interactive. No worksheets. Nothing to collect or grade. Just a group of editors, talking and editing. When you finish, your work should look something like the edited copy in Figure 10.10.

Author's Note

See the complementary texts *Creating Revisers and Editors,* Grades 2 and 3 (by Vicki Spandel, Pearson, Inc.), for editing lessons involving carets and delete marks, capitals, wrapping sentences, periods, question marks, exclamation points, capital "I," subjects and verbs, and more.

Author's Note

Some young writers may already be composing on the computer. But there is still value in teaching copyediting symbols. For one thing, they focus on the *kinds of corrections* copyeditors make, thereby suggesting things young editors should look for in their own work. For another, when young writers review their writing, they can make changes *without* having to copy over (unless a piece is going to be published). This is a welcome relief. And third, practice in editing hard copy helps young writers develop an editor's eye.

FIGURE 10.9

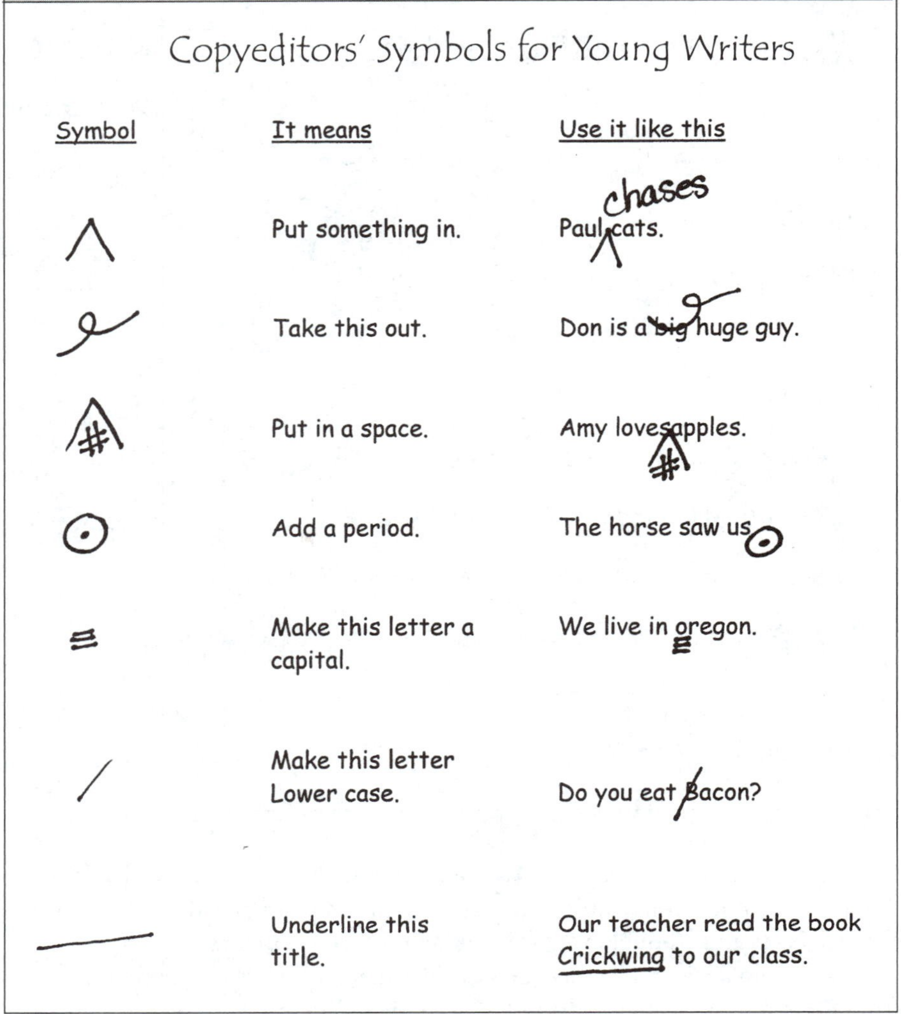

Copyeditors' Symbols for Young Writers

Symbol	It means	Use it like this
∧	Put something in.	Paul ∧ cats. (*chases*)
℘	Take this out.	Don is a ~~big~~ huge guy.
⩍#	Put in a space.	Amy loves apples.
⊙	Add a period.	The horse saw us ⊙
≡	Make this letter a capital.	We live in o̱regon.
/	Make this letter Lower case.	Do you eat B̸acon?
——	Underline this title.	Our teacher read the book <u>Crickwing</u> to our class.

FIGURE 10.10

Primary Editing Practice

The cat ate my fish.

The ∧ ate my fish. (*cat*)

The cat ate my fish ⊙

t̲h̲e̲ cat ate my fish.

The cat a∧te my fish. (*t*)

The C̸at ate my fish.

The cat ate ∕my fish. (#)

Did the cat eat my fish ∧? (#)

IDEA 11: READ AND CELEBRATE LITERATURE.

If you love to read aloud (and what teacher of writing doesn't?), you already have at your command the most powerful means available for teaching the traits to beginning writers—or really, *any* writers.

Following are a handful of books I frequently recommend for primary students, along with notes about special features. For a *much more extended* list of primary books (by trait), see *Creating Young Writers*, 3rd edition, 2011, Pearson Education, Inc.

Author's Note

I'm always reluctant to list books by trait since the minute I mention how wonderful a book might be for illustrating detail, someone will immediately cross it off the list for organization or voice or fluency—and of course, that makes no sense. The traits are an inherent part of writing and so *every book features every trait*. That's a given. Nevertheless, certain features of some books *do* jump out at readers, and that is what I mean to capture on this list.

Primary Books for Teaching IDEAS

Actual Size by Steve Jenkins. 2005. Boston: Houghton Mifflin.

Compare your hand to that of a gorilla, look a giant squid in the eye, or squint at the world's smallest fish—all in real-life size. This is one book in which illustrations outstrip text when it comes to presenting information.

Beaks! by Sneed B. Collard III. 2002. Watertown, MA: Charlesbridge.

Collard is a fine nonfiction writer who strives for clarity in every book he writes. This book shows how to take a central idea—all birds have beaks—and expand it by showing a wide range of examples.

Dog Loves Books by Louise Yates. 2010. New York: Alfred A. Knopf.

Dog loves books so much that he decides to open his own bookstore. There's just one small problem—no one comes. Luckily, dog has a surefire cure for the blues: reading.

Everybody Needs a Rock by Byrd Baylor. 1974. New York: Simon & Schuster.

Byrd Baylor gives us creative guidelines for finding just the right rock, and knowing what makes it different from all others. Wonderful for encouraging writers to take a close look at everything around them, even the humble rock.

The Quiet Book by Deborah Underwood. 2010. New York: Houghton Mifflin Harcourt.

Some words, such as quiet, can mean more than one thing: There's the "first one awake quiet," "don't scare the robin quiet," "last one to get picked up from school quiet," and . . . so many more.

Wilfrid Gordon McDonald Partridge by Mem Fox. 1984. New York: Kane/Miller.

In this classic story, based on true events, a sensitive young boy helps the elderly Miss Nancy recover her memory, showing how beloved objects can trigger profound personal connections. This book inspires writing about favorite personal treasures.

Once students learn to read as writers, then every act of reading has the potential to deepen their understanding of the craft of writing too.

—Katie Wood Ray
In Pictures and in Words, 2010, 61v

ADDITIONAL BOOKS WITH STRONG IDEAS . . .

- *Animal Dads* by Sneed B. Collard III
- *Courage* by Bernard Waber
- *Growing Frogs* by Vivian French
- *Go Away, Big Green Monster* by Ed Emberley
- *I'm in Charge of Celebrations* by Byrd Baylor
- *My Mouth Is a Volcano* by Julia Cook
- *Something Beautiful* by Sharon Dennis Wyeth
- *Some Things Are Scary* by Florence Parry Heide
- *Stars Beneath Your Bed* by April Pulley
- *Twilight Comes Twice* by Ralph Fletcher
- *Whoever You Are* by Mem Fox

Primary Books for Teaching ORGANIZATION

Amos and Boris by William Steig. 2004. New York: Farrar, Straus and Giroux.

This masterpiece of word choice offers a stunning conclusion that pays homage to the power of friendship and the importance of making memories.

An Egg Is Quiet by Dianna Aston. 2006. San Francisco: Chronicle Books.

This gorgeously illustrated informational text offers a wealth of information about eggs, provided along several informational "trails." You can page through the book simply looking at illustrations, or read the big ideas in big print—or small details in small print.

City Dog, Country Frog by Mo Willems. 2010. New York: Hyperion.

Time is a terrific organizational tool, and one of the easiest to use. Willems organizes his lovely tale of an unlikely friendship around the four seasons, and as you turn each transitional page, you will *feel* time move.

Press Here by Hervé Tullet. 2011. New York: Chronicle Books.

This highly imaginative, engaging book uses simple page by page directions to get readers personally involved in "arranging" a series of colorful dots.

What Do You Do When Something Wants to Eat You? by Steve Jenkins. 1997. Boston: Houghton Mifflin.

One central question can have many possible answers. This is an organizational structure young student writers can appreciate and use themselves—in many contexts.

When I Was Little: A Four-Year-Old's Memoir of Her Youth by Jamie Lee Curtis. 1993. New York: HarperCollins Publishers.

Here's an easy-to-imitate example of comparison-contrast: life way back when I was younger versus now. The paintings (by Laura Cornell) are whimsical and filled with voice.

Zoom by Istvan Banyai. 1995. New York: Puffin Books.

If you have ever looked through the zoom lens of a camera, you know the basic premise of this striking wordless book: The whole world changes as we move up close or pull back. Zooming in and out helps us appreciate both the big picture and the tiniest of details. Try taking the book apart and shuffling the pages. See if writers can use visual clues to put them back in order. (See also *Re-Zoom* by the same author.)

ADDITIONAL BOOKS WITH INTERESTING ORGANIZATION . . .

- *Dear Mr. Blueberry* by Simon James
- *Flotsam* by David Weisner
- *My Map Book* by Sara Fanelli
- *Previously* by Allan Ahlberg
- *Rain* by Manya Stojic
- *That's Good, That's Bad* by Margery Cuyler
- *The Tiny Seed* by Eric Carle
- *Tuesday* by David Weisner

Primary Books for Teaching VOICE

I Am Too Absolutely Small for School by Lauren Child. 2005. Cambridge, MA: Candlewick Press.

This is a delightful book for exploring the power of voice in persuasive writing. It can also open the door to discussions of new or uncomfortable situations. Perhaps some of your students have felt like Lola—intrigued by the idea of school, but not quite ready to go.

I'm Gonna Like Me by Jamie Lee Curtis. 2002. New York: HarperCollins.

The writer's honesty about her likeable—and less likeable—moments makes the voice come alive. Talk about ways illustrations also contribute to voice.

I'm Not by Pam Smallcomb. 2011. New York: Schwartz & Wade Books.

Evelyn seems to be everything the writer is not—she's mysterious and extraordinary, a born decorator, a fashion icon, and intrepid explorer. But as this narrator friend discovers, Evelyn cannot do *everything*—and she needs friends, too. Hilarious illustrations by Robert Weinstock. Do not miss the bios, back inside cover.

The OK Book by Amy Krouse Rosenthal. 2007. New York: HarperCollins.

It's not always imperative to be the BEST. Life is also meant to be enjoyed. Page by page, the author celebrates things she loves doing in an OK fashion—from roasting marshmallows to flipping pancakes or catching lightning bugs. Tom Lichtenheld's stick figure people formed from the letters O and K are fun and easy to imitate.

Parts by Tedd Arnold. 1997. New York: Puffin Books.

The young hero of this book is plenty worried—from hair on his comb to bits of skin peeling from his toes, he seems to be falling apart. Good grief! What's happening? Good thing Dad has plenty of masking tape.

Serious Farm by Egan, Tim. 2003. Boston: Houghton Mifflin.

Maybe there is "nothing funny about corn," but there's plenty to laugh about in this story of friendship. Farmer Fred has gotten too serious for his own good, and the animals, under the direction of Edna the cow, are determined to help. Enjoy their strategies—and facial expressions. Notice those eyebrows.

A Sick Day for Amos McGee by Philip C. Stead. 2010. New York: Roaring Brook Press.

Zookeeper Amos has a tender spot in his heart for each of the zoo's residents—and his affection is returned. Each finds a special way to provide comfort when Amos lands in bed with the sniffles. Award winning illustrations (by Erin E. Stead) touch the heart and add voice to this masterful story.

A Story for Bear by Dennis Haseley. 2002. San Diego, CA: Harcourt, Inc.

As Bear listens to the voice of the woman who gently shares stories with him, he falls in love with the sound of her voice. A great book for teaching what the concept of voice is really about.

ADDITIONAL BOOKS WITH STRONG VOICE . . .

- *A Bedtime for Bear* by Bonnie Becker
- *Dear Mrs. LaRue* by Mark Teague
- *Don't Let the Pigeon Drive the Bus* by Mo Willems
- *Enemy Pie* by Derek Munson

> I'm convinced that writing without passion is writing for oblivion.
>
> —Mem Fox
> *Dear Mem Fox, I Have Read All Your Books Even the Pathetic Ones,* 1992, 148

- *A Frog Thing* by Eric Drachman
- *Ish* by Peter H. Reynolds
- *I Will Never Not Ever Eat a Tomato* by Lauren Child
- *Koala Lou* by Mem Fox
- *Matilda* by Roald Dahl
- *Olivia* by Ian Falconer
- *Once Upon a Cool Motorcycle Dude* by Kevin O'Malley
- *Only One You* by Linda Kranz
- *The Pencil* by Allan Ahlberg
- *Piggie Pie* by Margie Palatini
- *This Land Is My Land* by George Littlechild
- *The Twits* by Roald Dahl
- *Where the Wild Things Are* by Maurice Sendak

Primary Books for Teaching WORD CHOICE

***Fables* by Arnold Lobel. 1980. New York: HarperTrophy.**

Arnold Lobel is both author and illustrator of these 20 original fables. You can use them to teach the trait of ideas, for each fable makes a point that is humorously reinforced by the illustrations. But in addition, they are rich with sophisticated language.

***Frederick* by Leo Leonni. 1967. New York: Alfred A. Knopf, Inc.**

While his friends are gathering grain and other staples for winter, little Frederick, the poet-mouse, gathers ideas, memories, and words. Are your writers word collectors, too? Are you? And where do you store your favorites?

***Lord of the Forest* by Caroline Pritcher. 2004. Great Britain: Frances Lincoln Children's Books.**

Dramatic artwork (by Jackie Morris) graces this masterful coming of age tale focused on young Tiger, who is seeking the elusive Lord of the Forest.

***Moon Bear* by Brenda Z. Guiberson. 2010. Illustrated by Ed Young. New York: Henry Holt and Company.**

Likely what you'll notice first about this remarkable book are the illustrations. They're stunning. Read it a second time to focus on the verbs, taking time to be impressed by how a writer weaves so much information into a few simple lines.

***Shades of Black: A Celebration of Our Children* by Sandra Pinkney. 2002. New York: Scholastic.**

This collage of photographs and poetic text celebrates the uniqueness of each child. The children pictured are not just "black," but "the creamy white frost in vanilla ice cream" or "the velvety orange in a peach." If ever there was a book to teach precision in word choice (and in thinking), this is it.

***Spiders and Their Websites* by Margery Facklam. 2001. Boston: Little, Brown and Company.**

This book, the fourth in Margery Facklam's impressive and acclaimed natural history picture book series, is a model of good informational writing: clear, precise, educational, and filled with voice. Her imagery takes us right into the spider's world.

Very young children need to know that nonfiction writing is varied, but at the core of all nonfiction writing is often a question, an observation, a passion fermenting in the author's mind and heart.

—Georgia Heard and Jennifer McDonough
A Place for Wonder, 2009, 58

Water Hole Waiting by Jane Kurtz. 2002. New York: HarperCollins.
Lee Christiansen's breathtaking illustrations and Jane Kurtz's elegant, powerful language work together to create a picture of dawn at an African water hole.

ADDITIONAL BOOKS WITH STRONG WORD CHOICE . . .

- *Amos and Boris* by William Steig
- *The Boy Who Loved Words* by Roni Schotter
- *Click, Clack, Moo: Cows That Type* by Doreen Cronin
- *Crickwing* by Janell Cannon
- *Dr. DeSoto* by William Steig
- *The Great Fuzz Frenzy* by Janet Stevens and Susan Stevens Crummel
- *I, Crocodile* by Fred Marcellino
- *Max's Words* by Kate Banks
- *Miss Alaineus* by Debra Frasier
- *Roberto, the Insect Architect* by Nina Laden
- *Stellaluna* by Janell Cannon
- *Verdi* by Janell Cannon
- *Walter Was Worried* by Laura Vaccaro Seeger

Primary Books for Teaching SENTENCE FLUENCY

Bat Loves the Night by Nicola Davies. 2004. Cambridge, MA: Candlewick Press.
This book's easy-to-read sentences carry a wealth of information and display incredible variety.

The Curious Garden by Peter Brown. 2009. New York: Little, Brown and Company.
An outstanding book for illustrating variety in sentence beginnings and lengths. You'll love reading this one aloud.

The Frog and Toad Collection Box Set by Arnold Lobel. 2004. New York: Harper Collins.
Whether flying kites, learning to swim, enjoying ice cream, or getting the shivers over scary stories, Frog and Toad make the most of life. Their always-humorous exchanges involve some of the best dialogue anywhere.

Insectlopedia by Douglas Florian. 2002. New York: Sandpiper.
Like Florian's other books, this one contains masterful, playful word choice presented in fluent poetry. Many poems are short and easy to memorize—or perform.

An Island Grows by Lola M. Schaefer. 2006. New York: Greenwillow Books.
The simplest of sentences, subject-verb, can tell a complex story: the growth of an island from its volcanic origins to thriving villages. Beginners and ELLs will appreciate the beauty of a book that reduces the complexities of English to its most basic core.

The Little Yellow Leaf by Carin Berger. 2008. New York: Greenwillow Books.
Use the story of the timid leaf to show that repetition isn't always a problem; sometimes it creates voice or helps reinforce meaning.

Oh, the Places You'll Go! **by Dr. Seuss. 1990. New York: Random House, Inc.**
This wise and humorous graduation speech from the grand sage himself is a celebration of life, and a wonderful send-off for explorers of all ages.

ADDITIONAL BOOKS WITH STRONG SENTENCE FLUENCY

- *Abel's Island* by William Steig
- *Beast Feast* by Douglas Florian
- *Come On, Rain!* by Karen Hesse
- *Creatures of Earth, Sea, and Sky: Poems* by Georgia Heard
- *Dinothesaurus* by Douglas Florian
- *Gentle Giant Octopus* by Karen Wallace
- *George and Martha* by James Marshall
- *Great Crystal Bear* by Carolyn Lesser
- *Old Black Fly* by Jim Aylesworth
- *One Tiny Turtle* by Nicola Davies
- *A Pocketful of Poems* by Nikki Grimes

Primary Books for Teaching CONVENTIONS & PRESENTATION

Because Chapter 8 includes a thorough review of books with extraordinary use of conventions and/or striking design, I will not include additional annotations here. However, let me offer the following summary lists of books that are especially useful with primary writers.

BOOKS WITH STRIKING USE OF CONVENTIONS . . .

- *Chester* by Melanie Watt (and Chester)
- *Hairy, Scary, Ordinary: What Is an Adjective?* by Brian P. Cleary
- *Knuffle Bunny* by Mo Willems
- *Leonard the Terrible Monster* by Mo Willems
- *Muncha! Muncha! Muncha!* by Candace Fleming
- *The Night I Followed the Dog* by Nina Laden
- *Nouns and Verbs Have a Field Day* by Robin Pulver
- *A Poke in the Eye: A Collection of Concrete Poems* by Paul B. Janeczko
- *Punctuation Takes a Vacation* by Robin Pulver
- *Roomeow and Drooliet* by Nina Laden
- *Silent Letters Loud and Clear* by Robin Pulver
- *Surprising Sharks* by Nicola Davies
- *What! Cried Granny* by Kate Lum
- *When Pigasso Met Mootisse* by Nina Laden
- *Yo! Yes?* by Chris Raschka

Books with Striking PRESENTATION . . .

- *An Egg Is Quiet* by Diana Aston, illustrated by Sylvia Long
- *Art & Max* by David Weisner
- *Beautiful Oops!* by Barney Saltzberg
- *Bones* by Steve Jenkins
- *Bruno Munari's Zoo* by Bruno Munari
- *Button Up! Wrinkled Rhymes* by Alice Schertle
- *Gentle Giant Octopus* by Karen Wallace, illustrated by Mike Bostock
- *Iggy Peck, Architect* by Andrea Beaty
- *The Lion & the Mouse* by Jerry Pinkney
- *No, David!* by David Shannon
- *The Other Side* by Istvan Banyai
- *A Poke in the Eye: A Collection of Concrete Poems* by Paul B. Janeczko, illustrated by Chris Raschka

Closing Note

Chances are very good that you have a favorite book that is not on this list. That's OK—just be very careful not to use it. I am kidding. Read what you love because you'll enjoy it more—and you'll read with passion. It's very hard to throw yourself into a book you find tedious. Don't take anything from my list or anyone else's that you don't love right down to your toes.

Assessing Young Writers

As Barry Lane explains so eloquently in his Foreword to my book *Creating Young Writers*, the word *assessment* comes from the Latin word *assidere,* "to sit beside." Good assessment is about carefully watching, listening, and coaching. It has very little to do with test scores and numbers. Tests and formal assessments (those that involve scoring writing samples, for instance) are shortcuts, efforts to make immediately visible what could take weeks or months of close observation to reveal. They are educational compromises.

Assessment shortcuts are such an integral part of our American educational landscape now that it is nearly impossible to imagine life without them. But we must never forget that they do not take the place of real assessment, particularly for primary writers. I say *particularly* because with primary writing, we must continually train ourselves to interpret what we see with intelligence and sensitivity. Young writers' work looks different from anything we ourselves produce—or anything we can reasonably hope to recall. It looks different from virtually everything we read outside of the primary classroom. So to interpret such writing meaningfully and fairly takes effort, diligence, perception, and time. No shortcuts can be allowed.

Let me suggest five things you can do to make assessment work in your primary classroom:

1. Look carefully at individual pieces of writing.
2. Observe children as they go about the business of being writers.
3. Ask children to talk with you about their writing process.

Author's Note

Do this in-depth assessment with a partner or a small group. What one of you misses, another might see. Your resulting list will be richer and more telling. And with each example, your ability to see beyond conventions to the knowledge and skills within will grow.

4. Keep portfolios so you have a way of tracking work over time.

5. If you do *any* formal assessment, be sure the tools you use are age-appropriate.

Let's consider these individually.

ASSESSMENT STEP 1: LOOKING CAREFULLY AT STUDENT WRITING

Early in this chapter, we considered a number of student samples, to see specifically how traits such as ideas, voice, or fluency look in the work of our youngest writers. What we did not do, however, is to ask ourselves, *What does this writer know about writing at this point?*

Taking time for such analysis allows you to know in a much more precise way just where your writers are right now. It will guide you in making helpful comments, constructing mini lessons, deciding what to model, and thinking about literature you might share. The process is simple—but carrying it out can be challenging.

Let's try one example from this book: Nicholas's paper, "I Like My Library," reproduced here as Figure 10.11. Reread this paper carefully, and make a list of all the things you feel Nicholas can do as a writer. (If you are teaching now, take the next step and use this same procedure with one or more samples from your own students' work.)

FIGURE 10.11

"I Like My Library"
by Nicholas (Grade 1)

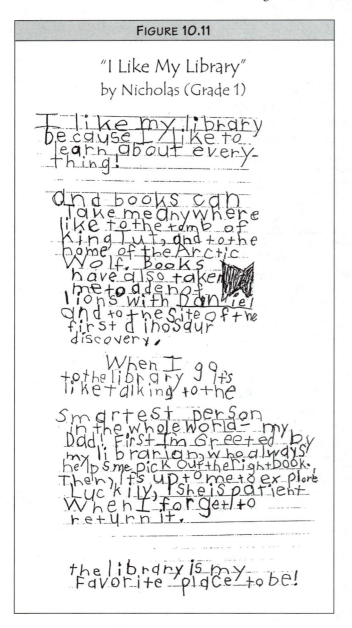

Author's Note

Make *your own list* before looking at mine. That way, my thinking won't influence you. Dig deep. See all you can in Nicholas's work. *Then* check to see if I noticed anything you did not.

Following are the things I feel this student currently knows or can do as a writer. Nicholas—

1. chooses a topic about which he feels strongly.

2. can "bend" a topic to suit his interests. When the teacher asked for a piece on "favorite place," he thought of how much he loves books—and that led him to the library. (He was the only student in the class to choose this *particular* place.)

3. begins with a forceful sentence that sums up his main point right away.

4. stays focused on one topic throughout the paper.

5. uses supporting details: books take the reader places, books are like talking to smart people, the librarian is helpful and kind).

6. speaks with a confident voice: "The library is my favorite place to be!"

7. writes left to right, up to down, on the page.

8. leaves large margins, which makes reading easier.

9. wraps his sentences, moving deftly down and left into the next line when he runs out of space.

10. uses capitals appropriately.

11. is comfortable with many punctuation marks
     (commas, periods, exclamation points, apostrophes, dashes), and uses them to
     influence meaning and voice.

12. breaks his writing into paragraphs—and begins them at the right spots.

13. begins sentences in many ways.

14. ends with a strong statement.

I noticed 14 things Nicholas can do. Perhaps you found more. As I do this kind of analysis, it occurs to me how superficial hasty assessment can be. We owe it to our children—and to their parents—to look within. To teach ourselves to see with "new eyes."

ASSESSMENT STEP 2: OBSERVING YOUNG WRITERS CAREFULLY

Writing assessment cannot focus only on the final product. We have to watch, listen to, and interact with students as they go about the business of being writers. The more you write yourself, the more you will see as you observe—and the better you will know what to watch for. If you do not write, you may find yourself relying too heavily on assessment of the product—the writing itself—and you will miss much of what your students are achieving.

Let me suggest some things you can watch for specifically—but please add to this list. You know your writers better than anyone else. You know what their personal writing process looks like. So use these questions as a starting point to suggest the *kinds of behaviors* that might be telling:

Before writing, a successful primary writer might—

- Choose her own topics—at least sometimes
- Modify an assigned topic to fit her experience
- Think about purpose or genre
- Envision how her final document will look
- Think about her audience
- Recognize when she needs more information
- Ask for help in getting that information
- Think about the topic for a time prior to writing
- Think about an illustration prior to drawing/painting
- Talk or draw to get started

As she drafts, a successful primary writer might—

- Make art part of her whole composition
- Use technology to compose
- Think carefully about the order of details
- Write various leads and pick a favorite
- Think about the reader as she composes
- Use paragraphing or other devices to divide her writing into sections
- Borrow ideas from literature
- Continue her writing from one day to the next
- Read aloud to check the voice or flow of ideas

The real voyage of discovery consists not in seeking new landscapes, but in having new eyes.

—Marcel Proust

- Write various endings and choose a favorite
- Wait to write her title last—to make sure it's right
- Share her writing with someone else to get a reaction
- Try something new
- Make adjustments (revisions) as she works

As she revises or edits, a successful primary writer might—

- Read her own writing aloud to herself and/or others
- Use arrows to move pieces within the text
- Do additional prewriting
- Change her mind about something
- Take information out
- Put new information in
- Add a detail
- Change wording
- Check resources—dictionary, thesaurus, word cards, etc.
- Ask for help from a partner, teacher, or other writing coach
- Imitate strategies used by other writers
- Make stylistic choices about design
- Use technology to help with final editing or formatting

Please *do not* use this as a checklist. No child would reasonably do all these things—and I am not suggesting they should. You want to look for *any* behavior that says "I am using what I've learned about process to be a more effective writer." By observing, we come to see our writers as problem solvers. And we discover what lessons they are learning from modeling and from participation in writing workshop. That makes it so much easier to design useful instruction.

ASSESSMENT STEP 3: ASKING CHILDREN TO TALK ABOUT THEIR PROCESS

Even if we're champion observers, we can miss worlds of information if we don't ask children to talk about the reasons behind their choices. We'll wind up making assumptions based on what we would do, or why we would do it. We need to ask questions like these:

- Does this writing feel like it's going OK—or do you need help?
- What will your next step be?
- How did you happen to make *this* particular choice? (In reference to anything from the title to the overall format or any other specific choice.)
- What do you love, or want a reader to love, about this writing?

Remember Connor's piece called "My Winter Vacation"? It is reproduced for you here as Figure 10.12. Like many teachers, I was concerned about organization when I first read this paper, thinking Aunt Helen had arrived right on the heels of the paramedics. But then, I was thinking *chronological order,* and that was blinding me to other possibilities.

Luckily, I had a chance to talk with Connor about his writing process. He told me he thought a long time about how to organize what he wanted to say, and he made a

CHAPTER 10   Exploring the World of BEGINNING WRITERS

FIGURE 10.12

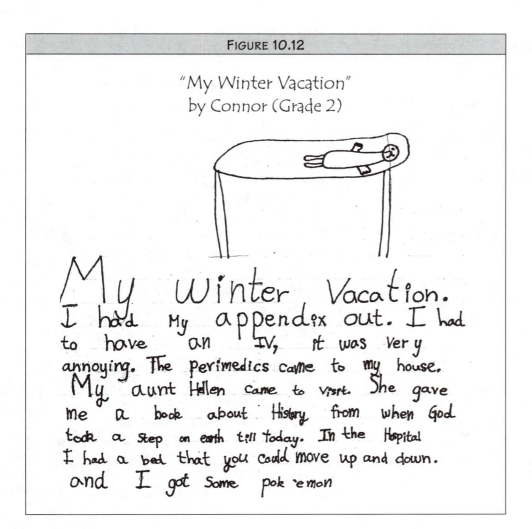

"My Winter Vacation"
by Connor (Grade 2)

My Winter Vacation.
I had My appendix out. I had
to have an IV, it was very
annoying. The perimedics came to my house.
My aunt Hellen came to visit. She gave
me a book about History from when God
took a step on earth till today. In the Hospital
I had a bed that you could move up and down.
and I got some pok'emon

definite choice *not* to tell it as a story. He said, "I was trying to explain the parts I *didn't* like so much and then the parts that were pretty good." That is a good organizational choice for this topic, and makes me enjoy the part about Aunt Helen's gift even more. When I reread the piece with this new perspective, I see that it is in fact not a story at all (even though I had been thinking of it that way—habit, you see). It is a comparison of the "annoying" parts (paramedics, IV, oversized books) and the good parts (moveable bed, games). The story *behind* the writing is often as interesting—and revealing—as the writing itself.

ASSESSMENT STEP 4: KEEPING PORTFOLIOS

Portfolios don't have to include every piece of writing the writer produces. They are more like photo albums, in which the writer saves "snapshots" of his or her favorite (for whatever reason) work. Everything is dated, and the pieces together tell a visual story of the writer's growth, a story no grades or scores (or even narratives) can match.

Edward, a second language student from South Korea, kept a portfolio throughout his third-grade year. He chose all the pieces for the portfolio himself. He kept it in the classroom until the end of the year, but enjoyed sharing it with his parents when they came to school for conferences. Poetry was his favorite genre. (It was also his teacher's favorite, which may have been a strong influence.)

FIGURE 13.a

Edward's Early Poetry

There Is a Dragon
By Edward

There is a dragon in a

white small world.

Then it gets filled with wide

dark color.

Nothing else.

Not so bad.

FIGURE 13.b

Edward's Later Poetry

Myself
By Edward

I am a wind blowing under a bright sky.
I am a player who jumps up and shoots
  for the victory.
I am the orange of a burning volcano
  in dinosaur times.
I am a rare mouse who runs for health
  every day.
I am a canyon with large minds.
I am a sunflower shining like sun
  every morning.
I am a statue standing tall and still.
I am moonlight,
  coming out with friendly stars.
I am South Korea,
  south from the battling guns.
I am the sweat of heat after a long game.
I am a son, cousin, and friend.
I am lucky to be me.

See Figures 10.13a and 10.13b for just two samples, fall and spring, of Edward's work. Read them aloud to hear the changes. By spring, Edward writes more easily and expansively. His vocabulary has grown markedly, and he is able to reach for the words he wants and create vivid images, metaphors, and similes. He is now *thinking* metaphorically, in fact: "I am the orange of a burning volcano in dinosaur times." He writes in fluent, rhythmic sentences, and uses conventions with impressive skill.

In Figures 10.14a and 10.14b, you will see two samples written by Max, a first grader. The first was written in September, the second in January. Again, the differences are striking. In September, Max is writing one sentence (even though it is punctuated as two): *This is a very small dog I'd like to have*. He is off to a good start, expressing a thought we can understand and experimenting with conventions, notably periods. He is still working on distinguishing between upper and lower case, and we might not recognize the dog in his drawing without the words to give us a clue.

By January . . . what a difference! Max is creating a drawing we can readily interpret; the characters are even labeled. He is writing multiple sentences—going on and on, we might say. His writing is filled with distinctive details about each member of the family, and his closing sentence, which definitely wraps up the writing, begins with the expressive *But most of all*. Max's conventions have come a very long way. He spells many words correctly and is so close on others that we can read his writing without difficulty, and without his help. He has a much better sense of the difference between capital and lower case letters, and is using commas and exclamation points, as well as periods. Not everyone gets excited about commas. But writing teachers? You bet.

FIGURE 10.14a

Max's September Writing

This is a vane smole dog. ID Lick to hav.

FIGURE 10.14b

Max's January Writing

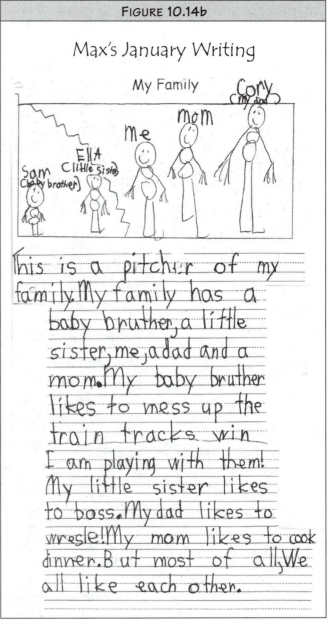

This is a pitcher of my family. My family has a baby bruther, a little sister, me, a dad and a mom. My baby bruther likes to mess up the train tracks win I am playing with them! My little sister likes to boss. My dad likes to wresle! My mom likes to cook dinner. But most of all, We all like each other.

Just summarizing these changes in the writings of Max or Edward could never generate the impact of seeing their work for yourself. Nothing—absolutely nothing—matches the power of the portfolio when it comes to assessment.

ASSESSMENT STEP 5: USING AGE-APPROPRIATE TOOLS FOR ASSESSMENT

Many districts do not require grades for primary writers, but offer narrative summaries of performance instead. I applaud this idea wholeheartedly. If this is an option for you, you may not need to do any assessment (of primary writers) that involves numbers—and that would be a very good thing. As we have seen, assessing the work of young writers is extraordinarily complex. What they know, what they can do, is very difficult (all but impossible) to capture in minimalistic scores or grades.

AVOID SCALES INTENDED FOR OLDER WRITERS

If you do, however, find yourself wanting a scale or continuum by which to measure growth, do not use the scales presented in Chapters 3 through 8 of this book unless you have a writer who is performing well above grade level. Those scales are inappropriate for use with *most* primary writers because they assume too much—and because they do not recognize art as an essential component of the message.

You can, however, use either of two options: the Early Guides (Figure 10.2) or Primary Continuums. Let me briefly explain the differences.

EARLY GUIDES TO TRAITS

The Early Guides (Figure 10.2) were adapted from the scales for older writers. They can be used with or without numbers. If you use them without numbers, you still provide an important record of the writing skills demonstrated in each performance—especially if the guide is attached to the performance itself.

If you wish to use numbers, provide a point for each check. Students should routinely receive at least three or four points. If this is not happening, use the Primary Continuums (see the next section) until the student is ready for assessment on this Early Guide.

Please note that it is not necessary (or even, in many cases, desirable) to assess a primary writing sample on *every trait*. Be flexible. Consider what is important for *that piece*, and assess accordingly. You might *just* look at ideas, or ideas and organization, or fluency and conventions. Let's assess two examples just for the trait of ideas, to see how the Early Guides work.

Example 1: *Mr. Bear Is Loving*

The first is Andrew's one-line message about Mr. Bear, reproduced for you here as Figure 10.15. I'm going to assess it only for ideas. This piece is not ready for assessment in other traits because it is simply too short. It doesn't make sense to talk about organization or fluency in a single sentence, and Andrew is not yet using enough words to make assessment of word choice meaningful. Nor would I put a score on this piece. But I can use the checklist to see how Andrew is progressing in his ability to convey ideas to a reader. Here's how I would respond to this writing. Does Andrew

- Create a message, decodable or not, on paper? (*Yes.*)
- Express a message the reader can understand without help? (*No—not quite. Without the teacher's addition of the word "loving," I have only part of the message. He's close, though.*)
- Provide details through words or art? (*Yes—I learn something important about Mr. Bear.*)
- Include sensory details? (*No—not yet. But I am confident he's fully capable of this, and I expect to see it in future writing.*)
- Show knowledge of this topic? (*Yes. Even with one sentence, I can tell that he and Mr. Bear share a special relationship.*)
- Use details that are original, unusual, striking, or memorable? (*Yes—that word "loving" is most unusual for a kindergarten writer, and it will stay with me for a long while.*)

So Andrew receives four checks out of six (or three of six if you do not allow credit for focusing on the central message). You could turn this number into a score, yes. But in Andrew's case, I would tuck it into a portfolio, then assess another piece of work down the road so I would have a very visual record of his growth. My comment to Andrew: *Your choice of the word* loving *was wonderful. It caught my attention.*

FIGURE 15

"Mr. Bear Is Loving"
by Andrew (Kindergarten)

Mᴾ br is / Loving

Example 2: *Jamey the Cat*

Let's look now at a very different piece, "Jamey the Cat," reproduced here as Figure 10.16. This is a highly sophisticated sample—and could *probably* be assessed using the Teacher Writing Guide for Ideas. But for now, let's keep our assessment at primary level. Does Veronica:

- Create a message, decodable or not, on paper? (*Yes.*)
- Express a message the reader can understand without help? (*Absolutely. It's not only clear, but it also amuses us and makes us think.*)
- Provide details through words or art? (*Yes—both. The drawing of the unhappy, de-clawed cat adds tremendously to both meaning and voice.*)
- Include sensory details? (*Yes. It's a highly visual piece. We picture the cat on the windowsill and Sarah having her picnic. With a bit of a stretch, we can even sense how good that picnic food smells and tastes.*)
- Share details that show knowledge of the topic? (*And how. This writer has exceptionally sophisticated understanding of how little things create jealousy or tension between friends.*)
- Use details that are original, unusual, striking, or memorable? (*Oh, yes—the notion of the cat who plots her revenge is unforgettable. This piece has drama.*)

PRIMARY CONTINUUMS

The Primary Continuums (see Figure 10.17) are intended only for use in the classroom, where the teacher can observe students on a day-to-day basis. They reflect performance over time, rather than performance on one piece of writing.

Continuums are a little different from writing guides in that they (1) have no numbers; (2) allow for observations of the *writer* (not just the writing) that relate to such things as listening skills or ability to discuss the traits; and (3) take writing process—notably revising—into account.

Like the Early Guides, these continuums focus on the positive, on what students *can* do—and also view art as an integral part of the total composition. Each continuum spans five stages:

- The *Beginner* (left column) understands that marks on paper have significance and meaning.
- The *Borrower* notices environmental print and uses it to enrich and expand his or her text.
- The *Experimenter* continues to borrow, but is becoming independent, daring to invent when no helpful text is readily available.
- The *Meaning Maker* creates text that is generally interpretable by a reader with no assistance from the writer. This writer's text is expanded and developed.
- The *Experienced Writer* is in control of his or her writing, constantly stretching, and to an extent, managing his or her own writing process.

FIGURE 10.16

"Jamey the Cat"
by Veronica (Grade 2)

My name is Jamey. I am a cat. I like this window sill. I can see a lot from here. Sarah is outside. She is having a picnic with a friend. I love Sarah. I love outside. But I can't go outside now. I've been fixed. That means I can't have kittens anymore. I didn't want kittens anyway. They are a lot of hard work. My nails were pulled too. If I go outside I will get clawed till I die. So I don't go outside. I'd like to, but I don't. I love Sarah, but I want to picnic too. When Sarah comes home I'm not letting her pet me!

by Veronica
Grade 2
St. Wilfrid

Author's Note

This writer is probably ready for assessment on the Teacher Writing Guide (Figure 1.7). You might try assessing "Jamey the Cat" using that guide to compare. Which scale provides better information for you? How about for the writer?

FIGURE 10.17

Primary Continuum for IDEAS

Beginner	Borrower	Experimenter	Meaning Maker	Experienced Writer
☐ Makes marks on paper	☐ Uses "words" and pictures to express ideas	☐ Uses text/art to create interpretable messages	☐ Creates clear message via text or text plus art	☐ Creates a clear, detailed message though text/art
☐ "Reads" own writing, invents meaning	☐ Uses imitative/ borrowed print to create signs, lists, rules, notes, etc. (not always interpretable without help)	☐ Expresses clear main message/idea in one or more sentences	☐ Expresses complex, extended thoughts	☐ Uses multiple sentences to enrich ideas or extend story
☐ Dictates a clear message/story	☐ Likes to come up with personal ideas for writing	☐ Can "reread" text shortly after writing it	☐ Uses multiple sentences to add detail	☐ Incorporates significant detail to enhance meaning
☐ Uses art to convey message/story	☐ Notices detail in read-aloud text and in art from picture books	☐ Creates decodable lists, labels, notes, statements, short summaries, "all about" or "how-to" pieces and/or poems	☐ Connects images/text to main idea	☐ Creates writing that explains, gives directions, tells a story, expresses an opinion, describes, etc.
☐ Recognizes that print has meaning/ significance		☐ Can talk about main ideas and details based on picture book text/art	☐ Creates images that show detail: eyes, expressive faces, fingers and toes, leaves and grass, etc.	☐ Can adapt text to suit the needs of various readers—and is highly aware of the reader
☐ Hears detail in stories read aloud		☐ Likes to choose own topics	☐ Creates writing that is fully decodable by independent reader	☐ Can summarize own or others' text
			☐ Can "reread" text after several days	☐ Can recognize and comment on detail or main message in text of others
			☐ Adds stories to repertoire	☐ Chooses personally important topics
			☐ Can think about and choose personal writing topic from several choices	☐ Can revise own text by adding detail
			☐ Can interpret or retell message from picture book	
			☐ Frequently chooses own topics	

FIGURE 10.17

Primary Continuum for ORGANIZATION

Beginner	Borrower	Experimenter	Meaning Maker	Experienced Writer
☐ Fills space randomly	☐ Can create art and text that go together	☐ Creates text/art with balanced look	☐ Creates balanced, pleasing layout	☐ Connects all text/art to main message
☐ Can dictate sequential story or how-to piece	☐ Creates layout with more purpose/balance	☐ Consistently creates images and text that complement each other	☐ Writes multiple sentences or images that suggest development/ sequencing	☐ Uses thoughtful titles
☐ Can point to illustrations that go with text	☐ May use two or more drawings to express story or message that has extended meaning and continuity	☐ Can arrange or create a sequence of drawings to convey a story or extended message	☐ Sometimes uses art to express sequence of events	☐ Writes a true lead (usually, the opening sentence)
☐ Can "hear" beginnings/endings in stories read aloud	☐ Recognizes titles as beginning points	☐ Writes more than one sentence on the same topic	☐ Uses connecting words: *first, next, then, once, after, and, but, or, so, because*	☐ Provides closure (usually with final sentence)
	☐ Recognizes THE END as a signal of closure	☐ May use title or THE END to signify beginning/ending	☐ Uses identifiable beginning and ending sentences	☐ Follows logical order/ sequence
		☐ Stays focused on message	☐ Creates organized lists, stories, descriptions, or recipes	☐ Creates easy-to-follow text
		☐ Often creates labels/lists	☐ Can make predictions based on text of others	☐ Connects idea
		☐ Can organize recipes, all about and how-to-pieces, directions, and simple stories		☐ Uses elaborate transitions: *After a while, The next day, Because of this, The first thing, Finally*
				☐ Creates organized stories, summaries, how-to pieces, short essays, and other forms
				☐ Can use variety of organizational patterns: e.g., step by step, chronological, comparison, problem-solution, main idea and detail
				☐ Can revise own text for order, lead, ending

FIGURE 10.17

Primary Continuum for VOICE

Beginner	Borrower	Experimenter	Meaning Maker	Experienced Writer
❑ Creates bold lines	❑ Incorporates voice into art through color, images, facial features, etc.	❑ Uses expressive language	❑ Creates some text recognizable as "this child's piece"	❑ Creates lively, engaging, personal text/art
❑ Uses color	❑ Uses exclamation points/underlining to show emphasis	❑ Often incorporates definite tone/flavor	❑ Writes/draws with personal style	❑ Creates writing that is FUN to read aloud
❑ Expresses voice in dictation	❑ Uses BIG LETTERS to show importance, strong feelings	❑ Creates expressive art	❑ Creates individual text, art	❑ Is able to sustain voice
❑ Responds to voice in text read aloud	❑ Shows preference for text/art with voice	❑ Creates tone that reflects feelings	❑ Elicits emotional response in reader	❑ Provokes strong reader response
	❑ Borrows strong "voice" words, e.g., LOVE	❑ Puts moments of voice throughout text	❑ May use conventional devices (exclamation points, underlining) to enhance voice	❑ Uses voice to influence meaning
		❑ Recognizes voice in text of others, can describe personal response: e.g., "I liked it," "It was funny."	❑ Shows beginning awareness of audience: use of *you*, conversational tone, direct questions: *Do you like cats?*	❑ "Speaks" to audience
			❑ Shows preference for certain types of voice in read-aloud pieces	❑ Creates voice that is easy to describe: *Joyful, Funny, Moody, Sarcastic, Fearful, Angry, Wistful*
			❑ Often comments on voice in others' text/art: e.g., "That has voice," or "I want to hear that again."	❑ Shows growing awareness of own voice and is beginning to control quality and strength of voice
				❑ Can rate extent of voice in others' text/art
				❑ Can revise own text to strengthen voice

FIGURE 10.17

Primary Continuum for WORD CHOICE

Beginner	Borrower	Experimenter	Meaning Maker	Experienced Writer
☐ Scribbles	☐ Borrows recognizable letter shapes from environment	☐ Writes easy-to-read letters/numbers	☐ Writes easy-to-read words	☐ Uses vivid, expressive language
☐ Creates letter "shapes"	☐ Borrows simple words	☐ Writes words with consonant sounds and some vowels	☐ Writes with variety—dares to try new, less familiar words	☐ Writes with vocabulary that may extend well beyond spelling ability
☐ Uses favorite words in dictation	☐ Labels pictures	☐ Uses titles on text	☐ Loves descriptive words and phrases	☐ Sometimes uses striking unexpected phrases: *"I felt like a once contented and proud swan who lost its feathers."*
☐ Responds positively to text with strong word choice	☐ Creates letter strings that contain one- or two-letter words: *lk* (like), *dg* (dog), *hs* (house), *m* (my)	☐ Writes decodable words/ sentences	☐ Uses some strong verbs	☐ Uses many strong verbs
	☐ Chooses favorite words from read-aloud text	☐ Uses many simple, familiar words	☐ Uses words to create images or add clarity, detail	☐ Keeps extensive personal dictionary
	☐ Repeats "comfort" (familiar) words in own text	☐ Uses sight words frequently	☐ Stretches for the "right word"	☐ Repeats words only for emphasis/effect
	☐ Guesses at word meanings from read-aloud text	☐ Has personal bank of favorite words	☐ Keeps growing personal dictionary of meaningful words	☐ Can revise own text to add descriptors
		☐ Attempts new or unfamiliar words in personal text	☐ Selects some "just right" words to express meaning	☐ Can revise own text to strengthen verbs
		☐ Adds new words to personal dictionary	☐ Repeats only for effect	☐ Can recognize and describe strong word choice in text of others
		☐ Repeats some words	☐ Uses language that creates imagery or sensory impressions	
		☐ Identifies favorite words from read-aloud text	☐ Favors literature with strong word choice	

FIGURE 10.17

Primary Continuum for SENTENCE FLUENCY

Beginner	Borrower	Experimenter	Meaning Maker	Experienced Writer
☐ Dictates a sentence	☐ Creates letter strings that suggest sentences: *nohtipdin*	☐ Writes letter strings that form readable sentences: *I lik skl.* (I like school.) *I HA DOG.* (I have a dog.)	☐ Creates easy-to-read text	☐ Can write two short paragraphs or more
☐ Enjoys poetry, rhythmic language			☐ Consistently writes multiple sentences	☐ Consistently writes complete sentences
☐ Enjoys music with a beat	☐ Writes text with a "sentence look" that may not be translatable	☐ Writes more than one sentence.	☐ Writes complete sentences	☐ Creates text that sounds fluent read aloud
☐ Enjoys marching, dancing, clapping to rhythmic beat	☐ Dictates multiple sentences	☐ Usually writes sentences that complete a thought	☐ Writes longer (complex or compound) sentences	☐ May use fragments for effect: *Wow! Crunch!*
	☐ Can hear rhythm, rhyme, and variety in read-aloud text	☐ Attempts longer sentences	☐ Begins to show variety in sentence lengths, patterns, beginnings	☐ Creates text that is easy to read with expression
		☐ Dictates a whole story or essay		
	☐ Can hear patterns—and may try imitating them	☐ Favors patterns: *I can pla.* *I can rid my bik.* *I can red.* (I can play. I can ride my bike. I can read.)	☐ May experiment with poetry—rhyming or free verse	☐ Often experiments with poetry/dialogue
	☐ Can memorize simple poems for group recitation		☐ May experiment with dialogue	☐ Can read own/others' text aloud with inflection
		☐ Likes to repeat text read aloud with inflection	☐ Reads aloud with inflection	☐ Can combine sentences
		☐ Likes to memorize and recite simple poetry	☐ Favors text with complex or varied sentence patterns	☐ Can revise by changing word order
				☐ Can revise by varying sentence beginnings
				☐ Can recognize and comment on fluency in others' text

FIGURE 10.17

Primary Continuum for CONVENTIONS & PRESENTATION

Beginner	Borrower	Experimenter	Meaning Maker	Experienced Writer
☐ May create left to right imitative text	☐ Imitates print: letters, "cursive flow (eee)," punctuation marks	☐ Uses capitals and lower case—not ALWAYS correctly	☐ Uses capitals and lowercase with fair consistency	☐ Uses wide range of conventions skillfully and accurately
☐ Can point to conventions in print	☐ Writes own name	☐ Uses periods, question marks, commas, and exclamation points (often correctly)	☐ Uses periods, commas, exclamation points, question marks correctly	☐ Creates easy-to-read text with few errors
☐ Plays with letter or number shapes	☐ Writes one to several sight words	☐ Puts spaces between words	☐ Sometimes uses paragraphs	☐ Uses paragraphs, often in the right places
☐ May "write" first letter (or more) of own name	☐ Loves to copy environmental print	☐ Spells many sight words	☐ Correctly spells ever-growing range of sight words and some challenging words	☐ Spells most sight words and many challenging words correctly
☐ May spell own name orally	☐ Creates letters that face the right way	☐ Creates readable, phonetic versions of harder words	☐ Uses some difficult conventions correctly: e.g., quotation marks, ellipses, dashes, parentheses	☐ Uses conventions to reinforce voice/meaning
☐ Knows what letters are, what writing is	☐ Can name/describe many punctuation marks: e.g., period, capital, comma, question mark	☐ "Plays" with more difficult conventions: dashes, ellipses, quotations marks	☐ Makes corrections in own text	☐ Consistently checks/edits own text for many conventions
☐ Draws to convey meaning	☐ May use periods or other punctuation marks randomly in own text	☐ Can name/describe numerous conventions	☐ Writes left to right, notices margins	☐ Writes left to right, top to bottom; wraps text and respects margins
☐ Attempts "words" of personal significance	☐ Asks about conventions	☐ Shows concern for correctness in own text	☐ Writes top to bottom	☐ Is careful with layout and formatting
☐ Responds to striking art/presentation	☐ Often writes left to right	☐ Writes left to right	☐ Wraps text easily	☐ Can edit own text for end punctuation, subject-verb agreement, capitalization, spelling of high-frequency words
	☐ Often writes top to bottom on page	☐ Writes top to bottom	☐ Places title or illustrations thoughtfully on page	☐ Can edit simple text of others
	☐ Can write on a line	☐ Is beginning to "wrap" text (down and left) to form the next line		☐ Knows simple copy editors' symbols
	☐ Imitates art or other presentation features	☐ Enjoys playing with document design		

A student who is *consistently* at the Experienced Writer level, across traits and across performances, is probably ready for assessment on the Teacher Writing Guide (Chapter 1, Figure 1.7).

The idea of a continuum is *not* to categorize students, placing them in one slot or another (Andrew's an Experimenter, but Veronica's an Experienced Writer), but rather to highlight *each thing* that each writer can do across the whole range of performance, so a given writer might have performance indicators highlighted in several columns. That way, you can make assessment personal and individual. I suggest using continuums—

- As part of a portfolio, attaching them to specific samples of writing incrementally through the year, to record students' progress.
- In parent conferences to help identify the skills a young writer has attained or is working toward.

Closing Thoughts

When my dear friend Lois Burdett began teaching Shakespeare to second graders, parents gasped. Many protested. Some requested a different teacher, believing that second grade was too young to be exposed to something so advanced. Five years later, so many parents were demanding to have Mrs. Burdett as their child's teacher that most had to be turned down—and the local theater was putting her children's writing and art on T-shirts and coffee mugs. Their work continues to thrill teachers (and many older students, too) in the *ShakespeareCanBeFun* series that has since made Lois famous.

When I asked Lois her secret, she said without hesitation, "We have to take the lid off. We have to believe our children can do *anything*." That philosophy underlies everything Lois does, and it has given her students courage to write poetry, history, letters in character, and drama. It has spurred them to perform Shakespeare for their school—and other schools in the U.S.

The thing is, Lois really *does* believe young children can do anything—and they know it. Her confidence is infectious. And when *children* believe they can do anything, make way.

STUDY GROUP

Interactive Questions and Activities

1. **Activity and Discussion.** Modeling is important with all students—but especially at the primary level. Which of the following things do you model (or plan to model) with or for your primary writers? Check each one that applies; then, with your group, consider what else you might add to this list:

   ___ Coming up with a topic

   ___ Writing a good lead or ending

   ___ Adding important details to a drawing or text

   ___ Double spacing to leave room for additions later

   ___ Using arrows or carets

   ___ Coming up with a good title

   ___ Using conventions correctly

   ___ Reading your own writing aloud

   ___ Revising wording or sentences

2. **Activity and Discussion.** Without referring to any text or guide, see if you can describe in your own words how each trait looks at the primary level. If you teach now, illustrate your definitions with samples from your own students' work.

3. **Activity and Discussion.** Choose one paper from your own classroom, and with your group, do an in-depth analysis, listing things that the writer can do (see pages 346–347 and the example with Nicholas's piece, "I Like My Library").

4. **Activity and Discussion.** Choose a book you might share with primary writers and build a lesson around it by: (1) selecting read-aloud passages (or reading the whole book) to reinforce a particular trait; (2) thinking of questions you might ask to help students see how such things as detail, voice, or word choice work in the text; or (3) extending students' learning by asking them to write, using one small lesson they have learned from the book. Present your lesson or idea to your group.

5. **Activity and Discussion.** As a group, choose any paper from this chapter—or from your own students' work—and assess it using one or more of the Early Guides (Figure 10.2). Discuss the results. Do you see the student's performance in similar ways?

6. **Activity and Discussion.** If you work with challenged writers at any grade level, choose two (or more) writing samples and, as a group, assess them using the Teacher Writing Guide from Chapter 1 (pick *one trait* on which to focus) and the corresponding Early Guide from this chapter. Which feels more appropriate? Which offers a more accurate profile of what the student can do?

7. **Activity and Discussion.** If you teach primary writers, you may wish to extend your study group discussions using all or part of *Creating Young Writers*, 3rd edition (Spandel, 2011), discussing the book's instructional strategies and philosophy about assessing primary writers.

8. **Discussion.** Check each of the following statements with which you agree. Then discuss your responses with your group.

___ Writers in grades K through 2 should never be formally assessed.

___ Numbers tell only a small part of the story when it comes to primary assessment.

___ Much of what we teach primary writers we teach by sharing good literature.

___ Modeling is essential with primary writers.

___ A person who writes makes a better teacher of writing.

___ Primary students' work should be thoroughly edited and corrected by a teacher.

___ When it comes to assessment, process is as important as product.

___ We often underestimate what our primary writers can do.

Coming Up

In Chapter 11, we'll look at ways of communicating about student writing, through comments, conferences, and writing response groups. In Chapter 12, we'll consider the foundations of quality writing assessment, building on the discussion initiated in this chapter to cover writers at all grade levels.

> My strange writing took a different form when in second grade my teacher got mad at me because I wrote too much (as if there is such a thing). She did not approve of my twenty-or-so-paged stories with the gorgeous pictures I drew for them. I understand that she expected five pages, but I took the time to write twenty! And no, I couldn't have shortened the story. . . . If you do that, it's not the same story.
> —Meghan Eremeyeff, student writer

COMMUNICATING about Students' Writing

I tell people all the things I like about their piece—how wonderful the atmosphere is, for instance, and the language—and also point out where they got all tangled up in their own process. We—the other students and I—can be like a doctor to whom you take your work for a general checkup.

ANNE LAMOTT
Bird by Bird, 1995, 153

My hope is that as teachers we respond to all students' writing with astonished, appreciative, awestruck eyes. But we can't create this kind of writing response if we don't first "fall in love" with our students' quirky, unconventional, and culture-infused texts.

KATHERINE BOMER
Hidden Gems, 2010, 7

Don't tell me what I did wrong. Tell me what I did right. Just having the courage to put something on the blank surface is miraculous enough. To express something from my own inner thoughts—that in itself is an achievement.

SAMANTHA ABEEL, Student
in "An Open Letter to An Assessor," The 9 Rights of Every Writer, 2005, 112

A few years ago I was both amused and distressed to hear Grant Wiggins tell a large group of conference attendees about a new teacher who was saying farewell to her students after what had seemed a highly successful term. One of the students, Wiggins explained, paused to whisper a question she'd been too timid to ask earlier: "You've written this on so many of my papers, but I don't understand. What is 'va-goo'?" "Va-goo" (*vague*) all too often describes *us* as we try to clarify our expectations for students.

In this chapter I will talk about three important ways of communicating about writing: through comments, conferences, and sharing. I'll close with some suggestions for bringing parents into the conversation. Let's begin with comments, both spoken and written.

Comments

Can you recall the most positive thing anyone ever said to you about your own writing? It might have come from a teacher or perhaps a friend, colleague, parent, child, editor, or anyone—a comment that inspired you and gave you confidence. Now turn the tables. Try to remember the most negative comment you ever received on your work—one that momentarily bumped you off the path or perhaps even stunned you, or discouraged you from writing. If you recall it still, it must have hurt deeply.

Here are two examples from my personal experience.

In eleventh grade, I spent five days writing an essay on *The Great Gatsby*. I didn't know nearly enough about life to appreciate the book at that time. Like many sixteen-year-olds, I thought classics were inherently dull, but I'd worked hard on my essay, particularly the symbolism involving light. I received only one comment, written at the end: "Your most irritating habit is your relentless, *persistent* misuse of the semicolon. Please revise!" Relentless? Persistent? What an angry man to envision me plotting the strategic placement of semicolons to create maximum annoyance (I wasn't that clever)—not to mention the startling phrase "*most* irritating habit." Apparently, out of my vast array of annoying habits, this was the one—this semicolon thing—that provoked him most.

A few years ago, a struggling fourth grader named Rocky wrote a heartfelt piece about a school employee, Harry, who had befriended him. Harry talked to Rocky, taught him to play the guitar, and coached him academically—and as a result, Rocky's grades soared. Rocky's paper ended with this line: "The day Harry and I stop being friends is the day I die, and that's a long time from now." I recall well the day I phoned Rocky's mother to seek permission to print Rocky's writing in *Creating Writers* (it appeared in two previous editions). Rocky answered the phone—so naturally, I told him the reason for my call, and let him know how touched I was by what he'd written. He dropped the phone, but I could hear him running, calling to his mother, "She says *I'm a writer!* I'm going to be in a book!" If a few words from a stranger can have such impact, imagine how much *your* words mean to the students who are an intimate part of your writing world.

I have often asked other teachers to recall positive or negative comments and am always struck by how long some comments have stayed in their minds.

Teachers Recall the Good Times . . .

- *You show remarkable insight.*
- *You have a creative soul!*
- *You made me want to keep reading—even at 11 P.M.*

- *This sounds so much like you that I had to keep looking over my shoulder to see if you were in the room.*
- *I like the way you say what you have to say and then quit. Bravo!*
- *I began this paper believing one thing, and though you haven't totally turned me around, you have really made me think.*
- *You told me you couldn't write. You can. This proves it.*
- *Thank you for sharing your poem. It spoke to me.*
- *You took a technical, hard-to-penetrate idea and made it reader-friendly. You made me feel like an insider.*

And the Not So Good Times . . .

- *I can't believe what I see here. There is nothing of worth, except that the documentation is perfect. It is only the documentation that boosts this paper to a D–.* [Boosts?]
- *I think you may have it in you to write competently, but not brilliantly.*
- *In looking at this paper again, I believe it is even worse than I originally thought.*
- *Reading this has depressed me more than I can say.*
- *I do not have time to read this much. Please be more concise.*
- *You simply don't know how to write.*
- *This is basically verbal vomit.*
- *No one would read this who was not paid to read it.*
- *Lay off the exclamation points. This isn't that exciting.*
- *What in the world are you trying to say? Just spit it out.*
- *You will never, ever be an author.*
- *You missed the point completely. F.*
- *Do the world a favor. Don't write.*
- *I do not believe you wrote this. This is not your work.*
- *Your writing reminds me of a porcupine—many points leading in meaningless directions.*

One teacher's comment came in the form of a gesture: Her teacher shredded her paper and returned it to her in a paper bag. It takes only seconds to create a lifetime memory.

When I share some of the preceding negative comments in workshops, the gasps are audible. People fold their hands over their hearts, instinctively shielding themselves. In *Hidden Gems*, author-teacher Katherine Bomer notes that some would-be writers never do recover from vitriolic pronouncements that deny their talent, their thinking, their voice. "Writers are rare," she suggests, "who pursued their craft despite, or perhaps because of, the critical comments. Most adults would rather dig a ditch beside a highway in the August sun than write something" (2010, 16).

But . . . We *Meant* Well!

While some of the preceding comments seem bitter and rancorous, *most* teacher comments are, from teachers' perspectives at least, well intentioned. Sometimes, though, good intentions are not enough to bridge the communications gap. Abbreviated or cryptic comments ("awk," "syn," "punc," "diction") often make no sense to students. And as the following examples (from middle school writers) show clearly, students' internal responses to our comments are often nothing like what we had hoped for:

When the teacher wrote "Needs work,"
students responded this way . . .

- *Kind of rude. Work on what?*
- *This is so harsh. It makes me feel hopeless.*
- *I have to ignore this or I'll wind up hating the teacher.*

When the teacher wrote, "Use examples to illustrate your point,"
students responded this way . . .

- *If I have to give examples on every little detail, I'll never get the point across.*
- *I did use examples. You mean more examples?*
- *I don't have any other examples.*

When the teacher wrote, "You need to be more concise,"
students responded this way . . .

- *I'm confused. What do you mean by "concise"?*
- *I'm not Einstein. I can't do everything right.*
- *I thought you wanted details and support. Now you want "concise." Which is it?*

When the teacher wrote, "Be more specific,"
students responded this way . . .

- *You be specific. What exactly do you want? Give me an example!!*
- *It's going to be too long then. What happened to concise?*
- *Maybe you need to read more closely. Maybe it's you not paying attention.*

When the teacher wrote, "You need stronger verbs,"
students responded this way . . .

- *I lack verby power.*
- *I knew it. I should have used the thesaurus.*
- *I don't know any other verbs. Give me some examples.*

When the teacher wrote, "Weak ending,"
students responded this way . . .

- *Weak? No way! That's a great ending. Read it again.*
- *I know I need a better conclusion, but I have no idea how to write one.*
- *Teach me about endings! <u>Teach</u> me!!!!!*

Research by George Hillocks, Jr. (*Research on Written Composition*, 1986) confirms that these responses are not isolated examples, but are, in fact, typical of students who become defensive or overwhelmed by comments they do not understand—or comments they perceive as negative. In fact, writers who routinely received corrective comments wrote less and less over time, and often hid their papers from others, tore them up, or destroyed them (163).

It might seem on the face of it that one of the best ways to help a budding writer is to point out what he or she is doing wrong. Yet the truth is that this usually *doesn't* help; it causes the writer to retreat and sometimes to avoid writing altogether.

We must speak to our students with an honesty tempered by compassion: Our words will literally define the ways they perceive themselves as writers.

—Ralph Fletcher
What a Writer Needs, 1993, 19

But . . . We *Meant* Well!

365

Encouraging Comments +
Modeling = Path to Success

What *does* help is (1) to point out what is going well so that the writer builds on that and then (2) to follow up by modeling ways of dealing with problems. Let's begin with the comments.

This seems like the easy part, doesn't it? It's not. Good comments must be truthful and very specific. It's one thing to say, "Good job, Alex." That's not going to crush anyone's spirit, but no one appreciates mindless approval. Generalities won't tell Alex what worked—or give him even a hint about what to do next time. We need to take our own advice and "be specific" with comments like these:

- *Your examples about chocolate-covered marshmallows really hit home! I felt like I was reading about myself!*
- *I think you were horrified at the idea of freeze-drying a cat, but I had the feeling you were laughing right along with your readers. You really know how to connect with an audience.*

In Figure 11.1, kindergartener Isabelle writes an end-of-year reflection on what she has enjoyed most: the reward of making friends. It's not a treasure, she tells us, and not just candy either, but the joy of knowing you have—or *think* you have—a friend for life. I love many things about this piece—the fluency, the voice (!), the discovery that a true friend can sometimes be "annoying." Most of all, I appreciate the comment from the sensitive "Mrs. Woody" (affectionate nickname for Mrs. Woodfield) who does not zero in on conventions, but writes as if to a colleague: "I loved the way you talked about 'friends for life.' It made me cry." A comment like that says, "You are a writer. Your words touched me."

What if you don't like the paper very much? There's not much there—or what *is* there doesn't seem to say anything. Don't give up. Look again—look deeper. Take your time. *Listen.* Find one thing you enjoyed—just one: a good topic choice, a new convention used correctly, a detail that caught you by surprise, an opening line that holds promise (even if there's no follow-up), a moment—just a hint, a faint echo—of voice. If you look hard, you will find *something*. Make a *very big deal* of it. Write a long and elaborate comment. Next time there will be another something and then another after that.

Comments aren't important only for struggling writers or for those who need significant coaching. They are vital to skilled, experienced writers, too. If you were a proficient writer in school, you would be unusual if you could not recall at least one instance where you received an A—but had *no idea* why. Most likely you expressed yourself clearly. Your conventions were probably good. But that's not enough to distinguish your writing from "The Redwoods." And a grade (or score) all by itself won't tell you what you ache to hear: *What made your piece stand out from others? What made it worth reading?* Don't leave your students wondering. Tell them what moved or impressed you.

In "Making Feedback Work," Susan M. Brookhart (*Virginia Journal of Education,* April 2011) describes good feedback as descriptive, positive, clear, and specific. She suggests beginning by pointing out a strength the student did not even recognize in his or her own work, and then directing the student toward a next step (2). With the "Redwoods" writer, I might say, "Your affection for your family comes through very clearly—and that's where I'm starting to hear your voice. You could make that voice even stronger by helping us see some of the personal characteristics that make each person lovable. I'm curious to know who did the cooking, who had a sense of humor, who was a good sport." With struggling students, Brookhart notes, suggestions for next

I genuinely believe it is possible to find something good in each piece of writing, and I think you'll find it becomes an acquired skill that is central to being a constructive critic.

—Barry Lane
After THE END, 1993, 126

Whether or not feedback is effective depends on what students need to hear, not what you need to say.

—Susan M. Brookhart
"Making Feedback Work," 2011, 1

CHAPTER 11 COMMUNICATING about Students' Writing

FIGURE 11.1

"What I Enjoyed" by Isabel
(With Teacher Comments)

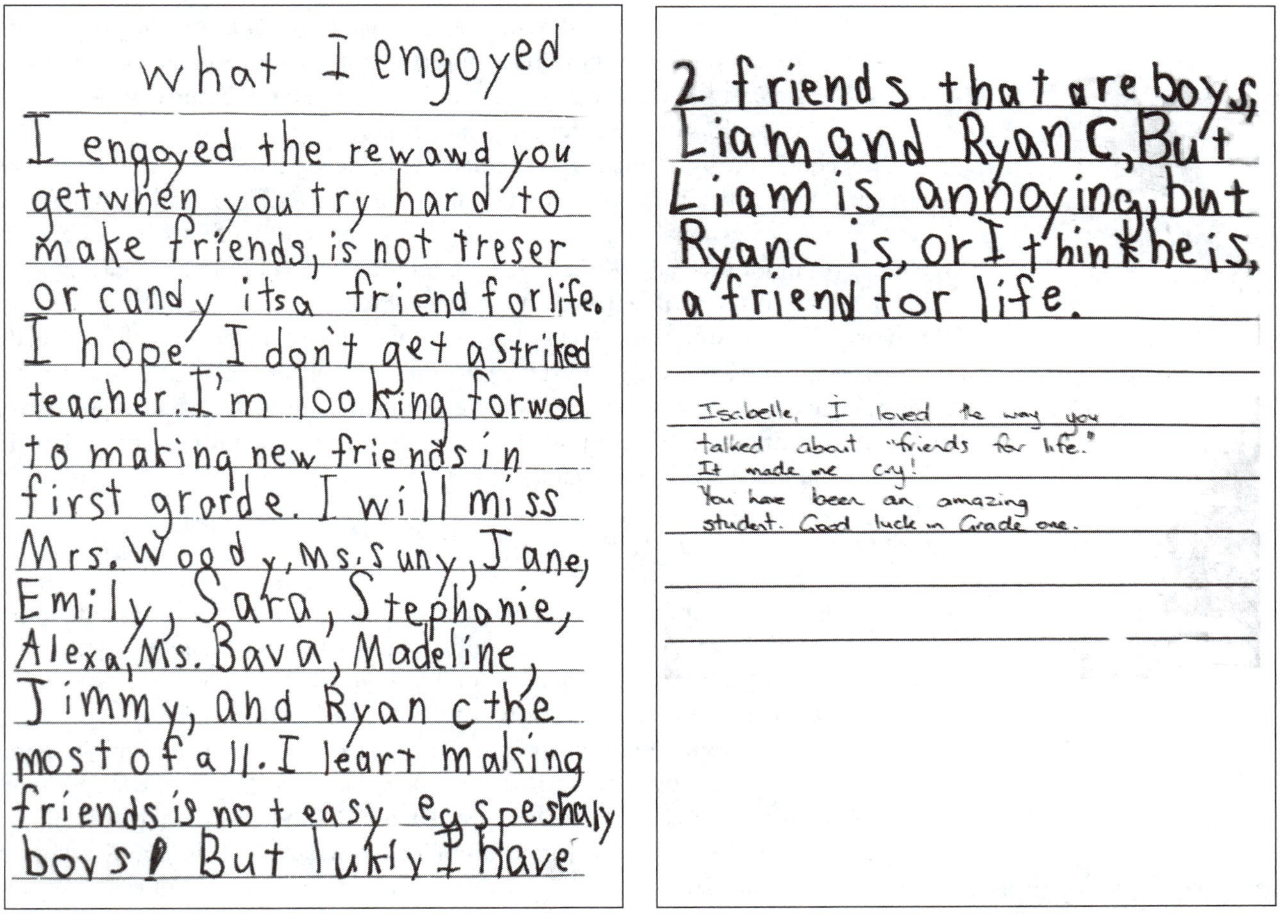

what I engoyed

I engoyed the rewawd you
get when you try hard to
make friends, is not treser
or candy its a friend for life.
I hope I don't get a striket
teacher. I'm looking forwod
to making new friends in
first grorde. I will miss
Mrs. Woody, Ms. Suny, Jane,
Emily, Sara, Stephanie,
Alexa, Ms. Bava, Madeline,
Jimmy, and Ryan c the
most of all. I leart maksing
friends is not easy egspeshaly
boys! But lukly I have

2 friends that are boys,
Liam and Ryan C, But
Liam is annoying, but
Ryanc is, or I think he is,
a friend for life.

Isabelle, I loved the way you
talked about "friends for life."
It made me cry!
You have been an amazing
student. Good luck in Grade one.

steps should be small and focused, targeting just one thing at a time (2). With writing, possibilities might include—

- Adding one detail
- Combining two sentences
- Replacing one verb with something stronger
- Having a character speak
- Revising a title

OFFER SUGGESTIONS THROUGH MODELING

Instead of scribbling a cryptic marginal note—"You need more detail here"—*show* the writer what this means. You might say, "Close your eyes. Now notice what happens in your mind when I change 'dog' to 'old black lab with one inside-out ear, nursing a limp in his right front leg.' Can you picture the difference? Making that kind of picture is what I mean by specific detail."

Encouraging Comments + Modeling = Path to Success

Or, "Here you are talking about the different parts of an atom—the *nucleus*, the *protons* and *neutrons*, and the *electrons*. You are probably thinking someone reading this knows all these terms very well. But what if they don't? What if they're hearing them for the very first time? See how you could put a small box in your writing [creating box on scratch paper] and tuck a definition right inside the text? Think how handy that would be for your reader. Or . . . consider using an illustration of an atom [creating a rough sketch] with all these parts labeled. When we did creative writing, we talked about vivid images. Images are just as important in informational writing as they are in poetry. Your readers might not picture anything but black and empty outer space—until *you* make a picture with your definitions and illustrations."

Modeling works like magic if we remember to "teach small," focusing on just one thing at a time. My all-time favorite teaching story comes from Don Graves (2003), about a golf professional helping him learn the game. On the first lesson, he simply told Graves to hit the ball. Minutes later, he told the new golfer to keep hitting—only this time with his head down, eye on the ball. Gradually, he added one more skill . . . then one more. "Before a few weeks were out," says Graves, "he had quietly attended to my grip, shoulder level, and follow through. A few years later I realized with a start that every single one of my problems was visible on the first lesson. If he had attended to all of them that first day, I would probably have missed the ball entirely and resigned in disgust from ever playing golf again" (314–315).

COMMENTS *PLUS* RUBRICS

The comments (on student writing) that appear throughout this book are intended to suggest *some* of the things you (or someone) might write on a student's paper—things you want to tell the writer that are not found in a writing guide. Some teachers would prefer to have comments replace writing guides or rubrics altogether.

As Katherine Bomer explains in her book *Hidden Gems*, "rubrics cannot begin to describe the complex joys and sorrows of a piece of writing . . ." (2010, 26). She is right, of course, and I couldn't agree more. There is a limit to what a rubric or writing guide—by itself—can achieve in terms of both assessing and communicating with students. But I disagree—strongly—with the idea of abandoning rubrics altogether. Here's why.

First, writing guides make what we believe public. There's an honesty and openness about this that I like. They push us to commit, to share what we value with students and with everyone else. For years, this was a mystery, and students had to guess. Grades came as a surprise. So, often, did comments. Do we really want to go back to those days? Writing guides take the mystery away. By sharing them openly with students, we say, "Welcome to the writing community. This is your language, too."

Second, as I read Katherine Bomer's book (*Hidden Gems*, 2010), I think how wonderful it is to have a sensitive teacher who takes extensive time to confer with students, who reads their writing with meticulous care, who looks—*always*—for the positive, thinks through each comment, and above all, appreciates students' writing as one treasures any great gift. But does this—*will* this—happen in every classroom with every teacher and student on every assignment?

What if some children get the teacher who isn't fully comfortable with conferences yet—or who cannot find time for lengthy comments or isn't sure what to say? Then what? A well-written writing guide, though it admittedly doesn't tell *everything*, does help a writer to know generally where his or her work stands, where the strengths lie, what most needs revision. It also reminds us, as teachers, what to look for—and how

Author's Note

It's important to keep in mind that it is quite possible to teach the traits of writing without using rubrics or writing guides *at all*. What matters is to teach the *concept* behind the words: What it means to write with clear ideas, to organize information effectively, to speak from the heart. A rubric, or writing guide, gives a beginning point that makes describing or teaching these concepts easier. And make no mistake: If you teach writing, you will *talk about* ideas, organization, voice, words, sentences, and conventions—whether you use rubrics or not.

to recognize it. Will we, with practice and experience, teach ourselves to read beyond the rubric? I should hope so. But that doesn't make it less helpful to have a beginning point. And I would also add that comments, no matter how insightful or brilliant, don't tell the writer everything either. As Susan M. Brookhart states, "Effective feedback compares work with criteria. Students should know the criteria for good work before they begin an assignment. A description of student work against criteria helps students see where they are now relative to where they intended to go" (2001, 2).

In addition, it is a myth that some people assess without using a guide or rubric. No one does this. Some rubrics simply aren't written down. They only exist in the mind of the assessor—and they're subject to change on a whim. We have to infer what these people value, through their responses, their preferences. This takes both time and intuitive acuity, and the process of discovery can be costly for the person being assessed. We should not play this game with students. We should be as open as possible about our expectations. It's only fair.

And finally, the true value of *any* rubric or writing guide lies not in the document itself, but in the development—in figuring out *for yourself* what makes writing work. That is why, throughout this book, I urge you to refine and revise any writing guide (whether from me or *any* source) according to the discoveries about writing that you and your writers make together. And whenever possible, develop writing guides or checklists of your own.

In my view, people often dislike or distrust writing guides because of how they are used—and misused. They're often viewed as iron-clad rules that must be interpreted literally and without exception. This is ridiculous—and dangerous. Our writing guides do not exist independently from us; they are an extension of our thinking. They don't control us; we control them. We should review them regularly, interpret and apply them with flexibility and sensitivity—not to mention common sense—and revise them to reflect our most current thoughts, understandings, and values about writing. Any time these things fail to happen, whether at the classroom, district, or state level, our assessment falls short of what it could be.

We should also recognize that writing guides can't say everything we want or need to say—they aren't "fast enough or huge enough to catch the winds of writing" (Bomer, 2010, 25). That's beautifully said. And it's true. But it overlooks the many positive things *well-written* writing guides can do. Writing guides give us a basis for ongoing, extended conversation—not only about one piece of writing, but about writing in general. Written criteria give us a consistency from assessor to assessor and from document to document that we never, ever had before. They give our students a visible goal to aim for. They document the "why" behind the elusive letter grade. And *combined with comments,* they give writers extremely thorough information about their work.

When you use a writing guide, and when your students know it well, some things are said for you. You don't have to write *everything about everything*. Then you can spend your precious teacher time writing what no scoring guide can ever convey: why and how someone's writing has touched you.

Quick Practice

Are you adept at saying (or writing) what your writers need to hear? To some people it comes very easily, while others need to practice a bit to feel fluent as assessors and responders. It helps if you abandon formalities. Take off your teacher hat for a moment, and just think about what you want to say, writer to writer. Instead of making judgments, create descriptions.

Teach like a doctor, not a judge.
—Jim Burke
Effective Instruction, 2008, 76

Read "Waters of Death" (Figure 11.2) and/or "The Bathroom" (Figure 11.3). Imagine you are reading a piece written by a colleague, rather than a student. Then write what you think, what you feel about each sample. I've put my own comments at the end of this chapter so you won't be influenced by them as you work. Here are six things to think about as you write your comments:

- Work on your own for this exercise because that is what you most likely will be doing as you respond to your students' work. Later, though, share comments with a partner or group so you can compare your reactions and perspectives.
- Read each paper more than once. Read aloud, listening for the voice, for the writer within the words.
- Look *first* for what is strong, what is done well—or what has promise. You will likely notice small problems. But for a moment, try to look beyond them to see what *is* working, and what the paper could become.

FIGURE 11.2

Waters of Death (Well, Not Quite) by Michael
Narrative, Grade 5

As soon as we left the stables, I knew it wouldn't be a good day for horseback riding. It had just rained a couple nights before and the trail was pretty muddy. All of the other riders were slipping all over the trail on their horses. My horse Buddy was surfooted. He didn't slide anyware. The air was making me cold but I was starting to relax. I was trying to spot deer through the trees.

When we were about half way done with the trail ride we came to a streem in the middle of the trail it really wasn't gentle anymore because it had just rained. It was about two feet deep. None of the other riders in front of me could get their horses to cross the streem. Not even the trail guide could get her horse to cross. She was kicking her horse in the side and she even got off her horse to push him but that horse wouldn't even budge.

All of a sudden my horse plunged into that streem. I felt like my head was going to fly off. I felt like I was going to fly off more like it. It seemed like forever but finally I got to the other side of the streem. While I was about to fall off my horse. My horse just stood their eating grass like nothing had ever happened.

Author's Note

Extend this practice by reviewing papers from your own students if you are currently teaching. It is helpful to write comments and score papers (for one, two, or more traits), and then to ask: *What does each form of response provide that the other does not?*

FIGURE 11.3

The Bathroom by Brett
(Narrative, Grade 8)

My summer vacation at my old house in California was going great, just relaxing and having a good time with friends until my mom came up to me and said, "I'm going on a trip up Highway 1. Wanna go?" I started thinking about it for a few minutes and then said, "I'm in, when are we leaving?" She told me it's still early in the morning and we should go right now.

Now if you don't know, Highway 1 is one of the most extraordinary places in California, going right along the coast. I said goodbye to my friends and we took off. About an hour and a half later, I found myself forging through the walls of pollution in the city of San Francisco, which were as thick as a veil of snow in a New York blizzard. We finally made it to Highway 1 and started driving down the never ending road of twists and curves. Well after several bottles of water and a couple of sodas, I told my mom I had to go to the bathroom.

We pulled over at a scenic rest stop and started heading for the bathroom. I stopped and gazed at the view from atop a hill, watching the whitecaps slapping the rocks and waited for my mom to go so I could have my turn. While I was standing there listening to the seagulls and inhaling the fresh ocean air I noticed a gigantic map of California to my left. It displayed the whole magnificent state including our microscopic town of Brentwood. After a few seconds of waiting, my mom came out of the bathroom. I inquired as to why she came out so quickly and although the look on her face said a lot she replied "that place was the sickest and most foul place I've ever seen, it's even worse than your room!!"

"That must be pretty bad then" I joked back. As I started my curious venture to the bathroom she yelled to me, "BRETT!" As I turned around she gave me a you're-not-really-going-in-there-are-you look. I told her I have to go and when you gotta go you gotta go! She turned in disgust and started walking toward the car. I started heading towards the bathroom.

Before I even reached the door I smelled it, the foul smell of roadkill and a bad case of someone who had eaten a lot of beans, all mixed in one. I plugged my nose and headed into the bathroom. I was not prepared for what then hit me. Even with my nose plugged the putrid smell still penetrated my nostrils. The place reeked like nothing I had ever smelled before. I took a look around and saw the dust covered sink and floor, the tiles are all cracked and I could see the dirt beneath them. I walked over to the toilet, took a look inside, and turned my head away so fast my neck cracked. I finished as fast as possible, avoided touching anything, and got out of there as fast as I could. I made a promise to myself to NEVER go back there again.

My summer vacation at my old house in California was going great, just relaxing and having a good time with my friends until my mom came up to me and said, "I'm going on a trip up Highway 1. Wanna go?"

- Describe what you see or hear in the writing. Be specific: Refer to particular words, lines, or images. Quote from the paper (in your comments) if you can.
- Come up with one small next step to help the writer revise with purpose and confidence and/or write more effectively next time.
- Think carefully about the words you write. Your words could influence deeply how the writer thinks of him- or herself *as a writer*.

Conferences

The very word *conference* can be horrifying to teachers who are already pressed for time. This is often so because they think that

1. They must control everything that happens during the conference.
2. They must use the conference as an opportunity to "fix" the writing.
3. A good conference has to be long—at least 20 minutes.

Think of a conference as a chat. Sometimes there's an opportunity for "small" modeling or teaching—but that doesn't have to be part of a conference. I like Tommy Thomason's analogy (in *Writer to Writer: How to Conference Young Authors*, 1998, pp. 62–64) to two neighbors talking about gardening. One is a veteran gardener, and one is a novice. The veteran might answer a question one day about when to plant lettuce. Another day he offers a suggestion on how to keep the flowers from falling off the tomato plants. But he never takes over the garden or delivers lectures on "How to Garden Properly." And if he did, it's a good bet the novice gardener would stop showing up.

Like the veteran, we confer best when we take time to "talk writing" with our students. Successful conferences can look very different. The way you confer with writers reflects your own style of teaching, as well as your students' needs. Maybe your style is casual and humorous. Maybe it's more formal and businesslike. But despite differences in approach, there are certain characteristics common to *most* successful conferences. Let's consider them individually.

Even if we feel our teaching falls short of what we wish it could be in a conference, it is still so significant that we sit down and talk to a child about his or her writing. No one ever did that with me when I was in school.

—Katie Wood Ray
The Writing Workshop, 2001, 156

A GOOD CONFERENCE . . .
BEGINS WITH *LISTENING*

That seems simple enough. But the truth is, we have to train ourselves, most of us, to be good listeners. For one thing, listening well is an art. And for another, we haven't had, for the most part, very good models ourselves.

Once you learn to listen, teaching a child how to write is easy.

—Cindy Marten
Word Crafting, 2003, xiii

Ralph Fletcher and JoAnn Portalupi (*Writing Workshop: The Essential Guide*) point out that "few of us had teachers who truly listened to us when we were kids" (2001, 49). This experience can imprint upon us a traditional paradigm of teachers doing all the talking while students listen—and, carried to an extreme, this can result in a culture where students are reluctant to voice any opinions for fear they may not coincide with the teachers' expectations.

To confer well—which is to say, to get the results we want—we need to stand that paradigm on its head. That means more than sitting passively as students read their work. We need to listen *actively*, concentrating on how we feel or what we see in our minds as each writer shares his or her work, and then describing those feelings or images as clearly as we can. Writers need to know the impact of their writing on a reader, but they won't know that if we spend our listening time thinking of the teaching points we are going to make. To gain students' trust, we must show them that we are deeply interested in what they have to say. Our eyes, our facial expressions, our body language must all say, "You, the writer, are at the center of my universe at this moment."

. . . IS ALSO SHORT.

How short? Well, as Katie Wood Ray reminds us (*The Writing Workshop*, 2001), a good conference *can* be as short as two minutes—and usually does not run more than six or seven. Ray points out the practical need for brevity when "we have lots of individuals to teach" (158).

Short conferences *are* a boon for the teacher with many students. But I also believe short is just better—in most cases. That's because a short conference tends to focus on just one or two writer's questions or trouble spots instead of three, four, or a dozen. We easily overwhelm writers, particularly beginners or struggling writers, by trying to do too much at one time. Indeed, we can turn the conference into something students will dread.

Donald Murray (2004) admitted that many of his conferences would run as long as fifteen minutes, though he considered five minutes ample time to get the "central business" of the conference—student comments and a teacher's response to those comments—finished (173). Murray went on to say that when he modeled conferences in teacher seminars, he usually averaged about 90 seconds, even though the participants observing were often surprised by how much was accomplished in so short a time. He also timed teachers as they responded to each other's writing, and rarely did they want to go much beyond two minutes. This experience led Murray to dub the two-minute conference "amazingly possible" (173).

Realistically, though, what can you hope to accomplish in two minutes? A lot, actually, if your whole attention is focused on the writer—*and* if you allow the student and his or her needs to direct the conference. Making *the paper* perfect, after all, is not the goal. What you really want to achieve is improving *the writer's skill* in solving writing problems—and not just for this paper, either, but for all that future writing he or she will do when you're not around. See Figure 11.4 for a list of things you can do in *under two minutes*.

> Teach one thing, no more . . . Overteaching means the child leaves the conference more confused than when he entered.
> —Donald H. Graves
> *Writing: Teachers and Children at Work,* 2003, 146

. . . PUTS *THE WRITER* IN CONTROL.

We can't usually anticipate what questions or difficulties will arise for our students as they go through their writing process. Therefore, we can't plan conferences the way we plan lessons. Some teachers find this nerve-wracking, while others find it stimulating.

But learning to love surprise means allowing the conference to take a course we cannot predict—a course set by the writer's needs. It also means getting comfortable with the notion that writers might ask us questions for which we have no immediate answers. We might need time to think, to read a second time, or to look something up. So what? Give yourself space to breathe, to reflect, or even to change your mind about how you see a piece of writing. Give yourself permission to not come up with "the answer" right away. Working toward understanding is part of *your process* as a teacher.

You can put the writer in control right from the first moment. A conference often begins with the teacher reading the student's work. Or the teacher may ask a leading question: *How are things going with your writing?* While I don't think either of these is a wrong approach, the conference can be even more effective when the writer initiates

> The important thing to realize is that students can be our teachers.
> —Lucy McCormick Calkins
> *The Art of Teaching Writing,* 1994, 54

FIGURE 11.4

Two-Minute Conference Topics

- Together, brainstorm two possible leads—or endings
- Brainstorm three possible titles
- Identify the MAIN thing that happens in each paragraph—and see if that's the path the writer really wants the reader to follow
- Identify the MAIN idea of the piece
- Identify each spot where the writer wanders from the main track
- Identify three spots where more detail is needed—information, expansion, an image—and insert a caret with a question mark in those spots
- Ask one question that will help the writer "fill in" informational holes
- Use sounds, smells, textures, or tastes to strengthen one moment or scene
- Identify one place where the writer could "shrink" time and improve the pacing of the piece
- Identify one place where the writer could *slow time down* to help the reader reflect on what is happening—or take in a technical concept
- Identify one moment of strong voice—and one where voice fades
- Replace two flat verbs with something stronger
- Get rid of one "There is," "There are," or "It is" sentence beginning
- Add one line of realistic dialogue to bring a character to life

- Identify one moment where a strong quotation would enliven an informational or persuasive piece
- Connect two choppy sentences to form one smooth sentence
- Disconnect one long, entangled sentence to form two or three easy-to-read sentences
- Cross out one line or phrase that is not needed
- Rewrite one sentence three different ways—then choose the best
- Show how a semicolon works
- Show how to put periods or commas inside quotation marks
- Brainstorm four alternatives to "said"—then choose the one that fits the mood
- Brainstorm four alternatives to "ran" or "walked" or "went"—then choose the one that creates the right mood and image
- Highlight the first four words of each sentence to check for variety
- Turn the last sentence of one paragraph into a transitional sentence that leads right into the next paragraph
- Highlight every "tired" word (*nice, good, great*) in the piece, and brainstorm alternatives for one or two
- Show how one strong verb (*raced*) can replace a weaker verb and adverb: *ran quickly*

the conversation, or even comes to the conference with something to say—a question to ask, a problem to solve. Writers can jot their questions down prior to the conference (*as they think of them*). Or, they can put an asterisk in the margin beside a passage they wish to discuss—one they're unsure about, one that just isn't working. Then the structure of the conference goes something like this:

- The student raises a question or problem—or just talks about the writing.
- The teacher says, "Let's have a look," and reviews the writing, or part of it.
- The teacher offers a response, short modeling, questions, or a suggestion.
- The student responds with more comments or questions.
- Together, teacher and student plan a next step.

This list is not intended as a "recipe" for the perfect conference. I am only trying to show how natural the flow can be when the student kicks things off. When students enter the conference prepared, it saves time, gives the conference focus, and helps ensure that what you discuss will be useful to the writer right away.

. . . IS FLEXIBLE.

Your writers (probably) are not experts in structuring conferences, and so you are learning together, shaping the conference to suit yourselves. For example, you might frequently wish to hear the student's writing in his or her own voice, and so ask students to read their work to you. Sometimes, though, you might want the student to hear how the piece sounds—and so *you* need to be the reader. There's no need for a rule on this. Vary things to keep your conferences fluid and interesting.

If you work with older writers whose work may run three or four pages or more, you may not want (or need) to read the whole piece each time. You can scan, or better yet, have the student identify the section he or she most wants to focus on.

Don't assume students will know the kinds of questions that make a good basis for a conference. You may need to model this. Ask a volunteer to confer with you—about your own writing. And have a very specific question in mind—something like one of these:

- *Do you think my lead is working?*
- *Is my main idea clear? If you put it in your own words, what would you say?*
- *Do I have one main idea—or two?*
- *I think this is wordy—but I'm not sure what I could cut. Can you help?*
- *Can you help me think of a different title?*
- *Does this voice sound like me?*
- *When you read the description in this paragraph, what do you picture?*
- *Is this easy to read aloud? Try a paragraph and tell me what you think.*
- *Does this ending work?*

You won't ask *all* of these questions about one piece, of course, so you will need to model more than once. You can also list some possible questions to help writers get the idea. It isn't essential for writers to come to a conference with a question, but it is undeniably helpful. Ralph Fletcher puts it this way: "I can help you be a problem solver in your writing. But it will help me if you are a problem *finder*" (*Writing Workshop*, 2001, 57).

Sometimes the writer doesn't have a question so much as a situation:

- *I can't get started.*
- *I don't know what to write next.*
- *This topic just isn't working for me.*

You may be thinking, "I don't know what to do about these things, either—other than the usual pep talk: Come on! You can do it!" Guess what? That might be the answer. Think about it. *If* you have been modeling writing (this is important) and *if* your writers have been engaged in workshop for at least a short while, learning from one another, then you have every right to expect that they will problem solve for themselves—at least some of the time. It's OK to toss the ball back in their court, at least temporarily (*if* the issue is one you've already discussed in workshop):

- *What are some things a writer can do to get started? Remember when we talked about that—and I showed you a few things I try? Reading? Drawing? Making notes? Which one of those do you think could work for you?*
- *So this topic isn't working for you . . . How can you "bend" it just a little to fit your experience? Remember—a million people have written about Disneyland. Is there a place right here in this neighborhood that you'll still have good memories about 30 years from*

> ### Author's Note
> When you model good conference questions, do it in front of the whole class, not just one student. You will, however, need one willing volunteer to take on the role of coach.

now? Think about that, and I'll check back. If you think of more than one, make a list and we'll talk.

- *So—you're feeling stuck and not sure what to write next. That happens to writers a lot. Remember how I made a quick list of the main things I wanted to tell the reader—and then read over what I'd written so far? Could that work for you? Give it a try and we'll talk again.*

We don't want to leave writers floundering. But we do not want to jump in like super heroes every time there's a tiny bump in the road. The point is not to crank out one brilliant draft after another. The point is to create a classroom full of proficient, creative problem solvers. We do that, in part, by giving writers practice in articulating their own writing process: what's going well and what isn't.

We also want to push writers toward independence. A conference has two purposes, really. One is to allow the writer a chance for one-on-one coaching from a more experienced writer (the teacher). The other is to help the writer get better at teaching him- or herself. When we sense the second is happening, we need to get out of the way.

Sharing: Connecting with an Audience

Criterion-based feedback, then, tells you how your writing measures up, reader-based feedback tells you what it does to readers.

—Peter Elbow
Writing with Power, 1998, 241

On January 30, 2011, television journalist Rita Braver did a Sunday Profile (for CBS's *Sunday Morning*) on actor Geoffrey Rush. Rush had just been nominated for an Oscar for his performance as speech therapist Lionel Logue in *The King's Speech.*

In the course of the interview, it came out that the very successful Australian film actor was currently putting on his own make-up for nightly performances of Gogol's classic tale "The Diary of a Madman"—in a small Sydney theater. Why? "My L.A. agent actually defined it best, in a very, kind of brisk, effective way," Rush replied. "He said, 'Oh, I understand why you're doing that; sometimes you gotta go and sharpen the knife.'"

Sharing is like that—a chance to "sharpen the knife" by playing to a live audience. Writers—all writers—need this. Learning to share and respond well is part of learning to be a writer. Here are ten things you can do to make sharing a more successful (and enjoyable) experience for everyone:

10 Things You Can Do to Make Sharing More Successful

1. Help students develop good listening skills.

Writers learn to be listeners first by having someone listen *to them*. In conferences, we must model what we hope to see.

2. Think about logistics.

Writers sometimes share with the whole class—say, from an author's chair. This is a terrific way to celebrate a finished piece. It is somewhat less successful for pieces *in process*, for two reasons. First, once a writer has shared with the whole class, the motivation to return to the piece is diminished—unless the writing is also going to an outside audience, such as a newspaper. But if you and the other students are the *only* audience, then revising and reading aloud again feels like retelling a joke everyone has already heard. Second—and this is equally important—when the whole class is involved as an audience, there is often only time to hear from three or four writers.

On the other hand, if you divide your class into writing groups (sometimes called writing circles) of three or four students, everyone can share. And everyone can respond in a personal way. In addition, whatever feedback is given to the writer can be used to revise the draft before *everyone* gets to hear it.

Think about how groups are structured, as well. There are many ways to organize writing groups. Early on, you may allow students to group themselves so that they work with people they know and are comfortable with sharing their writing (teachers in workshops like this, too). But as time goes on, you'll want to change things up. You might group students by strength or interest. For example, if you put strong editors or designers in one group, you'll get one take on a piece of writing. Another group, the poets in the class, will have another take entirely—and such diversity creates intriguing conversations. Some of your students are analysts, some visionaries. As you learn more about their strengths, you may wish to group them to achieve a mix.

3. Define roles clearly.

We often assume that students know precisely how to interact during sharing time. Often this is far from the case. No one is sure who should read first or whether writers must read their whole piece. What kinds of responses should listeners give? Are they responsible for the quality of the writer's revision?

The writer's role. The writer needs to take control of the group *for the time he or she is reading aloud.* First, the writer should give the text the best interpretive reading possible, keeping in mind that it is fine to focus on just one portion. For example, it's fine to read just the lead or the first entry in a journal, or just the explanation of black holes, the description of the sunken ship, or the dialogue between two characters. Second, the writer should tell listeners exactly what to listen for:

- *Tell me if this dialogue sounds real.*
- *Tell me if you can picture the ship under water.*
- *Let me know if this lead would make you keep reading.*
- *Tell me what questions you still have about black holes.*
- *Does this journal entry help you understand what life was like during the Revolution?*

The responder's role. Responders often feel on the spot, wondering if the ultimate fate of the paper rests in their hands. It doesn't. Help them understand that revising is the *writer's* job. Listening thoughtfully, then offering supportive, sensitive, honest feedback is their job. It's not their responsibility to tell the writer what to do, but rather to offer feedback that helps *the writer* figure out what to do.

4. Model what *not* to do.

Ask a volunteer to read aloud a short piece of writing: the writer's own or one you provide (e.g., "The Redwoods"). Then illustrate the kinds of responses that do not work: staring at the ceiling, laughing inappropriately, making a negative remark ("How is it even *possible* to write with so little voice?"), or taking over the revision yourself: "Don't be so vague. Tell us what the Redwoods looked like, *where* you hiked, and what you saw. *Describe* your brother. Add some dialogue so we don't fall asleep." Ask the volunteer to let you know how this kind of prescriptive and/or negative response makes him or her feel. Then discuss more helpful ways of responding.

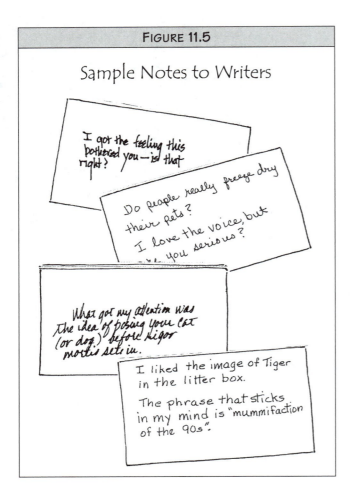

FIGURE 11.5

Sample Notes to Writers

I got the feeling this bothered you—is that right?

Do people really freeze dry their pets? I love the voice, but are you serious?

What got my attention was the idea of posing your cat (or dog) before rigor mortis sets in.

I liked the image of Tiger in the litter box.

The phrase that sticks in my mind is "mummifaction of the 90s".

5. Write notes.

This tip comes from a fine and creative teacher, Rosey Dorsey, who taught both of my children. Rosey suggests that writers brave enough to share their writing should receive something for their efforts, so she encourages each listener to write a brief comment on a 3 × 5 note card, all of which then go to the writer. In a group, writers can hold their cards until everyone has shared; then they all read responses together. Writers of all ages treasure written feedback and quickly learn what kinds of notes are most helpful and most appreciated (see Figure 11.5 for samples).

6. Encourage responders to "begin with *I*."

We can teach students to frame negative responses in positive terms by beginning with "I," as in "I felt . . ." or "I had difficulty with . . ." or "I didn't understand . . ." This shifts the focus from the flaws with the writing to the difficulties experienced by the reader. It's not only a gentler way of giving feedback, but it's more accurate. We cannot say, definitively, what is right or wrong about a piece of writing. We can only offer opinions. But we can say with great precision and accuracy how a piece of writing affects us, whether we want to hear more, whether we feel confused, whether the writing creates a strong image or impression or makes us gasp or shudder. See Figure 11.6 for some sample criticisms revised as "I comments."

> Suggestions for how to fix something may be valuable, but should be offered respectfully. Even if you're sure you see just how it ought to be changed, this [writing] belongs to the author, not you.
>
> —Ursula K. LeGuin
> *Steering the Craft*, 1998, 154

7. Participate.

Join a response group or writing circle as a responder—and share your own writing, too. Not every time—but now and then. Model how it looks when you ask for the kinds of responses you'd like; give the kinds you'd like your students to give you. (See Chapter 2 for an outstanding example of how middle school teacher Barbara Andrews models this for her students: *Learning to "Read" Each Other's Writing.*)

8. Don't apologize—and don't overreact.

So often we feel compelled to apologize for weaknesses, real or perceived, in our performance—especially when it comes to writing. "Remember," we say, "this is just a rough draft. I wrote this during a storm, and the computer was down. I had to use a crayon on butcher paper, and the neighbor's dog was howling." This says to the audience, "Never mind the writing; pay attention to *me*. I need approval." Most audiences will leap to the rescue—and forget all about the writing.

Don't create a distraction. When you share your writing aloud, just plunge in. If students fail to notice your courage, you can point it out—and tell them, "You do this, too. Be brave. Read your text with confidence so that the feedback you get will be more about your writing and less about you."

Also remind students not to overreact to feedback or suggestions. They should try to be as open as possible to comments, but should not feel obligated to take any suggestion that simply does not work for them. The writing belongs to the writer, always.

> Reading your words out loud is scary and many people invariably mumble or read too softly or too fast. We shrink from such blatant showing of our wares. But that is just what helps most.
>
> —Peter Elbow
> *Writing with Power*, 1998, 23

FIGURE 11.6

Converting Criticisms to "I" Comments

This criticism . . .	Becomes . . .
Your title doesn't go with your paper.	*I had a hard time connecting the title to the rest of your paper. I kept listening for something about the Redwoods.*
You are writing about two topics. That's really confusing.	*I wasn't sure if you were trying to explain why writing was important—or show how to be a good writer—or both.*
Your paper bounces all over the place!	*I couldn't tell for sure if you thought cartoons were too violent—or not. Could you talk about that?*
First you talk about one thing—then you switch to something else!	*I felt confused when you switched your three themes from fairness, <u>justice</u>, and courage to fairness, <u>respect</u>, and courage.*
You need some examples.	*I kept waiting for an example that would show how it felt to make a hard decision. I think that could help me understand what you're saying.*
You need to explain things more.	*I was so intrigued when you said gorillas are super intelligent. I would love to have some examples showing how we know that.*
Don't use terms you don't define.	*I waited for you to explain what an* accolade *is. I don't know that word.*
Your paper just stops like you fell off a cliff.	*After you said castles were "built for defense," I thought you might talk more about that. That comment made me curious, and I was surprised when that was your last sentence.*
You need quotations to back up your main points.	*I kept listening for a quotation that would help me remember how or when Atticus was brave.*

9. Make it real—by sharing what you picture, how you feel.

Many teachers feel more comfortable with a rule that says, "Each responder will make one positive comment followed by a suggestion." This can become very formulaic—and it can backfire, too: First, say something nice to get the writer's guard down; then slam her with the necessary criticism to ensure improvement.

Our responses to writing do not have to be couched in positives and negatives unless we choose to do that. And why would we? Our first impression is more likely to center on where the writing takes us mentally or emotionally as we listen.

A student said one day in response to a piece I'd written on a very tense, confrontational family Thanksgiving, "Your family seems very argumentative. *Very.* When you talked about staring into the candlelight reflecting off your mother's blue glass plates, I thought you were trying to escape. I used to do that." I had never before thought of myself as "escaping," but of course that is precisely what I was doing.

Even very young children can listen and look for one colorful word or the most exciting sentence or a line that has interesting sounds or the scariest phrase.

—Marjorie Frank
If You're Trying to Teach Kids How to Write . . . You've Gotta Have This Book!
1995, 140

Sharing: Connecting with an Audience

This very honest, spontaneous response was much more revealing to me than if the student had said, "I loved your vivid description of the candlelight reflecting on the plates." A compliment makes us feel good for a moment; an insight keeps us thinking for hours—sometimes forever.

10. Keep it snappy.

Sharing and responding is, by nature, a reflective activity, and we must respect that. On the other hand, allowing too much time for sharing can make students feel pressured to say more than they have to say, and soon the conversation drifts to unrelated topics. Try this (adjusting if the timing does not work for you):

Put students into groups of four. Let students know that they need to stay focused and make comments that are to the point. Ask them to decide who will go first, second, and third. Then give each student about 3 minutes to read his or her work. Allow responders about 2 minutes to give a focused, clear, concise response to each reader's piece, either orally or on note cards. The whole process will take under 20 minutes—and *everyone* will get to speak.

Debriefing

Once everyone has had a chance to share, take five minutes to debrief the process. Ask writers,

- *Who got a response that was really helpful today? What was it?*
- *How many of you have a strong sense right now of how you will go about revising your work?*
- *Did anyone get a response you plan to override—because you feel you know better?*
- *Was there anything else you would have found helpful?*
- *Will you know next time how to ask for the feedback you personally need?*

When writers take charge and ask for the feedback they need most, and when responders listen and offer heartfelt comments, response groups can make a world of difference.

Communicating with Parents or Other Caregivers

Parents are used to letter grades and—perhaps—heavily corrected copy. Suddenly, here you are with scores, continuums, writing guides, strengths and weaknesses, and the rest. How do you explain it all?

> **Author's Note**
>
> I have done a number of after-school sessions for parents through the years. They have all been extraordinarily well attended. The most common comment I receive from parents is, "I wish we'd had this [meaning the traits] when I was in school."

Perhaps the best way, if you have the luxury of a little time, is an after-school session in which you summarize the six traits and even have parents attempt to score a paper or two. You might also ask them to write a short paragraph and assess their own writing—not with *numbers*, but simply by identifying the traits they feel are strongest in their writing, and those they find challenging. Nothing brings the traits so vividly into focus as looking at your own work! Parents are good at this, enjoy it, and often remark that they have never before been asked to consider *any* aspect of their writing other than conventions.

Also invite family members to talk about how their own writing was assessed when they were in school, and the comments—helpful or not so helpful—that they recall. How many of them remember:

- One-on-one conferences with teachers?
- Comments (oral or written) that gave them confidence or encouraged them to write more?
- Grades that came as a surprise?
- Grades that did not match their own expectations?
- Heavily corrected copy?
- Teachers who made expectations in writing crystal clear?
- Teachers who did not make expectations clear—forcing students to guess?

Use their responses to these or similar questions as a basis for comparing their experiences with your writing instruction in a classroom that features traits, workshop, and process, all working together.

Parents who attend a short workshop on the traits almost always ask, "What can I do at home to help my child become a stronger writer?" See Figure 11.7 for a list of suggestions you can share with them. Please revise or expand this list to suit your needs.

> **Author's Note**
>
> If you share writing guides with parents (and I hope you do), I recommend sharing the student version. It is a little easier to navigate and parents will be able to use that guide with their children in reviewing work at home, if they wish to do so. With experience, some parents may want to help coach other students in your class.

FIGURE 11.7

Tips for Parents and Guardians

You may be wondering what you can do at home to help your child become a stronger writer. There are many things, actually. Here are a few suggestions.

1. Read to your child.

When you read aloud to your child, you do many things: show that books are exciting and enjoyable to share, expand your child's vocabulary and "sentence sense," and help him or her to understand why writing matters—as a way of communicating to readers. When you read, put all the passion you can into it. Have fun! If your child is beyond primary age, you may think he or she is too old for read-alouds. On the contrary. Even adults love being read to—and benefit from hearing wonderful words read by someone who is engaged and enthusiastic.

2. Encourage your child to read to you.

Students who read aloud (from books or other sources) learn to read for meaning. They also develop an ear for voice and fluency—two vital qualities of strong writing. A child who reads with expression learns to write with expression, too.

> NOTE: When we think of reading aloud, we usually think of books first. But there are countless other options: blogs, newspapers, film or book reviews, product reviews, advertisements, letters, emails — and on and on. We want students to read aloud from a variety of genres because each one has its own purpose and voice.

3. Explore topics together.

Many students have difficulty coming up with topics to write about. You can help. Talk with your child about experiences and interests you have shared. What do you like to do together? Have you overcome a frightening, sad, or challenging experience? Talk it through. Have you laughed together about something? Visited an interesting place? Talk about your memories. Share family stories your child may have forgotten or may not know, including stories of his or her own childhood (and yours). Families make a great resource for writing topics. A family photo album or scrapbook (if you keep one) can be a good place to begin. Perhaps a sibling, aunt or uncle, or grandparent has stories to share. Other general topic areas include: places or people you remember, hobbies, sports, pets, school experiences, work, friends, interesting people, holiday traditions, moving, chores, favorite or least favorite foods.

FIGURE 11.7 *(continued)*

Tips for Parents and Guardians

4. Be a listener.

Ask your child to share his or her writing—even if it is unfinished. Don't feel that you have to be a grammarian, teacher, or coach. Relax. Don't worry about making corrections. Don't even ask to *see* the paper. Just curl up on the couch and listen. Listen as you would to a cherished letter from a friend you had not seen in a long while. Respond to the content from your heart. Tell the student what you hear; what you love; what you picture in your mind; what you feel, think of, or remember; and what makes an impression on you. Ask questions. Be curious. Tell the writer what you'd like to hear more of. Be your writer's number one fan.

5. Write.

Let your child see you write—a note to a friend, a thank-you letter, an invitation, a blog or email, a résumé or job application letter, an evaluation or report, a letter to the editor, a recipe, a list. Each time you write, even if it's only a line or two, you show your child that writing is an important life skill and that it has many purposes.

6. Ask your child to write.

Are you planning a family get-together? Are you putting together an album or scrapbook? Are you sending greeting cards—by mail or electronically? Writing an online review? Let your child write (or help you write) captions, letters, notes, explanations, product assessments, or invitations. If he or she is very young, you can do some of the writing or keyboarding as your child comes up with ideas. When you do this, the child is still doing the *thinking* part of the writing—the most important part.

7. Let your child be your teacher.

Writers and editors learn by teaching. So let your child be your teacher. Ask him or her to coach you on the "right" voice for business correspondence, or help you to rewrite a sentence to make it shorter or more clear. Ask for help coming up with the right word, the best way to begin a letter, a correct spelling, or a just-right ending. If you're seeking employment, an older child may be able to proof your résumé or cover letter. If you're doing a PowerPoint presentation, he or she might provide tips on slides or transitions. If you're writing a speech or giving a presentation, perform it for your child first—get his or her feedback. You'll find that one of the best things you can do is to seek your child's help. Writing coaches learn quickly.

8. See your child as a writer.

Nothing you can do has more power and impact than believing in your child's ability to write. If possible, make the tools of writing available—a dictionary or handbook, journal, special pen, books to read. Take every opportunity you can to encourage your child and to say to him or her, in your own words, "You are a writer."

"Waters of Death" (Figure 11.2)

I loved your opening: "As soon as we left the stables, I knew it wouldn't be a good day for horseback riding." I immediately had a wonderful sense of anticipation, wondering what was going to go wrong. You pull the reader right in when you set a story up like that. You did a terrific job of getting us relaxed in the first paragraph—right before the trouble hits in paragraph 2. Your title is perfect. It seems to echo your mixed feelings of playfulness—plus a little bit of fear and anxiety. A question: Would you go again? Or was that experience enough? I couldn't quite tell how you felt at the end, and thought you might add just a sentence or two to make that clear. I loved that image of Buddy just munching grass "like nothing had ever happened." Your humor is very understated. I like that!

"The Bathroom" (Figure 11.3)

It intrigued me that your opening and ending were identical. You seemed to be saying, "This is how I got into this mess!" My favorite part was the image of you standing nonchalantly looking at the California map when your mom came rushing out to tell you the restroom was "worse than your room!" And you had a comical response. That dialogue works very well. It also works well when your mom tries to stop you with one look—but of course "when you gotta go you gotta go!" Your description of the restroom is very vivid—but I was surprised that you said things were coated with "dust." I would imagine a word like "grime" or "filth." I also pictured—even though you didn't say this—used towels and tissue everywhere. Am I using too much imagination here? Your pacing, beginning with paragraph 3, is very strong. The story clips right along. Before that, I had a sense you were searching for the true beginning. I'd love for you to read this again and just ask yourself, "Where does this really start?" I also sense—and I could be wrong—just a little hesitation. I think if you would "let go," your voice would explode from the page. You're a natural comic. Let it happen.

STUDY GROUP

Interactive Questions and Activities

1. **Discussion.** Put a check by each of the following with which you agree. Then discuss your responses with your group.

___ It is important to comment on every piece of student writing.

___ Negative comments can be very damaging to writers.

___ Comments, if thorough enough, can replace scores or grades.

___ Rubrics or writing guides prevent teachers from saying what they really think or feel about a piece of writing.

___ Rubrics and comments are both important and complement each other.

___ Conferences are essential to the teaching of writing.

___ It is important to confer with every writer about every *major* piece of writing.

___ What the student says in a conference is more important than what the teacher says.

___ Students gain valuable feedback through participation in response groups.

___ The configuration of response groups should change frequently to give students feedback from a number of different people.

___ A writer who disagrees strongly with feedback, whether from a conference or a response group, has every right to resist making changes in his or her writing.

2. **Activity and Discussion.** What is the most positive or negative comment you have ever received on your own writing? How did it influence you? Can you recall any positive or negative comments you have given to student writers? Do you think the student responded as you hoped he or she would? Would you write something different now?

3. **Activity and Discussion.** With your group, discuss your responses to "Waters of Death" or "The Bathroom" (or to any other piece of student writing on which you have written comments). Did you see the writing in the same way? How helpful is it to hear the comments of other teachers?

4. **Discussion.** If you are teaching now, do you confer with your writers? Talk about this with your group. Some specific questions you might address: How often do you confer with students? How long do your conferences typically run? Do you think it's realistic to make them shorter without diminishing their effectiveness? Who kicks off the conference—you or the student?

5. **Activity and Discussion.** (Try this OR Activity 6.) Bring in short samples of your own writing and practice conferring with your colleagues. Work with just one partner, and trade off roles so that each person has a chance to receive some coaching. As the "student," initiate the conference with one legitimate question or concern you have about your writing. As the "teacher," respond as you would with any student in your classroom, but talk "writer to writer." Don't assess the writing in any way. Keep track of *approximately* how long your conferences run. Does the time surprise you? Debrief your responses. Talk about what was especially helpful to each of you as a writer. What do you learn from this experience that you could use with writers in your classroom?

6. **Activity and Discussion.** Divide your larger study group into writing circles of 3 or 4. (If you have fewer than 7 people in your group, just remain in one circle.) Within each group, take turns sharing your writing while others act as a response group for you. Ask them to write their comments on 3 × 5 cards, which will be handed to you after you read. Talk about the most helpful responses you receive. Is this a response approach you might try with your own writers?

Coming Up . . .

Chapter 12 offers suggestions for maximizing the effectiveness of classroom or large-scale writing assessment.

> There were edits on my paper regarding grammar and syntax, which is the most I would have expected of any teacher. But Mrs. Morgan had also typed page-by-page remarks on my dialogue use, plot, and historical facts that I needed to keep in mind. I don't remember what score I got, much less if I even received one. I was young and a good grade was still important to me. But my concern for them decreased significantly after that. There was someone who enjoyed reading what I wrote as much as I enjoyed writing it. That meant the most to me, and no score or grade could ever give me a similar feeling. I was writing for the reader. And I was writing for myself. To me, writing isn't the means to a happy ending of a good grade. Writing is the end in itself.
>
> —Simona Patange, student writer

ASSESSING
Our Students Well

I've often wondered who in our national, state, or local government keeps an eye on the type of learner we are trying to develop in our public schools. Until we can begin to agree on what basics make up this ideal learner, it will be difficult to consider the best assessment approaches to tell us if our schools are succeeding.

DONALD H. GRAVES
Testing Is Not Teaching, 2002, 23

There is an epidemic of teaching to the test—and anyone who denies this is simply not facing reality.

THOMAS NEWKIRK
Holding On to Good Ideas in a Time of Bad Ones, 2009, 4

The key assessment question comes down to this . . . Do I know the difference between successful and unsuccessful performance and can I convey that difference in meaningful terms to my students?

RICK STIGGINS
Student-Involved Classroom Assessment, 2001, 196

When my son was in third grade, he taught me something important about interpreting assessment results. He had taken a standardized reading test, and when I opened the results sent home to parents, the world seemed to spin away. I grasped the kitchen counter, staring at the paper, knowing there had to be a mistake. My son was in the third percentile. Not *thirty-third*. Third. I was stunned, speechless—and frantic. Any minute now, I thought, the phone will ring. Someone from the school will say, "We saw the results. You must be devastated, but not to worry. We're on it." They never phoned, of course. So I phoned them. They hadn't noticed the scores and (even more disarming) didn't seem overly concerned—but they did promise to work with Michael.

I met with a reading specialist who agreed to help. For weeks we were deluged with little fat-cat-sat-flat-on-the-mat sorts of books, which we dutifully read. I was committed to turning this situation around. We did phonics and flash cards, as recommended, and I labeled everything in the house from COUNTER to LAMP to SINK. We didn't just count on the fat cat, either. We read every book I could get my hands on—selections from Arnold Lobel, Judy Blume, Mem Fox, Roald Dahl, William Steig, and countless others. When we read Gary Paulsen's *Harris and Me*, Michael didn't want me to stop. "Keep going!" he urged, holding his sides, tears of laughter squirting from his eyes. I cheerfully agreed, and we stayed up to read the whole book in one night. Surely this was helping.

The next spring, new scores were sent out. I bit my lip, prayed, and ripped open the envelope, peeking through one eye. He was at the *sixty-eighth percentile*. A score that would have dismayed many a parent had me shouting from the rooftops. I cheered! I danced! We had done it! Then, as I was making dinner, Michael tore in from outside—baseball in one hand, glove on the other, as always. "Mom!" he shouted out of the blue, "you know that reading test we worried about? I did something different this year."

Something clutched inside me as I asked him what was different. "I read the questions," was his cheery reply. Clouds parted. But of course, I had to know—"Why did you not read the questions before?" I asked. His reply was logical enough: "There wasn't time," he said, shaking his head. "I sat by Curtis, and you know how fast he is. I could barely keep up just marking all the letter A's. I didn't even get to all the questions!" So there you have it: how to achieve the lowest score possible. But the lesson was clear: Behind every score or grade is a face—and a story.

Good assessment, whether at state or classroom level, does not just happen. It takes planning. Tests are not inherently good, nor is assessment inherently beneficial, meaningful, or even helpful. The purpose of this chapter is to consider ways of making both large-scale and classroom writing assessment the very best they can be.

Making Large-Scale Writing Assessment All It Can Be

We often expect assessment, especially large-scale assessment, to magically improve performance, when the reality is that only instruction can do that. If assessment alone were the key, we would need only to weigh ourselves to lose weight. Would that it were so.

Large-scale writing assessment cannot replace instruction. But when it is carefully designed, it can *reflect* instruction—and right now, that isn't happening. We should not, in the twenty-first century, be "teaching to the writing test" any longer. We know too much about teaching writing well. We must turn the current situation around, using what we know to create a vision of success, then designing an assessment that shapes itself to that vision. Here are twelve steps for making that happen.

STEP 1: HAVE A CLEAR PURPOSE.

Why are we assessing writers? What do we hope to learn? Until this is crystal clear in our minds, we cannot make decisions about prompts, procedures, use of data—anything. It all begins here. We must consider, for example, whether we want to assess first-draft writing or revised writing, whether we care about genre, whether content matters as much as writing skill per se, and above all, whether we care about measuring the impact of writing process or just want a snapshot of performance under controlled conditions.

Most large-scale writing assessment involves first drafts only, and that is appropriate if the ability to write "on demand" is precisely what we wish to assess. There are times in life, in college or on the job, when it is necessary to write quickly, and without much preparation. College essay exams are a form of on-demand writing, for example. In addition, an employer may request a summary, a quick evaluation, a press release, or a response letter—any of which may need to be completed within minutes. It is reasonable therefore to measure students' readiness to meet the requirements of these situations.

We want to be careful, though, not to generalize, imagining that on-demand writing is the approach we should *always* use. After all, many situations call for writing over time, writing that is carefully planned and revised virtually up to the moment of publication. Examples of such writing include books, reports, drama, poetry, scripts, speeches, legal arguments, contracts, and more.

We must also take care not to assess in one way (through on-demand writing), and then interpret scores as if we had assessed *another way*—as if students had carefully planned, drafted, revised, and edited, when in fact nothing approaching true process has occurred. This happens more frequently than we might like to think, and it is a major flaw in our large-scale assessment approach.

Note that the Common Core Standards (in Standard 10) do distinguish between these two broad purposes for writing, requiring that students be able to—

10. Write routinely over extended time frames (time for research, reflection, and revision) and shorter time frames (a single sitting or a day or two) for a range of tasks, purposes, and audiences.
(http://www.corestandards.org) © 2010. National Governors Association Center for Best Practices and Council of Chief State School Officers. All rights reserved.

In other words, sometimes students must know how to self-assess and revise—the very strategies that trait-based instruction emphasizes above all else. But they must also be prepared to write spontaneously, with little or no preparation or opportunity for revision.

Until *we* have internalized this distinction, we cannot hope to assess with a clear purpose, and we cannot hope to create large-scale writing assessments that reflect true commitment to writing process. But—here's a question: *Can* we assess "writing over extended time frames" on a large-scale basis? Is that even an option? Or can we *only* do that in the classroom? See Step 2 for an innovative suggestion.

STEP 2: DESIGN AN ASSESSMENT TO MATCH OUR VISION OF SUCCESS.

Donald Graves suggests (in *Testing Is Not Teaching*) that we can reformat our writing assessment procedures to more closely align with our classroom vision of writing success—at least when assessing at the state, district, or building level. His inspired proposal (2002, 46) calls for students to explore topics throughout the year, settle on five

Currently, we are testing what we value, quick thinking. But what about long thinking? Can we discern thinkers like Thomas Jefferson, Albert Einstein, and Charles Darwin, who were self-professed long, slow thinkers? Can we identify and encourage the children who can formulate a question, find the information, design the evaluation, and know whether they have answered the original question?

—Donald H. Graves
Testing Is Not Teaching, 2002, 34

or six on which they feel qualified to write, then choose two final topics in conference with the teacher. Students would write on *both* topics, and teachers would be involved as assessors (although external assessors might score some papers to validate ratings).

Such an approach is dramatically different from anything that occurs in large-scale testing currently—to my knowledge. It is well worth considering as it offers numerous benefits:

- By including prewriting and other planning, drafting, research, sharing, revision, editing, and possibly document design, such an approach would help us answer the question, "Is process-based instruction working the way we would like it to?"
- Students would be engaged in topic selection over a long period of time; this would allow them to explore and think deeply about their choices.
- Students would have a chance to write in more than one genre, thereby expanding what we learn about their skills.
- Two pieces of writing would provide a more reliable picture of performance—not as telling as a notebook or portfolio, by any means, but still better than a single sample.
- The writing samples assessed would be *revised* writing—not just rough drafts—and so would almost certainly be more representative of students' true writing skills.
- Writing produced under such circumstances would be more likely to reflect deep thinking.

Author's Note

So many of the procedures surrounding large-scale writing assessment stem from a fear that students will somehow "cheat" by bringing text from home or copying text online. A *very* few *might* do that. But—let's take the chance. What we lose by isolating students from the world, having them effectively quarantined while they write, is so much greater than the risk we take by opening that world to them, and allowing them to draw from it as real world writers do. It's time to be less afraid, more inventive, and more open to learning how well our instruction is working.

Step 3: Match the Assessment Approach to the Task.

Most large-scale writing assessment today involves *direct assessment,* a form of performance assessment that requires students to actually write. *Indirect assessment* is, as its name implies, a somewhat more roundabout way of getting at *writing-related skills,* through fill-in or multiple choice questions, such as the examples shown in Figure 12.1.

Although indirect assessment of writing is rare these days, it is still used as a shortcut in instances where assessors want to save time and expense. The rationale given is that indirect assessment will be a good predictor of performance on direct writing assessment. This is not necessarily true. Indirect assessment measures knowledge of writing conventions and practice. This is not the same thing at all as writing ability. Knowing how many tablespoons are in a cup won't make me a chef.

Even when it is no longer used, indirect assessment's inherent emphasis on conventions (and speed) continues to influence many *direct* tests of writing. Because it is far easier to write multiple choice test items about grammar and punctuation than about concepts like voice and organization, indirect assessments have traditionally tended to favor conventions. And this over-weighting still affects the way some rubrics or writing guides are constructed—and the way many writing samples are scored.

What is more, assessors have searched for years for ways of quantifying writing in order to make scoring fast and simple: counting sentences, counting words within sentences, and so on—as

Figure 12.1

Sample Multiple-Choice Question

Which of the following is not a complete sentence?

1. As of February 1, his projection seemed accurate.
2. How accurate could that February 1 projection be?
3. Accurate: That was the word for the February 1 projection.
4. An accurate projection, no doubt, as of February 1.*
5. All of the above are complete sentences.

if such factors have *anything* to do with writing quality. In his brilliant book *Holding On to Good Ideas in a Time of Bad Ones*, Thomas Newkirk argues that "graphite-based assessment cannot touch some of the more important qualities we strive for in education, and even when human readers must be used, writing has to be bent out of recognition to be tested." He adds that "The new technological tools to 'rate' writing without human readers are testaments to how far we have advanced toward mechanized literacy" (2009, 4).

We must beware of shortcuts. If we seriously do not wish to invest the considerable time and effort required to read students' writing with care and concentration, we should leave it to those who do that best: classroom teachers.

Forms of Direct Assessment

Of the three most frequently used scoring methods for direct assessment, *analytical scoring* (of which the six-trait model is one example) has become the most popular because, most assessors agree, it provides the richest information for the time invested—and because it's easy to teach from. To best appreciate the advantages of this approach, it is worth looking at it in comparison with two other scoring methods: *holistic* and *primary trait*.

Holistic Assessment

Holistic assessment is based on the premise that the whole is more than the sum of its parts and that the most valid assessment of writing will consider how all components—ideas, mechanics, voice, and so forth—work in harmony to achieve an overall effect. See Figure 12.2 for an example of a holistic scoring scale.

As you can see, a holistic scale implies, by the way it is constructed, that strengths or problems move up or down the scale *together*. Sometimes they do. But many writers (notably beginning writers or those learning a second language) show great strength in one area—such as ideas or voice—while sentence fluency or conventions are less developed. The holistic scale makes no allowances for such differences, and in assigning a score, the rater must choose whether to weight the apparent strengths or the problems. Obviously, this makes "compromise" scores ("On the whole, it's a 3") difficult to interpret later. It is also more difficult to teach from a holistic scale because the traits are not defined in detail. All the same, because of its appealing simplicity, holistic scoring remains popular for some large-scale assessments. Many districts choose it, thinking (erroneously) that scoring holistically will be far faster than scoring analytically. They overlook the fact that most of a rater's time is spent reading the paper—and this must occur regardless of the scoring method.

Primary-Trait Assessment

Primary-trait assessment is based on the premise that in any piece of writing, there's a primary—most important—trait that determines the success of that writing. In a political speech, it might be voice; in a set of directions, organization; in a proposal, ideas—and so on.

Primary-trait assessment has never really caught on in large-scale state or district writing assessments because many educators feel that it is too limited in scope to provide all the feedback they want. On the other hand, it can be useful in the classroom. For instance, if students are learning to write good business letters, the teacher might ask them to focus on word choice or format. The same effect can be achieved, however, simply by weighting traits within an analytical model.

FIGURE 12.2

Focused Holistic Scale

Holistic Six-Trait Scale*

Strengths Outweigh Problems at the 4 to 6 Level

Problems Outweigh Strengths at the 1 to 3 Level

6

- Clear, focused main idea enriched with telling, unusual details
- Inviting lead, satisfying conclusion, reader never feels lost
- Irresistible voice that asks to be shared
- Vivid, memorable, precise words—no wasted words
- Clear, fluent sentences that make expressive reading easy
- Only minimal touch-ups needed prior to publication

5

- Clear, focused main idea with striking details
- Strong lead and conclusion, structure that guides the reader
- Individual, confident voice speaks to readers
- Accurate, well-chosen words that make meaning clear
- Clear, fluent sentences that make expressive reading possible
- Very light editing needed prior to publication

4

- Clear main idea, supported by details (description, examples, etc.)
- Functional lead and conclusion, reader can follow story/discussion
- Moments of strong voice speak to readers
- Functional, clear language carries general message
- Clear sentences that can be read without difficulty
- A good once-over needed prior to publication

3

- Main idea can be inferred—a broad, unexpanded overview
- Some details/elements could be relocated—lead and conclusion are present, structure may be formulaic
- Voice comes and goes—or not always a good fit with audience
- Marked by tired, overused words, phrases—OR overwritten
- Limited variety in sentence length, structure
- Thorough editing needed prior to publication

2

- Reader must guess at main idea—few details or just a list
- Hard to follow, lead and/or conclusion missing
- Distant voice—writing to get it done
- Filled with tired, overused language—OR overwritten, wordy
- Problems with repetitive, awkward, or run-on sentences
- Line-by-line editing needed prior to publication

1

- No main idea yet—random collection of thoughts
- Reader consistently goes back—no apparent link thought to thought
- Hard to "hear" the writer in the text
- Word choice confusing, general, repetitive, vague, or incorrect
- Hard to tell where sentences begin or end—many problems
- Word-by-word editing needed prior to publication

*Please note that a perfect match is not necessary. Choose the set of descriptors that best fits a given writing sample.

Analytical Assessment

Because of its strong, natural link to revision, analytical assessment has become far and away the most preferred form of direct writing assessment. Analytical scoring takes a holistic view of writing as well, but it also assumes that for *instructional* purposes, we need to not only describe individual features very thoroughly, but actually get inside and analyze each one. Instead of saying, "Get organized," we need to take the trait of organization apart and show students what's inside: strong lead, thoughtful transitions, logical and interesting order, good pacing, occasional surprises, a satisfying conclusion. This kind of descriptive analysis makes two things happen: (1) it allows us to teach a trait such as organization effectively because we know what we're teaching, and (2) when we give a high score in organization, it has meaning because it's backed with descriptive language.

STEP 4: DESIGN RUBRICS OR WRITING GUIDES WITH CARE.

The scoring criteria should be authentic, with points awarded or taken off for essential successes and errors, not for what is easy to count or observe.

—Grant Wiggins
"Creating Tests Worth Taking,"
1992, 27

This means several things: (1) assessing what matters, (2) backing scores with examples to show how performance would look at various levels, and (3) avoiding language that labels either performances or writers.

In *Reflections on Assessment*, Kathleen and James Strickland caution that "many rubrics we use are invalid because we don't score what's important in the real-world application of the content being assessed. Instead we design rubrics to assess what's easiest to describe rather than what really matters" (1998, 81).

Grant Wiggins encourages us to focus on "the most salient characteristics" of performance—those things, in other words, that would truly cause us to score a performance higher or lower, such as clarity of ideas or organization—versus superficial qualities such as neatness or length. He also suggests linking criteria to "wider-world" expectations. In other words, we need to ask, *Does what we are teaching and emphasizing lead to successful performance in a broader educational sense—out there in the competitive real world?*

Wiggins (1992, 30) also reminds us that to the extent possible, "scoring criteria should rely on descriptive language, not on evaluative and/or comparative language such as 'excellent' or 'fair.'" Such words are impossible to define from rater to rater and they promote inconsistencies in scoring. In addition, it's sometimes tempting to use such words as labels; doing this causes us to forget that it is the performance—not the writer—we should be describing.

Most important, descriptors such as *excellent* or *poor* indicate a fundamental misunderstanding of how writing works. It does not start out being *poor* and suddenly become *good*. It begins with a small idea, like the planting of a seed, then expands, refocuses, and reshapes itself as the writer's understanding of the topic grows. A score of 1 should not say, "This is *poor* writing—you failed," but rather,

"You got some first thoughts on paper. Now let's see what this early idea might grow into."

How do you distinguish between the good rubrics—and the not-so-good ones? One excellent way to determine whether a scoring guide is well written is to ask, *Could the most important evaluator—the writer—use this language to self-assess and improve his or her performance?* At present, many writing guides are written to simplify assessment for the rater. This should not be our priority. Writing guides should be designed to serve students first, raters second. See Figure 12.3 for some guidelines that will help you recognize good criteria, whether they appear in a scoring guide or any other format.

STEP 5: BE THOUGHTFUL ABOUT PROMPTS.

Although we don't want to use "It was the prompt!" as an automatic excuse for less than stellar performances, prompts are frequently troublesome—for any or all of the following reasons:

- Students don't understand the prompt.
- It isn't appealing or motivating to writers.
- The prompt is experientially biased: *Write about your best memory with your family.*
- The prompt is linguistically biased: *Explain how ecology affects all of us.*
- It's too long, complex, and prescriptive, leaving no room for personal thought.
- It has an implied "right" answer: *Should more women serve as corporate CEOs?*
- The prompt is written in a way that confusingly blends genres: *Think of your best adventure. Explain why it was the best.* (It's unclear whether the prompt is requesting a story or explanation.)

FIGURE 12.3

Qualities of Well-Written Criteria

Well-written criteria for assessing writing are . . .

- **Clear**—easy to understand and apply
- **Complete**—supported by examples that illustrate strong and weak performance (e.g., "Redwoods" and "Mouse Alert")
- **Focused on what matters, not trivia**—*organization* versus *margin size*
- **Respectful and reflective of how writing works**—from *beginning levels* . . . through *developing* . . . to *strong*
- **Worded in a positive manner**—free from demeaning labels such as "fair" or "poor," and worded to help students think about themselves and their work in positive terms
- **Descriptive**—making it easy to identify strengths
- **Qualitative, not quantitative**—free from requirements that call for specific numbers of features: e.g., *three details*, or *no more than four errors*
- **Easy to teach from**—written in language students can easily use in revising their writing
- **Generalizable across many tasks**—so it isn't necessary to invent brand-new criteria for *every* assignment
- **Flexible**—open to interpretation and the revision demanded by new thinking

© 2012. Vicki Spandel

Often the problem isn't evident until the results come in. A few years ago, young writers in Hawaii were asked to imagine they were a pair of shoes, and to write about one exciting adventure they had had with their owner. Thanks to Hawaii's incredible climate, many children do not wear shoes every day. Paper after paper read, more or less, like this: "I live on a shelf and never get to go anywhere."

Another state assessment required third graders to compare two animals of their choice. Developers wanted writers to (1) create an expository piece (versus narrative), and (2) show that they could make comparisons in writing. They apparently did not think about how difficult it can be to write confidently or expansively on such a topic *completely from your own experience.*

Many students spent most of their allotted writing time trying to choose which animals they might write about. One writer sagely settled for the familiar cat and dog, but quickly ran out of things to say, and by page 2, his essay began to sound like this:

When they really want to be good they really want to be good when they really want to be. When they really want to be good when they are doing it they want to be good. When they really want to be good they really want to be.

It is almost impossible to imagine how punchy one becomes after reading several pages of this. But I have to hand it to this writer. He tried. He filled four pages. (Writers had been given four-page booklets, and though they were not told to fill them, many assumed they *should*.)

A paper like this should not be scored, of course, but maybe it teaches us a thing or two about good assessment: The prompt must make sense to the writer. We should never make length a trait, either directly or implicitly (by handing out long booklets). And if possible, we should allow our writers—particularly our younger writers—some reflection, reading, and discussion time to prepare for topics that demand knowledge and deep thought. Other prompts that looked good on paper, but yielded disappointing (sometimes mind-numbing) results:

- *Explain what it takes to be a good leader.* (Responses were vague, general, and predictable.)
- *Describe your favorite dinner.* (The expressions on the faces of the raters told it all.)
- *Write a persuasive letter to the principal arguing for or against school uniforms.* (As this was not a real situation, students did not take it seriously—and responses were profoundly voiceless.)
- *You wake up one morning and you've turned into Jello.* (Many students detest writing fantasy—and wrote notes to tell us so. On the plus side, *that* writing had voice.)

Some Better Options

In all fairness to prompt writers everywhere (I have been one myself and have written my share of losers), let me say at the outset that writing good prompts is very hard. There are countless variables: age, experience, appeal to both sexes, freedom from bias, genre, understandable language, and so on. By the time a prompt is poked and prodded into something that "appeals to everyone," it no longer appeals to anyone.

Still, some assigned prompts are far superior to others. See Figure 12.4 for a list of "better than average" prompts. I would call them *functional*. None of them will cause students to cry out, "Quick! A pen!" Yet each has potential to elicit strong writing. Notice the **boldfaced print** that offers students a clue about the *kind* of writing asked for. (One legitimate reason for imposing a prompt is to guide the writer into a particular genre—expository, persuasive, narrative.)

Most prompts are overwritten. My friend and colleague Barry Lane (*The Reviser's Toolbox*,1999, 56) gets around this problem with a single-word or phrase approach. See Figure 12.5 for a brief list of his favorites. The picture prompt (an excellent option) goes even further. If you have ever asked your students to write in response to *The Mysteries of Harris Burdick* (Van Allsburg, 1996), for example, you know how powerful and provocative a picture can be. Picture prompts stimulate thought and invite voice. Regardless of the approach you take, writing good prompts is a challenge, however. See Figure 12.6 for a few rules of the road to keep in mind.

FIGURE 12.4

A Few Good Prompts

1. Think of something you own that means a lot to you that was NOT purchased in a store. **Explain** why it is important to you—**OR, write a story** connected to this object.

2. Can very young and very old people be friends? Use your experience and judgment to **write a convincing paper** that answers this question for your reader.

3. Some people think pets are essential to happiness. Others think they are mostly a nuisance. Which side are you on? **Write an essay** that would **convince readers** to agree with you.

4. Think of a place so important to you that you would like to return to it many times. **Describe it** so clearly a reader can see, hear, and feel what it is like to be there.

5. Imagine it is ten years in the future. **Write any report** you think might appear on the front page of a major newspaper.

6. Think of a story (funny, sad, frightening, or embarrassing) that you might still enjoy telling to friends when you are older. **Write your story** as if it will be published in a magazine.

7. Think of a teacher (friend, family member) you will never forget. **Tell one story** that comes to mind when you think of what makes this person unforgettable.

8. Some people feel that video games and other electronic media have decreased our ability to concentrate and learn. Do you agree—or not? **Write a convincing paper** based on your experiences and observations.

9. Imagine you are a historian living 100 years in the future. You are **writing a description** of planet Earth in the year 20__. Think carefully about what you will say because your writing will be published in a science **textbook.**

10. What is it like to be in your place in your family—youngest child, oldest, middle, only, twin, or whatever? **Write a persuasive essay** that defends your position as best, worst, or just OK.

11. What might be the title and subject of the best-selling fiction or nonfiction book twenty years from now? **Write copy** that could be used on a **book jacket** to **help sell** the book.

12. The year is 2050. You have been asked to **write an updated version of the story** "Goldilocks and the Three Bears" [or substitute any story or fable]. Make sure your story contains details that make it authentic for the time. Think of how the characters speak, dress, and act.

13. What if you could spend one day with any person, real or fictional, from the past or present? Who would you choose and why? **Write an account of your time together** as if it has already happened.

14. The year is 2075. **Write an editorial protesting** the threatened extinction of an animal no one—not even scientists—ever thought would be endangered. **Convince** readers to take steps.

Whenever possible, we should do one of two things: (1) offer students the option of choosing their own writing topics, thereby challenging them to think like writers while simultaneously increasing the odds of strong voice; or (2) at a minimum, offer students a choice from two or more prompts.

STEP 6: ABOLISH FOREVER THE DREADED "OFF TOPIC" LABEL.

Our misguided reverence for prompts causes us to judge a high number of student papers as "off topic," meaning that the writer has changed the topic—or written about something else. Such papers (which often receive low scores) may be highly individual, even ingenious responses to a topic that was vague or uninspiring to begin with.

FIGURE 12.5

Barry's Prompts

1. Lost
2. Running away
3. Big fat nuisance
4. No longer a child
5. Funny now—not then
6. Unbelievable
7. The other side
8. The one thing
9. The key
10. I just couldn't
11. Better than I thought
12. Who knew?
13. On sale
14. Just think . . .
15. A courageous moment
16. Lines
17. I remember . . .
18. Garbage
19. Let's face it
20. It bugs me
21. Footprints
22. Home

Prompts are not holy writ. They are invitations to write, nothing more. Do we really, *seriously*, want to penalize students for thinking in an original manner, the very thing our instruction seeks (or should seek) to promote? Through the act of writing, writers discover what they think, and often write their way onto the real topic. Unless content matters (*What are your three goals as a future educator?*), we should happily go along on the journey of discovery, celebrating the fact that for once the *impossible* happened: *the prompt worked*.

STEP 7: BECOME TRULY SKILLED ASSESSORS.

Effective assessment does not only depend upon how students perform. It depends upon how *we* perform. Are we up to the task? It is no longer enough to be meticulous editors. That may have served us well in decades gone by, but not now. The National Commission on Writing (2003, 16) tells us that we need students who can create "precise, engaging, coherent prose." Our state standards, the Common Core Standards, and our own writing guides echo these goals, and this is a good thing. Maybe, deep in our hearts, we want even more. Maybe we want our students to rock the boat, give us chills, upset traditional thinking, make a difference. These are not easy things to incorporate into standards—or writing guides, for that matter—but we want them just the same, don't we?

The problem is, when we raise the bar for our students—whether through standards or heartfelt goals—we raise it for ourselves as *assessors*, too. We can no longer slide by with an ages-old definition of quality writing. We must know the precise from the imprecise, the engaging from the voiceless, the coherent from the disorganized. Do we? We must not ask of our students what we are not prepared to assess perceptively, performance after performance.

STEP 8: TEACH ON-DEMAND WRITING AS A GENRE UNTO ITSELF.

Face it. On-demand writing is different. Writers don't (usually) choose their topics (though we can change this if we want to). They often have time limits. They write to strangers. Sharing is not allowed—nor is talking. Unless we take radical steps to change these procedures (and I am wholly, passionately in favor of this), almost nothing about on-demand writing has the comforting familiarity of writing process or workshop. We can help students navigate this unfamiliar territory, however, by teaching them how to prewrite on their own, how to "read" prompts, how to write for an audience of strangers, and how to use their precious time wisely.

FIGURE 12.6

Rules of the Road for Writing Prompts

1. Consider the grade level and experience of the student writers. The topic should be reasonably familiar because they won't have time or opportunity for research. It should also be *interesting*—unless you want voiceless responses.

2. Do not give students any prompt you would not wish to write on yourself. The revenge factor is built in—you'll have to read the results.

3. Ask a question to which you don't already know the answer—and one that each respondent will likely answer differently: *What things were easier—or harder—for the previous generation?*

4. Avoid issues that are likely to trigger emotional response: *Explain why you think the United States is or is not ready for a woman president.*

5. Avoid prompts that can be answered with a simple yes or no: *Should the driving age in your state be lowered to fourteen?*

6. Avoid "helpful hints" that make it hard for the writer to use *any* imagination: *Write about a time you will always remember. It could be a happy or sad time; a funny, embarrassing, or exciting experience; a memory from long ago or something recent. Include sights, sounds, smells, and feelings to put your reader right at the scene.* (Oops—time's up and we've only read the prompt.)

7. Does it matter if students write a narrative, expository, or persuasive piece? If it does, be very careful to word the prompt in a way that cues them in:

   For narrative: Tell the story, Tell about a time when, Give an account, Tell the story of

   For expository: Explain, Give directions for, Analyze, Tell how, Help the reader understand, Teach someone

   For persuasive: Persuade, Convince, Make an argument for, Share your position/opinion/view

   For descriptive: Describe, Help your reader picture, Make a movie in the reader's mind, Put the reader at the scene

8. Whenever possible, allow students to select *their own topics.* Their ability to do so can be part of what you assess.

9. At a minimum, *give students choices.* Just having a choice often helps students feel more positive about the whole assessment process.

Prewriting on Your Own

In on-demand writing situations, students probably will not be allowed to brainstorm or talk with partners. Most of the time, they won't be able to read from favorite books or other such sources, either. But they can make a quick sketch on scratch paper. They can use webbing or listing. Practice these strategies and model them for students, keeping in mind that if you have only thirty minutes to write, prewriting probably needs to take no more than five of those minutes.

Responding to Prompts

Many writing difficulties could be averted if students took time to read prompts with care. *Practice this.* Here are several things to look for and to ask yourself *as a writer:*

- What is the intended genre? Story? Explanation? Argument? Or—?
- What is the *heart* of the question being asked—the most important thing?

- Can I twist or squeeze the prompt *just a little* to make this question fit *my* experience?
- What do I know from personal experience that I *can* use?
- How can I make my response different from those of others so it will be interesting to read?

Author's Note

Have *students* hunt for effective—or ineffective—prompts online. Talk about those that would be most fun to write about, and those that present challenges. One of my favorite sites is http://www.canteach.ca/elementary/prompts. You needn't be teaching at elementary level to love this list; it works for everyone. The prompts are minimalist (which I favor), and many are stimulating enough to get you writing almost at once.

Have an in-class "prompt day," during which you and your students play the guessing game "What does the prompt writer want?" You can access hundreds of prompts online by typing in "student prompts" or, for older students, check out the book *411 SAT Writing Questions/Essay Prompts,* published by Learning Express. I'm not suggesting writing to these prompts, which eats up an inordinate amount of valuable instructional time. Just discuss them. Talk about what is called for and how to begin. Write and share just first lines (they're the toughest ones anyway). Participate with your students and share your own responses.

A helpful thing to model is how to personalize a prompt. If asked to write about a "friend," for instance, think creatively. A friend might be a good buddy your own age. But it could also be a neighbor, grandparent or other close relative, a teacher, a coach—even a pet. A favorite "place" could be the bleachers at a baseball game, the top of the Ferris wheel, the corner booth in a favorite restaurant, a bridge overlooking a river or bay, the top of a tree—or as a teacher suggested one day, "inside my grandson's eyes."

In *Crunchtime* (2009, 14–15), teacher-authors Gretchen Bernabei, Joyne Hover and Cynthia Candler include a lesson on "banking" experiences—a way of teaching students to tap their memories for the strong writing topics we all carry with us, but do not always recognize or recall when presented with a prompt. They separate experiences into four levels, providing ample examples for all but those at level four (the most personal):

- Level 1: Experiences shared by nearly everyone: e.g., the first day of school
- Level 2: Stories you might tell a group of friends: e.g., a time you lost something important
- Level 3: Experiences you would only share with a trusted friend: e.g., a time you took something from a parent without permission
- Level 4: Things too personal to write about

The authors suggest avoiding Level 1 (so that your paper will not sound like everyone else's), and focusing on Levels 2 and 3. They provide a chart for triggering memories to help a writer brainstorm a whole list of level 2 and 3 experiences (Bernabei, Hover, and Candler, 2009, 12).

2-Minute Planning

When time is limited, you need to think carefully about how you will use it. Here's some practical advice for students: Imagine that you have thirty minutes for responding. Use the first two for getting acquainted with the prompt. It helps to read it more than once and to just take a thinking minute before writing *anything*. This reflective time can help you come up with a much better response than if you just plunge in.

Next, make a list of three or four details OR key questions to answer. This only takes about a minute, and gives you something to look at as you write.

Guess what? You're only four minutes in—and all your planning is done! Take two more minutes to write a killer lead. It's well worth the extra time. Then draft for twenty minutes, making sure to cover those three or four questions or points. Take two of your remaining four minutes to write a fabulous but surprising conclusion—and the last two to think of the perfect title.

Writing for Those Mysterious Raters

We always say to students, "Think about your audience," but when it comes to writing assessment, do we tell them who it is? In on-demand writing, it will *not* be a patient teacher who will come to the end of a piece he or she has already spent ten minutes on and say, "I'd better read that again—maybe I missed something."

Picture a tired reader, pressured from having to read too many essays too quickly, distracted by the hundreds of other readers around her, weary from a thousand overly structured responses to a prompt that she doesn't like one bit better than the students did, having two minutes (tops) to spend, and longing for a paper that (1) states the main idea clearly and boldly, right up front, and (2) treats the reader to a moment of voice that allows a precious mental break. Once you've got that image vividly imprinted in your mind, you're in a much better position to write something to brighten this person's day. I often tell students, "Picture yourself on a rescue mission. Think of your writing as a gift to cheer up someone who can really use it."

See Figure 12.7 for twelve writing tips that can be helpful in a formal, large-scale testing situation.

FIGURE 12.7

Twelve Tips for Succeeding on Writing Tests

1. **Read the prompt carefully.** Figure out the main focus (what the prompt writers want you to talk about) and the best form (story, expository essay, persuasive argument, description) to use.

2. Take a minute to settle on the **main thing you want to say.** Express it in one sentence and say it to yourself—on scratch paper or aloud.

3. **Make a general plan** to follow in a flexible way—not the very things you will say, but the kinds of things you will say. For example, if you're writing a persuasive essay, your plan might look like this: (1) A lead that lays out the issue in an interesting way, (2) What I believe, (3) Reasons I believe as I do, (4) How the other side sees things—and why, (5) Flaws in the opposition's arguments, (6) The serious consequences of not coming to the "right" conclusion.

4. In a persuasive or expository piece, **state your main idea outright**—and right up front. Don't make a tired reader guess. Make sure everything in your piece relates to that main point or argument. Don't wander from the path even if you have something interesting to say. Save that kind of writing for when you get published.

5. Spend time on a **strong lead and conclusion.** Use the lead to wake your reader up—and set up what follows.

6. In your conclusion, don't summarize or review old ground. **Cite something significant** (perhaps unexpected) **you gained** from your experience or observations.

7. **Don't try to tell everything.** Choose two or three key events in a story (including a *turning point*), and three or four key points in an essay or argument. Choose what is most interesting—and what the reader is *least likely to know already*.

8. If your writing includes characters, **have them speak** and make what they say important. If it doesn't, quote someone—even if it's someone you know.

9. If your writing includes a setting, focus on **sensory details**—sounds, smells—that not everyone might notice.

10. Think of adjectives and adverbs as salt and pepper. Use them sparingly. Let precise **nouns and active verbs carry the weight** of meaning.

11. **Tell the truth.** When it comes to putting voice in writing, there is no substitute for saying just what you mean.

12. Think carefully about your title and **write it last**. It will look as if your piece flowed right out of the title—when just the opposite is true.

Making Large-Scale Writing Assessment All It Can Be

STEP 9: MINIMIZE BIAS.

Bias involves basing a writing assessment score or grade on some factor unrelated to actual writing performance, e.g., length of the document, choice of topic, and so on. In large-scale writing assessment, raters may overreact to issues such as neatness, conventional correctness, or the student's use of raw language or violent content, or they may base their rating on personal preference; e.g., "This student wrote a science fiction piece, and I just don't like science fiction." Not surprisingly, many of these same factors influence teacher grading at the classroom level.

Isn't *Subjectivity* Just Another Word for Bias?

Actually, no. We often use the word *objective* in everyday conversation to mean *fair* or free from personal bias. In the world of testing, objectivity means that *no human judgment is involved*. Similarly, *subjectivity* refers not to bias, but simply to the application of human judgment—not *unfair* human judgment, but *any* human judgment.

In multiple choice tests, human judgment is applied *during test construction*. That's because someone must determine which questions are significant enough to bother asking in the first place, how those questions will be worded, and which answers will be considered correct. These are all *subjective* judgments: humans making decisions. But once the test is constructed, the opportunity for human judgment is over. The "right" or "best" answer is clearly identified, and frequently the tests are machine scored. Thus, no human judgment is applied *during scoring*.

In direct writing assessment (where students actually write), judgments are made both *during test construction* (selection and wording of prompts, definition of procedures) and *during scoring* (as raters apply criteria); such assessment is therefore *subjective* during both construction and scoring.

This common misperception about *objectivity* is important because it causes some assessors as well as the general public to place undue faith in certain testing approaches, such as multiple choice tests, because they seem somehow more "scientific." This is nonsense, of course. *All* tests are subjective. They don't fall from the sky. They're created by humans. Humans decide what to test, how to test, and what to consider best or right or strong or acceptable.

STEP 10: CONSIDER MULTIPLE SAMPLES.

Hoping one writing sample will "tell all" is risky. Reviewing multiple samples collected over time (and across forms of writing) gives us a far more accurate picture of student proficiency and helps to minimize bias. Such an approach is particularly important in high-stakes decisions such as graduation, entrance into college, or calculating a grade.

The value of this multi-sample approach is confirmed by Alan Purves' (1992) ten-year study of primary and secondary writing within fourteen international school systems, including those in the United States, England, Finland, Wales, Italy, Chile, Nigeria, New Zealand, and others. Among this study's many intriguing findings is this conclusion: "To make any assessment of students' [overall] writing ability, one at least needs multiple samples across the domain" (112).

In *The Neglected "R"* (2003, 21), The National Commission on Writing offers this recommendation: "Since single assessments are unlikely to be able to show the range of a student's abilities—and cannot conceivably measure growth—a writing assessment, ideally, should rest on several pieces of writing, written for different audiences and on different occasions." They add, "Writing assessment is a genuine challenge."

Even though people often think of selected response tests as objective measures of learning, selecting the content for the test is itself a subjective exercise . . . . It is a matter of professional judgment, just as is determining how to teach the material in the first place.

—Richard J. Stiggins, Judith A. Arter, Jan Chappuis and Stephen Chappuis *Classroom Assessment for Student Learning*, 2006, 133

Careful research shows us what common sense tells us is obvious: no matter how trustworthily we may evaluate any sample of student's writing, we lose all that trustworthiness if we go on to infer from just that one sample the student's actual skill in writing.

—Peter Elbow *Embracing Contraries*, 1986, 37

It can be convincingly argued, of course, that multiple-sample writing assessment is not affordable at the district or state level. This argument is almost impossible to refute, given the time required to read writing samples thoroughly—much less examine portfolios. But this reality should caution us to be *very* careful in *interpreting* large-scale writing assessment results or making any significant decisions on the basis of single samples produced under timed conditions.

STEP 11: ENSURE THAT ASSESSMENTS ARE RELIABLE AND VALID.

When the criteria are highly refined and explicit, and when the raters are thoroughly trained and they feel confident in applying those criteria (so confident that they could score a paper without even looking at the criteria, but they look anyway), the likelihood of their scoring consistently increases dramatically. We say their assessment has *reliability*. Or to put it another way, the score a student receives depends mostly on his or her actual performance—not on which person happens to read the paper.

A good assessment of writing is also said to have *validity,* the closest possible connection with the knowledge or skills we wish to assess. To determine whether a writing assessment has validity—in other words, whether it's really measuring good *writing* performance (versus something else)—we should ask questions like these:

1. Would a student who performed well on this assessment also do well in other writing contexts—in a college course, for example, or in a job demanding strong writing skills?

2. Would a student who did well on this assessment perform well on other well-constructed writing assessments—whether at the state, district, or classroom level?

3. Would a student participating in this assessment have a chance to demonstrate the kinds of skills considered essential to writing competence?

4. Would a teacher or professional writer or editor looking at this assessment say, "Yes! That's *exactly* what we should be testing"?

STEP 12: MAKE WRITING A PRIORITY.

Getting students comfortable with the act of writing, in every conceivable situation, is the very best thing we can do to prepare them for any assessment on the planet. Yet often it seems to be the last thing we think of. All the standards and objectives and assessments in the world won't help us if students do not have sufficient time to write . . . and write . . . and write.

Writing needs to feel as natural, vital, and integral to the curriculum as reading. We certainly don't assess students' reading skills each time they reach for something in print. We see reading as a natural way of accessing information they will use in thousands of ways. But when students create a piece of writing—any piece—we can hardly suppress

---

As is the case with many other things people do, getting better at writing requires doing it—a lot. This means actual writing, not merely listening to lectures about writing, doing grammar drills, or discussing readings . . . writers learn from each session with their hands on a keyboard or around a pencil as they draft, rethink, revise, and draft again.

—Writing Study Group of the NCTE Executive Committee
NCTE Beliefs about the Teaching of Writing
National Council of Teachers of English, 2004, 1–2

the urge to pounce on it and whip out a rubric. Let's remind ourselves that writing provides access, too. The act of writing helps students think, understand, remember, and make connections they would not have thought of in any other way. It makes their thinking visible, thereby allowing them to analyze and reshape it. To encourage this kind of learning, we must have students write much more than we assess.

Making Classroom Writing Assessment All It Can Be

In the more intimate, more personal writing environment we create for our students and ourselves, we have greater control over assessment procedures than in most large-scale venues. But we must still begin with a vision of success—then follow nine more steps.

STEP 1: DEFINE OUR PERSONAL VISION OF SUCCESS.

Jim Burke tells us that "we all need a map to guide us and a destination in mind to give us some means by which to make decisions, to evaluate the importance of different information" (*Effective Instruction*, 2008, 39). Sometimes, of course, the map and destination may be very clear in *our* minds. We're the "drivers," after all. At any given time though, within your classroom, do *students* know the destination? Could they articulate your primary objectives in their own words? If not, think about what you can do to make them clear.

Your objectives (your personal vision of success) are likely defined, to an extent, by Common Core Standards and by state or district standards as well. They might also be defined, in part, by the traits of writing since you may spend a certain amount of time on lessons relating to ideas, let's say, or organization (both of which are essential components of the Common Core Standards). And these, in turn, are refined by your personal goals for helping writers to be successful.

Objectives have to be far more precise than "improving organization" or "understanding ideas," however. They should help students picture *exactly* what they will be doing. For example, let's say you were working on the trait of organization. You might have one or more of the following objectives for a given lesson or set of lessons:

- Discussing and assessing design in various publications
- Listing possible organizational designs
- Connecting design to purpose (in narrative, informational writing, or argument)
- Reordering details
- Identifying strong leads in literature
- Writing or revising a lead
- Identifying transitions in literature
- Revising to strengthen transitions
- Defining good "pacing"
- Revising pacing by slowing or speeding up the flow of the writing
- Identifying strong endings in literature
- Writing or revising an ending

Without . . . an instructional compass, we feel like Yogi Berra who warned, "If you don't know where you are going you will end up somewhere else."

—Jim Burke
Effective Instruction, 2008, 39

You could voice your objectives aloud. But you might wish to go a step further and write them out, keeping them visible for as long as a lesson or set of lessons lasts—whether that's a day or a week. This helps provide the "map" Jim Burke reminds us is so essential for maintaining our focus.

We also need to have clear criteria for defining strong performance. Again, I am an advocate of making these criteria visible—and that means using such tools as checklists or writing guides. You certainly do not need to use the ones in this book. You can create your own, or you can modify the ones provided with the help of your students, adding or revising criteria as you explore your own writing and published writing together. Just make sure students do not need to read your mind to figure out what you expect.

STEP 2: LET THE WRITING TELL ITS OWN STORY.

We are obsessed with numbers in our society. But numbers, regardless of how precise, can tell us only so much. To assess students well, we must find ways to preserve actual performance. We need a visual record of each writer's journey. And we can only get that through writing notebooks and portfolios. These ordered collections of work show how writers met goals—and set new ones—over a period of time. A portfolio, if carefully assembled to include dated pieces chosen by the writer and reflections on the reasons for each choice, tells that writer's story as nothing else can. And thanks to technology, a portfolio can now appear online, enhanced by video. Reflections can be recorded so we hear the writer's voice, guiding us through the work.

STEP 3: THINK PROCESS—NOT JUST PRODUCT.

Good writing assessment focuses on behaviors as well as on products. Observe your writers as they

- Prewrite and plan, draft, revise, edit, and format their own work
- Conduct research
- Employ technology
- Discuss the work of others
- Evaluate literature
- Work in response groups
- Coach one another

The closer you look, the more you will see.

As in Chapter 10 ("Exploring the World of Beginning Writers"), I will suggest some things you can watch for specifically—and as before, I invite you to add to this list, with your students' help. This list is different from the primary version in Chapter 10 because, of course, older writers have an expanded repertoire of skills—and a wider awareness of the possibilities open to them.

Prior to writing, a successful writer might—

- Elect to choose her own topics—at least sometimes
- Explore several topics prior to making a final choice
- Use technology (Internet, online feeds) to identify a topic of interest
- Explore a range of informational sources, technological and otherwise
- Try various forms of prewriting: listing, webbing, etc.

- Borrow ideas from literature
- Think about and redefine purpose or genre
- Create a mock-up or other physical representation of the writing
- Conduct multiple forms of research

During the process of writing, a successful writer might—

- Think reflectively about what readers want or need
- Combine drafting and revising, continually expanding and changing text
- Continue her writing from one day to the next
- Continuously add, revise, or delete information
- Use various devices to section text: paragraphs, lines, bullets, boxes, headings, etc.
- Experiment with leads, titles, or conclusions
- Read aloud to check the organizational flow or voice
- Add other "voices" through quotations or references
- Consult resources—dictionary, thesaurus, handbook, informational sources
- Share her writing with others

After drafting, a successful writer might—

- Read aloud to do a final check of wording, fluency, or conventions
- Share her writing with others prior to formally publishing
- Explore design possibilities
- Imitate the look or style of an existing publication
- Review her final design
- Make editorial changes
- Use technology (spell checker, online thesaurus) to help with editing
- Use technology to aid in design or publishing
- Work with others in producing a final product
- Seek ways of expanding her audience—possibly through technology

Again, this is not a checklist. The purpose of listing writing behaviors is to heighten our own awareness of how writers personalize various writing processes to suit their own needs. Observational assessment doesn't normally result in a grade; it does, however, inform *teaching*. It suggests puzzle pieces that might be missing for some writers—things we could model or coach them on. It helps us to move writers toward success.

STEP 4: ASSESS SOME PIECES DEEPLY, TO SEE WHAT STUDENTS CAN DO.

Analytical scores tell us a great deal about student performance. But obviously, scores do not reveal everything. While it is impractical to thoroughly analyze every piece of student writing, it is useful to analyze representative pieces to discover more precisely what students can do—and what they are not yet able to do. Such analysis can form the basis for personal comments, and can also inspire wonderful lessons based on actual student work. I did this kind of analysis in Chapter 10 with a primary sample ("My Library"). But the work of older writers will (usually) look quite different, so I offer another example here.

The writing in Figure 12.8, "Bad Decision," has a number of notable strengths—and you may also see some need for revision, but this makes the piece interesting to

FIGURE 12.8

Bad Decision (Grade 7, Persuasive Argument)

Everyone makes bad decisions now and then. But some bad decisions have more serious consequences than others. One of the worst decisions anyone can make is adopting (or capturing) a wild animal for a pet. It is bad for the animal, the owner, and the environment. What happens is that poachers kill the mother and then capture the baby to sell it. You might be surprised how easy it is to buy a baby gorilla or tiger—or even an elephant! What is NOT easy is taking care of it.

Wild animals and domestic animals are very different. This sounds obvious, but surprisingly, some people don't even think of it. Think about the difference between a wolf and a dog, for example. One hunts for its dinner while the other waits for you to dish it up. Wild animals need to live outdoors—not in cages or little houses. Most of them do not bond with their owners. They have special dietary needs, which the owner may not understand. Some wild animals, such as tigers or wolves, need to hunt and kill prey. You can't just take them to the park. It may also be hard to recognize signs of illness in a wild animal. Would you know how a sick boa constrictor looks—or when a monkey isn't feeling her best? In addition, it can be hard to find a vet who is willing to treat a wild animal. Most vets are used to seeing dogs and cats plus an occasional rat or hamster. They may not be all that excited about a visit from your leopard or iguana.

Keeping a wild animal can be hard on the owner, too. For one thing, it's extremely expensive. You will need special food and a lot of it. You will need a way of keeping the animal contained, like a fence. Besides that, most wild animals carry diseases. Most owners do not even think of this when looking at an adorable baby cheetah or chimpanzee. They're just so cute with those big eyes and fluffy fur. But their diseases can be harmful or even fatal to humans. In addition, wild animals are dangerous. They become tame enough to tolerate humans, but that does not mean they feel affectionate toward us or that they won't attack us. Even a young chimpanzee or lion can easily overpower a human. Many exotic pets have injured owners, owners' children, or unsuspecting neighbors. If you have other pets, be careful. They could get eaten! To your new "pet" they are just prey. Some people have an animal declawed or have its teeth removed to make it less dangerous. Think how cruel this is! In addition, once you do that, you can never set the animal free because now it can't defend itself.

Taking a wild animal from its native habitat can upset the ecological balance of its home area. Having one less predator around allows prey animals to overpopulate and destroy too much vegetation. Wild animals can also upset the ecological balance of their new environment, especially if they break free. For example, alligators have invaded sewer systems, and monkeys have been known to hide out in suburban forests for months, raiding gardens and terrorizing pets and children. Extremely dangerous animals such as tigers, bears, or large snakes may have to be hunted down and killed.

Think how you would feel if someone captured you in a net, stuffed you in a cage, and transported you to another country, then fed you food you didn't recognize and couldn't digest. Sound like a nightmare? Exactly! If you want a pet, consider an animal that is domesticated, happy to live in a house, apartment, or yard, and friendly toward humans. Get a pet you know you can feed and house, an animal you're not afraid to sleep in the same house with, one that won't terrify your veterinarian or stalk your kids and neighbors. Let wild animals remain wild and free.

analyze. Don't worry about *scoring* the paper. Just read it carefully and make a two-column list on scratch paper: *Things the Writer Knows*, and *Things That Need Work*. Take your time, and when you finish, look through my comments (below) to see if they are similar to yours.

Some Things the Writer Knows

- How to achieve the right voice for a persuasive piece
- How to set up a discussion—moving from bad decisions to adopting exotic pets
- The importance of choosing a topic she knows well and feels passionate about
- The importance of good strong examples (e.g., *Would you know how a sick boa constrictor looks?*)
- The need to offer more than one reason in support of an argument
- The visual appeal of multiple paragraphs
- How to create strong transitions with sentence openings (*For one thing, Besides that*)
- How to use a conversational style to create voice
- How to use questions and other rhetorical techniques to bring the reader right into the discussion
- The importance of a strong ending—especially in a persuasive piece

Things That Need Work

- *Exploring the problem* (Although the writer acknowledges that exotic pets are "cute" and appealing, we don't get a real analysis of what motivates someone to want such a pet or how widespread this problem really is.)
- *More strong verbs* (Notice how *many* the writer uses in the final two paragraphs—and how the writing literally gathers momentum in this section.)
- *Specifics* (This writer offers excellent examples, but they are general—it would be helpful to have specific exotic pet stories to show not only what *can* go wrong, but what *has* gone wrong.)
- *Following up* (The writer raises some fascinating questions—but we might like more information on whether it's really easy to adopt exotic pets, what laws might exist to prevent this, and the ramifications of releasing alligators into the sewer system, or monkeys into suburban forests.)

How to Use This Information

Every strength in this paper—and there are many—can be used (with the writer's permission, of course) as an example to show other writers interesting things they might try. For example, I would like other students to notice how the writer asks the reader to put him- or herself in the place of a captured exotic animal—in the final paragraph. This rhetorical device can be very powerful in winning a reader's support.

I could use the writer's shifting voice to create a lesson as well (again, with her permission). First, I would want to discuss whether students hear this voice as "right" for a persuasive piece. I do. I think it hits the right note of passionate *and* professional. Yet unmistakably, it gains power in the final paragraphs. I'd want to see if students hear this shift, and if so, if they can identify the cause. (It's partly that rhetorical strategy of asking the reader to imagine how a captured animal feels—but it's also the abundance of strong verbs that breathe life into this section.)

Author's Note

You certainly don't need to do this kind of deep assessment with *every* piece of writing. But many wonderful examples and minilessons emerge when you do. This in-depth analysis also provides an excellent foundation for a writing conference. And it helps ensure that what you teach is directly relevant to students' immediate needs.

STEP 5: PROVIDE BOTH
FORMATIVE *AND* SUMMATIVE ASSESSMENT.

Formative assessment happens during learning, and is intended to provide information that helps both learner and teacher make adjustments. This is critical because writers need ongoing feedback—not just comments or grades when the writing is finished. Formative writing assessment occurs, for example, when you stop by to see how a writer is doing or talk about a draft in a conference. Or, it can be more formal—checking learning by asking a student to edit or revise a short sample, for instance. Formative instruction helps students gauge their progress and assists teachers in redirecting instruction.

> We need to teach students by using the concept that gamers have used so well: Failure is OK as long as it leads to learning. There is a reset button in education. It's called formative assessment.
>
> —Debra J. Dirksen
> "Hitting the Reset Button," 2011, 31

Summative assessment happens at the close of the learning process and is designed to show both learner and teacher what the student has gained from instruction during a specified period. With respect to writing, summative assessment usually involves concluding (perhaps publishing) a major piece of writing, or finishing a series of writings.

Both forms of assessment are important. But it is easy to focus heavily on summative assessment, and to overlook the value of providing ongoing feedback *as students write*.

Author's Note

Teacher and author Jim Burke (*Effective Instruction*, 2008, 36ff.) also points out the importance of *diagnostic assessment*, which occurs prior to instruction and is designed to identify the academic skills students currently have and what they might need to learn to succeed in a particular program. Diagnostic assessment is especially important in the case of ELLs or other students who might, for example, benefit from having special course-related vocabulary—or coaching in writing-related skills such as note taking, brainstorming, webbing, listing, editing, or quoting.

STEP 6: ASSESS WHAT
MATTERS—NOT WHAT'S OBVIOUS.

We've discussed how important this is in large-scale assessment. It's equally important at the classroom level.

Barry Lane (author of *After THE END* and *The Reviser's Toolbox*) tells the story of a high school teacher who commented on one piece of his writing, "It's nice to read typewritten work." Yes, it is. But it's even more rewarding to read work that reflects thinking. The obvious and easy thing to assess is not always what we value most. It is critical to distinguish between the two because what we assess is what we'll get more of—every time.

As teachers of writing, we usually mean well. We start out in pursuit of content, voice, fluency, or organization (and even go so far as to tell students that this is what we will be looking for), but we get bushwhacked by a pet peeve and wind up basing the grade on neatness, spelling, choice of topic, use of a pen rather than a pencil, or how closely the writer follows the assignment. One teacher actually gave an F to a third-grade student who had written a clever, original fairy tale—in purple ink; the teacher did not consider this color appropriate for a serious writing assignment. We might counter that giving a low grade for such a superficial reason is not appropriate in serious assessment.

STEP 7: TEACH STUDENTS TO
EVALUATE THEIR OWN WORK.

"Current approaches to evaluation," Donald Graves tells us, "have it backwards. At the moment, the most important evaluator is some person out of town who knows nothing of the teaching situation. In fact, the student, who is closest to the work in progress . . .

Author's Note

When students assess their own writing, they do not *score* it. They simply look for strengths—or for what needs revision. Self-assessment is a precursor to revision. The new writing guides, with their "leap the river" design, are formatted to make this kind of self-assessment that much easier. See Chapter 1, teaching strategy 13, for more ideas on having students do their own formative assessment.

ought to be and is the most important evaluator" (2002, 28). This statement underlies the most important thing we hope to achieve with trait-based instruction: *for students to be skilled evaluators of their own work.*

Think of the power this encompasses. A student who knows whether he or she has done a good job—quite aside from what anyone else says—has the knowledge and insight to revise with purpose, to set personal goals, and to experience the independence that *only* comes with knowing when and why your writing is working.

You can encourage self-evaluation in a number of ways. One, of course, is to provide students with their own writing guides, and to give them experience in assessing work other than their own. *Every paper in this book* is intended for sharing with students. The discussions that emanate from this sharing will raise countless issues of what it means to write well—and will give students new perspective about their own work.

Even without a writing guide, though, students can identify strengths and problems. In *Testing Is Not Teaching*, Donald Graves describes a process that author and teacher Linda Reif used with her students, in which she asked them to rank sixteen papers written by students from another town, then to say what was especially good about the top three and what could be done to improve the bottom three (2002, 28).

Reif later followed up this initial exercise with more papers—and even compared her students' rankings with those of professional writers and other teachers. You might consider trading sets of papers with another teacher and doing this.

Notice that this sort of ranking and rating directly parallels the process by which the six traits of writing were identified in the first place (see Chapter 1 and Appendix 1). It is an excellent way for students (or anyone) to identify the qualities that contribute to writing excellence.

Self-evaluation is enhanced dramatically when writers look at more than one piece at a time. Students might, for instance, look at early and late drafts within their portfolios to see what strengths they have gained, or which things they still need to work on. To help your students become strong evaluators, consider:

- Modeling how self-evaluation can look, using samples of your own writing
- Routinely providing time for students to reflect on their writing
- Coaching students about the *kinds of things* to look for, using samples such as "Bad Decision"
- Asking students to write down personal goals—and to bring those goals to a writing conference
- Providing key questions to help students reflect on specific pieces of work (see Figure 12.9)

STEP 8: MAKE PERSONAL COMMENTS A MAJOR PART OF ANY FEEDBACK.

Personal comments do not replace scores. They enhance them by revealing what scores cannot: what is unique about a piece of writing, where the potential lies, what a writer might try next, what happened in our minds or hearts as we read the piece. Writing is different from many kinds of performance in that it is deeply personal. Garrison Keillor once said, "When your true love writes *Dear Light of My Life, Joy of My Heart, O Lovely Pulsating Core of My Sensate Life,* some response is called for" (1989, 138). And so it is with our students' writing.

FIGURE 12.9

Self-Reflection Questions for Students

> Write freely and openly in response to each question. This sheet will not be graded. It is intended to help you reflect on your own writing, and to set goals.

1. What worked really well for you as you were writing this piece?

   _____

   _____

2. Was there anything you struggled with?

   _____

   _____

3. Would you do anything differently next time?

   _____

   _____

4. As you read over your work now, what is one thing you really like?

   _____

   _____

5. What have you learned that you could use to help other writers?

   _____

   _____

6. What's the most important thing you want to work on as a writer?

   _____

   _____

© 2012. *Creating Writers*, 6th edition, by Vicki Spandel. May be copied for classroom instruction.

STEP 9: BE FLEXIBLE ABOUT GENRE AND FORMAT.

Chapter 8 discusses expanding our definition of writing to incorporate twenty-first century literacies and multi-media compositions. We need to expand our definition of assessment in the same way, encouraging students to work from their strengths—to show organization through a slide show, perhaps, or voice through a podcast, or appreciation of detail through video. The options are right there before us. We have only to seize them.

As basic tools for communicating expand to include modes beyond print alone, "writing" comes to mean more than scratching words with pen and paper. Writers need to be able to think about the physical design of text, about the appropriateness and thematic content of visual images, about the integration of sound with a reading experience, and about the medium that is most appropriate for a particular message, purpose, and audience.

—The Writing Study Group of the NCTE Executive Committee *NCTE Beliefs about the Teaching of Writing,* November 2004, 9

Clearly, we face a challenge: to become proficient multi-media communicators ourselves. But the investment will be worth it if we can give a voice to students who are learning right this moment to speak through visual or auditory media.

STEP 10: ENCOURAGE STUDENTS TO DEVELOP "HABITS OF MIND" ESSENTIAL FOR SUCCESS.

The year 2011 saw the publication of a document that has, I believe, the potential to change the way we think about writing instruction and assessment. It is titled "Framework for Success in Postsecondary Writing," and is a collaborative effort by the Council of Writing Program Administrators, the National Council of Teachers of English, and the National Writing Project.

This document reviews the central role that writing (together with reading and critical analysis) plays in helping students learn to think, to develop those "habits of mind" that enable them to function as literate citizens not only in college or another academic setting, but throughout their lives. The introduction states, "This document takes as a central premise that teaching writing and learning to write are central to education and to the development of a literate citizenry" (2011, 2).

The specific habits of mind described in detail in this document (along with suggestions for helping writers to develop each of them) include such things as curiosity, openness, engagement, creativity, persistence, flexibility, and metacognition.

While it is impossible to do justice to this analysis in a few words, it is recommended that students develop these habits of mind through activities such as these:

- Using inquiry to develop research questions
- Listening effectively
- Taking risks
- Committing to long-term, challenging writing tasks
- Working with others
- Seeking new information
- Reading diversely
- Reflecting on one's own and others' work
- Composing in multimedia environments

This list represents only a tiny portion of the whole—which you must read for yourself. As you will see, this summary encourages independent thinking, stamina, love of learning, and a perspective that embraces all experience as a potential learning environment. The document deals, obviously, with instruction, not assessment. But it encourages us to provide new and different opportunities that go far beyond what many of us have previously taught as "writing." And in so doing, it asks us to look for behaviors we may never have thought to notice before, and to assess in ways that not only *allow* but *invite* students to break from tradition. Expect barriers to be broken.

Standardized writing curricula or assessment instruments that emphasize formulaic writing for nonauthentic audiences will not reinforce the habits of mind and the experiences necessary for success as students encounter the writing demands of postsecondary education.

—Council of Writing Program Administrators
—National Council of Teachers of English
—National Writing Project
"Framework for Success in Secondary Writing," 2011, 3

Grading

As Barry Lane (1993) tells us, "For a writing teacher who believes in encouraging revision, graded papers are nothing less than a curse. Low grades discourage and high grades imply that a piece is done. Even worse, students begin writing to improve their grade instead of finding out what they have to say" (p. 129). Donald M. Murray (2004) calls grades the "terminal response," meaning that once a grade is assigned to a piece of writing, the writing virtually dies, for the student will not look at it again.

In his book, *Punished by Rewards*, Alfie Kohn (1993, 203) talks openly about the naïveté of imagining we can motivate students to strive for excellence with a simplistic carrot-and-stick, A-to-F grading system. A student's inner world, he assures us, is far too complex for this. When grades dominate the classroom environment, Kohn argues, students tend to

1. Place minimal value on things learned and care only about the grade earned.
2. Become dependent on the reward, allowing themselves to be controlled by the threat of the grade.
3. Become unwilling to take any risk, however promising, that might jeopardize their grade point average (GPA).

Kohn suggests that comments are more meaningful and more motivational than grades and are far more likely to inspire excellent performance.

Grades are a choice, not a necessity. Nevertheless, they may be a reality for you, like it or not. If you're like many educators, you would prefer a different method of documenting student performance (portfolios, narrative records)—but may feel you have no choice. This section offers some perspectives on grading, plus an easy process for converting analytical scores into grades.

> Learning and teaching can take place just fine without grades.
> —Richard J. Stiggins, Judith A. Arter, Jan Chappuis, and Stephen Chappuis
> *Classroom Assessment for Student Learning,* 2006, 301

WHAT GRADES MEAN TO STUDENTS

Ask *students* what grades mean, and you're likely to get some startling answers. Many will tell you that A's are mostly for parents (or for precollege records)—and sometimes translate into money, the right to drive the car, or other tangible rewards.

Do you think C means average and F means failure? Think again. Many students will tell you that the *worst* grade to receive is a C because while an F means that you didn't try or didn't care (this can even be a badge of honor), a C indicates that you did your best but *still* failed—and that's depressing.

What's more, though many of us hate admitting this, grades have no universal meaning beyond the most general level. To *most* teachers, an A signifies a job well done; an F, significant problems with performance. However, some teachers refuse ever to assign a D or an F because of the potential damage to self-esteem. One teacher I knew assigned grades of A, AA, AAA, and so on, to avoid any confidence-diminishing "lower grades." It didn't work, of course. Within a very short time, his students unraveled the code and were devastated to receive the low grade of "A."

In a workshop one day I asked teachers to define what B minus meant to them. Here are just some of their intriguing, diverse answers:

- *You tried hard, but it needed work.*
- *Good job! Just needed that little something more.*
- *Close to what I expected—almost!*
- *Average work. It's what used to be a C.*

- *Between 80 and 82 percent—it's pure mathematics.*
- *I tried to like your paper, but I couldn't.*

Given these diverse responses, can we ever hope to achieve consistency, a clear definition of performance goals, and all-around fairness? We can. Indeed, we must. By connecting grades to criteria, we say to students, "We will define what we mean by various levels of performance, and we will apply those definitions as consistently as human nature will allow."

HOW AND WHAT TO GRADE

Student achievement (performance, that is) lies at the heart of most grading systems. Does that make sense? Should other factors be considered as well? Let's take a closer look.

Achievement

If we grade on achievement, we tell students, in effect, that those who attain a higher level of writing proficiency will receive higher grades. To many people, this seems a fair approach to grading, and I agree. After all, demand for high-level achievement is a reality of life, both in and out of the classroom.

Writers whose work no one wants to read do not get published, nor do they get hired as journalists, technical writers, communications specialists, or editors. Performance counts everywhere, not just in school. Having said that, we must determine what kinds of achievement we wish to measure and how we will go about it.

Much of this book is devoted to defining and promoting a performance assessment approach that judges the quality of students' writing based essentially on the writing itself. However, achievement must also include the writer's ability to use the processes of prewriting, drafting, revising, and editing. Some of this is implied by the quality of the final product, of course, but we can bolster this assessment tremendously by carefully observing our students. Through observation we learn which students are comfortable with writing processes and are continually experimenting with new ways to plan, write, revise, edit, or design a variety of compositions.

Effort

Teachers define "effort" very differently—and this creates inconsistencies. Further, the notion of grading on effort implies that the performance itself is unsuccessful. That's not necessarily true at all. Haven't we all known people whose specialty was making the next to impossible look easy? When it's working, effort is *invisible*. And when it isn't, it undermines performance—big time. Do we want to reward that? Nobody wants to eat at the restaurant where the cook makes an effort. No one wants to see a film or play in which the actors all try hard.

On the other hand, if we *don't* grade on effort, what will become of students who really *are* trying but cannot seem to succeed? What, other than rewarding effort, will rescue these students from failure? The answer lies in reshaping the task:

- Lengthen the time allowed to complete the assignment.
- Have the student choose another topic or approach this topic in different way.
- Change the genre—perhaps a concrete poem instead of an essay, or photojournalism instead of the standard research paper.
- Allow the student to dictate part of the piece or to provide some or all information through photos, audio, or video.

- Provide help with research: Point out promising sources or suggest interviews, site visits, surveys, and other alternatives that require minimum technical reading.
- Assemble a mini dictionary with key words or terms.
- Ask the student to do independent editing on only a portion of the whole piece; provide help with the rest.
- Have the writer work with a partner or as part of a team.

Let's find a way to help writers succeed with the business of writing. Then we won't hear ourselves saying to students, via artificially inflated grades (which fool no one), "I see that you cannot make it as a writer, but here are some points for trying."

Attitude

I write virtually every day, but my attitude fluctuates. On days when the words come readily, my attitude is just superior. First-rate. Once, however, when I was working on an economics textbook (far from my favorite topic), the computer "ate" a large chunk of the chapter I had been struggling with for two weeks. On that day I became, at heart, Mad Max. I did, nevertheless, finish that chapter . . . and the seven after it as well.

Keeping at it when you don't feel like it is my definition of good attitude. Another teacher-assessor will look for classroom participation, voluminous writing, or willingness to embrace technology. The point is, we can't really define good attitude—any more than we can recognize effort. Better to reward both with appreciative comments and not figure either into our grades.

Growth Over Time

Some teachers like to focus on recent performance because it reflects what the writer has learned or can do *following instruction*. I agree with this practice. There are several ways to do it. You might, for example, simply toss out an early performance—or even more than one. Look on them as "warm-ups," so to speak. Or weight the scores of later performances more heavily. And finally, you might consider giving credit for the extent of growth by looking at the conceptual "distance" between early and later drafts. Has the writer set important and measurable goals all along—and achieved each one? Is the writer aware of his or her achievement? In other words, can the writer review and assess his or her own work—and recognize specific indicators of growth? Please note that growth is easy to assess when students keep portfolios, and far more difficult if they do not.

GRADING AS A CONTROL ISSUE

It's no secret: teachers hold the trump card. Grades can be used to manipulate students, to motivate them, and to control them.

We don't want to use grades to control students. We want to use grades to *communicate*—and their *only* intrinsic value lies in their capacity to do that. Many people would argue that we are already communicating with students through analytical scores and comments, and that grades add little of value. I agree. But until we can stop asking, "How will this figure into a grade?" and until students stop asking, "What grade did I get?" we are not prepared to do away with them.

Some people think grades are addictive. Do you agree? Perhaps you recall with some pride the A's you received as a student. Do you recall grades more than comments? And each time you received an A, did it make you try even harder to get another? Did you ever *fear* receiving a low grade? And did you define "low" as "anything other than an A"?

> A low grade for effort is more likely to be read as "You're a failure even at trying." On the other hand, a high grade for effort combined with a low grade for achievement says "You're just too dumb to succeed."
> —Alfie Kohn
> *Punished by Rewards*, 1993, 208–209

> When achievement is cumulative over time, base the grade on the most recent work.
> —Judith A. Arter and Jan Chappuis
> *Creating and Recognizing Quality Rubrics*, 2006, 125

> Where do children learn to be grade-grubbers? From this: "You'd better listen up, folks, because this is going to be on the test." And from this: "A B-minus? What happened, Deborah?" And from this: "I take pride in the fact that I'm a hard grader. You're going to have to work in here."
> —Alfie Kohn
> *Punished by Rewards*, 1993, 205

Think about what grades mean to you as a teacher. Maybe they seem closer to the "truth" than scores or comments. Maybe you hold A's in reserve for certain performances that have a quality difficult to articulate. *It's an A performance: What more is there to say?* Until we can answer that question, until we have *supreme confidence* in our ability to communicate through comments, scores, or both, we cannot say goodbye to grades.

Translating Analytical Scores into Grades

Analytical scores do not convert *directly* into grades. This is because a score (on the six-trait writing guide, anyway) represents an assessment of *one writing trait*—not the writing as a whole. Therefore, it does not make sense to say a 6 is an A, a 5 is a B, and so forth.

Assessment specialist Richard Stiggins reminds us that the whole point of having a rubric in the first place is to provide the student (or anyone) with much richer, more detailed information than any grade can offer: "If the objective is to communicate thoroughly about student achievement, then don't convert rubric scores to letter grades at all if you can help it. Rather, communicate using the points on the rubric" (2006, 316).

Sometimes, of course, you *cannot* help it. Grades—like it or not—are required. In that case, begin by developing for yourself and for your students a "big picture." Spell out, in very specific terms, which tasks, assignments, or tests will affect students' grades and what percentage of the total grade will hinge on each. Be sure that students are familiar with the explicit criteria that you will use to assess performance. And follow some guidelines.

1. Base any grade on a body of work—not just one sample.

One or two samples are not enough. When we assess five or six samples of writing, though, we see a *body* of work; that allows us to feel confident that our assessment is meaningful.

2. Do not grade individual pieces of writing *at all.*

When you score a piece of writing analytically, you create a performance profile that shows where relative strengths or weaknesses lie—for that piece. That performance profile goes away once you average those scores. Moreover, if students know the traits and the writing guides well, and if you are offering your own personal comments in addition to scores alone, you are already providing significant, meaningful feedback. A grade adds nothing new.

3. Don't assess *everything.*

Ideally, you want students to write every day. If you assess everything they write, you create a logistical nightmare. During a given grading period, ask students to select samples they believe are worth taking all the way through the writing process; others remain practice drafts—good for developing skills but never assessed.

4. For any given assignment, score those traits that are most relevant.

You do not need to assess all six traits every time, although you can if this kind of "full picture" approach makes you more comfortable. Consider, though, that in a piece of technical writing, ideas, conventions, and word choice may be more important than, say, fluency or voice. For a persuasive essay, you may value ideas and voice more than other traits. Topic, genre, and audience, considered together, help determine what is vital.

If you grade a body of work, you will give students a better picture of their overall strengths and weaknesses.

—Barry Lane
After THE END, 1993, 128

5. Give students the option to revise further *after a score is assigned.*

Students who are unsatisfied with their performance on any piece of writing should have the option to revise and thereby improve that performance—and likely raise scores, too. This option reinforces the value of revision. One teacher with whom I worked refused to assign *any* score lower than a 3. Instead of looking at 1s and 2s as "weak performance," she regarded them as "not yet ready for assessment." She conferred with students whose scores fell below the 3 level, and together they made a plan for raising the scores. Another teacher friend simply chopped the 1 and 2 level scores off her writing guides. She didn't want her students (or parents) to see that anything lower than a 3 was possible.

6. Calculate grades based on an average.

This is perhaps the simplest way to compute grades, and I have come to favor it because calculating percentages based on a continuum is very tricky business. Along a continuum, a score of, say 5, actually represents a *range* of possible scores, from 5.0 to 5.9. No one wants to get *that* precise ("Wow, Josh! A 5.4 in organization!") because a score is an impression, an approximation to begin with. We're not measuring temperature, weight, or distance, after all. So for this edition, I am recommending that grades be based on an average—keeping in mind that you will not grade individual papers, but a collection of at least five or six. Here's how to do it:

> Total the <u>points earned</u> (on all papers, all traits) across a span of time, and divide by the number of <u>traits assessed</u>. Please note that the number of *traits* assessed is very different from the number of *papers* assessed. For any given paper, you may score from one to six traits—more if you score presentation and/or genre separately.

Let's say that students have completed five pieces of writing, each of which is scored on <u>six traits</u>. One student—Pat—receives (for the sake of simplicity) all <u>5s</u> (on a 6-point scale) on <u>three</u> of the writings and all <u>4s</u> on the other <u>two</u>.

Pat's total *points earned* equal $6 \times 5 \times 3$ (or 90) plus $6 \times 4 \times 2$ (or 48), for a total of 138.

How many *traits* have been assessed altogether? The answer to this is five assignments $\times$ six traits, or 30. So Pat's average, for this period, is 138 (total points) divided by 30 (the total number of individual *traits* assessed on all five papers). The resulting score is 4.6.

What grade is this? Actually, that's entirely up to you. I look at it this way: A 5-level performance really meets all criteria that define strength in a given trait. A 6 means "met the criteria and then some." (That extra *something* is one of the things you want to capture in your comments.) In other words, students who are routinely achieving at the 5 level should, I feel, be getting A's. You may disagree—and that's fine. Make yourself a chart, like the one that follows, with grade cutoffs that suit you. Remember, this chart is *only a model;* yours may look very different. And notice also that I am recommending not grading performance below the 2.8 level. Instead, provide time for revision if you can.

Possible Grade Equivalents for a Six-Point Scale (The one used for Pat)

5.2 A	4.2 B	3.2 C
4.8 A–	3.8 B–	2.8 C–*
4.4 B+	3.4 C+	

*Anything below this average will require revision of selected pieces.

Final Thoughts . . .

In the end, quality assessment is quality communication. It demands that we find different ways to collect information—through everyday observations, assessment of on-demand and long-term writing tasks, and in-depth analysis of *some* writing samples. It also means offering students multiple ways of demonstrating proficiency—through traditional writing, portfolios, and multi-media genres. And finally, it means finding varied ways to share information—not only through scores or grades, but through comments as well. By combining scores and comments and supplementing both with actual samples of student performance, we ensure that we create a rich, vibrant, representative picture of what students can do. We must continually ask ourselves not only *What did we learn about students' performance?* but equally important—*What did we miss that we should be celebrating?* Until students have every opportunity to demonstrate what they can do, our assessments are not all that they can be. Further, until *students*—not policy makers—can use the results of an assessment to improve their performance, assessment has failed to fulfill its most important reason for being.

STUDY GROUP

Interactive Questions and Activities

1. **Discussion.** In *Testing Is Not Teaching* (2002, 46), Donald Graves presents an alternative writing assessment plan in which students would have time to explore personally important topics, and, with the teacher's help, choose two on which to write. Compare this approach to the on-demand assessment favored by most districts or states that assess writing. What would we gain from this approach that we do not learn from current assessments? How would our view of assessment need to change in order to support Graves' plan?

2. **Discussion.** What is your personal vision of success within your own classroom? Is it defined (in part) by

   ___ the Common Core Standards?

   ___ other state standards?

   ___ the traits?

   ___ your own definitions of successful writing performance?

   Discuss this vision with your group. Compare your thoughts at this point to the vision of success you entered in your writing notebook at the close of Chapter 1. Revise or expand what you first wrote.

3. **Activity.** With your class or group, have a "prompt day." Look up prompts online (just type in "student writing prompts" for numerous lists, including picture prompts). Identify some of the best—and worst. Discuss what each prompt seems to require, and how (as a writer) you could approach it successfully. As a teacher, what do you learn from this review?

4. **Activity and Discussion.** Check each of the following that is part of your current classroom assessment. Discuss responses with your group.

   ___ Assessing multiple samples (a body of work)

   ___ Having students keep portfolios

   ___ Observing students as they engage in writing process

   ___ Doing in-depth analysis of selected writings to discover strengths (or problems) that go beyond a rubric

   ___ Asking students to evaluate themselves as writers

5. **Discussion.** Which factors (performance, growth, effort, etc.) do you feel should figure into a student's grade in writing? With your group, discuss various ways of calculating grades.

6. **Activity and Discussion.** In this chapter, you had a chance to take an in-depth look at one piece of writing: "Bad Decision." Choose any other paper and do a similar analysis. It might be one from this book, or one from your own class. Work with a partner to see how many strengths you can identify. What potential do you see in the writing? What lessons could you share with other students based upon this writing?

7. **Activity and Discussion.** Put a check by each of the following statements with which you agree. When you finish, discuss your responses with your group.

___ Large-scale writing assessment provides valuable information we need to make important educational decisions.

___ In any writing assessment, students should have the option of coming up with their own topics.

___ When students do not perform well on a writing assessment, the prompt is *often* the problem.

___ Procedures within large-scale writing assessment should be revised to more closely match the way in which writing is taught and assessed in a process- and workshop-based classroom.

___ At the classroom level, students should have the option to demonstrate writing proficiency in a variety of ways, including the use of technology.

___ Student self-assessment is more important than any other form of assessment.

___ Grades are of limited value and should eventually disappear.

___ The most important function of assessment is to communicate about performance.

8. **Activity and Discussion.** Download the article *Framework for Success in Postsecondary Writing* (you can find it by simply entering the title). Read and discuss it with your group in light of its potential impact on classroom writing instruction and assessment. If we followed the implied recommendations in this article, what implications might they have for large-scale assessment as we now know it?

Most of all, I write to soar. To soar through the clouds of imagination, dreams and possibilities. To soar on the words of hope. I am an eagle, catching the air and rising up to greatness.

—Maegan Rowley, student writer

Who knows? I just might make millions of dollars writing books. I might be the next J. R. R. Tolkien. Would that be sweet or what?

—Carl Matthes, student writer

When first entering this galaxy of writing, you fear doing something wrong, of messing up, of being a bad writer. It takes a while to let that go, to just rocket off and take what comes.

—Elisabeth Kramer, student writer

Looking Forward
Expanding the Vision

Think about your favorite teachers from your youth: the ones who changed your life. Chances are, these were the teachers with a gift for improvisation . . . Chances are, they didn't teach from a script.

LINDA PERLSTEIN
Tested, 2007, 50

When my students and I discover uncharted territory to explore, when the pathway out of a thicket opens up before us, when our experience is illuminated by the lightning life of the mind—then teaching is the finest work I know.

PARKER J. PALMER
The Courage to Teach: Exploring the Inner Landscape of a Teacher's Life, 1998, 1

Let us put our heads together and see what life we will make for our children.

TATANKA IOTANKS (SITTING BULL, LAKOTA)
New Horizons, 1995

A test-obsessed environment makes shortcuts seductive—almost irresistible. We still pay homage to the wisdom of those strong and fearless voices—Donald Graves, Donald Murray, Lucy Calkins, Georgia Heard, Regie Routman, Katie Wood Ray, Tom Romano, and others—who taught us that writing is thinking, that it is a process or multiple processes, that we can teach it better by creating a workshop setting where writers learn together, by sharing fine literature (where the lessons lie), and by being writers ourselves.

Yet an agonizing worry gnaws at us: *What if teaching writing this way takes too long?* The test, after all, is coming. It is *always* coming. We must make better writers of our students this year, this month, now. We cannot wait. *Someone* out there *surely* has the secret to quick success. *What is it?* Six traits? Seven? Eight? New rubrics? *No rubrics?* Technology? Conferences? Genres? Writing circles? Writing across the curriculum?

The truth is, all shortcuts are a lie. The answer to teaching writing well lies within *you*, and within the vision *you create* from process, workshop, traits, genre, literature, conferencing—all of it, *all* working together. Instead of allowing yourself to drown in a sea of numbers that seem to tell so much and yet offer us so little, step back, take a deep breath, and reflect. Remember why you became a teacher. Build for yourself a *true* vision of success based on eight core beliefs.

1. BELIEVE IN THE VOICES THAT ONCE LED US.

Writing itself is the key. We can strengthen process by putting it in a workshop setting, by adding modeling and conferences, by surrounding writers with the best literature of our time—and we should do all these things. But at the core remains this fundamental truth: People learn to write by writing—and by living and working within a community of writers who can share their experience and their growing expertise. Writers do not learn to write overnight or through shortcuts. Learning to write takes a lifetime, and to any writer's journey each of us adds not *the* answer, but whatever wisdom we can draw from our own experience of being writers ourselves.

I hate to tell ya, but there's no easy answer. If you want discipline you have to keep slowly adding, building, and staying with it until one day, doing it feels better than not doing it. It's like doing push-ups.

—Nancy Slonin Aronie
Writing from the Heart, 1998, 13

2. BELIEVE THAT THE HUMAN SPIRIT IS TOO ELUSIVE, TOO VAST, AND TOO DIVERSE TO BE DEFINED BY A SINGLE ASSESSMENT.

Assessment gives us useful information (sometimes) and helps us to know where to put our teaching energy (sometimes). A single assessment cannot tell us whether a student can write or whether a teacher can teach.

In his last years of public school, a young man received these comments on his writing:

- "This boy is an indolent and illiterate member of the class."
- "Ideas limited."
- "A persistent muddler."
- "I have never met a boy who so persistently writes the exact opposite of what he means."

Some years later, in the early 1940s, this "persistent muddler" wrote an article about his military experiences, an article for which he received a then-amazing sum of $1000 from the *Saturday Evening Post*, and this encouraging comment from the novelist C. S. Forester: "You were meant to give me notes, not a finished story. I'm bowled over. Your piece is marvelous. It is the work of a gifted writer" (*The Wonderful Story of Henry Sugar*, 2000, pp. 187–188, 198–199).

At the very least [we ought to] make it clear to every child . . . that our judgment of students' intellect and character and ultimate potential will have no connection with the numbers tabulated by a person who is not an educator, and has never met them, working in a test-score factory 1,000 or 3,000 miles away.

—Jonathan Kozol
Letters to a Young Teacher, 2007, 129

The young man was Roald Dahl, and had he allowed those early assessments to define how he saw himself forever, think what we might have missed.

In your class there's almost certainly a Roald Dahl—or a Nikki Giovanni, Gary Paulsen, Nicola Davies, Maya Angelou, Billy Collins, Jon Scieszka, or Sandra Cisneros. Your words can encourage that writer to share his or her voice—no matter what the test scores say.

3. BELIEVE THAT WE CAN CREATE ASSESSMENT TO MATCH OUR VISION OF GOOD WRITING INSTRUCTION.

In the David Mamet film *Heist*, Gene Hackman's character, Joe, explains how he manages to appear more intelligent and clever than he really is: "I try to imagine a fella smarter than myself, and then I try to imagine, 'What would *he* do?'" Let's adopt Joe's strategy. Let's imagine the world's best assessment, 50 years or 100 years from now, run by somebody smarter than we are. What would it look like? Would it be fast and slick, a model of stunning efficiency? Or might today's "rush to judgment" approach be replaced by a more reflective style, tempered by a sense of compassion, which is to say, a genuine desire to help writers?

We are capable of so much more when it comes to writing assessment—but it all comes back to vision. Do we believe—*really believe*—that writing is thinking? If we do, we must stop focusing *all* our assessment energies on quick drafts written in response to meaningless topics. We must stop asking students to create purposeless writing for faux audiences of writers paid to read drafts in which they have no vested interest. Instead, let's design—and carry out—the kind of writing assessment that measures the effectiveness of process-based instruction.

In such an assessment, students would not only be allowed, but *required*, to choose their own topics. They would spend time exploring, researching, gathering information, talking to others, reflecting, and identifying questions *they* considered worthy of investigation. Armed with real information, a sense of direction, and the confidence these things provide, they would be given extended time in which to compose a first draft. They would have access to resources, including technology—the kind of support all professional writers take for granted.

Students would set their work aside for a time in order to gain the mental distance essential for good revision. During this time, they could, of course, do additional exploration. Real-world writers, after all, do most of their work away from their desks.

At some point, they would have an opportunity to share their writing with fellow writers. Using feedback selectively and thoughtfully is *very hard to do well*. It needs to be built into our assessment because it helps young writers understand how to use audience response wisely. Only nonwriters think that people in a response group can give you the "secret" by telling you what and how to write. In truth, learning to sift through a sea of voices to filter out what is useful takes both an open mind and thoughtful judgment.

Inspired by feedback and by their own reflective thinking, students would then *revise* their work. Imagine. Not just touch it up during the final five minutes of allotted writing time, but *really* revise: rethink the message, reorganize, release the voice. And in so doing, they would outrageously increase the odds that assessors would find what they had written both enlightening and engaging.

Speaking of assessors . . . we could then turn writing assessment on its head by asking *teachers*—the people who really care how the students perform—to assess their work. *But wait . . . Wouldn't external reviewers be more objective?* It's hard to believe that

Given only 25 minutes to write the SAT essay (30 minutes for the ACT essay), students will likely produce a kind of writing that is necessarily formulaic and superficial—writing that is very different from the lengthier, in-depth, and complex writing expected by most college instructors, who tend to discourage rapid, unrevised writing especially because it encourages rote organization and superficial thinking.

—NCTE Task Force
The Impact of the SAT and ACT Timed Writing Tests, April 2005, 3

Writing needs a lot of time—not just the time it takes to put the words down on the page, but time to reflect, to ponder an idea, to read, to stare out a window, to go for a walk, to gather courage and strength. All of this requires immeasurable amounts of time. When people ask me how long it took to write my first book I say, "It took four years to think about it and another year to write."

—Georgia Heard
Writing Toward Home, 1995, 21

Looking Forward: Expanding the Vision

anyone asks this question seriously. But they do. We might ask in return, Who is assessing our students *most* of the time?

Teachers have great insight when it comes to assessing student writing. They have experience. They know how writing process works within the classroom. And most important of all, teachers know how to dig for what Katherine Bomer calls the "hidden gems" inside students' writing. Teachers cry, wince, shiver, explode with laughter, shake their heads, close their eyes and remember—all when reading students' poems, stories, and essays. Where else will we find readers so appreciative of students' work? Nowhere. We have spent untold fortunes hunting for the flaws in student writing. Aren't we the least bit curious to discover what our writers *can* do? Teachers—like you—must be the ones to point out what students do well. Then we can follow the advice of the great Donald Murray and help our writers build upon those strengths.

4. BELIEVE THAT STUDENTS CAN WRITE.

Plenty of people will tell you otherwise. They cannot *wait* to tell you the many things that children cannot do in 25 minutes—forgetting that for many professional writers, the first 25 minutes of a writing work day involves pouring tea or coffee, looking out the window, reflecting on what the day will bring, reading a favorite poem or passage, and gathering thoughts in *preparation* for writing.

True enough, many student writers struggle. But I personally encounter students every year whose writing both moves and teaches me—so, I suspect, do you. Some truly fine student work—such as the poem by fourth grader Corinne (Figure 1), fifth grader Thomas's tribute to the teacher he will soon be leaving (Figure 2), or the witty, multi-layered celebration of individuality by high school senior Simona (Figure 3)—appears in this book. Much of it is stunning. You will not see their talent or success lauded in the newspaper, probably because, as a reporter told me once, "Kids writing well? *That's* not news. People want to hear about the *problems*." Rubbish. The much-guarded secret that countless American students write somewhere between functionally and brilliantly is beyond newsworthy—a story worth telling. Certainly it would be reassuring to parents desperate for their children to succeed in college or at the workplace. It would be emotionally lifesaving to teachers grading papers at 11 P.M. and wondering how else they can help their students "get it."

FIGURE 1

"Family"
by Corinne (Grade 4)

Without family you would be
a lone wolf
You'd be a stranger
to yourself
You would be the last leaf on the tree
Without family

FIGURE 2

"Mine"
by Thomas (Grade 5)

Her lips curve into a smile
As the day's first laugh engulf her.
"Uh-oh, math is hard," her frown at the book tells us—
But she congratulates us for our hard work.

She is the watering can of knowledge
Quenching my everlasting thirst,
Dripping and cooling you on a hot day.
Torn away, soon to be twice.
The second I dread
For it will be even more painful
Than the first.

But my heart never leaves her—
Always staying with her,
Part of my heart into hers
Forever and for eternity.

She is clearing lit by sunshine
When you're lost in a dark forest,
A path that provides clarity
In a blurry, unmarked land.
She is the barrier
That keeps me on track,
And she is my teacher.

Mine.

Author's Note

Thomas had the same teacher for grades 3 and 5. He was thrilled when she was transferred to grade 5, but heartbroken when he had to leave her for the second time—as his second stanza shows.

FIGURE 3

"A Bad Apple"
by Simona (Grade 12)

A Bad Apple

will spoil the bunch, the farmers say,
misbehavior spreads easily among fruit; more likely
the apple was just rebellious
and ripened faster, growing up to a different rhythm
from the rest
and incurring the wrath of the farmers.
Misbehavior among apples was a serious problem
in the days of candles and spinning wheels.

These days there are fewer mistakes.
Seeds are taken to labs
of polyethylene and electron microscopes.
Like the elements
people once thought that the seed
was the smallest entity of life.
But science has dissected the psyche of the seed.
Strands of protein are the secret of life,
chemicals that can be created on a Petri dish—
snip snip copy paste into the seed they go
a package of genetic perfection.
This is called scientific breakthrough.

The seeds are injected with codes for sweet red
    immortality.
An evil stepmother couldn't do better.
There is a new alarm clock that prods the seed to
    blossom, grow,
and ripen for maximum profit.
Pluck, pluck zip zip into little bags they go
a package of commercial perfection.
This is called economics.

The trees grow at the same rate creating an orchard
hideout in eleven point seven months.
Apples grow in perfect bunches
saccharine sweet and red
all at the same time
all the same

the same
each
one.

But once in a while there is one who hears the strains
of a cosmic melody
and a deeper life to be lived.
It is the first blossom to be kissed by the bee
before the others are even awake.
It delights in the adventures of the children who come
    to play
and learns of a world beyond the orchard,
of adventure and fairies in disguise and magic mirrors
    and wishes that come true.

The petals fall, the fruit begins to grow,
and the apple forgets about the polyethylene
and being genetically correct.
It hears rainstorms and marvels
at the brilliance of a butterfly
and whispers with fireflies
of midsummer night dreams.

The apple lives as an apple should,
becoming older, wiser, riper than the others—
and yes, a little bruised.
It tells the others that life
is not about lab-injected alarm clocks
mindlessly following the farmer
rushing from one point to the next.
Life is one juicy adventure.
Those who stop to savor it
risk getting bruised and wrinkled
and falling off the tree altogether.
But that doesn't stop them.
And they become more divine as a result.
Perhaps bad apples really are the sweetest.

5. Believe you can make a difference.

Admittedly, not *all* our student writers are achieving at a level that we can feel good about. But we have many options for changing this situation. Here are just a few things you can do . . .

Get involved . . .

. . . as a parent—or an educator. If you have children in school, read to them and listen to their writing. If you have an idea for improving writing instruction or assessment, share it. Start a blog. Talk with your school board. Don't assume others know more than you do about how things should be done. You test lessons, strategies, and literature every day, don't you? You make discoveries worth sharing—discoveries that could light the way for someone else. Make your voice heard.

Don't give up . . .

. . . even if your students seem to dislike writing. Read to them. Show them the many ways other writers have found to share their ideas with the world. Write with them and show them how you come up with ideas, how you write that first challenging line or come up with a title. Be surprised, shocked, overwhelmed, ecstatic when you read your students' work. Make sure they know your goal is not to be their best critic, but their most devoted reader.

Create your own vision of writing success.

Start with what *you* know to be true about writing. Trust yourself. If you write, you know more than you think. Don't stop there, though.

Familiarize yourself with the Common Core Standards of Writing—but don't assume *everything* will be captured in standards. While they provide an important beginning, no set of standards in the world is broad or insightful enough to inspire everything you'll want to do in your classroom.

To expand your own vision, review the strategies summarized by Steve Graham and Dolores Perin in *Writing Next* (2007) (see Chapter 1 of this book). Ask how many of these you currently incorporate—or could incorporate—into your instruction. Review the "habits of mind" summarized in the 2011 *Framework for Success in Postsecondary Writing* (see Chapter 12 of this book). Ask yourself, *How can I encourage habits of mind such as flexibility, persistence, curiosity, or engagement* in my classroom?

Take time to review the NCTE (National Council of Teachers of English) Beliefs about the Teaching of Writing. How close do they come to matching what *you* believe about writing instruction? How many of them fit your vision? (See www.ncte.org/positions/statements/writingbeliefs for a thorough explanation of each of NCTE's ten fundamental beliefs.)

Get comfortable with technology.

The fear goes away; the advantages don't. Technology allows writers to reach a broader audience than ever before in history, and gives new meaning to "finding a personal voice." For many students, it provides a world in which their comfort exceeds ours; they become *our* teachers, and in so doing, gain a measure of confidence and motivation previously unknown. Composing via technology prepares students for the flexibility they need to be communicators in a twenty-first century world—where "a writer might be asked to write a traditional essay, compose a webpage or video, and design a print brochure all based on similar information" (*Framework for Success*, 2011, 10).

I have no doubt that when you think about it, you are also a teacher-researcher. You just need to make the mental shift to thinking like one. And then, take another risk. Think about speaking out and writing. We need to have much more writing by teachers for teachers.

—Regie Routman
Literacy at the Crossroads, 1996, 169

Be a reader.

Almost nothing you can do as a teacher of writing will help you more than this simple thing. Read trade books, of course: picture books, chapter books, nonfiction, poetry, drama. Share what you love with students. Read books by the best educators of our time, as well. In Figure 4, you'll find a list of books I frequently recommend. Add your own favorites to this list and share them with a teacher reading group.

Recommended Resources for Teachers of Writing

- *After THE END: Teaching and Learning Creative Revision by Barry Lane*. 1993. Portsmouth, NH: Heinemann.
- *Bird by Bird* by Anne Lamott. 1995. New York: Random House.
- *Crafting Authentic Voice* by Tom Romano. 2004. Portsmouth, NH: Heinemann.
- *The Curious Researcher: A Guide to Writing Research Papers* by Bruce Ballenger. 4th edition. 2004. New York: Pearson.
- *The Digital Writing Workshop* by Troy Hicks. 2009. Portsmouth, NH: Heinemann.
- *Effective Instruction* by Jim Burke. 2008. New York: Scholastic.
- *Embracing Contraries* by Peter Elbow. 1986. New York: Oxford University Press.
- *A Fresh Look at Writing* by Donald H. Graves. 1994. Portsmouth, NH: Heinemann.
- *Hidden Gems: Naming and Teaching from the Brilliance in Every Student's Writing* by Katherine Bomer. 2010. Portsmouth, NH: Heinemann.
- *Holding On to Good Ideas in a Time of Bad Ones* by Thomas Newkirk. 2010. Portsmouth, NH: Heinemann.
- *In Pictures and In Words* by Katie Wood Ray. 2012. Portsmouth, NH: Heinemann.
- *Into Writing: The Primary Teacher's Guide to Writing Workshop* by Megan S. Sloan. 2009. Portsmouth, NH: Heinemann.
- *Little Big Minds* by Marietta McCarty. 2006. New York: Penguin.
- *The 9 Rights of Every Writer* by Vicki Spandel. 2005. Portsmouth, NH: Heinemann.
- *No More "I'm Done!" Fostering Independent Writers in the Primary Grades* by Jennifer Jacobson. 2010. Portland, ME: Stenhouse.
- *On Writing: A Memoir of the Craft* by Stephen King. 2000. New York: Scribner.
- *On Writing Well*, 30th Anniversary Edition by William Zinsser. 2006. New York: HarperCollins.
- *A Place for Wonder* by Georgia Heard & Jennifer McDonough. 2009. Portland, ME: Stenhouse.
- *Radical Reflections* by Mem Fox. 1993. New York: Harcourt Brace & Company.
- *Room to Write: Daily Invitations to a Writer's Life* by Bonni Goldberg. 1996. New York: G. P. Putnam's Sons.
- *Talking, Drawing, Writing: Lessons for Our Youngest Writers* by Martha Horn and Mary Ellen Giacobbe. 2007. Portland, ME: Stenhouse.
- *Testing is Not Teaching: What Should Count in Education* by Donald H. Graves. 2002. Portsmouth, NH: Heinemann.
- *What a Writer Needs* by Ralph Fletcher. 1993. Portsmouth, NH: Heinemann.
- *The Write Direction: A New Teacher's Practical Guide to Teaching Writing and Its Application to the Workplace* by Fred S. Wolff and Lynna Garber Kalna. 2010. New York: Pearson Education.
- *Writing to Change the World* by Mary Pipher. 2006. New York: Penguin.
- *Writing Toward Home: Tales and Lessons to Find Your Way* by Georgia Heard. 1995. Portsmouth, NH: Heinemann.
- *The Writing Workshop: Working Through the Hard Parts (And They're All Hard Parts)* by Katie Wood Ray with Lester Laminack. 2001. Urbana, IL: National Council of Teachers of English.
- *A Writer Teaches Writing* by Donald M. Murray. 2nd Edition. 2004. Boston: Houghton Mifflin.

Note: This list is very different from that in Chapter 8, page 255. That list includes books excellent for teaching or learning conventions of writing. This list includes books that focus on the craft and/or teaching of writing.

Make writing a part of every content area.

If you are an elementary teacher, provide opportunities for your students to write in connection with social science, physical science, math, art, and other subjects. If you teach at the secondary level, work with colleagues to ensure students write in every area possible, with support to make the gathering of information easy (through libraries, RSS feeds, online searches, and other sources). Diverse writing teaches flexibility of thinking since students must move not only from subject to subject, but audience to audience—using different "languages" and conventions at the same time. As Rafael Heller and Cynthia L. Greenleaf (2007) state, "Every academic content area—and every nonacademic kind of text as well—has its own vocabulary, textual formats, stylistic conventions, and ways of understanding, analyzing, interpreting, and responding to words on the page" (8). Students who can move easily from human experience to scientific analysis will definitely have an edge in twenty-first century writing.

Flexibility is now perhaps the most prized goal of writing instruction because the fairly proficient writer can adapt to different contexts, formats, and purposes for writing.
—Steve Graham and Dolores Perin
Writing Next, 2007, 22

Help students find authentic audiences.

It isn't enough for writers to write just for us—or even for their peers. They need to write to businesses in your area, to the community in general, to the President, to Congress, to favorite authors or sports figures, to students in other states or parts of the world. They need to see their work published online or in physical format made possible by technology. They need an opportunity to share before gatherings of teachers, students, and community members who come not to assess but to celebrate what our writers can do.

It was and still is a wonder for me, what books are and how they become part of a reader's mind and soul. I thank all of the writers I've read and all of the readers who've read my books for allowing me the unending thrill of being a part of this crazy dance of words.
—Gary Paulsen, editor
Shelf Life: Stories by the Book, 2003, 9

Build a classroom your students will love.

Being a literate person isn't *all* about performance. If we do not help students to love reading and writing, nothing else we do will matter very much. Never miss a chance to share your love for books—or for any writing. The teacher who taught me to love Shakespeare read aloud to us every day. He played all the parts, Cleopatra to Hamlet, astonishing us with his repertoire of voices—and hilarious facial expressions. He threw himself into every role, shunning all dignity to become an outrageous Falstaff or a menacing Richard III. This teacher had found something to do in life that he loved, and he wanted us to love it, too. We did. To this day, I cannot attend a theatrical performance of any kind without thinking of him.

Make safety a priority.

This is more easily said than done in a social context where assessment is so highly valued, and where fear of "the test" is a way of life. Fear, though, is not conducive to learning. In his provocative book *Social Intelligence,* Daniel Goleman explores the conditions under which optimal learning can occur, and concludes that one requirement is security: "By offering a secure base, a teacher creates an environment that lets students' brains function at their best" (2006, 283).

Narrative writing is even discouraged in the first-year [university level] writing courses, even though one could argue that English departments are built upon narratives; they would not exist without narratives.
—Thomas Newkirk
Holding On to Good Ideas in a Time of Bad Ones, 2009, 54

Author's Note

Don't be afraid of narrative. Sometimes narrative is looked upon as a simple form, quickly mastered before students move on to the more "serious" writing of academic essays, informational reports, and persuasive arguments. In truth, narrative writing is extraordinarily challenging and teaches complex thinking through character development, plot (which requires both imagination and the most deft organizational skill of any genre), and the tension required to keep a reader engaged, continually anticipating events while never knowing *too* much.

How do we create this safety net? By being writers ourselves. By sharing our own writing first—and inviting comments. By tempering insight with compassion in any feedback we offer, looking always for what has potential and by implication, teaching students to do the same. By respecting our students as fellow writers. And by *loving* what they write. By letting students know we cannot get enough, that the words they write (in the language of one student) "joy our day."

6. BELIEVE THAT WRITING ISN'T JUST A SKILL FOR SCHOOL, BUT A SKILL FOR LIFE.

Learning to write takes a lifetime, not a semester. It is *hard*. When our students do not master it quickly, it is usually not for lack of testing, teaching, or effort. It is the complex and difficult nature of the task itself. Once we become writers, we recognize this. But the struggle is worth it.

A 2004 survey of more than 160 of America's top corporations conducted by the College Board suggests that almost nothing we do better prepares students for work than teaching them to write well. That report states that nearly all corporate executives look on writing as a "marker" of high skill, suggesting that "educational institutions interested in preparing students for rewarding and remunerative work should concentrate on developing graduates' writing skills" (19). One respondent summed it up this way: "You can't move up without writing skills" (3).

In *The Write Direction* (2010, 97) authors Fred Wolff and Lynna Garber Kalna identify six qualities that corporate America identifies as essential to success on the job—and link them directly to the six traits of writing: clarity (*ideas*), format (*organization*), tone (*voice*), vocabulary (*word choice*), style (*sentence fluency*), and error-free text + document design (*conventions & presentation*).

Graham and Perrin (2007) note that in college, most writing tasks are expository in nature—which they define as "reporting, summarizing and analyzing factual information, and expressing an opinion with the support of evidence" (23). While workplace writing also calls for informational writing skills, the forms writing takes in a work environment stretch far beyond what we see in many classrooms, and that, of course, must change.

We can help students make the leap into workplace writing by including in our classroom repertoire forms that writers *are* likely to produce on the job:

- proposals
- project evaluations
- predictions
- reviews
- book jackets
- summaries
- keynote speeches
- lessons
- letters and memos
- news summaries and analyses
- interpretive data analyses
- economic forecasts

- questionnaires
- product evaluations
- press releases
- brochures and other promo pieces
- technical instructions
- social commentary
- journalistic reports
- scripts
- websites
- wikis
- blogs
- videos

Are we out of our comfort zone with some of these writing forms? Probably. But we cannot ask students to write only what makes us comfortable—or even what makes them comfortable. We can't spend all our time writing for the test, either. We must spend a little of it writing for our lives.

7. BELIEVE THAT VOICE IS POWER.

"Divorcing voice from process," Donald Graves tells us, "is like omitting salt from stew, love from sex, or sun from gardening" (2003, 227). Voice is the reason for the writing.

Moreover, it is the primary reason—beyond the simple gathering of information—that most of us read. Voice is the human spirit, the essence of all that we feel and believe and know to be true. It is, ultimately, our ethnic, cultural, spiritual, and individual identity. Our verbal fingerprints.

Voice shakes our consciousness, awakens us, and causes us to see and act in new ways. To write with voice is to hold in our hands the power to shape destiny. Our children have this power. We can nurture it—or suppress it. We rob our children of voice when we:

- Consistently choose topics for them, requiring them to write about things in which they have no personal interest or about which they know little.
- Neglect to read deeply and widely ourselves, and to share contemporary voices—from a range of genres and cultures.
- Discourage students from expressing the truth as *they* see it, especially when it conflicts with what we view as acceptable or conventionally popular.
- Hide our innermost responses to literature, embarrassed to reveal how emotionally vulnerable writing can make us.
- Force students' ideas into universal, uninspired formulaic patterns that distort and camouflage rather than reveal thinking.
- Restrict options for presenting information because we do not feel as comfortable with new forms—podcasts, videos, or others—as we should.
- Seek convenient, rapid ways to assess instead of taking the time and effort required to read students' work with understanding and appreciation.
- *Correct* conventions instead of taking time to *teach* them.
- Hesitate to lose ourselves in the depths of students' writing, and let them see how much their writing touches us.

> We either teach our children it's okay to write and talk about the things they think to be the truth or else we teach them that it's more acceptable to silence their beliefs . . .
>
> —Jonathan Kozol
> *Letters to a Young Teacher,* 2007, 86

8. BELIEVE THAT YOU CAN TEACH.

It's what you were born to do, isn't it? Don't allow a test score or a whole battery of test scores to steal your rightful heritage from you. Remember, anyone can be a critic. Not everyone can teach. Only the brave teach.

Treasure that moment when you look out into a sea of faces and eyes look back at you with an unspoken message, "I understand." That moment (see Figure 5, the teacher's reply to fifth grader Thomas) is the most powerful assessment of a teacher's skill. So what if no one else sees or records it? Dare to value what cannot be measured.

Don't give in to the temptation of formulaic writing, which provides the illusion of writing success without any of the satisfaction or sense of achievement. Almost anyone can be taught to fill in blanks if we make the formula simple enough, just as almost anyone can paint by numbers. Formulaic writing may lift floundering students to mediocrity, but the price is high, for it fosters formulaic thinking. Students who write

FIGURE 5

"A Celebration of Thomas"
by Judy Mazur (5th Grade Teacher)

Eager eyes spark and he sits a little taller,
he learns.
"Something new," he seems to say—with quiet relish.
He rolls it around on his tongue, in his brain.
It belongs to him.

His pencil hovers
above the void
ready for any challenge
as he considers, mulls, knows.
Yes, he always knows.

Yet he cares about you,
really cares.
He listens with his heart
and wants you to share his contentment.
He knows peace.

A tree, growing skyward,
thirsty for knowledge—
offering you a spot to rest
in his shade, in his giving.
Always giving.

to fill in blanks rather than to express what they passionately believe will never lead others to new levels of understanding, compel hungry readers to turn pages, knock down barricades of prejudice, or land Oscars for screenwriting. What a hefty price to pay for a tiny formula that will be of use nowhere save on a test.

Teach students to be strong editors—not by correcting conventions, as was done for us—but by modeling twenty-first century conventions as they are now used by the best editors of our time. Check current and reliable handbooks (see Chapter 8 for a list). Read from these sources routinely. Provide students with extensive, frequent practice in editing text of all kinds: poetry, fiction, informational text, technical pieces, business writing, journalistic reports, blogs, websites—and your own writing. Don't edit for them. No one learns to swim by clinging to the side of the pool.

Celebrate students' successes, however small. When a student's writing moves you, don't tell a colleague or friend; tell the writer. Expect of yourself, because you *are* a teacher, that you can look deep within, that you can find even the smallest surprises that others would miss. In a tender and philosophical little book called *The Dot* (Reynolds, 2003), the young and blossoming author/artist Vashti can't bring herself to put more than a single dot on that huge white sheet of paper and is horrified by her own limitations—but she takes sudden pride in her work when her teacher asks if she will please *sign it*, and then posts her signed piece on the wall.

Believe that the best thing you have to give your students is *you*. You sharing the books you love, daring to read your words aloud, laughing, grimacing, struggling to say what you mean, never giving up, and just being a genuine, human presence in your writers' lives. No book, no set of lessons, no strategies gleaned from a seminar or conference can take the place of you being you. If all you had was blank paper and pencils, you could still teach students to write—*if you believed you could*.

Trust your heart. Believe that just around the bend is a new piece of writing to surprise and delight you. Never fear being too readily impressed. Never be ashamed of your unabashed joy at a student's success, however humble; it is the greatest gift you can give a young writer who longs for someone to love the words on the page. Believe that as a teacher you are doing the most important work anyone can do—opening doors to new thinking.

As Parker J. Palmer reminds us, no innovation, no reform movement, no amount of restructuring, and no set of standards will "transform education if we fail to cherish—and challenge—the human heart that is the source of good teaching" (1998, p. 3). Believe that every time you listen thoughtfully to your students' work, share your own writing (good or bad), express your sense of joy in discovering a new, fine piece of literature, or help a student writer hear a moment of voice in his or her writing that just a second ago that writer did not know was there, you are making a difference—for you are.

How to Be a Flower

I'll start out as a seed and become a colorful flower.

I will grow long roots to drink water.

I will remember to produce oxygen.

The bees will gather my pollen.

I will have a fragrant smell and stand up tall.

I will be a gift to people who like me.

When I die, my soul will become art.

—**Gail Robinson's Fourth Graders,**
Room 106,
Jeffrey Elementary School,
Kenosha, Wisconsin

Appendix 1 History of the Traits

It's widely believed that the six-trait model was developed by a publishing house, testing company, or national laboratory. Actually—it wasn't. The real history is far more interesting; I know because I was fortunate enough to be part of it.

The six traits are as grassroots as you can get. They were developed—over a period of some months—by a 17-member teacher team known as the Analytical Writing Assessment Development Committee (AWADC). The committee members were volunteer teachers, grades 3 through 12, from the Beaverton, Oregon, School District #48, just outside Portland. They were passionate about good assessment—but mostly, they were passionate about teaching writing, and believed that good assessment offered one key to doing it better. The committee began their research on existing models of analytical writing in 1984, and they felt ready to finalize a workable analytical scale of their own in 1985 (when I was invited to join the team to help with that part of the project). Once the final draft came together, all of us were excited about the work we had done—though none of us could envision at the time the reach this concept would have.

Paul Diederich: The Inspiration

Beaverton's innovative research design was based largely on work done in the 1960s by Paul Diederich (as documented in *Measuring Growth in English*, 1974). Diederich had been curious to know whether people could agree on what makes writing work and whether they could come up with language to describe what they found. His research method was ingenious in its simplicity. He assembled a group of fifty or so writers, editors, attorneys, business executives, and English, natural science, and social science teachers and asked them to read numerous student essays and rank them into three groups: effective, developing (about halfway home), and problematic. Then—this is the interesting part—they were asked to record their reasons for ranking the papers as they had. In the process, they discovered something rather striking: In most cases they were influenced by nearly identical qualities (traits) in the writing. Here (listed here in order of apparent influence) are the traits Diederich's team identified. Notice that these are *conceptually* nearly identical to the six traits identified by Beaverton, except that sentence structure (or what we called *fluency*) was included under mechanics:

- Ideas
- Mechanics (usage, sentence structure, punctuation, and spelling)
- Organization and analysis
- Wording and phrasing
- Flavor (voice, tone, and style)

Confirmation from Purves and Murray

Over the years, Diederich's method has been replicated by other researchers, including Donald Murray (1982) and Alan Purves (1992). Both Murray and Purves identified traits similar to those described by both Diederich and the Beaverton School District. In his work on international writing assessment, Purves and his team of raters identified the following significant traits:

- Content (what we call *ideas*)
- Organization
- Style and tone (what we call *voice, word choice*, and *sentence fluency*)
- Surface features (essentially *conventions*)
- Personal response of the reader (essentially, response to the quality we call *voice*)

In 1982, Donald Murray (66–67) identified these six traits—also closely aligned with those in this book:

- Meaning
- Authority
- Voice
- Development
- Design
- Clarity

Meaning and clarity equate with the trait of ideas, design with organization, voice and authority with voice.

Beaverton: The First Six-Trait Rubric

Beaverton had been conducting holistic writing assessment throughout the late 1970s and early 1980s—and they weren't happy with it. As indicated in Chapter 12, holistic scoring yields one score per paper, and because there is no way to know what problems or strengths are indicated by a given score, results can be difficult to interpret and therefore have little or no impact on instruction. The Beaverton teachers and administrators believed that if they could identify the salient characteristics that distinguish successful from unsuccessful writing, they could transform writing assessment (and instruction) in their classrooms.

Inspired by Diederich's research design, Beaverton's Analytical Assessment Development Committee set about to identify the qualities that make writing work. Carol Meyer (then director of evaluation and assessment for the district) and I were privileged to direct and work with this team. We spent weeks reading student papers at every grade level from 3 through 12, sorting them into high, middle, and beginning levels and documenting our reasons for ranking them as we did. Eventually, we arranged our documentation along a continuum of writing performance, and the result was a draft of what would eventually become the six-trait assessment model.

Footnote: Shortly thereafter, Portland Public Schools conducted a similar study—in which I also participated. Minus any collaboration with Beaverton, Portland came up with traits virtually identical to those of Beaverton, their list also closely matching that of Diederich. Since Portland had no knowledge of Beaverton's work or Diederich's, this similarity further reinforced our belief that teachers *do* in fact share common values about what is important in writing.

Field Testing: Beaverton and the Oregon Department of Education

Once the model was finalized, everyone was eager to put it to the test. In spring of 1985, Beaverton conducted a field test of their new six-trait model by analytically assessing the writing of approximately 5,000 students in grades 3, 5, 8, and 11 (1,250 papers per grade level). I was asked to be scoring director, and we recruited raters locally: teachers, part-time and retired teachers, and substitutes. They were extremely enthusiastic—and dedicated to improving students' writing. We routinely took time to read and discuss students' writing with one another—and also read from trade books that exemplified strong detail, voice, fluency, or word choice. At the end of our scoring time, people said it had been "like going to camp." They *all*, to a person, volunteered to return the following year—but they didn't have to wait that long to get more scoring experience.

Administrators from the Oregon Department of Education had come to observe us during the scoring, and liked what they saw. They noticed the camaraderie among raters, the enthusiasm they brought to their work, and—most of all—the extraordinary commitment to assessing students' work fairly and well. They decided to break a

ten-year holistic tradition and begin scoring students' writing for the Oregon State Assessment analytically. That first year, they focused on grade 8, but because they were so pleased with the results and the process, they gradually expanded, eventually assessing the writing of virtually all the state's students in grades 3, 5, 8, and 11. For the next several years, Oregon used the Beaverton model, at that time a five-point scale. Eventually, they moved to a six-point scale, and developed their own version of that scale—but they remained committed to analytical scoring.

The Oregon Department of Education sponsored training workshops throughout the state, and ultimately conducted scoring regionally through several Educational Service Districts (rather than in just one central location) in order to maximize participation by Oregon teachers who wanted to be readers for the state assessment. The Department felt strongly that such experience offered extremely beneficial professional development to teachers, and repeatedly, teacher-raters expressed how much insight they gained from seeing and discussing the writing of hundreds of students—not just those in their own classrooms.

Our experience in those early days bore *no resemblance* to the assembly-line process of today's high-powered scoring in out-of-town locations. Readers laughed and lingered over papers that told of memorable teachers, inspiring—or hovering—parents, pets gone wild, school musicals gone wrong, zany family get-togethers, improvisational Halloween costumes, wacky or devoted friends, first loves, loyal or mischievous pets, shoes that made the wearer feel grown up, a jacket that made the wearer feel he could fly, sports games where memories were made. They cried over tales of alcoholism, drug abuse, child abuse, divorce, unwanted moves, broken hearts, lost jobs, lost friends or loved ones, brave pets that didn't make it, grandparents no one could forget. Countless papers were shared aloud, and favorites were flagged for inclusion in a collection published by the Department every year at the close of the assessment. It was a time we cherished.

Oregon's switch to analytical scoring prompted enormous interest throughout the Northwest, and soon districts throughout the region were using the six-trait model and seeking workshops to support this development. Requests for workshops poured in from Alaska, Nevada, Washington, Idaho—and Kansas. Australian teachers called to ask for copies of our rubrics. Gradually, the model was adapted for use by at least one district in virtually every state. Teachers, administrators, and assessment specialists appreciated the opportunity to identify students' strengths; reports typically included not only average scores but so-called exemplar papers representing performance at various levels. Countless teachers incorporated these exemplars into their instruction. In time, the model's reputation spread, and it came to be used by teachers in every part of the world—but this happened largely in thanks to the creativity of teachers who had the foresight to take the traits into the classroom.

Teaching the Traits to Students

Two inspired teachers from Beaverton's AWADC took the lead in making the traits accessible to students. They were Ronda Woodruff (who taught grade four at the time), and Jocelyn Hoffman (who taught grades two and three). Together, they developed a "student friendly" version of the original scoring guide—and began sharing it with students in the classroom, together with sample papers. Ronda very kindly invited me to work with her and some of her students—an opportunity I enjoyed enormously. A few teachers had been skeptical that students could be taught to assess writing, or that the traits would significantly influence their writing or revising. Ronda and I quickly discovered, however, that students not only took to the traits but quickly learned to assess anything that wouldn't get up and run away: textbooks, encyclopedias, office memos—and more. At the time Ronda said, "They learn this faster than we do because they don't have all that teacher baggage—they're like fresh little slates." Indeed. Within weeks of beginning to use scoring guides, not only did students' drafts begin to explode with detail and voice, but they looked forward to revision—and began to read differently as well. When Ronda's students received their long-awaited pen pal letters from another country, they ripped them open with excitement they could not contain—and then their faces fell. Why? we wondered. As one student put it, "We wrote them 5s and they sent us back 3s." The face of writing had changed.

Reaching Out: The Northwest Regional Educational Laboratory (NWREL)

In 1990, just after being hired (for the fifth time) to direct scoring for the Oregon State Writing Assessment, I returned to work for the Assessment Department of the Northwest Regional Educational Laboratory in Portland Oregon. I took the six-trait model (now nearly six years old) with me, of course. NWREL embraced the model fully. Though they had played no role in its initial development, they enthusiastically supported creation of extensive workshop materials—and the sharing of those materials throughout the Northwest and the nation. We modified the original rubric somewhat, and also developed our own version of Beaverton's "student friendly" rubric (other student versions—like those in this book—were developed later).

The first edition of *Creating Writers* had just been released. That rather skinny edition was co-written by Rick Stiggins, also a Senior Associate with the Assessment Program at NWREL. Rick was a champion advocate of the six traits from the beginning, and although he had not participated in development of the six-trait criteria or rubrics, he saw the traits as a model of what good performance assessment could be. We did countless workshops together in which he emphasized quality assessment and I presented the traits as an example; from that experience grew the idea of co-authoring a book. Rick's portion of the book, which focused on the qualities of sound performance assessment, was written partly under the auspices of NWREL; my portion, focusing on writing and the analytical assessment of student samples, was written independently.

Our NWREL assessment staff conducted numerous six-trait workshops, and even did some training internationally. And it was during this period that I published, through NWREL, two additional books relating to the traits: *Seeing with New Eyes*, a book on primary writing, and *Dear Parent*, a resource for parents who wanted to support their students' trait-based instruction.

The Laboratory, in time, modified their version of the six-trait model, changing its name to "6+1" to accommodate presentation as an individual trait, rather than as part of conventions and publishing. The concept of presentation first gained prominence in the mid-90s when several members of the NWREL assessment staff worked to develop a technical writing workshop, and discovered what a vital role presentation can play in effective technical writing—particularly with respect to such elements as charts, diagrams, maps, or other graphics. Presentation is now recognized as vital to many forms of writing.

Research by NWREL

As an agency committed to research, NWREL was eager to show the impact of teaching the traits directly. They conducted several studies to this end—one of which I was part of. That study involved six fifth grade classrooms, and was conducted during the 1992–1993 school year. Several of us who knew the six-trait model well worked directly with teachers in three of the classrooms, teaching students as teachers observed, coaching teachers between sessions, and providing materials. Our instruction emphasized three traits: ideas, organization, and voice. Teachers in other classrooms taught writing as they had previously, without any coaching or special materials provided.

The students were assessed prior to and following the intervention in two genres: narrative and expository writing. Papers were coded and read blindly in the spring, following all trait-based instruction. The trained raters who scored the papers had no idea whether or not they were reading before or after samples, or whether the papers were from students in the six-trait classrooms. Results did show greater gains in writing performance in the three focus traits—ideas, organization, and voice—for those students who had received direct instruction in the six traits. (See Arter, J.A., Spandel, V., Culham, R., and Pollard, J., "The Impact of Training Students to Be Self-Assessors of Writing." Paper presented at the annual meeting of the American Educational Research Association. New Orleans.)

Results of this research, while compelling, are far from conclusive. There are simply too many variables to control in such a study, including differences in groups prior to any intervention, exposure to traits among both groups, and even similarities and differences in instruction during the study itself. It is quite possible (even probable), for example, that teachers in the "non-trait" classes actually did refer (quite innocently and unintentionally) to various traits, even without ever using the term *trait* or meaning to teach traits directly. Further there is no real way to know how much of the measurable difference was attributable to individual instructors' style, personal effectiveness, or ability to motivate students—or even to the inherent capabilities of the student writers themselves.

As I point out in every workshop, it is virtually impossible to teach writing *without* teaching the traits in some way, in some form. You certainly don't have to call them traits—and you don't have to use rubrics. But terms and rubrics are not the cornerstones of trait-based instruction. What's essential is the teaching of *concepts*: what it means to develop an idea, to organize information, to share one's voice with readers, and so on. And the teaching of such concepts is an inherent part of *any* good writing instruction. It is highly challenging—probably impossible—even for research purposes, to set up a writing classroom from which the traits are *totally* excluded. This realization should, in my view, temper our interpretation of any results. What the study probably *does* suggest is that giving students direct, repeated practice in applying various writing elements (detail, strong lead or conclusion, effective wording, voice) has a positive impact on their writing performance. In short, focused trait-based instruction

works. (This is basically what Ronda and I had observed in her fourth grade classroom.)

Over time, the Northwest Laboratory has conducted additional research relating to the efficacy of the traits. For information on procedures and outcomes, check out "Six Traits Research by Michael Kozlow and Peter Bellamy," online.

Great Source Education: New Lessons . . . and More

In 1997, I joined the staff of Great Source Education. Over the next several years, with the support and input of teachers throughout the country, we created entirely new six-trait writing guides, including guides for young students. In addition, we developed original lessons for teaching traits to students of all ages. These materials became the basis for a fresh round of workshops (under the banner *Write Traits*) that grew increasingly popular over the decade that followed. We assembled a team of trainers who took the traits throughout the country and beyond, continually adding their own innovations and literary recommendations.

For years, teachers had asked for published lesson sets—and through Great Source, we were able to respond to this need. My partner Jeff Hicks (the best co-writer with whom I've yet to work) and I put together the first *Write Traits Kits*, sets of lessons, trait by trait, that were grade-specific. This set, published by Great Source, was updated and expanded in 2010.

With so many resources now available, people often ask if there is conflict—or at least competition. Not really, no. After all, there is no limit to the number of lessons, strategies or literary resources for supporting writing—and so no need for one set of lessons to replicate another. And of course, since I have had a hand in writing various books and lesson sets, it has been one of my goals to ensure that the resources I help produce are complementary but unique, not repetitions of one another. I am grateful to the publishers and editors at both Pearson Education and Great Source Education (now part of Houghton Mifflin Harcourt) for their support in achieving this goal.

As of Now . . .

The six-trait model belonged first to Beaverton, but now it belongs to teachers *everywhere*, many of whom have contributed to its revision and expansion into multiple forms. In many states, it is very closely aligned to state standards—as well as to the Common Core Standards for Writing.

Its wide use is largely due to three things: First, it simply reflects the heart and soul of what good writing is about, with definitions expressed in clear, easy-to-understand language from which teachers can teach. Second, it has a kind of déjà vu feel to it, echoing what teachers themselves believe about good writing—and no wonder. It's written in their own words. Truly, the six traits are writing teachers' gift to themselves. And third, it is essentially a literature-based approach to writing that allows teachers to show students that writing is—as Donald Graves always said—the making of reading. No other approach to writing instruction that I know of makes such extensive use of literature or so closely links reading to writing.

Teachers who use this model continue to make it their own, creating lessons, discovering new books and other written materials that show how writing works, modifying writing guides and creating checklists with the help of their students. Many creative teachers have adapted the traits to art, video, or other forms of expression—and undoubtedly, new creative applications will emerge as composition expands well beyond the written page.

Appendix 2 Teacher Three-Level Writing Guide

Ideas and Development

5/6

The writing is clear, focused, and well developed, with many important, intriguing details.

- ❑ The writer is selective, avoiding trivia, and choosing details that keep readers reading.
- ❑ The topic or story is narrow, focused, and manageable.
- ❑ Details work together to clarify and expand the main idea.
- ❑ The writer's knowledge, experience, insight, and perspective lend the piece authenticity.
- ❑ The amount of detail is just right—not skimpy, not overwhelming.

3/4

The writer has made a solid beginning. It is easy to see where the piece is headed, though more expansion would be helpful.

- ❑ Global information provides the big picture, making the reader long for more specifics.
- ❑ Greater focus might help narrow or shape the topic.
- ❑ Intriguing details blend with common knowledge or generalities.
- ❑ Still, the writer draws from knowledge, experience, or research to make some important points.
- ❑ Sections feel a bit sketchy—or repetitive.

1/2

Sketchy, loosely focused information forces the reader to make inferences. Readers notice one or more of these problems:

- ❑ The topic or central idea is undefined or unclear.
- ❑ The topic is so big—*All About Earth*—that it is hard for the writer to focus in and say anything meaningful.
- ❑ The writer does not know enough about the topic.
- ❑ The writing fills space, but lacks substance.
- ❑ Everything seems as important as everything else. No MAIN message pops out at the reader.

Organization

5/6

The order, presentation, and structure of the piece are compelling and guide the reader purposefully through the text.

- ❑ A strong sense of balance gives main ideas center stage.
- ❑ The structure showcases ideas without dominating them.
- ❑ An inviting lead draws writers in; a satisfying conclusion provides closure and prompts thought.
- ❑ Details fit just where they are placed.
- ❑ Transitions are smooth, helpful, and natural.
- ❑ The writer knows just when to linger—and when to move along.

3/4

The order lets readers move through the text without undue confusion.

- ❑ Key ideas can be identified.
- ❑ Order may be predictable, but it is not random.
- ❑ The reader feels an urge to reorder or delete some information.
- ❑ Transitions are present—they may seem formulaic.
- ❑ The reader sometimes wants to speed ahead or slow down to reflect.

1/2

Ideas seem loosely or randomly strung together, creating confusion. Readers notice one or more of these problems:

- ❑ The writing lacks a sense of direction and balance.
- ❑ Structure is missing—or so formulaic it overpowers ideas.
- ❑ No true lead sets things up; no conclusion offers closure.
- ❑ The story or discussion is hard to follow.
- ❑ Missing or unclear transitions leave the reader to build bridges.
- ❑ The writer consistently dawdles, or speeds through what needs explaining.

Voice

5/6

The writer's passion for the topic drives the writing, making the text lively, expressive, and engaging.

- ❏ The tone and flavor of the piece are just right for the topic, purpose, and audience.
- ❏ The writing bears the clear imprint of *this* writer.
- ❏ The writer seems to know the audience and to anticipate their interests and informational needs.
- ❏ Narrative text is moving and honest; informational text is lively and engaging.
- ❏ This is a piece readers want to share aloud.

3/4

The writing communicates in a sincere, functional manner. It has lively moments.

- ❏ The tone and flavor are generally acceptable for purpose, topic, and audience.
- ❏ The writer has not fully found his/her voice, but is experimenting.
- ❏ On occasion, the writer reaches out to the audience.
- ❏ Voice comes and goes as the writer's engagement with the topic fluctuates.
- ❏ Readers may wish to share brief passages aloud.

1/2

The writer seems distanced from the audience, topic, or both. Readers notice one or more of these problems:

- ❏ The voice does not suit the topic, purpose, or audience.
- ❏ This writer's individual spirit is hiding behind an "anybody" voice.
- ❏ The reader has difficulty paying attention; the writer is not working to make the topic come alive for an audience.
- ❏ There is no person "at home" in the words.
- ❏ Moments of individuality or liveliness are missing or rare.
- ❏ The writing is not yet "asking" to be shared aloud.

Word Choice

5/6

Precise, vivid, natural language enhances the message and paints a clear picture in the reader's mind.

- ❏ The writer's meaning is clear throughout the piece.
- ❏ Phrasing is original—even memorable—yet the language is never overdone.
- ❏ Lively verbs lend the writing energy and power.
- ❏ Modifiers are effective and not overworked.
- ❏ The writer uses repetition only for effect.
- ❏ Striking words or phrases linger in the reader's memory.

3/4

The language communicates in a functional manner. It gets the job done.

- ❏ Most words are used correctly and convey a general message.
- ❏ Memorable phrases intermingle with overwritten—or underwritten—passages.
- ❏ A strong verb or two—the reader wishes for more!
- ❏ The writer may rely too heavily on modifiers—or clichés, overworked phrases, jargon. (Put the thesaurus away!)
- ❏ Some words or phrases are repeated—it's not a serious problem.
- ❏ Promising words or phrases catch the reader's attention.

1/2

The writer struggles to get the right words on paper. Readers notice one or more of these problems:

- ❏ Words are used incorrectly (*The bus impelled into the motel*).
- ❏ Vague words (*She was nice . . . The decision had impact*) convey only the most general messages.
- ❏ Modifiers weigh the text down—strong verbs are scarce or missing.
- ❏ Inflated language makes the text hard to penetrate.
- ❏ Word choice is repetitive, vague, unclear, or distracting.
- ❏ The words just don't speak to the reader.

Sentence Fluency

5/6

Easy flow and sentence sense make the text a delight to read aloud.

- ❏ Sentences are well crafted with a strong, varied structure that invites expressive oral reading.
- ❏ Striking variety gives language texture and interest.
- ❏ Purposeful sentence beginnings help connect thoughts.
- ❏ The writing has cadence, as if the reader hears the beat in his/her head.
- ❏ Fragments or repetition, if used, add style and punch; dialogue, if used, is natural and effective.

3/4

The text hums along with a steady beat. It is fairly readable.

- ❏ Most sentences are easy to read aloud with practice.
- ❏ The text shows some variety in sentence structure and length.
- ❏ Some sentences have purposeful beginnings: *After a while, As it turned out, On the other hand.*
- ❏ Graceful, natural phrasing intermingles with mechanical structure.
- ❏ Fragments or repetition are not always effective; dialogue does not always echo real speech.

1/2

An interpretive reading of this text takes practice. Readers notice one or more of these problems:

- ❏ Irregular or unusual word patterns hinder readability.
- ❏ It is hard to tell where sentences begin and end.
- ❏ Repetitive patterns or choppy sentences are common.
- ❏ Endless connecting phrases (*and then, so then, because*) create gangly word string "sentences" that leave readers breathless.
- ❏ The reader must reread or fill in words to create meaning.
- ❏ Fragments or repetition seem accidental; dialogue sounds forced—or is hard to pick out from other text.

Conventions & Presentation

5/6

The writer shows excellent control over a wide range of age-appropriate conventions and uses them to enhance voice and meaning.

- ❏ Errors are so few and minor a reader could skip right over them unless searching for them specifically.
- ❏ The text appears clean, edited, polished. It's easy to process.
- ❏ Only light touchups are needed for publication.
- ❏ Conventions bring out both meaning and voice.
- ❏ The presentation enhances and showcases the message.

3/4

The writer shows reasonable control over widely used, grade-appropriate conventions.

- ❏ Errors are noticeable, but the writer also handles some conventions well.
- ❏ The text is lightly edited; the reader must do a little "mental editing."
- ❏ Moderate to thorough editing is needed prior to publication.
- ❏ Conventional problems do not obscure the message.
- ❏ The presentation is adequate to support readability.

1/2

The writer demonstrates limited control even over widely used conventions. Readers notice one or more of these problems:

- ❏ Errors are frequent and/or serious enough to be distracting, even for patient readers.
- ❏ The text does not appear edited. The reader must frequently pause, reread, decode, or mentally edit (fill in, correct).
- ❏ Extensive line-by-line or word-by-word editing is needed prior to publication.
- ❏ Conventional problems slow the reader or obscure the message.
- ❏ The presentation needs work; it is distracting or not yet fully thought out.

Appendix 3 Student Three-Level Writing Guide

Ideas and Development

5/6

My writing is clear, focused, and filled with important, interesting details.

❑ I have a clear main message—or a story to tell.
❑ The topic is small and manageable and I stick to it.
❑ I chose intriguing details that expand my key ideas and answer a reader's questions thoroughly.
❑ I know this topic very well, and it shows.
❑ I cover what matters without burying the reader alive in trivia.

3/4

I have made a good beginning. You can see where I'm headed.

❑ I have a main message or a story. My writing makes sense.
❑ My topic might be a little big. Most of the time, I stay in bounds.
❑ I chose some interesting details—I might have included a few things you've heard before.
❑ I know some things about this topic—I wish I knew more.
❑ Sometimes I didn't tell enough—or I repeated myself.

1/2

I wrote something, but I really don't have a message or story in mind yet. I have one or more of these problems:

❑ I'm not sure what I'm trying to say.
❑ My topic is so big—*All About Earth*—that I can't tell where to begin.
❑ I just wrote to fill space. I didn't know what was important.
❑ I don't know enough about this topic to write.
❑ I repeated things. Or I wrote whatever came into my head.

Organization

5/6

This is so easy to follow it's like I drew you a road map.

❑ I know right where I'm going, beginning to end.
❑ The organization makes ideas easy to follow—but I wouldn't rule out a surprise twist or turn.
❑ My lead draws you right in. My conclusion wraps things up and leaves you thinking.
❑ Every detail comes at *just* the right moment.
❑ I connect ideas so you can tell how one thought leads to another.
❑ I explain what's complicated—but skip over things that aren't important to my topic or story.

3/4

You can follow this if you pay attention.

❑ I go down a few side roads—but you won't get lost.
❑ At times I followed a formula: *My first point, My second point . . .*
❑ I have a lead and conclusion. They could be stronger.
❑ It wouldn't hurt to change the order of some details.
❑ Some ideas are connected. Sometimes you have to make your own connections as you read.
❑ I spend too much time on some things—not enough on others.

1/2

Ideas are just thrown together with no real order or design. I have one or more of these problems:

❑ My writing wanders. I don't really know where I'm headed.
❑ There's no real plan here. It's a list or collection of thoughts.
❑ Lead? Conclusion? I just started—then stopped.
❑ The order is like a messy closet. My ideas are in there—*somewhere.*
❑ These ideas don't seem connected—to each other or any main idea.
❑ I couldn't tell what to spend time on.

Voice

5/6

I love this topic—and I want you to care about it, too.

❏ I feel this voice is ideal for my topic and my audience.

❏ This sounds like *me* and no one else. I hear myself in every line.

❏ I thought about my readers all the way through. It's like I'm having a conversation with them.

❏ My writing is honest; it's how I see the world. It's also lively; I worked to make this topic come alive for the reader.

❏ This is a piece a reader will want to share with someone else.

3/4

This is an OK topic. I think I sound interested—most of the time.

❏ The voice seems fine.

❏ At times, it sounds like me. Sometimes, it's an anybody voice (*blah, blah, blah*) or an encyclopedic voice (*fact, fact, fact*).

❏ Sometimes I reached out to the reader. Other times, I was just focusing on getting my ideas on paper.

❏ My voice comes and goes. You'll find moments of honesty or liveliness.

❏ You might want to share a line or two aloud.

1/2

I could not get into this topic, and just wrote to fill the page. I have one or more of these problems:

❏ I can't hear any voice—or else this is the wrong voice for my topic or audience.

❏ I don't think this sounds like me. It's just words on paper.

❏ I wasn't really "talking" to anyone. I wrote what came into my head.

❏ I'm not present in this piece. *Honest? Lively?* I felt bored when I wrote this.

❏ I don't really care if anyone shares this aloud. It's not me anyway.

Word Choice

5/6

I chose every word or phrase to make the message clear—or create a vivid picture (movie) in the reader's mind.

❏ My meaning is crystal clear from beginning to end.

❏ My words and phrases are fresh and accurate. I found *my own way* to say things.

❏ Lively verbs create energy and give my writing power.

❏ I went easy on the adjectives. I left out tired words (*nice, good, really*) that are overworked.

❏ If I repeated words, it was for effect.

❏ A few words or phrases might linger in your memory.

3/4

My words communicate. They get the job done.

❏ Most words are used correctly. You'll get the basic idea.

❏ My words aren't always original or memorable, but they make sense.

❏ I have a strong verb or two—guess I could use more!

❏ Some parts are too flowery—or too flat—maybe I used the thesaurus too much.

❏ I repeated words when I got tired or couldn't think of another way to say it.

❏ There are some good moments if you look.

1/2

I couldn't seem to find the words I needed. I have one or more of these problems:

❏ I don't know the meaning of some words. They might be incorrect.

❏ I used the first words that came into my head: *fun, nice, awesome, bad, cool, real*—you know, the usual words everybody uses all the time.

❏ I needed more verbs—and not so many adjectives.

❏ I overdid it at times: *The baseball game was superlative.*

❏ I repeated words without thinking: *A hard rain was falling hard.*

❏ I don't think these words will speak to my reader.

Sentence Fluency

5/6

My writing has rhythm, like music or poetry. It's easy to read aloud.

- ❏ You can read this with expression and voice. Try it and see.
- ❏ My sentences begin in different ways. Some are long, some short.
- ❏ I used sentence beginnings—*After a while, For the first time*—to show how ideas connect.
- ❏ You can almost hear the beat. You'll love the sound of it.
- ❏ If I used fragments, they work. If I wrote dialogue, it sounds like real people talking.

3/4

This writing hums along. It may not be musical, but you can read it without much trouble.

- ❏ It's pretty easy to read aloud—especially if you practice.
- ❏ My sentences aren't *all* the same length—and they don't *all* begin the same way.
- ❏ Connecting phrases? Like *For example?* I could use more of those.
- ❏ It's mechanical in spots—but it has some good moments, too.
- ❏ My fragments do not all work. My dialogue needs to sound more like conversation, less like robots talking.

1/2

This is hard to read aloud, even for me. I have one or more of these problems:

- ❏ It's hard to tell where my sentences begin and end.
- ❏ Too many sentences start exactly the same way.
- ❏ I need to combine some sentences and shorten others.
- ❏ I used words like *and, and then, so then,* or *because* so much that you can't read this without getting breathless.
- ❏ You might need to pause and reread or fill in missing words.
- ❏ Did I write sentences or fragments? I'm not sure. I'm not sure if I wrote any dialogue.

Conventions & Presentation

5/6

I know my conventions and it shows. I used them correctly and creatively to bring out voice and meaning.

- ❏ An editor would get bored looking for mistakes in my copy.
- ❏ This is edited thoroughly. Spelling, punctuation, grammar, capitals, and paragraphing are all correct.
- ❏ It might need light touchups—*if* I missed something.
- ❏ Strong conventions guide a reader right through my text.
- ❏ My presentation is eye catching and will help you access key information.

3/4

I know my conventions pretty well. You might catch a few errors.

- ❏ I see mistakes when I read this over, but I did some things well.
- ❏ This is edited lightly; you'll need to do a little "mental editing."
- ❏ I need to read this aloud, use a ruler to read line by line, and use a dictionary or spell checker to help catch everything.
- ❏ The mistakes are noticeable, but they don't get in the way of my message.
- ❏ My presentation might not be dazzling, but it's OK for my purpose.

1/2

I have trouble with conventions. You'll notice one or more of these problems:

- ❏ I have many mistakes. You'll need to read once just to decode.
- ❏ This paper isn't really edited yet. I have errors in spelling, punctuation, grammar, or capitals. My paragraphs don't start in the right spots.
- ❏ I need to read this aloud, word by word, pen in hand—with a coach to help me.
- ❏ This many mistakes will make a reader pause or reread. They could even get in the way of the message.
- ❏ Presentation? Oops. I need to work on that.

Appendix 4
Student Writing Guide in Spanish

Guía de escritura de 6 puntos del estudiante: IDEAS

6
- ❑ Mi texto es claro, se enfoca en el tema y está bien desarrollado. Seguro llamará la atención.
- ❑ Se puede saber exactamente cuál es mi mensaje.
- ❑ Conozco el tema de arriba a abajo.
- ❑ Ayudo a los lectores a aprender, pensar y comprender.
- ❑ Los detalles que incluyo despertarán tu curiosidad; es posible que te enseñen algo nuevo.

5
- ❑ Mi escrito es claro y se enfoca en el tema. Profundicé en algunos puntos clave.
- ❑ Pienso que el mensaje es claro.
- ❑ Sé mucho sobre este tema.
- ❑ Presento información importante e interesante en el texto.
- ❑ Escogí detalles que hacen que mi mensaje sea interesante.

4
- ❑ El texto es claro y se enfoca en el tema *casi* todo el tiempo.
- ❑ Puedes entender el mensaje.
- ❑ Sé algunas cosas sobre este tema.
- ❑ Presento *cierta* información novedosa.
- ❑ Incluyo algunos detalles y ejemplos.

3
- ❑ Escribí una lista de ideas: no desarrollé ninguna por completo.
- ❑ Puedes entender mi mensaje, o puedes no entenderlo.
- ❑ Me gustaría saber más sobre este tema.
- ❑ No sé qué más decir: fue muy difícil pensar qué información adicional podía incluir.
- ❑ Tuve dificultad para incluir detalles.

2
- ❑ Mi texto es confuso: no todo tiene sentido.
- ❑ Todavía no sé cuál es mi mensaje.
- ❑ NO sé suficiente de este tema como para escribir un texto.
- ❑ Escribí algunas cosas que no puedo probar o respaldar.
- ❑ No se me ocurrieron muchos detalles. ¿Está bien repetir cosas?

1
- ❑ No pude decidir qué quería decir. Aún no tengo un tema o una idea principal.
- ❑ Seguramente mi lector se quedó con miles de dudas.
- ❑ ¿Cómo puedo conseguir información? ¡No tengo un tema!
- ❑ Estas ideas no tienen orden.
- ❑ Sólo traté de llenar la hoja.

Guía de escritura de 6 puntos del estudiante: ORGANIZACIÓN

6
- ❑ El texto está tan bien organizado que no tendrás problemas para pasar de una idea a otra.
- ❑ La introducción atrapará tu atención; la conclusión te dejará pensando.
- ❑ Las transiciones presentan conexiones que no se te ocurrirían sin mi ayuda.
- ❑ Me detengo en donde hace falta: en los puntos importantes.
- ❑ Hay algunas sorpresas, pero en ningún momento te sentirás perdido.

5
- ❑ Mi organización del texto le da unidad al mensaje.
- ❑ Mi introducción es llamativa; mis conclusiones no dejan cabos sueltos.
- ❑ Mis transiciones muestran las conexiones entre las ideas.
- ❑ Dedico la mayor parte del tiempo a los puntos clave y no a aspectos incidentales.
- ❑ Puedes seguir mi argumento/relato sin dificultades.

4
- ❑ Mi organización es la adecuada para mi mensaje.
- ❑ Tengo una introducción y una conclusión. Las dos funcionan.
- ❑ Mis transiciones te guían de un punto al otro.
- ❑ A veces es difícil identificar qué es lo más importante.
- ❑ Puedes seguir el texto sin demasiada dificultad.

3
- ❑ Es una buena idea reorganizar algunas partes.
- ❑ Puedo trabajar más en la introducción y conclusión.
- ❑ Intenté usar transiciones. No estoy seguro de que muestren claramente las conexiones.
- ❑ Dediqué demasiado tiempo a cosas que el lector o ya sabe, o no necesita saber.
- ❑ Te puedes sentir perdido en el texto. ¡A veces, también, puedes saber *exactamente* qué es lo que sigue!

2
- ❑ Creo que debo reorganizarlo todo *¡de principio a fin!*
- ❑ No hay introducción o conclusión, o las que hay son más que conocidas por todos.
- ❑ No hay transiciones, o no tienen sentido.
- ❑ Es difícil identificar los puntos más importantes.
- ❑ Es difícil de seguir, incluso poniendo atención.

1
- ❑ Es como tratar de caminar por un bosque en la oscuridad.
- ❑ Simplemente empieza y acaba: no hay introducción o conclusión.
- ❑ ¿Transiciones? ¿Qué son? ¿Están conectados los diferentes puntos?
- ❑ Todo tiene la misma importancia.
- ❑ Nadie puede seguir el texto. Ni siquiera yo.

Guía de escritura de 6 puntos del estudiante: VOZ

6
- ❏ El texto tiene mi sello personal.
- ❏ Con toda seguridad querré leerlo a otras personas.
- ❏ Soy *yo*: lo que pienso, lo que siento.
- ❏ ¿Escuchas la pasión en mi voz? Me interesa que el lector quede prendado del tema.
- ❏ Una vez que comienzas a leerlo, no lo quieres dejar.

5
- ❏ Es un texto original y personal. Definitivamente soy *yo*.
- ❏ Creo que querré leerlo en voz alta.
- ❏ Logro transmitir mis pensamientos y sentimientos personales.
- ❏ La voz está llena de vida; transmite entusiasmo.
- ❏ Es evidente que pienso en mis lectores.

4
- ❏ Puedes reconocerme en el texto.
- ❏ Puedes leer una que otra línea en voz alta.
- ❏ Definitivamente estoy presente en el texto.
- ❏ Mi escritura es sincera. La impresión es que creo en lo que escribo.
- ❏ Pienso en mis lectores casi todo el tiempo.

3
- ❏ Mi voz aparece y desaparece. ¿Se nota que soy yo?
- ❏ Todavía no está listo para leerse en voz alta pero ¡falta poco!
- ❏ Necesito reforzar mi voz o usar una voz *diferente*.
- ❏ No me expresé en el texto: me contuve.
- ❏ No podía pensar todo el tiempo en mis lectores, ¿o sí?

2
- ❏ Me escondo tras las palabras: aún no soy yo.
- ❏ Hay algún indicio de voz en el texto, pero aún no está lista para comunicarse.
- ❏ No creo que el lector sepa quién soy después de leerlo.
- ❏ La voz es aburrida o, a lo mejor, parecida a la de una enciclopedia.
- ❏ Me preocupa que mis lectores se queden dormidos, o me abandonen.

1
- ❏ Me siento "incómodo" con este texto. Ni siquiera escucho un eco de mi voz real.
- ❏ No creo que alguien quiera leerlo en voz alta.
- ❏ Es una voz que puede ser "cualquiera". No soy yo.
- ❏ No logré emocionarme con este tema.
- ❏ ¿Lectores? ¿Qué lectores?

Guía de escritura de 6 puntos del estudiante: SELECCIÓN DE PALABRAS

6
- ❏ Escribí las cosas de manera original, creativa y clara.
- ❏ Me esforcé por encontrar la MEJOR manera de decir las cosas. ¡Hasta podrías citarme!
- ❏ Cada palabra es importante: no usé palabras innecesarias.
- ❏ Usé verbos expresivos: no dependí del uso excesivo de adjetivos.
- ❏ Mis palabras generan imágenes en tu mente, apelan a tus sentidos o te ayudan a comprender.

5
- ❏ Escribí para que el significado fuera claro, no para impresionar.
- ❏ Hay momentos que vale la pena recordar.
- ❏ Mi escritura es concisa.
- ❏ Usé verbos expresivos.
- ❏ Mis palabras te ayudan a comprender o visualizar las cosas.

4
- ❏ Mi escrito tiene sentido. Usé correctamente las palabras.
- ❏ Habrá algunos momentos que vale la pena subrayar o resaltar.
- ❏ Puede ser que en algún momento me exceda en verbosidad.
- ❏ Necesito *más* verbos expresivos, pero usé *algunos*.
- ❏ Los momentos expresivos superan a los problemáticos.

3
- ❏ Escribí lo primero que se me ocurrió, pero seguramente captarás la idea.
- ❏ En uno que otro lugar hay una frase que me gusta.
- ❏ Use más palabras de las necesarias, o repetí cosas.
- ❏ Necesito más verbos y tengo que alejarme de palabras trilladas como: *bonito, bueno, divertido, grandioso, genial.*
- ❏ Los problemas con las palabras superan los momentos expresivos.

2
- ❏ Cuidado con las palabras trilladas y ambiguas.
- ❏ Es difícil encontrar momentos para resaltar.
- ❏ Tengo problemas de verbosidad o repetición.
- ❏ Los verbos expresivos brillan por su ausencia. Predominan: *es, son, fue, fueron.*
- ❏ Debo esforzarme para encontrar palabras "adecuadas".

1
- ❏ Aunque mis palabras no sean las "correctas", llenan la página.
- ❏ Fue DIFÍCIL escribir este texto.
- ❏ Tuve que repetir; no se me ocurrieron palabras nuevas.
- ❏ Siempre usé las mismas palabras: *bonito, bueno, grandioso, divertido, maravilloso, genial, especial, de verdad, muy* . . .
- ❏ No creo que mi mensaje sea claro.

Guía de escritura de 6 puntos del estudiante: FLUIDEZ DE LAS ORACIONES

6
- ❏ Es fácil leerlo en voz MUY ALTA.
- ❏ Fluye como un buen guión de cine.
- ❏ No vas a creer la variedad de oraciones que incluí.
- ❏ Si usé fragmentos o repetición, éstos añaden énfasis.
- ❏ Mis diálogos son tan auténticos que son como escuchar una conversación en vivo.

5
- ❏ Se puede leer con expresividad.
- ❏ Me gusta el sonido cuando lo leo en voz alta.
- ❏ Mis oraciones empiezan de diferentes maneras. Algunas son largas y otras cortas.
- ❏ Si usé fragmentos o repetición, suenan bien.
- ❏ Mis diálogos son como si hablaran personas reales.

4
- ❏ Debe ser fácil leerlo en voz alta.
- ❏ Lo puedo leer en voz alta sin *demasiado* esfuerzo.
- ❏ Hay *alguna* variedad en la longitud y en el principio de las oraciones.
- ❏ Es cierto, hay algunos fragmentos y repetición, pero no representan un problema.
- ❏ Mi diálogo suena bien.

3
- ❏ Da trabajo pero, con esfuerzo, se puede leer.
- ❏ Es necesario hacer más fluidas algunas partes.
- ❏ Hay __ demasiadas oraciones cortas, __ demasiadas oraciones largas y __ demasiadas oraciones que empiezan igual.
- ❏ Hay __ demasiados fragmentos y __ demasiada repetición.
- ❏ El diálogo no parece real. Así no hablan las personas.

2
- ❏ Puedes leer esto *si practicas.*
- ❏ Hay __ encabalgamientos y __ oraciones interrumpidas.
- ❏ Hay __ demasiadas oraciones cortas, __ demasiadas oraciones largas y __ demasiadas oraciones que empiezan igual.
- ❏ Hay __ demasiados fragmentos y __ demasiada repetición.
- ❏ Este diálogo definitivamente NO funciona.

1
- ❏ Es difícil de leer, incluso para mí.
- ❏ Faltan palabras; o las oraciones simplemente no fluyen.
- ❏ Es difícil identificar dónde empiezan mis oraciones.
- ❏ Hay__ demasiadas oraciones cortas, __ demasiadas oraciones largas y __ demasiadas oraciones que empiezan igual.
- ❏ Hay __ demasiados fragmentos, __ demasiada repetición.
- ❏ ¿Es esto un diálogo? No estoy seguro.

Guía de escritura de 6 puntos del estudiante: CONVENCIONES & ORGANIZACIÓN

6
- ❏ Lo edité *bien.* Lo leí en silencio y en voz alta.
- ❏ La __ ortografía, la __ puntuación, la __ gramática, el __ uso de mayúsculas y la __ organización de los párrafos son *todos correctos.*
- ❏ Trabajé en el esquema. Llamará la atención.
- ❏ El trabajo está listo para ser publicado.

5
- ❏ Es posible que tenga algunos errores *menores:* voy a revisarlo otra vez.
- ❏ La __ ortografía, la __ puntuación, la __ gramática, el __ uso de mayúsculas y la __ organización de los párrafos son *todos correctos.*
- ❏ Trabajé en el esquema. Es bueno.
- ❏ El texto está *casi* listo para ser publicado.

4
- ❏ Encontré algunos errores que tengo que corregir.
- ❏ Debo revisar la __ ortografía, la __ puntuación, la __ gramática, el __ uso de mayúsculas y la __ organización de los párrafos.
- ❏ Trabajé en el esquema. Está bien, aunque podría hacerlo mejor.
- ❏ Debo revisar el texto una vez más y estará listo para ser publicado.

3
- ❏ Creo que el lector notará algunos errores en este texto.
- ❏ Tengo que revisar la __ ortografía, la __ puntuación, la __ gramática, el __ uso de mayúsculas y la __ organización de los párrafos.
- ❏ Necesito trabajar más en el esquema.
- ❏ Debo leerlo en silencio y en voz alta, con un bolígrafo a la mano.

2
- ❏ Los errores podrían impedir la comprensión de mi mensaje.
- ❏ Debo revisar la __ ortografía, la __ puntuación, la __ gramática, el __ uso de mayúsculas y la __ organización de los párrafos.
- ❏ Necesito trabajar más en el esquema.
- ❏ Tengo que leerlo en silencio y en voz alta, línea por línea.

1
- ❏ Los errores dificultan la lectura, ¡incluso para mí!
- ❏ Puedo editar __ la primera oración, __ el primer párrafo, __ TODO.
- ❏ Tengo que revisar la __ ortografía, __ la puntuación, __ gramática, el __ uso de mayúsculas y la __ organización de los párrafos.
- ❏ Voy a trabajar más en el esquema.
- ❏ Tengo que leerlo en silencio y en voz alta, palabra por palabra.

Appendix 5 Student Checklist in Spanish

Lista de revisión del estudiante

Ideas

- ❏ Mi escritura es clara y se enfoca en el tema.
- ❏ Los puntos clave están bien desarrollados.
- ❏ Es evidente que conozco este tema muy bien.
- ❏ Escogí los detalles con cuidado. Son interesantes e importantes.
- ❏ Resumí el tema para presentarlo en un tamaño accesible.

Organización

- ❏ Mi introducción atraerá al lector.
- ❏ Mi conclusión dejará pensando al lector.
- ❏ Las transiciones conectan claramente las ideas.
- ❏ El lector nunca se sentirá perdido al leerlo.

Voz

- ❏ En este texto se me puede reconocer; a mí y a nadie más.
- ❏ Es como si estuviera allí, conversando personalmente contigo.
- ❏ Es posible que quiera leer mi texto en voz alta a otras personas.
- ❏ Es un tema que me interesa y el lector lo notará.
- ❏ Una vez que *empiezas* a leerlo, querrás leer *hasta el final*.

Selección de palabras

- ❏ Encontré una manera personal de expresarme.
- ❏ Me esforcé en usar las MEJORES palabras, no las primeras que se me ocurrieron.
- ❏ Eliminé las palabras que eran innecesarias.
- ❏ Los verbos expresivos tienen más fuerza.
- ❏ *No* me excedí en el uso de adjetivos.
- ❏ Mis palabras ayudan a visualizar y sentir las cosas, o a comprender mi tema.

Fluidez de las oraciones

- ❏ Es un texto fácil de leer en voz alta *destacando la voz*.
- ❏ Es sorprendente la variedad de oraciones que usé.
- ❏ Lo leí en voz alta y me gusta cómo se oye.
- ❏ Cuando repetí frases o usé fragmentos fue para hacer énfasis.
- ❏ Mis diálogos son realistas. Son como conversaciones entre personas reales.

Convenciones & Organización

- ❏ Lo edité *bien*. Lo leí en silencio y en voz alta.
- ❏ Corregí errores de ortografía, puntuación, gramática, uso de mayúsculas y organización del párrafo.
- ❏ Este texto está listo para ser publicado.

Appendix 6 Requirements by Genre: Common Core Standards for Writing

Note: This is a summary of information that appears on the website: www.corestandards.org

Informational Writing
(Paraphrased from the Common Core Standards)

- Write informative/explanatory texts that examine a topic thoroughly and provide clear information on that topic.
- Introduce the topic clearly.
- Group details logically.
- Use illustrations and multi-media when helpful.
- Use sub-headings when helpful.
- Develop the topic through supporting details: facts, definitions, quotations, examples, etc.
- Use connecting words or phrases (e.g., *in contrast, on the other hand, for example*) to link ideas.
- Use precise word choice, including any relevant terminology, to help the reader understand the topic.
- Provide a relevant, satisfying conclusion.

Narrative Writing
(Paraphrased from the Common Core Standards)

- Write stories or other narratives based on real or imagined events, using effective style, detail, and sequencing to bring the writing to life.
- Set up the situation by introducing the setting, narrator, and/or characters.
- Order events in a natural, compelling manner.
- Use narrative techniques like dialogue, description, or pacing to unfold the plot or develop characters.
- Connect events clearly, through direct references or use of such transitional words as these: *after a while, the next year, later, just before that*, etc.
- Create vivid images and impressions, using sensory language or other effective techniques.
- Write a conclusion that wraps up events in a satisfying way.

Argument
(Paraphrased from the Common Core Standards)

- Write persuasive pieces, offering a clear argument and supporting it with relevant, convincing evidence.
- Introduce the topic clearly.
- State the opinion in a clear, unequivocal way.
- Give reasons for the point of view, and organize those reasons clearly.
- Support each reason with facts or other evidence.
- Connect each reason to the central argument using transitional words: *as a result, for example, to illustrate, more important, specifically, etc.*
- End with a logical and persuasive conclusion.

Abeel, Samantha. 2005. *My Thirteenth Winter*. New York: Scholastic.

Ackerman, Diane. 1995. *A Natural History of the Senses*. New York: Random House.

Anderson, Jeff. 2005. *Mechanically Inclined*. Portland, ME: Stenhouse.

_____. 2007. *Everyday Editing*. Portland, ME: Stenhouse.

Anderson, Richard C., Elfrieda H. Hiebert, Judith A. Scott, and Ian A. G. Wilkinson. 1985. *Becoming a Nation of Readers*. Washington, DC: U.S. Department of Education.

Aronie, Nancy Slonim. 1998. *Writing From the Heart: Tapping the Power of Your Inner Voice*. New York: Hyperion.

Aronson, Marc, and Marina Budhos. 2010. *Sugar Changed the World: A Story of Magic, Spice, Slavery, Freedom, and Science*. Boston: Houghton Mifflin Harcourt.

Arter, Judith A., and Jan Chappuis. 2006. *Creating and Recognizing Quality Rubrics*. Portland, OR: Educational Testing Service.

Atwell, Nancie. 1987. *In the Middle: Writing, Reading and Learning with Adolescents*. Portsmouth, NH: Boynton/Cook.

Avi. 1999. *Ragweed*. New York: HarperCollins.

Bernabei, Gretchen S., Jayne Hover, and Cynthia Candler. 2009. *Crunchtime*. Portsmouth, NH: Heinemann.

Ballenger, Bruce. 2004. *The Curious Researcher: A Guide to Writing Research Papers*, 4th ed. Boston: Allyn and Bacon.

Barry, Dave, and Ridley Pearson. 2004. *Peter and the Starcatchers*. New York: Hyperion Books.

Baylor, Byrd. 1995. *I'm in Charge of Celebrations*. New York: Aladdin.

Black, Paul. April 23, 2003. "A Successful Intervention—Why Did It Work?" Paper presented at the American Educational Research Association annual meeting, Chicago.

Black, Paul, and Dylan Wiliam. 1998. "Inside the Black Box: Raising Standards Through Classroom Assessment." *Phi Delta Kappan* (October), pp. 139–148.

Bomer, Katherine. 2010. *Hidden Gems: Naming and Teaching from the Brilliance in Every Student's Writing*. Portsmouth, NH: Heinemann.

Brandt, Ron. 1993. "On Teaching for Understanding: A Conversation With Howard Gardner." *Educational Leadership* 50 (September), pp. 4–7.

Brodie, Deborah. 1997. *Writing Changes Everything*. New York: St. Martin's Press.

Brookhart, Susan M. April 2011. "Making Feedback Work." *Virginia Journal of Education*. Richmond: Virginia Education Association.

Brown, John Seely. 1991. "Research That Reinvents the Corporation." *Harvard Business Review* (January–February), pp. 102–111.

Bryson, Bill. 2001. *In a Sunburned Country*. New York: Random House.

_____. 2010. *At Home: A Short History of Private Life*. New York: Doubleday.

Burdett, Lois. 2009. *A Child's Portrait of Shakespeare*. Richmond Hill, Ontario: Firefly Books.

Burke, Jim. 1999. *The English Teacher's Companion*. Portsmouth, NH: Heinemann.

_____. 2008. *Effective Instruction (The Teacher's Essential Guide Series)*. New York: Scholastic.

Cahill, Thomas. 1995. *How the Irish Saved Civilization*. New York: Doubleday.

Calkins, Lucy. 1994. *The Art of Teaching Writing*, rev. ed. Portsmouth, NH: Heinemann.

Cannon, Janell. 2000. *Crickwing*. New York: Harcourt Brace.

Capote, Truman. 1996. *A Christmas Memory, One Christmas, & The Thanksgiving Visitor*. New York: Random House.

Carle, Eric, editor. 2009. *Artist to Artist: 23 Major Illustrators Talk to Children about Their Art*. New York: Philomel Books.

Charlton, James, ed. 1992. *The Writer's Quotation Book*. New York: Penguin.

Chew, Charles. 1985. "Instruction Can Link Reading and Writing." In *Breaking Ground: Teachers Relate Reading and Writing in the Elementary School*. Edited by Jane Hansen, Thomas Newkirk, and Donald Graves. Portsmouth, NH: Heinemann.

Chicago Manual of Style, The. 16th edition. 2010. Chicago: University of Chicago Press.

Childs, Craig. 2007. *The Animal Dialogues: Uncommon Encounters in the Wild*. New York: Little, Brown and Company.

Cisneros, Sandra. 1991. *The House on Mango Street*. New York: Random House.

Clark, Roy Peter. 1987. *Free to Write: A Journalist Teaches Young Writers*. Portsmouth, NH: Heinemann.

_____. 2008. *Writing Tools: 50 Essential Strategies for Every Writer*. New York: Little, Brown and Company.

Codell, Esme Raji. 2004. *Sing a Song of Tunafish: A Memoir of My Fifth-Grade Year*. Illustrated by LeUyen Pham. New York: Hyperion.

Collard, Sneed B. III. 1997. *Creepy Creatures*. Watertown, MA: Charlesbridge.

_____. 2000. *Birds of Prey: A Look at Daytime Raptors*. New York: Franklin Watts.

_____. 2003. *The Deep-Sea Floor*. Watertown, MA: Charlesbridge.

_____. 2007. *Pocket Babies*. New York: Darby Creek Publishing.

_____. 2008. *Reign of the Sea Dragons*. Watertown, MA: Charlesbridge.

_____. 2010. *The World Famous Miles City Bucking Horse Sale*. Missoula, MT: Bucking Horse Books.

_____. 2012. *Lizards*. Watertown, MA: Charlesbridge.

Collins, James L. 1998. *Strategies for Teaching Struggling Writers*. New York: The Guilford Press.

Condry, John. 1977. "Enemies of Exploration: Self-Initiated vs. Other-Initiated Learning." *Journal of Personality and Social Psychology* 35, pp. 459–477.

Conlan, Gertrude, 1986. "Objective Measures of Writing Ability." 1986. In *Writing Assessment: Issues and Strategies*. Edited by Karen L. Greenberg, Harvey S. Wiener, and Richard A. Donovan. White Plains, NY: Longman.

Council of Writing Program Administrators, National Council of Teachers of English, and the National Writing Project. 2011. *Framework for Success in Postsecondary Writing*. http://www.wpacouncil.org

Cramer, Ronald L. 2001. *Creative Power: The Nature and Nurture of Children's Writing*. New York: Addison-Wesley Longman.

Crichton, Michael. 1988. *Travels*. New York: Random House.

Crystal, David. 2007. *Words, Words, Words*. New York: Oxford University Press.

Dahl, Roald. 1980. *The Twits*. New York: Penguin Books.

_____. 1988. *Matilda*. New York: Viking Kestrel.

_____. 2000. *The Wonderful Story of Henry Sugar*. New York: Penguin Books.

_____. 2009. *Boy: Tales of Childhood*. New edition. New York: Penguin Books.

Daniels, Harvey. December 2003. "Reading Like a Writer." In *Voices from the Middle*. Edited by Harvey Daniels. Volume 11, Number 2.

Davies, Nicola. 2003. *Surprising Sharks*. Cambridge, MA: Candlewick Press.

_____. 2004. *Bat Loves the Night*. Cambridge, MA: Candlewick Press.

_____. 2005. *One Tiny Turtle*. Cambridge, MA: Candlewick Press.

_____. 2006. *Extreme Animals: The Toughest Creatures on Earth*. Cambridge, MA: Candlewick Press.

_____. 2007. *What's Eating You?* Cambridge, MA: Candlewick Press.

_____. 2009. *Just the Right Size: Why Big Animals Are Big and Little Animals Are Little*. Cambridge, MA: Candlewick Press.

DiCamillo, Kate. 2000. *Because of Winn-Dixie*. Cambridge, MA: Candlewick Press.

_____. 2003. *The Tale of Despereaux*. Cambridge, MA: Candlewick Press.

Dickens, Charles. 1859. *A Tale of Two Cities*. Reprinted edition, 2011. New York: Penguin Classics.

Diederich, Paul B. 1974. *Measuring Growth in English*. Urbana, IL: National Council of Teachers of English.

Dirksen, Debra J. April 2011. "Hitting the Reset Button: Using Formative Assessment to Guide Instruction." *Phi Delta Kappan*. Volume 92, Number 7. Pages 26-31.

Elbow, Peter. 1973. *Writing Without Teachers*. New York: Oxford University Press.

_____. 1986. *Embracing Contraries*. New York: Oxford University Press.

_____. 1998. *Writing with Power*. New York: Oxford University Press.

Engle, Margarita. 2008. *The Surrender Tree: Poems of Cuba's Struggle for Freedom*. New York: Henry Hold and Company, LLC.

An English Grammar for Schools. 1883. Prescribed by the Council for Public Instruction. Halifax, Nova Scotia: A & W Mackinlay, Ltd., Publishers.

Erskine, Kathryn. 2010. *Mockingbird*. New York: Philomel Books.

Facklam, Margery. 2001. *Spiders and Their Web Sites*. New York: Little, Brown.

Fletcher, Ralph. 1993. *What a Writer Needs*. Portsmouth, NH: Heinemann.

_____. 2006. *Boy Writers: Reclaiming Their Voices*. Portland, ME: Stenhouse.

Florian, Douglas. 1998. *Insectlopedia*. New York: Harcourt.

Fox, Mem. 1989. *Wilfred Gordon McDonald Partridge*. New York: Kane/Miller.

_____. 1992. *Dear Mem Fox, I Have Read All Your Books, Even the Pathetic Ones*. Sidney: Mariner Books.

_____. 1993. *Radical Reflections*. New York: Harcourt Brace.

Frank, Marjorie. 1995. *If You're Trying to Teach Kids How to Write . . . You've Gotta Have This Book!* 2nd ed. Nashville: Incentive Publications.

Fraser, Jane, and Donna Skolnick. 1994. *On Their Way: Celebrating Second Graders As They Read and Write*. Portsmouth, NH: Heinemann.

Gardner, Howard. 1993. "Educating for Understanding." *The American School Board Journal* (July), pp. 20–24.

George, Twig C. 2000. *Jellies*. Minneapolis: Millbrook Press.

_____. 2003. *Seahorses*. Brookfield, CT: Millbrook Press.

Gilbert, Elizabeth. 2009. *Stern Men*. Reprint edition. New York: Penguin.

Glenn, David. April 11, 2007. "College Board Researchers Defend New Essay Component of SAT." *The Chronicle of Higher Education*. http://chronicle.com/daily/2007/04/2007041104n.htm.

Goldberg, Bonni. 1996. *Room to Write: Daily Invitations to a Writer's Life*. New York: G.P. Putnam's Sons.

Goleman, Daniel. 2006. *Social Intelligence: The Revolutionary New Science of Human Relationships*. New York: Random House.

Gordon, David George. 1996. *The Compleat Cockroach*. Berkeley, CA: Ten Speed Press.

Graham, Steve, and Dolores Perin. 2007. *Writing Next: Effective Strategies to Improve Writing of Adolescents in Middle and High School (A report to Carnegie Corporation of New York)*. Washington, DC: Alliance for Excellent Education.

Graves, Donald H. 1994. *A Fresh Look At Writing*. Portsmouth, NH: Heinemann.

_____. 1999. *Bring Life Into Learning*. Portsmouth, NH: Heinemann.

_____. 2002. *Testing Is Not Teaching*. Portsmouth, NH: Heinemann.

_____. 2003. *Writing: Teachers and Children At Work*. 20th Anniversary edition. Portsmouth, NH: Heinemann.

Graves, Donald H., and Virginia Stuart. 1987. *Write from the Start: Tapping Your Child's Natural Writing Ability*. New York: NAL Penguin.

Hairston, Maxine. 1986. "On Not Being a Composition Slave." In *Training the New Teacher of College Composition*. Edited by Charles W. Bridges. Urbana, IL: National Council of Teachers of English.

Hale, Constance. 2001. *Sin and Syntax: How to Craft Wickedly Effective Prose*. New York: Random House.

Heard, Georgia. 1995. *Writing Toward Home*. Portsmouth, NH: Heinemann.

_____. 2002. *The Revision Toolbox: Teaching Techniques That Work*. Portsmouth, NH: Heinemann.

Heard, Georgia, and Jennifer McDonough. 2009. *A Place for Wonder: Reading and Writing Nonfiction in the Primary Grades*. Portland, ME: Stenhouse Publishers.

Heller, Rafael, and Cynthia L. Greenleaf. June 2007. "Literacy Instruction in the Content Areas: Getting to the Core of Middle and High School Improvement." Washington, DC: Alliance for Excellent Education.

Hemingway, Ernest. 1995. *The Old Man and the Sea*. New York: Scribner.

Hesse, Karen. 1996. *The Music of Dolphins*. New York: Oxford University Press.

Hicks, Troy. 2009. *The Digital Writing Workshop*. Portsmouth, NH: Heinemann.

Hillenbrand, Laura. 2001. *Seabiscuit*. New York: Ballantine Books.

Hillman, Ben. 2008. *How Fast Is It?* New York: Scholastic.

Hillocks, George, Jr. 1986. *Research on Written Composition: New Directions for Teaching*. Urbana, IL: ERIC Clearinghouse on Reading and Communications Skills.

_____. 2002. *The Testing Trap: How State Writing Assessments Control Learning*. New York: Teachers College Press.

Hoose, Phillip, and Hannah Hoose. 1998. *Hey, Little Ant*. New York: Tricycle Press.

Horn, Martha, and Mary Ellen Giacobbe. 2007. *Talking, Drawing, Writing: Lessons for Our Youngest Writers*. Portland, ME: Stenhouse Publishers.

Huot, Brian. 1990. "The Literature of Direct Writing Assessment: Major Concerns and Prevailing Trends." *Review of Educational Research* 60 (Summer), pp. 237–263.

Iotanks, Tatanka (Sitting Bull, Lakota). 1995. *New Horizons*. Manhattan, KS: The Master Teacher, Inc.

Irving, John. 1990. *A Prayer for Owen Meany*. New York: Random House.

Jacobson, Jennifer. 2010. *No More "I'm Done!"* Portland, ME: Stenhouse.

Jago, Carol. 2009. *Crash! The Currency Crisis in American Culture*. A report from the National Council of Teachers of English. Urbana, IL: National Council of Teachers of English.

Jenkins, Steve. 2009. *Down, Down, Down: A Journey to the Bottom of the Sea*. New York: Houghton Mifflin Harcourt.

Johnson, Bea. 1999. *Never Too Early to Write.* Gainesville, FL: Maupin House.

Junger, Sebastian. 2000. *The Perfect Storm.* New York: HarperCollins.

Keillor, Garrison. 1987. *Leaving Home.* New York: Viking Penguin.

_____. 1989. *We Are Still Married.* New York: Viking Penguin.

King, Stephen. 2000. *On Writing.* New York: Scribner.

Kingsolver, Barbara. 2002. *Small Wonder.* New York: HarperCollins.

_____. 2007. *Animal, Vegetable, Miracle.* New York: HarperCollins.

Kloske, Geoffrey. 2005. *Once Upon a Time, the End (Asleep in 60 Seconds).* New York: Atheneum.

Kohn, Alfie. 1993. *Punished by Rewards.* Boston: Houghton Mifflin.

_____. 2000. *The Case Against Standardized Testing.* Portsmouth, NH: Heinemann.

Korda, Michael. September 1999. "Editing Explained." *Sky Magazine,* pp. 106–112. Reprinted with permission from Michael Korda. 1999. *Another Life.* New York: Random House.

Kozol, Jonathan. 2007. *Letters to a Young Teacher.* New York: Crown (an imprint of Crown Publishers).

Kurlansky, Mark. 2006. *The Big Oyster: History on the Half Shell.* New York: Random House.

_____. 2006. *The Story of Salt.* New York: G. P. Putnam's Sons.

Lamkin, Billie. April 2004. Personal interview by Vicki Spandel with teacher Billie Lamkin.

Lamott, Anne. 1995. *Bird By Bird.* New York: Bantam Doubleday Dell.

Lane, Barry. 1993. *After THE END.* Portsmouth, NH: Heinemann.

_____. 1996. "Quality in Writing." *Writing Teacher* 9(3), pp. 3–8.

_____. 1997. *Writing As a Road to Self-Discovery.* Shoreham, VT: Discover Writing Press.

_____. 1999. *Reviser's Toolbox.* Shoreham, VT: Discover Writing Press.

_____. 2002. *The Tortoise and the Hare . . . Continued.* Shoreham, VT: Discover Writing Press.

_____. 2003. *51 Wacky We-Search Reports.* Shoreham, VT: Discover Writing Press.

_____. 2011. In Vicki Spandel, *Creating Young Writers: Using the Six Traits to Enrich Writing Process in Primary Classrooms,* 3rd ed. Boston: Allyn and Bacon.

Lane, Barry, and Gretchen Barnabei. 2001. *Why We Must Run With Scissors Sometimes.* Shoreham, VT: Discover Writing Press.

LearningExpress Editors. 2006. *411 SAT Writing Questions and Essay Prompts.* LearningExpress.

Leavy, Jane. 2002. *Sandy Koufax: A Lefty's Legacy.* New York: HarperCollins.

Lederer, Richard, and Richard Dowis. 1995. *The Write Way.* New York: Simon and Schuster.

Lederman, Marie Jean. 1986. "Why Test?" In *Writing Assessment: Issues and Strategies.* Edited by Karen L. Greenberg, Harvey S. Wiener, and Richard A. Donovan. White Plains, NY: Longman.

Lee, Gus. 1991. *China Boy.* New York: Penguin.

Lee, Harper. 1960 (renewed 1988). *To Kill a Mockingbird.* New York: HarperCollins.

LeGuin, Ursula K. *Steering the Craft.* 1998. Portland, OR: Eighth Mountain Press.

Lunsford, Andrea A. 1986. "The Past—and Future—of Writing Assessment." In *Writing Assessment: Issues and Strategies.* Edited by Karen L. Greenberg, Harvey S. Wiener, and Richard A. Donovan. White Plains, NY: Longman.

_____. 2009. *Easy Writer.* 3rd edition. New York: Bedford/St. Martin's.

Mamet, David, writer/director. "Heist." A Warner Brothers film.

Marcus, Leonard S., editor. 2012. *Show Me a Story! Why Picture Books Matter.* New York: Candlewick Press.

Marrin, Albert. 2006. *Oh, Rats! The Story of Rats and People.* New York: Penguin.

_____. 2009. *Years of Dust: The Story of the Dust Bowl.* New York: Penguin.

Marten, Cindy. 2003. *Word Crafting: Teaching Spelling, Grades K–6.* Portsmouth, NH: Heinemann.

McCarty, Marietta. 2006. *Little Big Minds.* New York: Tarcher.

McCourt, Frank. 1999. *'Tis.* New York: Scribner.

McGraw, Phillip C. 1999. *Doing What Works, Doing What Matters.* New York: Hyperion.

Montgomery, Sy. 2006. *Quest for the Tree Kangaroo.* New York: Houghton Mifflin Harcourt.

_____. 2007. *The Good, Good Pig: The Extraordinary Life of Christopher Hogwood.* New York: Ballantine Books.

_____. 2010. *Birdology: Adventures with a pack of hens, a peck of pigeons, cantankerous crows, fierce falcons, hip hop parrots, baby hummingbirds, and one murderously big living dinosaur.* New York: Free Press.

Morrison, Toni. In Murray, Donald M. 1990. *Shoptalk.* Portsmouth, NH: Heinemann.

Murray, Donald M. 1982. *Learning By Teaching.* Portsmouth, NH: Boynton/Cook.

_____. 1984. *Write to Learn.* New York: Holt, Rinehart and Winston.

_____. 1990. *Shoptalk.* Portsmouth, NH: Boynton/Cook.

_____. 1998. *The Craft of Revision.* 3rd ed. New York: Harcourt Brace College Publishers.

_____. 2004. *A Writer Teaches Writing.* 2nd ed. Boston: Houghton Mifflin.

Myers, Walter Dean. 2008. *Slam!* New York: Scholastic.

Myspace Community, with Jessica Taudte. 2008. *Our Planet: Change Is Possible.* New York: HarperCollins Publishers.

Nagin, Carl, and the National Writing Project. 2006. *Because Writing Matters.* Revised edition. New York: Jossey Bass.

National Commission on Writing. 2003. *The Neglected "R": The Need for a Writing Revolution.* New York: College Entrance Examination Board.

_____. September 2004. *Writing: A Ticket to Work . . . Or a Ticket Out: A Survey of Business Leaders.* New York: College Entrance Examination Board.

National Council of Teachers of English (NCTE) Task Force. April 2005. "The Impact of SAT and ACT Timed Writing Tests." Urbana, IL: NCTE.

Newkirk, Thomas. 1989. *More Than Stories.* Portsmouth, NH: Heinemann.

_____. 2009. *Holding On to Good Ideas in a Time of Bad Ones.* Portsmouth, NH: Heinemann.

Nye, Bill. 1993. *The Science Guy's Big Blast of Science.* Mercer Island, WA: TV Books.

O'Brien, Tony, and Mike Sullivan. 2008. *Afghan Dreams: Young Voices of Afghanistan.* Photographs by Mike Sullivan. New York: Bloomsbury Children's Books.

O'Conner, Patricia T. 1999. *Words Fail Me.* New York: Harcourt Brace.

_____. 2010. *Woe Is I.* Third edition. New York: Putnam.

_____. 2010. *Origins of the Specious.* New York: Random House.

Ohanian, Susan. 1999. *One Size Fits Few.* Portsmouth, NH: Heinemann.

Olshansky, Beth. *Picturing Writing: Fostering Literacy Through Art* and *Image-Making Within the Writing Process.* University of New Hampshire. www.picturingwriting.com.

Oregon Shakespeare Festival Association. *The Language Archive.* Playbill, 2011.

Oregon Statewide Assessment Final Report. October 1985. Salem, OR: Oregon Department of Education.

Palatini, Margie. 2009. *Lousy Rotten Stinkin' Grapes.* New York: Simon & Schuster.

Palmer, Parker J. 1998. *The Courage to Teach: Exploring the Inner Landscape of a Teacher's Life.* San Francisco: Jossey-Bass.

Paulsen, Gary. 1989. *The Winter Room.* New York: Dell.

_____. 1993. *Dogteam.* New York: Delacorte Press.

_____. 1994. *Winterdance*. Orlando: Harcourt Brace & Company.

_____. 2001. *Guts*. New York: Delacorte Press.

_____. 2007. *Hatchet*. 20th anniversary edition. New York: Simon & Schuster.

_____, editor. 2003. *Shelf Life: Stories by the Book*. New York: Simon and Schuster.

Perlstein, Linda. 2007. *Tested: One American School Struggles to Make the Grade*. New York: Holt.

Pipher, Mary. 2006. *Writing to Change the World*. New York: Penguin.

Pirie, Bruce. 1997. *Reshaping High School English*. Urbana, IL: National Council of Teachers of English.

Plotnik, Arthur. 2007. *Spunk & Bite: A Writer's Guide to Bold, Contemporary Style*. New York: Random House Reference.

Poe, Edgar Allan. 1996. *Poe: Tales of Mystery and Imagination*. Illustrated by Gary Kelley. New York: Harcourt.

Polacco, Patricia. 2009. *January's Sparrow*. New York: Philomel.

Potter, Beatrix. 2003. *Squirrel Nutkin*. Centenary edition. New York: Frederick Warne Publishers, Ltd.

Provost, Gary. 1985. *100 Ways to Improve Your Writing*. New York: Penguin.

Pukite, John. 2002. *A Field Guide to Pigs*. New York: Penguin Books.

Purves, Alan C. 1992. "Reflections on Research and Assessment in Written Composition." *Research in the Teaching of English* 26 (February), pp. 108–122.

Quammen, David. 1996. *The Song of the Dodo*. New York: Scribner.

_____. 1998. *Wild Thoughts From Wild Places*. New York: Scribner.

_____. 2000. *The Boilerplate Rhino*. New York: Simon & Schuster.

Ray, Katie Wood. 1999. *Wondrous Words*. Urbana, IL: National Council of Teachers of English.

_____. 2002. *What You Know By Heart: How to Develop Curriculum for Your Writing Workshop*. Portsmouth, NH: Heinemann.

_____. 2010. *In Pictures and in Words*. Portsmouth, NH: Heinemann.

Ray, Katie Wood, and Matt Glover. 2008. *Already Ready: Nurturing Writers in Preschool and Kindergarten*. Portsmouth, NH: Heinemann.

Ray, Katie Wood with Lester L. Laminack. 2001. *The Writing Workshop: Working through the Hard Parts (And They're All Hard Parts)*. Urbana, IL: National Council of Teachers of English.

Reynolds, Peter H. 2003. *The Dot*. Cambridge, MA: Candlewick Press.

Romano, Tom. 1987. *Clearing the Way: Working With Teenage Writers*. Portsmouth, NH: Heinemann.

_____. 1995. *Writing With Passion*. Portsmouth, NH: Boynton/Cook.

_____. 2004. *Crafting Authentic Voice*. Portsmouth, NH: Heinemann.

Rosenthal, Amy Krouse. 2005. *Encyclopedia of an Ordinary Life*. New York: Three Rivers Press.

Routman, Regie. 1996. *Literacy At the Crossroads*. Portsmouth, NH: Heinemann.

_____. 2000. *Conversations: Strategies for Teaching, Learning, and Evaluating*. Portsmouth, NH: Heinemann.

r.w.t. Magazine for Writing Teachers K–8. San Antonio: ECS Learning Systems.

Ryan, Pam Munoz. 2010. *The Dreamer*. New York: Scholastic.

Rylant, Cynthia. 1993. *The Relatives Came*. New York: Aladdin Paperbacks.

_____. 1998. *Scarecrow*. New York: Harcourt Inc.

Sachar, Louis. October 16, 1999. Keynote address: Author's Luncheon. Florida Reading Association. Orlando.

Sachar, Louis. 2010. *The Card Turner*. New York: Delacorte.

Sagan, Carl. 1980. *Cosmos*. New York: Random House.

Salinger, J.D. 1951. *The Catcher in the Rye*. New York: Little, Brown & Company.

Samway, Katharine Davies. 2006. *When English Language Learners Write*. Portsmouth, NH: Heinemann.

Schmidt, Gary D. 2004. *Lizzie Bright and the Buckminster Boy*. Boston: Houghton Mifflin Company.

_____. 2007. *The Wednesday Wars*. New York: Houghton Mifflin Harcourt.

_____. 2011. *Okay for Now*. New York: Houghton Mifflin Harcourt.

Scieszka, Jon. 1996. *The True Story of the 3 Little Pigs*. New York: Puffin.

_____. 2008. *Knucklehead*. New York: Viking.

Scieszka, Jon, ed. 2002. *Guys Write for Guys Read*. New York: Penguin Group.

_____. 2010. *Guys Read Funny Business*. New York: HarperCollins.

Seife, Charles. 2000. *Zero: The Biography of a Dangerous Idea*. New York: Penguin Books.

Selznick, Brian. 2007. *The Invention of Hugo Cabret*. New York: Scholastic.

Seinfeld, Jerry. 1993. *SeinLanguage*. New York: Bantam Books.

Shaughnessy, Mina P. 1977. *Errors and Expectations*. New York: Oxford University Press.

Shusterman, Neal. 2004. *The Schwa Was Here*. New York: Puffin Books.

Sidman, Joyce. 2010. *Ubiquitous: Celebrating Nature's Survivors*. Illustrated by Beckie Prange. New York: Houghton Mifflin Harcourt.

Silver, Donald. 1997. *One Small Square: Backyard*. New York: McGraw-Hill.

Simon, Seymour. 2004. *Dogs*. New York: HarperCollins/Smithsonian.

_____. 2007. *Our Solar System*. Revised edition. New York: HarperCollins/Smithsonian.

_____. 2009. *Gorillas*. New York: HarperCollins/Smithsonian.

Sloan, Megan. 2009. *Into Writing*. Portsmouth, NH: Heinemann.

Smith, Frank. 1984. "Reading Like a Writer." In *Composing and Comprehending*. Edited by Julie M. Jensen. Urbana, IL: ERIC Clearinghouse on Reading and Communication Skills.

Spandel, Vicki. 2005. *The 9 Rights of Every Writer*. Portsmouth, NH: Heinemann.

_____. 2008a. *Creating Revisers and Editors, Grade 3*. Boston: Allyn and Bacon (an imprint of Pearson Education, Inc.).

_____. 2008b. *Creating Revisers and Editors, Grade 4*. Boston: Allyn and Bacon (an imprint of Pearson Education, Inc).

_____. 2011c. *Creating Young Writers*, 3rd ed. Boston: Allyn and Bacon.

Spandel, Vicki, and Jeff Hicks. 2008. *Write Traits Kindergarten: Bringing the Traits to Kinderwriters*. Boston: Great Source Education Group, a division of Houghton Mifflin Harcourt.

_____. 2010. *Write Traits Kits for Grades 1 through 8*. Revised edition. Boston: Great Source Education, a division of Houghton Mifflin Harcourt.

Steele, Bob. 1998. *Draw Me a Story*. Winnipeg, Manitoba, Canada: Peguis Publishers.

Stegner, Wallace. 2002. *On Teaching and Writing Fiction*. New York: Penguin.

Steig, William. 1971. *Amos and Boris*. 2004, reissued edition. New York: Puffin Books.

_____. 1987. *Abel's Island*. Toronto: Collins.

_____. 2011. *Brave Irene*. New edition. New York: Farrar, Straus and Giroux.

Stiggins, Richard J. 2001. *Student-Involved Classroom Assessment*, 3rd ed. Upper Saddle River, NJ: Prentice-Hall.

Stiggins, Richard J., Judith A. Arter, Jan Chappuis, and Stephen Chappuis. 2006. *Classroom Assessment for Student Learning: Doing It Right—Using It Well*. Portland, OR: Educational Testing Service.

Strickland, Kathleen, and James Strickland. 1998. *Reflections on Assessment*. Portsmouth, NH: Boynton/Cook.

Strong, Richard, Harvey F. Silver, and Amy Robinson. 1995. "What Do Students Want?" *Educational Leadership* 53 (September), pp. 8–12.

Strunk, William, Jr., and E. B. White. 2008. *The Elements of Style*, 50th anniversary edition. Boston: Longman.

Teachers Are the Center of Education: Writing, Learning and Leading in the Digital Age. 2010. Conceptualized and written by the College Board, the National Writing Project, and Phi Delta Kappa International.

Thomas, Dylan. [1978] 1993. *A Child's Christmas in Wales*. London: Orion House.

Thomason, Tommy. 1993. *More Than a Writing Teacher*. Commerce, TX: Bridge Press.

_____. 1998. *Writer to Writer: How to Conference Young Authors*. Norwood, MA: Christopher-Gordon.

_____. 2003. *WriteAerobics: 40 Workshop Exercises to Improve Your Writing Teaching*. Norwood, MA: Christopher-Gordon.

Thomason, Tommy, and Carol York. 2000. *Write on Target: Preparing Young Writers to Succeed on State Writing Achievement Tests*. Norwood, MA: Christopher-Gordon.

Tredway, Linda. 1995. "Socratic Seminars: Engaging Students in Intellectual Discourse." *Educational Leadership* 53 (September), pp. 26–29.

Trimble, John R. 2000, *Writing With Style*. 2nd ed. Upper Saddle River, NJ: Prentice-Hall.

Truss, Lynne. 2006. *Eats, Shoots & Leaves*. New York: G. P. Putnam's Sons.

Van Allsburg, Chris. 1996. *The Mysteries of Harris Burdick*. Boston: Houghton Mifflin.

Walsh, Bill. 2004. *The Elephants of Style*. New York: McGraw-Hill.

Wasserstein, Paulette. 1995. "What Middle Schoolers Say About Their Schoolwork." *Educational Leadership* (September), pp. 41–43.

White, E. B. 1980. *Charlotte's Web*. New York: Harper Trophy.

Wiggins, Grant. 1992. "Creating Tests Worth Taking." *Educational Leadership* (May), pp. 26–33.

Williams, Joseph M. 2002. *Style: Ten Lessons in Clarity and Grace*, 7th ed. New York: Pearson Longman.

Wolcott, Willa, with Sue M. Legg. 1998. *An Overview of Writing Assessment: Theory, Research, and Practice*. Urbana, IL: National Council of Teachers of English.

Wolff, Fred S., and Lynna Garber Kalna. 2010. *The Write Direction: A New Teacher's Practical Guide to Teaching Writing and Its Application to the Workplace*. Boston: Allyn & Bacon.

Woodford, Chris et al. 2005. *Cool Stuff and How It Works*. New York: DK Publishing.

Write Source Handbooks for Students. Wilmington, MA: Great Source Education Group:

Writing Spot. (Kindergarten). Elsholz, Carol, Patrick Sebranek, and David Kemper.

Write One. (Grade 1). Kemper, David, Carol Elsholz, and Patrick Sebranek.

Write Away. (Grade 2). Kemper, David, Ruth Nathan, Patrick Sebranek, and Carol Elsholz.

Write on Track. (Grade 3). Kemper, David, Ruth Nathan, Patrick Sebranek, and Carol Elsholz.

Writers Express. (Grades 4–5). Kemper, David, Ruth Nathan, Patrick Sebranek, and Carol Elsholz.

Write Source 2000. (Grades 6–8). Sebranek, Patrick, David Kemper, and Verne Meyer.

All Write. (Grades 6–8). Kemper, David, Patrick Sebranek, and Verne Meyer.

Write Ahead. (Grades 9–10). Kemper, David, Patrick Sebranek, and Verne Meyer.

Writers Inc. (Grades 9–12). Sebranek, Patrick, David Kemper, and Verne Meyer.

School to Work. (Grades 9–12). Sebranek, Patrick, David Kemper, and John Van Rys.

Write for College. (Grades 11–12). Sebranek, Patrick, David Kemper, and Verne Meyer.

Writing Study Group of the NCTE Executive Committee. November 2004. NCTE Beliefs about the Teaching of Writing. Urbana, IL: National Council of Teachers of English.

Ziegler, Alan. 1981. *The Writing Workshop*. Vol. 1. New York: Teachers and Writers Collaborative.

Zinsser, William. 2006. *On Writing Well*. 30th Anniversary edition. New York. HarperCollins.

Index